th

hamlyn

crossword
dictionary

General Editor

John Bailie

This revised and updated edition published in 2001 by
Hamlyn, an imprint of Octopus Publishing Group Ltd
2–4 Heron Quays, London E14 4JP

First published in 1932
Revised 1963, 1978
Reprinted in 1992, 1993, 1994, 1996 (twice), 1997, 1998
and 1999

Distributed in the United States and Canada by
Sterling Publishing Co., Inc.
387 Park Avenue South, New York, NY 10016-8810

ISBN 0 600 60246 X

A CIP catalogue record for this book is available from
the British Library

Printed and bound in Great Britain by Mackays of
Chatham PLC, Chatham, Kent

10 9 8 7 6 5 4 3 2 1

Contents

CONTENTS

ARMED FORCES
Air force ranks and appellations: British and U.S.

2 – 4

F.O.
L.A.C.
W.A.A.F.
W.R.A.F.

5

major (U.S.)
pilot

6

airman
fitter
rigger

7

aviator
captain (U.S.)
colonel (U.S.)

general (U.S.)
private (U.S.)

8

armourer
corporal
mechanic
observer
sergeant

9

air gunner
bomb aimer
drum-major
navigator

10

air marshal
apprentice
balloonist
bombardier (U.S.)
nose gunner
rear gunner

tail gunner

11

aircraftman
belly gunner
second pilot

12

air commodore
group captain
major general (U.S.)
pilot officer

13

flying officer
master aircrew
sergeant major (U.S.)
staff sergeant (U.S.)
wing commander

14

air vice marshal
flight engineer

flight mechanic
flight sergeant
master sergeant (U.S.)
squadron leader
warrant officer

15

air chief marshal
chief technician
first lieutenant (U.S.)

16 AND OVER

brigadier general (U.S.)
(16)
flight lieutenant (16)
junior technician (16)
leading aircraftman
(18)
second lieutenant
(U.S.) (16)
senior aircraftman (17)

Battles and sieges

3 AND 4

Acre
Aden
Agra
Alma (The)
Amoy
Caen
Gaza
Guam
Hué
Ivry
Jena
Kiev
Kut
Laon
Loos
Lys (The)
Maas
Metz
Mons
Nile (The)
Taku

Tet
Trak
Uhm
Yser (The)
Zama

5

Aduwa
Aisne (The)
Alamo (The)
Anzio
Arcot
Arras
Basra
Boyne (The)
Bulge (The)
Cadiz
Cairo
Crécy
Crete
Delhi
Douai
Douro

El Teb
Eylau
Genoa
Herat
Issus
Kabul
Kandy
Kursk
Liège
Ligny
Luzon
Maida
Malta
Marne (The)
Meuse
Miami
Paris
Patay
Pusan
Rhine
Sedan
Selle
Sluys

Somme (The)
Tagus (The)
Texel (The)
Tours
Valmy
Ypres

6

Actium
Aleppo
Amiens
Arbela
Argaon
Armada (The)
Arnhem
Assaye
Atbara (The)
Bagdad
Barnet
Bataan
Berlin
Burgos
Busaco

Calais
Camden
Campen
Cannae
Chusan
Coruña
Dargai
Delium
Dunbar
Ferrol
Ghazni
Guarda
Havana
Isonzo (The)
Jattoo
Jhansi
Lützen
Madras
Madrid
Majuba
Málaga
Maldon
Manila

Mantua
Midway
Mileto
Minden
Moscow
Mukden
Nagpur
Narvik
Naseby
Nicaea
Oporto
Orthez
Ostend
Peking
Plevna
Quebec
Rabaul
Rhodes
Rivoli
Rocroi
Sadowa
Saigon
Saints (The)
Shiloh
Tarifa
Tobago
Tobruk
Toulon
Towton
Tudela
Tugela (The)
Ushant
Verdun
Vienna
Wagram
Warsaw

7

Aboukir
Abu Klea
Alamein
Albuera
Algiers
Alkmaar
Almansa
Almeida
Antioch
Antwerp
Badajoz
Baghdad
Bapaume
Bautzen
Bousaco
Brienne

Britain
Bull Run
Cambrai
Cape Bon
Cassino
Chalons
Coimbra
Colenso
Cordova
Coronel
Corunna
Dresden
Dunkirk
Edghill
El Obeid
Erzurum
Falkirk
Flodden
Granada
Gujerat
Gwalior
Iwo Jima
Java Sea
Jutland
Kharkov
Khe Sanh
La Hogue
Leipzig
Lemberg
Lepanto
Leuthen
Lucknow
Magdala
Magenta
Marengo
Matapan
Megiddo
Minorca
Moselle
Moskowa (The)
Nam Dong
Nations (The)
Newbury
Nivelle (The)
Okinawa
Orleans
Plassey
Poltava
Preston
Salamis
Salerno
Sobraon
Solebay
St. Kitts

St. Lucia
Taranto
Vimeiro
Vitoria

8

Antietam
Ardennes
Atlantic (The)
Ayacucho
Bastille (The)
Beresina (The)
Bhurtpur
Blenheim
Borodino
Bosworth
Calcutta
Carthage
Cawnpore
Coral Sea
Culloden
Drogheda
Ebro Riva
Edgehill
Flanders
Flushing
Fontenoy
Fort Erie
Granicus
Hastings
Hydaspes
Inkerman
Jemappes
Kandahar
Khartoum
Lake Erie
Le Cateau
Mafeking
Malakoff (The)
Marathon
Maubeuge
Medellin
Messines
Metaurus
Montreal
Navarino
Nieuport
Normandy
Omdurman
Overlord
Philippi
Poitiers
Potidaea
Pretoria

Przemysl
Salsette
Saratoga
Smolensk
Spion Kop
St. Albans
St. Mihiel
St. Pierre
Stirling
Suvla Bay
Syracuse
Talavera
Tiberias
Toulouse
Tsushima
Valencia
Waterloo
Yorktown
Zaragoza

9

Algeciras
Arginusai
Balaclava
Barcelona
Belle Isle
Bluff Cove
Caporetto
Caxamarco
Chaeronea
Champagne
Charleroi
Ctesiphon
Dettingen
El Alamein
El Mansura
Falklands (The)
Festubert
Friedland
Gallipoli
Gaugamela
Gibraltar
Hyderabad
Jerusalem
Kasserine
Kimberley
Ladysmith
Laing's Nek
Leningrad
Leyte Gulf
Louisburg
Magdeburg
Mauritius
Melagnano

Mobile Bay
Nashville
Oudenarde
Pharsalus
Port Mahon
Princeton
Ramillies
Rodriguez
Salamanca
Saragossa
Sedgemoor
Singapore
Solferino
St. Quentin
St. Vincent
Stormberg
Stromboli
Tarragona
Tourcoing
Trafalgar
Vicksburg
Vimy Ridge
Wakefield
Walcheren
Worcester
Zeebrugge

10

Adrianople
Ahmednagar
Alexandria
Appomattox
Austerlitz
Brandywine
Brownstown
Bunker Hill
Camperdown
Cerro Gordo
Chevy Chase
Copenhagen
Corregidor
Dogger Bank
Fort George
Gettysburg
Gravelotte
Guadeloupe
Heligoland
Imjin River
Kut-el-Amara
La Rochelle
Les Saintes
Malplaquet
Martinique
Montevideo

Montfaucon
New Orleans
Nördlingen
Paardeburg
Petersburg
Port Arthur
Porto Praya
Quatre Bras
River Plate
Sevastopol
Shrewsbury
Stalingrad
Tannenberg
Tel-el-Kebir
Tewkesbury
Tinchebray

11

Bannockburn
Bismarck Sea
Breitenfeld
Bunker's Hill

Cape Matapan
Chattanooga
Chilianwala
Dardanelles (The)
Dien Bien Phu
Fort Niagara
Guadalcanal
Hohenlinden
Isandhlwana
Jameson Raid (The)
Londonderry
Marston Moor
Masulipatam
Modder River
Pearl Harbor
Philiphaugh
Philippines (The)
Pieter's Hill
Pondicherry
Port Stanley
Prestonpans
Quiberon Bay

Rorke's Drift
Schoneveldt
Thermopylae
Ticonderoga
Vinegar Hill

12 AND OVER

Antietam Creek (13)
Battle of Britain (15)
Bloemfontein (12)
Cape St. Vincent (13)
Cedar Mountain (13)
Chalgrove Field (14)
Chancellorsville (16)
Ciudad Rodrigo (13)
Constantinople (14)
Delville Wood (12)
Falkland Islands (15)
Flodden Field (12)
Fredericksburg (14)
Fuentes de Oñovo (14)
Harper's Ferry (12)

Killiecrankie (13)
Lake Champlain (13)
Little Bighorn (13)
Magersfontein (13)
Mariana Islands (14)
Messines Ridge (13)
Neuve Chapelle (13)
Neville's Cross (13)
Passchendaele (13)
Philippine Sea (13)
Plains of Abraham (15)
San Sebastian (12)
Seringapatam (12)
Solomon Islands (14)
Spanish Armada
   (The) (13)
Stamford Bridge (14)
Trichinopoly (12)
Tsushima Strait (14)
Vittorio Veneto (14)
White Mountain (13)

Military ranks and appellations

2 AND 3

A.D.C.
A.T.S.
C.O.
C.S.M.
G.I.
M.P.
N.C.O.
O.C.
R.A.
R.E.
R.S.M.
R.T.O.
S.A.S.

4

naik
para
peon
R.A.O.C.
R.E.M.E.
W.A.A.C.
W.R.A.C.
Zulu

5

cadet

fifer
Jäger
Jerry
major
piper
poilu
scout
sepoy
sowar
spahi
Tommy
Uhlan

6

archer
askari
batman
bomber
bowman
bugler
cornet
driver
ensign
gunner
Gurkha
hetman
hussar
lancer

marine
ranger
ranker
sapper
sutler
yeoman
Zouave

7

captain
colonel
Cossack
dragoon
drummer
farrier
flanker
general
hoplite
jemadar
lancers
marines
marshal
militia
officer
orderly
pikeman
pioneer
private

recruit
redcoat
regular
reserve
saddler
samurai
sappers
soldier
subadar
trooper
vedette
veteran
warrior

8

adjutant
armourer
bandsman
cavalier
chasseur
commando
corporal
decurion
deserter
doughboy
dragoons
fencible
fugelman

fusilier
havildar
infantry
janizary
Landwehr
marksman
messmate
muleteer
mutineer
partisan
rifleman
sentinel
sergeant
spearman

9

beefeater
berserker
brigadier
cannoneer
cannonier
centurion
combatant
commander
conscript
drum-major
estafette
field rank

fife-major
grenadier
guardsman
guerrilla
Home Guard
irregular
Janissary
junior N.C.O.
lance-naik
lifeguard
man-at-arms
musketeer
paymaster
pensioner
pipe-major
Roundhead
senior N.C.O.
signaller
subaltern
tactician
town major
tradesman
trumpeter
vexillary
voltigeur
volunteer

10

aide-de-camp
bandmaster
bombardier
carabineer
cavalryman
commandant
cuirassier
drummer-boy
file-leader
footguards
halberdier
instructor
Lansquenet
lieutenant
Life Guards
militiaman
other ranks
paratroops
roughrider
serviceman
skirmisher
strategist

11

arquebusier
artillerist
auxiliaries
bashi-bazouk
bersaglieri

condottiere
crack troops
crossbowman
enlisted man
gendarmerie
horse guards
infantryman
Landsknecht
moss-trooper
parachutist
paratrooper
Tommy Atkins
top sergeant

12

armour-bearer
artilleryman
brigade-major
camp follower
ensign-bearer
field marshal
field officer
horse soldier
major-general
master gunner
officer cadet
P.T. instructor
Royal Marines
Royal Signals
sharpshooter
staff officer

storm-trooper
territorials

13

army commander
barrack-master
color sergeant
corporal-major
dispatch-rider
drill sergeant
first sergeant
foreign legion
generalissimo
gunner officer
lance-corporal
lance-sergeant
Life Guardsman
light infantry
machine-gunner
mounted rifles
prisoner of war
quartermaster
sapper officer
sergeant major
staff-sergeant

14

colonel-in-chief
colour-sergeant
liaison officer
master sergeant

medical officer
military police
orderly officer
provost-marshal
Royal Artillery
Royal Engineers
Royal Tank Corps
signals officer
standard bearer
warrant officer

15

adjutant-general
corporal-of-horse
first lieutenant
gentleman-at-arms
honorary colonel
household troops
mounted infantry
national service
orderly corporal
orderly sergeant
ordnance officer
provost sergeant

17 AND OVER

lieutenant-colonel (17)
lieutenant-general (17)
quartermaster-sergeant
(21)

Military terms (including fortifications)

2 – 4	file	lay	raze	ward	butts
	fire	levy	rear	wing	cadre
aim	flag	line	rout	zero	corps
ally	flak	loot	ruse		decoy
ammo	foe	man	sack	**5**	depot
arm	foot	map	sap	abort	ditch
arms	form	mess	shot	agent	draft
army	fort	mine	slay	alarm	dress
A.W.O.L.	gas	moat	slug	alert	drill
band	gun	N.A.T.O.	spur	annex	enemy
base	ha-ha	O.C.T.U.	take	A.N.Z.A.C.	enrol
belt	halt	park	tank	armed	equip
blip	host	plan	tent	armor	feint
camp	hut	post	tilt	array	field
defy	impi	P.O.W.	trap	baton	fight
draw	jam	push	turn	beret	flank
duck	jeep	raid	unit	beset	flare
duel	kern	ramp	van	booty	foray
fife	kit	rank	war	busby	fosse

front	strap	donjon	pursue	air-raid	fatigue
gazon	talus	double	raider	archery	fortify
gorge	track	dugout	ransom	armoury	fortlet
guard	troop	embark	rapine	arsenal	forward
guide	truce	encamp	rappel	assault	fourgon
herse	unarm	engage	ration	baggage	foxhole
horse	waste	enlist	recall	barrack	gallery
khaki	wheel	ensign	recoil	barrage	guérite
lager	wound	epaule	reduce	basenet	gunfire
lance	yield	escape	relais	bastion	gunnery
lines		escarp	relief	battery	gunshot
march	**6**	escort	report	besiege	half-pay
medal		Fabian	resist	bivouac	harness
mêlée	abatis	firing	retake	bombard	holster
mount	ack-ack	fleche	retire	brigade	hostage
mufti	action	foeman	review	bulwark	hostile
onset	affray	fraise	riddle	caltrop	hutment
order	allies	gabion	rideau	canteen	jamming
party	ambush	glacis	roster	carbine	Kremlin
peace	archer	guards	saddle	caserne	liaison
pivot	armour	helmet	salute	cavalry	looting
pouch	assail	hot war	sconce	chamade	lunette
prime	attack	hurter	second	charger	maniple
radar	bailey	impact	signal	chevron	martial
rally	banner	inroad	sniper	citadel	megaton
range	barbed	invade	sortie	cold war	moineau
ranks	battle	invest	square	colours	mounted
redan	beaten	kitbag	stores	command	neutral
relay	billet	laager	strife	company	nuclear
repel	blow up	legion	strike	conquer	on guard
rifle	brevet	limber	stripe	counter	outpost
round	bunker	maquis	stroke	coupure	outwing
route	cartel	merlon	subdue	crusade	outwork
royal	casern	mining	submit	curtain	overrun
sally	castle	mobile	supply	debouch	parados
salvo	centre	muster	target	defence	parapet
scale	charge	mutiny	tattoo	degrade	pennant
scarp	cohort	number	tenail	destroy	phalanx
S.E.A.T.O.	colour	occupy	thrust	détente	pillage
seize	column	oppose	trench	detrain	pillbox
S.H.A.E.F.	combat	orders	trophy	disband	platoon
shako	convoy	outfit	vallum	dismiss	plongée
shell	cordon	outgun	valour	dispart	postern
shock	corral	parade	victor	draw off	priming
shoot	curfew	parley	volley	drawn up	provost
siege	débris	parole	walled	dungeon	quarter
snipe	decamp	patrol	war-cry	echelon	rampart
sonar	defeat	pennon	zareba	enguard	rations
sonic	defend	permit	zigzag	entrain	ravelin
spoil	defile	picket		envelop	Red Army
squad	deploy	plonge	**7**	epaulet	redoubt
staff	desert	pompom		fallout	refugee
stand	detach	pompon	abattis	fanfare	regular
storm	detail	primer	advance	fascine	remblai
	disarm		airlift		

5

remount
repulse
reserve
retaken
retreat
reverse
salient
sandbag
section
service
sniping
spurred
standby
subvert
support
tactics
take out
tambour
tenable
tilting
trailer
triumph
unarmed
uncased
uniform
victory
ward off
warfare
wargame
warlike
warpath
warsong
wartime
warworn
wheeler
wounded

8

accoutre
admiralty
advanced
air force
airborne
alarm gun
alliance
armament
armature
armorial
arms race
Army List
baldrick
barbette
barbican
barracks

bartizan
bearskin
billeted
blockade
bull's eye
camisade
camisado
campaign
casemate
casualty
chivalry
civil war
collapse
conquest
cornetcy
crusader
decimate
decisive
defended
defender
defilade
demi-lune
demolish
despatch
detonate
disarray
dismount
dispatch
division
doubling
drumhead
duelling
embattle
enceinte
enfilade
ensigncy
entrench
equipage
escalade
eyes left
fastness
fatigues
field day
fighting
flanking
fortress
furlough
garrison
gauntlet
gendarme
guerilla
half-moon
hedgehog
herisson

hill fort
horn-work
invasion
knapsack
last post
lay siege
lay waste
limber up
lodgment
loophole
magazine
Mameluke
mantelet
marching
mark time
matériel
mess bill
militant
military
mobilize
movement
muniment
musketry
mutinous
on parade
on parole
opponent
ordnance
outflank
outguard
overkill
palisade
partisan
password
pay corps
petronel
pipe-clay
prisoner
punitive
quarters
railhead
ramparts
re-embark
rear line
rear rank
rearward
recharge
regiment
remounts
reprisal
retrench
reveille
ricochet
rifle-pit

roll-call
sabotage
saboteur
saluting
scout-car
seconded
security
sentry-go
services (the)
shabrack
shelling
shooting
shot-belt
siege-war
skirmish
soldiery
spotting
squadron
stampede
standard
stockade
storming
straddle
strategy
strength
struggle
supplies
surprise
surround
sword arm
tactical
tenaille
time-fuse
tortoise
total war
training
transfer
traverse
trooping (the
    colour)
unbeaten
unlimber
uprising
vanguard
vanquish
vexillar
victuals
warhorse
warpaint
war-whoop
watch-box
wheeling
yeomanry
zero hour

9

aggressor
alarm post
ambuscade
armistice
armouries
army corps
artillery
assailant
atomic war
attrition
ballistic
bandolier
banquette
barricade
barricado
battalion
batteries
battle-cry
beachhead
beleaguer
bellicose
billeting
bodyguard
bombproof
bombsight
bugle call
bulldozer
cannonade
caponiere
captaincy
cashiered
cavalcade
ceasefire
challenge
chevalier
colonelcy
combatant
conqueror
covert-way
crossfire
crow's foot
crown-work
defection
defensive
demi-gorge
desertion
devastate
discharge
disengage
dismantle
earthwork
elevation

embattled
embrasure
encompass
encounter
enfiladed
enrolment
epaulette
equipment
espionage
esplanade
eyes front
eyes right
fencibles
field rank
fire power
fire-drill
firefight
flagstaff
forage cap
form fours
fortalice
fusillade
gabionade
gas attack
gladiator
guardroom
guerrilla
haversack
homograph
housewife
incursion
interdict
invalided
irregular
land force
Landsturm
legionary
lifeguard
logistics
Luftwaffe
manoeuvre
march-past
mercenary
musketoon
Mutiny Act
objective
offensive
onslaught
operation
overpower
overshoot
overthrow
overwhelm
pack train

packdrill
palladium
parachute
predictor
pregnable
presidial
pressgang
projector
promotion
protector
provender
provision
re-enforce
re-entrant
rearguard
rebellion
reconquer
red ensign
refortify
reinforce
reprimand
revetment
revictual
revictual
safeguard
sally-port
scrimmage
semaphore
sentry-box
slaughter
slope arms
slow-march
stack arms
stand fast
stratagem
strategic
subjugate
surrender
sword-knot
taskforce
terrorist
unguarded
uniformed
unopposed
unscathed
unsheathe
unwarlike
war office
watchword
Wehrmacht
white flag
withstand
zigzagged

10

action left
aggressive
air defence
ammunition
annexation
annihilate
arbalister
armipotent
battlement
blitzkrieg
blockhouse
breastwork
brevet rank
bridgehead
camel corps
camouflage
cantonment
capitulate
ceremonial
challenger
color guard
commandeer
commissary
commission
covered-way
crenulated
dead ground
decampment
defensible
demobilize
demolition
deployment
despatches
detachment
detonation
direct fire
dismounted
dispatches
divisional
dragonnade
drawbridge
encampment
enfilading
engagement
enlistment
ensignship
epaulement
epauletted
escalation
escarpment
expedition
fieldworks

first strike
garrisoned
glasshouse
ground fire
guardhouse
hand-to-hand
heliograph
indecisive
Indian file
inspection
investment
invincible
leadership
light horse
light-armed
limited war
line of fire
manoeuvres
map-reading
martial law
militarism
musketeers
muster book
muster roll
night-watch
no man's land
nuclear war
occupation
odd numbers
operations
opposition
outgeneral
over the top
patrolling
point blank
portcullis
presidiary
prison camp
projectile
protection
quartering
quick-march
raking fire
raw recruit
re-entering
reconquest
recruiting
regimental
rencounter
rendezvous
reorganize
reparation
resistance
respirator

retirement
revolution
rifle range
route march
rules of war
sabretache
sentry beat
sentry duty
sentry post
shell-proof
short-range
sick parade
siegecraft
siege-train
signalling
slit trench
soldiering
squad drill
state of war
stronghold
subjection
submission
submissive
subsection
subversion
surrounded
sword-fight
table money
terreplein
tirailleur
trajectory
trench foot
undefended
unlimbered
unmolested
unsheathed
vanquisher
victorious
volunteers
vulnerable
war-council
watchtower

11

action front
action right
barking iron
barrack room
battle-array
battledress
battlefield
belligerent
besiegement
bombardment

7

bulletproof
button-stick
castellated
colour party
countermand
countermine
defenceless
demi-bastion
disarmament
disbandment
double-march
drawn swords
dress parade
embarkation
emplacement
envelopment
even numbers
fatigue duty
firing party
firing squad
flag of truce
flying party
foot-soldier
forced march
forlorn hope
form two deep
fortifiable
generalship
germ warfare
guerilla war
hostilities
impregnable
machicoulis
mobile force
orderly room
penetration
postern gate
present arms
range-finder
rank-and-file
reconnoitre
recruitment
review order
running-fire
safe conduct
searchlight
shock troops
skirmishing
smokescreen
stand-to-arms
supply depot
trained band
trench fever
trous-de-loup

trumpet call
unfortified
unprotected
unsoldierly
unsupported
war memorial

12

advance guard
advanced base
annihilation
anti-aircraft
Bailey bridge
battlemented
break-through
bush-fighting
capitulation
casualty list
civil defence
commissariat
commissioned
conscription
counterforce
countermarch
court-martial
covering fire
disaffection
dropping fire
encirclement
entrenchment
fatigue party
field colours
field officer
field-kitchen
flying column
foot barracks
friendly fire
garrison town
guard forces
guerrilla war
headquarters
heavy brigade
hollow square
horse-and-foot
indefensible
intelligence
invulnerable
irresistible
landing party
light brigade
light cavalry
line-of-battle
machicolated
Maltese cross

mobile column
mobilization
outmanoeuvre
platoon drill
plunging fire
protectorate
quarter-guard
remount depot
retrenchment
rocket attack
running fight
ruse-de-guerre
saluting base
shock tactics
shoulder-belt
shoulder-knot
siege tactics
siege warfare
staff college
surveillance
truce-breaker
ungarrisoned
unobstructed
white feather
working party

13

accoutrements
active service
advanced guard
armored column
articles of war
assault course
carrier pigeon
cheval-de-frise
circumvallate
co-belligerent
column-of-route
counterattack
fatigue parade
field equipage
field hospital
field of battle
fighting force
flying colours
fortification
guards' brigade
interior lines
machicolation
martello tower
mass formation
Military Cross
Military Medal
mounted police

mushroom cloud
order of battle
order of the day
ordnance depot
pontoon-bridge
radiolocation
rallying point
re-embarkation
re-enforcement
regular troops
reinforcement
running battle
shoulder-strap
splinter-proof
storming-party
strategically
striking force
swordsmanship
trench warfare
unarmed combat
urban guerilla
Victoria Cross
war department

14

action stations
airborne forces
ammunition dump
armored brigade
armoured column
auxiliary force
blockade-runner
castrametation
chevaux-de-frise
demobilization
field allowance
field ambulance
freedom fighter
general reserve
liaison officer
marching orders
mechanized army
medical officer
military school
miniature-range
musketry course
musketry school
nuclear warfare
pincer movement
Pyrrhic victory
reconnaissance
reinforcements
reorganization
standing orders

8

supreme command
urban guerrilla
volunteer force
winter quarters

15

armoured brigade
auxiliary forces
casualty station

circumvallation
clearing station
contravallation
counter approach
creeping barrage
discharge papers
dressing-station
entrenching tool
guerilla warfare

married quarters
military academy
military college
military funeral
non-commissioned
observation post
operation orders
rearguard action
regimental march

substantive rank
turning movement

16 AND OVER

collateral damage (16)
counter-insurgency (17)
counter-offensive (16)
flanking movement (16)
guerrilla warfare (16)

Naval (British and U.S.), Fleet Air Arm, Merchant Navy (Merchant Marine) ranks and appellations

3 AND 4

cook
C.P.O.
mate
Wren
W.R.N.S.

5

bosun
cadet
diver
middy
pilot

6

cooper
ensign
gunner
lascar
marine
master
purser
rating
reefer
seaman
snotty
stoker
topman
writer
yeoman

7

admiral
armorer
artisan
captain
deck boy

fireman
greaser
jack-tar
lookout
messman
recruit
shipman
skipper
steward
surgeon

8

armourer
cabin boy
chaplain
coxswain
engineer
flag rank
gun-layer
helmsman
messmate
ship's boy

9

artificer
boatswain
commander
commodore
cook's mate
navigator
paymaster
ropemaker
sailmaker
ship's cook
signalman
tugmaster

10

able seaman
apprentice
coastguard
lieutenant
midshipman
shipmaster
ship's baker
shipwright

11

air mechanic
chief stoker
electrician
flag captain
flag officer
foremastman
gunner's mate
port admiral
port officer
post captain
rear-admiral
vice-admiral
watchkeeper

12

cabin steward
chief officer
chief steward
first officer
fleet admiral
junior seaman
master gunner
master-at-arms
petty officer
powder monkey
second master

senior purser
telegraphist
third officer

13

armourer's mate
chief armourer
chief engineer
fourth officer
harbourmaster
leading seaman
leading stoker
marine officer
privateersman
quartermaster
radio operator
sailing master
second officer
ship's corporal
signal officer
sub-lieutenant
third engineer

14 AND OVER

admiral of the fleet (17)
boarding officer (15)
boatswain's mate (14)
chief petty officer (17)
first lieutenant (15)
flag-lieutenant (14)
fourth engineer (14)
leading steward (14)
lieut.-commander (14)
ordinary seaman (14)
second engineer (14)
ship's carpenter (14)
warrant officer (14)

Weapons and armour

3 AND 4

ABM
ammo
arm
arms
axe
ball
bill
bolt
bomb
bow
butt
cane
club
Colt
cosh
dag
dart
dirk
epée
foil
goad
gun
helm
ICBM
kris
mace
mall
mere
meri
mine
MIRV
pike
ram
Scud
shot
tank
taws
TNT
tuck
Uzi
whip

5

A-bomb
aegis
armet
armor
arrow
bilbo
birch

bolas
crest
estoc
flail
fusee
fusil
H-bomb
jereed
jerid
knife
knout
kukri
lance
lasso
lathi
Luger
Maxim
Minié
panga
pilum
rifle
sabre
salvo
shell
skean
skene
sling
spear
staff
stake
stave
stick
sword
targe
tawse
visor
vizor

6

ack-ack
airgun
armlet
armour
barrel
basnet
bodkin
bullet
cannon
casque
cudgel
dagger
dualin
dumdum

Exocet
glaive
gorget
gusset
heaume
helmet
jereed
kreese
lariat
lorica
mailed
Mauser
morion
mortar
musket
muzzle
napalm
parang
pellet
petard
pistol
pom-pom
popgun
powder
primer
rapier
rocket
sallet
scutum
scythe
Semtex
shield
sickle
stylet
swivel
target
tonite
tulwar
weapon
Webley
womera
zipgun

7

assagai
assegai
bar-shot
basinet
bayonet
bazooka
beldric
Bren gun

buckler
bundook
calibre
caliver
caltrop
car bomb
carbine
cordite
corslet
cuirass
curtana
cutlass
dudgeon
ejector
elf-bolt
firearm
firepot
fougade
gas mask
Gatling
greaves
grenade
gunport
gunshot
hackbut
halberd
halbert
handgun
harpoon
hatchet
hauberk
haubert
holster
javelin
long tom
longbow
lyddite
machete
megaton
missile
nuclear
Patriot
Polaris
poleaxe
poniard
priming
quarrel
shotgun
side-arm
sjambok
Skybolt
Spandau

Sten gun
surcoat
teargas
torpedo
trident
warhead
woomera

8

arbalist
arbelest
Armalite
arquebus
atom bomb
aventail
ballista
basilisk
blowpipe
bludgeon
broadaxe
Browning
burganet
burgonet
canister
carabine
catapult
cavalier
chamfrom
chamfron
chanfron
chausses
claymore
corselet
crossbow
culverin
dynamite
eel-spear
elf-arrow
falchion
falconet
field-gun
firearms
fireball
firebomb
firelock
fireship
fougasse
gas shell
gauntlet
gunsight
half-pike
haquebut

howitzer
jazerant
landmine
langrage
Lewis gun
linstock
magazine
mangonel
mantelet
Maxim gun
Oerlikon
ordnance
paravane
partisan
partizan
petronel
pistolet
plastron
portfire
pyroxyle
repeater
revolver
ricochet
ringmail
scabbard
scimitar
scorpion
shrapnel
siege-gun
skean-dhu
slow fuse
spontoon
stiletto
time bomb
tomahawk
tommy gun
vambrace
vamplate
whinyard
whiz-bang
yataghan

9

ack-ack gun
angel-shot
arrowhead
artillery
automatic
backpiece
balistite
ballistic
bandoleer

bandolier
battleaxe
Big Bertha
blackjack
Blue Water
boar-spear
Bofors gun
bombshell
bombsight
boomerang
Brown Bess
brownbill
carronade
cartouche
cartridge
chain-mail
chain-shot
chamfrain
chassepot
damascene
defoliant
derringer
deterrent
detonator
doodle-bug
equalizer
face-guard
fish-spear
fléchette
flintlock
gelignite
grapeshot
guncotton
gunpowder
habergeon
half-track
harquebus
headpiece
matchlock
Mills bomb
Minuteman
munitions
needle-gun
poison gas
quaker-gun
rerebrace
sling-shot
slow-match
small arms

small-bore
smoke-bomb
spring-gun
starshell
stinkbomb
sword-cane
trebuchet
troopship
truncheon
turret gun
whizz-bang
xyloidine

10

ammunition
Blue Streak
bowie knife
broadsword
cannon-shot
cannonball
coat of mail
demi-cannon
field-piece
flick knife
flying bomb
Gatling gun
knobkerrie
Lee-Enfield
letter bomb
limpet mine
machine-gun
Minié rifle
mustard-gas
pea-shooter
petrol bomb
powder horn
projectile
recoilless
safety-fuse
shillelagh
Sidewinder
six-shooter
smallsword
smoothbore
sticky bomb
swordstick
touchpaper
Winchester®

11

air-to-ground
antitank gun
armoured car
balistraria
basket sword
blockbuster
blunderbuss
bow and arrow
breastplate
cluster bomb
contact-mine
depth-charge
elephant gun
Garand rifle
germ warfare
gun carriage
hand-grenade
Kalashnikov
neutron bomb
powder flask
powder-chest
safety-catch
scale-armour
snickersnee
Snider rifle
stern-chaser

12

acoustic mine
armour-plated
Armstrong gun
battering ram
battery piece
breech-loader
cartridge-box
conventional
demi-culverin
double-charge
flame-thrower
fowling-piece
guided weapon
hydrogen bomb
landing craft
magnetic mine
mine detector
mitrailleuse
muzzle-loader

quarterstaff
rifle grenade
sword-bayonet
tracer bullet
trench mortar

13

aerial torpedo
armaments race
armor-piercing
ball-cartridge
cartridge-case
cruise missile
guided missile
high-explosive
knuckleduster
life preserver
percussion cap
poisoned arrow
semi-automatic
submachine-gun
thermonuclear
two-edged sword

14 AND OVER

air-to-air missile (15)
anti-aircraft gun (15)
armour-piercing (14)
ballistic missile (16)
blank cartridge (14)
chemical warfare (14)
duelling pistol (14)
field artillery (14)
heat-seeking
    missile (18)
heavy artillery (14)
horse artillery (14)
incendiary bomb (14)
miniature rifle (14)
Molotov cocktail (15)
nitroglycerine (14)
nuclear weapons (14)
plastic explosive (16)
powder-magazine (14)
rocket launcher (14)
sawn-off shotgun (14)
small-bore rifle (14)

BUSINESS, PROFESSIONS AND OCCUPATIONS
Business, trade and commerce

2 AND 3

A1
AVC.
bid
B.O.T.
buy
C.A.
C.O.D.
cut
due
dun
E.C.
ECU
fee
F.O.B.
G.D.P.
G.N.P.
H.P.
I.O.U.
ISA
job
lot
Ltd
M.B.A.
net
owe
par
pay
PEP
r.d.
rig
S.E.T.
sum
tax
tip
V.A.T.

4

agio
back
bail
bank
bear
bill
bond
boom
bull
call
cash

cess
chip
coin
cost
deal
dear
debt
deed
dole
dues
dump
duty
earn
easy
E.F.T.A.
even
fees
FIFO
fine
firm
fisc
free
fund
gain
G.A.T.T.
gild
gilt
giro
glut
gold
good
hire
idle
kite
lend
levy
lien
loan
long
loss
mart
mint
nett
note
owed
paid
P.A.Y.E.
peag
perk
poll

pool
post
puff
punt
ramp
rate
rent
ring
risk
ruin
safe
sale
scot
sell
sink
sold
spot
stag
swap
tare
term
turn
vend
wage

5

agent
angel
assay
asset
at par
audit
award
baron
batch
bears
bid up
block
board
bonds
bonus
brand
bribe
bulls
buy in
buy up
buyer
by-law
cargo
cheap

check
chips
clear
clerk
costs
cover
crash
cycle
debit
dough
draft
entry
Ernie
ex cap.
ex div.
float
folio
funds
gilts
gnome
goods
gross
hedge
'House'
index
issue
labor
lease
limit
MIRAS
money
notes
offer
order
owing
panic
paper
payee
payer
pound
price
proxy
quota
quote
rally
rates
remit
repay
rhino
rider

scalp
scoop
score
scrip
share
shark
short
sight
slash
slump
snake
spend
stake
stock
tally
talon
taxes
teind
TESSA
tight
tithe
token
trade
trend
truck
trust
usury
value
wages
worth
yield

6

accept
accrue
advice
agency
amount
assets
assign
at cost
avails
backer
bailee
bailor
banker
barter
bazaar
bearer
borrow

bought
bounce
bounty
bourse
branch
broker
bubble
budget
burden
bursar
buy out
buying
by-laws
cartel
cash in
change
charge
cheque
client
corner
coupon
credit
crisis
cum. div.
deal in
dealer
debtor
defray
demand
dicker
docket
drawee
drawer
equity
estate
excise
expend
export
factor
figure
fiscal
freeze
gazump
go slow
godown
growth
hammer
hawker
holder
honour

import	rebate	wind up	endorse	on trust	trade in
in cash	recoup	worker	engross	out tray	trading
in debt	redeem	**7**	entrust	package	traffic
income	refund		ex-bonus	partner	tranche
indent	remedy	account	expense	pay cash	trustee
insure	rental	actuary	exploit	pay rise	utility
in-tray	rentes	advance	exports	pay slip	vending
job lot	report	allonge	factory	payable	venture
jobber	resale	annuity	failure	payment	war bond
labour	resign	arrears	fall due	payroll	war loan
ledger	retail	at sight	feedback	pension	warrant
lender	retire	auction	finance	per cent	way bill
liable	return	auditor	flutter	poll tax	welfare
Lloyd's	salary	average	for sale	portage	workday
lock-up	sample	backing	forward	pre-empt	wound up
margin	save up	bad debt	freebie	premium	write up
market	saving	balance	freight	prepaid	
mark-up	sell in	banking	funding	pricing	**8**
mature	sell up	bargain	futures	pro rata	above par
merger	set off	bidding	gearing	product	acceptor
minute	settle	bonanza	go under	profits	accounts
moneys	shares	bullion	haulage	promote	act of God
nem. con.	shorts	bursary	hedging	pyramid	after tax
notice	silver	buy back	holding	realize	agiotage
octroi	simony	cambist	imports	realtor	amortize
office	specie	capital	imprest	receipt	ante-date
on call	spiral	cashier	in funds	refusal	appraise
on tick	spread	ceiling	in trust	reissue	assignee
oncost	staple	certify	indorse	release	assigner
one off	stocks	charter	inflate	renewal	auditing
option	strike	coinage	insured	reserve	back bond
outbid	supply	company	interim	returns	bailment
outlay	surety	consols	invoice	revenue	bank bill
outlet	surtax	convert	jobbers	rigging	bank giro
output	syndic	corn pit	jobbing	royalty	bank loan
packet	tariff	crossed	kaffirs	salable	bank rate
parity	taxman	customs	killing	salvage	bankbook
pay out	teller	cut-rate	launder	sell-out	banknote
pay-day	tender	damages	lay days	selling	bankroll
paying	ticket	day book	leasing	service	bankrupt
pay-off	tithes	dealing	lending	sold out	barratry
payola	trader	declare	limited	solvent	basic pay
picket	tycoon	default	lockout	spinoff	below par
pledge	unload	deficit	lottery	squeeze	berthage
plunge	unpaid	deflate	lump sum	stipend	blue chip
policy	usance	deposit	manager	storage	book debt
profit	usurer	dockage	mint par	striker	borrower
public	valuta	douceur	minutes	subsidy	bottomry
punter	vendor	draw out	name day	surplus	business
purvey	vendue	due bill	nest egg	swindle	buying in
quorum	volume	dumping	net gain	takings	carriage
racket	wampum	duopoly	no funds	tax free	cash down
rating	wealth	economy	on offer	taxable	cash sale
realty		embargo	on order	tonnage	cashbook

13

clearing	increase	scarcity	borrowing	free trade
commerce	indebted	schedule	brand name	fully paid
consumer	industry	security	brokerage	garnishee
contango	interest	shipment	by-product	gilt-edged
contract	investor	shipyard	call money	going rate
credit to	kitemark	showcase	call price	guarantee
creditor	lame duck	showroom	carry over	guarantor
cum bonus	manifest	sideline	certified	hard money
currency	manpower	sinecure	chartered	hush money
customer	mark down	soft sell	charterer	import tax
cut-price	markings	solvency	clearance	in arrears
day shift	maturing	spending	commodity	incentive
dealings	maturity	spot cash	cost price	income tax
defrayed	merchant	sterling	cum rights	indemnity
delivery	monetary	straddle	death duty	indenture
director	monopoly	supertax	debenture	inflation
disburse	mortgage	swindler	debit note	insolvent
discount	net price	takeover	deck cargo	insurance
dividend	net worth	tax dodge	deduction	inventory
drawings	novation	taxation	defaulter	knock down
dry goods	on credit	taxpayer	deflation	late shift
earnings	on demand	trade gap	demurrage	leasehold
embezzle	on strike	transfer	depletion	liability
employee	operator	Treasury	depositor	liquidate
employer	ordinary	turnover	direct tax	liquidity
emporium	overhead	underbid	directors	list price
endorsee	overtime	undercut	dishonour	long-dated
endorser	par value	unquoted	easy money	lossmaker
entrepot	passbook	wage rate	easy terms	luxury tax
equities	pawn shop	warranty	economics	mail order
estimate	pay talks	watchdog	economies	marketing
evaluate	pin money	wharfage	economize	means test
ex-gratia	post paid	windfall	emolument	middleman
ex-rights	poundage	write off	endowment	mortgagee
exchange	price cut	**9**	exchequer	mortgagor
expenses	price war		excise tax	near money
exporter	proceeds	actuarial	exciseman	negotiate
finances	producer	ad valorem	executive	net income
fine gold	property	aggregate	export tax	night safe
flat rate	purchase	allotment	extortion	on account
gold pool	quit rent	allowance	face value	on the tail
goodwill	rack rent	annuitant	fair price	order book
gratuity	rag trade	ante-dated	fair trade	outgoings
hallmark	receipts	anti-trust	fiat money	outworker
hammered	receiver	appraisal	fiduciary	overdraft
hard cash	recovery	appraiser	financial	overdrawn
hard sell	reinvest	arbitrage	financier	overheads
hardware	rent free	arrearage	fine paper	packaging
hoarding	reserves	assurance	firm offer	pari passu
hot money	retailer	averaging	firm price	paymaster
huckster	retainer	bank stock	first call	pecuniary
importer	salaried	blank bill	first cost	petty cash
in arrear	saleroom	book value	flotation	piecework
in the red	salesman	bordereau	franchise	piggy bank

portfolio
preferred
price list
price ring
price rise
prime cost
principal
profiteer
promotion
purchaser
put option
quittance
quotation
ratepayer
ready cash
recession
redundant
reflation
reimburse
repayable
repayment
resources
restraint
reversion
royalties
sell short
shift work
shop floor
short bill
short time
shortfall
sight bill
slush fund
sold short
sole agent
speculate
spot price
stamp duty
statement
stock list
stockpile
strike pay
subscribe
subsidize
surcharge
sweat shop
syndicate
tax return
ticket day
trade fair
trade name
trademark
tradesman
traveller

treasurer
undersell
unit trust
unskilled
utilities
valuation
vendition
viability
wage claim
warehouse
wealth tax
wholesale
winding up
work sheet
work study
workforce
World Bank

10

acceptance
account day
accountant
accounting
accumulate
active bond
added value
adjustment
advice note
appreciate
assessment
assignment
attachment
auctioneer
automation
average out
bank credit
bank return
bankruptcy
bear market
bearer bond
bill broker
bill of sale
block grant
bondholder
bonus issue
bonus share
bookkeeper
bottom line
bucket shop
bulk buying
bull market
calculator
call option
capitalism

capitalist
capitalize
capitation
chain store
chargeable
chequebook
closed shop
closing bid
collateral
colporteur
commercial
commission
compensate
consortium
contraband
conversion
cost centre
credit bank
credit card
credit note
credit slip
cumulative
defalcator
defrayment
del credere
department
depository
depreciate
depression
direct cost
dirty money
drawn bonds
elasticity
encumbered
end product
engrossing
ergonomics
estate duty
eurodollar
euromarket
evaluation
ex dividend
excise duty
first offer
fiscal year
fixed costs
fixed price
fixed trust
floor price
forced sale
forwarding
free market
funded debt
green pound

gross value
ground rent
growth area
honorarium
import duty
in the black
income bond
industrial
insolvency
instalment
investment
issue price
job hunting
joint stock
lighterage
liquidator
living wage
long period
loss leader
management
marked down
marketable
mass market
meal ticket
mercantile
monetarism
monetarist
money order
monopolist
monopolize
moratorium
negotiable
never never
night shift
no par value
nonpayment
note of hand
obligation
open cheque
open credit
open market
open policy
opening bid
option rate
overcharge
paper money
pawnbroker
peppercorn
percentage
plough back
pre-emption
preference
prepayment
price index

price level
production
profitable
profits tax
prospector
prospectus
prosperity
prosperous
provide for
purchasing
pure profit
pyramiding
quarter day
ready money
real estate
real income
recompense
redeemable
redemption
redundancy
remittance
remunerate
repurchase
rock bottom
sales force
scrip issue
second-hand
securities
selling day
selling out
serial bond
settlement
share index
short bonds
short-dated
smart money
sole agency
speculator
statistics
stock split
stockpiles
subscriber
tape prices
tax evasion
ticker tape
tight money
trade cycle
trade price
trade union
ultra vires
underwrite
unemployed
upset price
wage freeze

wage policy
Wall Street
wholesaler
work to rule
working day
written off

11

account book
accountancy
acquittance
advance note
advertising
arbitration
asking price
at face value
auction ring
auction sale
average bond
bank account
bank balance
bank holiday
bank manager
bank of issue
bear squeeze
beneficiary
betting shop
big business
bill of entry
billionaire
bimetallism
black market
blank cheque
bond washing
bonded goods
bonus scheme
book-keeping
budget price
businessman
capital gain
cash account
central bank
certificate
circulation
closing down
co-operative
commitments
commodities
common stock
competition
competitive
comptometer
consignment
consumerism

consumption
corporation
cost-benefit
counterfeit
cover charge
cum dividend
customs duty
danger money
days of grace
defence bond
demand curve
demand draft
demutualize
deposit rate
deposit slip
devaluation
direct debit
discounting
dishonoured
distributor
dividend tax
double entry
down payment
economic law
economic man
endorsement
estate agent
expenditure
fixed assets
fixed charge
fixed income
floor trader
fluctuation
foreclosure
free on board
freight note
Gresham's Law
gross income
high finance
hypermarket
hypothecate
income stock
indemnified
indirect tax
industrials
job analysis
joint return
legal tender
life savings
liquidation
loan capital
manufacture
market overt
market place

market price
mass-produce
merchandise
middle price
millionaire
minimum wage
money-lender
negotiation
net interest
net receipts
open account
option price
outstanding
overpayment
overtrading
package deal
partnership
pay on demand
physiocrats
pocket money
point of sale
postal order
poverty line
poverty trap
premium bond
price fixing
price freeze
property tax
purchase tax
Queer Street
raw material
realization
reinsurance
reserve bank
retiring age
revaluation
rights issue
risk capital
safe deposit
sales ledger
sales person
savings bank
seigniorage
self service
sell forward
shareholder
single entry
sinking fund
small trader
sold forward
speculation
stagflation
stake holder
stock market

stockbroker
stockjobber
stockpiling
stocktaking
subsistence
supermarket
syndicalism
take-home pay
takeover bid
time deposit
time sharing
tracker fund
trading post
transaction
travel agent
undercharge
undervalued
underwriter
with profits

12

above the line
account payee
ad valorem tax
amalgamation
amortization
appreciation
assembly line
balance sheet
banker's draft
banker's order
bargain price
below the line
bill of lading
board meeting
Board of Trade
bond creditor
bonded stores
bottomry bond
branch office
bridging loan
buyer's market
callable bond
capital gains
capital goods
capital stock
carpet bagger
carry-over day
carrying over
cash and carry
cash register
caveat emptor
charter party
clearing bank

closing price
common market
compensation
contract note
cost of living
credit rating
current price
current ratio
customs union
Defence Bonds
denomination
depreciation
differential
direct labour
disbursement
discount rate
disinflation
distribution
Dutch auction
early closing
earned income
econometrics
economy drive
embezzlement
entrepreneur
exchange rate
export credit
first refusal
fiscal policy
fixed capital
floating debt
frozen assets
gate receipts
general store
going concern
gold standard
haberdashery
hard currency
hire purchase
indirect cost
interest rate
invoice clerk
irredeemable
joint account
keep accounts
labour market
laissez-faire
life interest
liquid assets
manufacturer
marginal cost
mass-produced
maturity date
mercantilism

merchant bank
mixed economy
monetization
money changer
national bank
national debt
nearest offer
nominal price
nominal value
official list
opening price
overcapacity
pay as you earn
pay in advance
paying-in slip
policy holder
present worth
price ceiling
price control
price current
price rigging
productivity
profit margin
profit motive
profit taking
profiteering
public sector
rate of growth
raw materials
redeployment
remuneration
remunerative
reserve price
retaining fee
rig the market
rising prices
running costs
sale or return
sales gimmick
sales manager
salesmanship
severance pay
share capital
shareholding
sliding scale
social credit
soft currency
specie points
state lottery
statistician
sterling area
stock in trade
stockjobbery
stockjobbing

street market
surplus value
tax avoidance
tax collector
tax exemption
terms of trade
trade balance
trade barrier
trading stamp
transfer deed
travel agency
Treasury bill
treasury bond
treasury note
trial balance
trustee stock
underwriting
unemployment
valued policy
welfare state
works council

13

acceptilation
allotment note
appropriation
articled clerk
asset stripper
average clause
backwardation
bank overdraft
bank statement
blank transfer
budget surplus
bullion market
business cycle
cash dispenser
cash in advance
clearance sale
clearing house
consumer goods
contract curve
cost-effective
credit account
credit control
credit squeeze
crossed cheque
current assets
discount house
discount store
dividend yield
dollar premium
Dow-Jones index
effective rate

excess profits
exchequer bill
financial year
fire insurance
free trade area
fringe benefit
futures market
gross receipts
guarantee fund
impulse buying
incomes policy
interim report
issued capital
life assurance
life insurance
livery company
Lombard Street
long-dated bill
making-up price
multinational
multiple store
non-cumulative
not negotiable
options market
ordinary share
outside broker
overhead price
paid-up capital
par of exchange
participating
payment in kind
penalty clause
premium income
private sector
profit and loss
profit sharing
profitability
protectionism
public company
purchase price
quota sampling
rateable value
sales forecast
seller's market
service charge
settlement day
share transfer
small business
specification
standing order
Stock Exchange
subcontractor
switch selling
tax-deductible

taxable income
trade discount
trading estate
value added tax
vendor's shares
wasting assets
wheeler-dealer
works councils

14

accident policy
account current
advance freight
apprenticeship
balance of trade
bearer security
bill of exchange
blocked account
break-even point
bureau de change
capital account
capital gearing
capitalization
command economy
consumer credit
convertibility
corporation tax
cost accountant
cost accounting
current account
current balance
debenture stock
decimalization
deferred rebate
deferred shares
deposit account
discount market
economic growth
featherbedding
fiduciary issue
finance company

floating charge
founders' shares
fringe benefits
full employment
garnishee order
general average
general manager
half-commission
holder for value
holding company
hyperinflation
imprest account
inertia selling
infrastructure
inscribed stock
insider dealing
insider trading
invisible trade
joint stock bank
letter of credit
limited company
liquidity ratio
Lloyd's Register
loan conversion
macro-economics
managing agents
market research
merchant banker
micro-economics
monthly account
monthly payment
mortgage broker
national income
new issue market
nominal capital
option dealings
ordinary shares
over the counter
overproduction
oversubscribed
preferred stock

private economy
production line
progress chaser
promissory note
pyramid selling
quality control
random sampling
rate of exchange
rate of interest
receiving order
revenue account
shopping centre
short-term gains
simple interest
social security
superannuation
surrender value
trading account
uberrimae fidei
unearned income
venture capital
working capital

15 AND **16**

average adjuster
bargain basement
bonded warehouse
building society
business manager
business studies
capital employed
capital gains tax
closing down sale
commission agent
company director
consignment note
consumer durable
cottage industry
deferred annuity
demutualization
department store

dividend warrant
early retirement
endowment policy
ex-gratia payment
exchange control
family allowance
foreign exchange
golden handshake
insurance broker
insurance policy
interim dividend
investment trust
labour-intensive
lightning strike
liquidity ratios
marine insurance
national savings
nationalization
no-claim discount
non-contributory
non-profit making
personal pension
political science (16)
preference bonds
preference share
preference stock
preferred shares
public ownership
public relations
purchasing power
rationalization
redemption yield
reducing balance
reserve currency
secured creditor
service industry
sleeping partner
sterling balance
supply and demand
suspense account
unissued capital

Journalism, printing and publishing

2	s.c.	cub	run	book	etch
ad	w.f.	cut	set	bulk	face
em	**3**	die	sub	caps	film
en		imp	web	comp	flap
MS	ads	ink		copy	font
o.p.	bed	mat	**4**	cyan	grid
pi	box	out	back	dash	hack
	cap	pie	body	demy	ISBN
	crc	pot	bold	edit	lead

leaf
limp
mode
news
open
page
pica
puff
pull
quad
read
ream
ruby
rule
sewn
sink
slug
stet
take
trim
type
word

5

beard
black
bleed
block
blurb
cameo
canon
caret
cased
chase
chill
cloth
clump
cover
crown
daily
devil
Didot
draft
dummy
extra
flong
folio
forme
fount
gloss
index
leads
libel
linen

litho
metal
paper
pearl
plate
point
press
print
proof
punch
quire
quote
recto
reset
roman
rough
royal
run-on
scoop
serif
sigla
solid
sorts
spine
stone
story
tilde
title
verso
xerox

6

back-up
banner
binder
boards
ceriph
cliché
coated
cock-up
column
delete
editor
errata
flimsy
format
galley
indent
italic
jacket
keep up
layout
leader
linage

lock up
makeup
margin
mark up
marked
masked
matrix
matter
minion
morgue
octavo
offset
period
précis
quarto
quotes
random
review
revise
rotary
run off
screen
serial
series
set-off
sketch
spiked
splash
umlaut
uncial
weekly
weight

7

article
artwork
binding
bled off
brevier
bromide
bumping
capital
capsule
caption
cast off
cedilla
chapter
clicker
desk-top
diamond
display
edition
English

engrave
erratum
etching
feature
flyleaf
fold-out
Fraktur
full out
gravure
gripper
heading
imprint
in print
italics
journal
justify
leading
literal
masking
measure
monthly
mortice
net sale
overrun
overset
pen name
preface
prelims
printer
profile
publish
release
reprint
rewrite
section
sits vac
subedit
tabloid
typeset
woodcut
wordage

8

art board
ascender
biweekly
bleeding
boldface
book club
bookends
bookmark
bookshop
city desk
co-author

colophon
contents
cut flush
cuttings
dateline
deadline
designer
endpaper
foolscap
footnote
fudge box
full stop
hairline
halftone
handbook
hardback
headband
headline
hot metal
imperial
intaglio
keyboard
ligature
linotype
longhand
magazine
misprint
monotype
obituary
offprint
paginate
photoset
print run
printers
printing
register
reporter
slipcase
softback
streamer
tailband
textbook
turnover
type area
type size
typeface
verbatim
vignette
woodpulp

9

ampersand
art editor
bimonthly

book trade
bookplate
bookstall
bookstore
bourgeois
box number
brilliant
broadside
casebound
clippings
co-edition
collating
columnist
condensed
copypaper
copyright
crossword
descender
editorial
exclusive
facsimile
freelance
furniture
half title
hard cover
idiot tape
laminated
late extra
lightface
line break
lineblock
lower case
make ready
marked set
marking up
necrology
newspaper
newsprint
nonpareil
overprint
page proof
paperback
paragraph
photocopy
photostat
pressroom
print shop
proofread
pseudonym
publisher
quarterly
sans serif
shorthand
signature

small pica
soft cover
stonehand
subeditor
symposium
tear sheet
the morgue
title page
upper case
watermark
web-offset
woodblock
wrong font

10

annotation
assembling
blockmaker
body matter
bookbinder
bookseller
broadsheet
casting box
casting-off
catch title
city editor
compositor
copy edition
copyholder
copytaster
copywriter
dead matter
dirty proof
feuilleton
film critic
four colour
house style
imposition
impression
imprimatur
interleave
jacket copy
journalese
journalism
journalist
leader page
lithograph
long primer
manuscript
monochrome
news agency
news editor
nom-de-plume

out of print
overmatter
pagination
paraphrase
periodical
plagiarism
press agent
proof stage
publishing
reverse out
separation
short story
stereotype
subheading
supplement
syndication
title verso
trade paper
typescript
typesetter
typography
vignetting
wrong fount
xerography

11

advance copy
advertising
agony column
circulation
copy-editing
copyfitting
crown octavo
cub reporter
display type
fortnightly
galley proof
ghostwriter
great primer
gutter press
half measure
late edition
letterpress
line drawing
lithography
night editor
platemaking
printer's ink
proofreader
publication
rotary press
rotogravure
running
    head

section-sewn
unjustified

12

advance proof
block letters
book reviewer
contents list
cross heading
early edition
facing matter
feature story
first edition
fourth estate
frontispiece
illustration
keep standing
leader writer
London editor
magazine page
newspaperman
perfect bound
photogravure
press release
repagination
running title
sports editor
telegraphese
works manager

13

advertisement
composing room
editor-in-chief
foreign editor
justification
literary agent
pocket edition
spiral binding
stop press news
typographical
wire stitching

14 AND OVER

banner headline (14)
calendered paper (15)
camera-ready copy (15)
coffee table book (15)
colour separation (16)
colour supplement (16)
desk-top publishing (17)
double-page
    spread (16)
dramatic critic (14)

features editor (14)	line illustration (16)	perfect binding (14)	proof correction (15)
half-title verso (14)	literary editor (14)	personal column (14)	running headline (15)
leading article (14)	managing editor (14)	photolithography (16)	
limited edition (14)	offset printing (14)	proof correcting (15)	

Officials (including titles and religious designations)

2 – 4

abbé, aga, agha, aide, amir, babu, beak, bey, C.E.O., cid, curé, czar, dean, dey, doge, don, duce, duke, earl, emir, Graf, head, imam, inca, J.P., khan, king, lady, lama, lord, M.C., miss, M.P., page, peer, pope, rani, rex, shah, sir, sire, tsar, tzar, ward, whip

5

abbot, agent, ameer, baboo, baron, bedel, begum, board, boyar, calif, canon, chair, chief, count, dewan, divan, donna, doyen, edile, elder, emeer, envoy, ephor, friar, hakim, imaum, judge, junta, junto, jurat, laird, laity, liege, macer, mahdi, mayor, mufti, mulla, nabob, nawab, nizam, noble, pacha, padre, pasha, porte, prior, queen, rabbi, rajah, ranee, reeve, ruler, sahib, sheik, staff, suite, synod, thane, title, vakil, vicar, wazir, witan

6

abbess, aedile, alcade, archon, ataman, bailie, barony, bashaw, beadle, bigwig, bishop, brehon, bursar, caesar, caliph, cantor, censor, childe, consul, curate, custos, datary, deacon, deputy, despot, donzel, duenna, dynast, eparch, ephori, exarch, Führer, gauger, hakeem, herald, hetman, judger, Kaiser, keeper, khalif, knight, legate, lictor, mikado, misses, mullah, nuncio, police, préfet, pretor, primus, prince, puisne, rabbin, ranger, rector, regent, sachem, satrap, senate, serang, sexton, sheikh, sherif, shogun, sirdar, squire, sultan, syndic, tanist, umpire, verger, vestry, vizier, warden, warder

7

alcaide, alcalde, apostle, armiger, attaché, bailiff, baronet, bellman, bencher, burgess, cacique, caloyer, commère, compère, consort, coroner, council, curator, czarina, dauphin, dowager, duchess, duumvir, effendi, elector, embassy, emperor, empress, equerry, equites, esquire, Fuehrer, Gaekwar, Gestapo, grandee, hangman, head boy, headman, hidalgo, infanta, infante, jemadar, justice, khalifa, khedive, kinglet, maestro, magnate, mahatma, majesty, marquis, marshal, monarch, muezzin, nomarch, notable, officer, paladin, peeress, podestà, pontiff, praetor, prefect, prelate, premier, primate, proctor, prophet, provost, referee, regency, retinue, Sea Lord, sea-king, senator, shereef, sheriff, skipper, speaker, steward, subadar, subdean

sultana
supremo
tribune
tsarina
tzarina
vaivode
vavasor
viceroy
voivode

8

adjutant
alderman
archduke
autocrat
banneret
baroness
Black Rod
burgrave
canoness
cardinal
caudillo
chairman
chaplain
cicerone
co-bishop
co-regent
czarevna
deemster
delegate
dictator
diocesan
diplomat
director
douanier
duumviri
duumvirs
emeritus
emissary
ethnarch
guardian
head girl
headsman
heptarch
hierarch
highness
hospodar
imperial
interrex
laureate
lawgiver
lawmaker
lay elder
legation

licenser
life peer
lordling
maharaja
manciple
mandarin
margrave
marquess
marquise
martinet
mayoress
minister
monocrat
myrmidon
nobility
nobleman
noblesse
official
oligarch
overlord
overseer
Padishah
palatine
placeman
pontifex
princess
prioress
quaestor
recorder
register
resident
sagamore
seigneur
seignior
summoner
suzerain
tetrarch
tipstaff
triarchy
tribunal
triumvir
tsarevna
tzarevna
verderer
viscount
zamindar
zemindar

9

archdruid
authority
bodyguard
Carmelite
castellan

catchpole
celebrant
cellarist
centurion
chevalier
chief whip
chieftain
chiliarch
commander
commodore
constable
Cordelier
cupbearer
custodian
Dalai Lama
deaconess
decemviri
diaconate
dictatrix
dignitary
diplomate
Directory
dominator
drum major
electress
escheator
estafette
exciseman
executive
Gold Stick
grand duke
incumbent
inspector
Jack Ketch
justiciar
landgrave
lifeguard
liveryman
lord mayor
magnifico
maharajah
majordomo
mandatary
mandatory
matriarch
moderator
monsignor
oligarchy
ombudsman
Orangeman
palsgrave
patriarch
patrician
pendragon

pentarchy
policeman
portreeve
potentate
precentor
presbyter
president
pretender
principal
proconsul
registrar
rural dean
sacristan
secretary
seneschal
sovereign
statesman
subdeacon
suffragan
timocracy
town clerk
town crier
treasurer
vestryman
waldgrave
whipper-in

10

aide-de-camp
ambassador
archbishop
archdeacon
archflamen
archpriest
Areopagite
bumbailiff
camerlengo
chancellor
chatelaine
commandant
commissary
controller
corporator
corregidor
coryphaeus
councillor
covenanter
crown agent
czarevitch
dauphiness
delegation
designator
doorkeeper
enumerator

episcopate
excellency
headmaster
hierophant
high master
high priest
inquisitor
institutor
justiciary
lay brother
legislator
lieutenant
lower house
mace-bearer
magistracy
magistrate
margravine
marquisate
midshipman
ministrant
noblewoman
postmaster
praeposter
prebendary
presbytery
procurator
prolocutor
proscriber
pursuivant
ringmaster
sea captain
upper house
vice-consul
vice-regent
vicegerent
war council

11

archduchess
aristocracy
burgomaster
cardinalate
chamberlain
comptroller
court jester
crown prince
diplomatist
directorate
earl-marshal
ecclesiarch
executioner
flag officer
functionary
grand vizier

grandmaster
gymnasiarch
intercessor
internuncio
landgravine
legislatrix
lord provost
marchioness
monseigneur
papal legate
papal nuncio
policewoman
prince royal
protonotary
puisne judge
queen mother
school board
squirearchy
stadtholder
subordinate
sword-bearer
tax assessor
tax gatherer
town council
triumvirate
viscountess
witenagemot

12

agent-general
ambassadress
armour-bearer
chief justice
chief of staff

churchwarden
civil servant
commissioner
constabulary
ecclesiastic
field officer
headmistress
heir apparent
House of Lords
inspectorate
jack-in-office
legislatress
lord temporal
maid of honour
mastersinger
metropolitan
notary-public
office-bearer
parish priest
peace officer
poet laureate
prince-bishop
Privy Council
prothonotary
queen-consort
queen-dowager
queen-regnant
remembrancer
staff officer
tax collector
vicar-general

13

administrator
archimandrite
army commander
color sergeant
consul-general
count palatine
county council
district judge
Elder Brethren
generalissimo
grand seigneur
high constable
judge-advocate
lord spiritual
mounted police
police officer
prime minister
Prince of Wales
Princess Royal
public trustee
states-general
vice-president

14

auditor-general
camp commandant
chief constable
chief inspector
colour sergeant
dowager duchess
gentleman-usher
high court judge

House of Commons
king's messenger
lord chancellor
lord lieutenant
lord of the manor
lords spiritual
medical officer
political agent
provost-marshal
revenue officer
superintendent
town councillor
vicar-apostolic
vice-chancellor

15

advocate-general
astronomer-royal
attorney-general
cabinet minister
chargé d'affaires
district officer
election auditor
governor-general
heir-presumptive
lords lieutenant
parliamentarian
plenipotentiary
privy councillor
queen's messenger
sheriff's officer
suffragan bishop
surveyor-general
vice-chamberlain

People

2 AND 3			4	
	fop	mob	rip	brat
	G.I.	M.P.	R.S.M.	buck
A.B.	gun	Mr.	she	bull
ace	guy	Mrs.	sir	chap
ass	hag	mug	son	chum
B.A.	ham	mum	sot	clan
boy	hex	N.C.O.	spy	co-ed
B.Sc.	imp	nun	tar	colt
cad	kid	oaf	us	cove
D.D.	kin	oik	wag	crew
dad	lad	pa	we	dame
deb	M.A.	pal	wit	dear
dux	ma	pet	ye	demy
elf	man	Ph.D.	yob	doer
fag	me	pig	you	doll
fan	men	rat		dolt

doxy	peer	bairn	flirt	mummy	sizar
drip	peon	beast	flock	nanny	skier
duck	pimp	being	fogey	Negro	snail
dude	prig	belle	fraud	niece	sneak
dupe	rake	bigot	freak	ninny	sower
feed	roué	biter	gamin	noddy	spark
file	runt	black	gaper	nomad	sport
folk	sage	blade	gazer	nymph	squab
fool	salt	blood	genii	odist	squaw
funk	scab	booby	ghost	ogler	staff
gaby	sect	bride	giant	owner	stoic
gang	seer	broad	giber	pacer	stray
gawk	self	brute	gipsy	pagan	swam
girl	sept	bully	giver	party	swell
goer	serf	cadet	goose	pater	taker
Goth	shot	cheat	grass	patsy	tenor
grub	silk	child	groom	payee	thief
gull	sire	choir	guest	payer	toady
haji	slut	chump	guide	peach	tommy
heel	snob	churl	harpy	pigmy	toper
heir	soak	clown	hater	pin-up	tramp
herd	star	crank	heavy	piper	troop
hero	swot	crone	hewer	poser	trull
hick	tart	crony	hiker	posse	trump
hobo	team	crook	hussy	proxy	twins
host	them	crowd	idiot	prude	uncle
hunk	thug	cynic	idler	pryer	vixen
hype	tike	dandy	in-law	puker	voter
idol	tiro	darky	issue	pupil	wally
jack	toff	decoy	jingo	puppy	wench
jade	tool	deist	joker	pygmy	whore
jill	Tory	devil	Judas	quack	whoso
jilt	twin	dicer	juror	queen	widow
jury	twit	diver	knave	queer	wight
kith	tyke	do-all	lamia	racer	witch
lass	tyro	donor	lazar	raver	women
liar	user	doter	leper	rebel	wooer
loon	vamp	dozer	limey	rider	yahoo
lout	waif	droll	local	rival	yobbo
lush	ward	drone	locum	rogue	yokel
magi	Whig	dummy	loser	rough	youth
male	wife	dunce	lover	rover	
mama	wimp	duper	macho	rower	**6**
mate	wino	dwarf	madam	sahib	abuser
mess	yogi	enemy	maker	saint	admass
mime	zany	exile	mamma	scamp	adorer
minx		extra	mater	scion	agnate
miss	**5**	fakir	mimic	scold	air ace
mite	adept	felon	minim	scout	albino
monk	adult	fence	minor	screw	allies
mute	alien	fiend	miser	shark	alumna
mutt	angel	fifer	moron	shrew	Amazon
ogre	argus	firer	mouse	silly	ambler
papa	aunty	flier	mover	siren	angler

24

apache	dipper	helper	masher	paynim	second
au pair	dodger	hepcat	master	pedant	seeker
auntie	dotard	hermit	matron	pedlar	selves
backer	double	hippie	medium	peeler	sender
bad egg	dragon	hoaxer	member	peeper	senior
bandit	drawee	holder	menial	penman	sentry
barfly	drawer	hopper	mentor	penpal	sexist
batman	driver	hoyden	mestee	person	shadow
Bayard	drudge	humbug	midget	piecer	shaker
beater	dry-bob	hunter	minion	pigeon	shaman
beauty	duffer	hussar	misses	player	sharer
beldam	egoist	hymner	missis	Pommie	shaver
better	envier	iceman	missus	poseur	sheila
bibber	escort	infant	mister	prater	shrimp
bidder	eunuch	inmate	mocker	public	sinner
bilker	expert	jester	modist	pundit	sister
blacks	faggot	Jesuit	Mohock	punter	sitter
blonde	family	jet set	moiler	puppet	skater
bomber	father	jogger	molder	purger	skiver
boozer	fawner	jumper	monkey	purist	sloven
bowler	fellow	junior	moppet	pusher	smiler
buster	female	Junker	mortal	Quaker	smoker
cadger	fencer	junkie	mother	rabbit	snarer
caller	Fenian	keeper	mugger	rabble	sniper
camper	fiancé	killer	mulier	racist	snorer
captor	fibber	lancer	mummer	ragtag	solver
carper	finder	lassie	mustee	raider	spouse
carver	foeman	layman	myself	railer	square
casual	friend	leader	nagger	rammer	squire
client	gaffer	league	nation	ranter	stooge
clique	gainer	leaser	native	rapist	stroke
co-heir	gammer	lecher	nephew	rascal	sucker
co-star	gasbag	legist	nipper	rating	suitor
coaxer	gay dog	lender	nitwit	reader	surety
codger	geezer	lessee	nobody	reaper	talker
conman	genius	lessor	noodle	relict	tartar
coolie	gentry	limner	novice	rhymer	taster
copier	getter	loafer	nudist	ringer	tearer
cottar	gigolo	lobber	nutter	rioter	teaser
cousin	gillie	lodger	ogress	ripper	teller
coward	godson	looker	old boy	risker	tenant
craven	golfer	loonie	old man	roamer	Teuton
creole	gossip	looter	oracle	rocker	theist
cretin	granny	lubber	orator	Romany	thrall
cueist	griper	lurker	orphan	rookie	throng
damsel	grouch	lyrist	outlaw	rotter	toiler
dancer	grower	madcap	pander	rouser	tomboy
dauber	gunman	madman	pandit	runner	tosser
debtor	gunner	maiden	papist	rustic	toy boy
defier	gusher	maniac	parent	sadist	truant
delver	harlot	marine	pariah	savage	tutrix
denier	healer	marker	patron	savant	tyrant
deputy	hearer	maroon	pauper	scorer	umpire
digger	hedger	martyr	pawnee	scouse	uniter

urchin	atheist	comrade	drifter	floater	heretic
vandal	athlete	consort	driller	flouter	heroine
varlet	avenger	convert	drinker	fondler	hipster
vendee	babbler	convict	dropout	fopling	hoarder
vendor	bag lady	copycat	drubber	forager	homager
vestal	ballboy	Cossack	dualist	founder	hoodlum
viator	bastard	coterie	dueller	freeman	hostage
victim	batsman	coxcomb	dullard	frisker	hostess
victor	beatnik	crawler	dweller	fuddler	hothead
viewer	bedmate	creator	edifier	fumbler	hotspur
Viking	bedouin	creeper	egghead	gabbler	humbler
virago	beldame	cringer	egotist	gallant	hurrier
virgin	beloved	cripple	ejector	gambler	husband
votary	best man	croaker	elector	garbler	hustler
voyeur	bigshot	crooner	elegist	general	hymnist
walker	blabber	crybaby	empiric	gentile	imagist
wanton	boarder	cuckold	emptier	giggler	imbiber
washer	boaster	culprit	enactor	glutton	imposer
waster	bookman	curioso	endower	gobbler	imputer
wearer	bouncer	cyclist	endurer	goodman	inciter
weeder	bounder	dabbler	enticer	gormand	inducer
weeper	breeder	dabster	entrant	gossoon	infidel
wet-bob	brother	dallier	epicure	gourmet	infuser
whiner	bucolic	damosel	erecter	grandam	ingrate
winner	buffoon	darling	eremite	grandma	inhaler
wisher	bumpkin	dastard	escapee	grantee	injurer
wittol	bungler	dawdler	escaper	granter	insured
wizard	burgher	daysman	exacter	grantor	insurer
worker	bushman	debaser	exactor	grasper	invader
worthy	caitiff	debater	exalter	griffin	invalid
wretch	captain	defacer	exegete	groupie	inviter
writer	captive	defamer	exposer	grouser	jack-tar
yapper	casuist	defiler	faddist	growler	jackass
yeoman	caveman	defunct	failure	grown-up	Jacobin
zealot	changer	delator	fair sex	grubber	Jezebel
zombie	chanter	deluder	fall guy	grudger	Joe Soap
	Charlie	denizen	fanatic	grunter	jostler
7	charmer	derider	fancier	guesser	juggler
abetter	cheater	desirer	fantast	guzzler	jumbler
abettor	checker	devisee	fascist	gymnast	juryman
accuser	Chindit	deviser	fathead	habitué	Kantian
admirer	citizen	devisor	faulter	haggler	killjoy
adviser	climber	devotee	favorer	half-wit	kindler
aircrew	clipper	diarist	feaster	handler	kindred
almsman	clubman	dibbler	feoffee	hangdog	kingpin
also-ran	co-rival	diehard	feoffor	hard man	kinsman
alumnus	cockney	divider	fiancée	has-been	kneeler
amateur	cognate	diviner	fiddler	hatcher	knocker
amorosa	colleen	divorcé	fielder	haunter	knoller
amoroso	colonel	doubter	filcher	heathen	know-all
ancient	combine	dowager	flapper	heckler	laggard
anybody	commons	dragoon	flasher	heiress	leaguer
ascetic	company	dreader	fleabag	hellcat	learner
assizer	compère	dreamer	fleecer	hellion	legatee

liberal	Oxonian	rebuker	shedder	stealer	trouper
loather	paddler	reciter	shifter	stentor	trudger
lookout	papoose	recluse	shooter	stepson	trustee
lorette	paragon	redhead	shopper	sticker	tumbler
lounger	partner	redskin	shouter	stinger	twirler
lowbrow	parvenu	reducer	show-off	stinker	twister
Luddite	patcher	referee	shyster	stirrer	upstart
lunatic	patient	refugee	sibling	stooper	usurper
lurcher	patriot	refuser	skimmer	stopper	utopian
magnate	Paul Pry	refuter	skipper	strayer	utterer
mangler	peasant	regular	skulker	striker	vacuist
manikin	peruser	relater	slacker	striver	vagrant
mankind	pervert	remover	slammer	stroker	vampire
marcher	piercer	renewer	slasher	student	vaulter
marplot	pilgrim	repiner	sleeper	studier	vaunter
Marxist	pincher	replier	slinger	stumper	veteran
meddler	pioneer	rescuer	slitter	stylist	villain
menacer	plaiter	reserve	smasher	subduer	villein
mestizo	planner	retaker	snapper	subject	visitor
metrist	playboy	retinue	snarler	suicide	vouchee
milksop	pleadee	reverer	sniffer	suspect	voucher
mingler	pleader	reviver	snipper	swagman	voyager
minikin	pleaser	rhymist	snoozer	swearer	vulture
misdoer	plenist	roadhog	snorter	sweeper	waddler
mobster	plodder	royalty	snuffer	swiller	wakener
modiste	plotter	ruffian	society	swimmer	waltzer
monitor	plucker	ruffler	soloist	swinger	warbler
moulder	plumper	runaway	someone	tackler	warlock
mounter	plunger	rustler	soother	tattler	wastrel
mourner	pop idol	sad sack	sophist	taunter	watcher
Mr. Right	pounder	saluter	soprano	templar	waterer
mudlark	praiser	sandman	spaniel	tempter	waverer
mugwump	presser	saviour	spanker	thinker	weigher
mulatto	prinker	scalder	speaker	thriver	welcher
mumbler	private	scalper	speeder	thrower	welsher
Negress	prodigy	sceptic	speller	thumper	wencher
nibbler	progeny	schemer	spender	tickler	whipper
niggard	protégé	scholar	spiller	tippler	widower
niggler	prowler	scoffer	spitter	toddler	wielder
nominee	puncher	scolder	spoiler	tomfool	windbag
oarsman	punster	scooper	sponger	toppler	wise guy
obligee	puritan	scorner	sponsor	tosspot	witling
obliger	pursuer	scraper	sporter	tourist	witness
obligor	puzzler	Scrooge	spotter	trainee	wolf cub
oddball	quaffer	sculler	spouter	trainer	worrier
offerer	queller	seceder	sprayer	traitor	wounder
old fogy	querent	sectary	spurner	treader	wrapper
old girl	querist	securer	spurrer	treater	wrecker
old maid	quieter	seducer	stabber	tricker	wringer
old salt	quitter	seminar	stalker	trifler	yielder
oppidan	radical	service	stand-by	tripper	younker
opposer	rambler	settler	stand-in	trollop	Zionist
orderer	reacher	shammer	starlet	trooper	
outcast	realist	sharper	starter	tropist	

27

8

	bestower	coquette	embracer	galloper
	betrayer	corporal	emigrant	gamester
abdicant	big noise	cottager	emulator	gaolbird
abductor	bigamist	courtier	encloser	garroter
absentee	blackleg	crackpot	enforcer	gatherer
academic	blighter	creditor	enhancer	geometer
accepter	bluecoat	criminal	enquirer	giantess
acceptor	bohemian	crusader	enslaver	godchild
achiever	bookworm	customer	ensnarer	goodwife
adherent	borderer	dalesman	Ephesian	gourmand
adjutant	borrower	daughter	Erastian	gownsman
adulator	boy scout	deadhead	eschewer	graduate
advocate	braggart	deaf-mute	espouser	grandson
aesthete	brethren	debutant	eulogist	great man
agitator	brunette	deceased	euphuist	grisette
agnostic	busybody	deceiver	Eurasian	grumbler
alarmist	cabalist	defector	everyman	guerrilla
allottee	caballer	defender	everyone	habitant
allotter	canaille	deferrer	evildoer	hanger-on
alter ego	cannibal	democrat	evocator	harasser
altruist	canoeist	demoniac	examinee	hardener
ancestor	carouser	departer	examiner	harridan
ancestry	castaway	deponent	excepter	harrower
anchoret	catamite	deportee	executor	hastener
antihero	Catholic	depraver	expiator	hazarder
antipope	caviller	depriver	explorer	hectorer
apostate	celibate	derelict	exponent	hedonist
appellee	cenobite	deserter	extoller	helpmate
appellor	champion	deserver	fancy man	helpmeet
approver	chaperon	despiser	fanfaron	highbrow
arranger	children	detainee	fatalist	hijacker
aspirant	chiliast	detainer	favourer	hinderer
assassin	chuckier	detector	feminist	homicide
assembly	cicerone	devourer	ferreter	hooligan
assertor	cicisbeo	diffuser	figurant	horseman
assignee	civilian	diner-out	finalist	huckster
assignor	claimant	dirty dog	finisher	Huguenot
assuager	clansman	disciple	flaunter	humanist
attacker	clincher	disponee	flincher	humorist
attestor	clodpoll	disponer	folk-hero	humpback
audience	co-surety	disposer	follower	idealist
aularian	co-worker	disputer	fomenter	idolater
bachelor	cognizee	ditheist	fondling	idolizer
balancer	cognizer	diverter	foregoer	idyllist
bankrupt	colonial	divorcee	forgiver	imaginer
banterer	colonist	divorcer	franklin	imbecile
baritone	combiner	divulger	freedman	imitator
barrator	commando	do-gooder	freshman	immortal
beadsman	commoner	dogsbody	fribbler	impairer
beginner	commuter	drencher	front man	imparter
beguiler	complier	dribbler	fugitive	impeller
believer	consumer	drunkard	funny man	implorer
bellower	convener	duellist	futurist	impostor
benedict	conveyer	duettist	gadabout	improver

impugner	litigant	offender	provoker	returner
inceptor	livewire	old woman	punisher	revealer
indictee	logician	old-timer	purifier	reveller
indicter	loiterer	onlooker	Puseyite	revenger
indigene	looker-on	operator	pythoness	revolter
inductee	loyalist	opponent	quadroon	rewarder
inductor	luminary	optimist	quaverer	riffraff
indulger	lunarian	oratress	quibbler	rigorist
infector	lutenist	outsider	quidnunc	romancer
inferior	lyricist	pacifier	quietist	Romanist
inflamer	macaroni	pacifist	Quisling	romantic
informer	malapert	paleface	rakehell	rotarian
initiate	maligner	pamperer	ransomer	royalist
innocent	man-hater	paramour	ratifier	runagate
inquirer	mandarin	parasite	ravisher	saboteur
insister	mannikin	parcener	reasoner	satanist
inspirer	marauder	pardoner	rebutter	saucebox
insulter	marksman	parodist	receiver	sciolist
intended	martinet	partaker	recliner	scourger
intimate	may-queen	partisan	recoiler	scrawler
intruder	medalist	passer-by	recorder	scuffler
investor	mediator	patentee	recreant	seafarer
islander	messmate	pelagian	redeemer	searcher
jabberer	mistress	penitent	reformer	seconder
jackaroo	modalist	perjurer	refunder	selector
Jacobite	molester	pesterer	regicide	sentinel
jailbird	monsieur	pharisee	rejecter	sergeant
Jehovist	mooncalf	picaroon	rejoicer	shrieker
jingoist	moralist	pilferer	relapser	shrimper
John Bull	Moravian	pillager	relation	shrinker
Jonathan	motorist	plagiary	releasee	shuffler
joy-rider	murderer	playgoer	releaser	sidekick
Judaizer	murmurer	playmate	releasor	sidesman
juvenile	mutineer	plebeian	reliever	simoniac
kinsfolk	mutterer	poisoner	remarker	simperer
lady-love	namesake	polluter	reminder	skeleton
lame duck	narrator	poltroon	remitter	sketcher
lamenter	naturist	ponderer	renderer	skinhead
landsman	neophyte	popinjay	renegade	slattern
landsmen	nepotist	populace	repealer	slugabed
launcher	neurotic	prattler	repeater	sluggard
layabout	new broom	preparer	repeller	slyboots
laywoman	newcomer	presager	reporter	small fry
levanter	night owl	presumer	reprover	snatcher
leveller	nihilist	prisoner	repulser	snuffler
libellee	nuisance	prizeman	resenter	sodomite
libeller	numskull	prodigal	resident	solecist
liegeman	nursling	producer	resigner	solitary
linesman	objector	profaner	resister	somebody
lingerer	observer	promisee	resolver	son-in-law
linguist	obtainer	promiser	resorter	songster
listener	obtruder	promoter	restorer	sorcerer
literate	occupant	proposer	retarder	sorehead
literati	occupier	protégée	retorter	spinster

spitfire
splitter
spreader
springer
sprinter
spurrier
squasher
squatter
squeaker
squealer
squeezer
squinter
squireen
squirter
stickler
stitcher
stowaway
stranger
stripper
stroller
strutter
stumbler
suborner
suckling
sufferer
superior
superman
supposer
surmiser
survivor
swindler
sybarite
tacksman
talesman
Tartuffe
taxpayer
teddy boy
teenager
telltale
tenantry
testator
theorist
thrasher
threader
thruster
thurifer
thwarter
tightwad
top brass
torturer
townsman
traditor
traducer
trampler

trappist
trembler
triplets
truckler
truelove
turncoat
twaddler
twitcher
two-timer
underdog
unionist
upholder
upper ten
vagabond
vanguard
vapourer
venturer
verifier
vilifier
villager
violator
visitant
votaress
votarist
wallower
wanderer
war bride
wayfarer
waylayer
weakener
weanling
welcomer
Wesleyan
wheedler
whistler
whitener
whizz-kid
wiseacre
wrangler
wrestler
wriggler
yeomanry
yodeller
yokemate
yourself

9

abecedary
aborigine
absconder
abstainer
academist
accessory
acclaimer

addressee
addresser
addressor
adulterer
adversary
affirmant
aggressor
alcoholic
almswoman
analogist
anarchist
anchoress
anchorite
announcer
annuitant
apologist
appellant
applauder
applicant
appraiser
arch-enemy
assailant
associate
augmenter
authority
automaton
bacchanal
backbiter
banqueter
barbarian
bargainee
bargainer
battleaxe
bedfellow
bedlamite
beggarman
bel esprit
biblicist
bicyclist
blockhead
Bluebeard
blunderer
blusterer
bolsterer
bon vivant
bourgeois
boy wonder
boyfriend
bridesman
bystander
cabin crew
Calvinist
candidate
canvasser

careerist
carnalist
celebrity
chain-gang
chantress
chaperone
character
charlatan
charterer
chatterer
chiseller
Christian
churchman
classmate
clientele
co-heiress
co-nominee
co-patriot
coadjutor
coalition
cocklaird
cohabiter
colleague
collegian
combatant
comforter
commander
committee
committer
committor
communist
community
companion
concubine
confessor
confidant
conformer
Confucian
conqueror
conscript
consenter
consignee
consignor
conspirer
constable
consulter
consultor
contemner
contender
contralto
contriver
converter
corrector
corrupter

covergirl
crack shot
creatress
creditrix
cricketer
crookback
cut-throat
daredevil
dark horse
debauchee
debutante
declaimer
declarant
defaulter
defeatist
defendant
defrauder
deliverer
demagogue
demandant
demi-monde
dependant
depositor
depressor
depurator
designate
desperado
despoiler
destroyer
detractor
dialogist
disburser
discerner
disguiser
dispeller
disperser
displayer
disprover
disputant
disseisee
disseisor
dissenter
dissident
disturber
disuniter
do-nothing
dogmatist
dolly bird
driveller
dynamiter
dyspeptic
early bird
earthling
eccentric

Edwardian	free-liver	inamorato	matricide	patroness
emendator	freelance	increaser	medallist	peasantry
enchanter	freemason	incurable	mediatrix	Pecksniff
encomiast	fulfiller	indicator	messieurs	peculator
energumen	furtherer	indweller	Methodist	pen-friend
enfeebler	gainsayer	inebriate	metrician	pen-pusher
engrosser	garnishee	inflicter	middleman	pensioner
enlivener	garnisher	informant	millenary	perceiver
entangler	garreteer	infringer	miscreant	perfecter
entourage	garrotter	inhabiter	mitigator	performer
epicurean	gathering	inheritor	moderator	permitter
epileptic	gentleman	initiator	modernist	personage
epistoler	girl guide	innovator	modulator	personnel
euphemist	Girondist	inscriber	moneybags	persuader
evacuator	go-between	insolvent	monitress	perverter
everybody	godfather	insurgent	moonraker	pessimist
examinant	godmother	intestate	moralizer	pin-up girl
executant	Gothamite	intriguer	mortgagee	pinchfist
executrix	grandpapa	introvert	mortgagor	plaintiff
exhauster	grandsire	inveigher	mortifier	Platonist
exhibiter	gratifier	inveigler	Mrs. Grundy	plunderer
exhibitor	great-aunt	Jansenist	multitude	plutocrat
exploiter	greenhorn	jay-walker	muscleman	Plutonist
expositor	greybeard	jet setter	mutilator	poetaster
expounder	groomsman	jitterbug	mythmaker	possessor
exquisite	groveller	job hunter	Narcissus	posterity
extracter	guerrilla	job-seeker	neglecter	postponer
extractor	guest star	joint heir	neighbour	postulant
extravert	guinea pig	justifier	next of kin	pot-hunter
extremist	half-breed	kidnapper	night bird	practiser
extrovert	half-caste	kinswoman	nominator	prankster
falsifier	haranguer	lackbrain	non-smoker	precursor
family man	harbinger	ladies' man	nonentity	predicant
favourite	harbourer	lager lout	nourisher	predictor
fetishist	harebrain	landowner	novitiate	prelatist
fire-eater	harnesser	law-monger	nullifier	presbyope
first born	hearkener	lay reader	observant	presbyter
flag-waver	hell-hound	lazybones	occultist	presentee
flatterer	Hellenist	libellant	odd man out	presenter
flay-flint	highflier	liberator	offspring	preserver
forbidder	hillbilly	libertine	old master	pretender
forebears	honest man	lionheart	oppressor	preventer
foreigner	Hottentot	lip-reader	organizer	proceeder
forfeiter	household	liturgist	ourselves	profferer
forgetter	housewife	logroller	pacemaker	profiteer
formalist	hunchback	lost sheep	palaverer	projector
fortifier	hylozoist	loudmouth	panellist	prolonger
forwarder	hypocrite	lowlander	paralytic	proselyte
fossicker	ignoramus	make-peace	paranymph	prosodist
foster-son	immigrant	malthorse	parricide	protector
foundling	immolator	mammonist	part-owner	protester
foundress	impeacher	mammonite	passenger	purchaser
foxhunter	in-patient	mannerist	patrician	purloiner
free agent	inamorata	masochist	patricide	pussyfoot

31

pythoness	shaveling	sycophant	**10**	changeling
Quakeress	shortener	symbolist		chatterbox
qualifier	shoveller	syncopist	aboriginal	chauvinist
queer fish	sightseer	tactician	aborigines	cheesecake
rabbinist	simpleton	Talmudist	Abraham man	child bride
racketeer	skin-diver	Targumist	absolutist	churchgoer
raconteur	skinflint	temptress	accomplice	Cinderella
rainmaker	skylarker	termagant	admonisher	clodhopper
ransacker	slanderer	terminist	adulteress	co-operator
rapturist	slobberer	terrorist	adventurer	co-relation
ratepayer	slowcoach	testatrix	aficionado	coadjutant
recipient	slumberer	testifier	alcoranist	coadjutrix
recoverer	smart alec	theorizer	allegorist	cohabitant
rectifier	sniveller	thunderer	Anabaptist	collocutor
redresser	sob sister	toad-eater	ancestress	coloratura
regulator	socialist	tormentor	anecdotist	commonalty
rehearser	socialite	townsfolk	Anglo-Saxon	competitor
reinsurer	sojourner	traitress	Anglophile	complainer
renouncer	solicitor	traveller	Anglophobe	confessant
renovator	son-of-a-gun	traverser	antagonist	confidante
represser	sophister	trepanner	antecessor	contestant
reprobate	sophomore	tribesman	apologizer	controller
requester	Sorbonist	tributary	aristocrat	coparcener
respecter	spectator	trickster	assemblage	copyholder
rhymester	Spinozist	trigamist	assentient	counsellor
ridiculer	spiritist	tritheist	babe-in-arms	countryman
ritualist	spokesman	underling	baby-sitter	crackbrain
roisterer	sportsman	unitarian	bamboozler	criticizer
Romanizer	squabbler	valentine	beautifier	crosspatch
roughneck	stammerer	venerator	bedswerver	curmudgeon
routinist	star pupil	verbalist	Belgravian	daydreamer
rubrician	stargazer	versifier	benefactor	day-tripper
ruminator	stigmatic	Victorian	Benthamite	delinquent
Samaritan	straggler	vigilante	better half	demoiselle
Sassenach	strangler	visionary	big brother	depositary
satellite	stripling	volunteer	black sheep	depository
satisfier	strongman	Vulcanist	blackamoor	deprecator
saunterer	struggler	warmonger	blackguard	depredator
scapegoat	stutterer	warrantee	blasphemer	deputation
scarecrow	subaltern	warrantor	bobbysoxer	descendant
scavenger	submitter	wassailer	bogtrotter	dilettante
scholiast	subverter	whosoever	bold spirit	diminisher
schoolboy	succeeder	womanizer	bootlicker	directress
scoundrel	successor	womankind	borstal boy	discharger
scratcher	succourer	womenfolk	bridegroom	discourser
screwball	suggester	worldling	bridesmaid	discoverer
scribbler	sundowner	wrongdoer	bureaucrat	disparager
scrutator	suppliant	xenophobe	bushranger	dispraiser
sea-lawyer	supporter	yachtsman	campaigner	dissembler
sectarian	surfeiter	young lady	capitalist	distracter
separator	susceptor	youngling	caravanner	distrainer
serenader	sustainer	youngster	card-player	distrainor
sermonist	swaggerer		career girl	dramatizer
sexualist	swallower		centralist	drug addict

drug dealer
drug pusher
dunderhead
dunderpate
Dutch uncle
early riser
elaborator
electorate
elucidator
emblazoner
empiricist
encourager
encroacher
Englishman
enigmatist
enthusiast
enumerator
enunciator
epitaphist
epitomizer
equestrian
evangelist
expurgator
extenuator
extirpator
eye-witness
fabricator
fancy woman
federalist
filibuster
fire-raiser
flagellant
fly-by-night
footballer
footlicker
forefather
forerunner
forty-niner
fosterling
fraternity
fratricide
free-trader
freeholder
frequenter
fuddy-duddy
fund-holder
fund-raiser
gasconader
gastronome
gentlefolk
girl Friday
girlfriend
glacialist
goalkeeper

gold-digger
goodfellow
goody goody
grand juror
grandchild
grande dame
grandmamma
grandniece
grand-uncle
grass widow
great niece
great-uncle
half-sister
harmonizer
hatchet man
head hunter
heliolater
hellraiser
heresiarch
highjacker
highlander
hitch-hiker
human being
iconoclast
identifier
ideologist
idolatress
impenitent
importuner
imprisoner
incendiary
individual
inhabitant
inheritrix
inquisitor
insinuator
instigator
interceder
interferer
interloper
interposer
intervener
introducer
Ishmaelite
jackadandy
jackanapes
Jesus freak
jobbernowl
kith and kin
lady-killer
land-holder
landlubber
languisher
lawbreaker

leading man
left-winger
legitimist
liberty man
licentiate
lieutenant
loggerhead
lotus-eater
lower class
machinator
magnetizer
maiden aunt
maiden lady
malefactor
malingerer
man of straw
manoeuvrer
married man
marshaller
mastermind
matchmaker
merrymaker
metaphrist
Methuselah
middlebrow
militarist
mindreader
misogamist
misogynist
monarchist
moneyed man
monogamist
monologist
monomaniac
monopolist
monotheist
mountebank
mouthpiece
muddied oaf
multiplier
namby-pamby
ne'er-do-well
neutralist
nincompoop
nominalist
non-starter
notability
obstructor
old soldier
opium-eater
originator
orthoepist
out-patient
overturner

paedophile
painstaker
pall-bearer
panegyrist
paraphrast
past master
patronizer
peacemaker
pedestrian
Peeping Tom
pensionary
persecutor
persifleur
personator
petitioner
phenomenon
philistine
pinchpenny
plagiarist
polo player
polygamist
polyhistor
polytheist
population
positivist
pragmatist
pre-Adamite
prima donna
procreator
profligate
progenitor
prohibiter
promenader
pronouncer
propagator
prophesier
propounder
proprietor
prosecutor
Protestant
psychopath
pulverizer
Pyrrhonist
quarreller
questioner
rabblement
ragamuffin
rascallion
Rechabites
recidivist
reclaimant
recognizer
reconciler
reimburser

relinquent
reproacher
reproducer
republican
repudiator
restrainer
restricter
retributor
reverencer
revivalist
rhapsodist
ringleader
sacrificer
scapegrace
Scaramouch
schismatic
scrutineer
secularist
sensualist
separatist
sermonizer
seventh son
shanghaier
shoplifter
sinecurist
smart aleck
sneak thief
snuff-taker
solemnizer
solicitant
solifidian
son and heir
songstress
soothsayer
specialist
speculator
spoilsport
squanderer
starveling
stepfather
stepmother
stepsister
stimulator
stipulator
strategist
street arab
subscriber
substitute
subtracter
subtractor
sugar daddy
supplanter
supplicant
suppressor

surmounter
sweetheart
sworn enemy
syllogizer
syncopator
tale-bearer
tale-teller
tantalizer
taskmaster
tea-drinker
televiewer
temporizer
tenderfoot
textualist
themselves
thickskull
third party
threatener
timeserver
tramontane
transactor
transferee
transmuter
trespasser
troglodyte
troubadour
tub-thumper
tuft-hunter
tweedledee
tweedledum
unbeliever
undertaker
unemployed
upper class
upper crust
utopianist
vacillator
vanquished
vanquisher
vegetarian
vindicator
voluptuary
wallflower
well-wisher
white friar
whomsoever
widow-maker
wine-bibber
wirepuller
withdrawer
withholder
woman-hater
worshipper
yoke-fellow

young blood
Young Fogey
yourselves

11

abbreviator
abecedarian
academician
accompanier
accompanist
accumulator
adventuress
animal lover
aristocracy
association
beachcomber
beauty queen
belligerent
beneficiary
Bible reader
bibliolater
bibliophile
bird's-nester
blackmailer
bloodsucker
blue-eyed boy
blunderhead
bourgeoisie
braggadocio
breadwinner
brotherhood
calumniator
cattle thief
cave-dweller
centenarian
chain-smoker
chance-coiner
cheer leader
cheese parer
child minder
chucklehead
clairvoyant
cognoscenti
co-inheritor
commentator
complainant
condisciple
confiscator
conjecturer
connoisseur
conspirator
constituent
continuator
contributor

co-ordinator
couch potato
country girl
creationist
denominator
denunciator
depopulator
depreciator
diluvialist
dipsomaniac
discipliner
discourager
dishonourer
dissentient
dissertator
distributor
disunionist
doctrinaire
double agent
dram-drinker
drug peddler
eager beaver
electioneer
emancipator
embellisher
embroiderer
enchantress
encounterer
enlightener
enlisted man
enterpriser
entertainer
epigenesist
equilibrist
equivocator
establisher
exaggerator
faggot voter
father-in-law
fault-finder
femme fatale
fifth column
fighting man
first cousin
flat dweller
flying squad
foot soldier
forestaller
foster-child
francophile
francophobe
freethinker
galley slave
gallows bird

gatecrasher
gentlefolks
gentlewoman
ginger group
glue sniffer
god-daughter
gormandizer
grandfather
grandmaster
grandmother
grandnephew
grandparent
grave robber
guttersnipe
half-brother
hard drinker
harum-scarum
helping hand
high society
hobbledehoy
homo sapiens
hyperbolist
hypercritic
ideopraxist
imperialist
inaugurator
inheritress
interceptor
intercessor
interrupter
interviewer
intimidator
joint tenant
knucklehead
leading lady
leaseholder
libertarian
lickspittle
lilliputian
littérateur
living image
lycanthrope
manipulator
marrying-man
masquerader
materialist
matinee idol
maxim-monger
merry Andrew
middle class
millenarian
millionaire
misanthrope
misbeliever

misinformer
monopolizer
moonlighter
mother-in-law
mountaineer
Mrs. Malaprop
name dropper
nationalist
necessarian
neutralizer
night-walker
non-resident
nondescript
nosey-parker
opportunist
owner-driver
pacificator
panic-monger
parishioner
participant
pearly queen
pedobaptist
peripatetic
perpetrator
personality
perturbator
pettifogger
phenomenist
philanderer
philosopher
predecessor
prize-winner
probabilist
probationer
prodigal son
proletarian
proletariat
promulgator
propitiator
prosecutrix
protagonist
protectress
punchinello
punctualist
purgatorian
quacksalver
questionist
rank and file
rapscallion
rationalist
reactionary
recommender
recompenser
religionist

replenisher
reprehender
resuscitant
reversioner
right-winger
Rosicrucian
royal family
rugby player
sabbatarian
sacrilegist
sans-culotte
scaremonger
scoutmaster
scrutinizer
search party
self-made man
shareholder
simple Simon
sister-in-law
sleepwalker
soliloquist
spectatress
speech-maker
spendthrift
spindlelegs
stepbrother
stockholder
stonewaller
stool pigeon
storyteller
stump-orator
subordinate
suffragette
surrenderee
surrenderer
sympathizer
system-maker
systematist
tautologist
teacher's pet
teeny bopper
teetotaller
teleologist
telepathist
temporality
thanksgiver
theosophist
Tommy Atkins
torch-bearer
town-dweller
transferrer
trencherman
trend setter
undersigned

undervaluer
undesirable
Walter Mitty
war criminal
weathercock
wholehogger
withstander

12

abolitionist
acquaintance
advance party
antediluvian
appropriator
artful dodger
assassinator
awkward squad
baby snatcher
bachelor girl
backwoodsman
benefactress
bible-thumper
bibliomaniac
blabbermouth
blood brother
bluestocking
bond-creditor
bottle-washer
bounty hunter
brother-in-law
carpet-knight
chief mourner
church-member
co-respondent
coalitionist
collaborator
Colonel Blimp
commiserator
committeeman
communicator
complimenter
conquistador
conservative
contemplator
contemporary
controverter
convalescent
conventicler
convivialist
cosmopolitan
demimondaine
demonstrator
determinator
dialectician

disciplinant
disenchanter
disorganizer
dispossessor
disseminator
doppelgänger
double-dealer
eavesdropper
educationist
elocutionist
encumbrancer
enfranchiser
equestrienne
exclusionist
excursionist
exhibitioner
experimenter
expostulator
ex-serviceman
extemporizer
extensionist
exterminator
extinguisher
featherbrain
filibusterer
firstnighter
flower people
foster father
foster mother
foster parent
foster sister
foundationer
gastronomist
gesticulator
globe-trotter
grey eminence
guest speaker
hair-splitter
headshrinker
heir-apparent
holidaymaker
humanitarian
impersonator
impoverisher
improvisator
inseparables
intellectual
interlocutor
intermeddler
intermediary
interpolator
interrogator
investigator
kleptomaniac

knight-errant
landed gentry
leading light
legacy-hunter
letter-writer
lounge lizard
mademoiselle
man-about-town
married woman
mezzo-soprano
misinformant
modest violet
money grubber
morris dancer
natural child
near relation
neoplatonist
noctambulist
nonagenarian
obscurantist
octogenarian
old gentleman
paedobaptist
pantophagist
participator
peace-breaker
penitentiary
peregrinator
persona grata
philosophist
pillion-rider
poet laureate
poor relation
postdiluvian
postgraduate
pot-companion
precipitator
prevaricator
primogenitor
proprietress
proselytizer
public figure
quater-cousin
recriminator
redemptioner
relinquisher
remonstrator
residentiary
resolutioner
resuscitator
right-hand man
roller-skater
rolling stone
rough diamond

salvationist
scatterbrain
schoolfellow
second cousin
second fiddle
sequestrator
serial killer
sexagenarian
significator
single person
sister-german
sole occupant
somnambulist
somniloquist
spirit-rapper
spiritualist
stepdaughter
stormtrooper
straightener
street-urchin
stuffed shirt
sub-committee
sublapsarian
Sunday driver
swashbuckler
sworn enemies
system-monger
systematizer
theologaster
transgressor
transmigrant
transvestite
troublemaker
truce-breaker
ugly customer
ugly duckling
ultramontane
undermanager
unemployable
universalist
velocipedist
village idiot
wool gatherer
working class

13

administrator
Anglo-American
Anglo-Catholic
angry young man

annexationist
anthropophagi
antisocialist
bibliophilist
blood relation
brother-german
bureaucratist
castle-builder
child molester
co-religionist
conceptualist
conspiratress
correspondent
country cousin
daughter-in-law
deck passenger
deipnosophist
deserving poor
deuterogamist
devotionalist
discriminator
distinguisher
double crosser
exhibitionist
experimentist
first offender
foot passenger
fortune-hunter
foster brother
fresh-air fiend
good Samaritan
grand-daughter
guardian angel
hard bargainer
high churchman
hypochondriac
immaterialist
individualist
infant prodigy
irreligionist
Job's comforter
lady bountiful
latchkey child
laughing stock
life-annuitant
lunatic fringe
Machiavellian
millennialist
miracle-worker
misanthropist

mischief-maker
necessitarian
nonconformist
paterfamilias
perfectionist
philhellenist
philosophizer
predestinator
protectionist
proverbialist
revolutionary
rough customer
scandalmonger
social climber
speed merchant
spindleshanks
spiritualizer
state prisoner
strike-breaker
transmigrator
undergraduate
understrapper
wheeler dealer

14

armchair critic
backseat driver
beat generation
billiard-player
disciplinarian
disenchantress
doubting Thomas
elder statesman
foster daughter
galactophagist
good-for-nothing
ichthyophagist
improvisatrice
indifferentist
latitudinarian
male chauvinist
man in the street
matron of honour
ministerialist
misinterpreter
obstructionist
petit bourgeois
philanthropist
procrastinator
prognosticator

progressionist
prohibitionist
promise-breaker
psilanthropist
quadragenarian
requisitionist
restorationist
sabbath-breaker
Sacramentarian
salt of the earth
sensationalist
sentimentalist
septuagenarian
squandermaniac
stamp-collector
superior person
tatterdemalion
traditionalist
trencher-friend
troubleshooter
ultramontanist
undergraduette
valetudinarian
waifs-and-strays
weather prophet
whippersnapper

15

ambulance chaser
antitrinitarian
autograph hunter
circumnavigator
conservationist
cuckoo in the nest
emancipationist
experimentalist
flibbertigibbet
heir-presumptive
insurrectionary
insurrectionist
intellectualist
little Englander
manic depressive
snake in the grass
supernaturalist
Tom, Dick and Harry
tower of strength

Professions, occupations, trade, etc.

2 – 4	5	reeve	carter	hodman	priest
alma	actor	scout	carver	hooper	pruner
amah	ad-man	sewer	casual	hosier	purser
ayah	agent	shoer	clergy	hunter	querry
babu	augur	slave	cleric	intern	ragman
bard	baker	smith	coiner	issuer	ranger
boss	bobby	sower	con man	jailer	ratter
char	bonze	staff	coolie	jailor	reader
chef	boots	swami	cooper	jobber	reaper
cook	bosun	sweep	copper	jockey	rector
crew	caddy	tamer	coster	joiner	regent
diva	choir	taxer	cowboy	jurist	relief
doc	clerk	taxer	cowman	keeper	renter
don	clown	thief	critic	lackey	rigger
dyer	coach	tiler	cutler	lascar	robber
gang	comic	tuner	cutter	lawyer	roofer
G.P.	crier	tutor	dacoit	lector	rozzer
grip	crimp	ulmah	dancer	lender	runner
gyp	curer	usher	dealer	loader	sailor
hack	daily	valet	digger	lumper	salter
hand	dhobi	**6**	docker	master	salvor
head	envoy		doctor	matron	sartor
herd	extra	airman	dowser	medico	sawyer
hind	fakir	archer	draper	mender	scribe
lead	fence	artist	driver	menial	sea-dog
magi	fifer	aurist	drover	mentor	sealer
maid	filer	author	editor	mercer	seaman
mate	flier	bagman	factor	milker	seiner
M.D.	gipsy	bailee	farmer	miller	seizor
mime	gluer	bailor	fellah	minter	seller
M.O.	groom	bandit	fisher	monger	server
P.A.	guard	banker	fitter	mummer	setter
page	guide	barber	flayer	mystic	sexton
P.C.	guild	bargee	forger	notary	shrink
peon	gypsy	barker	fowler	oboist	shroff
P.M.	hakim	barman	framer	oilman	singer
poet	helot	batman	fuller	orator	skivvy
pro	hirer	bearer	gaffer	ostler	slaver
P.R.O.	leech	beggar	ganger	packer	slavey
rep	mason	binder	gaoler	parson	sleuth
ryot	medic	boffin	gaucho	pastor	snarer
seer	miner	bookie	gauger	pedant	sorter
serf	model	bowman	gilder	pedlar	souter
spy	navvy	brewer	gillie	penman	squire
syce	nurse	broker	glazer	picker	stager
thug	oiler	bugler	glover	pieman	stoker
tout	payer	bursar	graver	pirate	storer
vet	pilot	busker	grocer	pitman	sutler
ward	piper	butler	gunner	plater	tailor
whip	pupil	cabbie	hatter	porter	tanner
	quack	cabman	hawker	potboy	taster
		canner	healer	potter	teller
		carman			

tester
tiller
tinker
tinman
tinner
touter
tracer
trader
troupe
turner
tycoon
typist
usurer
vacher
vanman
vassal
vender
vendor
verger
viewer
waiter
warden
warder
weaver
weeder
welder
whaler
worker
wright
writer

7

abigail
acolyte
acrobat
actress
actuary
alewife
almoner
analyst
Arabist
arbiter
artisan
artiste
assayer
auditor
aviator
bailiff
barmaid
bellboy
bellhop
birdman
blender
boatman

bondman
bookman
bottler
bouncer
brigand
builder
burglar
butcher
buttons
callboy
cambist
carrier
cashier
cateran
caterer
caulker
cellist
chanter
chapman
chemist
cleaner
clicker
clippie
co-agent
co-pilot
coalman
cobbler
collier
copyist
coroner
corsair
counsel
courier
cowherd
cowpoke
crofter
cropper
curator
currier
danseur
dentist
ditcher
dominie
doorman
drayman
dresser
drummer
dustman
exegete
famulus
farrier
fiddler
fireman
flesher

florist
flunkey
flutist
footboy
footman
footpad
foreman
founder
friseur
frogman
furrier
gateman
glazier
gleaner
gleeman
grafter
granger
grazier
grinder
gymnast
hackler
harpist
haulier
herbist
herdman
higgler
hogherd
hostler
indexer
inlayer
janitor
juggler
junkman
knacker
knitter
laborer
linkboy
linkman
mailman
maltman
manager
marbler
mariner
marshal
matador
matelot
midwife
milkman
modiste
moulder
newsboy
oculist
orderly
packman

pageboy
painter
palmist
peddler
pianist
picador
planner
planter
pleader
plumber
poacher
poetess
pop star
postboy
postman
presser
printer
puddler
rancher
realtor
refiner
rentboy
riveter
roadman
rustler
saddler
sampler
samurai
scourer
servant
settler
sharper
shearer
shipper
shopboy
shopman
showman
shunter
skinner
skipper
smelter
socager
soldier
soloist
spencer
spinner
spotter
stamper
stapler
statist
steerer
steward
surgeon
swabber

sweeper
taborer
tallier
tapster
taxi-man
teacher
tipster
tracker
trainer
trapper
trimmer
trucker
trustee
tumbler
turnkey
vintner
violist
wagoner
warrior
webster
weigher
whetter
wireman
woodman
woolman
workman
wrapper

8

aeronaut
analyser
annalist
aphorist
apiarist
arborist
armorist
armourer
assessor
attorney
bagpiper
bandsman
bargeman
bedmaker
bleacher
boatsman
bondmaid
bondsman
boniface
brewster
cabin boy
callgirl
cellarer
ceramist
chandler

choirboy
clothier
coachman
co-author
codifier
collator
comedian
compiler
composer
conclave
conjurer
conjuror
coryphée
courtier
coxswain
croupier
cutpurse
dairyman
danseuse
deckhand
designer
director
domestic
doughboy
dragoman
druggist
editress
educator
embalmer
emissary
employee
employer
engineer
engraver
enroller
epic poet
essayist
examiner
exorcist
explorer
exporter
fabulist
factotum
falconer
farmhand
ferryman
figurant
film star
fishwife
flatfoot
flautist
fletcher
forester
gangster

gardener	milliner	salesman	watchman	chauffeur
gendarme	minister	satirist	waterman	cheapjack
glassman	minstrel	sawbones	wet nurse	chorister
goatherd	mistress	scullion	whaleman	clergyman
governor	modeller	sculptor	wigmaker	clinician
guardian	muleteer	sea-rover	winnower	clogmaker
gunsmith	musician	seamster	wool-dyer	coalminer
hammerer	neatherd	seedsman	workfolk	collector
handmaid	newshawk	sempster	wrestler	colourist
handyman	novelist	servitor		columnist
hatmaker	operator	shepherd	**9**	comprador
haymaker	optician	ship's boy		concierge
head cook	ordinand	shipmate	alchemist	conductor
headsman	organist	shopgirl	anatomist	conserver
helmsman	outrider	showgirl	annotator	cosmonaut
henchman	overseer	sidesman	announcer	cost clerk
herdsman	pargeter	sketcher	arbitress	costumier
hired man	parodist	smuggler	archeress	courtesan
hireling	penmaker	soldiery	architect	couturier
home help	perfumer	sorcerer	archivist	cowkeeper
hotelier	peterman	spaceman	art critic	cracksman
houseboy	pewterer	spearman	art dealer	craftsman
huckster	picaroon	speedcop	artificer	crayonist
huntsman	picklock	spurrier	astronaut	cymbalist
importer	pinmaker	stockman	attendant	daily help
improver	plagiary	storeman	authoress	dairymaid
inkmaker	polisher	stripper	balladeer	decorator
inventor	portress	stuntman	ballerina	decretist
japanner	potmaker	supplier	bank agent	desk clerk
jet pilot	preacher	surveyor	barrister	detective
jeweller	pressman	swindler	barrow boy	die-sinker
jongleur	procurer	tabourer	beefeater	dietitian
kipperer	promoter	tallyman	beekeeper	directrix
labourer	prompter	taverner	berserker	dispenser
landgirl	psalmist	teamster	biologist	dissector
landlady	publican	thatcher	Boanerges	distiller
landlord	pugilist	thespian	boatswain	doctoress
lapidary	purveyor	thresher	bodyguard	draftsman
Latinist	quarrier	tin miner	boilerman	dramatist
leadsman	raftsman	tinsmith	bondslave	drysalter
lecturer	ranchero	tipstaff	bondwoman	ecologist
linesman	rapparee	toymaker	bookmaker	embezzler
magician	receiver	tripeman	bootblack	enameller
magister	recorder	truckman	bootmaker	engineman
maltster	regrater	tutoress	buccaneer	engrosser
manciple	repairer	unionist	bus driver	errand boy
masseuse	reporter	valuator	cab driver	estimator
mechanic	restorer	vintager	café owner	examinant
medalist	retailer	virtuoso	cameraman	exchanger
melodist	retainer	vocalist	caretaker	exciseman
merchant	reviewer	waitress	carpenter	executive
milkmaid	rewriter	walker-on	catechist	exorcizer
millgirl	romancer	wardress	cellarman	eye doctor
millhand	rugmaker	warrener	chanteuse	fabricant
			charwoman	

39

fan dancer	lacquerer	physician	signalman	**10**
fashioner	lady's maid	physicist	Sinologue	
felt-maker	lampooner	planisher	soapmaker	able seaman
figurante	land agent	plasterer	solicitor	accoucheur
film actor	lap dancer	ploughboy	sonneteer	accountant
film extra	larcenist	ploughman	sorceress	advertiser
film-maker	launderer	pluralist	soubrette	aerologist
financier	laundress	poetaster	space crew	agrologist
fire-eater	legionary	pointsman	spiderman	agronomist
fish-curer	librarian	policeman	stableboy	air hostess
fish-woman	linotyper	pontonier	stableman	air steward
fisherman	lion-tamer	pop artist	stagehand	algebraist
flag-maker	liveryman	porteress	stationer	amanuensis
flyfisher	loan agent	portrayer	steersman	apothecary
freelance	lockmaker	postilion	stevedore	apple-woman
freighter	locksmith	postwoman	subeditor	apprentice
fruiterer	log-roller	poulterer	subworker	arbalester
furbisher	lumberman	precentor	succentor	arbalister
furnisher	machinist	preceptor	swineherd	arbitrator
gas fitter	major-domo	predicant	switchman	astrologer
gazetteer	male model	prelector	swordsman	astronomer
gem-cutter	male nurse	priestess	syndicate	auctioneer
geologist	man-at-arms	privateer	tablemaid	audit clerk
gladiator	mannequin	professor	tactician	ballet girl
gluemaker	medallist	publicist	tailoress	balloonist
goldsmith	mendicant	publisher	tap dancer	ballplayer
gondolier	mercenary	pulpiteer	tea-taster	bandmaster
gospeller	mesmerist	puppeteer	tentmaker	bank robber
governess	messenger	quarryman	test pilot	bassoonist
guitarist	metrician	racketeer	therapist	beadswoman
gun-runner	middleman	railmaker	theurgist	beautician
harlequin	mill-owner	recruiter	tire-woman	bell-ringer
harpooner	modelgirl	rehearser	toolsmith	bibliopole
harvester	mortician	ribbonman	town clerk	bill-broker
herb-woman	muffin-man	roadmaker	town crier	billposter
herbalist	musketeer	ropemaker	tradesman	biochemist
hired hand	musketoon	roundsman	tragedian	biographer
hired help	navigator	ruddleman	traveller	blacksmith
historian	negotiant	rum-runner	treasurer	blockmaker
homeopath	net-surfer	sacristan	trepanner	bluejacket
hop-picker	newsagent	safemaker	trumpeter	bombardier
hosteller	nursemaid	sailmaker	tympanist	bondswoman
housemaid	odd job man	scavenger	usherette	bonesetter
hygienist	office boy	scenarist	varnisher	bookbinder
hypnotist	operative	scholiast	versifier	bookkeeper
incumbent	orchestra	schoolman	vexillary	bookseller
innholder	osteopath	scientist	violinist	bootlegger
inscriber	otologist	scrivener	voltigeur	bricklayer
inspector	outfitter	sea-robber	washerman	bureaucrat
intendant	pantaloon	secretary	waxworker	butterwife
ironsmith	part-timer	ship's mate	winemaker	career girl
itinerant	paymaster	shipowner	zookeeper	cartoonist
kennelman	pedagogue	shoeblack	zoologist	cartwright
lacemaker	performer	shoemaker	zootomist	cat breeder

cat burglar
ceramicist
chargehand
charioteer
chirurgeon
chorus girl
chronicler
chucker-out
circuiteer
clapper boy
clockmaker
clog dancer
cloth maker
co-assessor
coachmaker
coalheaver
coastguard
colporteur
comedienne
compositor
contractor
controller
copyholder
copywriter
cordwainer
counsellor
customs man
cytologist
delineator
directress
disc jockey
dishwasher
dispatcher
dockmaster
dog breeder
dog-fancier
doorkeeper
dramaturge
dressmaker
drummer-boy
dry cleaner
enamellist
epitaphist
evangelist
eye-servant
fell monger
fictionist
film editor
firemaster
fishmonger
flight crew
flowergirl
folk singer
folk-dancer

forecaster
frame-maker
freebooter
fund raiser
game warden
gamekeeper
geisha girl
geneticist
geographer
glee-singer
gold-beater
gold-digger
grammarian
gunslinger
hall porter
handmaiden
harvestman
head porter
head waiter
highwayman
horn player
horologist
house agent
huckstress
husbandman
inoculator
institutor
instructor
ironmonger
ironworker
journalist
journeyman
kennelmaid
land-holder
laundryman
law officer
legislator
librettist
lighterman
lime-burner
linotypist
liquidator
lobsterman
lock-keeper
lumberjack
magistrate
management
manageress
manicurist
manservant
matchmaker
meat-hawker
medical man
militiaman

millwright
missionary
moonshiner
naturalist
nautch girl
negotiator
news editor
newscaster
newsreader
newsvendor
night nurse
nosologist
nurseryman
obituarist
oil painter
orchardist
osteologer
overlooker
panegyrist
pantrymaid
park-keeper
pastry-cook
pathfinder
pawnbroker
pearl-diver
pedicurist
penologist
perruquier
pharmacist
philologer
piano tuner
pickpocket
platelayer
playwright
politician
postillion
postmaster
prima donna
private eye
procurator
programmer
proprietor
prospector
quiz-master
railwayman
rat catcher
recitalist
researcher
ringmaster
roadmender
rope dancer
roughrider
safeblower
sales force

saleswoman
schoolmarm
scrutineer
sculptress
sea-captain
seamstress
seminarist
serving-man
sexologist
ship-broker
shipmaster
shipwright
shopfitter
shopkeeper
shopwalker
signwriter
silk-mercer
silk-weaver
Sinologist
slop seller
sneak thief
spin doctor
staff nurse
stewardess
stocktaker
stonemason
strategist
superviser
symphonist
tally clerk
taskmaster
taxi-dancer
taxi-driver
tea planter
tea-blender
technician
technocrat
theologian
theologist
timekeeper
tractarian
trade union
traffic cop
trafficker
tram-driver
translator
trawlerman
treasuress
troubadour
typesetter
undertaker
veterinary
victualler
vinegrower

vivandiere
wage-earner
wainwright
watchmaker
wharfinger
wholesaler
wine-waiter
winegrower
wireworker
woodcarver
woodcutter
woodworker
wool-carder
wool-comber
wool-grower
wool-sorter
wool-trader
wool-worker
workfellow
working man
workmaster
workpeople
yardmaster
zinc-worker
zymologist

11

accompanist
accoucheuse
acoustician
adjudicator
allopathist
annunciator
antiquarian
apple-grower
arbitratrix
army officer
arquebusier
artillerist
audio typist
auscultator
bag-snatcher
bank cashier
bank manager
bargemaster
basketmaker
beachcomber
bell-founder
Benedictine
bill-sticker
bird-catcher
bird-fancier
bird-watcher
boatbuilder

body servant
boilermaker
boilersmith
bondservant
broadcaster
bullfighter
businessman
candlemaker
car salesman
cat's-meat-man
cattle thief
chair-mender
chalk-cutter
chambermaid
chiffonnier
chiromancer
chiropodist
choirmaster
chronologer
coffin-maker
cognoscente
condisciple
condottiere
conductress
confederate
congressman
consecrator
conservator
constituent
conveyancer
coppersmith
cosmogonist
cosmologist
crane driver
cub reporter
cypher clerk
day-labourer
delivery man
demographer
dhobi wallah
dispensator
draughtsman
duty officer
electrician
embroiderer
entertainer
estate agent
ethnologist
etymologist
executioner
extortioner
face-painter
factory hand
faith healer

field worker
filing clerk
fire brigade
fire insurer
flax-dresser
fourbisseur
fruit picker
funambulist
galley-slave
genealogist
ghostwriter
glass-bender
glass-blower
glass-cutter
glass-worker
gouvernante
grass-cutter
grave-digger
greengrocer
haberdasher
hagiologist
hair stylist
hairdresser
head foreman
hierologist
histologist
horse doctor
horse trader
hospitaller
hotel-keeper
housekeeper
housemaster
housemother
hymnologist
illuminator
illusionist
illustrator
infantryman
interpreter
interviewer
iron-founder
ivory-carver
ivory-worker
kitchenmaid
lamplighter
land steward
laundrymaid
leading lady
ledger clerk
lifeboatman
lightkeeper
linen draper
lithologist
lithotomist

lollipop man
lorry driver
madrigalist
maidservant
master baker
mechanician
medicine man
memorialist
metal worker
miniaturist
money-broker
money-lender
monographer
mule-skinner
music critic
music master
mythologist
necrologist
necromancer
needlewoman
neurologist
night porter
night sister
nightworker
nomenclator
numismatist
office staff
onion-seller
opera singer
ophiologist
orientalist
orthopedist
osteologist
pamphleteer
panel-beater
pantomimist
paperhanger
parish clerk
parlourmaid
pathologist
pearl fisher
pedobaptist
penny-a-liner
petrologist
pettifogger
philatelist
philologist
phonologist
phytologist
piece worker
polyphonist
pork butcher
portraitist
preceptress

print-seller
probationer
promulgator
proofreader
property man
proprietrix
quacksalver
radiologist
rag merchant
rhetorician
roadsweeper
safebreaker
sandwich man
saxòphonist
scoutmaster
scrapdealer
secret agent
seditionary
servant girl
serving-maid
share-broker
sheepfarmer
shepherdess
ship's master
shipbreaker
shipbuilder
shop steward
silversmith
slaughterer
slave-driver
slave-trader
slaveholder
smallholder
sociologist
stake-holder
steeplejack
stereotyper
stipendiary
stockbroker
stockjobber
stonecutter
storekeeper
stripteaser
taxidermist
telegrapher
telephonist
ticket agent
toastmaster
tobacconist
topographer
torch-bearer
town planner
toxophilite
tragedienne

train-bearer
transcriber
transporter
travel agent
type-founder
typographer
underletter
underwriter
upholsterer
versemonger
vinedresser
washerwoman
watchkeeper
wax-chandler
wheelwright
witch-doctor
woman doctor
wool-stapler
xylophonist

12

accordionist
actor manager
ambulance man
anaesthetist
archeologist
artilleryman
artist's model
ballad singer
ballad-monger
ballet dancer
ballet master
bantamweight
bibliologist
bibliopegist
bibliopolist
body-snatcher
booking clerk
bus conductor
cabinet-maker
calligrapher
camp follower
caricaturist
carpet-bagger
carpet-fitter
cartographer
casual labour
cerographist
cheesemonger
chief cashier
chimney-sweep
chiropractor
chronologist
churchwarden

circuit rider
civil servant
clarinettist
clerk of works
cloth-shearer
coach-builder
coleopterist
commissioner
conchologist
confectioner
corn chandler
cosmographer
costermonger
craniologist
cryptogamist
dance hostess
deep-sea diver
demonologist
demonstrator
dendrologist
dramaturgist
ecclesiastic
Egyptologist
elecutionist
engine-driver
entomologist
entrepreneur
escapologist
ethnographer
experimenter
family doctor
farm labourer
film director
film producer
first officer
flying doctor
footplateman
geometrician
geriatrician
glass-grinder
glossologist
greasemonkey
gynecologist
hagiographer
harness-maker
head gardener
headshrinker
homeopathist
horse-breaker
hotel manager
house steward
house surgeon
housebreaker
housepainter

hydrographer
hydropathist
hypothecator
immunologist
instructress
invoice clerk
jerry-builder
joint-trustee
jurisconsult
juvenile lead
king's counsel
knife-grinder
knife-thrower
labouring man
leader-writer
legal adviser
lexicologist
lithographer
lollipop lady
longshoreman
loss adjuster
maître d'hôtel
make-up artist
malacologist
man of letters
manual worker
manufacturer
mass producer
master singer
metallurgist
mezzo-soprano
microscopist
mineralogist
miscellanist
money-changer
monographist
morris dancer
musicologist
mythographer
newspaperman
notary public
nutritionist
obstetrician
office junior
oneirocritic
orchestrator
organ-grinder
orthodontist
orthographer
ovariotomist
papyrologist
pattern-maker
pediatrician
photographer

phrenologist
physiologist
plant manager
ploughwright
plumber's mate
pornographer
postmistress
practitioner
press officer
prison warder
prize-fighter
professional
propagandist
proprietress
psychiatrist
psychologist
publicity man
pupil-teacher
puppet-master
pyrotechnist
quarry master
racing driver
radiographer
receptionist
remembrancer
restaurateur
riding-master
right-hand man
sales manager
scene-painter
scene-shifter
schoolmaster
screenwriter
scriptwriter
scullery-maid
seafaring man
seed-merchant
seismologist
sharecropper
sharpshooter
ship chandler
ship's husband
shoe-repairer
silver-beater
site engineer
slaughterman
snake-charmer
social worker
soil mechanic
special agent
speechwriter
spice-blender
sportscaster
sportswriter

stage manager
statistician
steel erector
stenographer
stonebreaker
stonedresser
street-trader
street-walker
sugar-refiner
tax-collector
technologist
telegraph boy
telegraphist
test engineer
therapeutist
thief-catcher
timber trader
toll-gatherer
tourist agent
toxicologist
tradespeople
transplanter
trichologist
trick cyclist
undermanager
underservant
veterinarian
waiting-woman
warehouseman
water diviner
wine merchant
wood-engraver
works manager
zincographer

13

administrator
agriculturist
antique dealer
arachnologist
archaeologist
arithmetician
articled clerk
Assyriologist
barber-surgeon
bibliographer
calico-printer
campanologist
chartographer
chicken-farmer
choreographer
chronographer
civil engineer
clearstarcher

coffee-planter
contortionist
contrabandist
cotton-spinner
counterfeiter
cryptographer
dancing master
dental surgeon
dermatologist
diagnostician
diamond-cutter
district nurse
draughtswoman
drawing-master
dress designer
drill sergeant
electroplater
encyclopedist
epigrammatist
estate manager
exhibitionist
family butcher
fencing-master
fortune-teller
freight-broker
glossographer
gynaecologist
harbour master
health visitor
hieroglyphist
hospital nurse
ichthyologist
industrialist
intelligencer
joint-executor
lady in waiting
lexicographer
lift attendant
lighthouse-man
maid-of-all-work
master builder
master mariner
mathematician
melodramatist
metaphysician
meteorologist
music mistress
night-watchman
office manager
old-clothes-man
ornithologist
orthographist
park attendant

pharmaceutist
physiognomist
physiographer
police officer
poultry farmer
printer's devil
prison visitor
privateersman
process-server
psalmographer
psychoanalyst
pteridologist
public speaker
queen's counsel
racing-tipster
rag and bone man
revolutionary
revolutionist
rubber-planter
sailing master
schoolteacher
science master
scrap merchant
ship's chandler
shop assistant
singing-master
station-master
stenographist
stereoscopist
stethoscopist
street-sweeper
sub-contractor
superintender
supernumerary
thaumaturgist
thimble-rigger
toll collector
trade unionist
traffic warden
tram conductor
tramcar-driver
ventriloquist
violoncellist
window-cleaner
window-dresser
woollen-draper

14

administratrix
anthropologist
autobiographer
bacteriologist
ballet mistress

billiard-player
black marketeer
casual labourer
charcoal burner
chimney-sweeper
citizen-soldier
classics master
clerical worker
colour sergeant
commissionaire
dancing partner
discount-broker
ecclesiologist
educationalist
encyclopaedist
exchange-broker
features editor
gentleman usher
grammaticaster
handicraftsman
heresiographer
horticulturist
house decorator
house furnisher
king's messenger
language master
leather-dresser
maintenance man
manual labourer
market-gardener
marriage broker
medical officer
merchant-tailor
mining engineer
miscellanarian
mother-superior
music publisher
nursing officer
pharmacologist
pneumatologist
prison governor
psalmographist
reception clerk
representative
schoolmistress
ship's-carpenter
siderographist
spectacle-maker
spectroscopist
sports reporter
station manager
store detective
street musician

superintendent
systems analyst
tallow chandler
troubleshooter
turf accountant
water-colourist
weather prophet

15

arboriculturist
assistant master
Bow Street runner
crossing-sweeper
crustaceologist
customs official
dancing mistress
diamond merchant
domestic servant
forwarding agent
funeral director
gentleman-farmer
gossip columnist
hackney coachman
heart specialist
helminthologist
hierogrammatist
historiographer
instrumentalist
insurance broker
jack-of-all-trades
musical director
numismatologist
ophthalmologist
palaeontologist
planning officer
platform-speaker
police constable
police inspector
portrait-painter
prestidigitator
professional man
programme seller
queen's messenger
railway engineer
resurrectionist
shorthand typist
sleeping partner
stretcher-bearer
ticket collector
tightrope walker
tonsorial artist
undercover agent

DOMESTIC
Clothes and materials

3

aba
abb
alb
bag
bib
boa
bra
cap
cop
cut
dye
fez
fur
hat
hem
kid
kit
lap
lei
mac
nap
net
obi
pin
PVC
rag
rep
rig
tag
tam
tee
tie
top
wig
zip

4

band
barb
batt
bead
belt
bias
boot
brim
burr
cape
clog
coat
coif
comb
cony
cope
cord
cowl
cuff
dart
down
drag
duck
duds
felt
fold
frog
garb
gear
geta
gimp
gore
gown
haik
heel
hide
hood
hoop
hose
jute
képi
kilt
knot
lace
lamé
lawn
leno
list
mask
maud
maxi
mesh
midi
mini
mink
mitt
mode
moff
muff
mule
mull
peak
pelt
poke
pump
repp
ring
robe
ruff
sack
sari
sark
sash
seam
shag
shoe
silk
slip
sock
sole
spur
stud
suit
tank
toga
togs
topi
trim
tuck
tutu
vamp
veil
vent
vest
warp
wear
weft
wool
wrap
yarn
yoke

5

baize
batik
beige
beret
boots
braid
busby
camis
chain
chaps
chino
cloak
clogs
cloth
clout
cotta
crape
crash
crêpe
cymar
denim
dhoti
dicky
dress
drill
ducks
ephod
ermin
fanon
fichu
fogle
frill
frock
gauze
get-up
gilet
glove
gunny
habit
hanky
heels
ihram
inkie
jabot
jeans
jupon
kapok
khaki
lacet
lapel
Levis
linen
liner
lisle
lungi
lurex
manta
mitre
mitts
moiré
mufti
mules
mutch
nappy
ninon
nylon
Orlon
orris
pants
parka
pique
plaid
plait
pleat
plume
plush
print
pumps
purse
rayon
robes
romal
ruche
rumal
sable
sabot
sagum
satin
scarf
serge
shako
shawl
sheer
shift
shirt
shoes
skirt
slops
smock
snood
spats
stays
stock
stole
stuff
suede
surah
tabby
tails
talma
tammy
terry
thrum
tiara
tibet
toile
topee
toque
train
trews
tulle
tunic
tweed
twill
V-neck
voile
weeds
welly
wigan

6

afghan
alpaca
angora
anklet
anorak
armlet
attire
banian
barège
barret
basque
beaver
bertha
biggin
bikini
blazer
blouse
boater
bob-wig
bodice
bolero
bonnet
bootee
bouclé
bow tie
bowler
braces

briefs
brogan
brogue
brolly
buckle
bum bag
burlap
burnet
buskin
bustle
button
byssus
caftan
calash
calico
camlet
canvas
capote
castor
cestus
chimer
chinos
chintz
chiton
choker
chopin
cilice
cloche
coatee
collar
collet
corset
cotton
cravat
crepon
crewel
curler
Dacron
damask
denier
diadem
diaper
dimity
dirndl
doiman
domett
domino
dowlas
duffel
ear-cap
edging
ermine
fabric
fag-end

faille
fedora
ferret
fillet
flares
fleece
fox-fur
frieze
fringe
gaiter
galosh
garter
girdle
guimpe
gurrah
gusset
hankie
hatpin
helmet
humhum
insole
jacket
jerkin
jersey
joseph
jubbah
jumper
kaftan
kersey
kimono
kirtle
lappet
lining
livery
madras
mantle
mantua
merino
mitten
mobcap
mohair
moreen
muslin
nankin
nutria
nylons
Oxford
Panama
parure
patent
patten
peltry
peplum
peruke

pleats
pomade
pompom
poncho
pongee
poplin
puttee
PVC mac
raglan
ratine
rebato
reefer
riband
ribbon
rigout
rochet
ruffle
russet

7

samite
sandal
sarong
satara
sateen
sendal
sequin
serape
shades
sheath
shoddy
shorts
shroud
ski cap
slacks
sleeve
smalls
sunhat
T-shirt
tabard
tartan
thibet
thread
tiepin
tights
tippet
tissue
top-hat
topper
torque
toupee
toupet
Tricel
tricot
trilby
trunks

tucker
turban
tussah
tuxedo
tweeds
ulster
velure
velvet
visite
waders
wampus
weeper
whites
wimple
wincey
woolly

7

Acrilan
acrylic
alamode
apparel
armband
art-silk
baldric
bandeau
batiste
biretta
blanket
blucher
bottine
brocade
brogans
buckram
burnous
cagoule
calotte
cambric
capuche
cassock
casuals
challis
chamois
chapeau
chaplet
chemise
chiffon
chimere
chlamys
civvies
clobber
clothes
coating
cockade

compact
coronet
corsage
costume
couture
cow-hide
crochet
culotte
cut-away
delaine
doeskin
doublet
drabbet
drawers
drip-dry
elastic
epaulet
falsies
felt hat
felting
fig leaf
filibeg
flannel
flat hat
flounce
foulard
frounce
fur coat
fustian
G-string
gaiters
galloon
garment
gingham
grogram
guipure
gumboot
gymslip
handbag
hat-band
hessian
hoggers
hogskin
holland
homburg
hopsack
hosiery
jaconet
lasting
latchet
layette
leather
legging
leghorn

leotard
loafers
mae west
maniple
mascara
Mechlin
miniver
modiste
monocle
montero
morocco
mozetta
mudpack
muffler
nacarat
nankeen
necktie
new look
nightie
non-iron
oilskin
organdy
organza
Orleans
orphrey
outsize
overall
padding
paisley
pajamas
paletot
pallium
panties
parasol
partlet
pattens
pegtops
pelisse
percale
periwig
petasus
pigskin
pillbox
pork-pie
pugaree
puttees
pyjamas
raiment
rompers
rosette
rubbers
sacking
satinet
sayette

scarlet	barracan	facepack	nainsook	sundress	comforter
silesia	bathrobe	Fair Isle	neckband	sunshade	Courtelle
silk hat	bearskin	fatigues	neckline	surplice	crinoline
singlet	bed linen	fillibeg	négligée	swanskin	Cuban heel
slicker	bedsocks	flannels	nightcap	swimsuit	cufflinks
slip-ons	berretta	footwear	nose ring	tabbinet	dalmatica
slipper	black tie	frilling	oilcloth	tailcoat	décolleté
soutane	bloomers	frippery	opera hat	tapestry	djellabah
spencer	bluchers	frontlet	organdie	tarboosh	dog collar
sporran	boat-neck	froufrou	osnaburg	tarlatan	drainpipe
stammel	bobbinet	furbelow	overalls	Terylene	dress coat
stetson	body-belt	galoshes	overcoat	trimming	dress suit
suiting	bonelace	gambeson	overshoe	trousers	duffel bag
sunsuit	bootlace	gambroon	paduasoy	two-piece	dungarees
surcoat	bottines	gauntlet	peignoir	umbrella	epaulette
surtout	breeches	glad rags	pelerine	vestment	fermillet
sweater	brodekin	gold lace	piccadil	war paint	fingering
tabaret	buckskin	gold lamé	pinafore	wardrobe	fleshings
tabinet	Burberry	gossamer	playsuit	whipcord	flipflops
taffeta	cameline	gumboots	plumelet	white tie	floss silk
tarbush	camisole	gymshoes	polo-neck	woollens	forage cap
tatting	capuchin	half-hose	ponyskin	wristlet	frockcoat
tea-gown	cardigan	hand-knit	prunella	zoot suit	full dress
textile	cashmere	headband	pullover		full skirt
ticking	Celanese	headgear	rag trade	**9**	fur collar
tiffany	chasuble	high heel	raincoat	Alice band	gabardine
top coat	chausses	hipsters	reticule	ankle-boot	gaberdine
top-boot	chenille	homespun	sandshoe	astrakhan	gambadoes
top-knot	cincture	hot pants	sarcenet	baby linen	garibaldi
topless	cloaking	jackboot	scapular	balaclava	gauntlets
tricorn	cloth cap	Jacquard	sealskin	bandolier	georgette
tunicle	clothing	jodhpurs	shagreen	beachwear	Glengarry
turn-ups	coiffure	jump suit	shalloon	bedjacket	greatcoat
tussore	collaret	kerchief	Shantung	billycock	grenadine
twinset	corduroy	knickers	sheeting	blond lace	grosgrain
undress	cordwain	knitwear	shirring	blue jeans	haircloth
uniform	corporal	lambskin	shirting	bombazine	hairpiece
vandyke	corselet	leggings	shoe horn	bowler hat	hairshift
velours	cosmetic	lingerie	shoelace	brassiere	headdress
vesting	creepers	lip salve	shot silk	broadbrim	headscarf
vesture	cretonne	lipstick	ski boots	bushshirt	high heels
webbing	crew-neck	lustring	ski pants	calamanco	hip pocket
wellies	culottes	mackinaw	skullcap	camelhair	hoop skirt
wetsuit	dalmatic	mantelet	slippers	caparison	horsehair
wiggery	day dress	mantilla	smocking	cassimere	housecoat
woollen	deerskin	material	snap brim	cerecloth	huckaback
worsted	diamanté	menswear	sneakers	chantilly	Inverness
yashmak	djellaba	moccasin	snowshoe	charmeuse	jack boots
	drilling	moleskin	sombrero	chaussure	jockey cap
8	dungaree	moquette	soutache	cheongsam	justi-coat
aigrette	dustcoat	muffatee	spun silk	chinstrap	kid gloves
appliqué	earmuffs	muslinet	spun yarn	clump boot	kirby grip
babouche	ensemble	musquash	stocking	coat-tails	knee socks
Balmoral	eyeshade	nail file	straw hat	cocked hat	lambswool

levantine
linen mesh
loincloth
long dress
long skirt
long socks
longcloth
macintosh
millinery
miniskirt
moiré silk
muffettee
neckcloth
nightgown
nightwear
off the peg
organzine
overdress
overshoes
panama hat
pantalets
pantaloon
paramatta
patchwork
pea jacket
peaked cap
percaline
persienne
petersham
petticoat
pina cloth
pinstripe
pixie hood
plimsolls
plus-fours
point lace
polo shirt
polonaise
polyester
pompadour
pourpoint
press stud
ready made
redingote
round-neck
sack dress
sackcloth
safety pin
sailcloth
sailor hat
sanbenito
sartorial
satinette
scapulary

school cap
scoop-neck
separates
sharkskin
sheepskin
shell suit
shirt-band
shirt-tail
shovel hat
shower cap
siren suit
sloppy joe
slouch hat
snowshoes
sou'wester
stockinet
stockings
stomacher
strapless
suede coat
sun helmet
sunbonnet
swansdown
sweatband
sword belt
tarpaulin
towelling
track suit
trilby hat
trousseau
undervest
underwear
velveteen
vestments
waistband
waistcoat
wedge heel
whalebone
wide-awake
wristband
zucchetto

10

ankle socks
balbriggan
ballet shoe
bathing cap
beaverteen
Berlin wool
black dress
blanketing
bobbin lace
bobbysocks
boiler suit

bombazette
broadcloth
brocatelle
bushjacket
buttonhole
candlewick
canonicals
chatelaine
chemisette
chinchilla
collar stud
collarette
court dress
court shoes
coverchief
crêpe soles
cricket cap
cummerbund
deshabille
dishabille
diving suit
drainpipes
dress shirt
dress shoes
dressmaker
embroidery
empire line
epauletted
Eton collar
Eton jacket
fancy dress
fascinator
fearnought
feather boa
flak jacket
florentine
flying suit
foresleeve
foundation
fustanella
Geneva gown
gold thread
grass cloth
grass skirt
habiliment
hair ribbon
halterneck
hodden-grey
hook and eye
horsecloth
Irish linen
jersey silk
jersey wool
kerseymere

khaki drill
life jacket
lounge suit
mackintosh
mess jacket
mock velvet
monk's habit
mousseline
needlecord
new clothes
nightdress
nightshirt
old clothes
opera cloak
overblouse
Oxford bags
pantaloons
parramatta
party dress
piccadilly
pilot-cloth
pinstripes
pith helmet
plastic mac
poke bonnet
powder puff
print dress
riding-hood
romper suit
roquelaure
sailor suit
scratch wig
seersucker
shirt front
shoe string
shoebuckle
sleeveless
slingbacks
solar topee
sport shirt
sportscoat
sportswear
string vest
suede shoes
Sunday best
sunglasses
suspenders
sweatshirt
three piece
thrown silk
toilinette
trench coat
trousering
turtle-neck

tussah silk
underpants
undershirt
waterproof
windjammer
wing collar
wraparound

11

Anthony Eden
Aran sweater
battledress
bellbottoms
best clothes
black patent
boiled shirt
boutonnière
bovver boots
boxer shorts
candystripe
canvas shoes
cap and bells
cheesecloth
clodhoppers
cloth-of-gold
contact lens
crash-helmet
dark glasses
décolletage
deerstalker
diving dress
Dolly Varden
dreadnought
dress shield
dressmaking
espadrilles
evening gown
farthingale
flannelette
flared skirt
football cap
formal dress
hammer cloth
hand-me-downs
Harris tweed
herringbone
hobble skirt
Honiton lace
Kendal green
lawn sleeves
leather coat
leatherette
leg of mutton
leopardskin

matinee coat
Mechlin lace
middy blouse
morning coat
mortarboard
neckerchief
nettlecloth
pantalettes
panty girdle
Persian lamb
Phrygian cap
pilot jacket
ready-to-wear
regimentals
riding habit
shawl collar
shell jacket
shirt button
shoe leather
shoulder bag
slumberwear
spatterdash
stiff collar
suede jacket
swallow tail
tam-o'-shanter
tennis dress
tennis skirt
torchon lace
trencher cap
trouser suit
tussore silk
watered silk
wellingtons
white collar
widow's weeds
windcheater
Windsor knot
work clothes
yachting cap

12

acrylic fibre
bathing dress
billycock hat
birthday suit
body stocking
bolting cloth
bomber jacket
breast pocket
business suit
cardinal's hat
cavalry twill
chastity belt
chesterfield
circassienne
clothes horse
collar and tie
college scarf
combinations
crêpe-de-chine
dinner jacket
divided skirt
Donegal tweed
donkey jacket
dress clothes
dress uniform
dressing gown
Easter bonnet
evening dress
fatigue dress
full mourning
galligaskins
haberdashery
handkerchief
haute couture
Hessian boots
Indian cotton
knee breeches
leather skirt
lumber jacket

moiré antique
monkey jacket
morning dress
Paisley shawl
plain clothes
pleated skirt
pressure suit
raglan sleeve
reach-me-downs
service dress
shirtwaister
sleeping suit
sports jacket
stovepipe hat
underclothes
wedding dress

13

Bermuda shorts
cashmere shawl
casual clothes
chinchilla fur
cocktail dress
football boots
football scarf
hacking jacket
Hawaiian skirt
Highland dress
Inverness cape
leather jacket
linsey-woolsey
made to measure
matinee jacket
Norfolk jacket
patent leather
period costume
pinafore dress
platform soles
Russia leather
shoulder strap
smoking jacket

spatterdashes
sports clothes
swaddling band
underclothing

14

afternoon dress
antiperspirant
artificial silk
bathing costume
cardigan jacket
chamois leather
clerical collar
collar-attached
double-breasted
Fair Isle jumper
fully fashioned
hobnailed boots
knickerbockers
Morocco leather
off the shoulder
riding breeches
Shetland jumper
shooting jacket
three-piece suit
undress uniform
winter woollies

15

balaclava helmet
cardigan sweater
civilian clothes
crease-resistant
maribou feathers
mourning clothes
ostrich feathers
sheepskin jacket
swimming costume
tarpaulin jacket
wellington boots

Dances

3

bop
fan
hay
hop
jig
pas

4

ball
clog
frug
haka
hula
jive
jota

juba
reel
step

5

bebop
caper
conga
fling

galop
gigue
gopak
limbo
mambo
pavan
pavin
polka
rumba

samba
shake
stomp
tango
twist
valse
volta
waltz

6

Apache
bolero
boston
bourée
canary
cancan
cha-cha

chassé	planxty	cha-cha-cha	saltarello
flurry	roundel	clog dance	strathspey
gallop	sardana	cotillion	sword-dance
minuet	shuffle	écossaise	tarantella
morris	two-step	eightsome	torch dance
pavane	watutsi	farandole	turkey-trot
redowa		folkdance	
rhumba	**8**	gallopade	**11**
shimmy	bunny-hug	jitterbug	black bottom
valeta	cachucha	line dance	contredanse
veleta	cake-walk	paso doble	floral dance
	capriole	passepied	Lambeth Walk
7	chaconne	Paul Jones	morris dance
	courante	polonaise	palais glide
beguine	fan-dance	poussette	rock and roll
bourrée	fandango	quadrille	schottische
carioca	flamenco	quickstep	square dance
choctaw	galliard	rock 'n' roll	varsovienne
czardas	habanera	siciliana	
forlana	hay-de-guy	tambourin	**12**
fox-trot	hornpipe	tripudium	country dance
gavotte	hulahula	zapateado	maypole dance
Helston	rigadoon		
hoedown	saraband	**10**	**13 AND OVER**
la volta	tap-dance		
lancers		boston reel	Boston two-step (13)
ländler	**9**	break dance	eightsome reel (13)
madison		charleston	Helston flurry dance
mazurka	allemande	Gay Gordons	(13)
measure	barn dance	hay-de-guize	Highland fling (13)
one-step	bossa nova	hokey-cokey	military two-step (15)

Drinks (wines, spirits, non-alcoholic beverages, etc.)

3	**4**	krug	wine	kvass	snort
		kvas	wort	lager	soave
ale	arak	lush		latte	stout
cha	Bass	marc	**5**	Macon	toddy
dop	beer	maté	booze	Médoc	Tokay
fix	bock	mead	broth	mocha	tonic
gin	bols	mild	Byrrh	negus	Vichy
jar	brut	milk	cider	noyau	vodka
kir	café	Moët	cocoa	oopak	water
mum	char	Mumm	cream	pekoe	
nip	coke	ouzo	cuppa	perry	**6**
nog	cola	port	drink	pinta	
rum	dram	raki	Evian	plonk	alegar
rye	fine	rosé	glass	punch	Alsace
sip	fino	sack	hooch	quass	amrita
sup	fizz	sake	hyson	Rioja	arrack
tea	flip	saki	Irish	shrub	Barsac
tot	grog	slug	Jerez	sirup	Beaune
vat	hock	soda	joram	sling	bishop
	kava	swig	julep	smash	bitter
					Bovril

brandy
bubbly
bumper
canary
cassis
caudle
chicha
claret
coffee
Cognac
congou
double
egg-nog
elixir
entire
geneva
grappa
Graves
hootch
kirsch
kumiss
kümmel
liquor
Malaga
muscat
nectar
noggin
oolong
pastis
Pernod
plotty
poison
porter
posset
poteen
potion
ptisan
pulque
Ribena
rickey
saloop
Saumur
Scotch
shandy
sherry
spirit
squash
stingo
Strega
swipes
tiffin
tipple
tisane
treble

Volnay
wallop
wherry
whisky

7

absinth
alcohol
aquavit
Bacardi
beef tea
bitters
bourbon
Campari
catawba
Chablis
Chandon
Chianti
cobbler
collins
cordial
curaçao
draught
dry wine
egg-flip
Falerno
gin fizz
gin sour
iced tea
koumiss
limeade
liqueur
low wine
mace ale
Madeira
Malmsey
Marsala
martini
mineral
Moselle
new wine
oloroso
Orvieto
pale ale
Perrier
pilsner
pink gin
Pomerol
Pommard
Pommery
Pouilly
ratafia
real ale
red wine

retsina
rosolio
Sangria
sherbet
sidecar
sloe gin
snifter
spirits
stinger
tequila
twankay
Vouvray
whiskey

8

absinthe
Adam's ale
advocaat
alicante
anisette
aperitif
beeswing
beverage
bock-beer
Bordeaux
brick tea
Burgundy
champers
China tea
ciderkin
Clicquot
Coca-Cola
cocktail
daiquiri
dog's nose
Drambuie
dry wines
Dubonnet
eau-de-vie
espresso
Florence
Frascati
fruit cup
gin-and-it
gin-sling
green tea
Guinness
herb beer
highball
Hollands
Horlicks
hydromel
lemonade
montilla

muscadel
near beer
nightcap
oopak tea
pekoe tea
pilsener
pink lady
Pol Roger
port wine
Punt y Mes
red biddy
red wines
Riesling
root beer
rosé wine
rosoglio
ruby port
rum punch
rum toddy
sack-whey
sangaree
Sauterne
schnapps
sillabub
skim-milk
small ale
souchong
sour milk
spritzer
St. Julien
strong ale
syllabub
tia maria
tincture
verjuice
vermouth
vin blanc
wish-wash

9

altar wine
angostura
applejack
aqua vitae
badminton
bitter ale
black beer
Bollinger
Buck's fizz
Budweiser
cappucino
Carlsberg
Ceylon tea
champagne

chocolate
claret cup
clary wine
Cointreau
Cuba libre
dry sherry
elder wine
Falernian
firewater
ginger ale
ginger pop
grenadine
gunpowder
Hall's wine
Heidsieck
Hermitage
hippocras
iced water
Indian tea
lager beer
lamb's wool
Lambrusco
limejuice
Manhattan
metheglin
Meursault
milk punch
milkshake
mint julep
Mochacino
moonshine
mulled ale
muscadine
oolong tea
orangeade
Rhine wine
Sauternes
Scotch ale
slivovitz
slivowitz
small beer
soda water
soft drink
St. Emilion
St. Raphael
sundowner
tarragona
tawny port
white lady
white port
white wine
Wincarnis

10

barley wine
Beaujolais
bitter beer
black-strap
bloody Mary
Bull's Blood
buttermilk
café-au-lait
caffe latte
canned beer
cappuccino
Chambertin
Chartreuse
clary-water
Constantia
cowslip tea
dry martini
Frontignac
ginger beer
ginger wine
horse's neck
iced drinks
Jamaica rum
lemon juice
malt liquor
malt whisky
malted milk
Manzanilla
maraschino
Mateus Rosé
Mickey Finn
Montrachet
Moselle cup
mulled wine
Munich beer
pale sherry
piña colada
raisin wine
Rhine wines
Rhône wines
rye whiskey
sack posset
shandygaff
soft drinks
spruce beer

still wines
stirrup cup
sweet wines
tanglefoot
Tom Collins
tonic water
twankay tea
usquebaugh
Vichy Water
vinho verde
whisky sour
white wines

11

aguardiente
amontillado
apple brandy
barley-water
Bénédictine
black coffee
black velvet
bottled beer
Bristol milk
cider-brandy
citron water
Courvoisier
cowslip wine
doch-an-doris
draught beer
Irish coffee
Irish whisky
John Collins
lemon squash
mountain dew
Niersteiner
orange juice
orange pekoe
peach brandy
Plymouth gin
potash water
Saint Julien
screwdriver
scuppernong
soda and milk
souchong tea
spring water
sweet sherry

tomato juice
vin de Graves
vintage wine
white coffee

12

champagne cup
cherry brandy
Côtes-du-Rhône
crème de cacao
Cyprus sherry
Fernet-Branca
ginger brandy
Grand Marnier
gunpowder tea
hot chocolate
ice-cream soda
India pale ale
Irish whiskey
kirschwasser
Malvern water
mulled claret
old fashioned
orange brandy
orange squash
peach bitters
Perrier-Jouet
red wine punch
Rhenish wines
Saint Emilion
Saint Raphael
sarsaparilla
Scotch whisky
seltzer water
supernaculum
treacle water
Valpolicella
vin ordinaire

13

aerated waters
apricot brandy
Château d'Yquem
Château Latour
Château-Lafite
cooking sherry
crème de menthe

dandelion wine
Darjeeling tea
Entre Deux Mers
Falernian wine
ginger cordial
instant coffee
Liebfraumilch
liqueur brandy
liqueur whisky
mild and bitter
mineral waters
Moët et Chandon
orange bitters
pink champagne
planters' punch
Pouilly Fuissé
prairie oyster
Seidlitz water
sherry cobbler
sparkling hock
sparkling wine
Veuve Clicquot

14

blended whiskey
champagne cider
champagne punch
Château-Margaux
elderberry wine
espresso coffee
French vermouth
Johannisberger
Napoleon brandy
pineapple juice
Piper-Heidsieck
sparkling wines
vermouth cassis
white wine punch

15

champagne-cognac
grapefruit juice
green Chartreuse
Italian vermouth
martini cocktail
sacramental wine
sparkling waters

Food

3 AND 4

bap	beef	brie	chop	dal	Edam
bean	blin	bun	chow	dhal	egg
	bran	cake	curd	dip	fare

fat	whey	melba	brains	muffin	beef tea
feta	yolk	melts	breast	mutton	biltong
fish		mince	brunch	noodle	biriani
flan	**5**	offal	burger	nougat	biryani
fool	aioli	pasta	butter	noyeau	biscuit
fowl	aspic	paste	canapé	nut oil	bloater
game	bacon	pasty	casein	oliver	borscht
ghee	blini	patty	catsup	omelet	botargo
grub	blood	pilaf	caviar	oxtail	bouilli
ham	board	pilau	cereal	paella	Boursin
hare	bombe	pilaw	cheese	panada	brioche
hash	borsh	pitta	coburg	pastry	brisket
herb	brawn	pizza	collop	pepper	broiler
ice	bread	prune	comfit	pickle	brownie
jam	brose	pulse	cookie	pilaff	cabbage
junk	broth	purée	cornet	pillau	calipee
kai	cakes	roast	course	polony	caramel
kale	candy	salad	croute	potage	catchup
lamb	capon	salep	crowdy	potato	caviare
lard	chili	salmi	crumbs	quiche	chapati
lean	chips	sauce	cutlet	rabbit	cheddar
leg	clove	scoff	dainty	ragout	chicken
loaf	cream	scone	dinner	raisin	chicory
loin	crêpe	scrag	dragée	rasher	chiffon
lung	crumb	shank	éclair	relish	chowder
meal	crust	shape	entrée	saddle	chutney
meat	curds	snack	faggot	salami	compote
menu	curry	spice	fillet	samosa	confect
milk	dough	split	flitch	sea-pie	corncob
mint	dulse	steak	fodder	simnel	cracker
mush	filet	stock	fondue	sorbet	crumble
nan	flank	sugar	fumado	sowens	crumpet
Oxo	flour	sushi	gammon	sponge	cupcake
paté	fruit	sweet	garlic	squash	currant
pie	fudge	syrup	gateau	staple	custard
poi	gigot	table	gelato	sundae	dessert
pork	glaze	taffy	giblet	supper	faggots
puff	Gouda	tansy	ginger	sweets	falafel
rice	gravy	toast	grease	tiffin	fig cake
roe	gruel	torte	greens	tit-bit	fritter
roll	gumbo	tripe	grouse	toffee	galette
roti	heart	viand	haggis	tongue	game pie
roux	honey	wafer	hot dog	trifle	gelatin
rusk	icing	yeast	hot-pot	viands	giblets
sago	jelly		humbug	waffle	glucose
side	joint	**6**	hummus	walnut	gnocchi
soup	juice	almond	humous	yogurt	goulash
soy	kebab	banger	jujube		gruyère
stew	korma	batter	junket	**7**	gumdrop
suet	liver	biffin	kidney	aliment	haricot
tart	lolly	blintz	kipper	baklava	haslets
tuna	lunch	bonbon	leaven	bannock	jam roll
veal	manna	borsch	lights	banquet	jam tart
	matzo	Bovril	mousse	Bath bun	ketchup

lasagne
Madeira
Marmite
matzoth
meat pie
mustard
oatcake
oatmeal
pancake
paprika
pavlova
pickles
plum jam
plum pie
polenta
popcorn
pork pie
pottage
poultry
praline
pretzel
pudding
ramekin
rarebit
ratafia
ravioli
rhubarb
rice bun
ricotta
risotto
rissole
rum baba
sapsago
sausage
saveloy
savoury
seafood
sherbet
sirloin
soufflé
Stilton
strudel
sucrose
tabasco
tapioca
tartlet
teacake
treacle
truffle
venison
vinegar
yoghurt
yule log

8

acid drop
allspice
ambrosia
angelica
apple jam
apple pie
bath chap
béchamel
Bel Paese
bouillon
bull's eye
chapatti
chestnut
chop suey
chow mein
clambake
coleslaw
conserve
consommé
coq au vin
couscous
cracknel
cream bun
cross bun
croutons
dainties
date roll
déjeuner
delicacy
doughnut
dressing
dripping
dumpling
Emmental
escalope
flapjack
flummery
fried egg
frosting
fruit pie
frumenty
hardbake
hazelnut
hung beef
ice cream
iced cake
Julienne
kedgeree
kickshaw
lamb chop
loblolly
loin chop

lollipop
luncheon
macaroni
macaroon
marzipan
meatball
meatloaf
meringue
mince pie
mishmash
molasses
moussaka
mushroom
olive oil
omelette
Parmesan
pastrami
pemmican
peperoni
plum cake
plum duff
poppadum
pork chop
porridge
pot roast
preserve
ramequin
rice cake
rigatoni
rock cake
rollmops
roly poly
rye bread
salad oil
salpicon
salt beef
salt fish
salt junk
salt pork
sandwich
scrag-end
seedcake
shoulder
sillabub
skim milk
slapjack
soda cake
soy sauce
squab pie
steak pie
stuffing
tiramisu
tortilla
turnover

undercut
victuals
vindaloo
yoghourt

9

angel cake
antipasto
appetizer
arrowroot
banquette
beefsteak
boiled egg
breakfast
bridecake
bubblegum
Camembert
cassareep
casserole
cassoulet
chipolata
chocolate
chump chop
comfiture
condiment
confiture
corn bread
corn salad
crackling
cream cake
cream puff
croissant
croquette
drop scone
Easter egg
enchilada
entremets
fairy cake
forcemeat
fricassee
fried eggs
fried fish
fried rice
fruit cake
fruit tart
galantine
Genoa cake
giblet pie
gravy soup
hamburger
honeycomb
Irish stew
lemon curd
loafsugar

lobscouse
lump sugar
macedoine
madeleine
marchpane
margarine
marmalade
mincemeat
mint sauce
mutton ham
mutton pie
nutriment
petit four
pigeon pie
Port Salut
potato pie
potpourri
pound cake
puff paste
raccahout
rillettes
Roquefort
rump steak
sage Derby
schnitzel
Scotch egg
seasoning
shellfish
shortcake
soda bread
sour cream
sourdough
spaghetti
spare ribs
stirabout
succotash
sugarloaf
sugar-plum
sweetmeat
Swiss roll
tipsy cake
vol-au-vent
white meat
wholemeal
wild honey

10

apple sauce
apricot jam
baked beans
Bath oliver
bêche-de-mer
beefburger
blancmange

blanquette
Bombay duck
bread sauce
breadfruit
breadstuff
bridescake
brown bread
buttermilk
Caerphilly
candy floss
cannelloni
cheesecake
Chelsea bun
comestible
confection
corned beef
cornflakes
cottage pie
currant bun
custard pie
Danish blue
delicacies
Eccles cake
egg custard
fettucine
fig pudding
frangipane
French loaf
fricandeau
fruit salad
garlic salt
giblet soup
ginger cake
girdle cake
Gloucester
Gorgonzola
grape sugar
ground rice
guava jelly
ham and eggs
hodge-podge
hotch-potch
ice pudding
Indian corn
jugged hare
lamb cutlet
maple sugar
marrowbone
mayonnaise
minced meat
minestrone
mock turtle
mortadella
mozzarella

mutton chop
peach Melba
pepper cake
peppermint
piccalilli
poached egg
Pontefract
potted fish
potted meat
provisions
pudding pie
puff pastry
raisin loaf
rhubarb pie
rolled oats
saccharine
salmagundi
sauerkraut
shish kebab
shortbread
shortcrust
silverside
simnel cake
sponge cake
stewed meat
sugar candy
sweetbread
tea biscuit
temse bread
tenderloin
tinned food
tortellini
turtle soup
veal cutlet
vermicelli
water gruel
white bread
white sauce
zabaglione

11

baked Alaska
baked potato
banana split
Banbury cake
barley sugar
black pepper
bonne bouche
brandy sauce
cassava cake
chiffon cake
chilli sauce
comestibles
cottage loaf

cream cheese
curry powder
dressed crab
frankfurter
French bread
gammon steak
garlic bread
gingerbread
golden syrup
green pepper
griddle cake
ham sandwich
hollandaise
hors d'oeuvre
hot cross bun
iron rations
jam turnover
leg of mutton
luncheon meat
Madeira cake
marshmallow
meat pudding
medlar jelly
milk pudding
olla podrida
oyster patty
peppermints
petits fours
plum pudding
potato crisp
potato salad
raisin bread
refreshment
rice biscuit
rice pudding
roast potato
sago pudding
sausage roll
Scotch broth
short pastry
side of bacon
sliced bread
smörgasbord
spotted dick
stewed fruit
suet pudding
tagliatelle
tomato sauce
treacle tart
vichyssoise
wedding cake
Welsh mutton
Welsh rabbit
Wensleydale

wheaten loaf
wine biscuit

12

apfelstrudel
apple crumble
apple fritter
Bakewell tart
birthday cake
black pudding
brandy butter
breast of lamb
brown Windsor
burnt almonds
butterscotch
cheeseburger
chicken tikka
chip potatoes
clotted cream
corn-on-the-cob
Cornish pasty
creme caramel
curds and whey
Danish pastry
Dunmow flitch
eggs and bacon
finnan haddie
fromage frais
guarana bread
hasty pudding
julienne soup
liver sausage
lobster patty
maid of honour
millefeuille
mulligatawny
nutmeg butter
peanut butter
pease pudding
pickled onion
plum porridge
potato crisps
pumpernickel
quartern loaf
refreshments
Russian salad
salted butter
scrambled egg
shepherd's pie
sherry trifle
ship's biscuit
smoked salmon
steak pudding
sweet and sour

taramasalata
tripe de roche
Waldorf salad
water biscuit
Welsh rarebit

13

apple dumpling
apple fritters
apple turnover
béchamel sauce
bouillabaisse
cheddar cheese
cheese biscuit
chili con carne
Christmas cake
confectionery
cottage cheese
crêpes suzette
custard-coffin
flitch of bacon
French mustard
German sausage
gigot de mouton
ginger pudding
gruyère cheese
Oxford sausage
pease porridge
roll and butter
salad dressing
scrambled eggs
sirloin of beef
sponge pudding
Stilton cheese
summer pudding
toad-in-the-hole
veal-and-ham pie

14

almond hardbake
apple charlotte
banana fritters
beef stroganoff
bologna sausage
bread and butter
bread and cheese
caramel custard
charlotte russe
Cheshire cheese
French dressing
haunch of mutton
macaroni cheese
mashed potatoes
mock-turtle soup

Parmesan cheese
Pontefract cake
saddle of mutton
toasted teacake
treacle pudding

tripe and onions
Turkish delight
wholemeal bread
Worcester sauce

15

bakewell pudding
bubble and squeak
chicken Maryland

chocolate éclair
Devonshire cream
haunch of venison
ploughman's lunch
sausages and mash

Furniture, fittings and personal effects

3

bag
bar
bed
bin
can
cot
fan
hod
ink
mat
nib
nog
pad
ped
pen
pew
pin
rug
urn
vat

4

ambo
bath
bowl
bulb
bunk
butt
case
cask
cist
comb
crib
desk
door
etui
ewer
form
gong
hi-fi
lamp
mull
plug
poke
rack
sack
safe
seal
seat
sofa
tank
tape
tray
vase
wick

5

apron
arras
basin
bench
besom
bidet
blind
board
broom
chair
chest
china
cigar
clock
cloth
coign
couch
cover
crate
cruse
diner
divan
doily
duvet
flask
futon
glass
globe
grate
guard
Jesse
jorum
label
light
linen
mural
panel
paper
piano
poker
pouch
purse
quill
quilt
radio
razor
scrip
shade
shelf
slate
spill
stand
stool
stoup
strop
suite
swing
table
tapis
tongs
tools
torch
towel
traps
trunk
twine
vesta
watch

6

air-bed
ash-bin
ash-can
awning
basket
box-bed
bunker
bureau
burner
camera
candle
carafe
carboy
carpet
carver
casket
caster
castor
cheval
chowry
coffer
cradle
damper
day-bed
drawer
duster
fender
forfex
gas tap
geyser
goblet
goglet
hamper
handle
hat-box
hearth
heater
hookah
hussif
ice-box
ink-pot
jordan
kit-bag
ladder
locker
log bin
loofah
lowboy
mirror
mobile
napery
napkin
needle
noggin
pallet
patera
pelmet
pencil
piggin
pillow
plaque
pomade
pottle
pouffe
punkah
punnet
red ink
rocker
salver
scales
sconce
screen
settee
settle
shower
siphon
socket
sponge
switch
syphon
tablet
tea set
tea urn
teapot
teapoy
thread
tinder
toy box
tripod
trophy
valise
wallet
window

7

adaptor
amphora
andiron
armoire
ash-tray
baggage
bath mat
bathtub
bedding
beeswax
bellows
bibelot
blanket
blotter
bolster
brasier
bunk bed
cabinet
camp bed
canteen
chalice
chamois
charpoy
cistern
coaster
coir mat
commode
compact
console
counter
cue-rack
curtain
cushion
cutlery
deed box
door-mat
drapery
dresser
drugget
dust-pan
dustbin
epergne
fire-dog

flannel
flasket
fly-rail
fuse-box
gas ring
gas-fire
hair-oil
hammock
hassock
heating
high boy
hip bath
holdall
ink-horn
keyhole
lagging
lantern
lectern
lighter
matches
matting
monocle
oil-lamp
ottoman
padlock
pannier
parquet
pianola
picture
pin-case
playpen
pomatum
pot-hook
roaster
rush mat
sadiron
samovar
sampler
sand-box
satchel
scraper
shelves
shoebox
soap-box
sofa-bed
stopper
stopple
syringe
tallboy
tambour
tankard
tea-cosy
tea-tray
tent-bed

Thermos
thimble
toaster
tobacco
tool kit
trammel
trolley
truckle
tumbler
tun-dish
twin bed
valance
what-not
whisket
woodcut
work-bag
workbox
yule-log

8

ale bench
Ansafone
armchair
baluster
banister
barbecue
bassinet
bed cover
bed linen
bed quilt
bedstead
bird-bath
bird-cage
bookcase
bookends
card-case
cashbook
CD player
cellaret
chair leg
chair-bed
chattels
cigar box
clay pipe
coat-hook
computer
coverlet
crockery
cupboard
curtains
cuspidor
decanter
demi-john
ditty-box

divan bed
doorbell
doorknob
doorstep
endirons
eyeglass
fauteuil
field-bed
firewood
fly paper
foot-bath
fuse wire
gallipot
gas meter
handbell
hangings
hat-brush
hatstand
heirloom
hi-fi unit
hip flask
holdfast
inkstand
jalousie
jewel box
knapsack
lamp-wick
lanthorn
latchkey
linoleum
lipstick
loo table
love seat
matchbox
mattress
nail-file
notebook
oak chest
oilcloth
ornament
penknife
pipe-rack
postcard
pot plant
press-bed
quill-pen
radiator
reticule
scissors
sea chest
shoehorn
shoelace
showcase
sitz-bath

slop bowl
slop pail
snuffbox
soap dish
speculum
spittoon
stair-rod
stairway
suitcase
sun-blind
table leg
table top
table-mat
tabouret
tantalus
tape-line
tapestry
tea-caddy
tea-chest
tea-table
triptych
tweezers
umbrella
vestiary
wall-safe
wardrobe
watch-key
water bed
water-pot
wax cloth
wax light
wine rack
wineskin
wireless

9

barometer
bathtowel
bedspread
black-jack
bookshelf
book-stand
boot-brush
bric-à-brac
cakestand
camp-stool
cane chair
card-table
carpet rod
carpet-bag
carpeting
china bowl
chinaware
cigarette

club chair
coffee-cup
coffee-pot
container
corkscrew
davenport
deckchair
directory
dish-cover
dog-basket
dog-collar
dog-kennel
double bed
dust cloth
dust-sheet
Dutch oven
easy chair
eiderdown
face cloth
face towel
faldstool
fire-board
fire-brick
fire-guard
fire-irons
fireplace
flower-pot
foot-board
footstool
girandole
gold plate
hair tonic
hairbrush
hall stand
hall table
hand-towel
haversack
high chair
horsewhip
housewife
inventory
jack-towel
jewel case
lamp-shade
lampstand
letter-box
light bulb
loving-cup
marquetry
master-key
mouse-trap
muffineer
music book
nail brush

newspaper
nick-nacks
notepaper
ornaments
palliasse
paper clip
parchment
pewter pot
pier-glass
pier-table
piggy-bank
plate-rack
porringer
portfolio
pot-hanger
potpourri
pounce-box
powder-box
punchbowl
punkah fan
radiogram
rush-light
safety-pin
secretary
serviette
shakedown
shoe-brush
shower-cap
sideboard
side-light
side-table
single bed
slop-basin
sponge-bag
sprinkler
stair rods
steel wool
stopwatch
sword-cane
table lamp
tableware
telephone
timepiece
timetable
tinder-box
toothpick
underfelt
vanity box
wallpaper
wash-basin
wash-stand
water-butt
water-tank
wax candle

wax polish
window-box
wine glass
wing chair
work table

10

air-cushion
alarm clock
alarm watch
bedclothes
biscuit-box
boot polish
broomstick
brown paper
buck-basket
calefactor
candelabra
canterbury
ceiling fan
chandelier
chessboard
chiffonier
clothes peg
clothes pin
coal bucket
coal bunker
coat hanger
crumb cloth
crumb-brush
curtain rod
dumb-waiter
elbow-chair
escritoire
featherbed
finger-bowl
fire-basket
fire-bucket
fire-escape
fire-shovel
firescreen
floor-cloth
flower-bowl
fly-catcher
fly-swatter
folding bed
foot-warmer
fourposter
garbage-can
gas-bracket
gas-lighter
gramophone
grand piano
hair lotion

humidifier
jardinière
lead pencil
letter-rack
loose cover
marking ink
music-stand
music-stool
musical box
napkin ring
needle-book
needle-case
needlework
night-light
nutcracker
opera glass
overmantel
pack-thread
paper-knife
paper-stand
pencil-case
pewter dish
photograph
piano stool
pianoforte
pile carpet
pillowcase
pillowslip
pincushion
plate-glass
pocket-book
pouncet-box
prayer-book
razor-strop
riding-whip
scatter rug
sealing-wax
secretaire
shower-bath
soda syphon
spectacles
spirit lamp
stamp-album
stationery
step-ladder
strip light
table linen
tablecloth
television
thermostat
time-keeper
time-switch
tobacco-jar
toilet roll

toothbrush
toothpaste
transistor
truckle-bed
typewriter
upholstery
vapour-bath
warming-pan
wassail-cup
watch-chain
watch-glass
watch-guard
window-seat
wine bottle
wine-cooler
work basket
wristwatch

11

account book
address book
attaché case
basket chair
bed-hangings
billiard-cue
bolster-case
book matches
bookshelves
butter-print
butter-stamp
button-stick
candelabrum
candlestick
centrepiece
chafing-dish
cheese board
cheval-glass
clothes-line
coal-scuttle
coffee table
counterpane
curtain hook
curtain rail
curtain ring
dining-table
dinner-table
dispatch-box
dredging-box
firelighter
first-aid box
floor polish
fountain-pen
gaming-table
garden chair

hearth brush
king-size bed
knick-knacks
lamp-chimney
leather case
linen basket
mantelpiece
minute glass
minute watch
mosquito net
music centre
nutcrackers
ormolu clock
paperweight
picture-rail
pipe-lighter
pocket flask
pocket-glass
pocket-knife
portmanteau
primus stove
pumice-stone
reading lamp
roll-top desk
safety-razor
shopping bag
slate-pencil
stair-carpet
straw pillow
studio couch
table napkin
table-runner
tape-measure
tea-canister
thermometer
tissue paper
tobacco pipe
toilet-cover
toilet-table
tooth-powder
vacuum flask
wash-leather
water heater
watering-can
wicker chair
window blind
work station
work surface
writing-desk

12

adhesive tape
antimacassar
bedside light

bedside table
blotting book
bottle-opener
candle-sconce
candleholder
carpet beater
chaise longue
chesterfield
churchwarden
clothes drier
clothes-brush
clothes-horse
console table
cottage piano
cup and saucer
dessert-spoon
dispatch-case
dressing-case
drinking-horn
electric bulb
electric fire
electric iron
electric lamp
extractor fan
field-glasses
fitted carpet
flower-basket
folding stool
gate-leg table
Gladstone bag
hot-water tank
ironing board
kneehole desk
light fitting
looking-glass
nail-scissors
nest of tables
nutmeg-grater
opera-glasses
paraffin lamp
picnic basket
place setting
playing cards
postage stamp
reading glass
record-player
rocking chair
rocking horse
serving hatch
sheepskin rug
standard lamp
straw bolster
sweating-bath
table lighter

table service
tallow candle
tape recorder
Thermos flask
tin-lined case
toasting fork
tobacco pouch
toilette case
trestle table
turkey carpet
upright piano
visitors' book
walking-staff
Welsh dresser
wicker basket
Windsor chair
wine decanter
writing paper
writing table

13

billiard balls
billiard table
blotting paper

carpet sweeper
carriage clock
clothes basket
cribbage board
dinner service
dressing-table
drinks cabinet
drop-leaf table
electric clock
electric razor
feather pillow
feeding bottle
filing cabinet
Florence flask
folding screen
four-poster bed
medicine chest
newspaper rack
Persian carpet
petrol-lighter
ping-pong table
quizzing-glass
roulette table
sewing-machine

Sheraton chair
smoothing-iron
storage heater
straw mattress
styptic pencil
television set
umbrella stand
vacuum cleaner
Venetian blind
video recorder
visiting-cards
wash hand basin
washhand-stand

14

airing cupboard
Anglepoise lamp
billiard marker
breakfast table
central heating
chest of drawers
cocktail-shaker
electric geyser
electric shaver

feather bolster
glove-stretcher
hot water bottle
hot-water septum
insulating tape
meerschaum pipe
reclining chair
tobacco stopper
Venetian blinds

15

cocktail cabinet
dining room table
electric blanket
feather mattress
garden furniture
gate-legged table
Japanese lantern
knitting needles
occasional table
photograph album
pneumatic pillow
weighing machine

Games, sports and pastimes

2 AND 3	kit	try	deal	hole	pass
	lap	win	deck	hoop	pawn
ace	l.b.w.	won	dice	hunt	play
aim	let		dive	I-spy	polo
bat	lie	**4**	draw	iron	pool
bet	lob		duck	jack	puck
bid	loo	ante	duel	judo	punt
bob	nap	away	epée	king	putt
bow	oar	bail	fall	knur	quiz
box	out	bait	faro	lido	race
by	pam	ball	foil	love	reel
bye	par	beat	fore	ludo	ride
cap	peg	bias	form	luge	ring
cat	p.t.	bike	foul	lure	rink
cox	put	bite	gaff	main	rook
cue	rod	blow	gala	mate	ruff
cup	run	blue	game	meet	sail
dan	set	boat	gate	mime	seed
die	ski	bout	gear	miss	shot
fan	tag	bowl	goal	mora	sice
go	taw	brag	golf	Oaks	side
gym	tie	card	grab	oars	skip
hit	tig	chip	grip	odds	skis
hop	tir	club	hand	over	slam
jeu	top	crew	hike	pace	slip
k.o.	toy	crib	hold	pack	snap
		dart			

solo	coach	point	angler	go-kart	revoke
spar	court	poker	archer	golfer	riding
spin	craps	prize	ascent	googly	rowing
suit	cycle	queen	ballet	ground	rubber
sumo	dance	quits	banker	hammer	rugger
swim	darts	racer	basset	hazard	runner
tack	Derby	rally	battue	header	safari
team	deuce	reins	bidder	hearts	savate
toss	dicer	relay	birdie	hiking	scorer
tote	diver	rodeo	bishop	hockey	sculls
trap	dormy	rugby	bookie	hooker	second
trey	drama	rummy	bowled	hoopla	see-saw
trip	drawn	scent	bowler	hunter	shinny
trot	drive	score	bowman	hurdle	shinty
turf	dummy	scrum	boxing	jigger	skater
vole	evens	scull	brassy	jigsaw	ski-run
volt	event	serve	bridge	jockey	skiing
walk	extra	shoot	bunker	jumper	slalom
whip	fault	skate	caddie	karate	sledge
wide	feint	skier	cannon	knight	soccer
wing	field	skiff	casino	kung-fu	soirée
wood	fight	slice	castle	leg-bye	sports
yo-yo	final	slide	centre	loader	sprint
yoga	fives	slips	chukka	lobber	squash
	fluke	smash	circus	mallet	stakes
5	going	spade	conker	manege	stroke
	grass	spoon	corner	marble	stumps
alley	green	sport	course	marina	stymie
arena	gully	spurt	crambo	marker	tackle
bails	halma	stake	crease	mascot	tai chi
bandy	hobby	stalk	cruise	mashie	target
basto	joker	start	cup tie	mid-off	ten-pin
baths	joust	steer	curler	no-ball	tenace
baton	kayak	stump	dealer	not-out	tennis
bingo	kendo	stunt	discus	opener	tierce
blade	knave	swing	diving	paddle	tip-cat
bluff	links	tarot	domino	peg-top	torero
board	lists	throw	dormie	pelota	toss-up
bogey	loser	title	driver	piquet	trophy
bogie	lotto	touch	dry-fly	player	umpire
bowls	lunge	track	écarté	punter	venery
boxer	match	train	eleven	putter	versus
break	medal	trial	euchre	puzzle	victor
caddy	miler	trick	falcon	quarry	volley
canoe	monte	trump	fencer	quoits	wicket
capot	no bid	vault	finish	rabbit	willow
cards	ombre	venue	gallop	racing	winger
carom	Ouija	wager	gambit	racket	winner
catch	pacer	whist	gamble	raffle	xystus
chase	pairs	yacht	gaming	ramble	yorker
cheat	parry		gammon	rapier	
check	party	**6**	gillie	rattle	**7**
chess	piste		glider	record	
chips	pitch	abseil	gobang	replay	acrobat
clubs		aikido			also ran

amateur
ambs-ace
ames-ace
angling
archery
arm hold
athlete
average
balloon
barbell
bathing
batsman
batting
beagles
bezique
bicycle
bidding
boating
bowling
brassie
bruiser
camping
canasta
captain
cassino
century
charade
checker
chicane
chukker
circuit
classic
contest
cooncan
counter
crampon
cricket
croquet
cue ball
curling
cycling
cyclist
dancing
day trip
decider
declare
defence
diabolo
dice-box
discard
doubles
dribble
driving
end game

etching
fairway
fan club
fencing
fielder
fifteen
fine leg
fishing
fixture
fly half
forward
fowling
fox hunt
funfair
gallery
gambler
gliding
golf bag
golfing
grounds
gymnast
hairpin
harrier
hawking
hunting
hurdler
hurling
ice rink
innings
jackpot
javelin
jogging
joy-ride
ju-jitsu
jumping
keep fit
kick off
knock up
last lap
leg side
line-out
lottery
love all
mah-jong
marbles
matador
maypole
misdeal
net cord
netball
niblick
nine pin
oarsman
oarsmen

offside
old maid
on guard
outdoor
over par
overarm
pallone
partner
pastime
pat ball
penalty
pharaoh
picador
picquet
pinball
pinocle
pit stop
pitcher
play off
playing
pontoon
press-up
primero
putting
rackets
rebound
referee
regatta
reserve
reversi
rubicon
running
sailing
scratch
sculler
service
shot put
shuffle
singles
skating
ski jump
skid lid
snooker
snorkel
St. Leger
stadium
starter
striker
stumped
sub-aqua
surfing
The Oaks
tilting
tinchel

tombola
top spin
tourney
trainer
trapeze
tumbler
vantage
vaulter
walking
wargame
weights
whip top
workout
wrestle

8

aerobics
aqualung
aquatics
away game
baccarat
backhand
backspin
ballgame
baseball
baseline
biathlon
boat race
body blow
boundary
bull's eye
bullring
bully off
canoeing
carnival
castling
catapult
ceramics
champion
charades
chequers
chess set
chessmen
climbing
commerce
contract
counters
coursing
crap game
cribbage
crossbar
cup final
dead heat
deck golf

delivery
dominoes
doublets
drag-hunt
draughts
dressage
dropkick
duelling
dumb-bell
eurythmy
eventing
exercise
face card
fair play
falconer
falconry
field day
fielding
finalist
firework
five pins
flat race
flippers
foot race
football
forehand
forfeits
foul play
fox hound
full back
full toss
gambling
game laws
gin rummy
goal kick
goal post
golf ball
golf club
gym shoes
gymkhana
halfback
handball
handicap
harriers
hat trick
heelkick
high jump
home game
Hula-Hoop
huntsman
hurdling
jiu-jitsu
jousting
juggling

knockout
korfball
lacrosse
leapfrog
left back
left half
left hook
left-wing
leg break
linesman
long jump
long stop
love game
lucky dip
mah-jongg
marathon
marksman
monopoly
motoring
napoleon
natation
ninepins
no trumps
off break
Olympiad
Olympics
opponent
outfield
outsider
palestra
pall-mall
patience
pétanque
ping-pong
pinochle
pintable
pole jump
pony race
pool room
pope Joan
pugilism
pugilist
pyramids
quatorze
quiz game
racegoer
racquets
rambling
roulette
rounders
runner-up
sack race
scrabble
sculling

set point
shooting
short leg
sideline
ski slope
ski stick
skipping
skittles
sledding
sledging
snowball
softball
southpaw
sparring
speedway
sporting
stalking
stock car
swimming
team game
teetotum
The Ashes
third man
tie break
toboggan
trap ball
trial run
tric trac
tricycle
trotting
tug of war
tumbling
turf club
umpiring
underarm
uppercut
vaulting
walkover
wall-game
wrestler
yachting

9

advantage
agonistic
anchorman
archeress
athletics
Aunt Sally
badminton
bagatelle
ball games
beach ball
bicycling

big dipper
billiards
black belt
blackjack
bob cherry
bobsleigh
body punch
bull board
bull feast
bullfight
card trick
chair lift
challenge
checkmate
chess game
clock golf
clubhouse
cockfight
cockmatch
conjuring
contender
court card
cricketer
crossword
cupwinner
cycle race
dartboard
decathlon
deck games
decoy duck
dirt track
dog racing
drawn game
dribbling
dumbbells
equalizer
extra time
favourite
five-a-side
flyweight
foot fault
forty–love
free-style
full house
game point
gardening
gate money
go-karting
goal posts
gold medal
golf clubs
golf links
golf shoes
grand prix

grand slam
gumshield
gymnasium
gymnastic
handstand
hard court
hatha yoga
hopscotch
horserace
ice hockey
ice-skates
joyriding
loose ball
low volley
motocross
Newmarket
nine holes
orienteer
pacemaker
palaestra
panel game
Parcheesi
pelmanism
philately
pogo stick
pole vault
pot hunter
potholing
prize-ring
punchball
quadrille
racehorse
racetrack
racing car
relay race
right half
right hook
right wing
safety net
sand yacht
schnorkel
scorecard
scrum half
semi-final
shinguard
shrimping
singleton
skin-diver
skydiving
sleighing
solitaire
solo whist
speedboat
sportsman

square-leg
stalemate
stool ball
stopwatch
stroke oar
surfboard
test match
tip and run
torch race
touchdown
touchline
trial game
trial race
trump card
turnstile
twenty-one
vingt-et-un
water jump
water polo
whipper-in
whirligig
wrestling
yacht club
yacht-race
yachtsman

10

acrobatics
aerobatics
backgammon
backstroke
ballooning
basket-ball
battledore
blood sport
booby prize
boxing ring
challenger
chessboard
clay pigeon
coconut shy
competitor
cover point
cricket bat
cup-and-ball
deck quoits
deck tennis
discobolus
doll's house
drag racing
drop volley
dumb crambo
equitation
fairground

fast bowler
feathering
field event
field sport
fishing net
fishing rod
fisticuffs
fives court
flat racing
fly-fishing
footballer
fox-hunting
goalkeeper
golf course
grandstand
greasy pole
groundbait
gymnastics
half volley
half-nelson
handspring
handy-dandy
high diving
hippodrome
hobby horse
hockey ball
hockey club
hockey team
hot cockles
humming-top
hunting box
ice dancing
ice skating
indian club
indoor golf
injury time
inside left
isometrics
jockey club
karate chop
landing net
lansquenet
lawn tennis
masquerade
midget golf
Monte Carlo
outfielder
pancratist
pancratium
paper chase
pari mutuel
pentathlon
philopoena
playground

pot hunting
prize fight
punch drunk
queen's pawn
queen's rook
racecourse
raceground
real tennis
recreation
relaxation
riding whip
rifle range
roundabout
rowing club
rugby union
saturnalia
scoreboard
sea bathing
second half
seven-a-side
showjumper
shuffle cap
sidesaddle
silly mid-on
skateboard
ski running
skin diving
sky jumping
slow bowler
snapdragon
somersault
speed trial
spillikins
stamp album
stroke play
submission
substitute
surf riding
sweepstake
switchback
tauromachy
team spirit
tennis ball
thimblerig
thirty–love
timekeeper
title fight
tournament
trial match
twelfth man
volley ball
weighing-in
whist drive

11

accumulator
agonistical
barley-brake
baseball bat
bear baiting
bird nesting
bloodsports
bobsledding
boxing match
bronze medal
bull baiting
bumblepuppy
chariot race
chess player
close season
competition
competitive
county match
coup de grâce
crash helmet
cricket ball
cricket pads
croquet ball
croquet hoop
cup of honour
cycle racing
Derby winner
diving board
double fault
egg and spoon
eurythmics
fast bowling
field events
field sports
fifteen love
first eleven
fishing line
folk dancers
football fan
forward pass
gaming house
garden party
general post
goal-kick line
gymnasiarch
hang gliding
heavyweight
hide-and-seek
hockey match
hockey stick
home and away
horse racing

horse riding
hunt counter
hunting horn
ice yachting
inside right
inter-county
king's bishop
king's knight
league table
lightweight
love–fifteen
martial arts
motor racing
mountaineer
neck and neck
oarsmanship
outside left
penalty area
photo finish
picnic party
pillow fight
playing card
pole vaulter
pony trekking
prizewinner
quarterback
rabbit punch
race meeting
river sports
rouge-et-noir
royal tennis
rugby league
service line
show jumping
shuttlecock
sightseeing
silly mid-off
silver medal
single stick
skating rink
slot machine
slow bowling
spelling bee
spinning top
sportswoman
springboard
squash court
stag hunting
stonewaller
straight bat
sweepstakes
table tennis
tennis court
tennis match

theatre-goer
tiddlywinks
tobogganing
totalizator
touring club
toxophilite
track record
triple crown
uncontested
water skiing
water sports
whipping-top
wild-fowling
wing forward
winning post
winning side
winning team
world record
yacht racing

12

approach shot
bantamweight
batting order
billiard ball
billiard room
birdwatching
bobsleighing
body-building
bowling alley
bowling green
boxing gloves
brass rubbing
breast stroke
bullfighting
butterfly net
caber tossing
championship
changing room
climbing rope
cockfighting
consequences
crapshooting
cricket boots
cricket match
cricket pitch
cross-country
curling stone
deer stalking
double sculls
doubles match
draughtboard
drinking bout
Eton wall game

field glasses
figure skater
first service
flying tackle
fruit machine
game of chance
gamesmanship
horsemanship
housey-housey
huntsmanship
jigsaw puzzle
level pegging
long distance
magic lantern
marathon race
medicine ball
merry-go-round
mixed bathing
mixed doubles
nursery slope
obstacle race
Olympic games
opera glasses
orienteering
paddling pool
parallel bars
parlour games
pigeon racing
pitch-and-toss
playing cards
playing field
pleasure trip
point-to-point
pole position
pole vaulting
prize fighter
prize winning
professional
putting green
pyrotechnics
Pythian games
quarter-final
queen's bishop
record holder
riding school
rock climbing
roller skates
sand yachting
scotch-hopper
second eleven
shadow boxing
shrimping net
shuffle board
singles match

skipping rope
skittle alley
starting post
state lottery
steeplechase
sticky wicket
stilt walking
swimming gala
swimming pool
table rapping
table turning
tennis player
tennis racket
theatre-going
thoroughbred
tiddleywinks
treasure hunt
trick cyclist
weightlifter
welterweight
wicket keeper
winter sports

13

aquatic sports
auction bridge
billiard table
blind man's buff
bubble blowing
callisthenics
centre-forward
chuck farthing
coarse fishing
county cricket

cribbage board
cricket ground
cricket stumps
croquet mallet
cruiserweight
double or quits
entertainment
equestrianism
featherweight
figure skating
finishing post
fishing tackle
football match
Grand National
ground-angling
half-time score
hare-and-hounds
horizontal bar
Isthmian games
kiss-in-the-ring
morris dancing
musical chairs
nursery slopes
Olympian games
parlour tricks
pillion riding
prisoner's base
prize fighting
record breaker
roller skating
roulette table
rugby football
skateboarding
spirit rapping

sports stadium
sportsmanship
squash rackets
stalking horse
starting price
steeplechaser
straight flush
ten-pin bowling
three-day event
track and field
vantage ground
vaulting horse
victor ludorum
weight lifting
wicket keeping

14

all-in wrestling
billiard marker
billiard player
children's party
coin collecting
conjuring trick
contract bridge
discus-throwing
divertissement
ducks-and-drakes
football ground
golf tournament
greyhound Derby
grouse shooting
hunt-the-slipper
hunt-the-thimble
marathon runner

master of hounds
mountaineering
opening batsman
putting the shot
record breaking
shove-halfpenny
speedway racing
squash racquets
steeplechasing
stock-car racing
thimblerigging
three-card trick
weight training
winter Olympics
wrestling match

15

ballroom dancing
bodyline bowling
cross-country run
crossword puzzle
Derby sweepstake
dirt-track racing
egg and spoon race
greyhound racing
javelin throwing
king-of-the-castle
leg before wicket
shooting gallery
sparring partner
stamp collecting
swimming costume
three-legged race
youth hostelling

Jewellery, gems, etc.

3 AND 4

bead
clip
gaud
gem
gold
jade
jet
onyx
opal
ring
ruby
sard
stud
torc

5

agate
aglet
amber
badge
beads
beryl
bezel
bijou
bugle
cameo
carat
charm
clasp
coral

crown
ivory
jewel
lapis
links
nacre
paste
pearl
tiara
topaz
watch

6

albert
amulet
anklet

armlet
augite
bangle
bauble
brooch
corals
diadem
enamel
fibula
garnet
gewgaw
iolite
jargon
locket
olivet
pearls

pyrope
quartz
sequin
signet
silver
spinel
tiepin
torque
wampum
zircon

7

abraxas
adamant
annulet
armilla

asteria
cat's eye
chaplet
coronet
crystal
diamond
eardrop
earring
emerald
euclase
girasol
jacinth
jewelry
olivine
pendant
peridot
regalia
ringlet
sardine
sardius
sceptre
spangle
telesia
trinket

8

adularia
aigrette
amethyst
bracelet
carcanet

corundum
crucifix
filigree
fire-opal
gemstone
hallmark
hyacinth
intaglio
ligurite
necklace
pectoral
platinum
sapphire
sardonyx
scarf-pin
sparkler
sunstone

9

balas ruby
black onyx
black opal
breast-pin
brilliant
carbuncle
carnelian
cornelian
cufflinks
gold watch
grossular
jadestone

jewellery
marcasite
medallion
moonstone
moss-agate
paillette
press stud
rubellite
seed pearl
solitaire
starstone
thumb ring
trinketry
turquoise
water opal

10

amber beads
aquamarine
black pearl
bloodstone
chalcedony
chrysolite
coral beads
glass beads
lucky charm
rhinestone
signet ring
topazolite
tourmaline
watch-chain

watchstrap
wristwatch

11

aiguillette
alexandrite
cameo brooch
chalcedonyx
chrysoberyl
chrysoprase
crocidolite
lapis lazuli
wedding-ring

12 AND OVER

bead necklace (12)
chain bracelet (13)
charm bracelet (13)
coral necklace (13)
crystal necklace (15)
engagement ring (14)
eternity ring (12)
link bracelet (12)
mother-of-pearl (13)
mourning brooch (14)
mourning ring (12)
pearl necklace (13)
precious stone (13)

Kitchen utensils and requisites

3

bin
can
cup
hob
jar
jug
lid
mop
mug
pan
pot
tap
tin
tub
urn
wok

4

bowl
coal
cosy
dish
ewer
flue
fork
grid
hook
iron
lard
mill
oven
pail
peel
rack
sink

soap
soda
spit
suet
trap
tray

5

basin
besom
broom
brush
caddy
china
cover
crock
cruet
cruse
doily

dough
glass
grate
grill
hatch
knife
ladle
match
mixer
mould
plate
poker
range
scoop
shelf
sieve
spoon
steel
stove

table
timer
tongs
towel
whisk

6

ash-pan
beaker
beater
bleach
boiler
bottle
bucket
burner
candle
carver
cooker
cupful

drawer
duster
eggbox
eggcup
fender
filter
flagon
fridge
funnel
gas-jet
geyser
grater
haybox
heater
ice-box
jugful
juicer
kettle
larder

65

mangle
mincer
mortar
pantry
pestle
polish
posnet
Primus
recipe
salver
saucer
scales
shears
shovel
sifter
skewer
slicer
starch
tea-cup
tea-pot
teaset
tea-urn
trivet
tureen
vessel

7

blender
bluebag
broiler
cake-tin
canteen
chamois
chip pan
chopper
coal-box
creamer
cuisine
cutlery
dishmat
dishmop
drainer
dresser
dustbin
dust-pan
freezer
gas ring
griddle
griller
milk-jug
pie-dish

pitcher
platter
ramekin
roaster
saltbox
samovar
scuttle
seether
skillet
spatula
steamer
stewpan
stewpot
tea-cosy
tea-tray
terrine
toaster
tumbler
vinegar
wash-tub
worktop
wringer

8

bread bin
canister
cauldron
colander
cream-jug
crockery
cupboard
dish rack
egg-slice
eggspoon
egg-timer
eggwhisk
fish fork
flan case
flat-iron
gas stove
gridiron
hotplate
matchbox
meatsafe
oilcloth
oilstove
ovenware
saucepan
scissors
shoe box
sink unit

slop bowl
stockpot
strainer
tea caddy
teacloth
teaspoon
trencher
water jug

9

bain-marie
baking tin
cafetière
can-opener
casserole
chinaware
coffee cup
coffee pot
corkscrew
dish cover
dishcloth
egg beater
fire-irons
fireplace
fish knife
fish-slice
frying-pan
gas burner
gas cooker
gravy boat
kitchener
microwave
muffineer
pepper-box
pepper-pot
plate-rack
porringer
salad bowl
sauceboat
slop basin
soup spoon
spin-drier
steel wool
sugar bowl
tea kettle
tin opener
toast rack
washboard
wineglass

10

baking tray
biscuit tin
bread board
bread knife
broomstick
butter dish
chafing pan
chopsticks
coffee mill
deep-freeze
dishwasher
egg poacher
fish basket
fish carver
fish kettle
floor cloth
gas lighter
jelly mould
knife board
liquidizer
mustard pot
pan scourer
pepper mill
percolator
rolling pin
rotisserie
salt cellar
tablecloth
tablespoon
waffle iron

11

butter knife
cheesecloth
coal-scuttle
dinner plate
dripping pan
flour dredge
kitchen sink
kitchen unit
meat chopper
paring knife
pudding bowl
scouring pad
serving dish
water filter
water heater

12

breakfast-cup
carving knife
dessertspoon
double boiler
fish-strainer
flour dredger
ironing board
kitchen range
knife machine
measuring jug
nutmeg grater
porridge bowl
potato peeler
pudding basin
pudding cloth
refrigerator
Thermos flask
toasting fork

13

chopping board
coffee grinder
food processor
kitchen scales
lemon squeezer
microwave oven
saucepan brush
water softener

14

double saucepan
electric cooker
juice extractor
knife sharpener
mincing machine
pressure cooker
scrubbing brush
washing machine

15

electric toaster
immersion heater
vegetable cutter

EDUCATION
Educational terms

2 AND 3

B.A.
C.S.E.
cap
D.E.S.
don
Dr.
fag
G.C.E.
gyp
M.A.
Ph.D.
Pop

4

bump
cane
coed
cram
crib
dean
demy
digs
exam
fail
form
gate
G.C.S.E.
gown
grad
hall
head
hood
I.L.E.A.
mark
mods
oral
pass
poly
prep
prof.
quad
swot
taws
term
test

5

Backs
bedel
board
chalk
class
coach
D.Phil.
dunce
final
flunk
gaudy
grade
grant
house
learn
lines
major
merit
minor
paper
prize
pupil
scout
sizar
slate
staff
study
tawse
tutor
usher

6

A-level
alumna
alumni
beadle
bursar
campus
course
day boy
degree
docent
doctor
eights
fellow
finals
grades
greats

Hilary
incept
lector
locker
master
matron
novice
O-level
old boy
optime
primer
reader
rector
regent
regius
remove
report
school
sconce
senate
senior
tripos
truant
warden

7

academy
alumnae
alumnus
battels
boarder
bull-dog
burgess
bursary
captain
college
crammer
diploma
dominie
entrant
examine
faculty
failure
fresher
Great-go
head boy
honours
learner
lecture
lexicon

May week
monitor
nursery
old girl
prefect
primary
proctor
project
provost
qualify
reading
scholar
seminar
student
teach-in
teacher
torpids
tuition
varsity

8

academic
aegrotat
backward
bookworm
commoner
cramming
educator
emeritus
encaenia
examinee
freshman
glossary
graduand
graduate
guidance
half term
head girl
homework
inceptor
learning
lecturer
literacy
Little-go
manciple
mistress
notebook
numerate
Oxbridge
pass mark

postgrad.
red-brick
research
revision
roll-call
semester
seminary
send down
statutes
textbook
tuck-shop
tutorial
tutoring
vacation
viva voce
wrangler

9

alma mater
art master
art school
classmate
classroom
collegian
day school
doctorate
dormitory
education
fifth form
final year
first form
first year
governess
great hall
inspector
institute
law school
novitiate
pedagogue
playgroup
preceptor
prelector
preschool
president
principal
professor
qualified
refectory
refresher
registrar

scholarly
schoolboy
selection
sixth form
sophomore
speech day
staffroom
streaming
sub-rector
third form
third year
trimester

10

blackboard
chancellor
classicist
college boy
collegiate
common room
curriculum
day release
dining-hall
discipline
eleven-plus
exhibition
extra-mural
fellowship
fives court
form-master
fourth form
free period
headmaster
high school
illiteracy
illiterate
imposition
instructor
laboratory
lower sixth
Michaelmas
playground
playschool
prep school

quadrangle
quadrivium
report card
sabbatical
school meal
school year
schoolbook
schooldays
schoolgirl
schoolmarm
schoolmate
schoolroom
second form
second year
Sheldonian
sink school
university
upper sixth
vicegerent

11

board school
coeducation
convocation
crash course
examination
fellow pupil
former pupil
games master
grade school
head teacher
holiday task
housemaster
institution
invigilator
lecture room
lectureship
liberal arts
matriculate
mortarboard
music master
music school
night school
polytechnic

prizegiving
prizewinner
probationer
responsions
scholarship
school hours
teaching aid
writing desk

12

aptitude test
church school
congregation
exercise book
exhibitioner
form mistress
headmistress
infant school
junior school
kindergarten
master of arts
night classes
postgraduate
preselection
public orator
pupil-teacher
regent master
school dinner
schoolfellow
schoolmaster
senior school
Sunday school

13

adult learning
advanced level
baccalaureate
coeducational
comprehension
comprehensive
doctor of music
faculty of arts
grammar school
home economics

honours degree
infant prodigy
learning curve
matriculation
mature student
non-collegiate
nursery school
ordinary level
primary school
private school
Rhodes scholar
school-leaving
schoolteacher
science master
supply teacher
undergraduate
vice-principal

14

approved school
bachelor of arts
boarding school
common entrance
educationalist
honorary degree
junior wrangler
language master
Open University
sandwich course
schoolmistress
senior wrangler
vice-chancellor

15

doctor of science
extracurricular
higher education
master of science
open scholarship
school inspector
secondary modern

Oxford and Cambridge colleges

(C.) = Cambridge; (m.) = mixed
(O.) = Oxford; (p.p.h.) = permanent private hall; (w.) = women

3 – 5

Caius (C.) (Gonville and)

Clare (C.) (m.)
Green (O.)
Jesus (O.)

Jesus (C.) (m.)
Keble (O.)
King's (C.) (m.)

New (O.)
Oriel (O.)

6

Darwin (C.) (m.)
Exeter (O.)
Girton (C.) (m.)
Merton (O.)
Queen's (O.)
Queens' (C.)
Selwyn (C.) (m.)
Wadham (O.)

7

Balliol (O.)
Christ's (C.) (m.)
Downing (C.) (m.)
Kellogg (O.)
Linacre (O.)
Lincoln (O.)
New Hall (C.)
Newnham (C.)
St. Anne's (O.)
St. Cross (O.)
St. Hugh's (O.)
St. John's (C.) (m.)
St. John's (O.)
Trinity (C.) (m.)
Trinity (O.)
Wolfson (C.) (m.)
Wolfson (O.)

8

All Souls (O.)
Emmanuel (C.) (m.)
Hertford (O.)
Homerton (C.) (m.)
Magdalen (O.)
Nuffield (O.)
Pembroke (O.)
Pembroke (C.) (m.)
Robinson (C.) (m.)
St. Hilda's (O.) (w.)
St. Peter's (O.)

9 AND 10

Brasenose (O.) (9)
Churchill (C.) (m.) (9)
Clare Hall (C.) (m.) (9)
Greyfriars (O.)
   (p.p.h) (10)
Hughes Hall (C.)
   (m.) (10)
Magdalene (C.) (m.) (9)
Mansfield (O.) (p.p.h.) (9)
Peterhouse (C.) (m.) (10)
Somerville (O.) (10)
St. Antony's (O.) (9)
St. Edmund's (C.) (m.) (9)
Templeton (O.) (9)

University (O.) (10)
Worcester (O.) (9)

11 AND 12

Blackfriars (O.) (p.p.h.) (11)
Campion Hall (O.) (p.p.h.) (11)
Christ Church (O.) (12)
Fitzwilliam (C.) (m.) (11)
Regent's Park (O.) (p.p.h.) (11)
Rewley House (O.) (11)
Sidney Sussex (C.) (m.) (12)
St. Benet's Hall (O.) (p.p.h.) (12)
St. Catharine's (C.) (m.) (12)
St. Catherine's (O.) (12)
St. Edmund Hall (O.) (12)
Trinity Hall (C.) (m.) (11)
Wycliffe Hall (O.) (p.p.h.) (12)

13 AND OVER

Corpus Christi (O.) (13)
Corpus Christi (C.) (m.) (13)
Gonville and Caius
   (C.) (m.) (16)
Harris Manchester (O.) (16)
Lady Margaret Hall
   (O.) (w.) (16)
Lucy Cavendish (C.) (w.) (13)

Some boys' and girls' schools

(c.) = "College", as distinct from "School", in title

4 – 6

Abbey (5)
Bolton (6)
Durham (6)
Eltham (c.) (6)
Epsom (c.) (5)
Eton (c.) (4)
Exeter (6)
Fettes (c.) (6)
Forest (6)
Harrow (6)
Leys (The) (4)
Oakham (6)
Oundle (6)
Radley (c.) (6)
Repton (6)
Rugby (5)
St. Bees (6)

Stowe (5)
Trent (c.) (5)

7

Alleyn's
Bablake
Bedales
Bedford
Bloxham
Bristol
Clifton (c.)
Dulwich (c.)
Felsted
Lancing (c.)
Loretto
Malvern (c.)
Mercers'
Oratory
Roedean

Rossall
St. Bede's
St. John's
St. Paul's
Taunton
The Leys
Warwick

8

Abingdon
Ardingly (c.)
Brighton (c.)
Denstone (c.)
Downside
Highgate
Mill Hill
Sedbergh
St. Albans
Whitgift

9

Blundell's
Bradfield (c.)
Brentwood
Bryanston
Cranbrook
Cranleigh
Dean Close
Liverpool (c.)
Millfield
Sherborne
St. George's
Tonbridge
Uppingham

10

Ampleforth (c.)
Birkenhead
Bromsgrove
Cheltenham (c.)
Eastbourne (c.)
Leeds Girls'
Pangbourne
Shrewsbury
Stoneyhurst (c.)
Wellington (c.)
Winchester (c.)

11

Bedford High
Berkhamsted
Bury Grammar

Eton College
Framlingham (c.)
Giggleswick
Gordonstoun
James Allen's
Marlborough (c.)
Mary Erskine
Westminster

12

Charterhouse
Cheadle Hulme
City of London
King's College (School)
Monkton Combe
St. Paul's Girls'
Surbiton High

13

Bedford Modern
Bedford School
George Watson's (c.)
Wolverhampton

14

Hurstpierpoint (c.)
Manchester High
Wellingborough

15

Bradford Grammar
Christ's Hospital
King's, Canterbury
Magdalen College (School)
Merchant Taylors'

FAMOUS PEOPLE
Admirals

3 – 5

Anson (Lord)
Bart
Blake
Bligh
Broke
Byng
Dewey
Drake
Hawke
Hood (Lord)
Howe (Lord)
Jones
Keyes (Lord)
Mahan
Perry
Rooke
Scott
Sims
Stark
Togo
Tovey
Tromp
Tryon

6

Beatty (Lord)
Benbow

Colomb
Darlan
Dönitz
Duncan
Fisher (Lord)
Fraser
Halsey
Howard (Lord)
Jervis
Keppel
Nelson (Lord)
Nimitz
Parker
Porter
Raeder
Ramsay
Rodney (Lord)
Rupert (Prince)
Ruyter
Scheer
Shovel
Vernon

7

Dampier
Decatur
Doenitz
Exmouth (Lord)
Kolchak

Phillip
Raleigh
Seymour
Sturdee
Tirpitz
von Spee

8

Boscawen
Cochrane (Lord)
de Ruyter
Farragut
Jellicoe (Lord)
Richmond
Sandwich (Lord)
Saumarez
van Tromp
Yamamoto

9

Albemarle
Beresford (Lord)
Duckworth
Effingham
Frobisher
Grenville
St. Vincent (Lord)
von Hipper

10

Codrington
Cunningham
Kempenfelt
Mountevans (Lord)
Somerville
Villeneuve
von Tirpitz

11 AND 12

Collingwood (11)
Elphinstone (11)
Mountbatten
  (Lord) (11)

13 AND OVER

Cork and Orrery
  (Lord) (13)
Rozhdestvensky (14)

Celebrities past and present
1. The world of entertainment: theatre, opera, ballet, films, the circus, television, radio, music (classical, jazz, folk, pop, etc.)

3 AND 4

Baez, Joan
Ball, Lucille
Ball, Zoë
Bass, Alfie
Bilk, Acker
Bird, John
Bow, Clara
Bron, Eleanor
Bull, Deborah
Butt, Dame Clara
Cash, Johnny
Cobb, Lee J.
Coco (clown)
Cole, George
Cole, Nat King
Cook, Peter
Day, Doris
Day, Sir Robin
Dean, James
Dors, Diana
Duse, Eleonora
Fame, Georgie
Ford, John
Ford, Harrison
Fry, Stephen
Fury, Billy
Gaye, Marvin
Getz, Stan
Gish, Lillian
Gwyn, Nell
Hall, Henry
Hall, Sir Peter
Hay, Will
Hess, Dame Myra
Hill, Benny
Hird, Dame Thora
Hope, Bob
Joad, Cyril
John, Sir Elton
Kaye, Danny
Kean, Edmund
Kerr, Deborah
Lahr, Bert
Lang, Fritz
Lean, Sir David
Lee, Bruce
Lee, Christopher
Lee, Peggy

Lee, Gypsy Rose
Lent, Alfred
Lind, Jenny
Lynn, Dame Vera
Marx, brothers
Monk, Thelonious
More, Kenneth
Muir, Frank
Nunn, Trevor
Peck, Gregory
Piaf, Edith
Ray, Satyajit
Reed, Sir Carol
Reed, Lou
Reid, Beryl
Rice, Sir Tim
Rigg, Dame Diana
Rix, Lord
Ross, Annie
Ross, Diana
Sher, Antony
Sim, Alastair
Swan, Donald
Tati, Jacques
Thaw, John
Took, Barrie
Tree, Sir Herbert
Vigo, Jean
Wark, Kirsty
West, Mae
Wise, Ernie
Wise, Robert
Wood, Sir Henry
Wood, Natalie
York, Michael
York, Susannah

5

Adler, Larry
Allen, Chesney
Allen, Dave
Allen, Woody
Arden, John
Arrau, Claudio
Askey, Arthur
Badel, Alan
Baker, Dame Janet
Baker, Sir Stanley
Basie, Count
Bates, Alan

Benny, Jack
Berry, Chuck
Björk
Black, Cilla
Blair, Lionel
Bloom, Clair
Boult, Sir Adrian
Bowie, David
Boyer, Charles
Bragg, Melvyn
Brain, Dennis
Brand, Jo
Bream, Julian
Brice, Fanny
Brook, Peter
Brown, Pamela
Bruno, Walter
Bryan, Dora
Bülow, Hans von
Caine, Sir Michael
Capra, Frank
Carné, Marcel
Clair, René
Clark, Lord
Clark, Petula
Clary, Julian
Clift, Montgomery
Cline, Patsy
Close, Glenn
Cooke, Alistair
Cukor, George
Dando, Jill
Davis, Bette
Davis, Sir Colin
Davis, Miles
Davis, Sammy
Dench, Dame Judi
Dolin, Anton
Du Pré, Jacqueline
Dylan, Bob
Elton, Ben
Evans, Chris
Evans, Dame Edith
Evans, Sir Geraint
Evans, Gill
Faith, Adam
Feltz, Vanessa
Finch, Peter
Flynn, Errol
Fonda, Henry

Fonda, Jane
Frost, Sir David
Gabin, Jean
Gable, Clark
Gabor, Zsa Zsa
Gance, Abel
Garbo, Greta
Gibson, Mel
Gigli, Beniamino
Gobbi, Tito
Gould, Elliott
Gould, Glenn
Grade, Lord
Grant, Cary
Greco, Juliette
Green, Hughie
Greer, Germaine
Grove, Sir George
Haley, Bill
Hallé, Sir Charles
Handl, Dame Irene
Handy, W.C.
Hanks, Tom
Hardy, Robert
Hawks, Howard
Henry, Lenny
Hicks, Sir Seymour
Hines, Earl
Holly, Buddy
Horne, Kenneth
Horne, Lena
Irons, Jeremy
Ivory, James
James, Clive
James, Sid
Jones, Tom
Joyce, Eileen
Kazan, Elia
Kelly, Gene
Kelly, Grace
Kempe, Rudolf
Korda, Sir Alexander
La Rue, Danny
Lauren, Sophia
Leigh, Vivien
Lenya, Lotte
Lifar, Serge
Lloyd, Harold
Lloyd, Marie
Loach, Ken

Lorre, Peter
Losey, Joseph
Marks, Alfred
Mason, James
Masur, Kurt
Mayer, Louis B.
Melba, Dame Nellie
Melly, George
Miles, Lord
Mills, Bertram
Mills, Sir John
Moore, Dudley
Moore, Gerald
Mount, Peggy
Munch, Charles
Negus, Arthur
Neill, Sam
Niven, David
Ogdon, John
Ozawa, Seiji
Paige, Elaine
Patti, Adelina
Pears, Sir Peter
Petit, Roland
Popov (clown)
Power, Tyrone
Price, Vincent
Quinn, Anthony
Reith, Lord
Robey, Sir George
Scott, Terry
Sharp, Cecil
Simon, Paul
Smith, Bessie
Smith, Delia
Smith, Dame Maggie
Solti, Sir George
Somes, Michael
Starr, Ringo
Stern, Isaac
Swann, Michael
Sykes, Eric
Tatum, Art
Terry, Ellen
Teyte, Dame Maggie
Topol, Chaim
Tracy, Spencer
Tutin, Dorothy
Tynan, Kenneth
Vitti, Monica
Wajda, Andrzej
Wayne, John
Welch, Raquel
Wogan, Terry

Worth, Irene
Zappa, Frank

6

Adrian, Max
Antoine, André
Arnaud, Yvonne
Artaud, Antonin
Ashton, Sir Frederick
Atkins, Eileen
Bacall, Lauren
Balcon, Sir Michael
Barber, Chris
Bardot, Brigitte
Barnum, P.T.
Bassey, Dame Shirley
Battle, Kathleen
Baylis, Lilian
Beatty, Warren
Bechet, Sidney
Benson, Sir Frank
Bogart, Humphrey
Boulez, Pierre
Braden, Bernard
Brando, Marlon
Briers, Richard
Bryant, Michael
Buñuel, Luis
Burney, Fanny
Burton, Richard
Cagney, James
Callas, Maria
Callow, Simon
Cantor, Eddie
Caruso, Enrico
Casals, Pablo
Casson, Sir Lewis
Charles, Ray
Cibber, Colley
Cleese, John
Cobain, Kurt
Colman, Ronald
Colyer, Ken
Cooper, Gary
Cooper, Dame Gladys
Cortot, Alfred
Coward, Sir Noël
Cranko, John
Crosby, Bing
Cruise, Tom
Curran, Charles
Curtis, Tony
Curzon, Sir Clifford
Cusack, Cyril

De Niro, Robert
de Sica, Vittorio
Devine, George
Disney, Walt
Domino, Fats
Dowell, Anthony
Draper, Ruth
Dreyer, Carl
Duncan, Isadora
Fields, Gracie
Fields, W.C.
Finney, Albert
Fokine, Mikhail
Forman, Milos
Formby, George
Foster, Jodie
French, Dawn
Galway, James
Garcia, Jerry
Garson, Greer
Geldof, Bob
Godard, Jean-Luc
Gong Li
Goring, Marius
Graham, Martha
Greene, Sir Hugh
Groves, Sir Charles
Guitry, Sacha
Harlow, Jean
Herzog, Werner
Heston, Charlton
Hiller, Dame Wendy
Hislop, Ian
Hobson, Harold
Hotter, Hans
Howard, Leslie
Howard, Trevor
Howerd, Frankie
Irving, Sir Henry
Izzard, Eddie
Jacobi, Sir Derek
Jacobs, David
Jagger, Mick
Jarman, Derek
Jolson, Al
Joplin, Scott
Joplin, Janis
Jouvet, Louis
Keaton, Buster
Kemble, Fanny
Kendal, Felicity
Kenton, Stan
Kidman, Nicole
Kramer, Stanley

Lauder, Sir Harry
Lemmon, Jack
Lennon, John
Lillie, Beatrice
Lipman, Maureen
Maazel, Lorin
Marley, Bob
Martin, Mary
Massey, Daniel
Massey, Raymond
Mayall, Rik
McKern, Leo
Merman, Ethel
Miller, Glenn
Miller, Jonathan
Mingus, Charlie
Monroe, Marilyn
Moreau, Jeanne
Morley, Robert
Morton, Jelly Roll
Mostel, Zero
Mutter, Anne-Sophie
Nerina, Nadia
Newman, Nanette
Newman, Paul
Norden, Denis
Norman, Jessye
O'Toole, Peter
Oliver, King
Pacino, Al
Parker, Charlie
Parker, Dorothy
Parton, Dolly
Paxman, Jeremy
Powell, Dilys
Powell, Michael
Previn, André
Quayle, Sir Anthony
Rattle, Sir Simon
Renoir, Jean
Robson, Dame Flora
Rogers, Ginger
Rooney, Mickey
Savile, Sir Jimmy
Seeger, Peggy
Seeger, Pete
Sibley, Antoinette
Sinden, Sir Donald
Stacey, Kevin
Steele, Tommy
Streep, Meryl
Suzman, Janet
Talbot, Godfrey
Tauber, Richard

Taylor, Dame Elizabeth
Temple, Shirley
The Who
Tilley, Vesta
Turner, Tina
Waller, Fats
Waring, Eddie
Warner, Brothers
Warner, David
Waters, Muddy
Welles, Orson
Wilder, Billy
Wilder, Gene
Wolfit, Sir Donald
Wonder, Stevie
Zanuck, Darryl F.

7

Andrews, Eamon
Andrews, Dame Julie
Astaire, Fred
Baillie, Dame Isobel
Beckham, Victoria
Beecham, Sir Thomas
Bennett, Alan
Bennett, Jill
Bentine, Michael
Bentley, Dick
Bergman, Ingmar
Bergman, Ingrid
Bergner, Elisabeth
Berkoff, Steven
Bogarde, Sir Dirk
Branagh, Kenneth
Bremner, Rory
Bresson, Robert
Burbage, Richard
Caballé, Montserrat
Campion, Jane
Chabrol, Claude
Chaplin, Sir Charles
Chester, Charlie
Clapton, Eric
Cochran, Eddie
Cocteau, Jean
Colbert, Claudette
Coleman, Ornette
Collins, Joan
Compton, Fay
Connery, Sir Sean
Coppola, Francis Ford
Corbett, Harry
Cushing, Peter
De Mille, Cecil B.

Delfont, Lord
Deneuve, Catherine
Domingo, Plácido
Donegan, Lonnie
Donovan
Douglas, Kirk
Douglas, Michael
Durante, Jimmy
Edwards, Jimmy
Elliott, Denholm
Feldman, Marty
Fellini, Federico
Ferrier, Kathleen
Fonteyn, Dame Margot
Forsyth, Bruce
Garland, Judy
Garrick, David
Gielgud, Sir John
Gingold, Hermione
Giulini, Carlo Maria
Goldwyn, Sam
Goodman, Benny
Guthrie, Sir Tyrone
Guthrie, Woody
Haitink, Bernard
Hammond, Dame Joan
Hancock, Sheila
Hancock, Tony
Handley, Tommy
Harding, Gilbert
Hawkins, Jack
Hendrix, Jimi
Hepburn, Audrey
Hepburn, Katharine
Hoffman, Dustin
Holiday, Billie
Hopkins, Sir Anthony
Hordern, Sir Michael
Ingrams, Richard
Jackson, Glenda
Jackson, Mahalia
Jackson, Michael
Jacques, Hattie
Johnson, Dame Celia
Karajan, Herbert von
Karloff, Boris
Kennedy, Sir Ludovic
Kubelik, Rafael
Kubrick, Stanley
Langtry, Lillie
Lehmann, Lili
Lehmann, Lotte
Lympany, Moira
MacColl, Ewan

Madonna
Malcolm, George
Marceau, Marcel
Markova, Dame Alicia
Massine, Léonide
McQueen, Steve
Menuhin, Lord
Mercury, Freddie
Mitchum, Robert
Montand, Yves
Monteux, Pierre
Murdoch, Richard
Nilsson, Birgit
Novello, Ivor
Nureyev, Rudolf
Olivier, Lord
Paltrow, Gwyneth
Pavlova, Anna
Paxinou, Katina
Pickles, Wilfred
Plummer, Christopher
Poitier, Sidney
Portman, Eric
Presley, Elvis
Quilley, Denis
Rambert, Dame Marie
Rantzen, Esther
Redding, Otis
Redford, Robert
Richard, Sir Cliff
Richter, Hans
Roberts, Julia
Robeson, Paul
Rodgers, Richard
Rodgers, Joan
Rushton, William
Russell, Jane
Russell, Ken
Sargent, Sir Malcolm
Secombe, Sir Harry
Segovia, Andrés
Sellers, Peter
Seymour, Lynn
Shankar, Ravi
Shearer, Moira
Sherrin, Ned
Siddons, Sarah
Simmons, Jean
Sinatra, Frank
Solomon (Solomon Cutner)
Steiger, Rod
Stevens, Cat
Stewart, James

Stewart, Rod
Swanson, Gloria
Tarrant, Chris
Thibaud, Jacques
Ulanova, Galina
Ustinov, Sir Peter
Vaughan, Frankie
Vaughan, Sarah
Wheldon, Sir Huw
Whicker, Alan
Winfrey, Oprah
Winters, Shelley
Withers, Googie
Wynette, Tammy

8

Anderson, Dame Judith
Anderson, Lindsay
Anderson, Marian
Ansermet, Ernest
Ashcroft, Dame Peggy
Atkinson, Rowan
Baddeley, Hermione
Bakewell, Joan
Bancroft, Anne
Bankhead, Tallulah
Barrault, Jean-Louis
Beerbohm, Sir Max
Berkeley, Busby
Boulting, John
Boulting, Roy
Brambell, Wilfrid
Brasseur, Pierre
Buchanan, Jack
Bygraves, Max
Calloway, Cab
Campbell, Mrs Patrick
Carreras, José
Christie, Julie
Clements, John
Coltrane, John
Connolly, Billy
Crawford, Joan
Crawford, Michael
Davidson, Jim
de Valois, Dame Ninette
Dietrich, Marlene
Dimbleby, Sir Richard
Eastwood, Clint
Flagstad, Kirsten
Flanagan, Bud
Flanders, Michael
Fletcher, Cyril

Franklin, Aretha
Goossens, Leon
Grenfell, Joyce
Grierson, John
Grimaldi, Joseph
Guinness, Sir Alec
Harrison, George
Harrison, Sir Rex
Hayworth, Rita
Helpmann, Sir Robert
Hoffnung, Gerard
Holloway, Stanley
Horowitz, Vladimir
Iglesias, Julio
Kreisler, Fritz
Kurosawa, Akira
Lansbury, Angela
Laughton, Charles
Lawrence, Gertrude
Leighton, Margaret
Liberace
Lockwood, Margaret
Marsalis, Wynton
Matthews, Jessie
McDonald, Sir Trevor
McKellen, Sir Ian
Melchior, Lauritz
Mercouri, Melina
Milligan, Spike
Milstein, Nathan
Mitchell, Joni
Morrison, Jim
Morrison, Van
Mulligan, Gerry
Nijinski, Vaslav
Oistrakh, David
Oistrakh, Igor
Paganini, Niccolò
Peterson, Oscar
Pfeiffer, Michelle
Pickford, Mary
Polanski, Roman
Redgrave, Corin
Redgrave, Lynn
Redgrave, Sir Michael
Redgrave, Vanessa
Reynolds, Burt
Robinson, Edward G.
Robinson, Robert
Schnabel, Artur
Schumann, Elisabeth
Scofield, Paul
Scorsese, Martin
Selznick, David O.

Stephens, Sir Robert
Streeter, Fred
Stroheim, Erich von
Te Kanawa, Dame Kiri
Thompson, Emma
Travolta, John
Truffaut, François
Visconti, Luchino
Whitelaw, Billie
Williams, Andy
Williams, Hank
Williams, John
Williams, Kenneth
Zeppelin, Led
Ziegfeld, Florenz

9

Almodóvar, Pedro
Antonioni, Michelangelo
Armstrong, Louis
Ashkenazy, Vladimir
Bacharach, Burt
Barrymore, Ethel
Barrymore, John
Barrymore, Lionel
Belafonte, Harry
Beriosova, Svetlana
Bernhardt, Sarah
Betterton, Thomas
Brannigan, Owen
Cardinale, Claudia
Chaliapin, Fyodor
Chevalier, Maurice
Christoff, Boris
Courtenay, Tom
Dankworth, John
Davenport, Bob
Depardieu, Gérard
Diaghilev, Serge
Dolmetsch, Arnold
Du Maurier, Sir Gerald
Ellington, Duke
Fairbanks, Douglas
Fernandel
Feuillère, Edwige
Gillespie, Dizzy
Grappelli, Stéphane
Hampshire, Susan
Hitchcock, Sir Alfred
Humphries, Barry
Klemperer, Otto
Lancaster, Burt
Landowska, Wanda
Lyttelton, Humphrey

Mackerras, Sir Charles
MacMillan, Sir Kenneth
McCartney, Sir Paul
McCartney, Stella
Monkhouse, Bob
Morecambe, Eric
Nicholson, Jack
Parkinson, Michael
Pavarotti, Luciano
Peckinpah, Sam
Pleasence, Donald
Plowright, Joan
Preminger, Otto
Reinhardt, Django
Reinhardt, Max
Spielberg, Steven
Sternberg, Joseph von
Stokowski, Leopold
Streisand, Barbra
Tarantino, Quentin
Tarkovsky, Andrei
Thorndike, Dame Sybil
Tortelier, Paul
Toscanini, Arturo
Valentino, Rudolf
Zinnemann, Fred

10

Balanchine, George
Barbirolli, Sir John
Bertolucci, Bernardo
Boucicault, Dion
Carmichael, Hoagy
Carmichael, Ian
Courtneige, Dame Cecily
Cunningham, Merce
D'Oyly Carte, Richard
Eisenstein, Sergei
Fassbinder, Rainer
Fitzgerald, Ella
Galli-Curci, Amelita
Halliwell, Geri
Littlewood, Joan
Mengelberg, William
Michelmore, Cliff
Muggeridge, Malcolm
Paderewski, Ignacy
Richardson, Ian
Richardson, Sir Ralph
Rossellini, Roberto
Rubinstein, Artur
Rutherford, Dame Margaret
Stradivari, Antonio
Sutherland, Dame Joan

Tetrazzini, Luisa
Woffington, Peg
Zeffirelli, Franco

11 AND OVER

Attenborough, David (12)
Attenborough, Lord (12)
Beiderbecke, Bix (11)
Buffalo Bill (11)
De Havilland, Olivia (11)

Ffrangcon-Davies, Gwen (15)
Fischer-Dieskau, Dietrich (14)
Forbes-Robertson,
  Sir Johnston (15)
Furtwängler, Wilhelm (11)
Granville-Barker, Harley (15)
Hammerstein, Oscar (11)
Laurel and Hardy (14)
Mac Liammóir, Micheál (11)
Mastroianni, Marcello

Mistinguett (11)
Schlesinger, John (11)
Schwarzkopf, Elisabeth (11)
Springfield, Dusty (11)
Stanislavsky, Konstantin (12)
Stradivarius, Antonio (12)
Terry Thomas (11)

2. Sports and Games

ath. = athletics; *box.* = boxing; *ch.* = chess; *crc.* = cricket; *fb.* = football; *gf* = golf;
gym. = gymanstics; *hr.* = horseracing; *mr.* = motor-racing; *mt* = mountaineering;
sj. = showjumping; *sw.* = swimming; *ten.* = tennis; *yt.* = yachting

3 AND 4

Ali, Muhammad *box.*
Ashe, Arthur *ten.*
Best, George *fb.*
Borg, Björn *ten.*
Cash, Pat *ten.*
Cobb, Ty *baseball*
Coe, Sebastian *ath.*
Cram, Steve *ath.*
Duke, Geoffrey *motor-cycling*
Endo, Yukio *gym.*
Fox, Uffa *yt.*
Graf, Steffi *ten.*
Hill, Graham *mr.*
Hill, Damon *mr.*
Hoad, Lew *ten.*
Hunt, James *mr.*
Hunt, Sir John *mt.*
John, Barry *rugby*
Khan, Imran *crc.*
Khan, Jahangir *squash*
Kim, Nellie *gym.*
King, Billie Jean *ten.*
Lara, Brian *crc.*
Law, Denis *fb.*
Lock, Tony *crc.*
Lomu, Jonah *rugby*
Lyle, Sandy *gf*
May, Peter *crc.*
Moss, Sir Stirling *mr.*
Pelé *fb.*
Read, Phil *motor-cycling*
Ruth, 'Babe' *baseball*
Snow, John *crc.*
Wade, Virginia *ten.*

Webb, Capt. Matthew *sw.*

5

Amiss, Dennis *crc.*
Banks, Gordon *fb.*
Brown, Joe *mt.*
Bruno, Frank *box.*
Budge, Don *ten.*
Bueno, Maria *ten.*
Busby, Sir Matthew *fb.*
Clark, Jim *mr.*
Close, Brian *crc.*
Court, Margaret *ten.*
Curry, John *skating*
Davis, Fred *billiards*
Davis, Joe *billiards*
Evans, Godfrey *crc.*
Evert, Chris *ten.*
Faldo, Nick *gf*
Gooch, Graham *crc.*
Grace, Dr W.G. *crc.*
Greig, Tony *crc.*
Gunnell, Sally *ath.*
Hagen, Walter *gf*
Hobbs, Sir John *crc.*
Hogan, Ben *gf*
Jeeps, Dickie *rugby*
Jones, Ann *ten.*
Jones, Bobby *gf*
Knott, Alan *crc.*
Laker, Jim *crc.*
Lauda, Niki *mr.*
Laver, Rod *ten.*
Lendl, Ivan *ten.*
Lewis, Carl *ath.*
Lloyd, Clive *crc.*

Louis, Joe *box.*
Meade, Richard *sj.*
Moore, Bobby *fb.*
Nurmi, Paavo *ath.*
Ovett, Steve *ath.*
Owens, Jesse *ath.*
Perry, Fred *ten.*
Pirie, Gordon *ath.*
Prost, Alain *mr.*
Revie, Don *fb.*
Senna, Ayrton *mr.*
Smith, Harvey *sj.*
Smith, Stan *ten.*
Spitz, Mark *sw.*
Tyson, Mike *box.*
Wills, Helen *ten.*
Woods, Tiger *gf*

6

Agassi, André *ten.*
Becker, Boris *ten.*
Bedser, Alec *crc.*
Benaud, Richie *crc.*
Border, Allan *crc.*
Botham, Ian *crc.*
Broome, David *sj.*
Brough, Louise *ten.*
Bugner, Joe *box.*
Carson, Willie *hr.*
Cooper, Henry *box.*
Cruyff, Johan *fb.*
Dexter, Ted *crc.*
Drobny, Jaroslav *ten.*
Edberg, Stefan *ten.*
Edrich, John *crc.*
Fangio, Juan *mr.*

Finney, Tom *fb.*
Foster, Brendan *ath.*
Fraser, Dawn *sw.*
Gibson, Althea *ten.*
Hadlee, Sir Richard *crc.*
Hutton, Sir Len *crc.*
Kanhai, Rohan *crc.*
Karpov, Anatoly *ch.*
Keegan, Kevin *fb.*
Korbut, Olga *gym.*
Lillee, Dennis *crc.*
Liston, Sonny *box.*
Merckx, Eddy *cycling*
Norman, Greg *gf*
Palmer, Arnold *gf*
Peters, Mary *ath.*
Player, Gary *gf*
Ramsey, Sir Alf *fb.*
Rhodes, Wilfred *crc.*
Robson, Bryan *fb.*
Shankly, Bill *fb.*
Sheene, Barry *motor-cycling*
Smythe, Pat *sj.*
Sobers, Sir Gary *crc.*
Stolle, Fred *ten.*
Taylor, Roger *ten.*
Thoeni, Gustavo *skiing*
Titmus, Fred *crc.*
Tunney, Gene *box.*
Turpin, Randolph *box.*
Wilkie, David *sw.*
Wright, Billy *fb.*

7

Beckham, David *fb.*
Boycott, Geoffrey *crc.*
Brabham, Sir Jack *mr.*
Bradman, Sir Donald *crc.*
Cantona, Eric *fb.*
Carling, Will *rugby*
Carnera, Primo *box.*
Compton, Denis *crc.*
Connors, Jimmy *ten.*
Cowdrey, Sir Colin *crc.*
Dempsey, Jack *box.*
Elliott, Herb *ath.*
Emerson, Roy *ten.*
Eusebio, Silva *fb.*
Ferrari, Enzio *mr.*
Fischer, Bobby *ch.*
Foreman, George *box.*
Fosbury, Richard *ath.*
Frazier, Joe *box.*
Greaves, Jimmy *fb.*

Hammond, Wally *crc.*
Higgins, Alex *snooker*
Hillary, Sir Edmund *mt.*
Hopkins, Thelma *hockey*
Jacklin, Tony *gf*
Johnson, Earvin *basketball*
Johnson, Jack *box.*
Larwood, Harold *crc.*
Lenglen, Suzanne *ten.*
Lineker, Gary *fb.*
Mansell, Nigel *mr.*
McBride, Willie *rugby*
McEnroe, John *ten.*
Mottram, Buster *ten.*
Nastase, Ilie *ten.*
Paisley, Bob *fb.*
Piggott, Lester *hr.*
Reardon, Ray *snooker*
Sampras, Pete *ten.*
Shilton, Peter *fb.*
Souness, Graeme *fb.*
Spassky, Boris *ch.*
Stewart, Jackie *mr.*
Surtees, John *motor-cycling, mr.*
Trevino, Lee *gf*
Trueman, Freddy *crc.*
Whymper, Edward *mt.*
Winkler, Hans *sj.*
Worrell, Sir Frank *crc.*
Zatopek, Emil *ath.*

8

Abrahams, Harold *ath.*
Agostini, Giacomo *motor-cycling*
Atherton, Michael *crc.*
Brinkley, Brian *sw.*
Campbell, Sir Malcolm *mr.*
Campbell, Donald *mr.*
Chappell, Greg *crc.*
Chappell, Ian *crc.*
Charlton, Sir Bobby *fb.*
Charlton, Jack *fb.*
Christie, Linford *ath.*
Dalglish, Kenny *fb.*
DiMaggio, Joe *baseball*
Docherty, Tommy *fb.*
Elvstrom, Paul *yt.*
Ferguson, Alec *fb.*
Gligoric, Svetozar *ch.*
Graveney, Tom *crc.*
Hailwood, Mike *motor-cycling*
Hawthorn, Mike *mr.*
Kapil Dev *crc.*
Kasparov, Gary *ch.*

Korchnoi, Viktor *ch.*
Latynina, Larissa *gym.*
Lindwall, Ray *crc.*
Maradona, Diego *fb.*
Marciano, Rocky *box.*
McLaren, Bruce *mr.*
Mortimer, Angela *ten.*
Newcombe, John *ten.*
Nicklaus, Jack *gf*
Richards, Viv *crc.*
Robinson, Sugar Ray *box.*
Rosewall, Ken *ten.*
Thompson, Daley *ath.*

9

Bannister, Sir Roger *ath.*
Bonington, Sir Chris *mt.*
Botvinnik, Mikhail *ch.*
D'Oliveira, Basil *crc.*
Gascoigne, Paul *fb.*
Goolagong, Evonne *ten.*
Llewellyn, Harry *sj.*
Patterson, Floyd *box.*
Schmeling, Max *box.*
Scudamore, Peter *hr.*
Shoemaker, Willie *hr.*
Underwood, Derek *crc.*
Whitbread, Fatima *ath.*

10 AND OVER

Ballesteros, Severiano *gf* (11)
Barrington, Jonah *squash* (10)
Beckenbauer, Franz *fb.* (11)
Blanchflower, Danny *fb.* (12)
Capablanca, José *ch.* (10)
Carpentier, Georges *box.* (10)
Chichester, Sir Francis *yt.* (10)
Constantine, Sir Learie *crc* (11)
Culbertson, Ely *bridge* (10)
Fittipaldi, Emerson *mr.* (10)
Fitzsimmons, Bob *box.* (11)
Illingworth, Ray *crc.* (11)
Lonsbrough, Anita *sw.* (10)
Navratilova, Martina *ten.* (11)
Oosterhuis, Peter *gf* (10)
Ranjitsinhji, Prince *crc.* (12)
Schockemöhle, Paul *sj* (12)
Schumacher, Michael *mr.* (10)
Tenzing Norgay *mt.* (13)
Torvill and Dean
   ice skating (14)
Turischeva, Ludmila *gym* (10)
Weissmuller, Johnny *sw.* (11)
Wills Moody, Helen *ten.* (10)

3. Other prominent people

3 AND 4

Ayer, A.J. (Eng. philosopher)
Beit, Alfred
  (S. African financier)
Cid, El (Spanish hero)
Eddy, Mrs Mary Baker (U.S. founder of Christian Science)
Fox, George (Eng. preacher)
Fry, Elizabeth (Eng. social reformer)
Hall, Marshall (Eng. physiologist)
Hill, Octavia (Eng. social reformer)
Hill, Sir Rowland (Eng. pioneer in postal services)
Hume, David (Sc. philosopher)
Hus, Jan (Bohemian religious reformer)
Jung, Carl Gustav (Swiss psychoanalyst)
Kant, Immanuel (Ger. philosopher)
Kidd, Capt. William (Sc. pirate)
Knox, John (Sc. religious reformer)
Kun, Bela (Communist leader in Hungary)
Lee, Ann (Eng. founder of Society of Shakers)
Low, Sir David (N.Z.-born cartoonist)
Luce, Henry Robinson (U.S. publisher)
Luce, Clare Booth (U.S. journalist and politician)
Marx, Karl (Ger. philosopher and social theorist)
Mond, Ludwig (Ger.-born chemist)
Nash, Beau (Eng. social arbiter)
Penn, William (Eng. Quaker, founder of Pennsylvania)
Polo, Marco (It. explorer)
Salk, Jonas Edward (U.S. scientist)

5

Acton, Lord (Eng. historian)
Adams, Henry (U.S. historian)

Adler, Alfred (Austrian psychologist)
Amati, Nicolò (Italian violin-maker)
Astor, Jacob (U.S. millionaire)
Astor, Viscountess (first woman in Br. House of Commons)
Bacon, Roger (philosopher)
Baird, Logie (Sc. pioneer in TV)
Banks, Joseph (Eng. naturalist)
Barth, Karl (Swiss theologian)
Booth, William (founder of the Salvation Army)
Botha, Louis (Boer leader)
Clive, Robert (Indian Empire pioneer)
Freud, Sigmund (Austrian pioneer psychoanalyst)
Hegel, Friedrich (Ger. philosopher)
Herzl, Theodor (Hung.-born founder of Zionism)
Karsh, Yousuf (Armenian-born photographer)
Keble, John (Eng. divine)
Zeiss, Carl (Ger. optical instrument maker)

6

Alcock, Sir John William (pioneer aviator)
Attila (King of the Huns)
Barker, Sir Herbert Atkinson (Eng. specialist in manipulative surgery)
Baruch, Bernard Mannes (U.S. financier)
Batten, Jean (N.Z. aviator)
Beeton, Isabella (Eng. cookery writer)
Besant, Mrs Anne (Eng. theosophist)
Boehme, Jakob (Ger. theosophist)
Butler, Mrs Josephine (Eng. social reformer)
Calvin, John (Fr. theologian)
Capone, Al (U.S. gangster)
Caslon, William (Eng. typefounder)
Cavell, Nurse Edith (Eng. patriot)

Caxton, William (first Eng. printer)
Childe, Vere Gordon (Australian archaeologist)
Cicero, Marcus Tullius (Roman statesman and writer)
Dunant, Henri (Swiss founder of International Red Cross)
Fawkes, Guy (Eng. conspirator)
Fokker, Anton (Dutch aviation pioneer)
Graham, Billy (U.S. evangelist)
Halley, Edmond (Eng. astronomer)
Hearst, William Randolph (U.S. newspaper publisher)
Hobbes, Thomas (Eng. philosopher)
Keynes, John Maynard (Eng. economist)
Loyola, St. Ignatius (Sp. founder of Jesuit order)
Luther, Martin (Ger. church reformer)
Mellon, Andrew William (U.S. financier)
Mesmer, Friedrich Franz (Ger. hypnotist)
Morgan, John Pierpont (U.S. financier)
Murrow, Edward R. (U.S. journalist and broadcaster)
Petrie, William Flinders (Eng. archaeologist)
Pitman, Sir Isaac (Eng. inventor of shorthand)
Planck, Max (Ger. physicist – formulated quantum theory)
Reuter, Paul Julius (Ger. founder of Reuters news agency)
Sandow, Eugene (Ger. strong man)
Sartre, Jean-Paul (Fr. writer and philosopher)
Stopes, Dr Marie (Eng. pioneer in family planning)
Tagore, Rabindranath (Indian poet and philosopher)
Teresa, Mother (Albanian-born Catholic missionary in India)

Turpin, Dick (Eng. highwayman)

Wesley, John (founder of Methodism)

Wright, Orville (U.S. pioneer aviator)

Wright, Wilbur (U.S. pioneer aviator)

7

Abelard, Peter (Fr. philosopher)

Aga Khan (Ismaili leader)

Agassiz, Jean (Swiss-born U.S. palaeontologist)

Aquinas, St. Thomas (It. philosopher and theologian)

Atatürk, Kemal (Turkish soldier and statesmen)

Blériot, Louis (Fr. aviator)

Blondin, Charles (Fr. acrobat)

Boyd-Orr, John, Baron (Sc. nutritionist)

Buchman, Frank (U.S. founder of Moral Rearmament)

Cassini, Giovanni Domenico (It. astronomer)

Celsius, Anders (Sw. inventor of Centigrade thermometer)

Cuvier, Georges (Fr. anatomist)

Earhart, Amelia (U.S. aviator)

Ehrlich, Paul (Ger. bacteriologist)

Erasmus, Desiderius (Dutch religious reformer and theologian)

Eysenck, Hans (Ger.-born psychologist)

Haeckel, Ernest Heinrich (Ger. naturalist)

Houdini, Harry (Erich Weiss) (Hung.-born magician and escapologist)

Johnson, Amy (Eng. aviator)

Leblanc, Nicolas (Fr. chemist)

Lesseps, Ferdinand de (Fr. engineer and diplomat)

Linacre, Thomas (Eng. founder of Royal College of Physicians)

Lumière, August and Louis (Fr. pioneers of cinematography)

MacEwen, Sir William (Sc. surgeon)

Marcuse, Herbert (Ger.-born political philosopher)

Murdoch, Rupert (Australian-born U.S. media proprietor)

Russell, Bertrand (Eng. philosopher)

Russell, William Howard (Eng. journalist)

Spencer, Herbert (Eng. philosopher)

Spinoza, Benedict (Dutch philosopher)

Steiner, Rudolf (Hung.-born philosopher and educationalist)

Tussaud, Mme Marie (Swiss-born modeller in wax)

Wheeler, Sir Mortimer (Eng. archaeologist)

Woolley, Leonard (Eng. archaeologist)

8

Averroës (Arab philosopher)

Avicenna (Arab philosopher)

Baedeker, Karl (Ger. publisher of travel guides)

Bancroft, George (U.S. historian)

Berkeley, George (Irish philosopher)

Carnegie, Andrew (Sc.-born philanthropist)

Cousteau, Jean-Jacques (Fr. oceanographer)

Foucault, Michel (Fr. philosopher)

Gollancz, Victor (Eng. publisher)

Grimaldi, Joseph (Eng. clown)

Larousse, Pierre Athanase (Fr. encyclopaedist)

Mercator, Gerardus (Flemish geographer)

Negretti, Enrico (It.-born instrument-maker)

Nuffield, William Richard Morris, Viscount (motor manufacturer and philanthropist)

Scribner, Charles (U.S. publisher)

Sheraton, Thomas (Eng. cabinet-maker)

Socrates (Gr. philosopher)

Wedgwood, Josiah (Eng. potter)

Wycliffe, John (Eng. religious reformer)

9

Arbuthnot, Alexander (printer of first bible, 1579, in Scotland)

Aristotle (Greek philosopher)

Arkwright, Sir Richard (inventor)

Blackwell, Dr. Elisabeth (first Eng. registered woman doctor)

Blavatsky, Madame Helena (Russian-born theosophist)

Courtauld, Samuel (Eng. silk manufacturer)

Descartes, René (Fr. philosopher)

Gutenberg, Johannes (Ger. founder of movable type)

Heidegger, Martin (Ger. philosopher)

Lindbergh, Charles (U.S. aviator)

Lucretius (Roman philosopher and poet)

Macgregor, Robert 'Rob Roy' (Sc. rebel)

Max-Müller, Friedrich (Ger.-born philologist and orientalist)

Nietzsche, Friedrich (Ger. philosopher)

Pankhurst, Mrs. Emmeline (Eng. suffragette leader)

Santayana, George (Spanish-born U.S. philosopher)

10

Bernadotte, Jean Baptiste (Fr. general and king of Sweden)

Cagliostro, Alessandro (Giuseppe Balsamo)

Flammarion, Camille (Fr. astronomer)

Guggenheim, Meyer (U.S. financier)

Macpherson, Aimée Semple (U.S. evangelist)

Montessori, Maria (It. founder of Montessori educational method)

Richthofen, Manfred von (Ger. air ace)

Rothermere, Harold Sidney Harmsworth, Viscount (Eng. newspaper publisher)

Rothschild, Meyer Amschel (Ger. financier)

Rutherford, Daniel (Sc. discoverer of nitrogen)

Schweitzer, Dr. Albert (Alsatian musician and medical missionary)

Stradivari, Antonio (It. violin-maker)

Swedenborg, Emanuel (Sw. theologian)

Vanderbilt, Cornelius (U.S. financier)

11

Aristarchos (Greek astronomer)

Beaverbrook, William Maxwell Aitken, 1st Baron (Canadian-born newspaper publisher)

Chippendale, Thomas (Eng. furniture designer)

Hippocrates (Greek physician)

Kierkegaard, Soren (Danish philosopher)

Kraft-Ebing, Richard von (Ger. psychiatrist)

Machiavelli, Niccolò (It. political reformer)

Montesquieu, Charles de (Fr. writer and philosopher)

Nightingale, Florence (Eng. pioneer in training nurses)

Northcliffe, Alfred Harmsworth, Viscount (Irish-born newspaper owner)

Shaftesbury, Anthony Ashley Cooper, 7th Earl (Eng. philanthropist)

Wilberforce, Samuel (Eng. divine)

Wilberforce, William (Eng. abolitionist)

12

Krishnamurti, Jiddu (Indian mystic)

Schopenhauer, Arthur (Ger. philosopher)

Wittgenstein, Ludwig (Austrian-born philosopher)

Explorers

3 AND 4

Back
Bass
Bird
Byrd
Cam
Cano
Cook
Diaz
Eyre
Gama
Gann
Hore
Hume
Hunt
Kidd
Leif
Muir
Park
Pike
Polo
Rae
Ross (Sir John)
Rut

5

Anson (Lord)
Baker
Barth
Blyth
Brown (Lady)
Bruce (General)
Brulé
Burke
Byron
Cabot
Clark
Davis
Drake (Sir Francis)
Dyatt
Dyott (Commander)
Evans (Capt.)
Fuchs
Gomez
Hanno
Hedin
Lewis
Mosto
Nares (Sir George)
Necho
Newby
Oates (Capt.)
Ojeda
Parry (Admiral)
Peary (Admiral)
Penny (Capt.)
Prado
Scott (Capt.)
Serra
Smith (Capt.)
Speke
Start
Sturt
Sykes
Terry
Welzl
Wills

6

Andrée
Austin (Capt.)
Baffin
Balboa
Barnes
Barrow (Sir John)
Bellot
Bering
Brazza
Burton (Sir Richard)
Cabral
Carson
Conway (Sir Martin)
Cortés
Curzon
Da Gama
de Soto
Diemen
Eannes
Fermor
Fraser
Hanway
Hartog
Hobson
Hudson
Joliet
Kellas
Landor
Marcks
Mawson
Morton
Murphy
Nansen
Nobile (General)
Osborn
Philby
Philip
Selous
Smythe
Stuart
Tasman
Torres

7

Abruzzi
Almeida
Barents
Belzoni
Bingham
Burnaby
Cameron
Carpini
Cartier
Chapman
Charcot
Colbeck
Dampier (William)
Doughty
Fawcett (Col.)
Fiennes
Fleming
Francke
Frémont
Gilbert
Hakluyt
Hawkins (Sir John)
Herbert
Hillary (Sir Edmund)
Hovell
John Rae
La Salle
Maclean
Markham (Albert)
McClure (Sir Robert)
Niebuhr

Pizarro
Pythias
Raleigh (Sir Walter)
Selkirk
Severin
Stanley (Sir H. M.)
Watkins
Weddell
Wegener
Wilkins
Workman
Wrangel

8

Agricola
Amundsen
Bee-Mason
Champion
Clifford
Columbus
Coronado
de Torres
Diego Cam
Ericsson
Etherton
Filchner
Flinders
Franklin (Sir John)
Grenfell
Hovgaard
Humboldt
Jan Welzl
Johansen
Johnston
Kingsley
Lawrence

Magellan
Marchand
McGovern
Ommanney
Orellana
Radisson
Stanhope
Sverdrup
Thompson (David)
Tristram
Valdivia
Vespucci
William (Sir Hubert)

9

Africanus
Bonington
Cadamosto
Cavendish
Champlain
Cockerill
de Almeida
de Filippi
de Houtman
de Mendana
Emin Pasha
Fernández
Frobisher (Sir Martin)
Gonsalvez
Grenville
Heyerdahl
Iberville
Jenkinson
John Cabot
John Davis
John Smith (Capt.)

Kropotkin (Prince)
Lancaster
M'Clintock
Mackenzie
Marco Polo
Mungo Park
Rasmussen
Sven Hedin
Van Diemen
Vancouver
Velásquez
Vérendrye

10

Abel Tasman
Bransfield
Burckhardt
Chancellor
Clapperton
Diego Gomez
Dirk Hartog
Eric the Red
Herjulfson
Ibn Battuta
Inglefield
Kohl-Larsen
Leichhardt
Leigh Smith
Lewis Cabot
Mandeville
McClintock
Richardson (Sir James)
Richthofen
Shackleton
Stefansson
Thomas Gann

Tschiffley
Willoughby (Sir Hugh)

11

Admiral Byrd
Albuquerque
Captain Bird
Captain Cook
Jean Charcot
Kingdon-Ward
Leif Ericson
Livingstone
Ponce de León
Prince Henry
Vasco da Gama

12

Bougainville
Luis de Torres
Nordenskjöld
Piano Carpini
Przhevalski
St. John Philby
Younghusband

14

Bellingshausen
Blashford-Snell
Diego Velásquez
Dumont d'Urville
Fridtjof Nansen
Hanbury-Tenison
Pierre de Brazza
Sebastian Cabot

Generals, field marshals, air marshals, etc.

3 – 5

Alba
Baird
Bock
Botha
Bruce
Byng
Clark
Clive
Condé
Craig
Dayan
de Wet

Diaz
Foch
Giap
Gort
Gough
Haig
Hope
Ismay
Jodl
Junot
Keith
Kleist
Kluge
Lee

Leese
Maude
Milne
Model
Mola
Moore
Murat
Ney
Parma
Pile
Roon
Saxe
Slim
Smuts

Soult
Stark
Sulla
Tilly
Tojo
White
Wolfe
Wood

6

Arnold
Bayard
Buller
Butler

Caesar
Crerar
Cronje
Custer
Dundas
Dundee
Dunois
Eugene
Franco
French
Fuller
Giraud
Gordon
Göring

Graham	Fairfax	Marshall	Auchinleck
Granby	Gamelin	Montcalm	Belisarius
Greene	Jackson	Napoleon	Bernadotte
Harris	Lambert	O'Higgins	Chelmsford
Joffre	Leclerc	Pershing	Codrington
Keitel	Lyautey	Radetsky	Cornwallis
Kléber	Masséna	Sheridan	Cumberland
Koniev	Maurice	Skobelev	Eisenhower
Mangin	Metaxas	Stilicho	Enver Pasha
Marius	Mortier	Townsend	Falkenhayn
Moltke	Nivelle	Urquhart	Hindenburg
Moreau	Roberts	von Bülow	Kesselring
Murray	Sherman	von Kluck	Kuropatkin
Napier	Stewart	Wolseley	Ludendorff
Narses	Suvorov		Mannerheim
Outram	Turenne	**9**	Montgomery
Patton	Villars		Schlieffen
Paulus	Weygand	Alexander	Timoshenko
Pétain	Wingate	Bagration	Voroshilov
Plumer	Wrangel	Beresford	Wellington
Pompey		Boulanger	
Portal	**8**	Cambridge	**11**
Powell		Connaught	
Raglan	Anglesey	Dumouriez	Abercrombie
Rommel	Augereau	Dundonald	Albuquerque
Rupert (Prince)	Badoglio	Garibaldi	Baden-Powell
Scipio	Bertrand	Gneisenau	Beauharnais
Spaatz	Birdwood	Hasdrubal	Brauchitsch
Tedder	Browning	Kitchener	de Castelnau
Trajan	Burgoyne	Lafayette	Marlborough
Wavell	Campbell	MacArthur	Poniatowski
Wilson	Cardigan	Macdonald	Schwarzkopf
Zhukov	Cromwell	McClellan	Strathnairn
	De Gaulle	Miltiades	Wallenstein
7	Freyberg	Newcastle	
	Galliéni	Nicholson	**12 AND 13**
Agrippa	Gonzalvo	Rawlinson	
Allenby	Guderian	Robertson	Fabius Maximus (13)
Bazaine	Guesclin	Rundstedt	Hunter-Weston (12)
Berwick	Hamilton	Santa Anna	Smith-Dorrien (12)
Blücher	Hannibal	Trenchard	von Mackensen (12)
Bradley	Havelock	Wellesley	von Rundstedt (12)
Cadorna	Ironside	Willcocks	Younghusband (12)
Dempsey	Kornilov		
Denikin	Lockhart	**10**	**14 AND 15**
Douglas	MacMahon		Barclay de Tolly (14)
Dowding	Manstein	Alanbrooke	Garnet-Wolseley (14)
		Alcibiades	Napier of Magdala (15)

Politicians and statesmen: a selection

3 AND 4	Blum	Clay	Gore	King
	Burr	Díaz	Grey	Kohl
Amin	Cato	Foot	Hess	Lie
Benn	Chou	Fox	Hull	Meir

Nagy
Pitt
Pym
Rhee
Root
Rusk
Tito
Tojo
Tone
Tutu

5

Astor
Begin
Benés
Beria
Bevan
Bevin
Botha
Burke
Ciano
Cleon
De Wet
Debré
Desai
Ebert
Havel
Hiero
Hoare
Hoxha
Husak
Jagan
Kadar
Laval
Lenin
Lyons
Marat
Mboya
Menon
Nehru
Nkomo
Obote
Perón
Putin
Sadat
Simon
Smith
Smuts
Solon
Spaak
Sulla
Villa

6

Bhutto
Borden
Borgia
Brandt
Bright
Butler
Caesar
Castro
Cavour
Chiang
Chirac
Cicero
Cobden
Cripps
Cromer
Curzon
Deakin
Dubcek
Dulles
Erhard
Fleury
Franco
Gadafy
Gandhi
Göring
Grivas
Hitler
Horthy
Juárez
Kaunda
Kruger
Marcos
Marius
Mobutu
Mosley
Mugabe
Nasser
O'Neill
Pétain
Powell
Revere
Rhodes
Samuel
Stalin
Walesa
Zapata

7

Acheson
Allende

Atatürk
Batista
Bolívar
Bormann
Collins
Gaddafi
Gomulka
Grattan
Gromyko
Halifax
Hampden
Himmler
Hussein
Jenkins
Keating
Kennedy
Kinnock
Kosygin
Kreisky
Lumumba
Luthuli
Mandela
Masaryk
Mazarin
Mazzini
Menzies
Mintoff
Molotov
Nkrumah
Nyerere
Paisley
Parnell
Pearson
Ptolemy
Raffles
Reynaud
Salazar
Schmidt
Sukarno
Trotsky
Trudeau
Vorster
Webster
Whitlam
Yeltsin

8

Adenauer
Augustus
Ayub Khan
Bismarck
Brezhnev

Bulganin
Cosgrave
Cromwell
Crossman
Daladier
De Gaulle
De Valera
Dollfuss
Duvalier
Eichmann
Franklin
Goebbels
Harriman
Hastings
Hirohito
Holyoake
Honecker
Kenyatta
Khomeini
Lycurgus
Makarios
Malenkov
McCarthy
Montfort
Morrison
Napoleon
O'Higgins
Pericles
Pinochet
Podgorny
Poincaré
Pompidou
Quisling
Rasputin
Rawlings
Sihanouk
Sikorski
Ulbricht
Verwoerd
Waldheim
Welensky

9

Alexander
Ben Gurion
Bonaparte
Bourguiba
Chou En-Lai
Churchill
Clarendon
Dionysius
Gaitskell

Gorbachev
Ho Chi Minh
Kissinger
Luxemburg
Milosevic
Mussolini
Pankhurst
Richelieu
Salisbury
Stevenson
Strafford
Vishinsky

10

Alcibiades
Che Guevara
Clemenceau
Hindenburg
Khrushchev
Lee Kuan-Yew
Mao Tse-tung
Metternich
Mitterrand
Ribbentrop
Sekou Touré
Stresemann
Talleyrand
Voroshilov

11

Abdul Rahman
Boumédienne
Castlereagh
Chamberlain
Cleisthenes
Demosthenes
Diefenbaker
Machiavelli
Mountbatten
Robespierre
Shaftesbury

12

Bandaranaike
Hammarskjöld
Kemal Atatürk
Mendès-France
Papadopoulos
Shevardnadze
Themistocles

13 AND OVER

Chiang Kai-shek (13)
Giscard d'Estaing (15)
Haile Selassie (13)

Presidents of the United States

4 AND 5

Adams, John
Adams, John Quincy
Bush, George
Ford, Gerald
Grant, Ulysses S.
Hayes, Rutherford B.
Nixon, Richard M.
Polk, James K
Taft, William
Tyler, John

6

Arthur, Chester A.
Carter, Jimmy
Hoover, Herbert
Monroe, James
Pierce, Franklin
Reagan, Ronald
Taylor, Zachary
Truman, Harry S
Wilson, Woodrow

7

Clinton, William
Harding, Warren G.
Jackson, Andrew
Johnson, Andrew
Johnson, Lyndon B.
Kennedy, John F.
Lincoln, Abraham
Madison, James

8

Buchanan, James
Coolidge, Calvin
Fillmore, Millard

Garfield, James A.
Harrison, Benjamin
Harrison, William
McKinley, William
Van Buren, Martin

9

Cleveland, Grover
Jefferson, Thomas
Roosevelt, Franklin D.
Roosevelt, Theodore

10

Eisenhower, Dwight
Washington, George

Prime ministers of Great Britain

4 AND 5

Blair, Tony
Bute, Lord
Derby, Lord
Eden, Sir Anthony
Grey, Lord
Heath, Edward
Major, John
North, Lord
Peel, Sir Robert
Pitt, William (the Younger)

6

Attlee, Clement
Pelham, Henry
Wilson, Sir Harold

7

Asquith, Herbert
Baldwin, Stanley
Balfour, Arthur
Canning, George

Chatham, Lord (Wm Pitt the Elder)
Grafton, Duke of
Russell, Lord John
Walpole, Sir Robert

8

Aberdeen, Lord
Bonar Law, Andrew
Disraeli, Benjamin
Goderich, Lord
Perceval, Spencer
Portland, Duke of
Rosebery, Lord
Thatcher, Margaret

9

Addington, Henry
Callaghan, James
Churchill, Sir Winston
Gladstone, William
Grenville, George
Grenville, Lord

Liverpool, Lord
MacDonald, Ramsay
Macmillan, Harold
Melbourne, Lord
Newcastle, Duke of
Salisbury, Marquis of
Shelburne, Lord

10

Devonshire, Duke of
Palmerston, Lord
Rockingham, Marquis of
Wellington, Duke of
Wilmington, Lord

11 AND OVER

Beaconsfield, Lord (12)
Campbell-Bannerman, Sir Henry (17)
Chamberlain, Neville (11)
Douglas-Home, Sir Alec (11)
Lloyd George, David (11)

Scientists, engineers and mathematicians

3 AND 4

Abel
Airy
Auer
Bell
Benz
Bohr
Born
Bose
Burt
Davy
Eads
Ford
Gall
Gibb
Gold
Hale
Hero
Hess
Howe
Koch
Ohm
Otto
Paré
Ray
Reed
Ryle
Swan
Todd
Tull
Watt

5

Adams
Amici
Bacon
Baird
Banks
Bondi
Boole
Boyle
Bragg
Brahe
Chain
Crick
Curie
Debye
Dirac
Euler
Ewing
Fabre

Fermi
Frege
Galen
Galle
Gamow
Gauss
Gödel
Haber
Hardy
Henry
Hertz
Hooke
Hoyle
Jeans
Joule
Klein
Krebs
Libby
Lodge
Maxim
Monge
Monod
Morse
Nobel
Pauli
Pliny
Popov
Prout
Segrè
Soddy
Stahl
Tesla
Volta
White
Young

6

Adrian
Agnesi
Alfvén
Ampère
Bordet
Boveri
Bramah
Briggs
Brunel
Buffon
Bunsen
Calvin
Cantor
Carnot
Darwin

Diesel
Dunlop
Euclid
Fermat
Froude
Fulton
Galois
Halley
Harvey
Hubble
Hughes
Hutton
Huxley
Jacobi
Jenner
Joliot
Kekulé
Kelvin
Kepler
Kuiper
Landau
Liebig
Lister
Lorenz
Lovell
Lowell
Markov
Mendel
Morgan
Napier
Nernst
Newton
Olbers
Pascal
Pavlov
Penney
Perkin
Perutz
Planck
Proust
Ramsay
Réamur
Rennie
Roscoe
Sanger
Singer
Sloane
Stokes
Struve
Talbot
Taylor
Teller

Thales
Turing
Wallis
Watson
Wilson
Wright
Yukawa
Zeeman

7

Andrews
Audubon
Babbage
Babbitt
Banting
Bateson
Bergius
Braille
Brouwer
Buchner
Charles
Compton
Coulomb
Crookes
Da Vinci
Daimler
De Vries
Doppler
Faraday
Feynman
Fischer
Fleming
Fourier
Galileo
Galvani
Goddard
Gregory
Haeckel
Haldane
Hawkins
Helmont
Hilbert
Hodgkin
Hooker
Huggins
Huygens
Kapitsa
Kendrew
Lalande
Lamarck
Leibniz
Lockyer

Lorentz
Marconi
Maxwell
Medawar
Meitner
Moseley
Neumann
Oersted
Pasteur
Pauling
Peierls
Piccard
Ptolemy
Riemann
Röntgen
Rumford
Seaborg
Siemens
Szilard
Telford
Thomson
Tyndall
Vavilov
Venturi
Virchow
Wallace
Whitney
Whittle

8

Agricola
Angström
Avogadro
Bessemer
Bjerknes
Blackett
Calmette
Chadwick
Crompton
De Forest
De Morgan
Einstein
Foucault
Franklin
Gassendi
Goodyear
Guericke
Harrison
Herschel
Humboldt
Jacquard
Klaproth

Lagrange
Lawrence
Legendre
Leibnitz
Linnaeus
Lonsdale
Malpighi
Mercator
Millikan
Mitchell
Poincaré
Rayleigh
Sakharov
Sikorsky
Stirling
Thompson
Van Allen
Van't Hoff
Zeppelin

9

Arkwright
Armstrong
Arrhenius
Becquerel
Bernoulli
Berthelot
Berzelius
Bronowski
Cavendish
Cherenkov
Cockcroft
D'Alembert
De Broglie
Descartes
Eddington
Fibonacci
Flamsteed

Gay-Lussac
Heaviside
Helmholtz
Kirchhoff
Lankester
Lavoisier
Mendeleev
Michelson
Priestley
Ramanujan
Tinbergen
Wollaston
Zsigmondy
Zuckerman

10

Archimedes
Cannizzaro
Copernicus

Fahrenheit
Fitzgerald
Fraunhofer
Heisenberg
Hipparchus
Littlewood
Maupertius
Mendeleyev
Paracelsus
Rutherford
Stephenson
Swammerdam
Torricelli
Trevithick
Watson-Watt
Wheatstone

11 AND OVER

Chandrasekhar
   (13)
Eratosthenes (12)
Galileo Galilei (14)
Grosseteste (11)
Hero of
   Alexandria (16)
Joliot-Curie (11)
Le Châtelier (11)
Leeuwenhoek (11)
Montgolfier (11)
Oppenheimer (11)
Schrödinger (11)
Szent-Györgyi (12)
Tsiolkovski (11)
Van der Waals (11)

GEOGRAPHY
Abbreviations for geographical lists

Adr. Adriatic Sea
Aeg. Aegean Sea
Af. Africa
Afghan. Afghanistan
Alb. Albania
Alg. Algeria
Am. America
Ang. Angola
Antarc. Antarctic (Ocean)
Arab. Arabia, Arabian Sea
Arc. Arctic (Ocean)
Arg. Argentina
Arm. Armenia
Asia M. Asia Minor
Atl. Atlantic Ocean
Aust. Austria
Austral. Australia
Azer. Azerbaijan
Balt. Baltic (Sea)
Bangla. Bangladesh
Bela. Belarus
Belg. Belgium
Boliv. Bolivia
Bos. Bosnia-Hercegovina
Braz. Brazil
Bulg. Bulgaria
Bur. Burundi
Burk. Burkina Faso
C. Am. Central America
Can. Canada

Cen. Af. Rep. Central African
   Republic
Ch. Is. Channel Islands
Col. Colombia
Congo, Dem. Rep. Democratic
   Republic of the Congo
Congo, Rep. of Republic of the
   Congo
Cors. Corsica
Cze. Czech Republic
Den. Denmark
E. Af. East Africa
E. I. East Indies
Eng. England
Est. Estonia
Eth. Ethiopia
Eur. Europe
Fin. Finland
Fr. France
Geo. Georgia
Ger. Germany
Gr. Greece
Green. Greenland
Him. Himalayas
Hung. Hungary
Ind. India, Indian Ocean
Indo. Indonesia
Ire. Ireland, Republic of Ireland
Isr. Israel
It. Italy

Jam. Jamaica
Jap. Japan
Jord. Jordan
Kaz. Kazakhstan
Kyr. Kyrgyzstan
Lat. Latvia
Lith. Lithuania
Mac. Macedonia
Mad. Madagascar
Malay. Malaysia
Med. Mediterranean (Sea)
Mex. Mexico
Mold. Moldova, Moldavia
Mon. Mongolia
Monte. Montenegro
Moroc. Morocco
Moz. Mozambique
N. Af. North Africa
N. Am. North America
N. Guin. New Guinea
N.I. Northern Ireland
N. Pac. North Pacific
N.Z. New Zealand
Nam. Namibia
Nep. Nepal
Neth. Netherlands
Nig. Nigeria
Nor. Norway
Oc. Oceania
Pac. Pacific Ocean

Pak. Pakistan
Pal. Palestine
Papua Papua New Guinea
Philip. Philippines
Pol. Poland
Port. Portugal
Pyr. Pyrenees
Red S. Red Sea
Rom. Romania
Rus. Russia
S.A. South Africa
S. Am. South America
S. Pac. South Pacific
Sard. Sardinia
Saudi Saudi Arabia

Scot. Scotland
Serb. Serbia
Sib. Siberia
Sic. Sicily
Slov. Slovakia
Sloven. Slovenia
Sp. Spain
Sri Sri Lanka
Swed. Sweden
Swit. Switzerland
Taj. Tajikistan
Tanz. Tanzania
Tas. Tasmania
Thai. Thailand
Trin. Trinidad

Tun. Tunisia
Turk. Turkey
Turkmen. Turkmenistan
U.A.E. United Arab Emirates
Ukr. Ukraine
Uru. Uruguay
Uzbek. Uzbekistan
Venez. Venezuela
Viet. Vietnam
W. Af. West Africa
W.I. West Indies
Yug. Yugoslavia
Zam. Zambia
Zim. Zimbabwe

Bays, bights, firths, gulfs, sea lochs, loughs and harbours

B. = Bay; Bi. = Bight; F. = Firth; Fi. = Fiord; G. = Gulf;
Har. = Harbour; L. = Loch (Scottish); Lou. = Lough (Irish); S. = Sea

2 – 4

Acre, B. of (Isr.)
Aden, G. of (Arab.)
Awe, L. (Scot.)
Clew B. (Ire.)
Ewe, L. (Scot.)
Fyne, L. (Scot.)
Gilp, L. (Scot.)
Goil, L. (Scot.)
Ise B. (Jap.)
Kiel, B. (Ger.)
Long, L. (Scot.)
Lorn, F. of (Scot.)
Luce B. (Scot.)
Lyme B. (Eng.)
Ob, G. of (Rus.)
Pigs, B. of (Cuba)
Riga, G. of (Lat.)
Siam, G. of (Asia)
Suez, G. of (Red S.)
Tay, F. of (Scot.)
Tees B. (Eng.)
Tor B. (Eng.)
Vigo, B. of (Sp.)
Wash, The (Eng.)

5

Algoa B. (S.A.)
Aqaba, G. of (Red. S.)
Benin, Bi. of (W. Af.)
Blind B. (N.Z.)

Broom, L. (Scot.)
Cadiz, B. of (Sp.)
Casco B. (U.S.A.)
Clyde, F. of (Scot.)
Dvina B. (Rus.)
Enard B. (Scot.)
Evans B. (N.Z.)
False B. (S.A.)
Forth, F. of (Scot.)
Foyle, Lou. (Ire.)
Fundy, B. of (Can.)
Genoa, G. of (It.)
Hawke B. (N.Z.)
Izmir, G. of (Turk.)
James B. (Can.)
Kutch, G. of (Ind.)
Leven, L. (Scot.)
Lyons, G. of (Med.)
Milne B. (Papua)
Moray F. (Scot.)
Omura B. (Jap.)
Osaka B. (Jap.)
Otago Har. (N.Z.)
Papua, G. of (N. Guin.)
Paria, G. of (S. Am.)
Table B. (S.A.)
Tampa B. (U.S.A.)
Tokyo B. (Jap.)
Tunis, G. of (N. Af.)
Vlöre B. (Alb.)

6

Aegina, G. of (Gr.)
Alaska, G. of (U.S.A.)
Ariake B. (Jap.)
Aylort, L. (Scot.)
Baffin B. (Can.)
Bantry B. (Ire.)
Bengal, B. of (Ind.)
Biafra, Bi. of (W. Af.)
Biscay, B. of (Fr., Sp.)
Botany B. (Austral.)
Broken B. (Austral.)
Callao. B. of (Peru)
Cambay, G. of (Ind.)
Cloudy B. (N.Z.)
Colwyn B. (Wales)
Danzig G. of (Pol.)
Darien, G. of (S. Am.)
Denial B. (Austral.)
Dingle B. (Ire.)
Drake's B. (U.S.A.)
Dublin B. (Ire.)
Galway B. (Ire.)
Gdansk, G. of (Pol.)
Guinea, G. of (W. Af.)
Hervey B. (Austral.)
Hudson B. (Can.)
Jervis B. (Austral.)
Linnhe, L (Scot.)
Lobito B. (Ang.)
Lübeck B. (Ger.)

Manaar, G. of (Ind.)
Mexico, G. of (Mex.)
Mobile B. (U.S.A.)
Mounts B. (Eng.)
Naples, B. of (It.)
Panama, G. of (C. Am.)
Plenty, B. of (N.Z.)
Ramsey B. (Eng.)
Sharks B. (Austral.)
Smyrna, G. of (Turk.)
Solway F. (Scot.)
St. Malo, G. of (Fr.)
Sunart, L (Scot.)
Swilly, Lou. (Ire.)
Sydney Har. (Austral.)
Tasman B. (N.Z.)
Tonkin, G. of (S. China S.)
Toyama B. (Jap.)
Tralee B. (Ire.)
Ungava B. (Can.)
Venice, G. of (It.)
Walvis B. (S.A.)
Zuider S. (Neth.)

7

Aboukir B. (Med.)
Argolis, G. of (Gr.)
Belfast Lou. (N.I.)
Boothia, G. of (Can.)
Bothnia, G. of (Swed.)
Bustard B. (Austral.)
Cape Cod B. (U.S.A.)

Chaleur B. (Can.)
Delagoa B. (S.A.)
Donegal B. (Ire.)
Dornoch F. (Scot.)
Dundalk B. (Ire.)
Finland, G. of (Eur.)
Florida B. (U.S.A.)
Fortune B. (Can.)
Halifax B. (Austral.)
Hudson's B. (Can.)
Kaipara Har. (N.Z.)
Khambat, G. of (Ind.)
Killala B. (Ire.)
Lepanto, G. of (Gr.)
Montego B. (Jam.)
Moreton B. (Austral.)
Pegasus B. (N.Z.)
Persian G. (Asia)
Poverty B. (N.Z.)
Salerno, G. of (It.)
Setúbal, B. of (Port.)
Snizort, L. (Scot.)
Swansea B. (Wales)
Taranto, G. of (It.)
Tarbert, L. (Scot.)
Thunder B. (Can.)
Trieste, G. of (Adr.)
Trinity B. (Can.)
Wexford B. (Ire.)
Wigtown B. (Scot.)
Youghal B. (Ire.)

8

Biscayne B. (U.S.A.)
Buzzards B. (U.S.A.)
Cagliari, G. of (It.)
Campeche, B. of (Mex.)
Cardigan B. (Wales)
Cochinos, B. of (Cuba)
Cromarty F. (Scot.)
Delaware B. (U.S.A.)
Dunmanus B. (Ire.)
Georgian B. (Can.)
Hammamet, G. of (Tun.)

Hangzhou B. (China)
Honduras, G. of (C. Am.)
Liaodong, G. of (China)
Martaban, G. of (Burma)
Pentland F. (Scot.)
Plymouth Har. (Eng.)
Portland B. (Austral.)
Portland Har. (Eng.)
Quiberon B. (Fr.)
Salonika, G. of (Gr.)
San Jorge, G. of (S. Am.)
San Pablo B. (U.S.A)
Spencer's G. (Austral.)
St. Bride's B. (Wales)
Thailand, G. of (Asia)
Tongking, G. of (S. China S.)
Tremadog B. (Wales)
Weymouth B. (Eng.)

9

Admiralty B. (N.Z.)
Broughton B. (Austral.)
Cambridge G. (Austral.)
Discovery B. (Austral.)
Encounter B. (Austral.)
Famagusta B. (Cyprus)
Frobisher B. (Can.)
Galveston B. (U.S.A.)
Gweebarra B. (Ire.)
Hermitage B. (Can.)
Inverness F. (Scot.)
Liverpool B. (Eng.)
Mackenzie B. (Can.)
Magdalena B. (Mex.)
Morecambe B. (Eng.)
Notre Dame B. (Can.)
Placentia B. (Can.)
Saint Malo, G. of (Fr.)
San Matías, G. of (S. Am.)
St. Austell B. (Eng.)
St. George's B. (Can.)
St. George's B. (S. Am.)
St. Vincent G. (Austral.)
Van Diemen G. (Austral.)

Venezuela, G. of (S. Am.)

10 AND OVER

Ballyteige B. (Ire.) (10)
Barnstaple B. (Eng.) (10)
Bridgwater B. (Eng.) (10)
Bridlington B. (Eng.) (11)
Caernarfon B. (Wales) (10)
Caernarvon B. (Wales) (10)
California, G. of (Mex.) (10)
Carmarthen B. (Wales) (10)
Canterbury Bi. (N.Z.) (10)
Carpentaria, G. of (Austral.) (11)
Chesapeake B. (U.S.A.) (10)
Christiania Fi. (Nor.) (11)
Conception B. (Can.) (10)
Corpus Christi B. (U.S.A.) (13)
Espíritu Santo, B. of (Mex.) (13)
Great Australian Bi.
  (Austral.) (15)
Guantánamo B. (Cuba) (10)
Heligoland Bi. (Ger.) (10)
Lutzow-Holm B. (Antarc.) (10)
Massachusetts B. (U.S.A.) (13)
Narragansett B. (U.S.A.) (12)
Pomeranian B. (Baltic S.) (10)
Port Jackson B. (Austral.) (11)
Port Philip B. (Austral.) (10)
Portsmouth Har. (Eng.) (10)
Princess Charlotte B.
  (Austral.) (17)
Ringkøbing Fi. (Den.) (10)
Robin Hood's B. (Eng.) (10)
Saint Vincent, G. (Austral.) (12)
San Francisco B. (U.S.A.) (12)
Southampton Water (Eng.) (16)
St. Lawrence, G. of (Can.) (10)
Tehuantepec, G. of (Mex.) (11)

Capes, headlands, points, etc.

C. = Cape; Hd. = Head or Headland; N. = Ness; Pt. = Point

3 AND 4

Aird Pt. (Scot.)
Ann, C. (U.S.A.)
Ayre Pt. (Eng.)

Baba, C. (Turk.)
Bon, C. (N. Af.)
Busa, C. (Crete)
Cod, C. (U.S.A.)
Cruz, C. (S. Am.)

East C. (NZ.)
East Pt. (Can.)
Farr Pt. (Scot.)
Fear, C. (U.S.A.)
Fife N. (Scot.)

Fogo, C. (Can.)
Frio, C. (Braz.)
Frio, C. (W. Af.)
Hoe Pt. (Scot.)
Horn, C. (S. Am.)

Howe, C. (Austral.)
Icy C. (Can.)
Krio, C. (Crete)
Loop Hd. (Ire.)
May, C. (U.S.A.)
Nao, C. (It.)
Naze (The) (Eng.)
Naze (The) (Nor.)
Nord, C. (Nor.)
Noss Hd. (Scot.)
Nun, C. (W. Af.)
Race, C. (Can.)
Roxo, C. (Can.)
Sima, C. (Jap.)
Slea Hd. (Ire.)
Soya, C. (Jap.)
Sur Pt. (S. Am.)
Toe Hd. (Scot.)
Turn N. (Scot.)
York, C. (Austral.)

5

Adieu, C. (Austral.)
Amber, C. (E. Af.)
Aniva, C. (Rus.)
Bauer, C. (Austral.)
Brims N. (Scot.)
Byron, C. (Austral.)
Clare, C. (Ire.)
Clark Pt. (Can.)
Corso, C. (Cors.)
Creus, C. (Sp.)
Gallo, C. (Gr.)
Gaspé C. (Can.)
Lopez C. (W. Af.)
Malia, C. (Gr.)
Mink, C. (W. Af.)
Negro, C. (W. Af.)
North C. (N.Z.)
North C. (Nor.)
Orme's Hd. (Wales)
Otway, C. (Austral.)
Quoin Pt. (S.A.)
Roray Hd. (Scot.)
Sable, C. (Can.)
Sable, C. (U.S.A.)
San Ho, C. (Viet.)
Sandy C. (Austral.)
Sheep Hd. (Ire.)
Slade Pt. (Austral.)
Sleat Pt. (Scot.)
Slyne Hd. (Ire.)
South C. (China)
Spurn Hd. (Eng.)

Start Pt. (Eng.)
Tavoy Pt. (Burma)
Troup Hd. (Scot.)
Verde, C. (W. Af.)
Wiles, C. (Austral.)
Worms Hd. (Wales)
Wrath, C. (Scot.)
Yakan, C. (Sib.)

6

Andres Pt. (S. Am.)
Bantam, C. (Indo.)
Barren, C. (Austral.)
Beachy Hd. (Eng.)
Blanco, C. (N. Af.)
Blanco, C. (S. Am.)
Branco, C. (S. Am.)
Breton, C. (Can.)
Buddon N. (Scot.)
Burrow Hd. (Scot.)
Burrow Pt. (Scot.)
Carmel, C. (Isr.)
Castle Pt. (N.Z.)
Comino, C. (Sard.)
Cuvier, C. (Austral.)
De Gata, C. (Spain)
De Roca, C. (Port)
Dodman Pt. (Eng.)
Dunnet Hd. (Scot.)
Egmont, C. (N.Z.)
Formby Hd. (Eng.)
Friars Pt. (U.S.A.)
Galley Hd. (Ire.)
Gallon Hd. (Scot.)
Glossa, C. (Turk.)
Lizard (The) (Eng.)
Orford N. (Eng.)
Palmas, C. (W. Af.)
Prawle Pt. (Eng.)
Recife, C. (S.A.)
Rhynns Pt. (Scot.)
Sambro, C. (Can.)
Sanaig Pt (Scot.)
Sidero, C. (Crete)
Soreli, C. (Austral.)
St. Abb's Hd. (Scot.)
St. Bees Hd. (Eng.)
St. Mary, C. (Can.)
St. Paul, C. (W. Af.)
Tarbat, N. (Scot.)
Tarifa, C. (Sp.)
Tolsta Hd. (Scot.)
Wad Nun, C.
   (N. Af.)

Whiten Hd. (Scot.)
Yerimo, C. (Jap.)

7

Agulhas, C. (S.A.)
Arisaig Pt (Scot.)
Bengore Hd. (N.I.)
Bismark, C. (Green.)
Bizzuto, C. (It.)
Blanche C. (Austral.)
Charles C. (U.S.A.)
Clogher Hd. (Ire.)
Colonna, C. (Gr.)
Comorin, C. (Ind.)
De Palos, C. (Sp.)
De Penas, C. (Sp.)
De Sines, C. (Port.)
Formosa C. (W. Af.)
Gregory, C. (Can.)
Gris-Nez, C. (Fr.)
Icy Cape (Can.)
Kataska, C. (Jap.)
Kennedy, C. (U.S.A.)
Leeuwin, C. (Austral.)
Matapan, C. (Gr.)
Milazzo, C. (Sic.)
Mondego, C. (Port.)
Mumbles Hd. (Wales)
Needles, The (Eng.)
Negrais, C. (Burma)
Orlando, C. (Sic.)
Ortegal, C. (Sp.)
Rattray Hd. (Scot.)
Romania, C. (Malay.)
Runaway, C. (N.Z.)
San Bias, C. (U.S.A.)
São Tomé, C. (Braz.)
Spartel, C. (Moroc.)
St. Lucia, C. (S.A.)
Strathy Pt. (Scot.)
Tegupan Pt. (Mex.)
Teulada, C. (Sard.)
The Horn (S. Am.)
The Naze (Eng.)
The Naze (Nor.)
Toe Head (Scot.)
Upstart, C. (Austral.)
Vincent, C. (U.S.A.)

8

Bathurst, C. (Can.)
Cambodia Pt. (Thai.)
Cap, Haïtien (Haiti)
East Cape (N.Z.)

Espicher, C. (Port.)
Fairhead, C. (N.I.)
Farewell, C. (Green.)
Farewell, C. (N.Z.)
Fife Ness (Scot.)
Flattery, C. (U.S.A.)
Foreland (The) (Eng.)
Gallinas Pt. (S. Am.)
Good Hope, C. of (S.A.)
Greenore Pt. (Ire.)
Hangklip, C. (S.A.)
Hartland Pt. (Eng.)
Hatteras, C. (U.S.A.)
Kaliakra, C. (Bulg.)
Kinnaird Hd. (Scot.)
Land's End (Eng.)
Loop Head (Ire.)
Maranhao, C. (Braz.)
Melville, C. (Austral.)
Palliser, C. (N.Z.)
Palmyras Pt. (Ind.)
San Diego, C. (S. Am.)
San Lucas, C. (Mex.)
São Roque, C. (Braz.)
Sidmouth, C. (Austral.)
Slea Head (Ire.)
Sordwana Pt. (S.A.)
St. Albans Hd. (Eng.)
St. David's Hd. (Wales)
St. George, C. (Can.)
St.-Gildas, Pointe du (Fr.)
St. Gowan's Hd. (Wales)
Strumble Hd. (Wales)
Sumburgh Hd. (Scot.)
Sur Point (U.S.A.)
Thorsden, C. (Arc.)
Turn Ness (Scot.)
Vaticano, C. (It.)

9

Bonavista, C. (Can.)
Brims Ness (Scot.)
Canaveral, C. (U.S.A.)
Carvoeira, C. (Port.)
Claremont Pt. (Austral.)
De la Hague, C. (Fr.)
De Talbert Pt. (Fr.)
Dungeness (Eng.)
East Point (Can.)
Esquimaux, C. (Can.)
Farr Point (Scot.)
Girardeau, C. (U.S.A.)
Granitola, C. (Sic.)
Inishowen Hd. (Ire.)

Mendocino, C. (U.S.A.)
Murchison, C. (Can.)
Nash Point (Wales)
North Cape (N.Z.)
North Cape (Nor.)
Ormes Head (Wales)
Roray Head (Scot.)
Saint Abb's Hd. (Scot.)
Saint Bees Hd. (Eng.)
Saint Mary, C. (Can.)
Saint Paul, C. (Ghana)
Sand Patch Pt. (Austral.)
Sandy Cape (Tas.)
Santo Vito, C. (Sic.)
Sheep Head (Ire.)
Slyne Head (Ire.)
South Cape (Hawaii)
Spurn Head (Eng.)
St. Francis, C. (Can.)
St. Vincent, C. (Port.)
Streedagh Pt. (Ire.)
The Lizard (Eng.)
Trafalgar, C. (Sp.)
Troup Head (Scot.)
Vaternish Pt. (Scot.)
Worms Head (Wales)

10

Beachy Head (Eng.)
Breakheart Pt. (Can.)
Buddon Ness (Scot.)
Burrow Head (Scot.)
Clark Point (Can.)
Conception Pt. (U.S.A.)
Duncansbay Hd. (Scot.)
Dunnet Head (Scot.)
Finisterre, C. (Sp.)
Galley Head (Ire.)
Gallon Head (Scot.)
Great Ormes Hd. (Wales)
Greenstone Pt. (Scot.)
Orford Ness (Eng.)
Palmerston, C. (Austral.)
Quoin Point (S.A.)
Rayes Point (S. Am.)
Saint Lucia, C. (S.A.)
San Antonio Pt. (Mex.)
San Lorenzo, C. (S. Am.)
Santa Maria, C. (Port.)
Selsey Bill (Eng.)
Slade Point (Austral.)
Sleat Point (Scot.)
Snettisham Pt. (Can.)
St. Margaret Pt. (Can.)

St. Matthieu Pt. (Fr.)
Start Point (Eng.)
Tarbat Ness (Scot.)
Tavoy Point (Burma)
The Needles (Eng.)
Tolsta Head (Scot.)
Walsingham, C. (Can.)
Washington, C. (Arc.)
Whiten Head (Scot.)

11

Andrés Point (S. Am.)
Bengore Head (N.I.)
Bridgewater, C. (Austral.)
Castle Point (N.Z.)
Catastrophe, C. (Austral.)
Clogher Head (Ire.)
Dodman Point (Eng.)
Downpatrick Hd. (N.I.)
Flamborough Hd. (Eng.)
Friars Point (U.S.A.)
Little Ormes Hd. (Wales)
Lizard Point (Eng.)
Mumbles Head (Wales)
Murraysburg, C. (S.A.)
Prawle Point (Eng.)
Rattray Head (Scot.)
Rhynns Point (Scot.)
Saint Albans Hd. (Eng.)
Saint David's Hd. (Wales)
Saint Gowan's Hd. (Wales)
Sanaig Point (Scot.)
The Foreland (Eng.)
Three Points, C. (W. Af.)
Tribulation, C. (Austral.)

12 AND OVER

Ardnamurchan Pt. (Scot.) (12)
Arisaig Point (Scot.) (12)
Breakheart Point (Can.) (15)
Cape of Good Hope (S.A.) (14)
Cayenne Point (E. Af.) (12)
Claremont Point (Austral.) (14)
Conception Point (U.S.A.) (15)
Downpatrick Head (N.I.) (15)
Duncansbay Head (Scot.) (14)
Flamborough Head (Eng.) (15)
Gracias a Dios, C. (C. Am.) (12)
Inishowen Head (Ire.) (13)
North Foreland (Eng.) (13)
Northumberland, C.
  (Austral.) (14)
Palmuras Point (Ind.) (13)
Portland Bill (Eng.) (12)

Saint Margaret Pt. (Can.) (13)   Strumble Head (Wales) (12)   Vaternish Point (Scot.) (14)
San Francisco, C. (S. Am.) (12)   Sumburgh Head (Scot.) (12)
Sand Patch Point (Austral.) (14)   Tegupan Point (Mex.) (12)

Capital cities of the world

3 AND 4

Apia (Samoa)
Baku (Azer.)
Bern (Swit.)
Dilí (East Timor)
Doha (Qatar)
Kiev (Ukr.)
Lima (Peru)
Lomé (Togo)
Male (Maldives)
Oslo (Nor.)
Riga (Latvia)
Rome (It.)
San'a (Yemen)
Suva (Fiji)

5

Abuja (Nig.)
Accra (Ghana)
Agana (Guam)
Ajman (Ajman)
Amman (Jordan)
Berne (Swit.)
Cairo (Egypt)
Dakar (Senegal)
Delhi (India)
Dhaka (Bangla.)
Dubai (Dubai)
Hanoi (Viet.)
Kabul (Afghan.)
La Paz (Boliv.)
Macao (Macao)
Minsk (Bela.)
Nauru (Nauru)
Paris (Fr.)
Praia (Cape Verde)
Quito (Ecuador)
Rabat (Moroc.)
Sana'a (Yemen)
Seoul (S. Korea)
Skopje (Mac.)
Sofia (Bulg.)
Tokyo (Jap.)
Tunis (Tunis.)
Vaduz (Liechtenstein)

6

Ankara (Turk.)
Asmara (Eritrea)
Asthana (Kaz.)
Athens (Gr.)
Bamako (Mali)
Bangui (Cen. Af. Rep.)
Banjul (Gambia)
Beirut (Lebanon)
Berlin (Ger.)
Bissau (Guinea-Bissau)
Bogotá (Colombia)
Dodoma (Tanz.)
Dublin (Ire.)
Harare (Zimbabwe)
Havana (Cuba)
Hobart (Tasmania)
Kigali (Rwanda)
Kuwait (Kuwait)
La'youn (W. Sahara)
Lisbon (Port.)
London (U.K.)
Luanda (Angola)
Lusaka (Zambia)
Madrid (Sp.)
Malabo (Equatorial
   Guinea)
Manama (Bahrain)
Manila (Philip.)
Maputo (Mozambique)
Maseru (Lesotho)
Monaco (Monaco)
Moroni (Comoro Is.)
Moscow (Russia)
Muscat (Oman)
Nassau (Bahamas)
Niamey (Niger)
Ottawa (Can.)
Panama (Panama)
Peking (China)
Prague (Cze.)
Riyadh (Saudi)
Roseau (Dominica)
Taipei (Taiwan)
Tawara (Kiribati)
Tehran (Iran)

Thimbu (Bhutan)
Tirana (Albania)
Vienna (Aust.)
Warsaw (Pol.)
Yangon (Burma)
Zagreb (Croatia)

7

Algiers (Alg.)
Baghdad (Iraq)
Bangkok (Thai.)
Beijing (China)
Belfast (N. Ire.)
Bishkek (Kyr.)
Caracas (Venez.)
Cardiff (Wales)
Colombo (Sri)
Conakry (Guinea)
Douglas (Isle of Man)
El Aaiún (W. Sahara)
Gangtok (Sikkim)
Honiara (Solomon
   Islands)
Jakarta (Indo.)
Kampala (Uganda)
Managua (Nicaragua)
Mbabane (Swaziland)
Nairobi (Kenya)
Nicosia (Cyprus)
Palikir (Micronesia)
Rangoon (Myanmar)
San José (Costa Rica)
São Tomé (São Tomé
   and Principe)
Sharjah (Sharjah)
St. John's (Antigua and
   Barbuda)
Stanley (Falkland Is.)
Tallinn (Est.)
Tbilisi (Geo.)
Teheran (Iran)
Tel Aviv (Isr.)
Thimphu (Bhutan)
Tripoli (Libya)
Vilnius (Lith.)
Yaoundé (Cameroon)
Yerevan (Arm.)

8

Abu Dhabi (U.A.E.)
Ashgabat (Turkmen.)
Asunción (Paraguay)
Belgrade (Yug.)
Belmopan (Belize)
Brasilia (Braz.)
Brussels (Belg.)
Budapest (Hung.)
Canberra (Austral.)
Cape Town (S.A.)
Castries (St. Lucia)
Chisinau (Mold.)
Damascus (Syria)
Djibouti (Djibouti)
Dushanbe (Taj.)
Freetown (Sierra
   Leone)
Fujairah (Fujairah)
Funafuti (Tuvalu)
Gaborone (Botswana)
Hamilton (Bermuda)
Helsinki (Fin.)
Khartoum (Sudan)
Kingston (Jamaica)
Kinshasa (Congo, Dem.
   Rep. of)
Lilongwe (Malawi)
Monrovia (Liberia)
N'Djaména (Chad)
New Delhi (Ind.)
Plymouth (Montserrat)
Pretoria (S.A.)
Santiago (Chile)
Sarajevo (Bos.)
St. Helier (Jersey)
Tashkent (Uzbek.)
Valletta (Malta)
Victoria (Seychelles)
Windhoek (Namibia)

9

Amsterdam (Neth.)
Bucharest (Rom.)
Bujumbura (Burundi)
Edinburgh (Scot.)

Grand Turk (Turks and
    Caicos Is.)
Islamabad (Pak.)
Jamestown (St. Helena)
Kingstown (St. Vincent
    and the Grenadines)
Ljubljana (Sloven.)
Mogadishu (Somalia)
Nuku'alofa (Tonga)
Phnom Penh (Cambodia)
Port Louis (Mauritius)
Porta Vila (Vanuatu)
Porto Novo (Benin)
Pyongyang (N. Korea)
Reykjavik (Iceland)
San Marino (San Marino)
Singapore (Singapore)
St. George's (Grenada)
Stockholm (Swed.)
The Valley (Anguilla)
Ulan Bator (Mon.)
Vientiane (Laos)

10

Addis Ababa (Eth.)
Basseterre (St. Christopher
    and Nevis)
Bratislava (Slov.)
Bridgetown (Barbados)
Copenhagen (Den.)
George Town (Guyana)
Georgetown (Cayman Is.)
Kuwait City (Kuwait)
Libreville (Gabon)
Luxembourg (Luxembourg)
Mexico City (Mexico)
Montevideo (Uruguay)
Nouakchott (Mauritania)
Ougadougou (Burk.)
Panama City (Panama)
Paramaribo (Surinam)
Washington (U.S.A.)
Wellington (N.Z.)

11 AND OVER

Andorra la Vella (Andorra) (14)
Antananarivo (Mad.) (12)

Bandar Seri Begawan
    (Brunei) (17)
Brazzaville (Congo, Rep. of) (11)
Buenos Aires (Arg.) (11)
Dalap-Uliga-Darrit (Marshall
    Islands) (16)
Guatemala City (Guatemala)
    (13)
Kuala Lumpur (Malay.) (11)
Port Moresby (Papua) (11)
Port of Spain (Trinidad and
    Tobago) (11)
Port-au-Prince (Haiti) (12)
Ras al-Khaimah (Ras al-
    Khaimah) (12)
San Salvador (El Salvador) (11)
Santo Domingo (Dominican
    Rep.) (12)
St. Peter Port (Guernsey) (11)
Tegucigalpa (Honduras) (11)
Ulaanbaatar (Mon.) (11)
Umm al-Qaiwain (Umm al-
    Qaiwain) (12)
Vatican City (Vatican City) (11)
Yamoussoukro (Ivory Coast) (12)

Channels, passages, sounds and straits

Ch. = Channel; P. = Passage; Sd. = Sound; St. (s) = Strait(s)
Note – The land references are to give a general idea as to location

3 AND 4

Bass St. (Austral.)
Coll, P. of (Scot.)
Cook St. (N.Z.)
Fox Ch. (Can.)
Jura Sd. (Scot.)
Mona P. (W.I.)
Nore (The) (Eng.)
Palk St. (Ind.)

5

Cabot St. (Can.)
Davis St. (Can.)
Dover, Sts. of (Eng.)
Johor, Sts. of (Malay.)
Kerch St. (Ukr., Rus.)
Korea St. (Jap.)
Menai Sts. (Wales)
Minch (The) (Scot.)
North Ch. (Scot.)

Puget Sd. (U.S.A.)
Sleat, Sd. of (Scot.)
Smith Sd. (Can.)
Sound (The) (Swed.)
Sumba St. (Indo.)
Sunda, St. of (Indo.)
Tatar St. (Rus.)

6

Achill Sd. (Ire.)
Bangka St. (Indo.)
Barrow St. (Can.)
Bering St. (Pac.)
Hainan St. (China)
Harris, St. of (Scot.)
Hecate St. (Can.)
Hormuz, St. of (Iran)
Hudson St. (Can.)
Lombok St. (Indo)
Madura St. (Indo.)
Nootka Sd. (Can.)

Panama Canal (C. Am.)
Queen's Ch. (Austral.)
Solent (The) (Eng.)
Taiwan St. (China)
Torres St. (Austral.)
Tromsø Sd. (Nor.)

7

Bristol Ch. (Eng.)
Denmark St. (Green.)
Dolphin St. (Can.)
English Ch. (Eng.)
Florida St. (U.SA.)
Foveaux St. (N.Z.)
Georgia, St. of (Can.)
Le Maire St. (Arg.)
Malacca St. (Malaya)
Malacca, St. of (Indo.)
Messina, St. of (It.)
Molucca P. (E.I.)
Øresund (Swed., Den.)

Otranto, St. of (It.)
Pamlico Sd. (U.S.A.)
The Nore (Eng.)
Yucatán Ch. (Mex.)

8

Colonsay, P. of (Scot.)
Kattegat (The) (Den.)
Mackinac, Sts. of
    (U.S.A.)
Magellan, St. of
    (S. Am.)
Makassar Sts. (Indo.)
Plymouth Sd. (Eng.)
Spithead (Eng.)
The Minch (Scot.)
The Sound (Swed.)
Windward P. (W.I.)

9

Belle Isle, St. of (Can.)
Bonifacio, St. of (Med.)
Bosphorus
  (The) (Turk.)
Gibraltar, Sts. of (Spain)
Great Belt (The) (Den.)
La Pérouse St. (Jap., Rus.)
Lancaster Sd. (Can.)
Scapa Flow (Scot.)
Skagerrak (Nor. and Den.)
St. George's Ch. (Eng.)

Suez Canal (Egypt)
The Solent (Eng.)

10

Dogger Bank (N. Sea)
Golden Gate (U.S.A.)
Golden Horn (Turk.)
Juan de Fuca, St. of (Can.,
  U.S.A.)
Kilbrennan Sd. (Scot.)
King George Sd. (Austral.)
Little Belt (The) (Den.)
Mozambique Ch. (Moz.)

11 AND OVER

Bab-el-Mandeb St. (Red S.) (11)
Caledonian Canal (Scot.) (15)
Corinth Canal (Gr.) (12)
Dardanelles (The) (Turk. (11)
Goodwin Sands (Eng.) (12)
Grand Union Canal (Eng.) (15)
Hampton Roads (U.S.A.) (12)
Northumberland St. (Can.) (14)
Pas de Calais (Fr.) (11)
Queen Charlotte Sd. (Can.) (14)
Saint George's Ch. (Eng.) (12)
The Bosphorus (Turk.) (12)
The Dardanelles (Turk.) (14)
The Great Belt (Den.) (12)
The Little Belt (Den.) (13)

Counties: United Kingdom and Republic of Ireland

(E) = England; (Ire.) = Republic of Ireland; (N.I.) = Northern Ireland; (S.) = Scotland; (W.) = Wales
Note – As the names of some counties are commonly used in shortened form, both full and shortened names are given in this list. It also includes county names no longer officially in use.

3 AND 4

Avon (E.)
Ayr (S.)
Beds (E.)
Bute (S.)
Cork (Ire.)
Down (N.I.)
Fife (S.)
I.O.W. (E.)
Kent (E.)
Leix (Ire.)
Mayo (Ire.)
Oxon (E.)
Ross (S.)

5

Angus (S.)
Banff (S.)
Berks (E.)
Bucks (E.)
Cavan (Ire.)
Clare (Ire.)
Clwyd (W.)
Derby (E.)
Devon (E.)
Dyfed (W.)
Elgin (S.)
Essex (E.)

Flint (W.)
Gwent (W.)
Hants (E.)
Herts (E.)
Hunts (E.)
Kerry (Ire.)
Lancs (E.)
Laois (Ire.)
Leics (E.)
Lincs (E.)
Louth (Ire.)
Meath (Ire.)
Moray (S.)
Nairn (S.)
Notts (E.)
Perth (S.)
Powys (W.)
Salop (E.)
Sligo (Ire.)
Wilts (E.)
Yorks (E.)

6

Antrim (N.I.)
Argyll (S.)
Armagh (N.I.)
Brecon (W.)
Carlow (Ire.)
Dorset (E.)

Dublin (Ire.)
Durham (E.)
Forfar (S.)
Galway (Ire.)
Gloucs. (E.)
Lanark (S.)
London (E.)
N. Yorks (E.)
Offaly (Ire.)
Orkney (S.)
Oxford (E.)
Radnor (W.)
Surrey (E.)
Sussex (E.)
Tyrone (N.I.)

7

Bedford (E.)
Berwick (S.)
Borders (S.)
Central (S.)
Cumbria (E.)
Denbigh (W.)
Donegal (Ire.)
Gwynedd (W.)
Kildare (Ire.)
Kinross (S.)
Leitrim (Ire.)
Lincoln (E.)

Norfolk (E.)
Peebles (S.)
Renfrew (S.)
Rutland (E.)
Selkirk (S.)
Suffolk (E.)
Tayside (S.)
Warwick (E.)
Wexford (Ire.)
Wicklow (Ire.)
Wigtown (S.)

8

Aberdeen (S.)
Anglesey (W.)
Ayrshire (S.)
Cardigan (W.)
Cheshire (E.)
Cornwall (E.)
Cromarty (S.)
Dumfries (S.)
Grampian (S.)
Hereford (E.)
Hertford (E.)
Highland (S.)
Kilkenny (Ire.)
Laoighis (Ire.)
Limerick (Ire.)
Longford (Ire.)

Monaghan (Ire.)
Monmouth (E.)
Pembroke (W.)
Roxburgh (S.)
Somerset (E.)
Stirling (S.)

9

Berkshire (E.)
Caithness (S.)
Cambridge (E.)
Cleveland (E.)
Connaught (Ire.)
Dunbarton (S.)
Edinburgh (S.)
Fermanagh (N.I.)
Glamorgan (W.)
Hampshire (E.)
Inverness (S.)
Leicester (E.)
Merioneth (W.)
Middlesex (E.)
Northants (E.)
Roscommon (Ire.)
Tipperary (Ire.)
Waterford (Ire.)
Westmeath (Ire.)
Wiltshire (E.)
Worcester (E.)
Yorkshire (E.)

10

Banffshire (S.)
Buckingham (E.)
Caernarvon (W.)
Carmarthen (W.)
Cumberland (E.)
Derbyshire (E.)
Devonshire (E.)
East Sussex (E.)
Flintshire (W.)
Gloucester (E.)
Haddington (S.)
Humberside (E.)
Huntingdon (E.)

Inverclyde (S.)
Kincardine (S.)
Lancashire (E.)
Linlithgow (S.)
Merseyside (E.)
Midlothian (S.)
Montgomery (W.)
Perthshire (S.)
Shropshire (E.)
Sutherland (S.)
West Sussex (E.)

11 AND 12

Argyllshire (S.) (11)
Bedfordshire (E.) (12)
Berwickshire (S.) (12)
Clackmannan (S.) (11)
Denbighshire (W.) (12)
East Ayrshire (S.) (12)
East Lothian (S.) (11)
Forfarshire (S.) (11)
Isle of Wight (E.) (11)
Kircudbright (S.) (12)
Lanarkshire (S.) (11)
Lincolnshire (E.) (12)
Londonderry (N.I.) (11)
Mid Glamorgan (W.) (12)
Oxfordshire (E.) (11)
Radnorshire (W.) (11)
Renfrewshire (S.) (12)
Strathclyde (S.) (11)
Tyne and Wear (E.) (11)
Warwickshire (E.) (12)
West Lothian (S.) (11)
West Midlands (E.) (12)
Western Isles (S.) (12)
Westmorland (E.) (11)

13 AND 14

Aberdeenshire (S.) (13)
Argyll and Bute (S.) (13)
Brecknockshire (W.) (14)
Cambridgeshire (E.) (14)
Cardiganshire (W.) (13)
Clackmannanshire (S.) (16)

Dumfriesshire (S.) (13)
Dunbartonshire (S.) (14)
East Renfrewshire (S.) (16)
Greater London (E.) (13)
Herefordshire (E.) (13)
Hertfordshire (E.) (13)
Inverness-shire (S.) (14)
Leicestershire (E.) (14)
Merionethshire (W.) (14)
Monmouthshire (E.) (13)
North Ayrshire (S.) (13)
North Lanarkshire (S.) (16)
North Yorkshire (E.) (14)
Northumberland (E.) (14)
Orkney Islands (S.) (13)
Pembrokeshire (W.) (13)
Perth and Kinross (S.) (15)
Scottish Borders (S.) (15)
Shetland Islands (S.) (15)
South Ayrshire (S.) (13)
South Glamorgan (W.) (14)
South Lanarkshire (S.) (16)
South Yorkshire (E.) (14)
Staffordshire (E.) (13)
West Glamorgan (W.) (13)
West Yorkshire (E.) (13)
Worcestershire (E.) (14)

15 AND 16

Buckinghamshire (E.) (15)
Caenarvonshire (W.) (15)
Carmarthenshire (W.) (15)
Gloucestershire (E.) (15)
Huntingdonshire (E.) (15)
Montgomeryshire (W.) (15)
Northamptonshire (E.) (16)
Nottinghamshire (E.) (15)
Ross and Cromarty (S.) (15)

Countries and continents

Note – This list includes the names of former countries

3 AND 4

Anam (Asia)

Asia
Bali (Asia)
C.I.S. (Asia, Eur.)

Chad (Af.)
Cuba (W.I.)
D.D.R. (E. Ger.)

Eire (Eur.)
Fiji (S. Pac.)
G.D.R. (E. Ger.)

Guam (Pac.)
Iran (Asia)
Iraq (Asia)

Java (Asia)
Laos (Asia)
Mali (Af.)
Nejd (Asia)
Oman (Arab.)
Peru (S. Am.)
Siam (Asia)
Togo (Af.)
U.A.R. (Af.)
U.S.A. (N. Amer.)
U.S.S.R.
 (Asia, Eur.)

5

Annam (Asia)
Assam (Asia)
Benin (Af.)
Burma (Asia)
Chile (S. Am.)
China (Asia)
Congo (Af.)
Egypt (Af.)
Fiume (Eur.)
Gabon (Af.)
Ghana (Af.)
Haiti (W.I.)
India (Asia)
Italy (Eur.)
Japan (Asia)
Kandy (Asia)
Kenya (Af.)
Khmer (Asia)
Korea (Asia)
Libya (Af.)
Lydia (Asia)
Macao (Asia)
Macáu (Asia)
Malta (Med.)
Natal (Af.)
Nauru (Pac.)
Nepal (Asia)
Niger (Af.)
Papua (E.I.)
Qatar (Arab.)
Samoa (Oc.)
Spain (Eur.)
Sudan (Af.)
Syria (Asia)
Tchad (Af.)
Tibet (Asia)
Timor (Indo.)
Tonga (Oc.)
Tunis (Af.)
Wales (Eur.)

Yemen (Arab.)
Zaïre (Af.)

6

Africa
Angola (Af.)
Arabia (Asia)
Azores (Atl.)
Belize (C. Am.)
Bhutan (Asia)
Brazil (S. Am.)
Brunei (E.I.)
Canada (N. Am.)
Cathay (Asia)
Ceylon (Asia)
Cyprus (Med.)
Epirus (Eur.)
Europe
France (Eur.)
Gambia (Af.)
Greece (Eur.)
Guinea (Af.)
Guyana (S. Am.)
Hawaii (Pac.)
Israel (Asia)
Johore (Asia)
Jordan (Asia)
Kuwait (Arab.)
Latvia (Eur.)
Malawi (Af.)
Malaya (Asia)
Mexico (N. Am.)
Monaco (Eur.)
Muscat (Asia)
Norway (Eur.)
Panama (C. Am.)
Persia (Asia)
Poland (Eur.)
Ruanda (Af.)
Russia (Eur., Asia)
Rwanda (Af.)
Serbia (Eur.)
Servia (Eur.)
Sicily (Eur.)
Sikkim (Asia)
Soudan (Af.)
Sweden (Eur.)
Taiwan (Asia)
Tobago (W.I.)
Turkey (Eur., Asia)
Tuvalu (Oc.)
Uganda (Af.)
Ulster (Eur.)
Zambia (Af.)

7

Albania (Eur.)
Algeria (Af.)
America
Andorra (Eur.)
Antigua (W.I.)
Armenia (Asia)
Ashanti (Af.)
Assyria (Asia)
Austria (Eur.)
Bahamas (W.I.)
Bahrain (Arab.)
Bavaria (Eur.)
Belarus (Eur.)
Belgium (Eur.)
Bermuda (Atl.)
Bohemia (Eur.)
Bolivia (S. Am.)
Britain (Eur.)
Burkina (Af.)
Burundi (Af.)
Comoros (Af.)
Croatia (Eur.)
Dahomey (Af.)
Denmark (Eur.)
Ecuador (S. Am.)
England (Eur.)
Eritrea (Af.)
Estonia (Eur.)
Faeroes (Atl.)
Finland (Eur.)
Formosa (Asia)
Georgia (Eur.)
Germany (Eur.)
Grenada (W.I.)
Holland (Eur.)
Hungary (Eur.)
Iceland (Eur.)
Ireland (Eur.)
Jamaica (W.I.)
Lebanon (Asia)
Lesotho (Af.)
Liberia (Af.)
Livonia (Eur.)
Macedon (Eur.)
Moldova (Eur.)
Morocco (Af.)
Myanmar (Asia)
Namibia (Af.)
Nigeria (Af.)
Prussia (Eur.)
Romania (Eur.)
Rumania (Eur.)

São Tomé (Atl.)
Sarawak (Asia)
Senegal (Af.)
Somalia (Af.)
St. Kitts (W.I.)
St. Lucia (W.I.)
Sumatra (E.I.)
Sumeria (Asia)
Surinam (S. Am.)
Tangier (Af.)
Tartary (Asia)
Tripoli (Af.)
Tunisia (Af.)
Ukraine (Eur.)
Uruguay (S. Am.)
Vanuatu (Oc.)
Vatican (Eur.)
Vietnam (Asia)

8

Barbados (W.I.)
Botswana (Af.)
Bulgaria (Eur.)
Burgundy (Eur.)
Cambodia (Asia)
Cameroon (Af.)
Colombia (S. Am.)
Djibouti (Af.)
Dominica (W.I.)
Ethiopia (Af.)
Honduras (C. Am.)
Hong Kong (Asia)
Kiribati (S. Pac.)
Malagasy (Af.)
Malaysia (Asia)
Maldives (Ind.)
Moldavia (Eur.)
Mongolia (Asia)
Pakistan (Asia)
Paraguay (S. Am.)
Portugal (Eur.)
Rhodesia (Af.)
Roumania (Eur.)
Salvador (C. Am.)
Sardinia (Med.)
Scotland (Eur.)
Slovakia (Eur.)
Slovenia (Eur.)
St. Helena (Atl.)
St. Vincent (W.I.)
Suriname (S. Am)
Tanzania (Af.)
Tasmania (Austral.)
Thailand (Asia)

Togoland (Af.)
Trinidad (W.I.)
Zanzibar (Af.)
Zimbabwe (Af.)
Zululand (Af.)

9

Argentina (S. Am.)
Argentine, The (S. Am.)
Australia
Babylonia (Asia)
Caledonia (Eur.)
Cameroons (Af.)
Cape Verde (Af.)
Costa Rica (C. Am.)
East Timor (E.I.)
Gibraltar (Eur.)
Greenland (Arc.)
Guatemala (C. Am.)
Hindustan (Asia)
Indochina (Asia)
Indonesia (E.I.)
Kampuchea (Asia)
Kirghizia (Asia)
Lithuania (Eur.)
Luxemburg (Eur.)
Macedonia (Eur.)
Manchuria (Asia)
Mauritius (Af.)
New Guinea (E.I.)
Nicaragua (C. Am.)
Nyasaland (Af.)
Palestine (Asia)
Pondoland (Af.)
San Marino (Eur.)
Singapore (Asia)
Swaziland (Af.)
The Gambia (Af.)
Transvaal (Af.)
Venezuela (S. Am.)

10

Antarctica
Azerbaijan (Asia)
Bangladesh (Asia)
Basutoland (Af.)
Belorussia (Eur.)
California (N. Am.)
Cape Colony (Af.)
Damaraland (Af.)
El Salvador (C. Am.)
Ivory Coast (Af.)
Kazakhstan (Asia)
Kyrgyzstan (Asia)

Luxembourg (Eur.)
Madagascar (Af.)
Mauretania (Af.)
Mauritania (Af.)
Micronesia (Oc.)
Montenegro (Eur.)
Montserrat (W.I.)
Mozambique (Af.)
New Zealand (Pac.)
North Korea (Asia)
Seychelles (Af.)
Shan States (Asia)
Somaliland (Af.)
South Korea (Asia)
South Yemen (Asia)
Tajikistan (Asia)
Tanganyika (Af.)
Upper Volta (Af.)
Uzbekistan (Asia)
Yugoslavia (Eur.)

11

Afghanistan (Asia)
Australasia
Baluchistan (Asia)
Burkina Faso (Af.)
Byelorussia (Eur.)
Cochin China (Asia)
Cook Islands (Pac.)
Côte d'Ivoire (Af.)
Dutch Guiana (S. Am.)
East Germany (Eur.)
French Congo (Af.)
Malay States (Asia)
Mashonaland (Af.)
Mesopotamia (Asia)
Namaqualand (Af.)
Netherlands (Eur.)
New Hebrides (Pac.)
Philippines (Asia)
Saudi Arabia (Arab.)
Sierra Leone (Af.)
South Africa (Af.)
Soviet Union (Asia, Eur.)
Switzerland (Eur.)
Transjordan (Asia)
Vatican City (Eur.)
West Germany (Eur.)

12

Bechuanaland (Af.)
Belgian Congo (Af.)
Cocos Islands (Ind.)
Faroe Islands (Atl.)

French Guiana (S. Am.)
Great Britain (Eur.)
Guinea-Bissau (Af.)
Indian Empire (Asia)
Matabeleland (Af.)
Newfoundland (N. Am.)
North America
North Vietnam (Asia)
Ruanda-Urundi (Af.)
South America
South Vietnam (Asia)
Tadzhikistan (Asia)
The Argentine (S. Am.)
Turkmenistan (Asia)
United States (N. Am.)
Western Samoa (Oc.)

13

Afars and Issas (Af.)
Barbary States (Af.)
Cayman Islands (W.I.)
Comoro Islands (Af.)
Czech Republic (Eur.)
Khmer Republic (Asia)
Liechtenstein (Eur.)
Norfolk Island (Pac.)
Trucial States (Asia)
United Kingdom (Eur.)
Western Sahara (Af.)

14

Cape of Good Hope (Af.)
Congo Free State (Af.)
Czechoslovakia (Eur.)
Gilbert Islands (Pac.)
Irish Free State (Eur.)
Maldive Islands (Ind.)
Mariana Islands (Pac.)
Papua New Guinea (Oc.)
Pitcairn Island (Pac.)
Society Islands (Pac.)
Solomon Islands (Oc.)

15

British Honduras (C. Am.)
Caroline Islands (Pac.)
Christmas Island (Pac.)
Falkland Islands (Atl.)
Holy Roman Empire (Eur.)
Marshall Islands (N. Pac)
Northern Ireland (Eur.)
Northern Nigeria (Af.)
Orange Free State (Af.)
Republic of Congo (Af.)

South-West Africa (Af.)
Southern Nigeria (Af.)

16 AND OVER

Antigua and Barbuda (W.I.) (17)
Bosnia-Hercegovina (Eur.) (17)

Cape Verde Islands (Af.) (16)
Dominican Republic (W.I.) (17)
Equatorial Guinea (Af.) (16)
Malagasy Republic (Af.) (16)
São Tomé and Príncipé (Af.) (18)
Trinidad and Tobago (W.I.) (17)

United Arab Emirates (Asia) (18)
United Arab Republic
    (Af., Asia) (18)
Vatican City State (Eur.) (16)

Geographical terms

2 AND **3**	dene	neck	wynd	firth	ridge
	dike	ness	zone	fjord	river
alp	doab	névé		flats	sands
alt	down	park	**5**	flood	sault
as	dune	pass	abyss	fosse	scarp
bay	dyke	peak	alley	geoid	scree
ben	east	peat	atlas	ghaut	shelf
bog	eyot	plat	atoll	ghyll	shire
cay	firn	pole	banat	glade	shoal
col	floe	pond	bayou	globe	shore
cwm	flow	pool	beach	gorge	slade
dam	ford	port	bight	grove	slope
dun	fork	race	bluff	gully	sound
fen	foss	reef	bough	haven	south
lea	ghat	rift	bourn	heath	state
lin	gill	rill	broad	hithe	swale
map	glen	road	brook	hurst	swamp
mud	gulf	rock	butte	hythe	sward
ria	head	sand	canal	inlet	talus
sea	hill	scar	chart	islet	tract
sod	holm	seam	chasm	karoo	veldt
tor	holt	seat	chine	kloof	weald
voe	hook	sial	cliff	knoll	wilds
	inch	sike	clime	kopje	
4	isle	silt	coast	lande	**6**
aber	kaim	sima	combe	levee	alpine
bank	kame	soil	coomb	llano	Arctic
beck	lake	spit	copse	loess	boreal
belt	land	spur	creek	magma	broads
berg	lane	sudd	crest	marsh	canton
bill	limb	tarn	croft	monte	canyon
bore	linn	town	delta	mound	cavern
brae	loam	tump	ditch	mount	clough
burn	loch	vale	donga	mouth	colony
bush	lock	vega	downs	north	colure
cape	marl	veld	drift	oasis	common
cave	mead	wadi	duchy	ocean	corrie
city	mere	wash	dunes	oxbow	coulee
clay	mesa	weir	erode	plain	county
comb	midi	well	esker	point	course
cove	mire	west	falls	polar	crater
crag	moor	wind	fault	poles	cuesta
dale	mull	wold	field	reach	defile
deli	naze	wood	fiord	rhine	desert

dingle	suburb	plateau	latitude	cisalpine
divide	summit	polders	lava flow	cliff face
domain	tropic	prairie	littoral	coalfield
empire	trough	rivulet	lowlands	coastline
eyalet	tundra	saltpan	mainland	continent
feeder	upland	satrapy	midlands	coral reef
forest	valley	savanna	monticle	epicentre
geyser	warren	seaport	moorland	everglade
glacis		seaside	mountain	fleet-dike
grotto	**7**	straits	neap-tide	foothills
gulley	alluvia	subsoil	northern	foreshore
hamlet	austral	thicket	Occident	geography
harbor	bogland	topsoil	oriental	heathland
icecap	caldera	torrent	prospect	highlands
icicle	channel	tropics	province	landscape
inland	clachan	village	quagmire	landslide
inning	commune	volcano	republic	longitude
island	compass	western	riparian	marshland
isobar	conduit		river bed	midstream
jungle	conflux	**8**	riverine	monticule
karroo	contour	affluent	salt lake	northeast
lagoon	country	alluvial	sand dune	northwest
maldan	crevice	alluvium	sandbank	northerly
margin	cuffing	altitude	sea level	northward
massif	deltaic	brooklet	seaboard	peneplain
meadow	drought	cantonal	seacoast	peninsula
morass	eastern	cataract	seashore	precipice
nullah	enclave	causeway	sediment	rainwater
orient	eparchy	crevasse	shallows	rockbound
pampas	equator	currents	sheading	salt-marsh
parish	estuary	district	snow-line	sand dunes
plains	exclave	dominion	southern	sandbanks
polder	georama	downland	sub-polar	shore-line
rapids	glacier	dustbowl	telluric	snowdrift
ravine	habitat	easterly	toparchy	snowfield
region	harbour	eastward	township	southeast
riding	highway	effluent	tropical	southwest
rillet	hillock	eminence	undertow	southerly
runlet	hilltop	eminency	volcanic	southmost
runnel	hornito	environs	westerly	southward
sarsen	hummock	eruption	westward	streamlet
schist	hundred	foreland	woodland	sub-alpine
seaway	iceberg	fracture		tableland
sierra	ice-floe	frontier	**9**	territory
sinter	icepack	headland	Antarctic	tetrarchy
skerry	incline	high road	antipodal	tidal flow
source	insular	highland	antipodes	trade wind
spinny	isthmus	hillside	avalanche	tributary
spruit	kingdom	icefield	backwater	up country
steppe	lakelet	interior	backwoods	wapentake
strait	lowland	isostasy	billabong	waste land
strath	midland	isthmian	boondocks	water-hole
stream	new town	landmark	cadastral	waterfall
street	oceanic	landslip	catchment	watershed

waterside
westwards
whirlpool

10

co-latitude
confluence
cordillera
county town
depression
earthquake
equatorial
escarpment
fluviatile
fresh water
frigid zone
garden city
geographer
Gulf Stream
headstream
headwaters
hemisphere
high ground
hinterland
hot springs
interfluve
landlocked
margravate
market town
meridional
metropolis
no-man's-land
occidental
palatinate
peninsular
plantation
polar-angle
population
presidency
projection

promontory
quicksands
rain forest
rift valley
river basin
sandy beach
seismology
spring tide
stratiform
subsidence
substratum
tidal creek
torrid zone
water spout
water table
wilderness

11

archipelago
back country
bergschrund
circumpolar
cisatlantic
continental
conurbation
coral island
countryside
earth tremor
equinoctial
mountainous
northwardly
polar circle
polar region
river course
river valley
septentrion
subtropical
territorial
tetrarchate
tidal waters

transalpine
transmarine
ultramarine
watercourse

12

Arctic Circle
equatorially
geographical
geomagnetism
glacial drift
glacial epoch
landgraviate
magnetic pole
mean sea level
mountain pass
mountain peak
northeastern
northwestern
principality
protectorate
rising ground
southeastern
southernmost
southwestern
stratosphere
subcontinent
subterranean
tropical zone
ultramontane
virgin forest

13

above sea level
active volcano
deltafication
drainage basin
eastnortheast
eastsoutheast
extratropical

geotechtonics
intertropical
magnetic north
Mediterranean
mother country
neighbourhood
northeasterly
northeastward
northwesterly
northwestward
polar distance
septentrional
southeasterly
southeastward
southwesterly
southwestward
temperate zone
transatlantic
virgin country
watering place

14 AND 15

acclimatization (15)
Antarctic Circle (15)
circummeridian (14)
circumnavigate (14)
irrigation canal (15)
magnetic equator (15)
Mercator's chart (14)
north frigid zone (15)
northeastwards (14)
south frigid zone (15)
southeastwards (14)
tropic of Cancer (14)

17

tropic of Capricorn

Islands

Arch = Archipelago; I. = Island; Is. = Islands; (v) = volcanic

2 – 4

Adi (Pac.)
Amoy (China)
Aran (Ire.)
Arru Is. (Indo.)
Bali (Indo.)
Bay Is. (C. Am.)

Be (Mad.)
Bere (Ire.)
Brac (Adr.)
Bua (Adr.)
Buru (Indo.)
Bute (Scot.)
Cebu (Philip.)

Ceos (Gr.)
Coil (Scot.)
Cook Is. (Pac.)
Cos (Gr.)
Cres (Cro.)
Cuba (W.I.)
Dago (Fin.)

Dogs, I. of (Eng.)
Eigg (Scot.)
Elba (Med.)
Ewe (Scot.)
Farm Is. (Eng.)
Faro (Balt.)
Fiji Is. (Pac.)

Fohr (Ger.)
Gozo (Med.)
Guam (Pac.)
Hall Is. (Pac.)
Herm (Ch. Is.)
High I. (Ire.)
Holy I. (Scot.)

Hoy (Scot.)
Hvar (Cro.)
Idra (Gr.)
Iona (Scot.)
Java (Indo.)
Jura (Scot.)
Kea (Gr.)
Kei Is. (Indo.)
Kish (Iran)
Low Arch. (Pac.)
Man, I. of (British Is.)
May, I. of (Scot.)
Milo (Gr.)
Moen (Den.)
Muck (Scot.)
Mull, I. of (Scot.)
Oahu (Pac.)
Paxo (Gr.)
Pine I. (U.S.A.)
Rat Is. (Pac.)
Ré (Fr.)
Rum (Scot.)
Saba (W.I.)
Sark (Ch. Is.)
Scio (Gr.)
Skye (Scot.)
Sulu Is. (Indo.)
Sylt (Ger.)
Syra (Gr.)
Tory (Ire.)
Uist (Scot.)
Ulva (Scot.)
Unst (Scot.)
Yap (Pac.)
Yell (Scot.)
Yezo (Jap.)
Zea (Gr.)
Zebu (Indo.)

5

Abaco (W.I.)
Aland Is. (Balt.)
Albay (Indo.)
Ambon (Indo.)
Arran (Scot.)
Bahía Is. (C. Am.)
Banca (Malay.)
Banda (Indo.)
Banks (S. Pac.)
Barra (Heb.)
Bioko (W. Af.)
Bonin Is. (Pac.)
Brach (Adr.)
Caldy (Wales)

Canna (Scot.)
Capri (It.)
Ceram (Indo.)
Cheja (Korea)
Chios (Gr.)
Clare (Ire.)
Clear (Ire.)
Cocos Is. (Ind.)
Corfu (Gr.)
Corvo (Atl.)
Crete (Med.)
Delos (Gr.)
Devon I. (Arc.)
Eagle I. (Ire.)
Ellis (U.S.A.)
Farne Is. (Eng.)
Fayal (Atl.)
Ferro (Atl.)
Foula (Scot.)
Funen (Den.)
Goree (Atl.)
Haiti (W.I.)
Hart's I. (U.S.A.)
Hondo (Jap.)
Hydra (Gr.)
Ibiza (Med.)
Irian (Indo.)
Islay (Scot.)
Iviza (Med.)
Leros (Gr.)
Lewis (Scot.)
Leyte (Philip.)
Lissa (Adr.)
Lobos Is. (S. Am.)
Lundy I. (Eng.)
Luzon (Philip.)
Malta (Med.)
Matsu (China)
Melos (Gr.)
Milos (Gr.)
Mores (Atl.)
Nauru (Pac.)
Naxos (Gr.)
Nevis (W.I.)
Oesel (Est.)
Ormuz (Iran)
Panay (Philip.)
Parry Is. (Arc.)
Pearl Is. (Pac.)
Pemba (Af.)
Perim (Af.)
Pines, I. of (Cuba)
Pines, I. of (Pac.)
Rhode I. (U.S.A.)

Rugen (Ger.)
Sable I. (Can.)
Samar (Philip.)
Samoa (Oc.)
Samos (Gr.)
Samsø (Den.)
Spice Is. (Indo.)
Sunda Is. (Indo.)
Texel (Neth.)
Thera (Gr.)
Timor (Indo.)
Tiree (Scot.)
Tonga (Oc.)
Turk's I. (W.I.)
Voorn (Neth.)
Wight, I. of (Eng.)
Zante (Gr.)

6

Achill (Ire.)
Aegina (Gr.)
Albany (Austral.)
Andros (Gr.)
Baffin I. (Can.)
Bahama Is. (W.I.)
Banana Is. (Atl.)
Bissau (Atl.)
Borkum (Ger.)
Borneo (Indo.)
Bounty Is. (N.Z.)
Brazza (Adr.)
Burray (Scot.)
Caicos I. (W.I.)
Canary Is. (Atl.)
Candia (Med.)
Cayman Is. (W.I.)
Cerigo (Gr.)
Cherso (Cro.)
Chiloé (Chile)
Chusan (China)
Comoro Is. (Af.)
Crozet Is. (Ind.)
Cyprus (Med.)
Djerba (Tun.)
Dursey (Ire.)
Easter I. (Pac.)
Ellice Is. (Pac.)
Euboea (Aeg.)
Faroes (Atl.)
Flores (Atl.)
Flores (Indo.)
Gilolo (Indo.)
Gomera (Can.)
Hainan (China)

Harris (Scot.)
Hawaii (Pac.)
Honshu (Jap.)
Hormuz (Iran)
Imbros (Turk.)
Inagna Is. (W.I.)
Ionian Is. (Med.)
Ischia (It.)
Ithaca (Med.)
Iturup (Rus.)
Jaluit (Pac.)
Jersey (Ch. Is.)
Jethou (Ch. Is.)
Kadavu (Oc.)
Kodiak (Alaska)
Kurile Is. (Pac.)
Kyushu (Jap.)
Labuan (Malay.)
Lambay (Ire.)
Lemnos (Aeg.)
Lesbos (Aeg.)
Lesina (Cro.)
Limnos (Gr.)
Lipari Is. (v.) (It.)
Lombok (v.) (Indo.)
Madura (Indo.)
Mahore Is. (Af.)
Maluka Is. (Indo.)
Marajó (S. Am.)
Negros (Philip.)
Oléron (Fr.)
Orkney Is. (Scot.)
Patmos (Aeg.)
Penang (Malay.)
Quemoy (Taiwan)
Rhodes (Aeg.)
Robben (S.A.)
Sangir Is. (Indo.)
Savai'i I. (Pac.)
Scarba (Scot.)
Scilly Is. (Eng.)
Sicily (Med.)
Skyros (Aeg.)
St. John (W.I.)
St. Paul (Alaska)
Staffa (Scot.)
Staten I. (U.S.A.)
Stroma (Scot.)
Tahiti (Pac.)
Taiwan (China)
Thanet, I. of (Eng.)
Tholen (Neth.)
Tobago (W.I.)
Tromsø (Nor.)

Tubuai Is. (Pac.)
Usedom (Ger.)
Ushant (Fr.)
Virgin Is. (W.I.)

7

Aeolian Is. (v.) (It.)
Amboina (Indo.)
Ameland (Neth.)
Anambas Is. (Indo.)
Andaman Is. (Ind.)
Antigua (W.I.)
Austral Is. (Pac.)
Bahamas (W.I.)
Bahrain (Arab.)
Balleny Is. (Antarc.)
Barents (Arc.)
Bermuda (Atl.)
Bernera (Scot.)
Bonaire (W.I.)
Cabrera (Med.)
Capraia (Med.)
Celebes (Indo.)
Channel Is. (Eng.)
Chatham Is. (Pac.)
Chinmen (Taiwan)
Comoros (Af.)
Corsica (Med.)
Curaçao (W.I.)
Curzola (Cro.)
Cythera (Gr.)
Dampier Is. (Austral.)
Eivissa (Med.)
Eriskay (Scot.)
Faeroes (Atl.)
Falster (Balt.)
Fanning (Pac.)
Fehmarn (Balt.)
Flannan Is. (Scot.)
Formosa (China)
Frisian Is. (North Sea)
Gambier Is. (Pac.)
Gilbert Is. (Pac.)
Gotland (Balt.)
Grenada (W.I.)
Hayling I. (Eng.)
Iceland (v.) (Atl.)
Ireland
Jamaica (W.I.)
Kalamos (Gr.)
Kamaran (Red S.)
Keeling Is. (Ind.)
Korcula (Cro.)
Kythira (Gr.)

Leeward Is. (W.I.)
Lefkada (Gr.)
Lofoten Is. (Nor.)
Lolland (Den.)
Loyalty Is. (Pac.)
Madeira (Atl.)
Majorca (Med.)
Maldive Is. (Ind.)
Mariana Is. (Pac.)
Massowa (Red S.)
Mayotte Is. (Af.)
Mindoro (Philip.)
Minicoy Is. (Ind.)
Minorca (Sp.)
Molokai (Pac.)
Mombasa (Af.)
Mykonos (Gr.)
Nicobar Is. (Ind.)
Norfolk I. (Austral.)
Nossi Bé (v.) (Mad.)
Oceania (Pac.)
Okinawa (Jap.)
Orkneys (Scot.)
Palawan (Philip.)
Phoenix Is. (Pac.)
Purbeck, I. of (Bng.)
Rathlin (N.I.)
Réunion (Ind.)
Roanoke (U.S.A.)
Rockall (Atl.)
Rotumah (Pac.)
Salamis (Gr.)
São Tomé (W.Af.)
Serifos (Gr.)
Sheppey, I. of (Eng.)
Sherbro (W. Af.)
Shikoku (Jap.)
Society Is. (Pac.)
Socotra (Yemen)
Solomon Is. (Pac.)
St. Agnes (Eng.)
St. Kilda (Scot.)
St. Kitts (W.I.)
St. Lucia (W.I.)
Stewart I. (N.Z.)
Sumatra (Indo.)
Sumbawa (Indo.)
Ternate (Indo.)
Tortola (W.I.)
Tortuga (W.I.)
Tuamotu (Pac.)
Watling I. (W.I.)
Whalsay (Scot.)
Wrangel I. (Arc.)

8

Alderney (Ch. Is.)
Aleutian Is. (Pac.)
Amirante Is. (Ind.)
Andamans (Ind.)
Anglesey (Wales)
Antilles Is. (W.I.)
Auckland Is. (N.Z.)
Balearic Is. (Med.)
Barbados (Is.) (W.I.)
Belitung (Indo.)
Belle Ile (Fr.)
Bermudas (Is.) (Atl.)
Berneray (Scot.)
Billiton (Indo.)
Bismarck Arch. (Pac.)
Bissagos Is. (W.Af.)
Bornholm (Den.)
Campbell I. (N.Z.)
Canaries (Atl.)
Caroline Is. (Pac.)
Colonsay (Scot.)
Copeland I. (N.I.)
Cyclades Is. (Gr.)
Desertas Is. (Atl.)
Dominica (W.I.)
Dugi Otok (Cro.)
Fair Isle (Scot.)
Falkland Is. (Atl.)
Flinders (Austral.)
Friendly Is. (Pac.)
Furneaux Is. (Austral.)
Gökçeada (Turk.)
Guernsey (Ch. Is.)
Hebrides (Scot.)
Hokkaido (Jap.)
Hong Kong (China)
Jan Mayen (Arc.)
Juventud, I. de la
  (Cuba)
Kangaroo Is. (Austral.)
Kermadec Is. (Pac.)
Krakatoa (v.) (Indo.)
Ladrones (Pac.)
Lord Howe Is.
  (Austral.)
Magerøya (Arc.)
Mallorca (Med.)
Manihiki Is. (Pac.)
Marianas (Pac.)
Marshall Is. (Pac.)
Melville I. (Austral.)
Melville I. (Can.)

Mindanao (Philip.)
Miquelon (Can.)
Mitylene (Gr.)
Moluccas (Indo.)
Mustique (W.I.)
Pitcairn Is. (Pac.)
Portland, I. of (Eng.)
Pribilov Is. (Pac.)
Príncipe (W.Af.)
Quelpart (S. Korea)
Sakhalin (Rus.)
Sandwich Is. (Pac.)
Sardinia (Med.)
Scillies (Eng.)
Seriphos (Gr.)
Shetland Is. (Scot.)
Skopelos (Gr.)
Somerset I. (Arc.)
Sri Lanka (Asia)
St. Helena (Atl.)
St. Martin (W.I.)
St. Thomas (W.I.)
Starbuck (Pac.)
Sulawesi (Indo.)
Tasmania (Austral.)
Tenerife (v.) (Atl.)
Thousand Is. (N. Am.)
Tortugas Is. (W.I.)
Trinidad (W.I.)
Unalaska (U.S.A.)
Valencia I. (Ire.)
Victoria I. (Can.)
Viti-Levu (Fiji)
Vlieland (Neth.)
Watlings I. (W.I.)
Windward Is. (W.I.)
Zanzibar (E. Af.)

9

Admiralty Is. (Pac.)
Anticosti, Ile d'
Ascension (Atl.)
Benbecula (Scot.)
Cape Verde Is. (Atl.)
Caribbees Is. (W.I.)
Carolines (Pac.)
Christmas I. (Pac.)
Christmas I. (Ind.)
Elephanta I. (Ind.)
Eleuthera (W.I.)
Ellesmere I. (Can.)
Erromango (Pac.)
Falklands (Atl.)
Galápagos Is. (v.) (Pac.)

Greenland (Arc.)
Halmahera (Indo.)
Inchkeith (Scot.)
Inishturk (Ire.)
Isle of May (Scot.)
Karpathos (Gr.)
Kerguelen Is. (Ind.)
Lampedusa (Med.)
Langeland (Den.)
Lanzarote (Atl.)
Louisiade Arch. (Pac.)
Manhattan (U.S.A.)
Margarita (W.I.)
Marquesas Is. (Pac.)
Marshalls (Pac.)
Mauritius (Ind.)
Melanesia (Pac.)
Nantucket (U.S.A.)
New Guinea (E.I.)
New Ireland (Pac.)
Norderney (Ger.)
Polynesia (Pac.)
Rarotonga (Pac.)
Rodrigues (Ind.)
Saint John (W.I.)
Saint Paul I. (Pac.)
Santa Cruz (Pac.)
Santa Cruz (Mex.)
Santa Cruz. I. (U.S.A.)
Santa Cruz Is. (Pac.)
Santorini (v.) (Gr.)
Scarpanto (Gr.)
Shetlands (Scot.)
Singapore (Asia)
St. Nicolas (Atl.)
St. Vincent (W.I.)
Stromboli (v.) (Med.)
Tabuaeran (Pac.)
Vancouver I. (Can.)
Vanua Levu (Fiji)
Walcheren (Neth.)
Wellesley Is. (Austral.)

10

Ailsa Craig (Scot.)
Bay Islands (C. Am.)
Calamianes (Indo.)
Cape Barren I. (Austral.)
Cape Breton I. (Can.)
Cephalonia (Gr.)
Dirk Hartog I. (Austral.)
Dodecanese (Med.)
Fernando Po (W. Af.)
Formentera (Med.)

Grenadines (W.I.)
Guadeloupe (W.I.)
Heligoland (N. Sea)
Hispaniola (W.I.)
Holy Island (Eng.)
Isle of Dogs (Eng.)
Isle of Mull (Scot.)
Isle of Skye (Scot.)
Kuria Muria Is. (Arab.)
Laccadives (Ind.)
Long Island (U.S.A.)
Madagascar (Af.)
Manitoulin I. (Can.)
Martinique (W.I.)
Micronesia (Pac.)
Montserrat (W.I.)
New Britain (Pac.)
New Zealand (Pac.)
North Devon I. (Arc.)
Philippine Is. (Asia)
Puerto Rico (W.I.)
Saint Agnes (Eng.)
Saint Kilda (Scot.)
Saint Kitts (W.I.)
Saint Lucia (W.I.)
Sandlewood I. (Malay.)
Seychelles (Ind.)
West Indies (Atl.)

11

Axel Heiberg (Arc.)
Cook Islands (Pac.)
Eagle Island (Ire.)
Gran Canaria (Atl.)
Grand Canary (Atl.)
Guadalcanal (Pac.)
Hall Islands (Pac.)
Hart's Island (U.S.A.)
Isle of Pines (Cuba)
Isle of Pines (Pac.)
Isle of Wight (Eng.)
Isola Grossa (Cro.)
Lakshadweep Is. (Ind.)
Lindisfarne (Eng.)
Lundy Island (Eng.)
Mascarenene Is. (Ind.)
Montecristo (It.)
New Hebrides (Pac.)
New Siberian Is. (Arc.)
North Island (N.Z.)
Pantelleria (Med.)
Philippines (Asia)
Rhode Island (U.S.A.)
Rottumeroog (Neth.)

Sable Island (Can.)
Saint Helena (Atl.)
Saint Thomas (W.I.)
Sainte Marie (Mad.)
San Salvador (W.I.)
Scilly Isles (Eng.)
Sint Maarten (W.I.)
South Island (N.Z.)
Southampton I. (Can.)
Spitsbergen (Arc.)

12

Baffin Island (Arc.)
Bougainville (Pac.)
British Isles
Devil's Island (S. Am.)
Easter Island (Pac.)
Great Britain (U.K.)
Isle of Thanet (Eng.)
Marie-Galante (W.I.)
New Caledonia (Pac.)
Newfoundland (Can.)
Novaya Zemlya (Arc.)
Prince Edward I. (Can.)
Puffin Island (Wales)
Saint Vincent (W.I.)
Savai'i Island (Pac.)
South Georgia (Atl.)
St. Barthélemy (W.I.)
Staten Island (U.S.A.)
Turks' Islands (W.I.)

13 AND OVER

D'Entrecastreaux Is.
  (Austral.) (15)
Friendly Islands (Pac.) (15)
Isle of Portland (Eng.) (14)
Isle of Purbeck (Eng.) (13)
Isle of Sheppey (Eng.) (13)
Juan Fernandez Is. (Pac.) (13)
Martha's Vineyard (U.S.A.) (15)
Norfolk Island (Pac.) (13)
Prince Edward Island
  (Can.) (18)
Prince of Wales I. (Malay.) (13)
Prince of Wales I. (Arc.) (13)
Prince Patrick I. (Arc.) (13)
Queen Charlotte Is. (Can.) (14)
Saint Eustatius (W.I.) (14)
Santa Catalina (Mex.) (13)
South Shetlands (Atl.) (14)
St. Bartholomew (W.I.) (13)
St. Christopher (W.I.) (13)
St. Michael's Mount (Eng.) (15)

Stewart Island (N.Z.) (13)   Tristan da Cunha (Atl.) (14)
Tierra del Fuego (Chile) (14)   Watling Island (Atl.) (13)

Lakes, inland seas, lochs, loughs, etc.

3 AND 4

Aral (Kaz. and Uzbek.)
Ard (Scot.)
Awe (Scot.)
Bala (Wales)
Bear (U.S.A.)
Bear (Can.)
Biwa (Jap.)
Chad (Af.)
Como (It.)
Dall (U.S.A.)
Derg (N.I.)
Dore (Can.)
Earn (Scot.)
Eil (Scot.)
Erie (Can. and U.S.A.)
Erne (N.I.)
Ewe (Scot.)
Eyre (Austral.)
Há Há (Can.)
Iseo (It.)
Key (Ire.)
Kivu (Af.)
Long (Scot.)
Mask (Ire.)
Mead (U.S.A.)
Nemi (It.)
Ness (Scot.)
Oahe (U.S.A.)
Ryan (Scot.)
Tana (Eth.)
Tay (Scot.)
Thun (Swit.)
Utah (U.S.A.)
Van (Turk.)
Zug (Swit.)

5

Abaya (Eth.)
Baker (Can.)
Clark (U.S.A.)
Elton (Rus.)
Etive (Scot.)
Foyle (N.I.)
Frome (Austral.)
Garda (It.)
Hamun (Afghan.)

Honey (U.S.A.)
Huron (Can. and U.S.A.)
Ilmen (Rus.)
Kossu (Af.)
Kyoga (Af.)
Leech (U.S.A.)
Léman (Swit.)
Leven (Scot.)
Lochy (Scot.)
Loyal (Scot.)
Mälar (Swed.)
Maree (Scot.)
Minto (Can.)
Mjøsa (Nor.)
Moore (Austral.)
Morar (Scot.)
Mweru (Cen. Af.)
Neagh (N.I.)
Nevis (Scot.)
Nyasa (Cen. Af.)
Onega (Rus.)
Payne (Can.)
Rainy (Can.)
Rainy (U.S.A.)
Shiel (Scot.)
Takoe (U.S.A.)
Taupo (N.Z.)
Tumba (Congo, Dem. Rep.)
Urmia (Iran)
Volta (Ghana)

6

Albert (Cen. Af.)
Arkaig (Scot.)
Assynt (Scot.)
Austin (Austral.)
Baikal (Sib.)
Biwako (Jap.)
Chilka (Ind.)
Chilwa (Malawi)
Corrib (Ire.)
Edward (E. Af.)
Ennell (Ire.)
Geneva (Swit.)
George (Uganda)
George (U.S.A.)
IJssel (Neth.)
Indian (U.S.A.)

Itasca (U.S.A.)
Kariba (Af.)
Khanka (Asia)
Kossou (Ivory Coast)
Ladoga (Rus.)
Lomond (Scot.)
Lop Nor (China)
Lugano (Swit.)
Malawi (Cen. Af.)
Martin (U.S.A.)
Nasser (Egypt)
Natron (Tanz.)
Nyanza (Bur.)
Oneida (U.S.A.)
Peipus (Est. and Rus.)
Placid (U.S.A.)
Poyang (China)
Quoich (Scot.)
Rideau (Can.)
Rudolf (Kenya)
Shasta (U.S.A.)
Shirwa (Malawi)
Simcoe (Can.)
St.-Jean (Can.)
St John (U.S.A.)
Stuart (Can.)
Te Anau (N.Z.)
Tuz Göl (Turk.)
Vänern (Swed.)
Viedma (Arg.)
Vyrnwy (Wales)
Wanaka (N.Z.)
Zürich (Swit.)

7

Abitibi (Can.)
Balaton (Hung.)
Belfast (N.I.)
Benmore (N.Z.)
Blanche (Austral.)
Caspian (Asia)
Chapala (Mex.)
Chilika (Ind.)
Dead Sea (Isr. and Jord.)
Etawney (Can.)
Fannich (Scot.)
Galilee (Isr.)
Hickory (U.S.A.)

Hirakud (Ind.)
Hjalmar (Swed.)
Idi Amin (Af.)
Iliamna (U.S.A.)
Katrine (Scot.)
Koko Nor (China)
La Croix (Can. and U.S.A.)
Loch Eil (Scot.)
Loch Tay (Scot.)
Lucerne (Swit.)
Muskoka (Can.)
Nipigon (Can.)
Nu Jiang (China and Burma)
Ontario (Can. and U.S.A.)
Perugia (It.)
Pyramid (U.S.A.)
Qinghai (China)
Quesnel (Can.)
Rannoch (Scot.)
Rosseau (Can.)
Rutland (Eng.)
Rybinsk (Rus.)
Sheelin (Ire.)
St. Clair (Can. and U.S.A.)
Tezcuco (Mex.)
Torrens (Austral.)
Turkana (Kenya)
Tyrrell (Austral.)
Ugashik (U.S.A.)

8

Balkhash (Kaz.)
Bear Lake (U.S.A.)
Becharof (U.S.A.)
Chiemsee (Ger.)
Chowilla (Austral.)
Clywedog (Wales)
Coniston (Eng.)
Dongting (China)
Drummond (U.S.A.)
Gairdner (Austral.)
Grasmere (Eng.)
Hirfanli (Turk.)
Humboldt (U.S.A.)
Issyk-Kul (Kyr.)
Kakhovka (Ukr.)
Kawartha (Can.)
Kootenay (Can.)
Loch Ness (Scot.)
Loch Ryan (Scot.)
Luichart (Scot.)
Maggiore (It.)

Manitoba (Can.)
Menindee (Austral.)
Michigan (U.S.A.)
Reindeer (Can.)
Seaforth (Scot.)
Stefanie (E.)
Superior (U.S.A.)
Tarawera (N.Z.)
Titicaca (Peru)
Tonle Sap (Cambodia)
Tungtin'g (China)
Victoria (Cen. Af.)
Wakatipu (N.Z.)
Winnipeg (Can.)

9

Argentino (S. Am.)
Athabasca (Can.)
Bangweulu (Zamb.)
Champlain (N. Am.)
Constance (Swit.)
Ennerdale (Eng.)
Great Bear (Can.)
Great Lake (Austral.)
Great Salt (U.S.A.)
Hindmarsh (Austral.)
Honey Lake (U.S.A.)
Killarney (Ire.)
Kuibyshev (Rus.)
Loch Leven (Scot.)
Loch Maree (Scot.)
Loch Nevis (Scot.)
Mai-Ndombe (Congo, Dem.
    Rep.)
Maracaibo (Venez.)
Mille Lacs (U.S.A.)
Moosehead (U.S.A.)
Neuchâtel (Swit.)
Nicaragua (C. Am.)
Nipissing (Can.)
Rutanzige (E. Af.)
Salton Sea (U.S.A.)
Sempacher (Swit.)
Teshekpuk (U.S.A.)
Thirlmere (Eng.)
Trasimeno (It.)
Tustumena (U.S.A.)
Ullswater (Eng.)
Wast Water (Eng.)
Winnebago (U.S.A.)
Wollaston (Can.)

10

Brokopondo (S. Am.)
Buttermere (Eng.)
Great Lakes (Can. and U.S.A.)
Great Slave (Can.)
Haweswater (Eng.)
IJsselmeer (Neth.)
Indian Lake (U.S.A.)
Loch Lomond (Scot.)
Lough Neagh (N.I.)
Michigamme (U.S.A.)
Mistassini (Can.)
Okeechobee (U.S.A.)
Rydal Water (Eng.)
Serpentine (Eng.)
Strangford (N.I.)
Tanganyika (E. Af.)
Windermere (Eng.)
Xochimilco (Mex.)

11 AND OVER

Albert Edward Nyanza (Af.)
    (18)
Albert Nyanza (Af.) (12)
Bassenthwaite (Eng.) (3)
Bitter Lakes (Egypt) (11)
Cabora Bassa (Af.) (11)
Coniston Water (Eng.) (13)
Derwent Water (Eng.) (12)
Diefenbaker (Can.) (11)
Grand Coulee (U.S.A.) (11)
Great Salt Lake (U.S.A.) (13)
Great Slave Lake (Can.) (14)
Lake of the Woods (Can. and
    U.S.A.) (14)
Lesser Slave Lake (Can.) (15)
Loch Katrine (Scot.) (11)
Neusiedler See (Aust. and
    Hung.) (13)
Pend Oreille (U.S.A.) (11)
Pontchartrain (U.S.A.) (13)
The Cooroong (Austral.) (11)
Timiskaming (Can.) (11)
Upper Klamath (U.S.A.) (12)
Victoria Nyanza (Af.) (14)
Vierwaldstättersee (Swit.) (18)
Virginia Water (Eng.) (13)
Winnibigoshish (U.S.A.) (14)
Winnipegosis (Can.) (12)
Yellowstone (U.S.A.) (11)

Mountains

H. = Hill; Hs. = Hills; M. = "Mountain", commonly used *after* name; Ms. = Mountains; Mt. = "Mount", "Monte", or "Mont", commonly used *before* name; (v) = volcanic

2 – 4

Abu, Mt. (Ind.)
Adam, Mt. (Falkland Is.)
Alps (Eur.)
Blue Ms. (Austral. and U.S.A.)
Caha Ms. (Ire.)
Cook, Mt. (N.Z.)
Ebal, Mt. (Jord.)
Etna, Mt. (v.) (Sic.)
Fuji, Mt. (v.) (Jap.)
Harz Ms. (Ger.)
Ida, Mt. (Crete)
Iron M. (U.S.A.)
Jura Ms. (Eur.)
K2 (Him.)
Kea (v.) (Hawaii)
Kibo, Mt. (Tanz.)
Meru, Mt. (Tanz.)
Naga Hs. (Ind.)
Ore Ms. (Ger.)
Ossa, Mt. (Gr., Tas.)
Ural Ms. (Rus.)
Zug M. (Ger.)

5

Adams, Mt. (U.S.A.)
Altai Ms. (Him.)
Andes (S. Am.)
Aripo M. (Trin..)
Athos, Mt. (Gr.)
Atlas Ms. (Af.)
Black Ms. (U.S.A.)
Black Ms. (Wales)
Blanc, Mt. (Alps)
Brown, Mt. (N. Am.)
Cenis, Mt. (Alps)
Coast Ms. (N. Am.)
Djaja, Mt. (Indo.)
Downs, The (Hs.) (Eng.)
Eiger (Swit.)
Elgon, Mt. (Uganda)
Galty Ms. (Ire.)
Ghats, The (Ms.) (Ind.)
Green Ms. (U.S.A.)
Hekla (v.) (Iceland)
Kenya, Mt. (E. Af.)
Logan, Mt. (Yukon)
Maipo (v.) (Arg.)

Minto, Mt. (Antarc.)
Ochil Hs. (Scot.)
Ozark Ms. (U.S.A.)
Pelée, Mt. (v.) (W.I.)
Potro M. (Chile)
Rocky Ms. (N. Am.)
Sinai, Mt. (Egypt)
Snowy Ms. (Austral.)
Table M. (S.A.)
Tabor, Mt. (Isr.)
Tatra Ms. (Slov. and Pol.)
Urals (Rus.)
White Ms. (U.S.A.)
Wolds, The (Hs.) (Eng.)

6

Ararat, Mt. (Turk.)
Balkan Ms. (Eur.)
Bogong, Mt. (Austral.)
Bonete, Mt. (Arg.)
Carmel, Mt. (Isr.)
Darwin Ms. (Chile)
Elbert, Mt. (U.S.A.)
Elbrus, Mt. (Rus. and Geo.)
Elburz Ms. (Iran)
Erebus, Mt. (v.) (Antarc.)
Hermon, Mt. (Syria)
Hoggar Ms. (Alg.)
Juncal (v.) (Chile)
Katmai, Mt. (v.) (Alaska)
Kazbek, Mt. (Geo.)
Koryak Ms. (Rus.)
Lennox Hs. (Scot.)
Lhotse, Mt. (Him.)
Makalu, Mt. (Him.)
Masaya (v.) (C. Am.)
Mendip Hs. (Eng.)
Mourne Ms. (Ire.)
Muztag (M.) (China)
Olives, Mt. of (Isr.)
Ortles (M.) (It.)
Ozarks (U.S.A.)
Pamirs (Asia)
Pelion (Gr.)
Pindus Ms. (Gr.)
Pissis, Mt. (Arg.)
Robson, Mt. (Can.)
Sidlaw Hs. (Scot.)
Sidley, Mt. (Antarc.)

Taunus Ms. (Ger.)
Taurus Ms. (Turk.)
Vosges Ms. (Fr.)
Zagros Ms. (Iran)

7

Belukha (M.) (Kaz.)
Ben More (Scot.)
Bermina (It.)
Big Horn Ms. (U.S.A.)
Brocken, Mt. (Ger.)
Cascade Ms. (N. Am.)
Cheviot Hs. (Eng. and Scot.)
Dapsang, Mt. (Him.)
Darling Ms. (Austral.)
Estrela (Ms.) (Port.)
Everest, Mt. (Him.)
Helicon, Mt. (Gr.)
Hoffman, Mt. (U.S.A.)
Illampu, Mt. (Boliv.)
Jaintia Ms. (Assam)
Kilauea (v.) (Pac.)
Lebanon, Mt. (Leb.)
Malvern Hs. (Eng.)
Mendips (Eng.)
Nan Ling Ms. (China)
Nan Shan Ms. (China)
Nilgiri Hs. (Ind.)
Olympus, Mt. (Gr.)
Orizaba (v.) (Mex.)
Palomar, Mt. (U.S.A.)
Preseli Ms. (Wales)
Rainier, Mt. (U.S.A.)
Rhodope Ms. (Turk.)
Rockies (N. Am.)
Roraima, Mt. (S. Am.)
Ruahine Ms. (N.Z.)
Ruapehu, Mt. (N.Z.)
San Juan Ms. (U.S.A.)
Siwalik Hs. (Ind.)
Skiddaw, Mt. (Eng.)
Snowdon, Mt. (Wales)
St. Elias Ms. (Can. and U.S.A.)
St. Elias, Mt. (Alaska)
Stanley, Mt. (Uganda and
    Congo, Dem. Rep.)
Sudetes (Cze. and Pol.)
Triglav, Mt. (Sloven.)
Vindhya Ms. (Ind.)

Whitney, Mt. (U.S.A.)

8

Aravalli Ms. (Ind.)
Ben Nevis (Scot.)
Ben Venue (Scot.)
Ben Wyvis (Scot.)
Cambrian Ms. (Wales)
Cameroon, Mt. (Cameroon)
Catskill Ms. (U.S.A.)
Caucasus Ms. (Eur.)
Cévennes (Ms.)France
Cheviots (Hs.) (Eng. and Scot.)
Chiltern Hs. (Eng.)
Cotopaxi (v.) (Ecuad.)
Cotswold Hs. (Eng.)
Cumbrian Ms. (Eng.)
Damavand, Mt. (Iran)
Flinders (Ms.) (Austral.)
Fujiyama (v.) (Jap.)
Goat Fell (Mt.) (Scot.
Hualapei Ms. (U.S.A.)
Illimani, Mt. (v.) (Bol.)
Jaya Peak (Indo.)
Jungfrau (Mt.) (Swit.)
Katahdin, Mt. (U.S.A.)
Kinabalu (v.) (Born.)
Krakatoa (v.) (Indo.)
McKinley, Mt. (Alaska)
Mitchell, Mt. (U.S.A.)
Mulhacén (Mt.) (Sp.)
Pennines (Hs.) (Eng.)
Pentland Hs. (Scot.)
Pyrenees Ms. (Eur.)
Quantock Hs. (Eng.)
Rajmahal Hs. (Ind.)
Rushmore, Mt. (U.S.A.)
Snaefell, Mt. (I. of Man)
Sulaiman Ms. (Pak.)
Tarawera, Mt. (N.Z.)
The Downs (Hs.) (Eng.)
The Ghats (Ms.) (Ind.)
The Wolds (Hs.) (Eng.)
Tien Shan Ms. (Asia)
Vesuvius (v.) (It.)
Whitmore Ms. (Antarc.)
Wrangell, Mt. (Alaska)

9

Aconcagua (v.) (Arg.)
Adam's Peak (Sri)
Allegheny Ms. (U.S.A.)
Annapurna (Him.)
Apennines (It.)

Ben Lawers (Scot.)
Black Dome (U.S.A.)
Blue Ridge Ms. (U.S.A.)
Carstensz (Indo.)
Chilterns (Hs.) (Eng.)
Cleveland Hs. (Eng.)
Communism (Taj.)
Cotswolds (Hs.) (Eng.)
Dolomites (It.)
Grampians (Ms.) (Scot.)
Helvellyn, Mt. (Eng.)
Himalayas (Ms.) (Asia)
Hindu-Kush (Ms.) (Asia)
Huascarán (v.) (Peru)
Karakoram (Ms.) (Asia)
Kosciusko, Mt. (Austral.)
Lafayette, Mt. (U.S.A.)
Lenin Peak (Kyr.)
Liverpool (Ms.) (Austral.)
Mont Blanc (Alps)
Mont Cenis (Alps)
Monte Rosa (Ms.) (Alps)
Naga Hills (Ind.)
Parnassus, Mt. (Gr.)
Pic du Midi (Pyr.)
Pikes Peak (U.S.A.)
Rakaposhi (Mt.) (Ind.)
Ras Dashan (Eth.)
Ruwenzori Ms. (Uganda and
    Congo, Dem Rep.)
Solfatara (v.) (It)
St. Bernard (Pass) (Swit.)
Stromboli (v.) (Med.)
Thian-Shan Ms. (Asia)
Tirich Mir (Mt.) (Pak.)
Tongariro, Mt. (v.) (N.Z.)
Tupungato (v.) (Arg.)
Weisshorn (Mt.) (Swit.)
Yablonovy (Ms.) (Rus.)
Zugspitze (Mt.) (Ger.)

10

Adirondack Ms. (U.S.A.)
Arakan Yoma Ms. (Burma)
Baker Butte (v.) (U.S.A.)
Ben Macdhui (Scot.)
Cader Idris (Mt.) (Wales)
Cairngorms (Scot.)
Cantabrian Ms. (Sp.)
Carpathian Ms. (Eur.)
Chimborazo (v.) (Ecuad.)
Dent du Midi (Swit.)
Dhaulagiri, Mt. (Him.)
Diablerets, Mt. (Swit.)

Erzgebirge (Ger.)
Graian Alps (Eur.)
Khyber Pass (Afghan., Pak.)
Kuh-i-Taftan (v.) (Iran)
Kunlun Shan Ms. (China)
Lammermuir Hs. (Scot.)
Laurentian Ms. (Can.)
Matterhorn, The (Alps)
Moel Fammau, Mt. (Wales)
Monte Corno (It.)
Ochil Hills (Scot.)
Pinlimmon, Mt. (Wales)
Pobeda Peak (China and Kyr.)
Saint Elias (Alaska)
Saint Elias Ms. (Can. and
    U.S.A.)
St. Gotthard (Pass) (Swit.)
Wetterhorn, The (Swit.)

11

Adirondacks (U.S.A.)
Alleghenies (U.S.A.)
Appalachian Ms. (U.S.A.)
Bernese Alps (Swit.)
Brenner Pass (Aust. and It.)
Brooks Range (Alaska)
Carpathians (Ms.) (Eur.)
Coast Ranges (N.Am.)
Corno Grande (It.)
Descabezado (v.) (Chile)
Dinaric Alps (Eur.)
Drachenfels (H.) (Ger.)
Drakensberg Ms. (S.A.)
Drakenstein, Mt. (S.A.)
Hochstetter, Mt. (N.Z.)
Kilimanjaro, Mt. (Tanz.)
Koryak Range (Rus.)
La Soufrière (v.) (W.I.)
Livingstone Ms. (Tanz.)
Livingstone Ms. (N.Z.)
Mendip Hills (Eng.)
Nanga Parbat (Him.)
Ortler Spitz (It.)
Owen Stanley (Ms.) (Papua)
Pennine Alps (Eur.)
Scafell Pike (Eng.)
Sierra Madre Ms. (Mex.)
Simplon Pass (Alps)
Splügen Pass (Swit.)
Swabian Alps (Ger.)
Vatnajökull (Iceland)

12

Appalachians (U.S.A.)
Cheviot Hills (Eng. and Scot.)
Citlaltépetl (Mex.)
Godwin Austen, Mt. (Him.)
Gran Paradiso (It.)
Ingleborough, Mt. (Eng.)
Kanchenjunga, Mt. (Him.)
Kinchinjunga, Mt. (Him.)
Malvern Hills (Eng.)
Maritime Alps (Fr., It.)
Monte Cassino (It.)
Nilgiri Hills (Ind.)
Peak District (Eng.)
Pennine Chain (Eng.)
Popocatépetl (v.) (Mex.)
Roncesvalles (v) (Pyr.)
Saint Gothard, Mt. (Swit.)
Schiehallion, Mt. (Scot.)
Sierra Nevada Ms. (Sp.)
Siwalik Hills (Ind.)

Slieve Donard (Mt.)N.I.
Tinguiririca (v.) (Chile)

13 AND OVER

Black Dome Peak (U.S.A.) (13)
Blue Mountains (Austral.) (13)
Blue Mountains (U.S.A.) (13)
Brecon Beacons (Wales) (13)
Carrauntuohil, Mt. (Ire.) (13)
Cerro de Mulhacén (Sp.) (14)
Cerro del Potro (Chile) (13)
Chiltern Hills (Eng.) (13)
Chirripó Grande (Costa Rica)
   (14)
Coast Mountains (N. Am.) (14)
Communism Peak (Taj.) (13)
Cotswold Hills (Eng.) (13)
Fichtelgebirge Ms. (Ger.) (14)
Finsteraahorn, Mt. (Swit.) (13)
Flinders Ranges (Austral.) (14)
Grossglockner (Aust.) (13)
Knockmealdown Ms. (Ire.) (13)

Macgillicuddy's Reeks
   (Ire.) (19)
Margherita Peak (Uganda and
   Congo, Dem. Rep. (14)
Massif Central (France) (13)
Mont Aux Sources
   (Lesotho) (14)
Mount of Olives (Isr.) (13)
Ojos del Salado (v.) (Chile and
   Arg. 13)
Pentland Hills (Scot.) (13)
Pidurutalagala (Sri) (14)
Rocky Mountains (N. Am.) (14)
Serra de Estrela (Ms.) (Port.)
   (14)
Sierra Maestra (Ms.) (Cuba)
   (13)
Stanovoy Range (Rus.) (13)
Sudeten Mountains (Cze. and
   Pol.) (16)
Table Mountain (S.A.) (13)
Tabor Mountain (Isr.) (13)

Oceans and seas

3 AND 4

Aral S. (Kaz., Uzbek.)
Azov, S. of (Ukr., Rus.)
Dead S. (Jord., Isr.)
Java S. (Indo.)
Kara S. (Rus.)
Red S. (Egypt, Arab.)
Ross S. (Antarc.)
Savu S. (Indo.)
Sulu S. (Philip.)

5

Banda S. (Indo.)
Black S. (Eur., Turk.)
Ceram S. (Indo.)
China S. (China)
Coral S. (Indo.)
Irish S. (Brit. Isles)
Japan, S. of (Jap.)
North S. (Eur.)
Timor S. (Indo.)
White S. (Rus.)

6

Aegean S. (Gr., Turk.)
Arctic O.

Baltic S. (N. Eur.)
Bering S. (Pac.)
Flores S. (Indo.)
Indian O.
Ionian S. (Gr.)
Laptev S. (Rus.)
Tasman S. (Austral.)
Yellow S. (China)

7

Andaman S. (Indo.)
Arabian S. (Ind.)
Arafura S. (Austral.)
Barents S. (Rus.)
Caspian S. (Eur., Asia)
Celebes S. (Indo.)
Marmora, S. of (Turk.)
Molucca S. (Indo.)
Okhotsk, S. of (Rus.)
Pacific O.
Weddell S. (Antarc.)

8

Adriatic S. (Med.)
Amundsen S. (Antarc.)
Atlantic O.
Beaufort S. (Can.)

Bismarck S. (Pac.)
Ligurian S. (It.)
Sargasso S. (Atl.)
Sulawesi S. (Indo.)

9

Antarctic O.
Caribbean S. (Am.)
East China S. (China)
Greenland S. (Green.)
Norwegian S. (Nor.)
Waddenzee (Neth.)
Zuider Zee (Neth.)
Zuyder Zee (Neth.)

10 AND OVER

Bellingshausen S. (Antarc.) (14)
East Siberian S. (Rus.) (12)
Mediterranean S. (Eur., Af.,
   Asia) (13)
South China S. (China) (10)
Tyrrhenian S. (W. Med.) (10)

Ports

3 AND 4

Acre (Isr.)
Aden (Yemen)
Akko (Isr.)
Baku (Azer.)
Bar (Monte.)
Bari (It.)
Cebu (Philip.)
Cobh (Ire.)
Cork (Ire.)
Deal (Eng.)
Elat (Isr.)
Erie (U.S.A.)
Hull (Eng.)
Ilo (Peru)
Kiel (Ger.)
Kobe (Jap.)
Lüda (China)
Okha (Rus.)
Oran (Alg.)
Oslo (Nor.)
Para (Braz.)
Pula (Cro.)
Riga (Latvia.)
Rye (Eng.)
Safi (Moroc.)
Suez (Egypt)
Tain (Scot.)
Tema (Ghana)
Wick (Scot.)

5

Akyab (Burma)
Amboy (U.S.A.)
Arica (Chile)
Barry (Wales)
Basra (Iraq)
Beira (Moz.)
Belém (Braz.)
Brest (Fr.)
Cadiz (Sp.)
Canea (Gr.)
Ceuta (Moroc.)
Colón (Panama)
Corfu (Gr.)
Dakar (Senegal)
Delft (Neth.)
Dover (Eng.)
Dubai (Dubai)
Eilat (Isr.)
Emden (Ger.)

Gaeta (It.)
Galle (Sri.)
Genoa (It.)
Haifa (Isr.)
Hanko (Fin.)
Havre (Le) (Fr.)
Izmir (Turk.)
Kerch (Ukr.)
Kochi (Jap.)
Kotor (Monte.)
Lagos (Nig.)
Larne (N. Ire.)
Leith (Scot.)
Lulea (Swed.)
Mahón (Minorca)
Malmö (Swed.)
Mocha (Yemen)
Osaka (Jap.)
Ostia (It.)
Palma (Sp.)
Palos (Sp.)
Poole (Eng.)
Pusan (S. Korea)
Rabat (Moroc.)
Reval (Est.)
Scapa (Scot.)
Split (Cro.)
Tiksi (Rus.)
Trani (It.)
Tunis (Tun.)
Turku (Fin.)
Varna (Bulg.)
Visby (Swed.)
Yaita (Ukr.)
Ystad (Swed.)

6

Agadir (Moroc.)
Ancona (It.)
Ashdod (Isr.)
Balboa (Panama)
Bastia (Cors.)
Beirut (Lebanon)
Bergen (Nor.)
Bilbao (Sp.)
Bombay (Ind.)
Boston (U.S.A.)
Bremen (Ger.)
Calais (Fr.)
Callao (Peru)
Cannes (Fr.)
Chefoo (China)

Cochin (Ind.)
Dairen (China)
Danzig (Pol.)
Darwin (Austral.)
Dieppe (Fr.)
Douala (Cameroon)
Dunbar (Scot.)
Dundee (Scot.)
Durban (S.A.)
Fdérik (Mauritania)
Fuzhou (China)
Gdansk (Pol.)
Gdynia (Pol.)
Haldia (Ind.)
Hankow (China)
Hobart (Tas.)
Izmail (Ukr.)
Jeddah (Saudi)
Kalmar (Swed.)
Kuwait (Kuwait)
Larvik (Nor.)
Lisbon (Port.)
Lobito (Angola)
London (Eng.)
Luanda (Ang.)
Lüshun (China)
Madras (Ind.)
Málaga (Sp.)
Manila (Philip.)
Matadi (Congo, Dem. Rep.)
Mtwara (Tanz.)
Mumbai (Ind.)
Naples (It.)
Narvik (Nor.)
Nelson (N.Z.)
Odense (Den.)
Odessa (Ukr.)
Oporto (Port.)
Ostend (Belg.)
Padang (Indo.)
Patras (Gr.)
Penang (Malay.)
Ramsey (I. of Man)
Recife (Braz.)
Rhodes (Gr.)
Rijeka (Cro.)
Santos (Braz.)
Sittwe (Burma)
Skikda (Alg.)
Smyrna (Turk.)
Suakin (Sudan)

Sydney (Austral.)
Tainan (Taiwan)
Tetuán (Moroc.)
Toulon (Fr.)
Tromsø (Nor.)
Venice (It.)
Weihai (China)
Wismar (Ger.)
Yantai (China)

7

Aalborg (Den.)
Abidjan (Ivory Coast)
Ajaccio (Cors.)
Algiers (Alg.)
Antwerp (Belg.)
Bangkok (Thai.)
Belfast (N.I.)
Bushehr (Iran)
Cardiff (Wales)
Cattaro (Monte.)
Cayenne (Fr. Guiana)
Chatham (Eng.)
Colombo (Sri)
Corunna (Sp.)
Cotonou (Benin)
Dampier (Austral.)
Detroit (U.S.A.)
Donegal (Ire.)
Dundalk (Ire.)
Dunkirk (Fr.)
Foochow (China)
Funchal (Port.)
Geelong (Austral.)
Gotland (Swed.)
Grimsby (Eng.)
Guaymas (Mex.)
Halifax (Can.)
Hamburg (Ger.)
Harwich (Eng.)
Hodeida (Yemen)
Horsens (Den.)
Houston (U.S.A.)
Izmayil (Ukr.)
Jakarta (Indo.)
Karachi (Pak.)
Keelung (Taiwan)
Kitimat (Can.)
Kowloon (Hong Kong)
La Plata (Arg.)
Larnaca (Cyprus)
Le Havre (Fr.)

Leghorn (It.)
Livorno (It.)
Marsala (It.)
Melilla (Moroc.)
Messina (It.)
Mogador (Moroc.)
Mombasa (Kenya)
New York (U.S.A.)
Norfolk (U.S.A.)
Okhotsk (Rus.)
Palermo (It.)
Petsamo (Fin.)
Piraeus (Gr.)
Rangoon (Burma)
Rosario (Arg.)
Rostock (Ger.)
Salerno (It.)
San Juan (Puerto Rico)
Seattle (U.S.A.)
Shantou (China)
Stettin (Pol.)
Swansea (Wales)
Tallinn (Est.)
Tangier (Moroc.)
Tianjin (China)
Tilbury (Eng.)
Trapani (It.)
Trieste (It.)
Tripoli (Libya)
Yingkou (China)
Youghal (Ire.)

8

Abu Dhabi (Abu Dhabi)
Adelaide (Austral.)
Alicante (Sp.)
Arrecife (Sp.)
Auckland (N.Z.)
Benghazi (Libya)
Bordeaux (Fr.)
Boulogne (Fr.)
Brindisi (It.)
Brisbane (Austral.)
Budapest (Hung.)
Calcutta (Ind.)
Cape Town (S.A.)
Cocanada (Ind.)
Coquimbo (Chile)
Cuxhaven (Ger.)
Damietta (Egypt)
Djibouti (Djibouti)
Dunleary (Ire.)
El Ferrol (Sp.)
Elsinore (Den.)

Falmouth (Eng.)
Flushing (Neth.)
Freetown (Sierra
    Leone)
Gisborne (N.Z.)
Göteborg (Swed.)
Greenock (Scot.)
Hakodate (Jap.)
Halmstad (Swed.)
Hangzhou (China)
Helsinki (Fin.)
Holyhead (Wales)
Honfleur (Fr.)
Hong Kong (China)
Honolulu (Hawaii)
Istanbul (Turk.)
Kakinada (Ind.)
Kingston (Jam.)
La Coruña (Sp.)
La Guaira (Venez.)
Llanelli (Wales)
Macassar (Indo.)
Makassar (Indo.)
Montreal (Can.)
Moulmein (Burma)
Murmansk (Rus.)
Nagasaki (Jap.)
Nakhodka (Rus.)
Newhaven (Eng.)
Newhaven (U.S.A.)
Nyköping (Swed.)
Pechenga (Rus.)
Pembroke (Wales)
Penzance (Eng.)
Plymouth (Eng.)
Port Said (Egypt)
Portland (Eng.)
Rosslare (Ire.)
Sandwich (Eng.)
Shanghai (China)
St. Helier (Ch. Is.)
Szczecin (Pol.)
Taganrog (Rus.)
Takoradi (Ghana)
Tamatave (Mad.)
Tientsin (China)
Veracruz (Mex.)
Weymouth (Eng.)
Yokohama (Jap.)

9

Algeciras (Sp.)
Amsterdam (Neth.)
Archangel (Rus.)

Ardrossan (Scot.)
Avonmouth (Eng.)
Baltimore (U.S.A.)
Barcelona (Sp.)
Cartagena (Sp., Col.)
Cherbourg (Fr.)
Churchill (Can.)
Cristóbal (Panama)
Devonport (Eng.)
Dubrovnik (Cro.)
Ermoupoli (Gr.)
Esquimalt (Can.)
Essaouira (Moroc.)
Europoort (Neth.)
Fishguard (Wales)
Flensburg (Ger.)
Fremantle (Austral.)
Galveston (U.S.A.)
Gibraltar (Med.)
Gravesend (Eng.)
Guayaquil (Ecuador)
Helsingör (Den.)
Hiroshima (Jap.)
Inhambane (Moz.)
Kagoshima (Jap.)
Kaohsiung (Taiwan)
King's Lynn (Eng.)
Kolobrzeg (Pol.)
Las Palmas (Sp.)
Leningrad (Rus.)
Liverpool (Eng.)
Lyttelton (N.Z.)
Marseille (Fr.)
Melbourne (Austral.)
Mossel Bay (S.A.)
Nantucket (U.S.A.)
Newcastle (Eng.,
    Austral.)
Owen Sound (Can.)
Pensacola (U.S.A.)
Port Klang (Malay.)
Port Louis (Mauritius)
Port Mahon (Sp.)
Port Natal (S.A.)
Port Royal (Jam.)
Port Sudan (Sudan)
Portmadoc (Wales)
Porto Novo (Benin)
Rotterdam (Neth.)
Scapa Flow (Scot.)
Sheerness (Eng.)
Singapore (Singapore)
Stavanger (Nor.)
Stockholm (Swed.)

Stornoway (Scot.)
Toamasina (Mad.)
Trondheim (Nor.)
Vancouver (Can.)
Zeebrugge (Belg.)

10

Alexandria (Egypt)
Barnstaple (Eng.)
Bridgeport (U.S.A.)
Casablanca (Moroc.)
Charleston (U.S.A.)
Chittagong (Ind.)
Constantza (Rom.)
Copenhagen (Den.)
East London (S.A.)
Felixstowe (Eng.)
Folkestone (Eng.)
George Town (Malay.)
Gothenburg (Swed.)
Hammerfest (Nor.)
Hartlepool (Eng.)
Jersey City (U.S.A.)
La Rochelle (Fr.)
Los Angeles (U.S.A.)
Marseilles (Fr.)
Montego Bay (Jam.)
Montevideo (Uruguay)
New Bedford (U.S.A.)
New Orleans (U.S.A.)
Nouadhibou
    (Mauritania)
Pernambuco (Braz.)
Port Arthur (China)
Port Kelang (Malay.)
Portsmouth (Eng.,
    U.S.A.)
Rock Harbor (U.S.A.)
San Juan Bay (Peru)
Simonstown (S.A.)
Sunderland (Eng.)
Teignmouth (Eng.)
Travemünde (Ger.)
Valparaíso (Chile)
Vlissingen (Neth.)
Whitstable (Eng.)

11

Bremerhaven (Ger.)
Buenos Aires (Arg.)
Cinque Ports (Eng.)
Dar es Salaam (Tanz.)
Grangemouth (Scot.)
Helsingborg (Swed.)

Hermoupolis (Gr.)
Pearl Harbor (Hawaii)
Pondicherry (Ind.)
Port Glasgow (Scot.)
Port Jackson (Austral.)
Port Moresby (Papua)
Port of Spain (Trinidad)
Saint Helier (Ch. Is.)
Shimonoseki (Jap.)
Southampton (Eng.)
St. Peter Port (Ch. Is.)
Trincomalee (Sri)
Vladivostok (Rus.)

12

Barranquilla (Col.)
Buenaventura (Col.)
Dun Laoghaire (Ire.)
Kota Kinabalu (Malay.)
Kristiansund (Nor.)
Masulipatnam (Ind.)
Milford Haven (Wales)
North Shields (Eng.)
Port Adelaide (Austral.)
Port Harcourt (Nig.)
Port Sunlight (Eng.)
Rio de Janeiro (Braz.)

San Francisco (U.S.A.)
St. Petersburg (Rus.)

13 AND 14

Constantinople (Turk.) (14)
Frederikshavn (Den.) (13)
Machilipatnam (Ind.) (13)
Middlesbrough (Eng.) (13)
Petropavlovsk (Kaz.) (13)
Port Elizabeth (S.A.) (13)
Puerto Cabello (Venez.) (13)
Puerto de Hierro (Venez.) (14)
Santiago de Cuba (Cuba) (14)
Trois-Rivières (Can.) (13)
Wilhelmshaven (Ger.) (13)

Provinces, cantons, districts, regions, dependent states, etc.

3 AND 4

A.C.T. (Austral.)
Aceh (Indo.)
Ain (Fr.)
Aube (Fr.)
Aude (Fr.)
Bali (Indo.)
Bari (It.)
Bern (Swit.)
Cher (Fr.)
Diu (Ind.)
Eure (Fr.)
Fars (Iran)
Gard (Fr.)
Gaza (Moz.)
Gers (Fr.)
Goa (Ind.)
Ica (Peru)
Iowa (U.S.A.)
Jaén (Sp.)
Java (Indo.)
Jura (Fr.)
Kano (Nig.)
Komi (Rus.)
León (Sp.)
Lima (Peru)
Lodz (Pol.)
Lot (Fr.)
Lugo. (Sp.)
Nord (Fr.)
Ohio (U.S.A.)
Oise (Fr.)
Ondo (Nig.)
Orne (Fr.)

Oudh (Ind.)
Pará (Braz.)
Pegu (Burma)
Perm (Rus.)
Pisa (It.)
Qom (Iran)
Qum (Iran)
Saar (Ger.)
Sind (Pak.)
Tarn (Fr.)
Tuva (Rus.)
Uri (Swit.)
Utah (U.S.A.)
Var (Fr.)
Vaud (Swit.)
Zug (Swit.)

5

Achin (Indo.)
Adana (Turk.)
Aisne (Fr.)
Altai (Rus.)
Anhui (China)
Anjou (Fr.)
Assam (Ind.)
Baden (Ger.)
Bahía (Braz.)
Banat (Eur.)
Basel (Swit.)
Basle (Swit.)
Bauchi (Nig.)
Béarn (Fr.)
Beira (Port.)
Benue (Nig.)
Berne (Swit.)

Berry (Fr.)
Bihar (Ind.)
Cadiz (Sp.)
Ceará (Braz.)
Daman (Ind.)
Delhi (Ind.)
Doubs (Fr.)
Drome (Fr.)
Eifel (Ger.)
Gansu (China)
Gilon (Iran)
Goiás (Braz.)
Hamar (Nor.)
Hebei (China)
Hejaz (Saudi)
Henan (China)
Herat (Afghan.)
Hesse (Ger.)
Honan (China)
Hopeh (China)
Hunan (China)
Hupeh (China)
Idaho (U.S.A.)
Indre (Fr.)
Isère (Fr.)
Jilin (China)
Johor (Malay.)
Judea (Isr.)
Jujuy (Arg.)
Kansu (China)
Karoo (S.A.)
Khiva (Asia)
Kirin (China)
Kwara (Nig.)
La Paz (Boliv.)

Lagos (Nig.)
Lazio (It.)
Liège (Belg.)
Loire (Fr.)
Maine (U.S.A.
and Fr.)
Marne (Fr.)
Meuse (Fr.)
Morea (Gr.)
Namur (Belg.)
Nubia (Sudan)
Opole (Pol.)
Oruro (Boliv.)
Otago (N.Z.)
Perak (Malay.)
Posen (Pol.)
Puglia (It.)
Rhône (Fr.)
Sabah (Malay.)
Sahel (Af.)
Salta (Arg.)
Savoy (Fr.)
Seine (Fr.)
Sivas (Turk.)
Somme (Fr.)
Tacna (Peru)
Texas (U.S.A.)
Tibet (China)
Tigre (Eth.)
Tomsk (Rus.)
Tyrol (Aust.)
Viseu (Port.)
Weald (The) (Eng.)
Yonne (Fr.)
Yukon (Can.)

6

Aargau (Swit.)
Adygea (Rus.)
Alaska (U.S.A.)
Allier (Fr.)
Alsace (Fr.)
Anhwei (China)
Apulia (It.)
Aragon (Sp.)
Ariège (Fr.)
Artois (Fr.)
Baffin (Can.)
Bengal (Ind. and
  Bangla.)
Borneo (Indo.)
Cracow (Pol.)
Creuse (Fr.)
Crimea (Ukr.)
Dakota (U.S.A.)
Danzig (Pol.)
Darfur (Sudan)
Emilia (It.)
Epirus (Gr.)
Faiyum (Egypt)
Fujian (China)
Fukien (China)
Gdansk (Pol.)
Geneva (Swit.)
Gerona (Sp.)
Ghilan (Iran)
Glarus (Swit.)
Guiana (S. Am.)
Hawaii (U.S.A.)
Huelva (Sp.)
Huesca (Sp.)
Johore (Malay.)
Judaea (Isr.)
Kansas (U.S.A.)
Karroo (S.A.)
Kerala (Ind.)
Kerman (Iran)
Kielce (Pol.)
Ladakh (Ind.)
Landes (Fr.)
Latium (It.)
Lérida (Sp.)
Levant (Sp.)
Loiret (Fr.)
Lozère (Fr.)
Lublin (Pol.)
Madras (Ind.)
Madura (Indo.)
Málaga (Sp.)

Manche (Fr.)
Mari El (Rus.)
Mercia (Eng.)
Mergui (Burma)
Molise (It.)
Murcia (Sp.)
Mysore (Ind.)
Nelson (N.Z.)
Nevada (U.S.A.)
Nièvre (Fr.)
Novara (It.)
Oaxaca (Mex.)
Oregon (U.S.A.)
Orense (Sp.)
Orissa (Ind.)
Oviedo (Sp.)
Pahang (Malay.)
Pampas (S. Am.)
Paraná (Braz.)
Poitou (Fr.)
Potosí (Boliv.)
Poznán (Pol.)
Punjab (Ind., Pak.)
Quebec (Can.)
Rivers (Nig.)
Sahara (Af.)
Sarthe (Fr.)
Saxony (Ger.)
Scania (Swed.)
Schwyz (Swit.)
Seyhan (Turk.)
Shansi (China)
Shanxi (China)
Shensi (China)
Sicily (It.)
Sikkim (Ind.)
Sokoto (Nig.)
Sonora (Mex.)
St. Gall (Swit.)
Styria (Aust.)
Swabia (Ger.)
Tasman (N.Z.)
Tehran (Iran)
Thrace (Gr.)
Ticino (Swit.)
Toledo (Sp.)
Tyumen (Rus.)
Ulster (N.I.)
Umbria (It.)
Upsala (Swed.)
Valais (Swit.)
Vendée (Fr.)
Veneto (It.)
Viborg (Den.)

Vienne (Fr.)
Vosges (Fr.)
Warsaw (Pol.)
Wessex (Eng.)
Yunnan (China)
Zamora (Sp.)
Zurich (Swit.)

7

Abruzzi (It.)
Alabama (U.S.A.)
Alagoas (Braz.)
Alberta (Can.)
Algarve (Port.)
Almeria (Sp.)
Antwerp (Belg.)
Arizona (U.S.A.)
Aveyron (Fr.)
Bavaria (Ger.)
Bohemia (Cze.)
Bokhara (Uzbek.)
Brabant (Belg.)
Bukhara (Uzbek.)
Cáceres (Sp.)
Castile (Sp.)
Chiapas (Mex.)
Córdoba (Sp.)
Córdoba (Arg.)
Corrèze (Fr.)
Côte-d'Or (Fr.)
Drenthe (Neth.)
Durango (Mex.)
Fergana (Uzbek.)
Florida (U.S.A.)
Galicia (Sp.)
Galicia (Pol. and Ukr.)
Galilee (Isr.)
Gascony (Fr.)
Gauteng (S.A.)
Georgia (U.S.A.)
Gotland (Swed.)
Granada (Sp.)
Grisons (Swit.)
Guienne (Fr.)
Guizhou (China)
Gujarat (Ind.)
Hanover (Ger.)
Haryana (Ind.)
Hérault (Fr.)
Hidalgo (Mex.)
Holland (Neth.)
Huánuco (Peru)
Indiana (U.S.A.)
Iquique (Chile)

Jalisco (Mex.)
Jiangsu (China)
Jiangxi (China)
Jutland (Den.)
Karelia (Rus.)
Kashmir (Ind. and
  Pak.)
Katsina (Nig.)
Kiangsi (China)
Kiangsu (China)
Lapland (Eur.)
Liguria (It.)
Limburg (Neth.)
Limburg (Belg.)
Logroño (Sp.)
Lucerne (Swit.)
Malacca (Malay.)
Manipur (Ind.)
Marches (It.)
Mayenne (Fr.)
Mendoza (Arg.)
Montana (U.S.A.)
Moravia (Cze.)
Munster (Ire.)
Navarre (Sp.)
New York (U.S.A.)
Ontario (Can.)
Ossetia (Rus.)
Paraíba (Braz.)
Perugia (It.)
Picardy (Fr.)
Prussia (Ger.)
Qinghai (China)
Ravenna (It.)
Riviera (The) (Fr. and
  It.)
Santa Fé (Arg.)
Sarawak (Malay.)
Segovia (Sp.)
Sennaar (Sudan)
Sergipe (Braz.)
Sevilla (Sp.)
Seville (Sp.)
Shaanxi (China)
Siberia (Rus.)
Sichuan (China)
Silesia (Pol.)
Sinaloa (Mex.)
Sondrio (It.)
Sumatra (Indo.)
Tabasco (Mex.)
Tanjore (Ind.)
Teheran (Iran)
Thurgau (Swit.)

Trabzon (Turk.)
Tripura (Ind.)
Tucuman (Arg.)
Tuscany (It.)
Uppsala (Swed.)
Utrecht (Neth.)
Venetia (It.)
Vermont (U.S.A.)
Vizcaya (Sp.)
Waikato (N.Z.)
Wroclaw (Pol.)
Wyoming (U.S.A.)
Yakutia (Rus.)
Yucatán (Mex.)
Zeeland (Neth.)

8

Alentejo (Port.)
Alicante (Sp.)
Amazonas (Braz., Col.,
   Peru and Venez.)
Anatolia (Turk.)
Ardennes (Fr.)
Arkansas (U.S.A.)
Asturias (Sp.)
Auckland (N.Z.)
Brittany (Fr.)
Bukovina (Eur.)
Burgundy (Fr.)
Buryatia (Rus.)
Calabria (It.)
Calvados (Fr.)
Campania (It.)
Campeche (Mex.)
Carniola (Sloven.)
Carolina (U.S.A.)
Caucasus (Rus., Geo.,
   Arm. and Azer.)
Charente (Fr.)
Chechnya (Rus.)
Chekiang (China)
Coahuila (Mex.)
Colorado (U.S.A.)
Columbia (U.S.A.)
Dagestan (Rus.)
Dalmatia (Cro.)
Dauphiné (Fr.)
Delaware (U.S.A.)
Dordogne (Fr.)
Ferghana (Uzbek.)
Finnmark (Nor.)
Flanders (Belg.)
Florence (It.)
Fribourg (Swit.)

Girgenti (It.)
Gisborne (N.Z.)
Guerrero (Mex.)
Hainault (Belg.)
Hannover (Ger.)
Haut Rhin (Fr.)
Holstein (Ger.)
Illinois (U.S.A.)
Kandahar (Afghan.)
Kemerovo (Rus.)
Kentucky (U.S.A.)
Khorasan (Iran)
Kordofan (Sudan)
Kweichow (China)
Labrador (Can.)
Leinster (Ire.)
Liaoning (China)
Limbourg (Belg.)
Limousin (Fr.)
Lombardy (It.)
Lorestan (Iran)
Lorraine (Fr.)
Lothians (The) (Scot.)
Lowlands (Scot.)
Lyonnais (Fr.)
Manitoba (Can.)
Maranhao (Braz.)
Maryland (U.S.A.)
Michigan (U.S.A.)
Missouri (U.S.A.)
Moldavia (Rom.)
Morbihan (Fr.)
Nagaland (Ind.)
Nebraska (U.S.A.)
Normandy (Fr.)
Oberland (Swit.)
Oklahoma (U.S.A.)
Palencia (Sp.)
Parahiba (Braz.)
Peshawar (Ind.)
Piacenza (It.)
Piedmont (It.)
Provence (Fr.)
Roumelia (Turk.)
Ruthenia (Ukr.)
Saarland (Ger.)
Salonika (Gr.)
Salzburg (Aust.)
São Paulo (Braz.)
Sardinia (It.)
Shandong (China)
Shantung (China)
Sinkiang (China)
Slavonia (Cro.)

Szechwan (China)
Taranaki (N.Z.)
Tarapaca (Chile)
Tasmania (Austral.)
Thessaly (Gr.)
Tlaxcala (Mex.)
Tongking (Asia)
Trentino (It.)
Tsinghai (China)
Udmurtia (Rus.)
Valdivia (Chile)
Valencia (Sp.)
Vaucluse (Fr.)
Veracruz (Mex.)
Victoria (Austral.)
Vila Real (Port.)
Virginia (U.S.A.)
Wallonia (Belg.)
Westland (N.Z.)
Xinjiang (China)
Zaragoza (Sp.)
Zhejiang (China)

9

Agrigento (It.)
Alto Adige (It.)
Andalusia (Sp.)
Appenzell (Swit.)
Aquitaine (Fr.)
Archangel (Rus.)
Asia Minor (Asia)
Astrakhan (Rus.)
Cantabria (Sp.)
Carinthia (Aust.)
Catalonia (Sp.)
Champagne (Fr.)
Chihuahua (Mex.)
Chuvashia (Rus.)
Connaught (Ire.)
Entre Rios (Arg.)
Franconia (Ger.)
Free State (S.A.)
Friesland (Neth.)
Gaza Strip (Pal.)
Groningen (Neth.)
Guangdong (China)
Guipúzcoa (Sp.)
Hadramaut (Arab.)
Hawkes Bay (N.Z.)
Highlands (Scot.)
Kamchatka (Rus.)
Karnataka (Ind.)
Khuzestan (Iran)
Krasnodar (Rus.)

Kwangtung (China)
Languedoc (Fr.)
Louisiana (U.S.A.)
Macedonia (Gr.)
Meghalaya (Ind.)
Melanesia (Pac.)
Michoacán (Mex.)
Minnesota (U.S.A.)
Mordvinia (Rus.)
Neuchâtel (Swit.)
New Forest (Eng.)
New Guinea (Indo.)
New Jersey (U.S.A.)
New Mexico (U.S.A.)
Nivernais (Fr.)
North-West (S.A.)
Northland (N.Z.)
Nuevo León (Mex.)
Oldenburg (Ger.)
Palestine (Asia)
Patagonia (S. Am.)
Polynesia (Pac.)
Pomerania (Ger. and
   Pol.)
Potteries (The) (Eng.)
Querétaro (Mex.)
Rajasthan (Ind.)
Rajputana (Ind.)
Rhineland (Ger.)
Saint Gall (Swit.)
Salamanca (Sp.)
Samarkand (Asia)
Saragossa (Sp.)
Schleswig (Ger.)
Southland (N.Z.)
Stavropol (Rus.)
Tamil Nadu (Ind.)
Tarragona (Sp.)
Tatarstan (Rus.)
Tennessee (U.S.A.)
Thuringia (Ger.)
Transvaal (S.A.)
Trebizond (Turk.)
Turkestan (Asia)
Turkistan (Asia)
Turkmenia (Asia)
Villa Real (Port.)
Wallachia (Rom.)
West Coast (N.Z.)
West Irian (Indo.)
Wisconsin (U.S.A.)
Zacatecas (Mex.)

10

Basilicata (It.)
Bessarabia (Mold. and Ukr.)
Burgenland (Aust.)
California (U.S.A.)
Canterbury (N.Z.)
East Africa
East Anglia (Eng.)
Eure-et-Loir (Fr.)
Gelderland (Neth.)
Griqualand (S.A.)
Guanajuato (Mex.)
Haute-Loire (Fr.)
Haute-Marne (Fr.)
Haute-Saône (Fr.)
Ingushetia (Rus.)
Khabarovsk (Rus.)
Lambayeque (Peru)
Loir-et-Cher (Fr.)
Mazandaran (Iran)
Micronesia (Pac.)
Montenegro (Yug.)
New Castile (Sp.)
Nova Scotia (Can.)
Old Castile (Sp.)
Overijssel (Neth.)
Palatinate (Ger.)
Pernambuco (Braz.)
Pontevedra (Sp.)
Queensland (Austral.)
Roussillon (Fr.)
Saxe-Coburg (Ger.)
Senegambia (Af.)
Slave Coast (Af.)
Sverdlovsk (Rus.)
Tamaulipas (Mex.)
Tenasserim (Burma)
Valladolid (Sp.)
Valparaíso (Chile)
Vorarlberg (Aust.)
Washington (U.S.A.)
Waziristan (Pak.)
West Africa
West Bengal (Ind.)
West Indies (Carib.)
Westphalia (Ger.)

11

Arkhangelsk (Rus.)
Baluchistan (Pak.)
Bay of Plenty (N.Z.)
Bourbonnais (Fr.)
Brandenburg (Ger.)

Buenos Aires (Arg.)
Connecticut (U.S.A.)
Côtes-du-Nord (Fr.)
Eastern Cape (S.A.)
Extremadura (Sp.)
Great Karroo (S.A.)
Guadalajara (Sp.)
Haute-Savoie (Fr.)
Haute-Vienne (Fr.)
Hautes-Alpes (Fr.)
Hercegovina (Bos.)
Hesse-Nassau (Ger.)
Île-de-France (Fr.)
Krasnoyarsk (Rus.)
Lower Saxony (Ger.)
Maharashtra (Ind.)
Marlborough (N.Z.)
Matto Grosso (Braz.)
Mecklenburg (Ger.)
Minas Gerais (Braz.)
Mississippi (U.S.A.)
North Africa
North Dakota (U.S.A.)
Northumbria (Eng.)
Pas de Calais (Fr.)
Peloponnese (Gr.)
Pondicherry (Ind.)
Quintana Roo (Mex.)
Rhode Island (U.S.A.)
Schwarzwald (Ger.)
South Dakota (U.S.A.)
Sudetenland (Cze.)
The Lothians (Scot.)
Unterwalden (Swit.)
Upper Karroo (S.A.)
Valle d'Aosta (It.)
Western Cape (S.A.)
White Russia
Württemberg (Ger.)

12

British Isles (Eur.)
Franche-Comté (Fr)
Haute-Garonne (Fr.)
Heilongjiang (China)
Hohenzollern (Ger.)
Huancavelica (Peru)
Indre-et-Loire (Fr.)
KwaZulu-Natal (S.A.)
Latin America
Little Karroo (S.A.)
Little Russia
Lot-et-Garonne (Fr.)
Lower Austria (Aust.)

New Brunswick (Can.)
New Hampshire (U.S.A.)
Newfoundland (Can.)
North Brabant (Neth.)
North Holland (Neth.)
Northern Cape (S.A.)
Pennsylvania (U.S.A.)
Rio de Janeiro (Braz.)
Saskatchewan (Can.)
Schaffhausen (Swit.)
Seine-et-Marne (Fr.)
South Holland (Neth.)
The Potteries (Eng.)
Transylvania (Rom.)
Upper Austria (Aust.)
Uttar Pradesh (Ind.)
West Virginia (U.S.A.)

13

Andhra Pradesh (Ind.)
Bashkortostan (Rus.)
Canary Islands (Sp.)
Emilia-Romagna (It.)
Espírito Santo (Braz.)
Ille-et-Vilaine (Fr.)
Inner Mongolia (China)
Madhya Pradesh (Ind.)
Massachusetts (U.S.A.)
New South Wales (Austral.)
North Carolina (U.S.A.)
Rhondda Valley (Wales)
Romney Marshes (Eng.)
San Luis Potosí (Mex.)
Santa Catarina (Braz.)
Saxe-Altenburg (Ger.)
Saxe-Meiningen (Ger.)
South Carolina (U.S.A.)
Tarn-et-Garonne (Fr.)
Witwatersrand (S.A.)

14 AND OVER

Alpes-Maritimes (Fr.) (14)
Alsace-Lorraine (Fr.) (14)
Baden-Württemberg (Ger.) (16)
Balearic Islands (Sp.) (15)
Basque Provinces (Sp.) (15)
Bihar and Orissa (Ind.) (14)
British Columbia (Can.) (15)
Central America (14)
Channel Islands (U.K.) (14)
District of Columbia
    (U.S.A.) (18)
Entre-Douro-e-Minho
    (Port.) (16)

Griqualand West (S.A.) (14)
Hautes-Pyrénées (Fr.) (14)
Himachal Pradesh (Ind.) (15)
Jammu and Kashmir (15)
Loire-Atlantique (Fr.) (15)
Lower California (Mex.) (15)
Manawatu-Wanganui (N.Z.) (16)
North Rhine-Westphalia
    (Ger.) (20)
North-West Frontier (Pak.) (17)
Northern Ireland (U.K.) (15)

Northern Territory
    (Austral.) (17)
Northwest Territories
    (Can.) (20)
Orange Free State (S.A.) (15)
Prince Edward Island
    (Can.) (18)
Rhenish Prussia (Ger.) (14)
Rio Grande do Sul (Braz.) (14)
Santa Catharina (Braz.) (14)
Saxe-Coburg-Gotha (Ger.) (15)

Schaumberg-Lippe (Ger.) (15)
Schleswig-Holstein (Ger.) (17)
South Australia (Austral.) (14)
Southern Africa (14)
United Provinces (Ind.) (15)
United Provinces (Neth.)15
Western Australia
    (Austral.) (16)
Yukon Territory (Can.) (14)

Rivers

R. = River, and is inserted where "River" commonly follows the name

1 – 3

Aar (Swit.)
Ain (Fr.)
Aln (Eng.)
Axe (Eng.)
Bug (Pol. and Ukr.)
Cam (Eng.)
Dee (Wales)
Dee (Scot.)
Don (Scot.)
Don (Rus.)
Ems (Ger.)
Esk (Scot.)
Esk (Eng.)
Exe (Eng.)
Fal (Eng.)
Fly (Papua)
Han (China)
Ili (Asia)
Ill (Fr.)
Inn (Aust.)
Ket (Sib.)
Kwa (Congo, Dem.
    Rep.)
Lea (Eng.)
Lee (Ire.)
Lek (Neth.)
Lot (Fr.)
Lys (Fr. and Belg.)
Nen (Eng.)
Ob (Sib.)
Oka (Rus.)
Po (It.)
Red R. (U.S.A.)
Rur (Ger. and Neth.)
Rye (Eng.)

Sid (Eng.)
Syr (Kaz.)
Taw (Eng.)
Tay (Scot.)
Tom (Sib.)
Ure (Eng.)
Usa (Rus.)
Usk (Wales)
Vah (Slov.)
Var (Fr.)
Vis (Nam., S.A.)
Wey (Eng.)
Wye (Eng.)
Wye (Wales)
Yeo (Eng.)
Yug (Rus.)
Zab (Turk.)

4

Adda (It.)
Adda (Sudan)
Adur (Eng.)
Aire (Eng.)
Alma (Ukr.)
Amur (Asia)
Arno (It.)
Arun (Eng.)
Avon (Eng.)
Bann (N.I.)
Beas (Ind.)
Bobr (Bela.)
Bobr (Pol.)
Bure (Eng.)
Cher (Fr.)
Cole (Eng.)
Dart (Eng.)
Doon (Scot.)

Earn (Scot.)
Ebro (Sp.)
Eden (Eng.)
Elbe (Ger.)
Emba (Kaz.)
Enns (Aust.)
Erne (Ire.)
Fish R. (Nam., S.A.)
Geba (W. Af.)
Gila (U.S.A.)
Gota (Swed.)
Isar (Aust. and Ger.)
Isis (Eng.)
Juba (E. Af.)
Kama (Rus.)
Kura (Asia)
Kwai (Thai)
Lähn (Pol.)
Lech (Aust. and Ger.)
Leie (Fr. and Belg.)
Lena (Sib.)
Loir (Fr.)
Lune (Eng.)
Maas (Neth.)
Main (Ger.)
Main (Ire.)
Milk R. (Jam.)
Milk R. (U.S.A.)
Miño (Sp.)
Mole (Eng.)
Neva (Rus.)
Nida (Pol.)
Nile (Af.)
Nith (Scot.)
Nith (Can.)
Oder (Cze, Ger. and
    Pol.)

Ohio (U.S.A.)
Oise (Fr.)
Ouse (Eng.)
Oxus (Asia)
Peel (Can.)
Pegu R. (Burma)
Prut (S.E. Eur.)
Ravi (Ind. and Pak.)
Rede (Eng.)
Roer (Ger. and Neth.)
Ruhr (Ger.)
Saar (Fr. and Ger.)
Salt R. (U.S.A.)
Sava (S.E. Eur.)
Save (Fr.)
Save (Moz. and Zim.)
Slov (Hung.)
Spey (Scot.)
Styr (Bel. and Ukr.)
Suck (Ire.)
Suir (Ire.)
Swan (Can.)
Taff (Wales)
Tajo (Sp.)
Tana (Kenya)
Tapi (Ind.)
Tara (Yug.)
Tarn (Fr.)
Tees (Eng.)
Tefé (Braz.)
Teif (Wales)
Tejo (Port.)
Test (Eng.)
Thur (Swit.)
Tisa (S.E. Eur.)
Towy (Wales)
Tyne (Eng.)

Uele (Congo, Dem. Rep.)
Ural (Rus. and Kaz.)
Vaal (S. Af.)
Vire (Fr.)
Waal (Neth.)
Wash (Eng.)
Wear (Eng.)
Wlén (Pol.)
Yalu (China and N. Korea)
Yana (Sib.)
Yare (Eng.)

5

Adige (It.)
Adour (Fr.)
Agout (Fr.)
Aisne (Fr.)
Aller (Ger.)
Argun (Rus. and China)
Avoca R. (Austral.)
Awash (Eth.)
Benue (W. Af.)
Bío-Bío (Chile)
Black R. (U.S.A.)
Blood R. (S. A.)
Boyne (Ire.)
Camel (Eng.)
Chari (Cen. Af.)
Clyde (Scot.)
Colne (Eng.)
Congo (Af.)
Deben (Eng.)
Desna (Rus.)
Donau (Eur.)
Douro (Port. and Sp.)
Dovey (Wales)
Drava (Cen. Eur.)
Drave (Hung.)
Drina (Yug.)
Duero (Sp.)
Dvina (Rus.)
Dvina (Rus., Bela. and Lat.)
Eider (Ger.)
Feale (Ire.)
Fleet (Eng.)
Forth (Scot.)
Foyle (Ire.)
Frome (Eng.)
Grand R. (Can.)
Grand R. (U.S.A.)
Green R. (U.S.A.)

Gumti (Ind.)
Havel (Ger.)
Huang (China)
Hugli (Ind.)
Hunza (Pak.)
Ikopa (E. Af.)
Indus (Asia)
Isère (Fr.)
Ishim (Kaz.)
James R. (U.S.A.)
Jumna (Ind.)
Juruá (Braz. and Peru)
Kabul (Afghan.)
Kafue (Zam.)
Karun (Iran)
Kasai (Ang. and Congo, Dem. Rep.)
Katun (Sib.)
Koros (Hung.)
Lagan (N. Ire.)
Lagan (Swed.)
Lagen (Nor.)
Liard (Can.)
Lippe (Ger.)
Loire (Fr.)
Marne (Fr.)
Maros (Rom. and Hung.)
Memel (N.E. Eur.)
Meuse (Belg.)
Minho (Port.)
Moose (Can.)
Moose R. (U.S.A.)
Mosel (W. Eur.)
Mures (Rom. and Hung.)
Neath (Wales)
Negro (S. Am.)
Neman (N.E. Eur.)
Neuse R. (U.S.A.)
Niger (W. Af.)
Nitra (Slov.)
Oglio (It.)
Onega (Rus.)
Osage R. (U.S.A.)
Otter (Eng.)
Peace R. (Can.)
Peace R. (U.S.A.)
Pearl R. (China)
Pecos R. (U.S.A.)
Perak (Malay.)
Piave (It.)
Plate (S. Am.)
Pruth (Rom.)

Pungo (U.S.A.)
Purus (S. Am.)
Rance (Fr.)
Reuss (Swit.)
Rhine (Ger., Neth. and Swit.)
Rhône (Fr. and Swit.)
Saale (Ger.)
Saone (Fr.)
Sarre (Fr. and Ger.)
Seine (Fr.)
Shari (Cen. Af.)
Shire (S.E. Af.)
Siang (S. Asia)
Siret (Rom. and Ukr.)
Snake R. (U.S.A.)
Snowy R. (Austral.)
Somme (Fr.)
Spree (Ger.)
Stour (Eng.)
Swale (Eng.)
Tagus (Port.)
Tamar (Eng.)
Tamis (Rom. and Yug.)
Tapti (Ind.)
Tarim (China)
Teifi (Wales)
Teign (Eng.)
Teith (Scot.)
Tiber (It.)
Tinto (Sp.)
Tisza (S.E. Eur.)
Traun (Aust.)
Trent (Can.)
Trent (Eng.)
Tweed (Scot.)
Usuri (China and Rus.)
Vitim (Rus.)
Volga (Rus.)
Volta (W. Af.)
Warta (Pol.)
Welle (Congo, Dem. Rep.)
Werra (Ger.)
Weser (Ger.)
White R. (U.S.A.)
Xingú (S. Am.)
Yonne (Fr.)
Yssel (Neth.)
Yukon (Can.)
Yuruá (Braz. and Peru)
Zaïre (Cen. Af.)

6

Agogna (It.)
Alagón (Sp.)
Albany (Can.)
Allier (Fr.)
Amazon (S. Am.)
Angara (Rus.)
Arinos (Braz.)
Atbara (N.E. Af.)
Barrow (Ire.)
Barwon R. (Austral.)
Beauly (Scot.)
Bolsas (Mex.)
Brazos R. (U.S.A.)
Buller (N.Z.)
Calder (Eng.)
Caroni (S. Am.)
Caroni R. (Trin.)
Carron (Scot.)
Chenab (Ind.)
Coquet (Eng.)
Crouch (Eng.)
Cuanza (Ang.)
Danube (Eur.)
Dihang (Ind.)
Donets (Rus. and Ukr.)
Elster (Cze. and Ger.)
Escaut (Belg. and Neth.)
Finlay (Can.)
Fraser (Can.)
French R. (Can.)
Gambia R. (W. Af.)
Gandak (Ind.)
Ganges (Ind.)
Glomma (Nor.)
Gomati (Ind.)
Grande (Bol.)
Grande (U.S.A. and Mex.)
Grande (Braz.)
Hawash (E. Af.)
Hudson (U.S.A.)
Humber (Eng.)
Hunter (Austral.)
Hunter (N.Z.)
IJssel (Neth.)
Irtish (Kaz. and Rus.)
Irwell (Eng.)
Itchen (Eng.)
Japura (Braz.)
Javari (Braz.and Peru)
Jhelum (Ind.)

Jordan (Isr., Jord. and Syria)
Kagera (Rwanda and Tan.)
Kaveri (Ind.)
Kennet (Eng.)
Kistna (Ind.)
Kolyma (Rus.)
Komati (E. Af.)
Kwanza (Ang.)
Leitha (Aust. and Hung.)
Liffey (Ire.)
Loddon (Austral.)
Lomami (Congo, Dem. Rep.)
Mamoré (S. Am.)
Medina (U.S.A.)
Medina R. (Rus.)
Medway (Eng.)
Mekong (Asia)
Mersey (Eng.)
Mincio (It.)
Mobile R. (U.S.A.)
Modder R. (S.A.)
Mohawk R. (U.S.A.)
Moldau (Cze.)
Monnow (Eng.)
Morava (Cze.)
Moskva (Rus.)
Muluya (Moroc.)
Murray R. (Austral.)
Neckar (Ger.)
Neisse (Ger. and Pol.)
Nelson (Can.)
Neutra (Slov.)
Niemen (N.E. Eur.)
Orange (S.A.)
Orwell (Eng.)
Ottawa (Can.)
Paraná (S. Am.)
Parret (Eng.)
Platte R. (U.S.A.)
Porali (Pak.)
Pungoè (Moz.)
Pungwe (Moz.)
Racket (U.S.A.)
Ribble (Eng.)
Roding (Eng.)
Rother (Eng.)
Rovuma (Moz. and Tanz.)
Rufiji (E. Af.)
Sabine R. (U.S.A.)
Salado (Arg.)
Sambre (Belg. and Fr.)
Santee R. (U.S.A.)
Sarthe (Fr.)
Scioto (U.S.A.)

Sereth (Rom. and Ukr.)
Severn (Can.)
Severn (Eng. and Wales)
Shilka (Rus.)
Slaney (Ire.)
Struma (Bulg. and Gr.)
Sunday (S.A.)
Sutlej (Ind. and Pak.)
Swilly (Ire.)
Tamega (Port. and Spain)
Tanaro (It.)
Teviot (Scot.)
Thames (Can.)
Thames (Eng.)
Theiss (S.E. Eur.)
Ticino (Swit.)
Tigris (Iraq and Turk.)
Tormes (Sp.)
Tornio (Fin. and Swed.)
Tugela (S.A.)
Tummel (Scot.)
Ubangi (Cen. Af.)
Ussuri (China and Rus.)
Vienne (Fr.)
Vilyay (Rus.)
Vltava (Cze.)
Wabash (U.S.A.)
Waihou (N.Z.)
Wandle (Eng.)
Warthe (Pol.)
Weaver (Eng.)
Wharfe (Eng.)
Wipper (Ger.)
Witham (Eng.)
Yavarí (Braz. and Peru)
Yellow R. (China)
Yellow R. (U.S.A.)

7

Abitibi (Can.)
Akagera (Rwanda and Tanz.)
Alabama (U.S.A.)
Berbice (Guyana)
Big Blue R. (U.S.A.)
Bighorn R. (U.S.A.)
Buffalo (U.S.A.)
Catawba (U.S.A.)
Cauvery (Ind.)
Chambal (Ind.)
Chelmer (Eng.)
Cubango (S.A.)
Darling (Austral.)
Derwent (Eng.)
Deveron (Scot.)

Dnieper (E. Eur.)
Dubawnt (Can.)
Dunajec (Pol.)
Durance (Fr.)
Ettrick (Scot.)
Feather R. (U.S.A.)
Fitzroy (Austral.)
Garonne (Fr.)
Genesee R. (U.S.A.)
Gilbert (Austral.)
Glenelg (Austral.)
Glommen (Nor.)
Guaporé (Bol. and Braz.)
Han Shui (China)
Helmand (Afghan.)
Hooghly (Ind.)
Huang He (China)
Juniata R. (U.S.A.)
Kanawha (U.S.A.)
Krishna (Ind.)
La Plata (Arg.)
Lachlan (Austral.)
Limpopo (S.E. Af.)
Lualaba (Cen. Af.)
Luangwa (Moz. and Zam.)
Lugenda (Moz.)
Madeira (Braz.)
Marañón (Peru)
Maritsa (S. Eur.)
Mattawa (Can.)
Mayenne (Fr.)
Meklong (Thail.)
Moselle (W. .)
Murghob (Taj.)
Narmada (Ind.)
Niagara (Can.)
Orinoco (S. Am.)
Orontes (Leb. and Syria)
Paraíba (Braz.)
Paraná (S. Am.)
Pechora (Rus.)
Potomac (U.S.A.)
Roanoke (Ind.)
Rubicon (It.)
Salween (Tibet and Burma)
San Juan (S. Am.)
San Juan (Mex.)
San Juan R. (U.S.A.)
Sankuru (Af.)
Schelde (Belg. and Neth.)
Scheldt (Belg. and Neth.)
Selenga (Asia)

Semliki (Uganda and Congo, Dem. Rep.)
Senegal (W. Af.)
Shannon (Ire.)
Spokane R. (U.S.A.)
St. Clair (Can. and U.S.A.)
Sungari (China)
Tapajós (S. Am.)
Thomsen (Can.)
Trinity R. (U.S.A.)
Tsangpo (S. Asia)
Ucayali (Peru)
Uruguay (S. Am.)
Vistula (Pol.)
Waikato (N.Z.)
Waitaki (N.Z.)
Warrego R. (Austral.)
Washita R. (U.S.A.)
Waveney (Eng.)
Welland (Eng.)
Wichita R. (U.S.A.)
Yangtze (China)
Yarkand (China)
Yenisei (Sib.)
Zambezi (S. Af.)

8

Amu Darya (Cen. Asia)
Arkansas R. (U.S.A.)
Beaulieu (Eng.)
Berezina (Bela.)
Big Black R. (U.S.A.)
Big Sandy R. (U.S.A.)
Big Sioux R. (U.S.A.)
Blue Nile (Eth. and Sudan)
Cape Fear R. (U.S.A.)
Cherweli (Eng.)
Cheyenne R. (U.S.A.)
Chindwin (Burma)
Clarence R. (Austral.)
Colorado R. (U.S.A.)
Columbia (Can. and U.S.A.)
Delaware R. (U.S.A.)
Demerara R. (Guyana)
Dniester (Ukr. and Mold.)
Dordogne (Fr.)
Eastmain (Can.)
Evenlode (Eng.)
Flinders R. (Austral.)
Gatineau (Can.)
Godavari (Ind.)
Goulburn R. (Austral.)
Great Kei (S.A.)
Guadiana (Sp. and Port.)

Huallaga (Peru)
Humboldt R. (U.S.A.)
Illinois R. (U.S.A.)
Itimbiri (Congo, Dem. Rep.)
Kankakee R. (U.S.A.)
Kelantan (Malay.)
Kennebec R. (U.S.A.)
Klondike R. (Can.)
Kootenai (Can. and U.S.A.)
Mahanadi (Ind.)
Manawatu (N.Z.)
Mazaruni R. (Guyana)
Missouri (U.S.A.)
Mitchell R. (Austral.)
Moulouya (Moroc.)
Nebraska (U.S.A.)
Okavango (S.A.)
Olifants (Nam.)
Olifants (S.A.)
Paraguay (S. Am.)
Parnaíba (Braz.)
Putumayo (S. Am.)
Red River (U.S.A.)
Rio Negro (S. Am.)
Rio Tinto (Sp.)
Saguenay (Can.)
Santiago (Peru)
Savannah (U.S.A.)
St. Claire (Can.)
Suwannee R. (U.S.A.)
Syr Daria (Kaz.)
Torridge (Eng.)
Wanganui (N.Z.)
Winnipeg (Can.)

9

Allegheny R. (U.S.A.)
Athabaska (Can.)
Byerezino (Bela.)
Chambeshi (Zamb.)
Churchill (Can.)
Crocodile R. (S.A.)
East River (U.S.A.)
Essequibo (Guyana)
Euphrates (Iraq., Turk. and Syria)
Gala Water (Scot.)
Great Ouse (Eng.)
Guadalete (Sp.)
Han Chiang (China)
Indigirka (Rus.)
Irrawaddy (Burma)
Kalamazoo R. (U.S.A.)
Mackenzie (Can.)

Macquarie R. (Austral.)
Macquarie R. (Tas.)
Magdalena (Col.)
Merrimack R. (U.S.A.)
Murchison R. (Austral.)
Paranaíba (Braz.)
Penobscot R. (U.S.A.)
Pilcomayo (S. Am.)
Porcupine R. (Can.)
Rede River (Eng.)
Rio Grande (Braz.)
Rio Grande (U.S.A. and Mex.)
Rio Grande (Bol.)
Saint John (Can. and U.S.A.)
Saint Paul (W. Af.)
Salt River (U.S.A.)
Tennessee R. (U.S.A.)
Tocantins (Braz.)
White Nile (Uganda and Sudan)
Wisconsin R. (U.S.A.)
Yarkant He (China)

10

Black River (U.S.A.)
Blackwater (Eng.)
Blackwater (Ire.)
Chang Jiang (China)
Chao Phraya (Thai.)
Dora Baltea (It.)
Frome Creek (Austral.)
Green River (U.S.A.)
Kizil Irmak (Turk.)
Manzanares (Sp.)
Missinaibi (Can.)
Mississagi (Can.)
Qezel Owzan (Iran)
Republican R. (U.S.A.)
Sacramento (U.S.A.)
Saint John's R. (U.S.A.)
San Joaquin R. (U.S.A.)
Shenandoah R. (U.S.A.)
Snake River (U.S.A.)
St. Lawrence (Can.)
Torneälven (Fin. and Swed.)
Torniojoki (Fin. and Swed.)
White River (U.S.A.)

11 AND OVER

Assiniboine (Can.) (11)
Big Black River (U.S.A.) (13)
Big Blue River (U.S.A.) (12)
Big Sandy River (U.S.A.) (13)
Big Sioux River (U.S.A.) (13)
Bighorn River (U.S.A.) (12)

Bonaventure (Can.) (11)
Brahmaputra (S. Asia) (11)
Desaguadero (Bol. and Peru) (11)
Dora Riparia (It.) (11)
Great Kanawka (U.S.A.) (12)
Guadalquivir (Sp.) (12)
Mississippi (U.S.A.) (11)
Modder River (S.A.) (11)
Murrumbidgee (Austral.) (12)

Paraíba do Sul (Braz.) (12)
Rappahannock R. (U.S.A.) (12)
Río de la Plata (Arg.) (12)
Saint Claire (Can.) (11)
Saint Lawrence (Can.) (13)
São Francisco (Braz.) (12)
Saskatchewan (Can.) (12)
Shatt al-Arab (Iraq) (11)
Songhua Jiang (China) (12)
Susquehanna R. (U.S.A.) (11)

Upper Paraná (S. Am.) (11)
Yangtse Kiang (China) (12)
Yarrowwater (Scot.) (11)
Yellow River (China) (11)
Yellowstone R. (U.S.A.) (11)

States of the USA (Abbreviations)

AK (Alaska)
AL (Alabama)
Ala (Alabama)
Alas (Alaska)
AR (Arkansas)
Ariz (Arizona)
Ark (Arkansas)
AZ (Arizona)
CA (California)
Cal (California)
CO (Colorado)
Colo (Colorado)
Conn (Connecticut)
CT (Connecticut)
DC (District of Columbia)
DE (Delaware)
Del (Delaware)
FL (Florida)
Fla (Florida)
GA (Georgia)
Ga (Georgia)
HA (Hawaii)
IA (Iowa)
ID (Idaho)
Ida (Idaho)
IL (Illinois)
Ill (Illinois)
IN (Indiana)
Ind (Indiana)

Kan (Kansas)
Ken (Kentucky)
KS (Kansas)
KY (Kentucky)
LA (Louisiana)
MA (Massachusetts)
Mass (Massachusetts)
MD (Maryland)
ME (Maine)
MI (Michigan)
Mich (Michigan)
Minn (Minnesota)
Miss (Mississippi)
MN (Minnesota)
MO (Missouri)
Mont (Montana)
MS (Mississippi)
MT (Montana)
N Dak (North Dakota)
N Mex (New Mexico)
NC (North Carolina)
ND (North Dakota)
NE (Nebraska)
Neb (Nebraska)
Nev (Nevada)
NH (New Hampshire)
NJ (New Jersey)
NM (New Mexico)
NV (Nevada)

NY (New York)
OH (Ohio)
OK (Oklahoma)
Okla (Oklahoma)
OR (Oregon)
Oreg (Oregon)
PA (Pennsylvania)
Penn (Pennsylvania)
RI (Rhode Island)
S Dak (South Dakota)
SC (South Carolina)
SD (South Dakota)
Tenn (Tennessee)
Tex (Texas)
TN (Tennessee)
TX (Texas)
UT (Utah)
VA (Virginia)
VT (Vermont)
W Va (West Virginia)
WA (Washington)
Wash (Washington)
WI (Wisconsin)
Wis (Wisconsin)
WV (West Virginia)
WY (Wyoming)
Wyo (Wyoming)

Towns and cities: United Kingdom

(e.) = England; (N.I.) = Northern Ireland; (S.) = Scotland; (W.) = Wales

3 AND 4

Alva (S.)
Ayr (S.)
Bala (W.)

Barr (S.)
Bath (E.)
Bray (E.)
Bude (E.)
Bury (E.)

Clun (E.)
Deal (E.)
Diss (E.)
Duns (S.)
Elie (S.)

Ely (E.)
Eton (E.)
Eye (E.)
Holt (E.)
Holt (W.)

Hove (E.)
Hull (E.)
Hyde (E.)
Ince (E.)
Kirn (S.)

Leek (E.)
Looe (E.)
Luss (S.)
Lydd (E.)
Mold (W.)
Nigg (S.)
Oban (S.)
Pyle (W.)
Reay (S.)
Rhyl (W.)
Ross (E.)
Ryde (E.)
Rye (E.)
Shap (E.)
Stow (S.)
Uig (S.)
Usk (E.)
Ware (E.)
Wark (E.)
Wem (E.)
Wick (S.)
Wick (E.)
Yarm (E.)
York (E.)

5

Acton (E.)
Alloa (S.)
Alton (E.)
Annan (E.)
Avoch (S.)
Ayton (S.)
Bacup (E.)
Banff (S.)
Beith (S.)
Blyth (E.)
Brora (S.)
Busby (S.)
Caine (E.)
Ceres (S.)
Chard (E.)
Cheam (E.)
Chirk (W.)
Clova (S.)
Colne (E.)
Corby (E.)
Cowes (E.)
Crail (S.)
Crewe (E.)
Cupar (S.)
Denny (S.)
Derby (E.)
Doagh (N.I.)
Dover (E.)

Egham (E.)
Elgin (S.)
Ellon (S.)
Epsom (E.)
Errol (S.)
Filey (E.)
Flint (W.)
Fowey (E.)
Frome (E.)
Fyvie (S.)
Glynn (N.I.)
Goole (E.)
Govan (S.)
Grays (E.)
Hawes (E.)
Hurst (E.)
Hythe (E.)
Insch (S.)
Keady (N.I.)
Keiss (S.)
Keith (S.)
Kelso (S.)
Lairg (S.)
Largs (S.)
Larne (N.I.)
Leeds (E.)
Leigh (E.)
Leith (S.)
Lewes (E.)
Louth (E.)
Louth (N.I.)
Luton (E.)
March (E.)
Nairn (S.)
Neath (W.)
Newry (N.I.)
Olney (E.)
Omagh (N.I.)
Otley (E.)
Perth (S.)
Poole (E.)
Reeth (E.)
Ripon (E.)
Risca (W.)
Rugby (E.)
Salen (S.)
Sarum (E.)
Selby (E.)
Stoke (E.)
Stone (E.)
Tebay (E.)
Tenby (W.)
Thame (E.)
Towyn (W.)

Tring (E.)
Troon (S.)
Truro (E.)
Wells (E.)
Wigan (E.)

6

Aboyne (S.)
Alford (E.)
Alford (S.)
Alston (E.)
Amlwch (W.)
Antrim (N.I.)
Ashton (E.)
Augher (N.I.)
Bangor (W.)
Bangor (N.I.)
Barnet (E.)
Barrow (E.)
Barton (E.)
Barvas (S.)
Batley (E.)
Battle (E.)
Bawtry (E.)
Beauly (S.)
Bedale (E.)
Belcoo (N.I.)
Belper (E.)
Biggar (S.)
Bo'Ness (S.)
Bodmin (E.)
Bognor (E.)
Bolton (E.)
Bootle (E.)
Boston (E.)
Bourne (E.)
Brecon (W.)
Bruton (E.)
Buckie (S.)
Bungay (E.)
Burton (E.)
Buxton (E.)
Carron (S.)
Caston (E.)
Clunes (S.)
Cobham (E.)
Comber (N.I.)
Comrie (S.)
Conway (W.)
Crieff (S.)
Cromer (E.)
Cullen (S.)
Darwen (E.)
Dollar (S.)

Dudley (E.)
Dunbar (S.)
Dundee (S.)
Dunlop (S.)
Dunnet (S.)
Dunoon (S.)
Durham (E.)
Dysart (S.)
Ealing (E.)
Eccles (E.)
Edzell (S.)
Epping (E.)
Exeter (E.)
Findon (S.)
Forfar (S.)
Forres (S.)
Girvan (S.)
Glamis (S.)
Goring (E.)
Hanley (E.)
Harlow (E.)
Harrow (E.)
Havant (E.)
Hawick (S.)
Henley (E.)
Hexham (E.)
Higham (E.)
Howden (E.)
Huntly (S.)
Ilkley (E.)
Irvine (S.)
Jarrow (E.)
Kendal (E.)
Killin (S.)
Lanark (S.)
Lauder (S.)
Leslie (S.)
Leyton (E.)
Linton (E.)
Lochee (S.)
London (E.)
Ludlow (E.)
Lurgan (N.I.)
Lynton (E.)
Lytham (E.)
Maldon (E.)
Malton (E.)
Marlow (E.)
Masham (E.)
Meigle (S.)
Moffat (S.)
Morley (E.)
Naseby (E.)
Nelson (E.)

Neston (E.)
Newark (E.)
Newent (E.)
Newlyn (E.)
Newton (E.)
Newton (S.)
Norham (E.)
Oakham (E.)
Oldham (E.)
Ossett (E.)
Oundle (E.)
Oxford (E.)
Penryn (E.)
Pewsey (E.)
Pinner (E.)
Pladda (S.)
Pudsey (E.)
Putney (E.)
Ramsey (E.)
Redcar (E.)
Reston (S.)
Rhynie (S.)
Ripley (E.)
Romney (E.)
Romsey (E.)
Rosyth (S.)
Rothes (S.)
Ruabon (W.)
Rugely (E.)
Ruthin (W.)
Seaham (E.)
Seaton (E.)
Selsey (E.)
Settle (E.)
Shotts (S.)
Slough (E.)
Snaith (E.)
St. Ives (E.)
St. Neot (E.)
Strood (E.)
Stroud (E.)
Sutton (E.)
Thirsk (E.)
Thorne (E.)
Thurso (S.)
Tongue (S.)
Totnes (E.)
Walmer (E.)
Walton (E.)
Watton (E.)
Welwyn (E.)
Weston (E.)
Whitby (E.)
Widnes (E.)

Wigton (E.)
Wilton (E.)
Wishaw (S.)
Witham (E.)
Witney (E.)
Woking (E.)
Wooler (E.)
Word (E.)
Yarrow (S.)
Yeovil (E.)

7

Airdrie (S.)
Alnwick (E.)
Andover (E.)
Appleby (E.)
Arundel (E.)
Ashford (E.)
Aylsham (E.)
Balfron (S.)
Balloch (S.)
Bampton (E.)
Banavie (S.)
Banbury (E.)
Barking (E.)
Beccles (E.)
Bedford (E.)
Belfast (N.I.)
Belford (E.)
Belleek (N.I.)
Berwick (E.)
Bewdley (E.)
Bexhill (E.)
Bilston (E.)
Bourton (E.)
Bowmore (S.)
Braemar (S.)
Brandon (E.)
Brechin (S.)
Bristol (E.)
Brixham (E.)
Brodick (S.)
Bromley (E.)
Burnley (E.)
Burslem (E.)
Caistor (E.)
Caledon (N.I.)
Carbost (S.)
Cardiff (W.)
Carluke (S.)
Carrick (N.I.)
Catford (E.)
Cawston (E.)
Charing (E.)

Chatham (E.)
Cheadle (E.)
Cheddar (E.)
Chesham (E.)
Chester (E.)
Chorley (E.)
Clacton (E.)
Clifton (E.)
Clogher (N.I.)
Crathie (S.)
Crawley (E.)
Croydon (E.)
Culross (S.)
Cumnock (S.)
Cwmbran (W.)
Datchet (E.)
Dawlish (E.)
Denbigh (W.)
Denholm (S.)
Dervock (N.I.)
Devizes (E.)
Dorking (E.)
Douglas (E.)
Douglas (S.)
Dundrum (N.I.)
Dunkeld (S.)
Dunmore (N.I.)
Dunning (S.)
Dunster (E.)
Elstree (E.)
Enfield (E.)
Epworth (E.)
Evanton (S.)
Everton (E.)
Evesham (E.)
Exmouth (E.)
Fairlie (S.)
Falkirk (S.)
Fareham (E.)
Farnham (E.)
Feltham (E.)
Fintona (N.I.)
Galston (S.)
Gifford (S.)
Gilford (N.I.)
Glasgow (S.)
Glenarm (N.I.)
Glencoe (S.)
Glossop (E.)
Golspie (S.)
Gosport (E.)
Gourock (S.)
Granton (S.)
Grimsby (E.)

Halifax (E.)
Halkirk (S.)
Hampton (E.)
Harwich (E.)
Haworth (E.)
Helston (E.)
Heywood (E.)
Hitchin (E.)
Honiton (E.)
Hornsea (E.)
Hornsey (E.)
Horsham (E.)
Ipswich (E.)
Ixworth (E.)
Jesmond (E.)
Kenmore (S.)
Keswick (E.)
Kilmory (S.)
Kilmuir (S.)
Kilsyth (S.)
Kington (E.)
Kinross (S.)
Kintore (S.)
Lamlash (S.)
Lancing (E.)
Langton (E.)
Larbert (S.)
Ledbury (E.)
Leyburn (E.)
Lincoln (E.)
Lisburn (N.I.)
Lybster (S.)
Macduff (S.)
Maesteg (W.)
Malvern (E.)
Margate (E.)
Matlock (E.)
Maybole (S.)
Melrose (S.)
Melvich (S.)
Meridan (E.)
Methven (S.)
Monikie (S.)
Moreton (E.)
Morpeth (E.)
Mossley (E.)
Mossley (N.I.)
Muthill (S.)
New Quay (W.)
Newbury (E.)
Newport (E.)
Newport (W.)
Newport (S.)
Newquay (E.)

Newtown (W.)
Norwich (E.)
Oldbury (E.)
Ormesby (E.)
Overton (E.)
Overton (W.)
Padstow (E.)
Paisley (S.)
Peebles (S.)
Penrith (E.)
Polmont (S.)
Poolewe (S.)
Portree (S.)
Portsoy (S.)
Poulton (E.)
Prescot (E.)
Preston (E.)
Rainham (E.)
Reading (E.)
Redhill (E.)
Redruth (E.)
Reigate (E.)
Renfrew (S.)
Retford (E.)
Romford (E.)
Royston (E.)
Runcorn (E.)
Saddell (S.)
Salford (E.)
Saltash (E.)
Sandown (E.)
Sarclet (S.)
Saxilby (E.)
Scourie (S.)
Seaford (E.)
Selkirk (S.)
Shifnal (E.)
Shipley (E.)
Shipton (E.)
Silloth (E.)
Skipton (E.)
Spilsby (E.)
St. Asaph (W.)
St. Neots (E.)
Staines (E.)
Stanley (S.)
Stanley (E.)
Stilton (E.)
Strathy (S.)
Sudbury (E.)
Sunbury (E.)
Swanage (E.)
Swansea (W.)
Swindon (E.)

Swinton (E.)
Swinton (S.)
Tarbert (S.)
Tarland (S.)
Taunton (E.)
Tayport (S.)
Telford (E.)
Tenbury (E.)
Tetbury (E.)
Thaxted (E.)
Tilbury (E.)
Torquay (E.)
Tranent (S.)
Turriff (S.)
Twyford (E.)
Ventnor (E.)
Walsall (E.)
Waltham (E.)
Wantage (E.)
Wareham (E.)
Warwick (E.)
Watchet (E.)
Watford (E.)
Weobley (E.)
Wickwar (E.)
Windsor (E.)
Winslow (E.)
Winster (E.)
Wisbech (E.)
Worksop (E.)
Wrexham (W.)

8

Aberavon (W.)
Aberdare (W.)
Aberdeen (S.)
Abergele (W.)
Aberlady (S.)
Abingdon (E.)
Abington (S.)
Ahoghill (N.I.)
Alfreton (E.)
Alnmouth (E.)
Amersham (E.)
Amesbury (E.)
Ampthill (E.)
Arbroath (S.)
Armadale (S.)
Arrochar (S.)
Auldearn (S.)
Aviemore (S.)
Axbridge (E.)
Bakewell (E.)
Ballater (S.)

Bamburgh (E.)
Banchory (S.)
Barmouth (W.)
Barnsley (E.)
Barrhill (S.)
Bearsden (S.)
Beattock (S.)
Bedworth (E.)
Berkeley (E.)
Beverley (E.)
Bicester (E.)
Bideford (E.)
Blantyre (S.)
Bolsover (E.)
Brackley (E.)
Bradford (E.)
Brampton (E.)
Bridgend (W.)
Bridport (E.)
Brighton (E.)
Bromyard (E.)
Broseley (E.)
Burghead (S.)
Caerleon (W.)
Camborne (E.)
Canonbie (S.)
Cardigan (W.)
Carlisle (E.)
Carnwath (S.)
Caterham (E.)
Chepstow (E.)
Chertsey (E.)
Clevedon (E.)
Clovelly (E.)
Coventry (E.)
Crediton (E.)
Creetown (S.)
Cromarty (S.)
Dalkeith (S.)
Dalmally (S.)
Dartford (E.)
Daventry (E.)
Debenham (E.)
Dedworth (E.)
Deptford (E.)
Dewsbury (E.)
Dingwall (S.)
Dirleton (S.)
Dolgelly (W.)
Dufftown (S.)
Dumfries (S.)
Dunbeath (S.)
Dunblane (S.)
Dungiven (N.I.)

Dunscore (S.)
Earlston (S.)
Ebbw Vale (W.)
Egremont (E.)
Eversley (E.)
Eyemouth (S.)
Fakenham (E.)
Falmouth (E.)
Findhorn (S.)
Fortrose (S.)
Foulness (E.)
Glenluce (S.)
Grantham (E.)
Grantown (E.)
Greenlaw (S.)
Greenock (S.)
Hadleigh (E.)
Hailsham (E.)
Halstead (E.)
Hamilton (S.)
Hastings (E.)
Hatfield (E.)
Hawarden (W.)
Helmsley (E.)
Hereford (E.)
Herne Bay (E.)
Hertford (E.)
Hilltown (N.I.)
Hinckley (E.)
Holbeach (E.)
Holyhead (W.)
Holywell (W.)
Holywell (E.)
Hunmanby (E.)
Ilkeston (E.)
Inverury (S.)
Jedburgh (S.)
Keighley (E.)
Kidwelly (W.)
Kilbride (S.)
Kilniver (S.)
Kilrenny (S.)
Kinghorn (S.)
Kingston (E.)
Kirkwall (S.)
Knighton (W.)
Lampeter (W.)
Langholm (S.)
Latheron (S.)
Lavenham (E.)
Lechlade (E.)
Leuchars (S.)
Leyland (E.)
Liskeard (E.)

Llanelli (W.)
Llanrwst (W.)
Loanhead (S.)
Longtown (E.)
Lynmouth (E.)
Markinch (S.)
Marykirk (S.)
Maryport (E.)
Maryport (S.)
Midhurst (E.)
Minehead (E.)
Moniaive (S.)
Monmouth (E.)
Montrose (S.)
Monymusk (S.)
Muirkirk (S.)
Nantwich (E.)
Neilston (S.)
Newburgh (S.)
Newhaven (E.)
Newmilns (S.)
Nuneaton (E.)
Ormskirk (E.)
Oswestry (E.)
Paignton (E.)
Pembroke (W.)
Penicuik (S.)
Penzance (E.)
Pershore (E.)
Peterlee (E.)
Petworth (E.)
Pevensey (E.)
Plaistow (E.)
Plymouth (E.)
Portrush (N.I.)
Pwllheli (W.)
Ramsgate (E.)
Redditch (E.)
Rhayader (W.)
Richmond (E.)
Ringwood (E.)
Rochdale (E.)
Rothbury (E.)
Rothesay (S.)
Saltburn (E.)
Sandgate (E.)
Sandwich (E.)
Sedbergh (E.)
Shanklin (E.)
Shipston (E.)
Sidmouth (E.)
Skegness (E.)
Sleaford (E.)
Solihull (E.)

Southend (E.)
Spalding (E.)
St. Albans (E.)
St. Fergus (S.)
St. Helens (E.)
Stafford (E.)
Stamford (E.)
Stanhope (E.)
Stanhope (S.)
Stanwell (E.)
Stirling (S.)
Stockton (E.)
Strabane (N.I.)
Stratton (E.)
Strichen (S.)
Surbiton (E.)
Swaffham (E.)
Talgarth (W.)
Tamworth (E.)
Thetford (E.)
Thornaby (E.)
Tiverton (E.)
Tredegar (W.)
Tregaron (W.)
Tunstall (E.)
Uckfield (E.)
Ullapool (S.)
Uxbridge (E.)
Wallasey (E.)
Wallsend (E.)
Wanstead (E.)
Westbury (E.)
Wetheral (E.)
Wetherby (E.)
Weymouth (E.)
Whithorn (S.)
Woodford (E.)
Woolwich (E.)
Worthing (E.)
Yarmouth (E.)

9

Aberaeron (W.)
Aberdovey (W.)
Aberfeldy (S.)
Aberffraw (W.)
Aberfoyle (S.)
Aldbrough (E.)
Aldeburgh (E.)
Aldershot (E.)
Allendale (E.)
Ambleside (E.)
Ardrossan (S.)
Ashbourne (E.)

Ashburton (E.)
Ashington (E.)
Avonmouth (E.)
Axminster (E.)
Aylesbury (E.)
Ballymena (N.I.)
Banbridge (N.I.)
Beaumaris (W.)
Bebington (E.)
Beckenham (E.)
Bettyhill (S.)
Blackburn (E.)
Blackburn (S.)
Blackpool (E.)
Blandford (E.)
Blisworth (E.)
Bracadale (S.)
Bracknell (E.)
Braintree (E.)
Brentford (E.)
Brentwood (E.)
Brighouse (E.)
Broadford (S.)
Broughton (E.)
Broughton (S.)
Broughton (W.)
Buckhaven (S)
Bushmills (N.I.)
Caerphilly (W.)
Callander (S.)
Cambridge (E.)
Carnarvon (W.)
Carnforth (E.)
Carstairs (S.)
Castleton (E.)
Chingford (E.)
Clitheroe (E.)
Coleraine (N.I.)
Colwyn Bay (W.)
Congleton (E.)
Cookstown (N.I.)
Craigavon (N.I.)
Cranbrook (E.)
Crewkerne (E.)
Criccieth (W.)
Cricklade (E.)
Cuckfield (E.)
Dartmouth (E.)
Devonport (E.)
Doncaster (E.)
Donington (E.)
Droitwich (E.)
Dronfield (E.)
Dumbarton (S.)

Dungannon (N.I.)
Dungeness (E.)
Dunstable (E.)
Edinburgh (S.)
Ellesmere (E.)
Faversham (E.)
Fishguard (W.)
Fleetwood (E.)
Fochabers (S.)
Gateshead (E.)
Godalming (E.)
Gravesend (E.)
Greenwich (E.)
Guildford (E.)
Halesowen (E.)
Harrogate (E.)
Haslemere (E.)
Haverhill (E.)
Hawkhurst (E.)
Holmfirth (E.)
Ilchester (E.)
Immingham (E.)
Inveraray (S.)
Inverness (S.)
Johnstone (S.)
Kettering (E.)
King's Lynn (E.)
Kingswear (E.)
Kingussie (S.)
Kircubbin (N.I.)
Kirkcaldy (S.)
Lambourne (E.)
Lancaster (E.)
Leadhills (S.)
Leicester (E.)
Lichfield (E.)
Liverpool (E.)
Llanberis (W.)
Llandudno (W.)
Llangadog (W.)
Lochgelly (S.)
Lochinver (S.)
Lockerbie (S.)
Longridge (E.)
Lowestoft (E.)
Lyme Regis (E.)
Lymington (E.)
Maidstone (E.)
Mansfield (E.)
Mauchline (S.)
Middleton (E.)
Milngavie (S.)
Moneymore (N.I.)
Morecambe (E.)

New Radnor (W.)
New Romney (E.)
Newcastle (E.)
Newcastle (N.I.)
Newmarket (E.)
Northwich (E.)
Otterburn (E.)
Pembridge (E.)
Penistone (E.)
Penkridge (E.)
Peterhead (S.)
Pickering (E.)
Pitlochry (S.)
Pontypool (E.)
Port Ellen (S.)
Portadown (N.I.)
Porthcawl (W.)
Portmadoc (W.)
Prestwick (S.)
Rasharkin (N.I.)
Riccarton (S.)
Rochester (E.)
Rostrevor (N.I.)
Rotherham (E.)
Salisbury (E.)
Saltfleet (E.)
Sevenoaks (E.)
Sheerness (E.)
Sheffield (E.)
Sherborne (E.)
Shieldaig (S.)
Slamannan (S.)
Smethwick (E.)
Southgate (E.)
Southport (E.)
Southwell (E.)
Southwold (E.)
St. Andrews (S.)
St. Austell (E.)
St. Fillans (S.)
Starcross (E.)
Stevenage (E.)
Stewarton (S.)
Stockport (E.)
Stokesley (E.)
Stornoway (S.)
Stourport (E.)
Stranraer (S.)
Stratford (E.)
Strathdon (S.)
Stretford (E.)
Strontian (S.)
Tarporley (E.)
Tavistock (E.)

Tenterden (E.)
Thornhill (S.)
Tobermore (N.I.)
Tobermory (S.)
Todmorden (E.)
Tomintoul (S.)
Tonbridge (E.)
Tovermore (N.I.)
Towcester (E.)
Tynemouth (E.)
Ulverston (E.)
Upminster (E.)
Uppingham (E.)
Uttoxeter (E.)
Wainfleet (E.)
Wakefield (E.)
Welshpool (W.)
Westerham (E.)
Weybridge (E.)
Wimbledon (E.)
Wincanton (E.)
Wokingham (E.)
Woodstock (E.)
Worcester (E.)
Wymondham (E.)

10

Abbotsford (S.)
Accrington (E.)
Achnasheen (S.)
Altrincham (E.)
Anstruther (S.)
Applecross (S.)
Ardrishaig (S.)
Auchinleck (S.)
Ballantrae (S.)
Ballyclare (N.I.)
Ballymoney (N.I.)
Ballyronan (N.I.)
Barnstaple (E.)
Beaminster (E.)
Bedlington (E.)
Bellingham (E.)
Berriedale (S.)
Billericay (E.)
Birkenhead (E.)
Birmingham (E.)
Bridgnorth (E.)
Bridgwater (E.)
Bromsgrove (E.)
Broxbourne (E.)
Buckingham (E.)
Caernarfon (W.)
Carnoustie (S.)

Canterbury (E.)
Carmarthen (W.)
Carshalton (E.)
Carsphairn (S.)
Castlederg (N.I.)
Castletown (S.)
Castletown (E.)
Chelmsford (E.)
Cheltenham (E.)
Chichester (E.)
Chippenham (E.)
Chulmleigh (E.)
Coatbridge (S.)
Coggeshall (E.)
Colchester (E.)
Coldingham (S.)
Coldstream (S.)
Cranbourne (E.)
Cullompton (E.)
Cushendall (N.I.)
Dalbeattie (S.)
Darlington (E.)
Donaghadee (N.I.)
Dorchester (E.)
Drumlithie (S.)
Dukinfield (E.)
East Linton (S.)
Eastbourne (E.)
Eccleshall (E.)
Farningham (E.)
Ffestiniog (W.)
Folkestone (E.)
Freshwater (E.)
Galashiels (S.)
Gillingham (E.)
Glenrothes (S.)
Gloucester (E.)
Haddington (S.)
Halesworth (E.)
Hartlepool (E.)
Haslingden (E.)
Heathfield (E.)
Horncastle (E.)
Hornchurch (E.)
Hungerford (E.)
Hunstanton (E.)
Huntingdon (E.)
Ilfracombe (E.)
Johnshaven (S.)
Kenilworth (E.)
Kilcreggan (S.)
Kilmarnock (S.)
Kilwinning (S.)
Kincardine (S.)

Kingsbarns (S.)
Kingsclere (E.)
Kirkmaiden (S.)
Kirkoswald (E.)
Kirkoswald (S.)
Kirriemuir (S.)
Launceston (E.)
Leamington (E.)
Lennoxtown (S.)
Leominster (E.)
Lesmahagow (S.)
Letchworth (E.)
Linlithgow (S.)
Littleport (E.)
Livingston (S.)
Llandovery (W.)
Llanfyllin (W.)
Llangollen (W.)
Llanidloes (W.)
Maidenhead (E.)
Malmesbury (E.)
Manchester (E.)
Markethill (N.I.)
Mexborough (E.)
Middlewich (E.)
Mildenhall (E.)
Milnathort (S.)
Montgomery (W.)
Motherwell (S.)
Nailsworth (E.)
Nottingham (E.)
Okehampton (E.)
Pangbourne (E.)
Patrington (E.)
Peacehaven (E.)
Pittenweem (S.)
Pontefract (E.)
Pontypridd (W.)
Port Talbot (W.)
Portaferry (N.I.)
Portishead (E.)
Portobello (S.)
Portsmouth (E.)
Potter's Bar (E.)
Presteigne (W.)
Ravenglass (E.)
Rutherglen (S.)
Saintfield (N.I.)
Saltcoates (S.)
Saxmundham (E.)
Scunthorpe (E.)
Shepperton (E.)
Sheringham (E.)
Shrewsbury (E.)

St. Leonards (E.)
Stalbridge (E.)
Stonehaven (S.)
Stonehouse (S.)
Stoneykirk (S.)
Stowmarket (E.)
Strangford (N.I.)
Sunderland (E.)
Tanderagee (N.I.)
Teddington (E.)
Teignmouth (E.)
Tewkesbury (E.)
Thamesmead (E.)
Torrington (E.)
Trowbridge (E.)
Tweedmouth (S.)
Tweedsmuir (S.)
Twickenham (E.)
Warminster (E.)
Warrington (E.)
Washington (E.)
Wednesbury (E.)
Wellington (E.)
West Calder (S.)
Westward Ho! (E.)
Whitchurch (E.)
Whitehaven (E.)
Whitstable (E.)
Whittlesey (E.)
Willenhall (E.)
Winchelsea (E.)
Winchester (E.)
Windermere (E.)
Wirksworth (E.)
Withernsea (E.)
Wolsingham (E.)
Woodbridge (E.)
Workington (E.)

11

Aberchirder (S.)
Abergavenny (E.)
Aberystwyth (W.)
Ballycastle (N.I.)
Ballygawley (N.I.)
Balquhidder (S.)
Bannockburn (S.)
Basingstoke (E.)
Berkhamsted (E.)
Bickley Moss (E.)
Blairgowrie (S.)
Bognor Regis (E.)
Bournemouth (E.)
Bridlington (E.)

Builth Wells (W.)
Buntingford (E.)
Campbeltown (S.)
Carrickmore (N.I.)
Charlestown (S.)
Cirencester (E.)
Cleethorpes (E.)
Cockermouth (E.)
Crickhowell (W.)
Crossmaglen (N.I.)
Cumbernauld (S.)
Downpatrick (N.I.)
Draperstown (N.I.)
Dunfermline (S.)
East Dereham (E.)
East Molesey (E.)
East Retford (E.)
Ecclefechan (S.)
Enniskillen (N.I.)
Farnborough (E.)
Fettercairn (S.)
Fort William (S.)
Fraserburgh (S.)
Glastonbury (E.)
Grangemouth (S.)
Great Dunmow (E.)
Guisborough (E.)
Haltwhistle (E.)
Hampton Wick (E.)
Hatherleigh (E.)
Helensburgh (S.)
High Wycombe (E.)
Ingatestone (E.)
Invergordon (S.)
Kirkmichael (S.)
Leytonstone (E.)
Littlestone (E.)
Llantrisant (W.)
Londonderry (N.I.)
Lossiemouth (S.)
Lostwithiel (E.)
Ludgershall (E.)
Lutterworth (E.)
Mablethorpe (E.)
Machynlleth (W.)
Magherafelt (N.I.)
Manningtree (E.)
Market Rasen (E.)
Marlborough (E.)
Maxwelltown (S.)
Much Wenlock (E.)
Musselburgh (S.)
New Brighton (E.)
Newton Abbot (E.)

Northampton (E.)
Oystermouth (W.)
Petersfield (E.)
Pocklington (E.)
Port Glasgow (S.)
Port Patrick (S.)
Portglenone (N.I.)
Portmeirion (W.)
Prestonpans (S.)
Pultneytown (S.)
Randalstown (N.I.)
Rathfriland (N.I.)
Rawtenstall (E.)
Scarborough (E.)
Shaftesbury (E.)
South Molton (E.)
Southampton (E.)
St. Margaret's (E.)
Stalybridge (E.)
Stourbridge (E.)
Strathblane (S.)
Toome Bridge (N.I.)
Wallingford (E.)
Walthamstow (E.)
West Molesey (E.)
Westminster (E.)
Woodhall Spa (E.)

12

Attleborough (E.)
Auchterarder (S.)
Ballachulish (S.)
Beaconsfield (E.)
Bexhill-on-Sea (E.)
Burnham-on-Sea (E.)
Castledawson (N.I.)
Castlewellan (N.I.)
Chesterfield (E.)
Christchurch (E.)
East Kilbride (S.)
Fivemiletown (N.I.)
Fort Augustus (S.)
Gainsborough (E.)
Garelochhead (S.)
Great Grimsby (E.)
Great Malvern (E.)
Hillsborough (N.I.)
Huddersfield (E.)
Innerleithen (S.)
Inverkeithny (S.)
Long Stratton (E.)
Loughborough (E.)
Macclesfield (E.)
Milton Keynes (E.)

North Berwick (S.)
North Shields (E.)
North Walsham (E.)
Ottery St. Mary (E.)
Peterborough (E.)
Port Sunlight (E.)
Portmahomack (S.)
Shoeburyness (E.)
Skelmersdale (E.)
South Shields (E.)
Stewartstown (N.I.)
Stoke-on-Trent (E.)
Strathpeffer (S.)
Tenbury Wells (E.)
Tillicoultry (S.)
West Bromwich (E.)

13

Allendale Town (E.)
Auchtermuchty (S.)
Barnard Castle (E.)
Bishop's Castle (E.)
Boroughbridge (E.)
Brightlingsea (E.)
Brookeborough (N.I.)
Burnham Market (E.)
Burton-on-Trent (E.)
Bury St. Edmunds (E.)
Carrickfergus (N.I.)
Castle Douglas (S.)
Chipping Ongar (E.)
Cockburnspath (S.)
Dalmellington (S.)
Derrygonnelly (N.I.)

East Grinstead (E.)
Godmanchester (E.)
Great Yarmouth (E.)
Haverfordwest (W.)
Higham Ferrers (E.)
Inverkeithing (S.)
Inverkeithnie (S.)
Kidderminster (E.)
Kirkby Stephen (E.)
Kirkcudbright (S.)
Kirkintilloch (S.)
Knaresborough (E.)
Leamington Spa (E.)
Littlehampton (E.)
Lytham St. Anne's (E.)
Market Deeping (E.)
Market Drayton (E.)
Melcombe Regis (E.)
Melton Mowbray (E.)
Merthyr Tydfil (W.)
Middlesbrough (E.)
Newton Stewart (S.)
Northallerton (E.)
Rothiemurchus (S.)
Saffron Walden (E.)
Shepton Mallet (E.)
Wolverhampton (E.)

14

Ashby de la Zouch (E.)
Berwick-on-Tweed (E.)
Bishop Auckland (E.)
Bishops Waltham (E.)
Chipping Barnet (E.)

Chipping Norton (E.)
Grantown-on-Spey (S.)
Hemel Hempstead (E.)
Kirkby Lonsdale (E.)
Market Bosworth (E.)
Mortimer's Cross (E.)
Newton Aycliffe (E.)
Newtown Stewart (N.I.)
Stockton-on-Tees (E.)
Stony Stratford (E.)
Sutton Courtney (E.)
Thornaby-on-Tees (E.)
Tunbridge Wells (E.)
Wellingborough (E.)
West Hartlepool (E.)
Wootton Bassett (E.)

15

Ashton-under-Lyne (E.)
Barrow-in-Furness (E.)
Burnham-on-Crouch (E.)
Burton-upon-Trent (E.)
Clifton-upon-Teme (E.)
Leighton Buzzard (E.)
Shipston-on-Stour (E.)
Sutton Coldfield (E.)
Weston-super-Mare (E.)

16

Bishop's Stortford (E.)
Littlestone-on-Sea (E.)
Saltburn-by-the-Sea (E.)
Welwyn Garden City (E.)

Towns and cities: United States

4

Erie
Gary
Mesa
Reno
Troy
Waco
Yuma

5

Akron
Boise
Bronx
Butte
Flint

Macon
Miami
Ogden
Omaha
Ozark
Plano
Salem
Selma
Tempe
Tulsa
Utica

6

Albany
Aurora
Austin

Bangor
Biloxi
Boston
Camden
Canton
Dallas
Dayton
Denver
Duluth
Durham
El Paso
Eugene
Fresno
Irvine
Irving
La Mesa

Laredo
Lowell
Mobile
Monroe
Nassau
Newark
Orange
Oxnard
Peoria
Pomona
Queens
Racine
St. Paul
Tacoma
Toledo
Topeka

Tucson
Urbana
Warren

7

Abilene
Anaheim
Atlanta
Boulder
Buffalo
Chicago
Concord
Detroit
El Monte
Fremont
Garland

Hampton
Hayward
Hialeah
Hoboken
Houston
Jackson
Key West
Lansing
Laramie
Lincoln
Livonia
Lubbock
Lynwood
Madison
Memphis
Modesto

123

New York
Norfolk
Oakland
Ontario
Orlando
Palm Bay
Phoenix
Pontiac
Raleigh
Reading
Roanoke
Saginaw
Salinas
San Jose
Seattle
Spokane
St. Louis
Vallejo
Wichita
Yonkers

8

Amarillo
Ann Arbor
Beaumont
Berkeley
Chandler
Columbia
Columbus
Dearborn
Glendale
Green Bay
Hannibal
Hartford
Honolulu
Lakeland
Lakewood
Las Vegas
Longview
Mesquite
Monterey
New Haven
Oak Ridge
Palo Alto
Pasadena
Paterson
Portland
Richmond
Rockford
San Diego
Santa Ana

Savannah
Scranton
Stamford
Stockton
Syracuse
Torrance
Wheeling
Whittier

9

Allentown
Anchorage
Annapolis
Arlington
Baltimore
Bethlehem
Cambridge
Champaign
Charlotte
Cleveland
Des Moines
Elizabeth
Escondido
Fairbanks
Fort Wayne
Fort Worth
Fullerton
Galveston
Henderson
Hollywood
Inglewood
Johnstown
Kalamazoo
Knoxville
Lafayette
Lancaster
Lexington
Long Beach
Manhattan
Milwaukee
Nashville
New London
Northeast
Oceanside
Pawtucket
Pine Bluff
Princeton
Rapid City
Riverside
Rochester
Santa Rosa

Sioux City
South Bend
Tombstone
Vicksburg
Waterbury
Worcester
Ypsilanti

10

Alexandria
Baton Rouge
Birmingham
Bridgeport
Charleston
Chesapeake
Chula Vista
Cincinnati
Evansville
Greensboro
Greenville
Harrisburg
Huntsville
Jersey City
Kansas City
Little Rock
Long Branch
Los Angeles
Louisville
Miami Beach
Montgomery
Naperville
New Bedford
New Orleans
Pittsburgh
Portsmouth
Providence
Richardson
Sacramento
Saint Louis
San Antonio
Scottsdale
Shreveport
Sioux Falls
Terre Haute
Tuscaloosa
Washington
Youngstown

11

Albuquerque
Bakersfield

Brownsville
Cedar Rapids
Chattanooga
Garden Grove
Grand Rapids
Lake Charles
Midwest City
Minneapolis
Newport News
Palm Springs
Schenectady
Springfield
Tallahassee

12 AND OVER

Atlantic City (12)
Beverly Hills (12)
Colorado Springs (15)
Corpus Christi (13)
Fayetteville (12)
Fort Lauderdale (14)
Huntington Beach (15)
Independence (12)
Indianapolis (12)
Jacksonville (12)
Lexington-Fayette (16)
Moreno Valley (12)
New Brunswick (12)
Newport Beach (12)
Niagara Falls (12)
Oklahoma City (12)
Overland Park (12)
Philadelphia (12)
Pompano Beach (12)
Poughkeepsie (12)
Rancho Cucamonga (15)
Salt Lake City (12)
San Bernardino (13)
San Francisco (12)
Santa Barbara (12)
Santa Clarita (12)
Saratoga Springs (15)
St. Petersburg (12)
Staten Island (12)
Sterling Heights (15)
Thousand Oaks (12)
Virginia Beach (13)
West Palm Beach (13)

Towns and cities: rest of the world

3 AND 4

Agra (Ind.)
Aix (Fr.)
Albi (Fr.)
Bâle (Swit.)
Bari (It.)
Bonn (Ger.)
Bray (Ire.)
Brno (Cze.)
Caen (Fr.)
Cali (Col.)
Cobh (Ire.)
Cork (Ire.)
Fez (Moroc.)
Gaza (Pal.)
Gera (Ger.)
Giza (Egypt)
Graz (Aust.)
Györ (Hung.)
Hama (Syria)
Homs (Syria)
Hue (Viet.)
Jaén (Sp.)
Jos (Nig.)
Juba (Sudan)
Kano (Nig.)
Kiel (Ger.)
Kobe (Jap.)
Köln (Ger.)
Kota (Ind.)
Lamu (Kenya)
Laon (Fr.)
Linz (Aust.)
Lodz (Pol.)
Lüda (China)
Lund (Swed.)
Lviv (Ukr.)
Lvov (Ukr.)
Lyon (Fr.)
Metz (Fr.)
Mons (Belg.)
Naas (Ire.)
Nice (Fr.)
Nis (Yug.)
Omsk (Rus.)
Oran (Alg.)
Orel (Rus.)
Osh (Kyr.)
Pará (Braz.)
Pau (Fr.)
Pécs (Hung.)

Pegu (Burma)
Perm (Rus.)
Pisa (It.)
Pune (Ind.)
Puno (Peru)
Sian (China)
Suez (Egypt)
Suhl (Ger.)
Tour (Fr.)
Troy (Asia M.)
Tula (Rus.)
Tver (Rus.)
Tyre (Lebanon)
Ufa (Rus.)
Vigo (Sp.)
Xian (China)
Yazd (Iran)

5

Adana (Turk.)
Ajmer (Ind.)
Akyab (Burma)
Alwar (Ind.)
Aosta (It.)
Arbil (Iraq)
Arles (Fr.)
Arras (Fr.)
Aswan (Egypt)
Asyut (Egypt)
Avila (Sp.)
Basel (Swit.)
Basle (Swit.)
Basra (Iraq)
Beira (Moz.)
Belém (Braz.)
Boyle (Ire.)
Braga (Port.)
Breda (Neth.)
Brest (Fr.)
Brest (Bela.)
Bursa (Turk.)
Cadiz (Sp.)
Cavan (Ire.)
Cuzco (Peru)
Davao (Phil.)
Delhi (Ind.)
Dijon (Fr.)
Ennis (Ire.)
Enugu (Nig.)
Essen (Ger.)
Evian (Fr.)
Fayum (Egypt)

Galle (Sri)
Genoa (It.)
Ghent (Belg.)
Gomel (Bela.)
Gorky (Rus.)
Haifa (Isr.)
Halle (Ger.)
Haora (Ind.)
Herat (Afghan.)
Izmir (Turk.)
Jaffa (Isr.)
Jinau (China)
Kabwe (Zamb.)
Kandy (Sri)
Kazan (Rus.)
Kells (Ire.)
Kirov (Rus.)
Konya (Turk.)
Kursk (Rus.)
Kyoto (Jap.)
Liège (Belg.)
Lille (Fr.)
Luxor (Egypt)
Lyons (Fr.)
Macon (Fr.)
Mainz (Ger.)
Malmö (Swed.)
Mbeya (Tanz.)
Mecca (Saudi)
Medan (Indo.)
Memel (Lith.)
Milan (It.)
Mosul (Iraq)
Namen (Belg.)
Namur (Belg.)
Nancy (Fr.)
Ndola (Zamb.)
Nîmes (Fr.)
Orange (Fr.)
Osaka (Jap.)
Ostia (It.)
Padua (It.)
Parma (It.)
Patna (Ind.)
Perth (Austral.)
Pinsk (Bela.)
Piura (Peru)
Poona (Ind.)
Posen (Pol.)
Pskov (Rus.)
Pusan (S. Korea)
Ramla (Isr.)

Reims (Fr.)
Rieti (It.)
Rouen (Fr.)
Sidon (Lebanon)
Siena (It.)
Simla (Ind.)
Sligo (Ire.)
Sohag (Egypt)
Split (Cro.)
Surat (Ind.)
Taegu (S. Korea)
Talca (Chile)
Tanta (Egypt)
Tomsk (Rus.)
Tours (Fr.)
Trent (It.)
Trier (Ger.)
Turin (It.)
Tuzla (Bos.)
Varna (Bulg.)
Vlöre (Alb.)
Worms (Ger.)
Wuhan (China)
Yalta (Ukr.)
Ypres (Belg.)

6

Aachen (Ger.)
Aarhus (Den.)
Abadan (Iran)
Agadir (Moroc.)
Aizawl (Ind.)
Aleppo (Syria)
Amiens (Fr.)
Ancona (It.)
Anshan (China)
Arklow (Ire.)
Arnhem (Neth.)
Bantry (Ire.)
Baroda (Ind.)
Bauchi (Nig.)
Bayeux (Fr.)
Berber (Sudan)
Bergen (Nor.)
Bhopal (Ind.)
Bilbao (Sp.)
Bochum (Ger.)
Bombay (Ind.)
Bremen (Ger.)
Bruges (Belg.)
Bukavu (Congo, Dem. Rep.)

Burgos (Sp.)
Calais (Fr.)
Callao (Peru)
Cannes (Fr.)
Canton (China)
Carlow (Ire.)
Cashel (Ire.)
Cassel (Ger.)
Chonju (S. Korea)
Cracow (Pol.)
Da Nang (Viet.)
Dairen (China)
Dalian (China)
Danzig (Pol.)
Darwin (Austral.)
Dieppe (Fr.)
Dinant (Belg.)
Dodoma (Tanz.)
Durban (S.A.)
Durrës (Alb.)
Erfurt (Ger.)
Fushun (China)
Galway (Ire.)
Gdansk (Pol.)
Geneva (Swit.)
Grodno (Bela.)
Harbin (China)
Hobart (Austral.)
Hohhot (China)
Howrah (Ind.)
Hrodna (Bela.)
Huambo (Ang.)
Huelva (Sp.)
Huesca (Sp.)
Ibadan (Nig.)
Ilorin (Nig.)
Imphal (Ind.)
Indore (Ind.)
Jaffna (Sri)
Jaipur (Ind.)
Jeddah (Saudi)
Jhansi (Ind.)
Jiddah (Saudi)
Juarez (Mex.)
Kaduna (Nig.)
Kalyan (Ind.)
Kanpur (Ind.)
Kassel (Ger.)
Kaunas (Lith.)
Khulna (Bangla.)
Kirkuk (Iraq)
Kisumu (Kenya)

125

Kohima (Ind.)
Kraków (Pol.)
Kurgan (Rus.)
Lahore (Pak.)
Le Mans (Fr.)
Leiden (Neth.)
Leyden (Neth.)
Lobito (Angola)
Lübeck (Ger.)
Lublin (Pol.)
Lüshun (China)
Madras (Ind.)
Málaga (Sp.)
Manaus (Braz.)
Manisa (Turk.)
Medina (Saudi)
Meerut (Ind.)
Meknès (Moroc.)
Modena (It.)
Mostar (Bos.)
Mukden (China)
Multan (Pak.)
Mumbai (Ind.)
Munich (Ger.)
Murcia (Sp.)
Mutare (Zim.)
Mwanza (Tanz.)
Mysore (Ind.)
Nagoya (Jap.)
Nagpur (Ind.)
Nakuru (Ken.)
Nanning (China)
Nantes (Fr.)
Napier (N.Z.)
Naples (It.)
Nelson (N.Z.)
Oaxaca (Mex.)
Odense (Den.)
Odessa (Ukr.)
Oporto (Port.)
Ostend (Belg.)
Panaji (Ind.)
Paraná (Arg.)
Patras (Gr.)
Pilsen (Cze.)
Poznán (Pol.)
Puebla (Mex.)
Quebec (Can.)
Quetta (Pak.)
Rampur (Ind.)
Recife (Braz.)
Reggio (It.)
Regina (Can.)
Rheims (Fr.)

Rostov (Rus.)
Samara (Rus.)
Samsun (Turk.)
Sendai (Jap.)
Seville (Sp.)
Shiraz (Iran)
Sittwe (Burma)
Smyrna (Turk.)
Sokoto (Nig.)
Soweto (S.A.)
Sparta (Gr.)
St. Gall (Swit.)
St. Malo (Fr.)
Sydney (Austral.)
Szeged (Hung.)
Tabora (Tanz.)
Tabriz (Iran)
Taejon (S. Korea)
Thebes (Gr.)
Thebes (Egypt)
Tobruk (Libya)
Toledo (Sp.)
Toulon (Fr.)
Toyota (Jap.)
Tralee (Ire.)
Trento (It.)
Trèves (Ger.)
Tromsø (Nor.)
Tsinan (China)
Tudmur (Syria)
Urumqi (China)
Venice (It.)
Verdun (Fr.)
Verona (It.)
Viborg (Den.)
Vyatka (Rus.)
Zurich (Swit.)
Zwolle (Neth.)

7

Aalborg (Den.)
Ajaccio (Cors.)
Alençon (Fr.)
Alkmaar (Neth.)
Antalya (Turk.)
Antwerp (Belg.)
Athlone (Ire.)
Avignon (Fr.)
Babylon (Iraq.)
Badajoz (Sp.)
Bandung (Indo.)
Bassein (Burma)
Bayonne (Fr.)
Benares (Ind.)

Bergamo (It.)
Bologna (It.)
Bolzano (It.)
Brescia (It.)
Breslau (Pol.)
Bryansk (Rus.)
Bushehr (Iran)
Calabar (Nig.)
Calgary (Can.)
Carrick (Ire.)
Catania (It.)
Chengdu (China)
Chongju (S. Korea)
Clonmel (Ire.)
Coblenz (Ger.)
Coimbra (Port.)
Cologne (Ger.)
Córdoba (Sp.)
Córdoba (Arg.)
Corinth (Gr.)
Corunna (Sp.)
Cottbus (Ger.)
Donetsk (Ukr.)
Dongola (Sudan)
Dresden (Ger.)
Dundalk (Ire.)
Dunedin (N.Z.)
Dunkirk (Fr.)
El Obeid (Sudan)
Elbasan (Alb.)
Entebbe (Ug.)
Erzerum (Turk.)
Ferrara (It.)
Fukuoka (Jap.)
Funchal (Port.)
Gangtok (Ind.)
Granada (Sp.)
Gwalior (Ind.)
Haarlem (Neth.)
Halifax (Can.)
Hamburg (Ger.)
Hanover (Ger.)
Hitachi (Jap.)
Holguín (Cuba)
Homburg (Ger.)
Homyyel (Bela.)
Irkutsk (Rus.)
Isfahan (Iran)
Jericho (Pal.)
Jodhpur (Ind.)
Kalinin (Rus.)
Karachi (Pak.)
Karbela (Iraq.)
Kenitra (Moroc.)

Kharkiv (Ukr.)
Kharkov (Ukr.)
Kildare (Ire.)
Koblenz (Ger.)
Kunming (China)
La Plata (Arg.)
Lanchow (China)
Lanzhou (China)
Latakia (Syria)
Le Havre (Fr.)
Leipzig (Ger.)
Lemberg (Ukr.)
Liepaja (Lat.)
Lifford (Ire.)
Limoges (Fr.)
Logroño (Sp.)
Lourdes (Fr.)
Lucerne (Swit.)
Lucknow (Ind.)
Malines (Belg.)
Mansura (Egypt)
Maramba (Zam.)
Mashhad (Iran)
Massawa (Eritrea)
Memphis (Egypt)
Mendoza (Arg.)
Messina (It.)
Miskolc (Hung.)
Mogilev (Bela.)
Mombasa (Kenya)
Morelia (Mex.)
München (Ger.)
Mycenae (Gr.)
Nanjing (China)
Nanking (China)
Nicosia (Cyprus)
Novi Sad (Yug.)
Orléans (Fr.)
Ostrava (Cze.)
Palermo (It.)
Palmyra (Syria)
Perugia (It.)
Pescara (It.)
Piraeus (Gr.)
Plovdiv (Bulg.)
Pompeii (It.)
Potsdam (Ger.)
Ravenna (It.)
Rosario (Arg.)
Rostock (Ger.)
Salerno (It.)
San Remo (It.)
Santa Fe (Arg.)
Sapporo (Jap.)

Setúbal (Port.)
St. John's (Can.)
Taiyuan (China)
Tangier (Moroc.)
Tel Aviv (Isr.)
Tétouan (Moroc.)
Tianjin (China)
Toronto (Can.)
Trieste (It.)
Tripoli (Leb.)
Tripoli (Libya)
Tucumán (Arg.)
Uppsala (Swed.)
Utrecht (Neth.)
Vitebsk (Bela.)
Vitoria (Sp.)
Wexford (Ire.)
Wicklow (Ire.)
Wroclaw (Pol.)
Yakutsk (Rus.)
Youghal (Ire.)
Zagazig (Egypt)

8

Acapulco (Mex.)
Adelaide (Austral.)
Agartala (Ind.)
Alicante (Sp.)
Amritsar (Ind.)
Auckland (N.Z.)
Augsburg (Ger.)
Benguela (Ang.)
Besançon (Fr.)
Biarritz (Fr.)
Bordeaux (Fr.)
Boulogne (Fr.)
Brisbane (Austral.)
Bulawayo (Zim.)
Cagliari (It.)
Calcutta (Ind.)
Camagüey (Cuba)
Carthage (N. Af.)
Cawnpore (Ind.)
Changsha (China)
Changzhi (China)
Chartres (Fr.)
Chemnitz (Ger.)
Chonqing (China)
Clontarf (Ire.)
Curitiba (Braz.)
Damietta (Egypt)
Debrecen (Hung.)
Dortmund (Ger.)
Drogheda (Ire.)

Edmonton (Can.)
El Faiyum (Egypt)
Florence (It.)
Göteborg (Swed.)
Grenoble (Fr.)
Haiphong (Viet.)
Hakodate (Jap.)
Hamilton (Can.)
Hannover (Ger.)
Ismailia (Egypt)
Istanbul (Turk.)
Jamalpur (Ind.)
Kandahar (Afghan.)
Karlstad (Swed.)
Kawasaki (Jap.)
Kilkenny (Ire.)
Kingston (Can.)
Klaipeda (Lith.)
Lausanne (Swit.)
Limerick (Ire.)
Listowel (Ire.)
Longford (Ire.)
Ludhiana (Ind.)
Mafeking (S.A.)
Mahilyou (Bela.)
Mandalay (Burma)
Mannheim (Ger.)
Matanzas (Cuba)
Mechelen (Belg.)
Medellín (Col.)
Monaghan (Ire.)
Montreal (Can.)
Murmansk (Rus.)
Nagasaki (Jap.)
Nazareth (Isr.)
Novgorod (Rus.)
Nürnberg (Ger.)
Omdurman (Sudan)
Pamplona (Sp.)
Peshawar (Pak.)
Port Said (Egypt)
Przemysl (Pol.)
Rajshahi (Bangla.)
Rathdrum (Ire.)
Salonica (Gr.)
Salvador (Braz.)
Salzburg (Aust.)
São Paulo (Braz.)
Schwerin (Ger.)
Semarang (Indo.)
Shanghai (China)
Shenyang (China)
Shillong (Ind.)
Shymkent (Kaz.)

Smolensk (Rus.)
Soissons (Fr.)
Srinagar (Ind.)
St. Tropez (Fr.)
Surabaya (Indo.)
Syracuse (It.)
The Hague (Neth.)
Tientsin (China)
Timbuktu (Mali)
Toulouse (Fr.)
Vadodara (Ind.)
Valencia (Sp.)
Varanasi (Ind.)
Veracruz (Mex.)
Victoria (Can.)
Vladimir (Rus.)
Voronezh (Rus.)
Winnipeg (Can.)
Yokohama (Jap.)
Zanzibar (Tanz.)
Zaragoza (Sp.)

9

Abbeville (Fr.)
Agrigento (It.)
Ahmadabad (Ind.)
Allahabad (Ind.)
Archangel (Rus.)
Astrakhan (Rus.)
Bangalore (Ind.)
Banja Luka (Bos.)
Barcelona (Sp.)
Beersheba (Isr.)
Benin City (Nig.)
Brunswick (Ger.)
Byzantium (Turk.)
Cartagena (Sp.)
Cartagena (Col.)
Castlebar (Ire.)
Changchun (China)
Changzhou (China)
Cherbourg (Fr.)
Cherkessk (Rus.)
Chungking (China)
Connemara (Ire.)
Darmstadt (Ger.)
Dordrecht (Neth.)
Eindhoven (Neth.)
El Mansura (Egypt)
Fortaleza (Braz.)
Frankfurt (Ger.)
Gazientep (Turk.)
Gibraltar (Eur.)
Groningen (Neth.)

Guangzhou (China)
Guayaquil (Ecuador)
Heraklion (Gr.)
Hiroshima (Jap.)
Hyderabad (Ind.)
Hyderabad (Pak.)
Innsbruck (Aust.)
Jalalabad (Afghan.)
Kaohsiung (Taiwan)
Karaganda (Kaz.)
Killarney (Ire.)
Kimberley (S.A.)
Kisangani (Congo,
    Dem. Rep.)
Krivoi Rog (Ukr.)
Kryvyy Rig (Ukr.)
Kuibyshev (Rus.)
Ladysmith (S.A.)
Las Palmas (Sp.)
Leningrad (Rus.)
Linköping (Swed.)
Ljubljana (Sloven.)
Magdeburg (Ger.)
Maiduguri (Nig.)
Maracaibo (Venez.)
Marrakech (Moroc.)
Marrakesh (Moroc.)
Marseille (Fr.)
Matsuyama (Jap.)
Melbourne (Austral.)
Montauban (Fr.)
Monterrey (Mex.)
Mullingar (Ire.)
Newcastle (Austral.)
Nuremberg (Ger.)
Palembang (Indo.)
Perpignan (Fr.)
Podgorica (Monte.)
Roscommon (Ire.)
Rotterdam (Neth.)
Samarkand (Uzbek.)
Santander (Sp.)
Saragossa (Sp.)
Saskatoon (Can.)
St. Étienne (Fr.)
Stavanger (Nor.)
Stavropol (Rus.)
Stuttgart (Ger.)
Tipperary (Ire.)
Trondheim (Nor.)
Tullamore (Ire.)
Vancouver (Can.)
Volgograd (Rus.)
Waterford (Ire.)

Wiesbaden (Ger.)
Wuppertal (Ger.)
Yaroslavl (Rus.)
Zamboanga (Phil.)
Zhengzhou (China)
Zonguldak (Turk.)

10

Alexandria (Egypt)
Bad Homburg (Ger.)
Baden Baden (Ger.)
Casablanca (Moroc.)
Chandigarh (Ind.)
Chittagong (Bangla.)
Concepción (Chile)
Cuernavaca (Mex.)
Darjeeling (Ind.)
Daugavpils (Lat.)
Diyarbakir (Turk.)
Düsseldorf (Ger.)
Faisalabad (Pak.)
Gothenburg (Swed.)
Gujranwala (Pak.)
Heidelberg (Ger.)
Jamshedpur (Ind.)
Kitakyushu (Jap.)
Klagenfurt (Aust.)
Königsberg (Rus.)
Lubumbashi (Congo, Dem. Rep.)
Maastricht (Neth.)
Marseilles (Fr.)
Montélimar (Fr.)
Port Arthur (China)
Port Laoise (Ire.)
Portoviejo (Ecuador)
Qaraghandy (Kaz.)
Rawalpindi (Pak.)
Sevastopol (Ukr.)

Shillelagh (Ire.)
Simonstown (S.A.)
Stalingrad (Rus.)
Strasbourg (Fr.)
Sverdlovsk (Rus.)
Thunder Bay (Can.)
Trivandrum (Ind.)
Valladolid (Sp.)
Valparaíso (Chile)
Versailles (Fr.)
Whitehorse (Can.)

11

Armentières (Fr.)
Bahia Blanca (Arg.)
Ballymurphy (Ire.)
Bandar Abbas (Iran)
Bhubaneswar (Ind.)
Campo Grande (Braz.)
Chelyabinsk (Rus.)
Dar es Salaam (Tanz.)
Fredericton (Can.)
Grahamstown (S.A.)
Guadalajara (Mex.)
Guadalajara (Sp.)
Helsingborg (Swed.)
Kaliningrad (Rus.)
Khorramabad (Iran)
Lillehammer (Nor.)
Montpellier (Fr.)
Novosibirsk (Rus.)
Porto Alegre (Braz.)
Puerto Montt (Chile)
Punta Arenas (Chile)
Rostov-on-Don (Rus.)
Saarbrücken (Ger.)
Sharpeville (S.A.)
Trincomalee (Sri)
Vladivostok (Rus.)

Yellowknife (Can.)

12

Alice Springs (Austral.)
Barranquilla (Col.)
Bloemfontein (S.A.)
Braunschweig (Ger.)
Cagayan de Oro (Phil.)
Christchurch (N.Z.)
Dun Laoghaire (Ire.)
Johannesburg (S.A.)
Niagara Falls (Can.)
Port Harcourt (Nig.)
Rio de Janeiro (Braz.)
San Sebastian (Sp.)
St. Petersburg (Rus.)
Thessaloniki (Gr.)

13 AND OVER

Aix-la-Chapelle (Ger.) (13)
Banská Bystrica (Slov.) (14)
Belo Horizonte (Braz.) (13)
Carrick-on-Shannon (Ire.) (16)
Ceske Budejovice (Cze.) (15)
Charlottetown (Can.) (13)
Clermont-Ferrand (Fr.) (15)
Constantinople (Turk.) (14)
Dnepropetrovsk (Ukr.) (14)
Karl-Marx-Stadt (Ger.) (13)
Nizhny Novgorod (Rus.) (14)
Pietermaritzburg (S.A.) (16)
Port Elizabeth (S.A.) (13)
Reggio di Calabria (It.) (16)
Reggio nell'Emilia (It.) (16)
s'-Hertogenbosch (Neth.) (14)
Santiago de Cuba (Cuba) (14)
Yekaterinburg (Rus.) (13)

Waterfalls: the largest

Angel (5) *Venez.*
Churchill (9) *Can.*
Gavarnie (8) *Fr.*
Giessbach (9) *Swit.*
Guaira (6) *Braz.*
Hamilton (8) *Can.*

Krimml (6) *Aust.*
Multnomah (9) *U.S.A.*
Niagara (7)
   Can.–U.S.A.
Ribbon (6) *U.S.A.*
Roraima (7) *Guyana*

Sete Quedas (10) *Braz.*
Stanley (7) *Zaïre*
Sutherland (10) *N.Z*
Trümmelbach (11)
   Swit.
Vettisfos (9) *Nor.*

Victoria (8) *Zambia,*
   Zimbabwe
Yosemite (8) *U.S.A*

Weather

3 AND 4

bise
bora
calm
cold
cool
damp
dark
dry
dull
east
fog
föhn
gale
gust
haar
hail
haze
hazy
heat
hoar
hot
ice
icy
mild
mist
rain
rime
smog
snow
sun
thaw
tide
veer
warm
west
wet
wind

5

blast
blowy
buran
chill
cirri
cloud
dusty
Eurus
flood
foehn
foggy

front
frost
gusty
heavy
humid
light
misty
muggy
north
rainy
sleet
snowy
south
storm
sunny
windy

6

Aeolus
arctic
aurora
auster
boreal
Boreas
breeze
breezy
brumal
chilly
cirrus
clouds
cloudy
colder
corona
degree
deluge
floods
freeze
frosty
haboob
hot day
isobar
isohel
mizzle
mizzly
nimbus
normal
red sky
samiel
serein
shower
simoom
solano

squall
starry
stormy
stuffy
sultry
torrid
trades
vortex
warmer
wet day
winter
wintry
zephyr

7

air-mass
aureole
backing
blowing
blue sky
bluster
chinook
clement
climate
clouded
cold air
cold day
coldish
cumulus
current
cyclone
drizzle
drizzly
drought
element
fogbank
freshen
fresher
freshet
gregale
grey sky
hailing
hottish
ice-cold
icy wind
isohyet
khamsin
meltemi
mistral
monsoon
pampero
pea soup

rainbow
raining
set fair
showery
sirocco
sizzler
snowing
squally
stratus
sub-zero
summery
sunspot
tempest
thunder
tornado
typhoon
veering
warm day
warmish
weather
wintery

8

autumnal
Beaufort
black ice
blizzard
clear day
climatic
cloud cap
cold wave
cold wind
cyclonic
dead calm
dewpoint
doldrums
downpour
east wind
easterly
elements
favonian
fireball
forecast
freezing
haziness
headwind
heat haze
heatwave
high wind
humidity
isothere
isotherm

levanter
libeccio
low cloud
lowering
meteoric
moderate
nubilous
occluded
overcast
pressure
rain belt
raindrop
rainfall
rainless
rainy day
scirocco
scorcher
snowfall
sunburst
sunlight
sunshine
thundery
tropical
west wind
westerly
wind cone
windless
windsock
windvane

9

anemology
barometer
below zero
blue skies
cloud bank
cloud over
cold front
corposant
drizzling
dry season
dust storm
fogginess
frostbite
gale force
hailstone
hailstorm
hard frost
harmattan
heavy rain
hoarfrost
hurricane

inclement
light rain
lightning
midday sun
mild spell
mistiness
moonlight
nor'easter
nor'wester
north wind
northeast
northerly
northwest
occlusion
overcloud
pea souper
rain gauge
raincloud
rainstorm
sandstorm
sea breeze
snowflake
snowstorm
sou'-wester
south wind
southeast
southerly
southwest
starlight
tidal wave
trade wind
turbulent
unclouded
unsettled
warm front
weak front
whirlwind
wind gauge
windstorm

10

anemograph
arctic cold
bitter cold
black frost
changeable
cloudburst
cloudiness
cool breeze
depression
euroclydon
freshening

frostbound
hailstones
hot climate
hot weather
hygrometer
land breeze
light winds
March winds
patchy rain
pouring-wet
Scotch mist
sharp frost
stormcloud
strong wind
sweltering
turbulence
waterspout
wet weather
white frost

11

anticyclone
cats and dogs
cold climate
cold weather
driving rain
dull weather
etesian wind
foul weather
fresh breeze
gale warning

ground frost
harvest moon
low pressure
lowering sky
mackerel sky
meteorology
mild weather
monsoon wind
northeaster
northwester
patchy cloud
pouring rain
precipitate
rain or shine
rainy season
showery rain
stiff breeze
summer cloud
temperature
tempestuous
thermometer
thunderbolt
thunderclap
warm weather
weathercock
weathervane
wind backing
wind veering

12

anticyclonic

April showers
atmospherics
bitterly cold
cirrocumulus
cirrostratus
cumulonimbus
easterly wind
equinoctials
freezing cold
freezing rain
high pressure
Indian summer
microclimate
offshore wind
shooting star
storm brewing
storm signals
thundercloud
thunderstorm
tropical heat
tropical rain
warm sunshine
weather chart
weather glass
westerly wind
wind velocity
windy weather

13 AND 14

aurora borealis (14)
autumn weather (13)

Beaufort scale (13)
cumulostratus (13)
frosty weather (13)
further outlook (14)
meteorological (14)
meteorologist (13)
moonlight night (14)
northeast wind (13)
northerly wind (13)
northwest wind (13)
sheet lightning (14)
southeast wind (13)
southerly wind (13)
southwest wind (13)
starlight night (14)
summer weather (13)
thunder-shower (13)
torrential rain (14)
weather prophet (14)
weather report (13)
weather station (13)
wintry weather (13)

15

forked lightning
meteoric showers
prevailing winds
summer lightning
tropical climate
weather forecast

LAW AND GOVERNMENT
Legal terms

2

J.P.
KC.
Q.C.

3 AND 4

abet
act
aka
bail
bar
bars
beak
bribe
case
dock
D.P.P.

fair
fee
feu
fine
g.b.h.
gaol
I.O.U.
jail
jury
law
lien
life
m'lud
not
oath
plea
quit
rape

rent
rob
seal
silk
soke
stay
sue
suit
tort
try
use
veto
will
writ

5

abjure
alias

alibi
alien
arson
award
bench
brief
bylaw
cause
claim
clerk
costs
court
crime
crook
false
felon
feoff
forge

fraud
guilt
in rem
judge
juror
lease
legal
libel
mulct
order
penal
plead
poach
prize
proof
quash
right
rules

steal
swear
thief
trial
trust
usher
usury
valid

6

access
action
affirm
amerce
appeal
arrest
asylum
attorn

bailee
bigamy
breach
caveat
censor
charge
commit
de jure
deceit
decree
delate
delict
disbar
duress
elegit
entail
equity
escrow
estate
felony
fiscal
forger
guilty
Hilary
holdup
incest
indict
injury
insult
junior
jurist
kidnap
lawful
lawyer
legacy
legist
lessee
lessor
lethal
malice
master
motion
motive
murder
on oath
outlaw
pardon
parole
piracy
police
prison
puisne
remand
repeal

robber
ruling
socage
suitor
surety
tenant
warder

7

abscond
accused
accuser
adjourn
alimony
amnesty
arbiter
arraign
assault
assizes
autopsy
bailiff
battery
bencher
bequest
binding
borstal
bribery
burglar
capital
case law
cashier
caution
charter
chattel
circuit
codicil
consent
convict
coroner
counsel
cruelty
custody
damages
de facto
defence
delator
demesne
deodand
divorce
escheat
estreat
ex parte
foreman
forfeit

forgery
garnish
hanging
harming
hearing
hearsay
illegal
illicit
impeach
inquest
inquiry
John Doe
juryman
justice
larceny
law lord
lawless
lawsuit
legatee
legator
licence
marshal
mens rea
neglect
non suit
offence
penalty
perjury
precept
probate
proctor
release
reserve
Riot Act
robbery
sheriff
sine die
slander
statute
summary
summons
suspect
swear in
tenancy
testate
testify
treason
trustee
verdict
warrant
witness

8

absolute
abstract
act of God
advocate
advowson
allodium
amortize
attorney
barratry
bottomry
burglary
canon law
chancery
civil law
coercion
contempt
contract
copyhold
covenant
criminal
deed poll
deponent
detainee
detainer
disorder
disseize
distrain
distress
domicile
drafting
embezzle
entailed
estoppel
estovers
eviction
evidence
executor
felo de se
fidelity
findings
forensic
foul play
genocide
gravamen
guardian
homicide
hung jury
in camera
indecent
informer
innocent
jailbird

judgment
judicial
law agent
law court
law lords
legal aid
licensee
litigant
litigate
majority
mandamus
mistrial
mittimus
mortmain
murderer
novation
nuisance
offender
peculate
penal law
penology
perjuror
petition
pleading
preamble
prisoner
promisee
promisor
rebuttal
rebutter
receiver
recorder
reprieve
Salic law
sedition
sentence
Shops Act
stealing
subpoena
sui juris
test case
testator
tipstaff
trespass
tribunal
Truck Act
true bill
unlawful
validity
war crime

9

abatement
abduction

accessory
acquittal
ademption
affidavit
agreement
allotment
annulment
appellant
appellate
attainder
barrister
blackmail
bona fides
bound over
care order
champerty
code of law
collusion
common law
copyright
courtroom
de son tort
defendant
desertion
discharge
dismissal
disseisin
distraint
doli capax
embezzler
embraceor
embracery
endowment
equitable
execution
executory
exonerate
extortion
fee simple
felonious
feoffment
Gaming Act
good faith
grand jury
guarantee
guarantor
high court
income tax
indemnity
innocence
intestacy
intestate
judiciary
jurywoman

justiciar
libellant
litigious
loitering
mala fides
mandatory
matricide
murderous
nisi prius
not guilty
not proven
objection
Old Bailey
open court
parricide
penal code
petty jury
pilfering
plaintiff
precatory
precedent
privilege
probation
procedure
pronounce
prosecute
receiving
refresher
registrar
remission
represent
reprimand
restraint
sanctions
servitude
smuggling
solicitor
statement
statutory
sub judice
summing up
surrender
testament
testatrix
testimony
title deed

10

alienation
appearance
assessment
assignment
attachment
attornment

bank robber
bankruptcy
breath test
certiorari
child abuse
civil wrong
confession
connivance
conspiracy
contraband
contravene
conveyance
conviction
copyholder
corruption
court of law
court order
crime sheet
crown court
decree nisi
deed of gift
defamation
delinquent
deposition
disclaimer
duty of care
enticement
estate duty
executrix
eye witness
finance act
forfeiture
fratricide
fraud squad
fraudulent
free pardon
gaming acts
gun licence
hard labour
illegality
impediment
in chambers
indictment
injunction
inter vivos
judicature
justiciary
King's Bench
land tenure
Law Society
legal right
legitimacy
limitation
liquor laws

litigation
magistrate
martial law
misconduct
misprision
negligence
next friend
out of court
petty theft
pickpocket
post mortem
prize court
procurator
prosecutor
respondent
revocation
separation
settlement
shoplifter
soliciting
statute law
title deeds
trespasser
ultra vires
witness box

11

advancement
affiliation
appointment
arbitration
assize court
attestation
Children Act
civil wrongs
Common Pleas
composition
concealment
condonation
coparcenary
county court
criminal law
death duties
debtors' acts
deportation
dissolution
disturbance
enabling act
enforcement
engrossment
escheatment
examination
extenuating
extradition

fair comment
false arrest
fingerprint
fleri facias
foreclosure
garnishment
high treason
higher court
house arrest
impeachment
incriminate
infanticide
issue of writ
king's pardon
law merchant
legal tender
libel action
maintenance
malpractice
market overt
mayor's court
obstruction
open verdict
prerogative
prosecution
puisne judge
Queen's Bench
requisition
restitution
root of title
royal assent
sheriff's act
shoplifting
stamp duties
stipendiary
subornation
suicide pact
third degree
trespassing
trial by jury
under arrest
Vagrancy Act
vesting deed
ward of court

12

adjudication
age of consent
amicus curiae
bill of rights
bona vacantia
breathalyzer
case of thorns
causa proxima

caution money
caveat emptor
charter party
chattels real
chief justice
circuit judge
co-respondent
Companies Act
compensation
compurgation
condemnation
confiscation
constabulary
conveyancing
court martial
cross-examine
crown witness
death penalty
disaffection
divorce court
embezzlement
encroachment
express trust
ferae naturae
first offence
grand assizes
guardianship
habeas corpus
hereditament
imprisonment
infringement
inherent vice
interpleader
intimidation
jail sentence
joint tenancy
jurisdiction
kerb crawling
king's proctor
legal fiction
life sentence
Lord Advocate
lord of appeal
manslaughter
mensa et thoro
misbehaviour
misdemeanour
misdirection
oral evidence
pendente lite
petty larceny
prescription
privy council
prostitution

Queen's Pardon
ratification
royal charter
royal warrant
sheriff clerk
supreme court
taxing master
testamentary

13

administrator
ancient lights
apportionment
appropriation
burden of proof
charging order
citizen's arrest
common assault
consideration
coroner's court
court of appeal
Court of Arches
criminal libel
cross-question
damage feasant
ejection order
Ground Game Act
hereditaments

housebreaking
illegal action
impersonation
interlocutory
judge advocate
justification
juvenile court
kangaroo court
letters patent
lord president
nolle prosequi
parliamentary
petty sessions
public trustee
quantum meruit
Queen's counsel
recognizances
right of appeal
search warrant
sharp practice
sitting tenant
statute barred
treasure trove
trial by combat
trial by ordeal
Witchcraft Act

14

act of indemnity
Admiralty Court
choses in action
civil liberties
common nuisance
common sergeant
conjugal rights
county judgment
court of inquiry
court of justice
criminal damage
criminal record
decree absolute
default summons
double jeopardy
ejusdem generis
exclusion order
false pretences
identification
identity parade
legally binding
lord chancellor
naturalization
penal servitude
plea bargaining
Queen's evidence

special licence
wrongful arrest

15

act of bankruptcy
act of Parliament
Act of Settlement
attorney-general
autrefois acquit
benefit of clergy
charitable trust
compound a felony
confidence trick
consistory court
contempt of court
coroner's inquest
detention centre
disorderly house
emergency powers
indecent assault
latent ambiguity
majority verdict
marriage licence
oyer and terminer
power of attorney
protection money
quarter sessions
stay of execution

Parliamentary and political

2	S.N.P.	pact	draft	6	member
	sit	pass	edict		motion
E.C.	T.U.C.	peer	elect	assent	nation
E.U.	tax	poll	enact	backer	picket
M.P.		rump	forum	ballot	policy
P.M.	4	seat	house	budget	putsch
U.N.	ayes	Sejm	junta	caucus	quorum
	bill	Tory	legal	clause	recess
3	coup	veto	lobby	colony	record
A.N.C.	D.O.R.A.	vote	Nazis	commie	reform
act	Dáil	Whig	order	Cortes	report
bar	Diet	whip	paper	decree	ruling
C.B.I.	Duma	writ	party	divide	satrap
C.I.A.	E.F.T.A.		Provo	enosis	secede
E.E.C.	gain	5	purge	Fabian	senate
E.T.A.	left	agent	rally	Führer	sirkar
gag	lord	amend	right	govern	speech
I.R.A.	mace	Boule	S.E.A.T.O.	heckle	strike
K.G.B.	N.A.T.O.	bylaw	sit-in	Labour	summon
O.A.U.	Nazi	chair	valid	leader	swaraj
P.L.O.	noes	clerk	voter	Majlis	tariff
red	oath	count		Maoism	

teller
tyrant

7

adjourn
Al Fatah
Althing
anarchy
barrack
borough
boycott
cabinet
canvass
censure
chamber
closure
cold war
Comecon
Commons
commune
council
deficit
détente
dissent
elector
embargo
fascism
fascist
federal
finance
gallery
Hansard
heckler
hot line
Knesset
liberal
lock out
mandate
Marxism
neutral
new left
opening
outvote
pairing
passage
politic
poor law
premier
primary
prolong
radical
reading
recount
re-elect

re-enact
Riksdag
senator
session
speaker
statute
Toryism
tribune
Tynwald
tyranny
vacancy
Zionism
Zionist

8

assembly
autarchy
autocrat
Black Rod
blockade
caudillo
chairman
Chiltern
    (Hundreds)
commissar
commoner
Congress
democrat
dictator
dissolve
division
dominion
ecclesia
election
elective
feminism
free vote
Gerousia
home rule
hustings
left-wing
Lok Sabha
majority
minister
ministry
minority
national
official
oligarch
politics
prorogue
republic
rollback
schedule

Sinn Féin
Sobranie
Storting
suffrage
Tanaiste
Treasury
triumvir
unionism
unionist
Whiggery
woolsack

9

amendment
anarchism
apartheid
autocracy
ballot box
Barebone's
bicameral
Bundesrat
Bundestag
coalition
Cominform
Comintern
committee
communism
communist
democracy
deterrent
Eduskunta
exchequer
first lord
Folketing
legislate
New Labour
oligarchy
ombudsman
politburo
Poujadist
president
red guards
Reichstag
right-wing
sanctions
secretary
shire-moot
show trial
socialism
socialist
Stalinism
Taoiseach
terrorism

10

aristocrat
block grant
by-election
capitalism
chancellor
collective
conference
devolution
filibuster
government
guillotine
invalidate
monarchism
Monday Club
opposition
parliament
Plaid Cymru
plebiscite
psephology
radicalism
Rajya Sabha
referendum
republican
resolution
revolution
scrutineer
sitting day
Third Reich
Third World
trade union
Trotskyism
unicameral
Warsaw Pact
White House
white paper

11

adjournment
aristocracy
backbencher
ballot-paper
bye-election
casting vote
co-operative
coexistence
congressman
constituent
containment
demarcation
dissolution
divine right
enfranchise

finance bill
front runner
imperialist
independent
legislation
legislative
legislature
McCarthyism
nationalist
Nationalrat
package deal
party leader
prerogative
private bill
reactionary
revisionism
statute book
suffragette
syndicalism
syndicalist
Tamil Tigers
Tammany Hall
Witenagemot
yeoman-usher

12

commissioner
Common Market
Commonwealth
Conservative
constituency
constitution
dictatorship
domino theory
favourite son
federal union
House of Lords
house of peers
invalidation
lord advocate
lord chairman
privy council
reading clerk
snap division
ways and means
welfare state

13

demonstration
deputy speaker
disengagement
division lobby
free trade area
home secretary

international
lord president
lord privy seal
prime minister
shadow cabinet
single chamber
States General
trade unionist
United Nations

vote of censure

14

constitutional
deputy chairman
deputy premier
deputy sergeant
gerrymandering
House of Commons

lord chancellor
representative
sergeant-at-arms
social democrat

15

attorney-general
cabinet minister
clerk of the house

general election
Marxist-Leninist
minister of state
people's republic
personality cult
social democracy
totalitarianism

LITERATURE AND THE ARTS
Art

2 AND 3

air
art
bur
del.
exc.
fec.
hue
inc.
inv.
key
mat
oil
op
pen
pop
sit

4

airy
arts
base
body
burr
bust
cast
chic
Dada
daub
draw
etch
flat
form
gild
halo
icon
kore
limn
line

lipo
mass
Merz
nude
oils
pinx.
pose
size
swag
tone
wash

5

batik
bloom
blush
board
brush
burn
cameo
carve
chalk
couch
delin.
donor
draft
easel
ember
Fauve
fecit
frame
genre
gesso
glair
glaze
glory
gloss
glyph
grave
hatch

inert
ivory
japan
lay-in
lumia
magot
model
mount
mural
Nabis
naive
Op Art
paint
panel
Pietà
prime
print
putto
rebus
resin
salon
scene
sculp
secco
sepia
shade
Stijl
study
stump
tondo
torso
trace
vertu
virtu

6

action
artist
ash-can
bistre

cachet
canvas
colour
crayon
Cubism
depict
design
dipper
doctor
ectype
emblem
emboss
enamel
engild
flambé
fresco
fylfot
gisant
Gothic
ground
incavo
kitcat
kitsch
kouros
limner
mastic
medium
megilp
mobile
mosaic
niello
nimbus
object
offset
ormolu
ox-gall
pastel
patina
pencil
pinxit

plaque
plaster
Pop Art
primer
Purism
reflex
relief
rhythm
rococo
school
sculpt
shadow
shippo
sitter
sketch
statue
stucco
studio
uncial
veduta
verism

7

abbozzo
academy
acrylic
amorino
archaic
Art Brut
Art Deco
atelier
aureole
bachiru
baroque
Bauhaus
biscuit
bitumen
bodegón
bottega
camaieu

cartoon
carving
cassone
cissing
classic
collage
contour
Dadaism
daubing
De Stijl
diagram
diorama
diptych
draught
drawing
écorché
etching
excudit
faience
Fauvism
felt tip
fine art
gilding
glazing
gouache
graphic
hot tone
impaint
impasto
Junk Art
lacquer
linocut
lost wax
lunette
modello
montage
mordant
Orphism
outline
painter

135

palette
picture
pigment
plastic
priming
profile
realism
relievo
remodel
replica
reredos
retable
rococco
scumble
sfumato
shading
sketchy
stabile
stencil
stipple
support
surlace
T-square
tableau
tempera
texture
touch up
tracery
tracing
vanitas
varnish
vehicle
woodcut

8

abstract
academic
acid bath
acrolith
airbrush
anaglyph
aquatint
armature
arriccio
Art Autre
artistic
Barbizon
Blue Four
bozzetto
caryatid
charcoal
concours
cool tone
diaglyph

drypoint
emulsion
engraver
figurine
fixative
freehand
frottage
Futurism
gargoyle
graffiti
graphics
grouping
half-tone
handling
hatching
idealism
intaglio
intarsia
intonaco
luminism
majolica
makimono
mandorla
maquette
Mogul Art
monotype
mounting
naive art
negative
oil paint
ornament
painting
panorama
pastiche
penumbra
plein air
pointing
portrait
pouncing
predella
Rayonism
repoussé
rocaille
romantic
seascape
seicento
statuary
symmetry
tachisme
tapestry
tectonic
tesserae
throwing
trecento

triglyph
triptych
vignette
warm tone

9

aesthetic
aggregate
alla prima
anti-cerne
appliqué
aquarelle
aquatinta
arabesque
asymmetry
ball-point
bas-relief
Blaue Vier
block book
bric-à-brac
cartouche
cartridge
cloisonné
colourist
crow quill
damascene
damaskeen
dichroism
Die Brücke
distemper
emblemata
embossing
encarnado
encaustic
engraving
facsimile
geometric
gradation
grisaille
grotesque
happening
highlight
hot colour
indelible
indian ink
intimisme
japanning
landscape
lay figure
life class
lithotint
low relief
mahlstick
Mannerism

marquetry
maulstick
mezzotint
miniature
Minoan Art
modelling
multiples
Nazarenes
Neo-Gothic
oil colour
old master
oleograph
painterly
pen and ink
phototype
plaquette
polyptych
primitive
ready-made
recession
red-figure
sculpture
scumbling
Serial Art
serigraph
sgrafitto
sketch pad
statuette
still-life
stippling
strapwork
stretcher
Symbolist
tailpiece
tattooing
Tenebrism
Totentanz
undercoat
Vorticism
woodblock
xylograph

10

accidental
achromatic
altarpiece
altogether
anaglyphic
anaglyptic
applied art
Archaic Art
Art Nouveau
Arte Povera
assemblage

atmosphere
automatism
avant-garde
background
biomorphic
body colour
caricature
cartellino
cartoonist
cerography
cire-perdue
Classicism
cool colour
cornucopia
craquelure
crosshatch
dead colour
drying oils
embossment
embroidery
fitch brush
flat colour
Florentine
foreground
full-length
glass print
graphic art
hair pencil
half-length
India paper
Jugendstil
Kinetic Art
linseed oil
lithograph
marouflage
metal point
mezzotinto
Minimalism
monochrome
Naturalism
night piece
organic art
paint brush
pantograph
pen and wash
pencilling
pentimento
photograph
pietra dura
plasticity
portcrayon
quadratura
Raphaelism
Raphaelite

repoussoir
Romanesque
Section d'Or
serigraphy
silhouette
silk screen
Surrealism
Synthetism
terracotta
turpentine
warm colour
water glass
xylography

11

Abstract Art
academician
alto-relievo
aquatinting
Art Informel
battle piece
Biedermeier
black-figure
Blaue Reiter
calligraphy
canvas board
chiaroscuro
chinoiserie
chromograph
cinquecento
Claude glass
colour print
composition
Concrete Art
connoisseur
conté crayon
Cosmati work
Divisionism
draughtsman
Eclecticism
electrotype
engravement
foreshorten
found object
french chalk
ground plane
Hague School
heliochrome
heliochromy
Hellenistic
iconography
Illusionism
imprimatura
life drawing

lithography
marqueterie
masterpiece
neo-romantic
objet trouvé
oil painting
papier collé
pavement art
perspective
photography
picturesque
Pointillism
portraiture
poster paint
Primitivism
Renaissance
restoration
Romanticism
scenography
stained glass
stereochromy
Suprematism
tracing linen
tracing paper
watercolour
wood carving

12

acrylic paint
alkyd colours
anamorphosis
Ash-can School
bird's eye view
Byzantine Art
camera lucida
Cloisonnisme
Eidophusikon
illustration
Newlyn School
palette knife
photomontage
Precisionism
quattrocento
scraper board
self-portrait
Superrealism
tessellation

13

black and white
camera obscura
complementary
Conceptual Art
crosshatching

daguerreotype
decorative art
degenerate art
etching needle
Expressionism
fête champêtre
figurative art
Flemish School
Glasgow School
glass painting
golden section
Impressionism
line engraving
Neoclassicism
neoplasticism
Norwich School
Pre-Raphaelite
primary colour
relief etching
Social Realism
tactile values
underpainting
wood engraving

14 AND OVER

Abstract Expressionism (21)
action painting (14)
cabinet painting (15)
Camden Town Group (15)
chromatography (14)
Constructivism (14)
conversation piece (17)
draughtsmanship (15)
Euston Road School (16)
Florentine School (16)
foreshortening (14)
history painting (15)
International Gothic (19)
Kitchen Sink School (17)
Neo-Impressionism (16)
Neo-Romanticism (14)
Neue Sachlichkeit (16)
pavement artist (14)
performance art (14)
picture gallery (14)
plaster of paris (14)
portrait painter (15)
Post-Impressionism (17)
representational (16)
silk-screen printing (18)
Socialist Realism (16)
steel engraving (14)
vanishing point (14)

Artists, architects, sculptors, cartoonists, etc.

3 AND 4

Adam
Arp
Bell
Bill
Bles
Bol
Bone
Both
Boyd
Bril
Bush
Cano
Capp
Caro
Cole
Cuyp
Dadd
Dali
Dick
Dine
Dix
Doré
Dou
Dufy
Dyce
Dyck
Egg
Emin
Etty
Eyck
Feti
Ford
Fry
Fyt
Gabo
Gill
Goes
Gogh
Gore
Goya
Gris
Gros
Guys
Hals
Hemy
Herp
Holl
Home
Hone
Hook
Hunt
Jack
John
Jorn
Judd
Kahm
Kalf
Kane
Kent
Kerr
Klee
Lam
Lamb
Lear
Lely
Lin
Loos
Low
Maes
Marc
May
Miró
Mola
Mor
Nash
Neer
Opie
Post
Rego
Reni
Rops
Rosa
Rude
Shaw
Soto
Tura
Vos
Wall
Wan
Ward
West
Wit
Witz
Wols
Wood
Wren
Zorn
Andre
Antal
Appel
Bacon
Baily
Banks
Barry
Barye
Beale
Beuys
Blake
Bosch
Bouts
Brown
Burra
Campi
Caron
Carrà
Corot
Cossa
Costa
Cotes
Crane
Credi
Crome
Daddi
Dalou
Danby
Dance
David
Davis
Degas
Denis
Devis
Dossi
Dürer
Duvet
Ensor
Ernst
Fink
Foley
Freud
Frith
Gaddi
Gaudí
Gibbs
Giles
Gorky
Goyen
Grant
Grosz
Hayez
Henri
Heron
Hirst
Homer
Hooch
Horta
Itten
Johns
Jones
Kahlo
Keene
Kelly
Kitaj
Klein
Klimt
Kline
Koons
Kupka
Leech
Leger
LeVau
Lewis
Lhote
Lippi
Lotto
Louis
Lowry
Macke
Manet
Marin
Maris
Matta
Mauve
Metsu
Monet
Moore
Moses
Mucha
Munch
Myron
Nervi
Nolan
Nolde
Orley
Orpen
Oudry
Pater
Peale
Penck
Pilon
Piper
Polke
Pozzo
Prout
Puget
Pugin
Redon
Repin
Ricci
Riley
Rodin
Rosso
Runge
Scott
Serra
Shahn
Smith
Soane
Speed
Stael
Steen
Steer
Stone
Stoss
Sully
Tacca
Tobey
Tonks
Velde
Vicky
Vouet
Vries
Watts
Wiens
Wyatt
Wyeth
Yeats

5

Aalto
Abbey
Allan

6

Abbate
Abbott
Albers
Allori
Archer
Audran
Ayrton
Batoni
Benson
Benton
Berman
Bewick
Braque
Bratby
Breuer
Buffet
Butler
Calder
Callot
Campin
Canova
Casson
Catlin
Cibber
Claude
Clouet
Cooper
Copley
Cosway
Cotman
Cousin
Coypel
Cozens
De Wint
Demuth
Derain
Dobell
Dobson
Dongen
Duccio
Dughet
Eakins
Flavin
Floris
Foster
Fraser
Fuller
Fuseli
Gelder
Gellée
Gérard
Gibson
Gilman
Gilpin
Ginner
Giotto
Girtin
Gleyre
Goujon
Greuze
Guardi
Guston
Hassam
Haydon
Hayman
Hayter
Heckel

Heyden
Hilton
Hodler
Holzer
Hopper
Houdon
Hudson
Hughes
Huysum
Ingres
Inness
Isabey
Ivanov
Jagger
Kaprow
Kettle
Keyser
Kiefer
Knight
La Tour
Laroon
Lasdun
Lavery
Le Nain
Lebrun
Legros
Lescot
Longhi
Lurçat
Mabuse
Man Ray
Mander
Marini
Martin
Masson
Massys
Matsys
McEvoy
Menzel
Mesdac
Metsys
Millet
Momper
Moreau
Morley
Moroni
Morris
Mytens
Nauman
Newman
Noland
Oliver
Orozco
Ostade

Pacher
Palmer
Panini
Parler
Paxton
Piombo
Pisano
Potter
Rainer
Ramsay
Renoir
Ribera
Rigaud
Rivera
Rivers
Robbia
Robert
Romney
Rothko
Rubens
Rublev
Ruskin
Sacchi
Sandby
Savery
Scarfe
Scorel
Searle
Seurat
Signac
Simone
Sisley
Sluter
Spence
Stella
Strube
Stuart
Stubbs
Tadema
Tamayo
Tanguy
Tàpies
Tatlin
Tissot
Titian
Troost
Turner
Varley
Vasari
Vernet
Villon
Voysey
Walker
Wardle

Warhol
Weenix
Weyden
Wilkie
Wilson
Wilton
Wright
Zeuxis

7

Alberti
Allston
Apelles
Audubon
Balthus
Barlach
Barocci
Bassano
Bateman
Bazille
Beechey
Behrens
Bellini
Bellows
Berchem
Bermejo
Bernini
Böcklin
Boldini
Bomberg
Bonheur
Bonnard
Bordone
Boucher
Boydell
Brouwer
Calvert
Cassatt
Cellini
Cézanne
Chagall
Chardin
Chirico
Christo
Cimabue
Clausen
Clodion
Collins
Corinth
Cornell
Cortona
Courbet
Coustou
Cranach

Da Vinci
Dalziel
Daniell
Daumier
De Hooch
De Maria
Delorme
Delvaux
Downman
Duchamp
Edwards
El Greco
Epstein
Flaxman
Fontana
Fouquet
Francia
Francis
Gauguin
Gertler
Gibbons
Gilbert
Gillray
Girodet
Gleizes
Gozzoli
Gropius
Guarini
Harding
Hartley
Hartung
Hayward
Herrera
Herring
Hobbema
Hockney
Hofmann
Hogarth
Hokusai
Holbein
Holland
Hoppner
Ictinus
Indiana
Israëls
Jackson
Johnson
Klinger
Kneller
Koninck
Kooning
L'Enfant
Lambert
Lancret

Lemoyne
Lievens
Limburg
Linnell
Llander
Lutyens
Maclise
Maderna
Maillol
Mansart
Manzoni
Maratta
Maratti
Marinus
Martini
Mathieu
Matisse
Memlinc
Michaux
Millais
Morandi
Morisot
Morland
Morrice
Murillo
Nasmyth
Nattier
Neumann
O'Keeffe
Orcagna
Ordóñez
Pasmore
Peruzzi
Pevsner
Phidias
Phil May
Phillip
Picabia
Picasso
Pigalle
Pollock
Poussin
Poynter
Prud'hon
Quercia
Rackham
Raeburn
Raphael
Redouté
Ribalta
Richter
Riviere
Roberts
Rouault

Russell
Sargent
Schiele
Seghers
Shannon
Sheeler
Shepard
Sherman
Sickert
Snyders
Solomon
Soutine
Spencer
Stanley
Stevens
Teniers
Tenniel
Thomson
Tibaldi
Tiepolo
Twombly
Uccello
Ugolino
Utrillo
Valadon
Van Dyck
Van Eyck
Van Gogh
Vermeer
Vignola
Vischer
Watteau
Westall
Woolner
Wynants
Zadkine
Zoffany
Zuccaro

8

Aaltonen
Ammanati
Angelico
Armitage
Avercamp
Baselitz
Beckmann
Beerbohm
Bellotto
Boccioni
Bramante
Brancusi
Brangwyn
Bronzino

Brueghel
Callcott
Carpeaux
Carracci
Carriera
Castagno
Chambers
Chantrey
Chillida
Christus
Cipriani
Coysevox
Daubigny
Delaunay
Deverell
Doesburg
Drysdale
Dubuffet
Eastlake
Evergood
Falconet
Fielding
Filarete
Flandrin
Frampton
Garofalo
Ghiberti
Giordano
Girardon
Goltzius
González
Gossaert
Gottlieb
Gravelot
Guercino
Hamilton
Hepworth
Herkomer
Highmore
Hilliard
Hodgkins
Ibbetson
Il Sodoma
Jacobsen
Jan Steen
Janssens
John Opie
Jordaens
Jouvenet
Kaufmann
Kienholz
Kirchner
Kokoshka
Kollwitz

Lairesse
Landseer
Lawrence
Leighton
Leonardo
Lipchitz
Lombardo
Lysippus
Magritte
Malevich
Mantegna
Marshall
Masaccio
Meegeren
Molenaer
Mondrian
Montalba
Mostaert
Mulready
Munkácsy
Munnings
Nevelson
Nevinson
Niemeyer
Overbeck
Palladio
Paolozzi
Patenier
Paul Nash
Perugino
Piranesi
Pissarro
Pontormo
Redgrave
Reynolds
Richmond
Ricketts
Robinson
Rossetti
Rousseau
Rugendas
Ruisdael
Rysbrack
Saarinen
Salviati
Sassetta
Schalken
Schinkel
Severini
Solimena
Soufflot
Stothard
Sullivan
Terborch

Tinguely
Topolski
Tournier
Trumbull
Van Goyen
Van Steen
Vanbrugh
Vasarely
Veronese
Vigeland
Vlaminck
Vuillard
Wheatley
Whistler
Williams
Wolgemut
Woollett
Zurbarán

9

Altdorfer
Antonello
Bakhuyzen
Bartholdi
Beardsley
Biederman
Bierstadt
Bonington
Borromini
Botticini
Bourdelle
Bourgeois
Burgkmair
Caldecott
Canaletto
Carpaccio
Cavallini
Cockerell
Collinson
Constable
Cornelius
Correggio
de Kooning
Delacroix
Delaroche
Donatello
Duquesnoy
Elsheimer
Fabritius
Farington
Feininger
Feuerbach
Fragonard
Franz Hals

Friedrich
Géricault
Giorgione
Gonçalves
Greenaway
Grünewald
Guido Reni
Hawksmoor
Honthorst
Jawlensky
Kandinsky
Kauffmann
Kokoschka
Lancaster
Lanfranco
Lissitzky
Louis Wain
Margarito
Martorell
Mestrovic
Mondriaan
Nicholson
Noliekens
Northcote
Oldenburg
Oppenheim
Pechstein
Piazzetta
Pisanello
Pordenone
Ravilious
Reinhardt
Rembrandt
Remington
Rodchenko
Roubiliac
Sansovino
Schlemmer
Siqueiros
Stanfield
Steenwyck
Thornhill
Vallotton
Velázquez
Vitruvius
Whiteread
Wouwerman

10

Alma-Tadema
Archipenko
Arcimboldo
Baumeister
Berruguete

Botticelli
Bouguereau
Bourdichon
Breenbergh
Burlington
Burne-Jones
Caracciolo
Caravaggio
Champaigne
Chassériau
Coldstream
Giacometti
Goncharova
Heartfield
Heemskerck
Holman Hunt
Jan van Eyck
Kennington
La Fresnaye
Liebermann
Lorenzetti
Mackintosh
Meissonier
Modigliani
Moholy-Nagy
Motherwell
Ochtervelt
Orchardson
Pollaiuolo
Polyclitus
Praxiteles
Richardson
Rowlandson
Schongauer
Schwitters
Signorelli
Squarcione
Sutherland
Tintoretto
Torrigiano
Van de Velde
Van der Goes
Van der Meer
Verrocchio
Waterhouse
Ysenbrandt

11

Abercrombie
Apollodorus
Bartolommeo
Butterfield
Callicrates
Castiglione

Chodowiecki
Della Robbia
Domenichino
Fra Angelico
Gentileschi
Ghirlandaio
Giambologna
Gislebertus
Hondecoeter
Hoogstraten
Le Corbusier
Lloyd Wright
Margaritone
Maulbertsch
Nam June Pike
Poelenburgh
Polycleitus

Polykleitos
Primaticcio
Saint-Phalle
Terbrugghen
Thorvaldsen
Van Ruisdael
Vigée-Lebrun

12 AND OVER

Andrea del Sarto (14)
Baldovinetti (12)
Baldung Grien (12)
Brunelleschi (12)
Claude Gellée (12)
Claude Lorraine (14)
de Loutherbourg (14)
Fantin-Latour (12)

Fischer von Erlach (16)
Ford Madox Brown (14)
Gainsborough (12)
Gaudier-Brzeska (14)
Geertgen tot Sint Jans (19)
Gilbert and George (16)
Giulio Romano (12)
Grandma Moses (12)
Guido da Siena (12)
Heath Robinson (13)
Joos van Cleve (12)
Leonardo da Vinci (15)
Lichtenstein (12)
Lucas van Leyden (14)
Master of Flémalle (16)
Master of Moulins (15)

Michelangelo (12)
Mies van der Rohe (14)
Palma Vecchio (12)
Parmigianino (12)
Piero della Francesca (19)
Piero di Cosimo (13)
Puvis de Chavannes (16)
Rauschenberg (12)
Rembrandt van Ryn (15)
Sassoferrato (12)
Schmitt-Rotluff (14)
Toulouse-Lautrec (15)
Van der Weyden (12)
Van Ochtervelt (13)
Winterhalter (12)

Authors, poets, dramatists, etc.

3 AND 4

Agee, Amis, Asch, Ayer, Baum, Bede, Behn, Bell, Benn, Blok, Böll, Bolt, Buck, Cary, Coke, Cole, Cruz, Dahl, Dana, Dane, Day, Dell, Eco, Eden, Elia, Eyre, Ford, Foxe, Fry, Fyfe, Gay, Gide, Glyn, Gray, Grey, Gunn, Hall, Hart, Hay, Hogg, Home, Hood, Hook, Hope, Hugo, Hunt, King, Knox, Kyd, Lamb, Lang, Lear, Lee, Levi, Livy, Loos, Loti, Lyly, Lynd, Mais, Mann, Marx, Mill, More, Muir, Nash, Nin, Ovid, Owen, Paz, Poe, Pope, Pugh, Pym, Read, Reid, Rhys, Roth, Rowe, Ruck, Sade, Saki, Sala, Sand, Seth, Shaw, Sims, Snow, Sue, Tate, Urfé, Vane, Vega, Wain, Ward, Webb, West, Wood, Wren, Zola

5

Acton, Adams, Aesop, Agate, Aiken, Albee, Arden, Arlen, Auden, Babel, Bacon, Barry, Barth, Bates, Behan, Benda, Benét, Betti, Beyle, Blake, Bloom, Blunt, Bowen, Brink, Bruce, Burke, Burns, Byatt, Byron, Cable, Caine, Camus, Capek, Carew, Clare, Colum, Corvo, Couch, Crane, Croce, Dante, Darío, Defoe, Donne, Doyle, Dumas, Duras, Eliot, Ellis, Elyot, Evans, Field, Frame, Frayn, Freud, Frost, Genet, Gibbs, Gogol, Gorki, Gosse, Gower, Grass, Green, Greer, Grimm, Hardy, Harte, Hasek, Heine, Henry, Henty, Herzl, Hesse, Heyer, Homer, Hulme, Ibsen, Innes, Irwin, James, Jarry, Jeans, Jones, Joyce, Kafka, Keats, Keith, Kesey, Keyte, Lewis, Locke, Lodge, Logue

141

Lorca	Tynan	Borges	Fuller	Motion	Thrale
Lowry	Tzara	Borrow	George	Munthe	Toller
Lucan	Udall	Braine	Gibbon	Murray	Traven
Lucas	Varro	Brecht	Godwin	Musset	Trevor
Marot	Verne	Breton	Goethe	Necker	Updike
Marsh	Vidal	Bridie	Gordon	Neruda	Uttley
Mason	Vigny	Brontë	Graeme	Nerval	Valéry
Milne	Waley	Brooke	Graves	Nesbit	Villon
Moore	Walsh	Brophy	Greene	O. Henry	Virgil
Murry	Waugh	Browne	Hallam	O'Brien	Walker
Musil	Wells	Bryant	Hamsun	O'Casey	Waller
Noyes	Welty	Buchan	Harris	Ogilvy	Walton
Odets	White	Bunyan	Haynes	O'Neill	Warren
O'Dowd	Wilde	Burney	Heaney	Orwell	Watson
O'Hara	Wolfe	Burton	Heller	Parker	Werfel
Opitz	Woolf	Butler	Hemans	Petöfi	Wesker
Orczy	Wyatt	Caesar	Hesiod	Pindar	Weyman
Orton	Yeats	Camões	Hilton	Pinero	Wilcox
Otway	Yonge	Capote	Hobbes	Pinter	Wilder
Ouida	Young	Carter	Holmes	Piozzi	Wilson
Paine	Zweig	Cather	Holtby	Plumer	Wotton
Pater		Cavafy	Horace	Porter	Wright
Paton	**6**	Céline	Howitt	Potter	
Peake		Chopin	Hughes	Powell	**7**
Peele	Adamov	Cibber	Ian Hay	Proust	
Péguy	Adcock	Cicero	Ibañez	Racine	Abelard
Pepys	Alcott	Clarke	Irving	Rohmer	Addison
Perse	Aldiss	Clough	Jacobs	Rowley	Aelfric
Plath	Algren	Conrad	Jerome	Runyon	Alarcón
Plato	Ambler	Cooper	Jonson	Ruskin	Alfieri
Pliny	Andric	Coward	Kaiser	Sandys	Angelou
Pound	Anstey	Cowley	Keller	Sapper	Anouilh
Powys	Aragon	Cowper	Kleist	Sappho	Aquinas
Queen	Arnold	Crabbe	Laclos	Sardou	Ariosto
Raine	Ascham	Cronin	Landor	Sartre	Balchin
Reade	Asimov	Darwin	Lao-Tse	Savage	Baldwin
Rilke	Atwood	Daudet	Larkin	Sayers	Ballard
Rolfe	Aubrey	Davies	Lawler	Scribe	Beckett
Sagan	Austen	Dekker	Lawson	Seneca	Beddoes
Scott	Azorín	Dowson	Le Fanu	Sidney	Beeding
Seton	Balzac	Dryden	Le Sage	Silone	Belasco
Shute	Barham	Dunbar	London	Singer	Bennett
Smart	Baroja	Duncan	Lowell	Sontag	Bentham
Smith	Barrès	Empson	Ludwig	Steele	Bentley
Spark	Barrie	Ennius	Lytton	Sterne	Birrell
Staël	Beeton	Ervine	Mailer	Stoker	Blunden
Stark	Bellay	Evelyn	Malozy	Storey	Boileau
Stein	Belloc	Fichte	Mannin	Strabo	Boswell
Stowe	Bellow	Fowles	Martyn	Surrey	Bridges
Swift	Benson	France	Miller	Symons	Brodsky
Synge	Besant	Frazer	Milton	Tagore	Büchner
Taine	Bierce	Frisch	Morgan	Taylor	Bunting
Tasso	Binyon	Froude	Mörike	Thomas	Burgess
Twain	Blixen	Fugard	Morris	Thorne	Caedmon
	Blyton				Calvino

Camoens
Carlyle
Carroll
Chapman
Chaucer
Cheever
Chekhov
Chénier
Cheyney
Claudel
Clayton
Clemens
Cobbett
Cocteau
Coetzee
Colette
Collins
Corelli
Crashaw
Da Ponte
Deeping
Delaney
Dickens
Diderot
Dinesen
Dodgson
Doughty
Douglas
Drabble
Drayton
Dreiser
Duhamel
Dunsany
Durrell
Emerson
Erasmus
Feydeau
Firbank
Flecker
Fleming
Fontane
Forster
Forsyth
Foscolo
Frankau
Freeman
Fuentes
Galileo
Gallico
Gardner
Garnett
Gaskell
Gautier
Gilbert

Gissing
Glossop
Golding
Goldoni
Haggard
Hakluyt
Hammett
Hartley
Hazlitt
Hellman
Herbert
Herrick
Heywood
Hichens
Hocking
Hopkins
Housman
Howells
Ibn Ezra
Ionesco
Jiménez
Johnson
Juvenal
Kastner
Kaufman
Kerouac
Kinross
Kipling
Kundera
Lardner
Laxness
Le Carré
Le Queux
Leacock
Lehmann
Lessing
Lindsay
Machaut
Mahfouz
Malamud
Malraux
Manning
Manzoni
Marlowe
Marquez
Marryat
Marston
Martial
Marvell
Maugham
Mauriac
Maurois
Maurras
Mencken

Mérimée
Meynell
Mishima
Mistral
Mitford
Molière
Montagu
Moravia
Murdoch
Nabokov
Naevius
Naipaul
Narayan
Newbolt
Novalis
O'Connor
Ogilvie
Osborne
Patmore
Peacock
Plautus
Prévert
Pushkin
Pynchon
Queneau
Ransome
Régnier
Renault
Rendell
Richler
Richter
Rimbaud
Rolland
Romains
Ronsard
Rostand
Rushdie
Rushkin
Russell
Sadleir
Sarasin
Saroyan
Sassoon
Scarron
Seferis
Service
Shaffer
Shelley
Simenon
Simonov
Sitwell
Skelton
Southey
Soyinka

Spencer
Spender
Spenser
Spinoza
Stevens
Strauss
Surtees
Tacitus
Terence
Thomson
Thoreau
Thurber
Tolkien
Tolstoy
Tutuola
Vaughan
Vicente
Wallace
Walpole
Webster
Wharton
Whitman

8

Anacreon
Andersen
Anderson
Andreyev
Apuleius
Asturias
Aumonier
Banville
Barbusse
Beaumont
Beauvoir
Beckford
Beerbohm
Benchley
Béranger
Bernanos
Berryman
Betjeman
Bjørnson
Bradbury
Brentano
Brookner
Browning
Bushnell
Calderón
Campbell
Cartland
Catullus
Chambers
Chandler

Christie
Congreve
Conquest
Constant
Crichton
Crockett
Crompton
Cummings
Davenant
Day Lewis
De la Mare
De Musset
Deighton
Disraeli
Donleavy
Drummond
Du Bellay
Etherege
Farquhar
Faulkner
Fielding
Firdausi
Flaubert
Fletcher
Fontaine
Forester
Ginsberg
Goncourt
Gordimer
Grierson
Hamilton
Han Suyin
Heinlein
Hochhuth
Hoffmann
Huysmans
Ishiguro
Jean Paul
Keneally
Kingsley
Koestler
Kotzebue
Laforgue
Lagerlöf
Langland
Lawrence
Leopardi
Lonsdale
Lovelace
Macaulay
MacNeice
Malherbe
Mallarmé
McCarthy

Melville
Menander
Meredith
Merriman
Michelet
Mitchell
Morrison
Mortimer
Nekrasov
Oliphant
Palgrave
Pattison
Perelman
Perrault
Petrarch
Plutarch
Proudhon
Quennell
Rabelais
Radiguet
Rattigan
Remarque
Richards
Rossetti
Rousseau
Sabatini
Salinger
Sandburg
Sarraute
Schiller
Schlegel
Shadwell
Sheridan
Sillitoe
Sinclair
Smollett
Spillane
Stendhal
Stoppard
Strachey
Sturgess
Suckling
Tennyson
Thompson
Tibullus
Tourneur
Traherne
Trilling
Trollope
Turgenev
Vanbrugh
Verlaine
Voltaire
Vonnegut

Wedekind
Wheatley
Whittier
Williams
Xenophon
Zane Grey
Zangwill

9

Adam Smith
Aeschylus
Ainsworth
Akhmatova
Aldington
Alec Waugh
Allingham
Anita Loos
Ayckbourn
Ben Jonson
Blackmore
Blackwood
Boccaccio
Bottomley
Bret Harte
Burroughs
Cervantes
Charteris
Churchill
Coleridge
Corneille
D'Annunzio
De la Roche
De Quincey
Descartes
Dickinson
Doolittle
Dos Passos
Du Maurier
Dudintsev
Eddington
Edgeworth
Ehrenberg
Euripides
Froissart
Giraudoux
Goldsmith
Goncharov
Greenwood
Hall Caine
Hauptmann
Hawthorne
Heidegger
Hemingway
Herodotus

Highsmith
Hölderlin
Isherwood
Jefferies
Kaye-Smith
Klopstock
La Bruyère
La Fayette
Lamartine
Lampedusa
Leigh Hunt
Lermontov
Linklater
Llewellyn
Lomonosov
Lord Byron
Lucretius
Mackenzie
Macrobius
Malaparte
Mansfield
Mark Twain
Martineau
Masefield
Massinger
McCullers
Middleton
Mitchison
Montaigne
O'Flaherty
Pasternak
Priestley
Pritchett
Quasimodo
Radcliffe
Robertson
Rochester
Sackville
Sax Rohmer
Schreiner
Shenstone
Sholokhov
Sophocles
Steinbeck
Stevenson
Sturluson
Suetonius
Swinburne
Thackeray
Tomlinson
Trevelyan
Turgeniev
Van Druton
Verhaeren

Wodehouse
Wycherley
Yourcenar

10

Bainbridge
Ballantyne
Baudelaire
Brett Young
Chatterton
Chesterton
Conan Doyle
Don Marquis
Dostoevsky
Drinkwater
Dürrenmatt
Elinor Glyn
Emil Ludwig
Fitzgerald
Galsworthy
Hungerford
Hutchinson
Jack London
Jane Austen
John Buchan
Jules Verne
La Fontaine
Lagerkvist
Longfellow
Lope de Vega
Lord Lytton
MacDiarmid
Mandelstam
Maupassant
Mayakovsky
McGonagall
Mickiewicz
Mrs. Gaskell
Noël Coward
Oscar Wilde
Pierre Loti
Pirandello
Propertius
Pryce-Jones
Quintilian
Richardson
Ronaldshay
Saint-Simon
Saintsbury
Schnitzler
Sean O'Casey
Strindberg
Tarkington
Theocritus

Thucydides
Van der Post
Victor Hugo
Williamson
Wordsworth

11

Abbé Prévost
Apollinaire
Callimachus
Demosthenes
Dostoievski
García Lorca
Grillparzer
Kazantzakis
Kierkegaard
Lautréamont
Maeterlinck
Montesquieu
Montherlant
Omar Khayyam
Pérez Galdós
Ravenscroft
Sainte-Beuve
Shakespeare
Sienkiewicz
Tocqueville
Vargas Llosa
Watts-Dunton
Yevtushenko

12

Aristophanes
Beaumarchais
Blasco Ibañez
Bulwer Lytton
Chesterfield
De Selincourt
Feuchtwanger
Hans Andersen
Hergesheimer
Hofmannstahl
López de Ayala
Martin du Gard
Matthew Paris
Quiller-Couch
Rider Haggard
Robbe-Grillet
Rose Macaulay
Saint-Exupéry
Solzhenitsyn
Storm Jameson
Wittgenstein
Wyndham Lewis

13

Andrew Marvell
Arnold Bennett
Baroness Orczy
Bertran de Born
Cecil Day Lewis
Chateaubriand
Edgar Allan Poe
Ford Madox Ford
Hilaire Belloc
Jeffrey Farnol

Jerome K. Jerome
Marie de France
Sackville-West
Sinclair Lewis
Stacy Aumonier
Upton Sinclair
Wilkie Collins

14

Agatha Christie
Compton-Burnett
Eden Phillpotts

Leconte de Lisle
Marcus Aurelius
Middleton Murry
Oehlenschläger
Rafael Sabatini
Rudyard Kipling
Warwick Deeping
Wollstonecraft

15 AND 16

Booth Tarkington (15)
Chrétien de Troyes (16)
Christine de Pisan (16)
Granville Barker (15)
La Rochefoucauld (15)
Millington Synge (15)
Pierre de Ronsard (15)
Somerset Maugham
  (15)
Washington Irving (16)

Building and architecture

2 AND 3	cage	jamb	sash	alley	facet
bar	cell	keep	seat	ambry	facia
bay	club	khan	shed	ancon	fence
cot	coin	kiln	shop	annex	flats
den	cote	kirk	sill	arena	floor
hip	cove	lath	silo	arris	flush
hut	cowl	lift	sink	atlas	flute
inn	crib	lock	site	attic	folly
kip	cusp	loft	slab	aulic	forum
loo	cyma	mart	slat	berth	fosse
mew	dado	maze	slum	block	foyer
pa	dais	mews	span	booth	gable
pub	digs	mill	stay	bothy	glass
pug	dike	mint	step	bower	glaze
rib	dome	moat	stoa	brace	glyph
spa	door	mole	stud	brick	grate
sty	drip	nave	tent	broch	griff
tie	drum	nook	term	build	groin
w.c.	eave	oast	tige	built	grout
won	exit	ogee	tile	cabin	gully
4	face	oven	toft	cella	gutta
	fane	pale	tomb	cheek	harem
adit	farm	pane	tope	choir	hatch
apse	flag	pave	town	close	helix
arch	flat	pier	trap	coign	hinge
area	flue	pile	vane	compo	hoist
balk	foil	plan	wall	congé	hotel
bank	fort	post	weir	court	house
barn	foss	quad	well	crypt	hovel
base	fret	quay	wing	dairy	hydro
bead	gaol	rail	xyst	depot	igloo
beam	gate	ramp	yard	domed	ingle
bema	grot	raze	**5**	Doric	Ionic
berm	haha	reed		drain	jetty
boss	hail	rink	abbey	drive	joint
byre	herm	roof	adobe	eaves	joist
café	home	room	agora	entry	jutty
	jail	ruin	aisle	erect	kiosk

kraal	stand	canopy	friary	mud hut
latch	stele	casino	frieze	museum
ledge	steps	castle	gablet	mutule
level	stile	cellar	garage	niched
lobby	stoep	cement	garret	Norman
lodge	stone	châlet	gazebo	office
manor	store	chapel	ghetto	outlet
manse	stove	church	girder	pagoda
mitre	stria	cilery	glazed	palace
motel	strut	cimbia	godown	paling
newel	study	cinema	Gothic	pantry
niche	stupa	cintre	gradin	parget
ogive	suite	circus	grange	parvis
order	talon	closet	griffe	paving
oriel	tepee	coffer	grille	perron
ovolo	thorp	coigne	grotto	pharos
paned	tiled	column	ground	piazza
panel	torii	concha	groyne	picket
patio	torus	coping	gutter	pigsty
plank	tower	corbel	hangar	pillar
plaza	tread	cordon	header	plinth
porch	truss	corona	hearth	podium
pound	Tudor	course	hostel	portal
putty	vault	coving	impost	prefab
pylon	villa	cranny	insula	priory
quirk	wharf	crèche	inwall	prison
quoin	works	crenel	Ionian	purlin
rails		cupola	kennel	putlog
ranch	**6**	dagoba	ladder	quarry
range		débris	lancet	rabbet
revet	abacus	dentil	larder	rafter
ridge	access	design	lean-to	rancho
riser	adytum	donjon	lierne	recess
Roman	alcove	dormer	lintel	refuge
salon	annexe	dosser	listel	reglet
scape	arbour	drains	lock-up	relief
serai	arcade	dry rot	locker	rococo
sewer	ashlar	dug-out	log-hut	rubble
shack	ashler	duplex	loggia	rustic
shaft	asylum	durbar	lounge	saloon
shelf	atrium	ecurie	louver	school
shell	aviary	Empire	louvre	scotia
slate	awning	enwall	lyceum	scroll
slatt	bagnio	estate	mantel	shanty
slums	bakery	exedra	marble	smithy
socle	barrow	façade	market	soffit
solar	batten	facing	metope	spence
spire	bedsit	fascia	mihrab	square
splay	belfry	fillet	mitred	stable
stack	billet	finial	module	stairs
stage	bistro	flèche	morgue	storey
stair	bourse	florid	mortar	stucco
stake	bricks	fluted	mosaic	studio
stall	bridge	fresco	mosque	suburb
	camera			

subway	beading	eustyle	mullion	shore up
taenia	bedroom	factory	munnion	shoring
tarsia	boudoir	fencing	narthex	shutter
tavern	boxroom	festoon	necking	slating
temple	bracket	fitment	new town	stadium
thatch	brewery	fixture	nogging	staging
tholos	builder	fluting	nunnery	station
thorpe	built-in	foundry	nursery	steeple
tiling	bulwark	gadroon	obelisk	storied
timber	butlery	galilee	offices	surgery
toilet	buttery	gallery	oratory	systyle
tolsey	cabaret	gateway	ossuary	tambour
torsel	cabinet	godroon	outwork	tannery
trench	calotte	gradine	paddock	taproom
trough	canteen	granary	palazzo	tayalot
tunnel	capitol	grating	pantile	tegular
turret	carving	Grecian	parapet	telamon
Tuscan	cassino	groined	parlour	terrace
unroof	cavetto	grounds	parquet	theatre
untile	ceiling	hallway	passage	thermae
vallum	chamber	hay loft	pendant	tie-beam
veneer	chancel	hip roof	pension	tracery
vestry	chantry	hospice	pergola	tracing
vihara	chapter	housing	piggery	transom
volute	château	hydrant	pillbox	trefoil
wattle	chevron	impasto	plaster	trellis
wicket	chimney	Islamic	portico	tumulus
wigwam	cistern	jib door	postern	unpaved
window	citadel	kennels	pugging	untiled
zareba	cob wall	keyhole	pyramid	upright
zenana	college	kitchen	quarrel	varnish
zoning	conduit	knocker	quarrel	vaulted
	contour	kremlin	railing	veranda
7	convent	lagging	rampart	viaduct
	cornice	landing	rebuild	village
academy	cortile	lantern	rectory	voluted
acroter	cottage	lathing	reeding	
air duct	crocket	lattice	rejoint	**8**
alcazar	cubicle	laundry	repairs	
almonry	culvert	lazaret	reredos	abat-jour
ancones	curtain	library	respond	abat-voix
annulet	De Stijl	lodging	rockery	abattoir
arcaded	deanery	low-rise	roofing	abutment
archlet	demesne	lunette	rooftop	acanthus
archway	dinette	mansard	rosette	air-drain
armoury	domical	mansion	rostrum	airtight
arsenal	doorway	marquee	rotunda	anteroom
asphalt	dovecot	masonry	sanctum	anthemion
astylar	dry wall	minaret	sawmill	apophyge
atelier	dungeon	minster	sea-wall	approach
balcony	echinus	moellon	section	aquarium
baroque	edifice	Moorish	shebeen	aqueduct
barrack	embassy	Mudéjar	shelter	arboured
bastion	entasis	mudsill	shelves	astragal
Bauhaus			shingle	atheneum

back door	doghouse	lathwork	sale room	well hole
backroom	dogtooth	lavatory	scaffold	well room
badhouse	domicile	legation	scullery	windmill
baguette	door jamb	lichgate	seminary	windowed
ballroom	door nail	lodgings	seraglio	woodwork
baluster	doorpost	log cabin	showroom	woodworm
banderol	doorsill	loghouse	shutters	workroom
banister	doorstep	lychgate	side door	workshop
bannerol	dovecote	madhouse	skewback	ziggurat
barbican	dovetail	magazine	skirting	
basement	dowel pin	martello	skylight	**9**
basilica	drainage	medieval	slop-shop	acropolis
bathroom	dwelling	memorial	smeltery	acroteria
bed-sitter	Egyptian	monolith	snack bar	aerodrome
brattice	elevator	monument	snuggery	alignment
building	emporium	Moresque	soil pipe	almshouse
bulkhead	entrance	mortuary	solarium	apartment
bungalow	entresol	moulding	spandrel	arabesque
buttress	epistyle	newsroom	spanroof	architect
caliduct	erection	ogee arch	stabling	archivolt
canephor	espalier	open-plan	stairway	archstone
capstone	excavate	openwork	stockade	art school
caryatid	fanlight	orangery	storeyed	ashlaring
casement	fireclay	outhouse	stuccoed	athenaeum
catacomb	fireside	overhang	subtopia	bakehouse
causeway	flagging	palisade	suburbia	banderole
cenotaph	flashing	panelled	sudatory	bas-relief
centring	flat roof	pantheon	sun-porch	bay window
cesspool	flooring	parclose	sun-proof	beadhouse
chapiter	fortress	parterre	taphouse	bell gable
chaptrel	freehold	pavement	tectonic	bell tower
cincture	fretwork	pavilion	tenement	belvedere
cloister	frontage	pedestal	terminal	blueprint
clubroom	fusarole	pediment	terminus	boathouse
cockloft	gable end	pilaster	terraced	bolection
coliseum	gargoyle	pinnacle	terminus	bow window
colossal	gatepost	plashing	toll-gate	box girder
comptoir	geodesic	platform	top floor	brick kiln
concrete	grillage	playroom	town hall	brickwork
contract	grouting	plumbing	transept	brutalist
corn loft	hacienda	pointing	trap door	bunkhouse
corridor	handrail	pothouse	traverse	butt joint
cow house	hen house	property	triglyph	Byzantine
crescent	high-rise	propylon	tympanum	cafeteria
cromlech	hoarding	quarters	underpin	calcimine
cross-tie	hospital	refinery	upstairs	campanile
crow step	hostelry	registry	vaulting	cartouche
cupboard	hothouse	rocaille	verandah	cathedral
curb roof	housetop	rockwork	vicarage	ceilinged
cymatium	ice house	rood loft	vignette	cellarage
dancette	intrados	roof tree	voussoir	centering
darkroom	jalousie	ropewalk	wainscot	chop house
decorate	keystone	sacristy	wardroom	clapboard
detached	kingpost	sail-loft	waxworks	classical

claustral
cloakroom
clubhouse
coalhouse
cofferdam
colonnade
colosseum
composite
construct
consulate
converted
copestone
courtyard
cross-beam
crown post
cubby hole
cubiculum
Cyclopean
cyma recta
decastyle
distemper
door frame
door panel
dormitory
dosshouse
dowelling
drainpipe
dripstone
dust stove
earthwork
elevation
embrasure
episenium
escalator
esplanade
estaminet
excavator
extension
farmhouse
file-drain
firebrick
fireplace
flagstone
flashings
floor plan
flophouse
floriated
foliation
forecourt
framework
front door
front room
gable roof
gatehouse

glory hole
gravel pit
green belt
groundsel
guardroom
guestroom
guildhall
guilloche
gymnasium
headpiece
headstone
hermitage
homestead
hood mould
houseboat
hypethral
hypocaust
hypostyle
infirmary
inglenook
inner city
ironworks
kerbstone
labyrinth
landscape
latticing
lazaretto
leasehold
letterbox
lift-shaft
linenfold
Mannerist
mausoleum
medallion
mezzanine
mock Tudor
modernist
modillion
monastery
Mozarabic
music hall
music room
neo-Gothic
Nissen hut
octastyle
orphanage
oubliette
outer door
outer gate
outskirts
paintwork
palladian
panelling
pargeting

parquetry
parsonage
parthenon
partition
party wall
pay office
penthouse
peristyle
pillarbox
playhouse
pleasance
pontlevis
poorhouse
pressroom
prize ring
promenade
quicklime
rail-fence
rainproof
reception
refectory
rendering
reservoir
residence
residency
revetment
ridgepole
ring-fence
roadhouse
roughcast
rusticate
sallyport
scagliola
scantling
scrimshaw
sectional
sepulchre
shopfront
slate roof
spare room
staircase
stanchion
stateroom
stillroom
stinktrap
stockroom
stonewall
stonework
storeroom
stretcher
structure
stylobate
sun-lounge
swing door

synagogue
tablature
tenements
threshold
tollbooth
tollhouse
tower-room
townhouse
treillage
triforium
turf-house
turnstile
undermine
underprop
vestibule
wallpaper
wall-plate
warehouse
wastepipe
watertank
whitewash
window box
windproof
windtight
wine vault
workhouse

10

antechapel
arc-boutant
arched roof
architrave
art gallery
auditorium
backstairs
ballflower
balustered
balustrade
bargeboard
bedchamber
bell-turret
brick earth
brick-built
brownfield
cantilever
catafalque
chimney cap
chimneypot
cinquefoil
clerestory
clock tower
coachhouse
coal cellar
coffee shop

common room
conversion
corbie step
Corinthian
court house
covered way
crenulated
cross-aisle
crown glass
crownpiece
damp-course
decoration
decorative
depository
dining hall
dining room
dispensary
distillery
doll's house
dome-shaped
Doric order
double lock
double-hung
dowel joint
drawbridge
drying room
Dutch tiles
earth house
earthworks
egg and dart
embankment
engine-room
excavation
facia panel
fan tracery
fire escape
first floor
fives court
flamboyant
flint glass
flock paper
footbridge
foundation
functional
garden city
garden wall
glasshouse
glebe house
grandstand
granny flat
Greek cross
greenfield
greenhouse
ground plan

groundsill
groundwork
guardhouse
habitation
hammer beam
hipped roof
hippodrome
hunting box
hypaethral
intramural
Ionic order
jerry-built
label mould
laboratory
lady chapel
lancet arch
Latin cross
lazar-house
lighthouse
living room
lumber-room
luxury flat
maisonette
manor house
manteltree
market town
mitre joint
necropolis
Norman arch
opera house
overmantel
panopticon
passageway
pebble dash
persiennes
pied-à-terre
plastering
plate glass
polychromy
Portakabin
portcullis
post office
power-house
proportion
propylaeum
proscenium
pycnostyle
quadrangle
quatrefoil
ranch house
real estate
repointing
repository
restaurant

retrochoir
ribbed arch
road bridge
robing-room
rock-temple
Romanesque
roof garden
rose garden
rose window
round tower
roundhouse
rubblework
rumpus room
sanatorium
sanitarium
settlement
sink estate
skew bridge
skyscraper
slaked lime
smokestack
split level
state house
storehouse
street door
stronghold
structural
sun parlour
terracotta
tetrastyle
tiring-room
tower block
trust house
Tudor style
tumbledown
undercroft
university
unoccupied
untenanted
varnishing
ventilator
vernacular
vestry room
watch-house
watch-tower
water-tower
way-station
wicket gate
window sash
windscreen
wine-cellar

11

antechamber
barge couple
barge course
barrel vault
caravansary
Carolingian
castellated
cementation
chain-bridge
cinquecento
coffee house
columbarium
compartment
concert hall
coping stone
corbel steps
cornerstone
counterfort
country seat
crazy paving
crenellated
curtail step
cyma reversa
distempered
door knocker
dovetailing
drawing room
dress circle
eating house
entablature
fan vaulting
fingerplate
florid style
foundations
gambrel roof
Graeco-Roman
ground floor
hearthstone
ichnography
kitchenette
lattice work
laundry room
lecture room
linen closet
load-bearing
louver-board
louvre-board
machicoulis
mansard roof
mantelpiece
mantelshelf
manufactory
market-cross

masonry arch
morning room
observatory
oeil-de-boeuf
office block
oriel window
outbuilding
paving stone
picket fence
picture rail
plasterwork
postern gate
public house
reading room
reconstruct
Renaissance
residential
restoration
Roman cement
roofing felt
sarcophagus
scaffolding
service lift
shooting box
sitting room
smoking room
stately home
stringboard
sub-contract
summerhouse
tessellated
tiled hearth
trelliswork
trussed beam
Turkish bath
Tuscan order
undercoated
unfurnished
uninhabited
urban sprawl
utility room
ventilation
wainscoting
waiting room
war memorial
water closet
water supply
weathercock
whitewashed
window frame
window glass
window ledge
wrought iron

12

amphitheatre
architecture
assembly hall
assembly room
auction rooms
billiard room
building line
building site
caravanserai
chapel of rest
chapter house
chimney shaft
chimney stack
chimneypiece
conservatory
construction
country house
covered court
dividing wall
dormer window
double-glazed
draught-proof
dressing-room
Early English
egg and anchor
egg and tongue
entrance hall
fluted column
folding doors
french window
frontispiece
garden suburb
geodesic dome
guest chamber
half-timbered
hôtel de ville
hunting lodge
inner sanctum
Ionian column
kitchen range
labour-saving
lake dwelling
lancet window
lightning-rod
lock-up garage
lodging house
louvre window
machicolated
main entrance
mansion house

meeting house
mission house
neoclassical
pantechnicon
parquet floor
penitentiary
plasterboard
power station
prefabricate
privy chamber
Purbeck stone
purpose-built
quattrocento
retiring room
rooming house
semi-detached
spiral stairs
stained glass
string course
substruction
substructure
subterranean
swinging post
thatched roof
town planning
tracing cloth
tracing linen
tracing paper
transitional
underpinning
unmodernized
unornamental
unornamented
untenantable
unventilated
urban renewal
wainscotting
weatherboard
weatherproof
winter garden

13

accommodation
amphiprostyle
ancient lights
architectonic
architectural
assembly rooms
back staircase
boarding house
breakfast room
building block

butler's pantry
chimney corner
compass window
contabulation
council estate
coursing joint
dormitory town
double glazing
Dutch clinkers
dwelling house
dwelling place
emergency exit
encaustic tile
entrance lobby
establishment
ferro-concrete
fire-resistant
fitted kitchen
floodlighting
furnished flat
Grecian temple
housing estate
lattice window
machicolation
martello tower
master builder
Norman doorway
owner-occupied
palais de danse
Perpendicular
picture window
Portland stone
postmodernism
prefabricated
public library
Purbeck marble
revolving door
satellite town
shooting lodge
skirting board
soundproofing
specification
sub-contractor
trading estate
triumphal arch
uninhabitable
vaulting shaft
venetian blind
vinyl emulsion
wattle and daub

14

airing cupboard
apartment house
architectonics
banqueting hall
bedsitting room
catherine wheel
central heating
consulting room
country cottage
drying cupboard
filling station
flying buttress
funeral parlour
lath and plaster
listed building
mezzanine floor
office building
picture gallery
Portland cement
powder magazine
reconstruction
slaughterhouse
superstructure
threshing floor
venetian window

15

air conditioning
clustered column
community centre
damp-proof course
discharging arch
dormitory suburb
feather-boarding
foundation stone
hydraulic cement
pleasure gardens
reception centre
refreshment room
spiral staircase
state apartments
unfurnished flat
Vitruvian scroll
weatherboarding
withdrawing room

Characters in literature

Some characters from **Ben Jonson**, **Charlotte Brontë**, **Lord Byron**, **Chaucer**, and **Congreve**. List of works from which the following characters are taken, with reference numbers.

Ben Jonson

Ref. No.	Title	
1.	Alchemist, The	(12 letters)
2.	Bartholomew Fayre	(16 letters)
3.	Cynthia's Revels	(14 letters)
4.	Devil is an Ass, The	(15 letters)
5.	Epicoene	(8 letters)
6.	Every Man in his Humour	(19 letters)
7.	Every Man out of his Humour	(22 letters)
8.	Magnetick Lady, The	(16 letters)
9.	New Inn, The	(9 letters)
10.	Poetaster, The	(12 letters)
11.	Sad Shepherd, The	(14 letters)
12.	Sejanus	(7 letters)
13.	Volpone	(7 letters)
14.	(Various)	

Lord Byron

Ref. No.	Title	
15.	Don Juan	(7 letters)
16.	(Various)	

Charlotte Brontë

17.	Jane Eyre	(8 letters)
18.	Professor, The	(12 letters)
19.	Shirley	(7 letters)
20.	Villette	(8 letters)

Chaucer (Geoffrey)

21.	Canterbury Tales	(15 letters)

Congreve (William)

22.	Double Dealer, The	(15 letters)
23.	Love for Love	(11 letters)
24.	Mourning Bride, The	(16 letters)
25.	Old Bachelor, The	(14 letters)
26.	Way of the World, The	(16 letters)

Note: The numbers in brackets indicate *the works* in which the characters appear

2 AND 3

Alp (16)
Anah (16)
Azo (16)
Baba (15)
Beck (20)
Busy (2)
Cash (6)
Cave (19)
Cob (6)
Cos (3)
Daw (5)
Dent (17)
Dudu (15)
Echo (3)
Ella (21)
Eyre (17)
Face (1)
Fly (9)
Gale (19)
Hall (19)
Hogg (19)
Home (20)
Hugo (16)
Inez (15)
Lara (16)
Lucy (25)
May (21)
Nero (12)
Otho (16)
Paul (18, 20)
Prue (23)
Pug (4)
Raby (15)
Rud (17)
Seyd (16)
Wasp (1)
Whit (2)
Zara (24)

5

Abbot (17)
Aesop (10)
Alken (11)
Arete (3)
Asper (7)
Beppo (16)
Betty (25)
Brisk (7, 22)
Burns (17)
Celia (13)
Chloe (10)
Cotta (12)
Cupid (3)
Donne (19)
Frail (23)
Froth (22)
Gabor (16)
Hedon (3)
Jenny (23)
Julia (10)
Kaled (16)
Laura (16)
Leila (15, 16)
Lloyd (17)
Lolah (15)
Lorel (11)
Lovel (9)
Lupus (10)
Manly (4)
Mason (17)
Minos (10)
Mitis (7)
Moore (19)
Moria (3)
Morus (3)
Mosca (13)
Neuha (16)
Osman (24)
Poole (17)
Pryor (19)
Roger (21)
Rufus (12)
Scott (19)
Selim (16)
Shift (7)
Snowe (20)
Steno (16)
Surly (1)
Tipto (9)
Topas (21)
Ulric (16)
Varro (12)
Waspe (2)
Whipp (19)
Yorke (19)

6

Albius (10)
Alison (21)
Arcite (21)
Arnold (16)
Asotus (3)
Bessie (17)
Caesar (10)
Canace (21)
Common (1)
Conrad (16)
Crites (3)
Damian (21)
Dapper (1)
Deliro (7)
Drusus (12)
Earine (11)
Emilia (21)
Ferret (9)
Foible (9)
Formal (6)
Gallus (10)
Gelaia (3)
Giaour (The) (16)

Graham (20)
Haidee (15)
Harold (16)
Hassan (16)
Horace (10)
Jaques (14)
Jeremy (23)
Kitely (6)
Lambro (15)
Legend (23)
Luscus (10)
Malone (19)
Mammon (1)
Marina (16)
Marino (16)
Maxime (21)
Medora (16)
Morose (5)
Myrrha (16)
Opsius (12)
Overdo (2)
Pliant (1)
Plyant (22)
Polish (8)
Reuter (18)
Setter (25)
Silvia (25)
Simkin (21)
St. John (Mr.) (17)
Subtle (1)
Symkin (21)
Tartar (dog) (19)
Tattle (23)
Temple (17)
Thopas (21)
Virgil (10)
Walter (21)
Werner (16)
Wittol (25)

7

Abolson (21)
Almeria (24)
Anaides (3)
Apicata (12)
Arbaces (16)
Astarte 16)
Azaziel (16)
Baillie (21)
Beleses (16)
Belinda (25)
Belmour (25)
Bertram (16)
Bobadil (6)

Boultby (19)
Bretton (20)
Buckram (23)
Buffone (7)
Clement (6)
Corvino (13)
Cutting (2)
Cynthia (3, 22)
Don José (15)
Don Juan (15)
Dorigen (21)
Drugger (14)
Emanuel (20)
Eudenus (12)
Eugenie (5)
Ezzelin (16)
Fainall (26)
Fairfax (17)
Faliero (16)
Foscari (16)
Fungoso (6, 7)
Gamelyn (21)
Giaffir (16)
Gulnare (16)
Harriet (20)
Hartley (19)
Hunsden (18)
John Daw (5)
Katinka (15)
Keeldar (19)
Kno'well (6)
Knockem (2)
Leonora (16)
MacTurk (19)
Marwood (26)
Matthew (6)
Mercury (3)
Mincing (26)
Minotti (16)
Mrs. Gale (19)
Mrs. Hogg (19)
Mrs. Reed (17)
Nunnely (19)
Olimpia (16)
Ovidius (10)
Palamon (21)
Placebo (21)
Plautia (10)
Regulus (12)
Samiasa (16)
Scandal (23)
Sejanus (12)
Sharper (25)
Sordido (7)

Stephen (6)
Sympson (19)
Theseus (21)
Tiburce (21)
Torquil (16)
Troilus (21)
Volpone (13)
Zuleika (16)

8

Abdallah (16)
Amorphus (3)
Angelica (23)
Araminta (25)
Argurion (3)
Caligula (12)
Camballo (21)
Careless (22)
Cordalus (7)
Custance (21)
Cytheris (10)
Donegild (21)
Edgworth (2)
Epicoene (5)
Griselda (21)
Gulbeyaz (15)
Helstone (19)
Hesperus (3)
Jane Eyre (17)
Joe Scott (19)
John Gale (19)
John Reed (17)
Laetitia (25)
Latiaris (12)
Loradano (16)
Mary Cave (19)
Maskwell (22)
Mecaenas (10)
Melibeus (21)
Mirabell (26)
Miss Prue (23)
Montanto (6)
Mooncalf (2)
Mrs. Frail (23)
Mrs. Poole (17)
Mrs. Pryor (19)
Mrs. Whipp (19)
Mrs. Yorke (19)
Murcraft (4)
Nicholas (21)
Parisina (16)
Pedrillo (15)
Petulant (26)
Prudence (21)

Quarlous (2)
Seacombe (18)
Sir Topas (21)
Suwarrow (15)
Sweeting (19)
Tiberius (12)
Trapland (23)
Tynedale (18)
Vainlove (25)
Valerian (21)
Waitwell (26)
Wishfort (26)
Witwould (26)

9

Angiolina (16)
Arviragus (21)
Ben Legend (23)
Brainworm (6)
Cambuscon (21)
Christian (16)
Clerimont (5)
Corbaccio (13)
Crispinus (14)
Cyril Hall (19)
Demetrius (10)
Dol Common (1)
Donna Inez (15)
Doricourt (26)
Downright (6)
Dr. Boultby (19)
Eglantine (21)
Eliza Reed (17)
Fitz-Fulke (15)
Foresight (25)
Francesca (16)
Goodstock (9)
Heartwell (25)
Hermegyld (21)
Josephine (16)
Lady Froth (22)
Littlewit (2)
Loadstone (8)
Lord Froth (22)
Lucy Snowe (20)
Macilente (7)
Marchmont (20)
Mark Yorke (19)
Meercraft (4)
Mellefont (22)
Millamont (26)
Miss Abbot (17)
Morphides (3)
Mrs. Polish (8)

Noll Bluff (25)
Oliver Cob (6)
Phantaste (3)
Philantia (3)
Pinchbeck (15)
Pomponius (12)
Prosaites (3)
Rochester (17)
Rose Yorke (19)
Scatcherd (17)
Seremenes (16)
Sir Thopas (21)
Steighton (18)
Terentius (12)
The Giaour (16)
Touchwood (22)
Valentine (23)
Wairavens (20)

10

Adam Overdo (2)
Aholibamah (16)
Aurora Raby (15)
Bailendino (14)
Crimsworth (18)
Don Alfonso (15)
Donna Julia (15)
Fondlewife (25)
Helen Burns (17)
Hiram Yorke (19)
Lady Plyant (22)
Lord Conrad (15)
Louis Moore (19)
Madame Beck (20)
Miss Temple (17)
Mrs. Bretton (20)
Mrs. Fainall (26)
Mrs. Fairfax (17)
Mrs. Marwood (26)
Paul Plyant (22)
Propertius (10)
Rev. Mr. Donne (19)
Sanguinius (12)
Sir Ezzelin (16)
Sir John Daw (5)
Thomas Cash (6)
Wife of Bath (The) (21)

11

Abel Drugger (14)
Barraclough (19)
Bertha Mason (17)
Captain Whit (2)
Colonel Dent (17)
Fitzdottrel (4)
Gerard Moore (19)
Jessie Yorke (19)
Lady Adeline (15)
Leatherhead (2)
Martin Yorke (19)
Michel Steno (16)
Mike Hartley (19)
Ned Careless (22)
Nightingale (2)
Paulina Home (20)
Robert Moore (19)
Roger Formal (6)
Simon Simkin (21)
Stralenheim (16)
Tom Quarlous (2)
Tribulation (1)

12

Asinius Lupus (10)
Brocklehurst (17)
Captain Bluff (25)
Carlo Buffone (7)
Childe Harold (16)
Harry Baillie (21)
John Seacombe (18)
Joseph Wittol (25)
Lady Wishfort (26)
Lord Tynedale (18)
Margaret Hall (19)
Matthew Yorke (19)
Monsieur Paul (18, 20)
Poore Persoun (The) (21)
Rev. Cyril Hall (19)
Richard Mason (17)
Sardanapalus (16)
St. John Rivers (17)
Symond Symkyn (21)

13

Dr. John Bretton (20)
Edward Belmour (25)
Edward Kno'well (6)
Epicure Mammon (1)
Georgiana Reed (17)
Hortense Moore (19)
Hugh of Lincoln (21)
Humphrey Waspe (2)
James Helstone (19)
James Loredano (16)
John Littlewit (2)
Lady Loadstone (8)
Lady Pinchbeck (15)
Lady Touchwood (22)
Lord Touchwood (22)
Magnetick Lady (The) (8)
Marino Faliero (16)
Master Stephen (6)
Miss Marchmont (20)
Miss Scatcherd (17)
Mrs. Crimsworth (18)
Philip Nunnely (19)
Rev. Mr. Sweeting (19)
Sir Paul Plyant (22)

14

Augustus Caesar (10)
Augustus Malone (19)
Captain Bobadil (6)
Captain Keeldar (19)
Edward Mirabell (22)
Francis Foscari (16)
Justice Clement (6)
Rev. Peter Malone (19)
Shirley Keeldar (19)
Wilful Witwould (26)

15

Anthony Witwould (26)
Clerk of Oxenford (21)
Ezekiel Edgworth (2)
Fastidious Brisk (7)
George Downright (6)
Hon. John Seacombe (18)
Madame Eglantine (21)
Sir Joseph Wittol (25)

Some characters from **Charles Dickens**

List of works from which the following characters are taken, with reference numbers.

Ref. No.	Title		Ref. No.	Title	
1.	Barnaby Rudge	(12 letters)	13.	Little Dorrit	(12 letters)
2.	Battle of Life, The	(15 letters)	14.	Martin Chuzzlewit	(16 letters)
3.	Bleak House	(10 letters)	15.	Master Humphrey's Clock	(20 letters)
4.	Chimes, The	(9 letters)	16.	Mudfog Papers, The	(15 letters)
5.	Christmas Carol, A	(15 letters)	17.	Nicholas Nickleby	(16 letters)
6.	Cricket on the Hearth, The	(21 letters)	18.	Old Curiosity Shop, The	(19 letters)
7.	David Copperfield	(16 letters)	19.	Oliver Twist	(11 letters)
8.	Dombey and Son	(12 letters)	20.	Our Mutual Friend	(15 letters)
9.	Edwin Drood	(10 letters)	21.	Pickwick, or The Pickwick Papers	(8 or 17 letters)
10.	Great Expectations	(17 letters)	22.	Sketches by Boz	(13 letters)
11.	Hard Times	(9 letters)	23.	Tale of Two Cities, A	(16 letters)
12.	Haunted Man, The	(13 letters)			

Note:: The numbers in brackets indicate *the works* in which the characters appear

2 – 4

Aged (The) (10)
Bell (16)
Bet (19)
Bray (17)
Bung (22)
Cobb (1)
Cute (4)
Dick (19)
Fang (19)
Fern (4)
Fips (14)
Fogg (21)
Gamp (14)
Gay (8)
Grip (bird) (1)
Grub (21)
Hawk (17)
Heep (7)
Hugh (1)
Jane (22)
Jip (dog) (7)
Jo (3)
Joe (21)
Jupe (11)
Kit (18)
Knag (17)
Mary (21)
Meg (4)
Mell (7)
Muff (16)
'Nemo' (3)

Peel (21)
Pell (21)
Peps (8)
'Pip' (10)
Pott (21)
Prig (14)
Pyke (17)
Riah (20)
Rosa (3)
Rugg (13)
Slug (16)
Slum (18)
Tigg (14)
Tim (5)
Tox (8)
Veck (4)
Wade (13)
Wegg (20)

5

Agnes (7)
Alice (15)
Bates (19)
Betsy (19)
Bevan (14)
Biddy (10)
Bloss (22)
Boxer (6)
Brass (18)
Brick (14)
Brown (8, 22)
'Caddy' (3)
Casby (13)

Chick (8)
Choke (14)
Clare (3)
Crupp (7)
Daisy (1)
Diver (14)
Drood (9)
Dumps (22)
Emily (7)
Evans (22)
Fagin (19)
Filer (4)
Fixem (22)
Flite (3)
Giles (19)
Gills (8)
Gowan (13)
Grace (2)
Green (22)
Gride (17)
Grove (18)
Guppy (3)
Gwynn (21)
Hardy (22)
Hicks (22)
Janet (7)
Jerry (18)
Jones (2)
Kenge (3)
Krook (3)
Lobbs (21)
Lorry (23)
Lupin (14)

Maggy (13)
Marks (15)
Miggs (1)
Mills (7)
Minns (22)
Molly (10)
Monks (19)
Mould (14)
Nancy (19)
Neddy (21)
Noggs (17)
Perch (8)
Pinch (14)
Pluck (17)
Price (17)
Pross (23)
Quale (3)
Quilp (18)
Rudge (1)
Sarah (22)
Scott (18)
Sikes (19)
Slyme (14)
Smart (21)
Smike (17)
Sophy (7)
Squod (3)
Stagg (1)
Tibbs (22)
Toots (8)
Tozer (8)
Trabb (10)
Trent (18)

Troll (22)
Tuggs (22)
Twist (19)
Venus (20)
Wosky (22)

6

Alfred (2)
Babley (7)
Badger (3)
Bagman (The) (21)
Bailey (14)
Bamber (21)
Bantam (21)
Barker (22)
Barkis (7)
Barley (10)
Barney (19)
Barton (22)
Beadle (13)
Bedwin (19)
Benton (15)
Bertha (6)
Bitzer (11)
Boffin (20)
Bowley (4)
Briggs (8, 22)
Bucket (3)
Budden (22)
Budger (21)
Bumble (19)
Bumple (22)

Bunsby (8)
Butler (22)
Buzfuz (21)
Calton (22)
Carker (8)
Carton (23)
'Cherub' (The) (20)
Codlin (18)
Cooper (22)
Corney (19)
Cousin (8)
Craggs (2)
Cuttle (8)
Dadson (22)
Danton (22)
Darnay (23)
Dartle (7)
Denham (12)
Dennis (1)
Dodson (21)
Dombey (8)
Dorrit (13)
Dounce (22)
Dowler (21)
Dr. Peps (8)
Durden (3)
Edkins (22)
Endell (7)
Etella (10)
'Fat Boy' (The) (21)
Feeder (8)
Folair (17)
George (3)
Gordon (1)
Graham (14)
Grueby (1)
Guster (3)
Harmon (20)
Harris (14, 18, 22)
Hawdon (3)
Helves (22)
Hexham (20)
Higden (20)
Hilton (22)
Hobler (22)
Hubble (10)
Hunter (21, 22)
Hutley (21)
Jarley (18)
Jasper (9)
Jingle (21)
Johnny (20)
Lammie (20)
Lumbey (17)

Magnus (21)
Marion (2)
Marley (5)
Martha (22)
Marton (18)
Maylie (19)
Merdle (13)
Milvey (20)
Mivins (21)
Moddle (14)
Morfin (8)
Mullet (14)
Muzzle (21)
Nathan (22)
Nipper (8)
Noakes (22)
Orlick (10)
Pancks (13)
Parker (22)
Pegler (11)
Peploe (22)
Perker (21)
Phunky (21)
Pipkin (21)
Pirrip (10)
Pocket (10)
Pogram (14)
Potter (22)
Purday (22)
Rachel (11)
Raddle (21)
Redlaw (12)
Rigaud (13)
Rogers (22)
Sapsea (9)
Sawyer (21)
Sleary (11)
Sloppy (20)
Strong (7)
Stubbs (22)
Tapley (14)
Timgon (22)
Toodle (8)
Tottle (22)
Tupman (21)
Tupple (22)
Varden (1)
Walker (22)
Warden (2)
Wardle (21)
Waters (22)
Weller (21)
Wilfer (20)
Willet (1)

Wilson (22)
Winkle (21)

7

Barbara (18)
Bardell (21)
Bazzard (9)
Blimber (8)
Blotton (21)
Bobster (17)
Boldwig (21)
Britain (2)
Brooker (17)
Browdie (17)
Bullamy (14)
'Charley' (3)
Chester (1)
Chillip (7)
Chivery (13)
Chuffey (14)
Cleaver (20)
Clenham (11)
Crackit (19)
Creakle (7)
Crewler (7)
Dawking (19)
Dedlock (3)
Defarge (23)
Dr. Wosky (22)
Drummle (10)
Edmunds (21)
Evenson (22)
Fleming (19)
Gargery (10)
Garland (18)
Gazingi (17)
General (13)
Granger (8)
Gridley (3)
Grimwig (19)
Grinder (18)
Groffin (21)
Heyling (21)
Hopkins (21)
Jackman (24)
Jackson (21)
Jaggers (10)
Jeddler (2)
Jellyby (3)
Jiniwin (18)
Jinkins (21)
Jobling (3, 14)
Jorkins (7)
Kenwigs (17)

Larkins (7, 22)
Lewsome (14)
Loggins (22)
Mackiln (22)
Manette (23)
Manners (22)
Meagles (13)
Mowcher (7)
Mrs. Heep (7)
Mrs. Pott (21)
Nadgeth (14)
Neckett (3)
Newcome (2)
Nubbles (18)
Nupkins (21)
O'Bleary (22)
Overton (22)
Pawkins (14)
Peecher (20)
Pipchin (8)
Plummer (6)
Podsnap (20)
Redburn (15)
Richard (4)
Sampson (20)
Scadder (14)
Scrooge (5)
Simpson (22)
Skewton (8)
Slammer (21)
Slowboy (6)
Slunkey (21)
Smangle (21)
Smauker (21)
Snagsby (3)
Snawley (17)
Snubbin (21)
Snuffin (17)
Sparsit (11)
Spenlow (7)
Squeers (17)
Stryver (23)
Swidger (12)
Taunton (22)
'The Aged' (10)
'Tiny Tim' (5)
Tippins (20)
Todgers (14)
Tom Cobb (1)
Tomkins (22)
Trotter (21)
Trundle (21)
Wackles (18)
Wemmuck (10)

Whimple (10)
Whisker (pony) (18)
Wickham (8)
Wilkins (22)
Wobbler (13)

8

Ada Clare (3)
Alphonse (17)
Aunt Jane (22)
Bachelor (The) (18)
Bagstock (7)
Barnacle (13)
Beckwith (12)
Beverley (22)
Blathers (19)
Brandley (10)
Bravassa (17)
Brittles (19)
Brownlow (19)
Bull's Eye (dog) (19)
Carstone (3)
Chadband (3)
Chitling (19)
Claypole (19)
Cleriker (10)
Cluppins (21)
Cratchit (5)
Crummles (17)
Crumpton (22)
Cruncher (23)
Crushton (21)
Dingwall (22)
Diogenes (dog)
Dr. Lumbey (17)
Dr. Strong (7)
Evrémond (23)
Fielding (6)
Finching (13)
Fladdock (14)
Flammell (22)
Fledgeby (20)
Gashford (1)
Haredale (1)
Harleigh (22)
Havisham (10)
Hortense (3)
Humphrey (15)
Jarndyce (3)
Jem Grove (18)
Jennings (22)
La Creevy (17)
Langford (12)
Ledbrain (16)

Ledbrook (17)
Lenvifie (17)
Littimer (7)
Lobskini (22)
Losberne (19)
Magwitch (10)
Micawber (7)
Miss Knag (17)
Miss Wade (13)
Mrs. Bloss (22)
Mrs. Crupp (7)
Mrs. Gowan (13)
Mrs. Lupin (14)
Mrs. Perch (8)
Mrs. Rudge (1)
Mrs. Tibbs (22)
Nicholas (22)
Nickleby (17)
Old Lobbs (21)
Peggotty (7)
Petowker (17)
Pickwick (21)
Plornish (13)
Robinson (22)
Skettles (8)
Skiffins (10)
Skimpole (3)
Slinkton (10)
Smithers (22)
Snitchey (2)
Sparkins (22)
Sparkler (13)
Stiggins (21)
Tetterby (12)
Toby Veck (4)
Tom Pinch (14)
Tom Scott (18)
Tom Smart (21)
Traddles (7)
Trotwood (7)
Uncle Tom (22)
Westlock (14)
Whiffers (21)
Will Fern (4)
Woolford (22)

9

Amy Dorrit (13)
Belvawney (17)
Betsy Prig (14)
Bill Sikes (19)
Blackpool (11)
Bob Sawyer (21)
Bounderby (11)

Boythorne (3)
Charlotte (19)
Cheeryble (17)
Chickweed (19)
'Cleopatra' (8)
Compeyson (10)
Dr. Blimber (8)
Dr. Jeddler (2)
Dr. Jobling (14)
Dr. Slammer (21)
Fleetwood (22)
Gattleton (22)
Gradgrind (11)
Gregsbury (17)
Grewgious (9)
Harthouse (11)
Headstone (20)
Jem Hutley (21)
Joe Willet (1)
Leo Hunter (21)
Lightwood (20)
Lillyvick (17)
'Lord Peter' (22)
Malderton (22)
Mantalini (17)
Maplesone (22)
Markleham (7)
Miss Flite (3)
Miss Gwynn (21)
Miss Miggs (1)
Miss Mills (7)
Miss Pross (23)
Mrs. Bedwin (19)
Mrs. Briggs (22)
Mrs. Budger (21)
Mrs. Corney (19)
Mrs. Craggs (2)
Mrs. Dadson (22)
Mrs. Dowler (21)
Mrs. Harris (14)
Mrs. Hubble (10)
Mrs. Hunter (21)
Mrs. Jarley (18)
Mrs. Lammle (20)
Mrs. Maylie (19)
Mrs. Merdle (13)
Mrs. Milvey (20)
Mrs. Parker (22)
Mrs. Pegler (11)
Mrs. Peploe (22)
Mrs. Raddle (21)
Mrs. Stubbs (22)
Mrs. Varden (1)
Mrs. Wilfer (20)

Murdstone (7)
Ned Dennis (1)
Nell Trent (18)
Old Orlick (10)
Pardiggle (3)
Pecksniff (14)
Phil Squod (3)
Potterson (20)
Riderhood (20)
Ruth Pinch (14)
Sam Weller (21)
Sarah Gamp (14)
Silas Wegg (20)
Sludberry (22)
Smallweed (3)
Smorltork (21)
Snodgrass (21)
Spruggins (22)
Swiveller (18)
Tackleton (6)
Tappertit (1)
'The Bagman' (21)
'The Cherub' (20)
'The Fat Boy' (21)
Tom Codlin (18)
Towlinson (8)
Uncle Bill (22)
Uriah Heep (7)
Veneering (20)
Verisopht (17)
Walter Gay (8)
Wickfield (7)
Will Marks (15)
Wisbottle (22)
Witherden (18)
Woodcourt (3)
Wrayburne (20)

10

Alice Brown (8)
Aunt Martha (2)
Ayresleigh (21)
Betsy Clark (22)
Bill Barker (22)
Bill Barley (10)
Billsmethi (22)
Bitherston (8)
Chevy Slyme (14)
Chuzzlewit (14)
'Cymon' Tuggs (22)
Dame Durden (3)
Doctor Peps (8)
Edwin Drood (9)
Emma Porter (22)

Flintwinch (13)
Heathfield (2)
Henry Gowan (13)
'Honest John' (22)
Jack Bamber (21)
Jack Bunsby (8)
Jem Larkins (22)
Job Trotter (21)
Joe Gargery (10)
John Carker (8)
John Dounce (22)
John Grueby (8)
John Harman (20)
John Willet (1)
'Kit' Nubbles (18)
Kittlebell (22)
Knight Bell (16)
Little Dick (19)
Little Paul (8)
MacStinger (8)
Mark Tapley (14)
Mary Graham (14)
Miss Benton (15)
Mrs. Bardell (21)
Mrs. Clenham (13)
Mrs. Crewler (7)
Mrs. Gargery (10)
Mrs. Garland (18)
Mrs. General (13)
Mrs. Grudden (17)
Mrs. Jellyby (3)
Mrs. Jiniwin (18)
Mrs. Kenwigs (17)
Mrs. Mackiln (22)
Mrs. Meagles (13)
Mrs. Nubbles (18)
Mrs. Parsops (22)
Mrs. Pipchin (8)
Mrs. Skewton (8)
Mrs. Sparsit (11)
Mrs. Squeers (17)
Mrs. Swidger (12)
Mrs. Taunton (22)
Mrs. Todgers (14)
Mrs. Wackles (18)
Mrs. Whimple (10)
Mrs. Wickham (8)
Paul Dombey (8)
Rosa Dartle (7)
Rose Maylie (19)
Rouncewell (3)
Sally Brass (18)
Sempronius (22)
Signor Jupe (11)

Simon Tuggs (22)
Sliderskew (17)
Sowerberry (19)
Stareleigh (21)
Steerforth (7)
Tattycoram (13)
Tony Weller (21)
Turveydrop (3)
Williamson (22)
Wititterly (17)

11

Abel Garland (18)
Arthur Gride (17)
Balderstone (22)
Bella Wilfer (20)
Betsey Quilp (18)
Betty Higden (20)
Bob Cratchit (5)
Cecilia Jupe (11)
Copperfield (7)
Daniel Quilp (18)
Doctor Wosky (22)
Dolge Orlick (10)
Dora Spenlow (7)
Edith Dombey (8)
Emily Wardle (21)
Emma Peecher (20)
Fanny Dombey (8)
Fanny Dorrit (13)
Frank Milvie (20)
Gabriel Grub (21)
'Game Chicken' (The) (8)
Ham Peggotty (7)
Harry Maylie (19)
Jack Hopkins (21)
Jack Redburn (15)
Jacob Barton (22)
James Carker (8)
Jarvis Lorry (23)
Jemima Evans (22)
Jesse Hexham (20)
John Browdie (17)
John Chivery (7)
John Dawkins (19)
John Edmunds (21)
John Evenson (22)
John Jobling (14)
John Podsnap (20)
John Smauker (21)
John Wemmock (10)
Joseph Tuggs (22)
Lady Dedlock (3)
Lady Tippins (20)

Linkinwater (17)
Little Emily (7)
Louisa Chick (8)
Lucretia Tox (8)
Miss Gazingi (17)
Miss Larkins (7)
Miss Mowcher (7)
Misses Brown (22)
Monflathers (18)
Mrs. Brandley (10)
Mrs. Clupping (21)
Mrs. Crummles (17)
Mrs. Dingwall (22)
Mrs. Fielding (6)
Mrs. Finching (13)
Mrs. Gummidge (7)
Mrs. Micawber (7)
Mrs. Nickleby (17)
Mrs. Plornish (13)
Mrs. Sparkler (13)
Mrs. Tetterby (12)
Newman Noggs (17)
Oliver Twist (19)
Percy Noakes (22)
Peerybingle (6)
Peter Magnus (21)
Polly Toodle (8)
Pumblechook (10)
Robin Toodle (8)
Slackbridge (11)
Snevellicci (17)
Solomon Pell (21)
Susan Nipper (8)
Susan Weller (21)
Sweedlepipe (14)
'The Bachelor' (18)
Tim Cratchit (5)
Toby Crackit (19)
Tom Chitling (19)
Tony Jobling (3)
Tracy Tupman (21)
Tulkinhorn (3)
Uncle George (22)
Uncle Robert (22)

12

Abel Magwitch (10)
Agnes Fleming (19)
Alderman Cute (4)
Alfred Jingle (21)
Alfred Lammle (20)
Amelia Martin (22)
'Artful Dodger' (The) (19)
Aunt Margaret (22)

Barnaby Rudge (1)
Bayham Badger (3)
Bully Stryver (23)
Charles Tuggs (22)
Charley Bates (19)
Colonel Diver (14)
Doctor Lumbey (17)
Doctor Strong (7)
Dr. Parker Peps (8)
Edith Granger (8)
Edward Cuttle (8)
Edward Dorrit (13)
Elijah Pogram (14)
Emily Taunton (22)
Emma Haredale (1)
Emma Micawber (7)
Esther Hawdon (3)
Fanny Cleaver (20)
Fanny Squeers (17)
Feenix Cousin (8)
George Gordon (1)
Grace Jeddler (2)
Honeythunder (9)
Horace Hunter (22)
Joe, the 'Fat Boy' (21)
John Jarndyce (3)
John Westlock (14)
Julia Manners (22)
Kate Nickleby (17)
Koeldwethout (17)
Little Dorrit (13)
Lizzie Hexham (20)
Lord Barnacle (13)
Lucie Manette (23)
Madeline Bray (17)
Major Pawkins (14)
Martha Endell (7)
Mary Fielding (6)
Matilda Price (17)
Milly Swidger (12)
Miss Bravassa (17)
Miss Havisham (10)
Miss La Creevy (17)
Miss Ledbrook (17)
Miss Skiffins (10)
Miss Willises (22)
Miss Woolford (22)
Montague Tigg (14)
Mrs. Gradgrind (11)
Mrs. Maplesone (22)
Mrs. Markleham (7)
Mrs. Pardiggle (3)
Mrs. Veneering (20)
Mulberry Hawk (17)

Noah Claypole (19)
'Peepy' Jellyby (3)
Philip Redlaw (12)
Philip Pirrip (10)
Sampson Brass (18)
Samuel Briggs (22)
Samuel Weller (21)
Solomon Daisy (1)
Solomon Gills (8)
Sophy Crewler (7)
Stoney Briggs (8)
Sydney Carton (23)
Thomas Sapsea (9)
Tilly Slowboy (6)
Tite Barnacle (13)
Tom Gradgrind (11)
Tom Malderton (22)
William Guppy (3)
William Sikes (19)

13

Alfred Tomkins (22)
Anabella Allen (21)
Arthur Clenham (13)
Augustus Minns (22)
Belinda Pocket (10)
Belinda Waters (22)
Benjamin Stagg (1)
Bertha Plummer (6)
'Bob the Grinder' (8)
Brook-Dingwall (22)
Captain Bunsby (8)
Captain Cuttle (8)
Captain Dowler (21)
Captain George (3)
Captain Hawdon (3)
Captain Purday (22)
Captain Waters (22)
Charles Darnay (23)
Charles Timson (22)
Charley Hexham (20)
Clara Peggotty (7)
Dick Swiveller (18)
Doctor Blimber (8)
Doctor Jeddler (2)
Doctor Jobling (14)
Doctor Manette (23)
Dodson and Fogg (21)
Dr. John Jobling (14)
Edward Chester (1)
Edward Plummer (6)
Emily Peggotty (7)
Emily Smithers (22)
Ernest Defarge (23)

Flora Finching (13)
Gabriel Varden (1)
George Swidger (12)
George Heyling (21)
George Nupkins (21)
George Sampson (20)
Harriet Beadle (13)
Harriet Carker (8)
Herbert Pocket (10)
Jane Murdstone (7)
Jerry Cruncher (23)
Joseph Overton (22)
Lavinia Wilfer (20)
Lord Verisopht (17)
Madame Defarge (23)
Maria Crumpton (22)
Marion Jeddler (2)
Mary Ann Raddle (21)
Matthew Pocket (10)
Mealy Potatoes (7)
Michael Bumple (22)
Michael Warden (2)
Minnie Meagles (13)
Miss Belvawney (17)
Miss Lillerton (22)
Miss Potterson (20)
Misses Kenwigs (The) (17)
Misses Wackles (The) (18)
Mistress Alice (15)
Mrs. Macstinger (8)
Mrs. Rouncewell (3)
Mrs. Sowerberry (19)
Mrs. Williamson (22)
Peg Sliderskew (17)
Philip Swidger (12)
Professor Muff (16)
Rachael Wardle (21)
Ralph Nickleby (17)
Richard Babley (7)
Sally Tetterby (12)
Samuel Slumkey (21)
Samuel Wilkins (22)
Septimus Hicks (22)
Seth Pecksniff (14)
Thomas Groffin (21)
Tumley Snuffim (17)
Watkins Tottle (22)
William Barker (22)
William Dorrit (13)

14

Abbey Potterson (20)
Agnes Wickfield (7)
Alexander Trott (22)

Allen Woodcourt (3)
Amelia Crumpton (22)
Anthony Jedder (2)
Augustus Cooper (22)
Augustus Moddle (14)
Barnet Skettles (8)
Bentley Drummle (10)
Betsey Cluppins (21)
Betsey Trotwood (7)
Captain Boldwig (21)
Caroline Wilson (22)
Cecilia Bobster (17)
'Charlotta' Tuggs (22)
Chickenstalker (4)
Daniel Peggotty (7)
'Dot' Peerybingle (6)
Edward Sparkler (13)
Edwin Cheeryble (17)
Florence Dombey (8)
Francis Spenlow (7)
Frank Cheeryble (17)
Frederick Trent (18)
General Scadder (14)
Harold Skimpole (3)
Hiram Grewgious (9)
Honoria Dedlock (3)
Isabella Wardle (21)
Jefferson Brick (14)
Johnny Tetterby (12)
Lavinia Spenlow (7)
Master Humphery (15)
Mercy Pecksniff (14)
'Merry' Pecksniff (14)
Monsieur Rigaud (13)
Mrs. Betty Higden (20)
Mrs. Copperfield (7)
Mrs. Peerybingle (6)
Mrs. Polly Toodle (8)

Mrs. Snevellicci (17)
Nicodemus Dumps (22)
Octavius Budden (22)
Reginald Wilfer (20)
Reuben Haredale (1)
Rev. Frank Milvey (20)
Roger Riderhood (20)
Samuel Pickwick (21)
Serjeant Buzfuz (21)
Signor Lobskini (22)
Simon Tappertit (1)
Sir John Chester (1)
Sophia Tetterby (12)
'The Game Chicken' (8)
Therese Defarge (23)
Thomas Traddles (7)
Tim Linkinwater (17)
William Swidger (12)

15

Alexander Briggs (22)
Alexander Budden (22)
Alfred Mantalini (17)
Benjamin Britain (2)
Caroline Jellyby (3)
'Cherry' Pecksniff (14)
Clarissa Spenlow (7)
Clemency Newcome (2)
Conkey Chickweed (19)
Cornelia Blimber (8)
'Dolphus Tetterby (12)
Dora Copperfield (7)
Ebenezer Scrooge (5)
Edward Murdstone (7)
Estella Havisham (10)
Eugene Wrayburne (20)
Frederick Dorrit (13)
General Fladdock (14)

Georgina Podsnap (20)
Godfrey Nickleby (17)
Henrietta Boffin (20)
Henry Wititterly (17)
Hon. Elijah Pogram (14)
Horatio Sparkins (22)
'Horatio St. Julien' (22)
James Steerforth (7)
John Peerybingle (6)
Jonas Chuzzlewit (14)
Josephine Sleary (11)
Josiah Rounderby (11)
Julia Wititterly (17).
Lavinia Dingwall (22)
Louisa Gradgrind (11)
MacChoakumchild (11)
Madame Mantalini (17)
Mary Peerybingle (6)
Miss Snevellicci (17)
Monsieur Defarge (23)
Mrs. Joseph Porter (22)
Nathaniel Pipkin (21)
Nathaniel Winkle (21)
Nicodemus Boffin (20)
Ninetta Crummles (17)
Paul Sweedlepipe (14)
Professor Mullet (14)
Richard Carstone (3)
Serjeant Snubbin (21)
Sir Joseph Bowley (4)
Sir Mulberry Hawk (17)
Smallweed Family (3)
Teresa Malderton (22)
'The Artful Dodger' (17)

17

Ferdinand Barnacle (13)

Some characters from **Dryden**, **George Eliot**, **Fielding**, and **Goldsmith**
List of works from which the following characters are taken, with reference numbers.

Dryden

Ref. No.	Title	
1. Absalom and Achitophel		(20 letters)
2. (Various)		

George Eliot

11. Adam Bede		(8 letters)
12. Clerical Life, Scenes from		(12 or 22 letters)
13. Daniel Deronda		(13 letters)
14. Felix Holt		(9 letters)
15. Middlemarch		(11 letters)
16. Mill on the Floss, The		(17 letters)
17. Romola		(6 letters)
18. Silas Marner		(11 letters)
19. Spanish Gipsy, The		(15 letters)

Fielding (Henry)

Ref. No.	Title	
3. Amelia		(6 letters)
4. Jonathan Wild		(12 letters)
5. Joseph Andrews		(13 letters)
6. Mock Doctor, The		(13 letters)
7. Pasquin		(7 letters)
8. Tom Jones		(8 letters)
9. Tom Thumb		(8 letters)
10. (Various)		

Goldsmith (Oliver)

20. Citizen of the World, The		(20 letters)
21. Good-Natured Man, The		(17 letters)
22. She Stoops to Conquer		(18 letters)
23. Vicar of Wakefield, The		(19 letters)
24. (Various)		

Note: The numbers in brackets indicate *the works* in which the characters appear

2 – 4

Agag (1)
Amri (1)
Arod (1)
Bath (3)
Bede (11)
Cass (18)
Cei (17)
Cora (1)
Dane (18)
Doeg (1)
Holt (14)
Iras (2)
Juan (19)
Juno (dog) (11)
Lisa (17)
Lyon (14)
Maso (11)
Moss (16)
Og (1)
Omri (1)
Rann (11)
Rock (20)
Saul (1)
Snap (4)
Tibs (20)
Wild (4)
Wyld (4)

5

Adams (5)
Amiel (1)
Balak (1)
Bardo (17)
Booby (5)
Booth (3)
Burge (11)
Caleb (I)
Calvo (17)
David (1)
Deane (16)
Dorax (2)
Edwin (24)
Eppic (18)
Fanny (5)
Garth (15)
Glegg (16)
Gomaz (2)
Guest (16)
Jakin (16)
Jonas (1)
Jones (8)
Kezia (16)
Lofty (21)
Macey (18)
Moody (2)
Nadab (1)
Nello (17)

Place (7)
Sagan (1)
Sheva (1)
Tessa (17)
Tibbs (20)
Vincy (16)
Wakem (16)
Whang (20)
Zadoc (1)
Zarca (19)
Zeis (20)
Zimri (1)

6

Abdael (1)
Adriel (1)
Alexas (2)
Amelia (3)
Antony (2)
Arnold (23)
Badger (10)
Barton (12)
Bennet (3)
Blaize (24)
Blifil (8)
Brooke (15)
Casson (11)
Crispe (23)
Dobson (16)
Dr. Rock (20)

Elvira (2)
Emilia (2)
Garnet (21)
Gilfil (12)
Hingpo (20)
Honour (8)
Irwine (11)
Jarvis (21)
Jasper (6)
Jerwyn (14)
La Ruse (4)
Marlow (22)
Marner (18)
Massey (11)
Melema (17)
Michal (1)
Morris (11)
Olivia (21)
Phaleg (1)
Pounce (5)
Poyser (11)
Pullet (16)
Quaver (10)
Romola (17)
Shimel (1)
Skeggo (23)
Sorrel (11)
Square (8)
Squint (20)
Supple (8)

Don Sebastian (2)
Featherstone (15)
Francesco Cei (17)
Friar Dominic (2)
Geoffrey Snap (4)
Hester Sorrel (11)
Jonathan Wild (4)
Jonathan Wyld (4)
Lady Chererel (12)
Lawyer Squint (20)
Lucy Goodwill (10)
Lydia Glasher (13)
Martin Poyser (11)
Miss Richland (21)
Monna Brigida (17)
Mrs. Allworthy (8)
Mrs. Heartfree (4)
Mrs. Partridge (8)
Squire Badger (10)
Stephen Guest (16)
Will Ladislaw (15)

13

Daniel Deronda (13)
Dolly Winthrop (18)
Harry Foxchase (7)

Janet Dempster (12)
Jonathan Burge (11)
Joseph Andrews (5)
Lady Bellaston (8)
Lady Thornhill (23)
Matthew Jermyn (14)
Maynard Gilfil (12)
Molly Straddle (4)
Moses Primrose (23)
Mrs. Hardcastle (22)
Mrs. Whitefield (8)
Nancy Lammeter (18)
Philip Debarry (14)
Pietro Cennini (17)
Romola di' Bardi (17)
Rosamond Vincy (15)
Sophia Western (8)
Squire Tankard (7)
Squire Western (8)
Theodosia Snap (4)
Thomas Thimble (4)

14

Adolphus Irwine (11)
Arabella Wilmot (23)
Carolina Skeggs (23)

Deborah Wilkins (8)
Dorothea Brooke (15)
Edward Casaubon (15)
Frederick Vincy (15)
George Primrose (23)
Harold Transome (14)
Jenny Tinderbox (20)
Kate Hardcastle (22)
Maggie Tulliver (16)
Maximus Debarry (14)
Miss Hardcastle (22)
Mrs. Cadwallader (15)
Mrs. Fitzpatrick (8)
Olivia Primrose (23)
Sophia Primrose (23)

15

Augustus Debarry (14)
Leontine Croaker (21)
Mrs. Lydia Glasher (13)
Olivia Woodville (21)
Parson Trulliber (5)
Sir James Chettam (15)
Squire Thornhill (23)
Thomas Heartfree (4)

Some characters from **Thomas Hardy**
List of works from which the following characters are taken, with reference numbers.

Ref. No.	Title		Ref. No.	Title	
1.	A Laodicean	(10 letters)	9.	The Mayor of Casterbridge	(22 letters)
2.	A Pair of Blue Eyes	(15 letters)	10.	The Return of the Native	(20 letters)
3.	Desperate Remedies	(17 letters)	11.	The Trumpet Major	(15 letters)
4.	Far from the Madding Crowd	(22 letters)	12.	The Woodlanders	(12 letters)
5.	Jude the Obscure	(14 letters)	13.	Time's Laughingstocks	(19 letters)
6.	Life's Little Cronies	(18 letters)	14.	Wessex Poems	(11 letters)
7.	Tess of the D'Urbervilles	(21 letters)	15.	Wessex Tales	(11 letters)
8.	The Hand of Ethelberta	(19 letters)			

Note: The numbers in brackets indicate *the works* in which the characters appear

4 – 6

Anna (6)
David (11)
Dr. Bath (9)
Hannah (13)
Laura (13)
Marion (7)
Meggs (14)
Michel (14)

Molly (11)
Sophy (6)
Unity (2)

7

Aguette (13)
Amos Fry (13)
Ann Dewy (13)
Barbree (14)
Bob Dewy (13)

Cawtree (12)
Charlie (10)
Cockton (1)
Dr. Chant (7)
Dr. Jones (12)
Haymoss (13)
Jim Caro (13)
Knowles (1)
Leverre (13)
Michael (13)

Mr. Cecil (13)
Mr. Hewby (2)
Rev. Glin (2)
Vilbert (5)

8

Boldwood (4)
Buzzford (9)
Cain Ball (4)
Car Darch (7)

Dick Dewy (13)
Dr. Breeve (8)
Fancy Day (13)
Humphrey (10)
Izz Huett (7)
Maitland (14)
Matt Grey (15)
Mr. Grower (9)
Mr. Lester (6)
Mrs. Edlin (5)
Mrs. Hurst (4)
Rev. P. Cope (6)
Uncle Joe (5)

9

Amos Graye (3)
Avice Caro (13)
Bannister (11)
Battersby (14)
Bessy Dewy (13)
Elijah New (15)
Henry Fray (4)
Jan Coggan (4)
Jane Smith (2)
Jim Clarke (15)
Jim Owlett (15)
Jim Weedle (6)
Jimmy Dewy (13)
John Biles (6)
John Green (15)
John Power (1)
John Smith (2)
John South (12)
Laban Tall (4)
Mark Clark (4)
Mr. Bollens (3)
Mr. Harnham (6)
Mr. Wilkins (1)
Mrs. Brooks (7)
Mrs. Martin (13)
Mrs. Morris (3)
Owen Graye (3)
Rev. Walker (6)
Sam Hobson (6)
Sarah Hall (15)
Stanidge (9)
Susan Dewy (13)
Tony Kytes (6)

10

Abner Power (1)
Angel Clare (7)
Anne Seaway (3)
Beck Knibbs (7)

Bob Loveday (11)
Captain Vye (10)
Chalkfield (10)
Dr. Charlson (15)
Emily Darth (6)
Fanny Robin (4)
Felix Clare (7)
Fred Shiner (13)
Gabriel Oak (4)
Helena Hall (15)
Henry Giles (6)
J. Appleseed (7)
Jack Dollop (7)
Jack Winter (6)
James Clare (7)
John Chiles (6)
John Upjohn (12)
Jude Fawley (5)
Lucy Savile (15)
Marty South (12)
Mercy Chant (7)
Milly Birds (1)
Mr. Cartlett (5)
Mrs. Dollery (12)
Mrs. Goodman (1)
Mrs. Palmley (6)
Nancy Darch (7)
Olive Pawle (6)
Olly Dowden (10)
Patty Beads (13)
Paula Power (1)
Philip Hall (15)
Reuben Dewy (13)
Rev. Melrose (15)
Rev. Twycolt (6)
Rhoda Brook (7) (15)
Sammy Blore (13)
Thomas Leaf (13)
Tim Tankens (14)

11

Abel Whittle (9)
Alfred Neigh (8)
Andrew Jones (15)
Anne Garland (11)
Charles Dewy (13)
Charles Raye (6)
Diggory Venn (10)
Dr. J. St. Cleeve (13)
Elias Spinks (13)
Esther Beach (11)
Eustacia Vye (10)
Faith Julian (8)
Farmer Groby (7)

Farmer Lodge (15)
Giles Martin (13)
Henry Knight (12)
Jacob Noakes (11)
Jane Vallens (6)
Jasper Clift (6)
Job Mitchell (11)
Julia Aspent (6)
Lucy Melbury (12)
Martha Sarah (15)
Matthew Moon (4)
Michael Mail (13)
Mr. Gradfield (3)
Mrs. Rolliver (7)
Nancy Weedle (6)
Nat Callcome (13)
Ned Hipcroft (6)
Oliver Giles (15)
Rev. A. Maybold (13)
Rev. Woodwell (1)
Robert Penny (13)
Robert Trewe (15)
Simon Burden (11)
Tabitha Lark (13)
Unity Sallet (6)
Wat Ollamore (6)
Wilf Latimer (15)
William Dare (1)
William Dewy (13)
William Worm (2)

12

Abraham Brown (3)
Alfred Somers (13)
Ann Avice Caro (13)
Anthony Green (13)
Arabella Donn (5)
Betty Privett (6)
Charles Downe (15)
Conjurer Fall (7) (9)
Damon Wildere (10)
Dr. E. Fitzpiers (12)
Edith Harnham (6)
Emily Hanning (6)
Felix Jethway (2)
Fred Beancock (12)
George Barnet (15)
Grace Melbury (12)
Henri Leverre (13)
James Comfort (11)
Jonathan Kale (7)
Levi Everdene (4)
Mary Ann Money (4)
Miss Bicknell (2)

Miss Fontover (5)
Mother Cuxsom (9)
Mrs. M. Pine-Avon (13)
Phyllis Grove (6)
Retty Priddle (7)
Rev. M. St. Cleeve (13)
Richard Crick (7)
Robert Dowdle (6)
Solomon Selby (6)
Sue Bridehead (5)
Susan Nonsuch (10)
Thomas Ballam (15)
Timothy Tanfs (12)
Tina Matthews (6)
Win. Marchmill (15)

13

Aeneas Manston (3)
Albert Feilmer (6)
Andrew Satchel (6)
Captain Flower (8)
Captain T. Hardy (11)
Charles Darton (15)
Clyn Yeobright (10)
Cuthbert Clare (7)
Cytherea Graye (3)
Dan Chickerell (8)
Donald Farfrae (9)
Elizabeth Leat (3)
Ella Marchmill (15)
Eunice Manston (3)
Farmer Jollice (6)
George Melbury (12)
Gertrude Lodge (15)
Grammer Oliver (12)
Hezekiah Biles (13)
Humphrey Gould (6)
Isaac Pierston (13)
James Everdene (4)
James Hardcome (6)
Johnny Nonsuch (10)
Joseph Lickpan (2)
Lady Petherwin (8)
Lizzy Newberry (15)
Lord Luxellian (2)
Louisa Menlove (8)
Martha Garland (11)
Miller Loveday (11)
Milly Richards (6)
Mrs. Goodenough (9)
Netty Sargeant (6)
Parson Thirdly (4)
Rev. Torkingham (13)
Robert Creedle (12)

Some characters from **Jane Austen**, **Charles Kingsley**, **Kipling**, and **Longfellow**
List of works from which the following characters are taken, with reference numbers.

Jane Austen

Ref. No.	Title	
1.	Emma	(4 letters)
2.	Lady Susan	(9 letters)
3.	Mansfield Park	(13 letters)
4.	Northanger Abbey	(15 letters)
5.	Persuasion	(10 letters)
6.	Pride and Prejudice	(17 letters)
7.	Sense and Sensibility	(19 letters)
8.	Watsons, The	(10 letters)

Charles Kingsley

16.	Alton Locke	(10 letters)
17.	Hereward the Wake	(15 letters)
18.	Two Years Ago	(11 letters)
19.	Westward Ho!	(10 letters)
20.	Yeast	(5 letters)
21.	(Various)	

Rudyard Kipling

Ref. No.	Title	
9.	Captains Courageous	(18 letters)
10.	Day's Work, The	(11 letters)
11.	Life's Handicap	(13 letters)
12.	Naulahka, The	(11 letters)
13.	Soldiers Three	(13 letters)
14.	Stalky and Co.	(11 letters)
15.	(Various)	

Longfellow

22.	Evangeline	(10 letters)
23.	Golden Legend, The	(15 letters)
24.	Hiawatha	(8 letters)
25.	Hyperion	(8 letters)
26.	Kavanagh	(8 letters)
27.	Miles Standish	(13 letters)
28.	(Various)	

Note: The numbers in brackets indicate *the works* in which the characters appear

3 – 5

Alden (27)
Algar (17)
Allen (4)
Basil (22)
Bates (1)
Brady (9)
Bukta (10)
Cary (19)
Chinn (10)
Croft (5)
Darcy (6)
Doone (13)
Drake (19)
Elsie (23)
Elton (1)
Emma (1)
Estes (12)
Fawne (10)
Felix (23)
Four (14)
'Foxy' (14)
Grant (3)
Hogan (13, 14)
Hurst (6)
Kamal (15)
Kim (15)
King (14)

Leigh (19)
Lewis (12, 21)
Locke (16)
M'Turk (14)
Mason (14)
Maxim (12)
Mowis (22)
Nixon (14)
Nolan (12)
O'Hara
　(13, 15)
Osseo (24)
Penn (9)
Platt (9)
Price (3)
Prout (14)
Scott (10)
Shadd (13)
Shott (15)
Slane (13)
Smith (4, 20)
Sneyd (3)
Titus (23)
Troop (9)
Tulke (14)
Uriel (23)
Ward (3)
White (14)
Yates (3)

Yeo (19)
Zouch (19)

6

Alfgar (17)
Ansell (14)
Arnoul (17)
Beetle (14)
Bennet (6)
Blayne (13)
Blazes (13)
Briggs (18)
Burton (21)
Carson (14)
Cheyne (9)
Clewer (14)
Conrad (21)
Coulan (13)
Dabney (14)
Elliot (5)
Elsley (18)
Folsom (10)
Gadsby (13, 15)
Gallio (13)
Godiva (17)
Godwin (17)
Harper (10)
Harvey (18)
Howard (8)

Hunter (8)
Hurree (15)
Jasoda (13)
Kinsey (9)
Lilian (16)
Maffin (13)
Mahbub (15)
Mannel (9)
Martin (1, 2, 9, 14)
Martyn (10)
McPhee (10)
Mellot (18)
Morton (7)
Mowgli (15)
Mutrie (12)
Norris (3)
O'Brien (8)
Palmer (7)
Raynes (10)
Sefton (14)
Stalky (14)
Steele (7)
Swayne (14)
Tarvin (12)
Thorpe (4)
Tilney (4)
Verney (17)
Vernon (2)
Watson (8)

Weston (1)
Willis (18)
Wilton (10)
Winter (19)

7

Baldwin (17)
Berkley (25)
Bertram (3)
Bingley (6)
Brandon (7)
Campian (19)
Coffins (6)
Corkran (14)
Curtiss (13)
De Sussa (13)
Dr. Grant (3)
Edwards (8)
Fairfax (1)
Ferrars (7)
Fleming (25)
Gilbert (28)
Gillett (14)
Hartopp (14)
Headley (18)
Heckler (12)
Holdock (10)
Huneefa (15)
Hypatia (21)

Johnson (2)
Learoyd (11, 13)
Leblanc (22)
Leofric (17)
Lilinau (22)
Lucifer (23)
Mackage (21)
Mackesy (13)
Manders (14)
Mildred (15)
Morland (4)
Mullins (13)
Nokomis (24)
Osborne (8)
Oweenee (24)
Oxenham (19)
Parsons (19)
Pelagia (21)
Perowne (14)
Pycroft (15)
Raleigh (19)
Rattray (14)
Salters (9)
Sheriff (12)
Simmons (13)
Vaughan (26)
Vaurien (20)
Wardrop (10)
Wenonah (24)

8

Aben-Ezra (21)
Basselin (28)
Bingleys (The) (6)
Campbell (14, 18)
Crawford (3)
Dan Troop (9)
Dashwood (7)
De Bourgh (6)
De Courcy (2)
Dick Four (14)
Dumachus (23)
Fastrada (23)
Felician (22)
Filomena (28)
Gardiner (6)
Gottlieb (23)
Grenvile (19)
Harrison (14)
Hereward (17)
Hiawatha (24)
Hyperion (25)
Jan Chinn (10)
Jennings (7)

Jervoise (13)
Kavanagh (26)
Lady Bath (19)
Limmason (11)
Long Jack (9)
Lynedale (16)
M'Cartney (10)
McRimmon (10)
Miss Carr (8)
Mrs. Allen (4)
Mrs. Blake (8)
Mrs. Estes (12)
Mrs. Hurst (6)
Mrs. Leigh (19)
Mrs. Price (3)
Mrs. Sneyd (3)
Mulvaney (13)
Musgrave (8)
Newbroom (20)
Ortheris (13)
Passmore (19)
Preciosa (28)
Salterne (19)
Schaefer (9)
Standish (27)
Stettson (14)
Threegan (13)
Thurnall (18)
Tom Platt (9)
Torfrida (17)
Treboaze (18)
Tregarva (20)
Vavasour (18)
Waltheof (1)
Will Cary (19)

9

Andromeda (21)
Armsworth (18)
Ashburton (25)
Azacanora (19)
Carmathan (12)
Churchill (1, 26)
Coffinson (14)
Creighton (15)
Dave Lewis (12)
Deercourt (13)
Elizabeth (21)
Finlayson (15)
Hitchcock (10)
John Alden (27)
John Chinn (10, 15)
Knightley (1)
Lavington (20)

Lightfoot (17)
MacDonald (9)
Mahbab Ali (15)
Maria Ward (3)
McAndrews (15)
Middleton (7)
Minnehaha (24)
Miss Bates (1)
Miss Sneyd (3)
Mrs. Cheyne (9)
Mrs. Harvey (18)
Mrs. McPhee (10)
Mrs. Mutrie (12)
Mrs. Norris (3)
Mrs. Palmer (7)
Mrs. Purvis (8)
Mrs. Vernon (2)
Mrs. Watson (8)
Mrs. Weston (1)
Nick Brady (9)
Priscilla (27)
Rushworth (3)
Sam Watson (8)
Stangrave (18)
The Mugger (15)
Tim Coulan (13)
Victorian (28)
Vieuxbois (20)
Wentworth (5)
Woodhouse (1)

10

Alton Locke (16)
Anne Elliot (5)
Arnyas Leigh (19)
Dinah Shadd (13)
Dirkovitch (11)
Disko Troop (9)
Dr. Thurnall (18)
Earl Godwin (17)
Emma Watson (8)
Evangeline (22)
Fanny Price (3)
Findlayson (10)
Godwinsson (17)
Jane Bennet (6)
John Briggs (18)
John Thorpe (4)
King Ranald (17)
Lady Godiva (17)
Lady Vernon (2)
Lajeunesse (22)
Lucy Steele (7)
Mainwaring (2)

Miss Kinzey (9)
Miss M'Kenna (13)
Miss Martin (10)
Miss Morton (7)
Mrs. De Sussa (13)
Mrs. Edwards (8)
Mrs. Holdock (10)
Mrs. Johnson (2)
Mrs. Mullins (13)
Prometheus (28)
Strickland (11)
Teshoo Lama (15)
Tom Bertram (3)
Villamarti (15)
Willoughby (7)

11

Alfred Chinn (10)
Barraclough (11)
Bracebridge (2)
Count of Lara (28)
Count Robert (17)
Dundas Fawne (10)
Earl Leofric (17)
Fanny Norris (3)
Frances Ward (3)
Harry Verney (20)
Henry Tilney (4)
Hinchcliffe (15)
James Burton (21)
Jane Fairfax (1)
Jerry Blazes (13)
John Gillett (14)
John Learoyd (11)
John Oxenham (19)
Kate Sheriff (12)
Lady Bertram (3)
Lady Osborne (8)
Lionel Chinn (10)
Lord Osborne (8)
Lucy Ferrars (7)
Lurgan Sahib (15)
Lydia Bennet (6)
Mary Edwards (8)
Megissogwon (24)
Mrs. Dashwood (7)
Mrs. Gardiner (6)
Mrs. Jennings (7)
Mudjekeewis (24)
Paul Fleming (25)
René Leblanc (22)
Rev. Mr. Howard (8)
Rev. Mr. Norris (3)
Shawondasee (24)

Susan Vernon (2)
Thomas Leigh (19)
Tom Musgrave (8)
Tom Thurnall (18)

12

Abbot Leofric (17)
Admiral Croft (5)
Brimblecombe (19)
Brugglesmith (10)
Captain Leigh (19)
Colonel Nolan (12)
Dick Grenvile (19)
Earl of Mercia (17)
Earl of Wessex (17)
Eustace Leigh (19)
Frank Headley (18)
Harriet Smith (4)
Harvey Cheyne (9)
Jack Thurnall (18)
Jasper Purvis (8)
John Dashwood (7)
Julia Bertram (3)
Lady de Bourgh (6)
Lady de Courcy (2)
Lady Grenvile (19)
Lord Lynedale (16)
Lucy Passmore (19)
Maria Bertram (3)
Mary Crawford (3)
Miss Bingleys (The) (6)
Miss Newbroom (20)
Miss Standish (27)
Mrs. Rushworth (3)
Pau-Puk-Keewis (24)
Paul Tregarva (20)
Robert Martin (1)
Robert Watson (8)
Rose Salterne (19)
Salvation Yeo (19)
Samuel Burton (21)

Sandy Mackage (16)
Uncle Salters (9)
William Price (3)

13

Admiral Winter (19)
Ali Baba Mahbub (15)
Alicia Johnson (2)
Bellefontaine (22)
Captain Gadsby (13, 15)
Captain Hunter (8)
Captain Maffin (13)
Captain O'Brien (8)
Captain Willis (18)
Colonel Dabney (14)
Corporal Slane (13)
Edmund Bertram (3)
Edward Ferrars (7)
Eleanor Tilney (4)
Emma Deercourt (13)
Emma Woodhouse (1)
Fanny Dashwood (7)
Father Campian (19)
Father Parsons (19)
Henry Crawford (3)
Henry Dashwood (7)
Humphrey Chinn (10)
John Middleton (7)
Julia Crawford (3)
Lady Middleton (7)
Lancelot Smith (20)
Little Mildred (15)
Lord Vieuxbois (20)
Major Campbell (18)
Mark Armsworth (18)
Mary Armsworth (18)
Mary Ashburton (25)
Miles Standish (27)
Raymond Martin (14)
Robert Ferrars (7)
Simon Salterne (19)

Thomas Bertram (3)
William Martin (10)

14

Captain Raleigh (19)
Cecilia Vaughan (26)
Colonel Brandon (7)
Earl Godwinsson (17)
Edward Thurnall (18)
Elinor Dashwood (7)
Emanuel Pycroft (15)
Father Felicien (22)
Frank Churchill (1)
Isabella Thorpe (4)
Miss Mainwaring (2)
Nicholas Tarvin (12)
Oliver Basselin (28)
Penelope Watson (8)
Rev. John Gillett (14)
Robert of Sicily (28)
Sir James Martin (2)
Thomas Thurnall (18)
Walter of Varila (21)

15

Amos Barraclough (11)
Catherine Vernon (2)
Elizabeth Bennet (6)
Elizabeth Watson (8)
Hereward the Wake (17)
Humphrey Gilbert (28)
Lady Susan Vernon (2)
Martin Lightfoot (17)
Private Mulvaney (13)
Private Ortheris (13)
Raphael Aben-Ezra (21)
Richard Grenvile (19)
Sergeant Mullins (13)
Sir Francis Drake (19)
Squire Lavington (20)
Valentia Headley (18)

Some characters from **Meredith**, **Milton** and **Thomas Moore**
List of works from which the following characters are taken, with reference numbers.

George Meredith

Ref. No.   *Title*

1. Beauchamp's Career   (16 letters)
2. Egoist, The   (9 letters)
3. Evan Harrington   (14 letters)
4. Harry Richmond   (13 letters)
5. Rhoda Fleming   (12 letters)
6. Richard Feverel   (14 letters)
7. One of our Conquerors   (18 letters)
8. Sandra Belloni   (13 letters)
9. Vittoria   (8 letters)
10. (Various)

John Milton

Ref. No.   *Title*

11. Comus   (5 letters)
12. Paradise Lost   (12 letters)
13. Paradise Regained   (16 letters)
14. (Various)

Thomas Moore

15. Lalla Rookh   (10 letters)

Note: The numbers in brackets indicate *the works* in which the characters appear

3 – 5

Alvan (10)
Azim (15)
Beppo (9)
Berry (6)
Camph (10)
Chloe (10)
Chump (8)
Comus (11)
Corte (9)
Dagon (12)
Dale (2)
Diana (10)
Drew (1)
Forey (6)
Forth (3)
Goren (3)
Hafed (15)
Hinda (15)
Kirby (10)
Kline (3)
Moody (5)
Mount (6)
Ople (10)
Pole (8)
Powys (9)
Rizzo (9)
Selim (15)
Uriel (12)

6

Abdiel (12)
Aliris (15)
Arioch (12)
Austin (1)
Azazel (12)
Azazil (12)
Barmby (7)
Barnes (3)
Belial (12)
Benson (6)
Blaize (6)
Boulby (5)
Burman (7)
Busshe (2)
Callet (7)
Corney (2)
Dacier (10)
Dalila (14)
Daphne (13)
Denham (1)
Durham (2)
Eccles (5)
Eglett (10)
Farina (10)
Gammon (5)
Graves (7)
Harley (6)
Kionis (4)
Laxley (3)
Lespel (1)
Lovell (5)
Lowton (3)
Manoah (14)
Nereus (11)
Noorka (10)
Oggler (1)
Oxford (2)
Pompey (13)

Radnor (7)
Raikes (3)
Romara (9)
Samfit (5)
Scipio (13)
Sedley (9)
Semele (13)
Strike (3)
Summer (8)
Syrinx (13)
Tethys (11)
Tinman (10)
Turbot (1)
Uploft (3)
Waring (5)
Zelica (15)

7

Ammiani (9)
Amymone (13)
Antiopa (13)
Asmadai (12)
Bagarag (10)
Barrett (8)
Beamish (10)
Belloni (8)
Beltham (4)
Billing (5)
Calisto (13)
Clymene (13)
Cougham (1)
Culling (1)
De Craye (2)
Durance (7)
Farrell (10)

Feverel (6)
Fleming (5)
Gambler (8, 9)
Gosstre (8)
Grossby (3)
Hackbut (5)
Halkett (1)
Harapha (14)
Jocelyn (3)
Killick (1)
Latters (5)
Lycidas (14)
Lydiard (1)
Mohanna (15)
Namouna (15)
Ottilia (4)
Parsley (3)
Pelleas 13)
Pempton (7)
Peridon (7)
Perkins (3)
Piavens (9)
Pierson (9)
Raphael (12)
Romfrey (1)
Sabrina (11)
Saracco (9)
Sedgett (5)
Shagpat (10)
Skepsey (7)
Sowerby (7)
Thyrsis (14)
Tuckham (1)
Warwick (10)
Weyburn (10)

Wicklow (5)
Zophiel (12)

8

Al Hassan (15)
Bakewell (6)
Blancove (5)
Blandish (6)
Braintop (8)
Crossjay (2)
De Saldar (3)
Dr. Corney (2)
Dunstane (10)
Fenellan (7)
Feramorz (15)
Ithuriel (12)
Lancelot (13)
Miss Dale (2)
Mortimer (6)
Mrs. Berry (6)
Mrs. Chump (8)
Mrs. Forey (6)
Mrs. Mount (6)
Patterne (2)
Pericles (8, 10)
Redworth (10)
Richmond (4)
Shrapnel (1)
Thompson (6)
Ugo Corte (9)
Vittoria (9)
Whitford (2)
Woodseer (10)

Some characters from **Sir Walter Scott**
List of works from which the following characters are taken, with reference numbers.

Ref. No.	Title		Ref. No.	Title	
1.	Abbot, The	(8 letters)	20.	Lay of the Last Minstrel, The	(23 letters)
2.	Anne of Geierstein	(16 letters)	21.	Legend of Montrose, The	(19 letters)
3.	Antiquary, The	(12 letters)	22.	Marmion	(7 letters)
4.	Aunt Margaret's Mirror	(19 letters)	23.	Monastery, The	(12 letters)
5.	Betrothed, The	(12 letters)	24.	Old Mortality	(12 letters)
6.	Black Dwarf, The	(13 letters)	25.	Peveril of the Peak	(16 letters)
7.	Bridal of Triermain, The	(20 letters)	26.	Pirate, The	(9 letters)
8.	Bride of Lammermoor, The	(20 letters)	27.	Quentin Durward	(14 letters)
9.	Castle Dangerous	(15 letters)	28.	Redgauntlet	(11 letters)
10.	Count Robert of Paris	(18 letters)	29.	Rob Roy	(6 letters)
11.	Fair Maid of Perth, The	(18 letters)	30.	Rokeby	(6 letters)
12.	Fortunes of Nigel, The	(18 letters)	31.	St. Ronan's Well	(12 letters)
13.	Guy Mannering	(12 letters)	32.	Surgeon's Daughter, The	(19 letters)
14.	Heart of Midlothian, The	(20 letters)	33.	Talisman, The	(11 letters)
15.	Highland Widow, The	(16 letters)	34.	Tapestried Chamber, The	(20 letters)
16.	Ivanhoe	(7 letters)	35.	Two Drovers, The	(13 letters)
17.	Kenilworth	(10 letters)	36.	Waverley	(8 letters)
18.	Lady of the Lake, The	(16 letters)	37.	Woodstock	(9 letters)
19.	Laird's Jock, The	(13 letters)			

Note: The numbers in brackets indicate *the works* in which the characters appear

3 AND 4

Adie (23)
Anna (Princess) (10)
Anne (Princess) (27)
Bean (36)
Beg (11)
Dods (31)
Eva (11)
Faa (13)
Gow (11)
Gray (8, 32)
Lee (37)
Lyle (21)
René (King) (2)
Tuck (16)
Weir (28)

5

Abney (37)
Allan (13)
Allen (24)
André (27)
Aston (37)
Aymer (16)
Bevis (horse) (22)

Binks (31)
Blair (11)
Block (2)
Blood (25)
Boeuf (16)
Brand (18)
Brown (29)
Caxon (3)
Clegg (25)
Croye (Countess) (27)
Deans (14)
Edgar (8)
Edith (Lady) (16)
Eppie (31)
Evans (25)
Ewart (28)
Glass (14)
Hadgi (33)
Hakim (33)
Hamet (16)
Harry (11)
Howie (36)
Irene (33)
Isaac (16)
Jabos (13)
Luira (dog) (18)

Mengs (2)
Nixon (28)
Norna (26)
North (Lord) (25)
Olave (26)
Penny (13)
Ralph (25)
Smith (17)
Timms (35)
Tinto (8, 31)
Troil (26)
Urgan (18)
Vanda (5)
Wamba (16)
Wilsa (12)

6

Airlie (Earl of) (21)
Alasco (17)
Alison (17)
Amelot (5)
Amoury (33)
Andrew (13)
Anselm (11)
Arnold (16)
Ashton (8)

Avenel (Lady of) (23)
Aylmer (37)
Badger (17)
Bailie (13)
Baliol (15)
Bayard (horse) (18)
Benjie (28)
Bennet (23)
Bertha (10)
Bibbet (37)
Blount (17)
Blower (31)
Bowyer (17)
Brakel (25)
Browne (34)
Bulmer (31)
Butler (14)
Caspar (2)
Cedric (16)
Copley (17)
Damien (16)
de Lacy (5)
de Vaux (7)
Elliot (6)
Empson (25)
Faggot (28)

Foster (17)
Foxley (28)
Geddes (28)
Glover (11)
Graeme (1)
Gyneth (7)
Halcro (26)
Hamako (33)
Happer (23)
Hastie (28)
Hector (21)
Hudson (25)
Inglis (24)
Jarvie (29)
Jin Yin (12)
Jobson (29)
Judith (12)
Lesley (27)
Louise (11)
Lumley (24)
MacIan (11)
Martha (10)
Martin (28)
Mattie (29)
Mervyn (13)
Mornay (27)
Morris (29)
Morton (Earl of)
   (1, 23, 24)
Norman (8)
Quitam (29)
Ramsay (12)
Red-Cap (12)
Rob Roy (29)
Robert (Count) (10)
Rowena (16)
Seyton (1)
Sharpe (24)
Stubbs (14)
Tacket (23)
Talbot (36)
Tormot (11)
Tyrrel (31)
Ulrica (10, 16)
Ursula (9)
Varney (17)
Vernon (29)
Vipont (16)
Warden (23)
Watley (25)
Wilson (14)
Winnie (8)

7

Abdalla (16)
Ackland (37)
Aikwood (3)
Aldrick (25)
Ambrose (1, 16, 28)
Anthony (9, 31)
Arnheim (2)
Baldwin (Count)
   (10, 16)
Balfour (24)
Barston (25)
Beaujeu (12, 36)
Berkely (lady) (9)
Bertram (13)
Berwine (5)
Bidmore (Lord) (31)
Bletson (37)
Bridget (1)
Brydone (23)
Bullseg (36)
Calista (33)
Cargill (31)
Corsand (13)
Crosbie (28)
de Boeuf (16)
de Bracy (16)
Dinmont (13)
Dorothy (11)
Douglas (18)
Dubourg (29)
Durward (27)
El Hadgi (33)
El Hakim (33)
Elspeth (3, 13)
Eustace (16, 23)
Feltham (12)
Fenella (25)
Fleming (1, 9, 14)
Francis (11, 27)
Glossin (13)
Godfrey (23)
Gosling (17)
Gourlay (8)
Grahame (24)
Guthrie (27)
Hartley (32)
Hayston (8)
Herries (Lord) (1)
Hesketh (35)
Hillary (32)
Hinchup (14)
Ivanhoe (16)

Joliffe (37)
Kennedy (13)
Kenneth (Sir) (33)
Langley (6)
Latimer (28)
Leopold (33)
MacEagh (21)
MacIvor (36)
MacTurk (31)
Malachi (28)
Margery (5)
Marmion (22)
Matilda (30)
Maxwell (12,24, 28)
Meg Dods (31)
Mertoun (26)
Mowbray (31)
Neville (3)
Nosebag (36)
Oldbuck (3)
Pacolet (26)
Peebles (28)
Peveril (25)
Ramorny (11)
Rattray (12)
Rebecca (16)
Redmond (30)
Robsart (17)
Ruthven (Lord) (1)
Saladin (33)
Sampson (13)
Scholey (26)
Sellock (25)
Shafton (23, 29)
Staples (17)
Stephen (16)
Taffril (3)
Tancred (10)
Tomkins (37)
Torquil (11)
Tresham (29)
Trotter (31)
Vanwelt (5)
Vincent (12)
Wakeman (25)
Waldeck (3)
Wayland (17)
Wenlock (5)
Wilfred (29)

8

Alberick (5, 33)
Alice Lee (37)
Anderson (31)

Argentin (2)
Baldrick (5)
Berenger (5)
Bohemond
   (Prince) (10)
Boniface (1, 23)
Burleigh (Lord) (21)
Campbell
   (14,15, 21, 28)
Cantrips (28)
Carleton (25)
Christie (12, 23)
Clifford (33,37)
Colkitto (21)
Conachar (11)
Dalgarno (Lord) (12)
Dalgetty (21)
Damiotti (4)
de Multon (33)
de Wilton (22)
Debbitch (25)
Dennison (24)
Engelred (16)
Evandale (Lord) (24)
Fairford (28)
Falconer (4, 36)
Fitzurse (Lord) (16)
Flammock (5)
Forester (4)
Geraldin (Lord) (3)
Guenevra (33)
Headrigg (24)
Henry Gow (11)
Henry Lee (37)
Hereward (10)
Hermione (12)
l'Hermite (2, 27)
Ingelram (23)
Jamieson (32)
Jellicot (37)
King René (2)
Lapraick (28)
Locksley (16)
Macaulay (21)
Macready (29)
Margaret (Ladye) (20)
Melville (1)
Menteith (Earl of) (21)
Meredith (28)
Misbegot (3)
Mrs. Allan (13)
Mrs. Glass (14)
Musgrave (20)
Nicholas (23)

Julian Peveril (25)
Kate Chiffinch (25)
Kettledrummle (24)
Lady Bellenden (24)
Ladye Margaret (20)
Lord Woodville (34)
Ludovic Lesley (27)
MacAnaleister (29)
Madge Wildfire (14)
Major Falconer (4)
Martin Waldeck (3)
Matthew Foxley (28)
Meg Murdochson (14)
Mother Bridget (1)
Nelly Christie (12)
Nigel Olifaunt (12)
O'Neale Redmond (30)
Peter Protocol (13)
Ralph de Wilton (22)
Ranald MacEagh (21)
Richard Walley (25)
Ringan Aikwood (3)
Robert of Paris (Count) (10)
Roger Wildrake (37)
Sir Bingo Binks (31)
Sir Hugo de Lacy (5)
Sir Jacob Aston (37)
Stephen Butler (14)
Thomas Ackland (36)
William Ashton (8)
Willie Johnson (13)

14

Adonbec el Hakim (33)
Augusta Bidmore (31)
Baldwin de Oyley (16)
Blondel de Nesle (33)
Brother Ambrose (16)
Captain Hillary (32)
Captain MacTurk (31)
Clement Dubourg (29)
Colonel Grahame (24)
Corporal Inglis (24)
Cuddie Headrigg (24)
Dame Whitecraft (25)
Davie Gellatley (36)
de Bois Guilbert (16)
Dirk Hatteraick (13)
Dominie Sampson (13)
Duncan Campbell (21)
Earl of Menteith (21)
Earl of Seaforth (21)
Edith Bellenden (24)
Edward Waverley (36)

Elspeth Brydone (23)
Eric Scambister (26)
Father Boniface (1)
Father Waltheof (11)
Geoffrey Hudson (25)
George Staunton (14)
Gilbert Glossin (13)
Grace Armstrong (6)
Harry Wakefield (35)
Heatherblutter (36)
Helen MacGregor (29)
Henry Cranstoun (20)
Jabesh Rentowel (36)
Jemima Forester (4)
Jessie Cantrips (28)
John Phillipson (2)
John Whitecraft (25)
Julia Mannering (13)
Lady Penfeather (31)
Maggie Steenson (28)
Major Bellenden (24)
Major Galbraith (29)
Malcolm Fleming (9)
Margaret Blower (31)
Margaret Ramsay (12)
Maria MacIntyre (3)
Martha Trapbois (12)
Nicholas Blount (17)
Nicholas Faggot (28)
Paulus Pleydell (13)
Peter Proudtext (24)
Philip Forester (4)
Piercie Shafton (23)
Prince Bohemond (10)
Quentin Durward (27)
Richard Grahame (24)
Robert Melville (1)
Runnion Rattray (12)
Sir Gibbs Amoury (33)
Sir John Ramorny (11)
Thomas de Multon (33)
Thomas Turnbull (28)
Wilkin Flammack (5)
William Crosbie (28)
William Maxwell (24)
Willie Steenson (28)
Zamet Maugrabin (27)
Zarah Christian (25)
Zilia de Moncada (32)

15

Abdallah el Hadgi (33)
Adam Craigdallie (11)
Adie of Aikenshaw (23)

Albert Malvoisin (16)
Archie Armstrong (12)
Arnold Biederman (2)
Augustus Bidmore (31)
Balfour of Burley (24)
Brother Nicholas (23)
Captain Campbell (15)
Captain Carleton (25)
Captain Porteous (14)
Captain Waverley (36)
Catherine Glover (11)
Catherine Seyton (1)
Claus Hammerlein (27)
Count Geierstein (2)
Countess of Croye (27)
Deborah Debbitch (25)
Duncan Galbraith (29)
Edgar Ravenswood (8)
Edward Christian (25)
Ephraim Macbriar (24)
Erminia Pauletti (12)
Eveline Berenger (5)
Father Howleglas (1)
Flibbertigibbet (17)
General Campbell (28)
Geraldin Neville (3)
Hamish MacGregor (29)
Hamish MacTavish (15)
Hector MacIntyre (3)
Hector of the Mist (21)
Hubert Ratcliffe (6)
Jeanie MacAlpine (29)
Joceline Joliffe (37)
Jonathan Oldbuck (3)
Lady Mary Fleming (1)
Lady Plantagenet (14)
Lady Rougedragon (28)
Lawrence Scholey (26)
Lawrence Staples (17)
Lawyer Clippurse (36)
Madame Cresswell (25)
Madge Murdochson (14)
Magdalene Graeme (1)
Malcolm Misbegot (3)
Miss Walkingshaw (28)
Monsieur Dubourg (29)
Mordaunt Mertoun (26)
Murdoch Campbell (21)
Peter Bridgeward (1, 23)
Philip Malvoisin (16)
Phoebe Mayflower (37)
Raymond Berenger (5)
Richard Musgrave (20)
Richard Waverley (36)

Rob-Roy MacGregor (29)
Robert MacGregor (29)
Rose Bradwardine (36)
Simon of Hackburn (6)
Sir Damian de Lacy (5)
Sir Randal de Lacy (5)

Sir Thomas Copley (17)
Squire Jnglewood (29)
Stephen Wetheral (16)
The Dougal Cratur (29)
Thomas Chiffinch (25)
Torquil of the Oak (11)

Tristan l'Hermite (2, 27)
Valentine Bulmer (31)
Wandering Willie (28)
Widow Flockheart (36)
Wilfrid Wycliffe (30)

Some characters from **Shakespeare**
List of plays from which the following characters are taken, with reference numbers.

Ref. No.	Title		Ref. No.	Title	
1.	All's Well that Ends Well	(20 letters)	19.	King Richard III	(10 or 14 letters)
2.	Antony and Cleopatra	(18 letters)	20.	Love's Labour's Lost	(16 letters)
3.	As You Like It	(11 letters)	21.	Macbeth	(7 letters)
4.	Comedy of Errors, A	(15 letters)	22.	Measure for Measure	(17 letters)
5.	Coriolanus	(10 letters)	23.	Merchant of Venice, The	(19 letters)
6.	Cymbeline	(9 letters)	24.	Merry Wives of Windsor	(19 letters)
7.	Hamlet (Prince of Denmark)	(6 letters)	25.	Midsummer Night's Dream, A	(21 letters)
8.	Julius Caesar	(12 letters)	26.	Much Ado About Nothing	(19 letters)
9.	King Henry IV, Part 1	(7 or 11 letters)	27.	Othello, The Moor of Venice	(7 letters)
10.	King Henry IV, Part 2	(7 or 11 letters)	28.	Pericles, Prince of Tyre	(8 letters)
11.	King Henry V	(6 or 10 letters)	29.	Romeo and Juliet	(14 letters)
12.	King Henry VI, Part 1	(7 or 11 letters)	30.	Taming of the Shrew, The	(19 letters)
13.	King Henry VI, Part 2	(7 or 11 letters)	31.	Tempest, The	(10 letters)
14.	King Henry VI, Part 3	(7 or 11 letters)	32.	Timon of Athens	(13 letters)
15.	King Henry VIII	(9 or 13 letters)	33.	Titus Andronicus	(15 letters)
16.	King John	(8 letters)	34.	Troilus and Cressida	(18 letters)
17.	King Lear	(8 letters)	35.	Twelfth Night; or, What You Will	(12 letters)
18.	King Richard II	(9 or 13 letters)	36.	Two Gentlemen of Verona	(20 letters)
			37.	Winter's Tale, The	(14 letters)

Note: The numbers in brackets indicate *the plays* in which the characters appear

(A.-B. of) = Archbishop of.   (B. of) = Bishop of.   (Card.) = Cardinal.   (C. of) = Count of.
(C'ess of) = Countess of.   (D. of) = Duke of.   (D'ess of) = Duchess of.   (E. of) = Earl of.
(K. of) = King of.   (M. of) = Marquis of.   (P. of) = Prince of.   (P'ess of) = Princess of.
(Q. of) = Queen of.

3 AND 4

Adam (3)
Ajax (34)
Anne (Lady) (19)
Bona (14)
Cade (13)
Cato (8)
Davy (10)
Dick (13)
Dion (37)
Dull (20)
Eros (2)
Fang (10)

Ford (24)
Ford (Mrs.) (24)
Grey (11)
Grey (Lady) (14)
Grey (Lord) (19)
Hero (26)
Hume (13)
Iago (27)
Iden (13)
Iris (31)
Jamy (11)
John (10)
John (Don) (26)
John (K.) (16)

Juno (31)
Kent (E. of) (17)
Lear (K.) (17)
Lion (25)
Luce (4)
Lucy (12)
Moth (20, 25)
Nym (11, 24)
Page (24)
Page (Mrs.) (24)
Peto (9, 10)
Puck (25)
Ross (Lord) (18)
Ross (21)

Say (Lord) (13)
Snug (25)
Time (37)
Vaux (13, 15)
Wart (10)
York (A.-B. of) (9, 10, 19)
York (D'ess of) (18, 19)
York (D. of) (11, 18, 19)

5

Aaron (33)
Abram (29)
Alice (11)

Angus (21)
Ariel (31)
Bagot (18)
Bates (11)
Belch (35)
Bigot (16)
Biron (20)
Blunt (9, 10)
Boult (28)
Boyet (20)
Bushy (18)
Butts (15)
Caius (6, 24)
Casca (8)
Celia (3)
Ceres (31)
Cinna (8)
Cleon (28)
Clown (22, 35)
Corin (3)
Court (11)
Curan (17)
Curio (35)
Denny (15)
Diana (1, 28)
Edgar (17)
Egeus (25)
Elbow (22)
Essex (E. of) (16)
Evans (24)
Flute (25)
Froth (22)
Ghost (7)
Gobbo (23)
Gower (10, 11, 28)
Green (18)
Helen (6, 34)
Henry (19)
Henry (K.) (9, 10, 11, 12, 13, 14, 15)
Henry (P.) (16)
Julia (36)
Lafeu (1)
Louis (Dauphin) (11, 16)
Louis (K.) (14)
Louis (Lord) (19)
Lucio (22)
March (E. of) (9)
Maria (20)
Melun (16)
Menas (2)
Milan (D. of) (36)
Mopsa (37)

Osric (7)
Paris (29, 34)
Pedro (Don) (26)
Percy (9, 10, 18)
Percy (Lady) (9)
Peter (13, 22)
Phebe (3)
Philo (2)
Pinch (4)
Poins (9, 10)
Priam (34)
Queen (6)
Regan (17)
Robin (24)
Romeo (29)
Rugby (24)
Sands (Lord) (15)
Snare (10)
Snout (25)
Speed (36)
Timon (32)
Tubal (23)
Varro (8)
Viola (35)
Wales (P. of) (9, 10, 19)

6

Adrian (31)
Aegeon (4)
Aeneas (34)
Albany (D. of) (17)
Alexas (2)
Alonso (31)
Amiens (3)
Angelo (4, 22)
Antony (2)
Armado (20)
Arthur (16)
Audrey (3)
Banquo (21)
Basset (12)
Bianca (27, 30)
Blanch (16)
Blount (19)
Bottom (25)
Brutus (5, 8)
Bullen (15)
Cadwal (6)
Caesar (2)
Caphis (32)
Cassio (27)
Chiron (33)
Cicero (8)
Clitus (8)

Cloten (22)
Cobweb (25)
Curtis (30)
Dennis (3)
Dorcas (37)
Dorset (M. of) (19)
Dromio (4)
Dumain (20)
Duncan (K.) (21)
Edmund (14, 17)
Edward (13)
Edward (K.) (19)
Edward (P. of Wales) (14, 19)
Elinor (16)
Emilia (27, 37)
Exeter (D. of) (11, 14)
Fabian (35)
Feeble (10)
Fenton (24)
France (K. of) (1, 17)
France (P'ess of) (20)
Gallus (2)
George (13, 14, 19)
Grumio (30)
Gurney (16)
Hamlet (7)
Hecate (21)
Hector (34)
Helena (1, 25)
Henry V (K.) (11)
Hermia (25)
Horner (13)
Imogen (6)
Isabel (11)
Jaques (3)
Juliet (22, 29)
Launce (36)
Le Beau (3)
Lennox (21)
Lovell (15)
Lucius (8, 32, 33)
Marina (28)
Morgan (6)
Morton (10, 19)
Mouldy (10)
Mr. Ford (24)
Mr. Page (24)
Mutius (33)
Nestor (34)
Oberon (25)
Oliver (3)
Olivia (35)
Orsino (35)

Oswald (17)
Oxford (D. of) (14)
Oxford (E. of) (19)
Pedant (30)
Philip (K.) (16)
Pierce (18)
Pistol (10, 11, 24)
Portia (8, 23)
Quince (25)
Rivers (Earl) (19)
Rivers (Lord) (14)
Rogero (37)
Rumour (10)
Scales (Lord) (13)
Scarus (2)
Scroop (9, 10, 18)
Scroop (Lord) (11)
Seyton (21)
Shadow (10)
Silius (2)
Silvia (36)
Simple (24)
Siward (21)
Strato (8)
Surrey (D. of) (18)
Surrey (E. of) (15, 19)
Talbot (12)
Talbot (Lord) (12)
Tamora (33)
Taurus (2)
Thaisa (28)
Thisbe (25)
Thomas (22)
Thurio (36)
Tranio (30)
Tybalt (29)
Tyrrel (19)
Ursula (26)
Venice (D. of) (23, 27)
Verges (26)
Vernon (9, 12)
Wolsey (Lord) (15)

7

Adriana (4)
Aemilia (4)
Agrippa (2)
Alarbus (33)
Alencon (D. of) (12)
Antenor (34)
Antonio (23, 26, 31, 35, 36)
Arragon (P. of) (23)
Aumerle (D. of) (18)

Bedford (D. of) (11, 12)
Berkley (Earl) (18)
Bertram (1)
Bourbon (D. of) (11)
Brandon (15)
Calchas (34)
Caliban (31)
Camillo (37)
Capulet (29)
Capulet (Lady) (29)
Cassius (8)
Catesby (19)
Cerimon (28)
Charles (3)
Charles (Dauphin) (11)
Charles (K.) (11)
Claudio (22, 26)
Conrade (26)
Costard (20)
Cranmer (A.-B.) (15)
Dauphin, The (12, 16)
Dionyza (28)
Don John (26)
Douglas (E. of) (9)
Eleanor (13)
Escalus (22,29)
Escanes (28)
Flavius (8,32)
Fleance (21)
Gloster (D'ess of) (18)
Gloster (D. of) (11, 14, 19)
Gloster (E. of) (12)
Gloster (P. of) (10)
Goneril (17)
Gonzalo (31)
Gregory (29)
Helenus (34)
Henry IV (K.) (9, 10)
Henry VI (K.) (12, 13, 14)
Herbert (19)
Horatio (7)
Hostess (30)
Hotspur (9, 10)
Iachimo (6)
Jessica (23)
Laertes (7)
Lavinia (33)
Leonato (26)
Leonine (28)
Leontes (37)
Lepidus (2)
Lincoln (B. of) (15)

Lord Say (13)
Lorenzo (23)
Lucetta (36)
Luciana (4)
Macbeth (21)
Macbeth (Lady) (21)
Macduff (21)
Macduff (Lady) (21)
Malcolm (21)
Marcius (5)
Mardian (2)
Mariana (1, 22)
Martext (3)
Martius (33)
Mercade (20)
Messala (8)
Michael (13)
Michael (Sir) (9, 10)
Miranda (31)
Montano (27)
Morocco (P. of) (23)
Mowbray (18)
Mowbray (Lord) (10)
Mrs. Ford (24)
Mrs. Page (24)
Nerissa (23)
Norfolk (D. of) (14, 15, 18, 19)
Octavia (2)
Ophelia (7)
Orlando (3)
Orleans (D. of) (11)
Othello (27)
Paulina (37)
Perdita (37)
Phrynia (32)
Pisanio (6)
Proteus (36)
Publius (8, 33)
Pucelle (12)
Pyramus (25)
Quickly (Mrs.) (9, 10, 11, 24)
Quintus (33)
Richard (13, 14, 19)
Richard (K.) (18, 19)
Salanio (23)
Salerio (23)
Sampson (29)
Setebos (31)
Shallow (10, 24)
Shylock (23)
Silence (10)
Silvius (3)

Simpcox (13)
Slender (24)
Solinus (4)
Stanley (13, 14)
Stanley (Lord) (19)
Suffolk (D. of) (13, 15)
Suffolk (E. of) (12)
Theseus (25)
Thryeus (2)
Titania (25)
Travers (10)
Troilus (34)
Ulysses (34)
Urswick (19)
Valeria (5)
Varrius (2, 22)
Vaughan (19)
Velutus (5)
Warwick (P. of) (10, 11, 12, 13, 14)
William (3)

8

Abhorson (22)
Achilles (34)
Aemilius (33)
Aufidius (5)
Auvergne (C'ess of) (12)
Baptista (30)
Bardolph (9, 10, 11, 24)
Bardolph (Lord) (10)
Bassanio (23)
Beatrice (26)
Beaufort (12)
Beaufort (Card.) (13)
Belarius (6)
Benedick (26)
Benvolio (29)
Bernardo (7)
Borachio (26)
Bouchier (Card.) (19)
Bullcalf (10)
Burgundy (D. of) (11, 12, 17)
Campeius (Card.) (15)
Canidius (2)
Capucius (15)
Charmian (2)
Clarence (D. of) (10, 19)
Claudius (8)
Claudius (K.) (7)
Clifford (13)

Clifford (Lord) (13, 14)
Colville (10)
Cominius (5)
Cordelia (17)
Cornwall (D. of) (17)
Cressida (34)
Cromwell (15)
Dercetas (2)
Diomedes (2, 34)
Dogberry (26)
Don Pedro (26)
Edward VI (K.) (19)
Eglamour (36)
Falstaff (9, 10, 24)
Fastolfe (12)
Florence (D. of) (1)
Florizel (37)
Fluellen (11)
Gadshill (9)
Gardiner (15)
Gargrave (13)
Gertrude (Q.) (7)
Gratiano (23, 27)
Griffith (15)
Harcourt (10)
Hastings (Lord) (10, 14, 19)
Hermione (37)
Humphrey (10, 13)
Isabella (22)
Jack Cade (13)
Jourdain (13)
King John (16)
King Lear (17)
Lady Anne (19)
Lady Grey (14)
Lawrence (29)
Leonardo (23)
Leonatus (6)
Lodovico (27)
Lord Grey (19)
Lord Ross (18)
Lucentio (30)
Lucilius (8, 32)
Lucullus (32)
Lysander (25)
Malvolio (35)
Margaret (12, 13, 19, 26)
Margaret (Q.) (14)
Marullus (8)
Mecaenas (2)
Menelaus (34)
Menteith (21)

178

Lady Capulet (29)
Lady Macbeth (21)
Lady Macduff (21)
Lord Mowbray (10)
Lord Stanley (19)
Mrs. Anne Page (24)
Mrs. Overdone (22)
Mustardseed (25)
Peasblossom (25)
Philostrate (25)
Plantagenet (12, 13, 14)
Prince Henry (16)
Robert Bigot (16)
Rosencrantz (7)
Westminster (A.-B. of) (18)
William Page (24)
Young Siward (21)

12

Decius Brutus (8)
Duke of Albany (17)
Duke of Exeter (11, 14)
Duke of Oxford (14)
Duke of Surrey (18)
Duke of Venice (23, 27)
Earl of Oxford (19)
Earl of Surrey (15, 19)
Falconbridge (16)
Falconbridge (Lady) (16)
Guildenstern (7)
Julius Caesar (8)
Junius Brutus (5)
King of France (1, 17)
Lady Montague (29)
Lady Mortimer (9)
Lord Bardolph (10)
Lord Clifford (13, 14)
Lord Hastings (10, 14, 19)
Lord Stafford (14)
Marcus Brutus (8)
Popilius Lena (8)
Sir Hugh Evans (24)
Sir Nathaniel (20)
Sir Toby Belch (35)
Thomas Horner (13)
Three Witches (21)
Titus Lartius (5)

Westmoreland (E. of)
(9, 10, 11, 14)
Young Marcius (5)

13

Alexander Iden (13)
Doll Tearsheet (10)
Duchess of York (18, 19)
Duke of Alencon (12)
Duke of Aumerle (18)
Duke of Bedford (11, 12)
Duke of Bourbon (11)
Duke of Gloster (11, 14, 19)
Duke of Norfolk (14, 15, 18, 19)
Duke of Orleans (11)
Duke of Suffolk (13, 15)
Earl of Douglas (9)
Earl of Gloster (17)
Earl of Suffolk (12)
Earl of Warwick (10, 11, 12, 13, 14)
Friar Lawrence (29)
Hubert de Burgh (16)
Joan la Pucelle (12)
King Henry VIII (15)
King Richard II (18)
Lord Fitzwater (18)
Owen Glendower (9)
Prince of Wales (10, 19)
Queen Margaret (14)
Sir Thomas Grey (11)
Young Clifford (13)

14

Cardinal Wolsey (15)
Christopher Sly (30)
Duke of Burgundy (11, 12, 17)
Duke of Clarence (10, 19)
Duke of Cornwall (17)
Duke of Florence (1)
Duke of Somerset (13, 14)
Earl of Pembroke (14, 16)
Earl of Richmond (19)
Edmund Mortimer (9, 12)
Hostess Quickly (9, 10)
Justice Shallow (10)
King Richard III (19)
Launcelot Gobbo (23)

Lord Willoughby (18)
Marcus Antonius (8)
Metellus Cimber (8)
Northumberland (E. of)
(9, 10, 14, 18)
Northumberland (Lady) (10)
Octavius Caesar (2, 8)
Peter of Pomfret (16)
Pompeius Sextus (2)
Prince Humphrey (10)
Queen Elizabeth (19)
Queen Katharine (15)
Sextus Pompeius (2)
Sir James Blount (19)
Sir James Tyrrel (19)
Sir John Stanley (13)
Sir Walter Blunt (9, 10)
Sir William Lucy (12)
Smith the Weaver (13)
Tullus Aufidius (5)
Walter Whilmore (13)

15

Aemilius Lepidus (8)
Bishop of Lincoln (15)
Dromio of Ephesus (4)
Duke of Lancaster (18)
Earl of Cambridge (11)
Earl of Salisbury
(11, 12, 13, 16, 18)
Earl of Worcester (9, 10)
Edmund of Langley (18)
Lord Abergavenny (15)
Margery Jourdain (13)
Marquis of Dorset (19)
Menenius Agrippa (5)
Prince of Arragon (23)
Prince of Morocco (23)
Robin Goodfellow (25)
Sicinius Volutus (5)
Sir Anthony Denny (16)
Sir Hugh Mortimer (14)
Sir John Falstaff (9, 10, 24)
Sir John Fastolfe (12)
Sir John Mortimer (14)
Sir Nicholas Vaux (15)
Sir Thomas Lovell (15)
Titus Andronicus (33)

Some characters from **Shelley**, **Sheridan** and **Smollett**
List of works from which the following characters are taken, with reference numbers.

Percy Bysshe Shelley

Ref. No.	Title	
1.	Cenci, The	(8 letters)
2.	Prometheus Unbound	(17 letters)
3.	Swellfoot the Tyrant	(18 letters)
4.	(Various)	

Richard Brinsley Sheridan

5.	Critic, The	(9 letters)
6.	Duenna, The	(9 letters)
7.	Pizarro	(7 letters)
8.	Rivals, The	(9 letters)

Ref. No.	Title	
9.	School for Scandal, The	(19 letters)
10.	St. Patrick's Day	(13 letters)
11.	Trip to Scarborough, A	(18 letters)

Tobias Smollett

12.	Count Fathom	(11 letters)
13.	Humphry Clinker	(14 letters)
14.	Peregrine Pickle	(15 letters)
15.	Roderick Random	(14 letters)
16.	Sir Launcelot Greaves	(19 letters)

Note: The numbers in brackets indicate *the works* in which the characters appear

3 AND 4

Asia (2)
Cora (7)
Crab (15)
Fag (8)
Ione (2)
Ivy (13)
Joey (15)
Lory (11)
Loyd (13)
Lucy (8)
Mab (4)
Puff (5)
Quin (13)
Rosy (10)
Trip (9)

5

Acres (8)
Cenci (1)
Clara (6)
Crowe (16)
Dakry (3)
Daood (4)
David (8)
Flint (10)
Frail (14)
Gawky (15)
Gomez (7)
Gwynn (13)
Jones (13)
Julia (8)
Lewis (13)
Lopez (6)

Maria (9)
Moses (3, 9)
Oakum (15)
Ocean (2)
Orano (7)
Pipes (14)
Probe (11)
Rifle (15)
Rolla (7)
Scrag (14)
Snake (9)
Sneer (5)
Strap (15)

6

Alonzo (7)
Amanda (11)
Andrea (1)
Apollo (2)
Banter (15)
Barton (13)
Bumper (9)
Clumsy (11)
Cythna (4)
Dangle (5)
Darnel (16)
Dr. Rosy (10)
Duenna (The) (6)
Elvira (7)
Emilia (14)
Fathom (12)
Ferret (16)
Gobble (16)
Hassan (4)
Hatton (5)

Hoyden (11)
Ianthe (4)
Jermyn (13)
Julian (4)
Louisa (6)
Mahmud (4)
Mammon (3)
Martin (13)
Marzio (1)
Morgan (15)
Murphy (13)
Norton (13)
Oregan (15)
Orsino (1)
Pallet (14)
Pickle (14)
Random (15)
Rattle (15)
Rowley (9)
Simper (15)
Teazle (9)
Thomas (8)
Townly (11)
Vandal (15)
Weazel 15)
Willis (13)
Zuluga (7)

7

Adonais (4)
Alastor (4)
Almagro (7)
Ataliba (7)
Baynard (13)
Bowling (15)

Bramble (13)
Bulford (13)
Buzzard (13)
Camillo (1)
Candour (9)
Celinda (12)
Clinker (13)
Coupler (11)
Cringer (15)
Davilla (7)
Dick Ivy (13)
Dr. Lewis (13)
Fashion (11)
Freeman (15)
Giacomo (1)
Gonzalo (7)
Greaves (16)
Griskin (13)
Gwyllim (13)
Hopkins (5)
Jackson (15)
Jenkins (13)
Macully (13)
Maddalo (4)
Melford (13)
Mendoza (6)
Mercury (2)
Milfart (13)
Mrs. Loyd (13)
O'Connor (10)
Olimpio (1)
Panthea (2)
Pizarro (7)
Raleigh (5)
Rattlin (15)

Savella (1)
Silenus (4)
Snapper (15)
Solomon (3)
Sparkle (15)
Surface (9)
Taurina (3)
Thicket (15)
Trounce (10)
Ulysses (4)
Wagtail (15)
Whiffle (15)

8

Absolute (8)
Backbite (9)
Bernardo (1)
Besselia (16)
Bob Acres (8)
Burleigh (5)
Campbell (13)
Careless (9)
Crabshaw (16)
Crabtree (9, 14)
Crampley (15)
Cropdale (13)
Dallison (13)
Dennison (13)
Hatchway (14)
Hercules (2)
Languish (8)
Las Casas (7)
Lauretta (10)
LaVarole (11)
Lavement (15)
Loveless (11)
Malaprop (8)
Marmozet (15)
Melville (8)
Mendlegs (11)
Molopoyn (15)
Mrs. Gawky (15)
Mrs. Gwynn (13)
Mrs. Jones (13)
Narcissa (15)
O'Donnell (15)
O'Trigger (8)
Orozembo (7)
Phillips (13)
Plagiary (5)
Purganax (3)
Queen Mab (4)
Rosalind (4)
St. Irvyne (4)

Staytape (15)
Straddle (15)
Swillpot (15)
Thompson (15)
Tom Pipes (14)
Trunnion (14)
Valverde (7)
Williams (15)

9

Ahasuerus (4)
Berinthia (11)
Credulous (10)
Don Carlos (6)
Don Jerome (6)
Dr. Wagtail (15)
Faulkland (8)
Ferdinand (6)
Gauntlett (14)
Hugh Strap (15)
Lady Frail (14)
Lismahago (13)
Mackshane (15)
Mary Jones (13)
Mrs. Dangle (5)
Mrs. Jermyn (13)
Mrs. Norton (13)
Mrs. Weazel (15)
Mrs. Willis (13)
Quiverwit (15)
Sneerwell (9)
Strutwell (15)
Swellfoot (3)
The Duenna (6)
Tilburing (5)
Zephaniah (3)

10

Constancia (4)
Count Cenci (1)
Demogorgon (2)
Doctor Rosy (10)
Don Antonio (6)
Donna Clara (6)
Father Paul (6)
Foppinton (11)
Helen Gwynn (13)
John Thomas (13)
Lady Teazle (9)
Lord Rattle (15)
Miss Hoyden (11)
Mitchelson (13)
Mrs. Bramble (13)
Mrs. Candour (9)

Mrs. Gwyllim (13)
Mrs. Jenkins (13)
Mrs. Snapper (15)
Prometheus (2)
Ritornello (5)
Rory Random (15)
Tom Bowling (15)
Tom Fashion (11)

11

Cadwallader (14)
Count Fathom (12)
Donna Louisa (6)
Dr. Mackshane (15)
Harry Bumper (9)
Jack Rattlin (15)
Jona Taurina (3)
Lady Bulford (13)
Lady Griskin (13)
Lefty Willis (13)
Miss Snapper (15)
Miss Sparkle (15)
Miss Withers (15)
Mrs. Lavement (15)
Mrs. Malaprop (8)
Peter Teazle (9)
Saint Ervyne (4)
Squire Gawky (15)
Tim Cropdale (13)

12

Captain Crowe (16)
Captain Oakum (15)
Count Maddalo (4)
Don Ferdinand (6)
Ensign Murphy (13)
Gosling Scrag (14)
Isaac Mendoza (6)
Lord Burleigh (5)
Lord Straddle (15)
Lord Swillpot (15)
Lydia Melford (13)
Master Rowley (9)
Miss Williams (15)
Mrs. Credulous (10)
Mrs. Mary Jones (13)
Whiskerandos (5)
Witch of Atlas (4)

13

Aurelia Darnel (16)
Captain Oregan (15)
Captain Weazel (15)
Colonel Townly (11)

Corporal Flint (10)
Earl Strutwell (15)
Father Francis (6)
Joseph Surface (9)
Julia Melville (8)
Justice Gobble (16)
Launcelot Crab (15)
Lady Sneerwell (9)
Lord Quiverwit (15)
Lydia Languish (8)
Mrs. Helen Gwynn (13)
Oliver Surface (9)

14

Captain Whiffle (15)
Charles Surface (9)
Clumsy Tunbelly (11)
Dougal Campbell (13)
Francesco Cenci (1)
Hawser Trunnion (14)
Humphry Clinker (13)
Justice Buzzard (13)
Laetitia Willis (13)
Lord Foppington (11)
Lucius O'Trigger (8)
Matthew Bramble (13)
Roderick Random (15)
Sir Harry Bumper (9)
Sir John Sparkle (15)
Sir Peter Teazle (9)
Squire Dallison (13)
Sunders Macully (13)
Tabitha Bramble (13)
Watkin Phillips (13)

15

Anthony Absolute (8)
Captain Absolute (8)
Cardinal Camillo (1)
Charles Dennison (13)
Earl of Leicester (5)
Emilia Gauntlett (14)
Father Augustine (6)
Ferdinand Fathom (12)
Peregrine Pickle (14)
Serjeant Trounce (10)
Timothy Crabshaw (16)
Tyrant Swellfoot (3)
Winifred Jenkins (13)

Some characters from **Southey**, **Spenser** and **Tennyson**
List of works from which the following characters are taken, with reference numbers.

Robert Southey

Ref. No.	Title	
1.	Curse of Kehama, The	(16 letters)
2.	Madoc	(5 letters)
3.	Roderick, the Last of the Goths	(8 letters)
4.	Thalaba the Destroyer	(19 letters)
5.	(Various)	

Edmund Spenser

Ref. No.	Title	
6.	Colin Clout's Come Home Again	(24 letters)
7.	Faerie Queene, The	(15 letters)
8.	Shephearde's Calender, The	(22 letters)
9.	(Various)	

Lord Tennyson

10.	Enoch Arden	(10 letters)
11.	Idylls of the King	(15 letters)
12.	(Various)	

Note: The numbers in brackets indicate *the works* in which the characters appear

3 AND 4

Alma (7)
Ate (7)
Atin (7)
Azla (1)
Azub (3)
Baly (1)
Cid (The) (5)
Dony (7)
Dora (12)
Dove (5)
Ebba (3)
Enid (11)
Flur (11)
Hoel (2)
Ida (12)
Lee (10)
Lot (11)
Lucy (7)
Mary (5)
Maud (12)
Ray (10)
Rose (12)
Una (7)

5

Alice (12)
Amias (7)
Anton (11)
Arden (10)
Aswad (4)
Balan (11)
Balin (11)
Belge (7)
Bleys (11)

Brute (7)
Celia (7)
Clare (12)
Cleon (7)
Clout (6)
Cuddy (8)
David (King) (2)
Dolon (7)
Doorm (11)
Edyrn (11)
Error (7)
Eudon (3)
Furor (7)
Guyon (7)
Indra (1)
Isolt (11)
Isond (11)
Laila (4)
Madoc (2)
Moath (4)
Odoar (3)
Orpas (3)
Pedro (3)
Phaon (7)
Talus (7)
Torre (11)
Tyler (5)
Urban (3)
Urien (2)
Willy (8)
Yamen (1)
Yniol (11)
Ysolt (11)

6

Abessa (7)
Action (6)
Adicia (7)
Alcyon (9)
Amavia (7)
Amidas (7)
Amoret (7)
Astery (9)
Aullay (1)
Aylmer (12)
Briana (7)
Burbon (7)
Cavall (dog) (11)
Coatel (2)
Diggon (8)
Donica (5)
Dubrie (11)
Duessa (7)
Elaine (11)
Elissa (7)
Favila (3)
Gareth (11)
Gawain (11)
Glauce (7)
Godiva (12)
Godmer (7)
Guisla (3)
Guizor (7)
Harold (12)
Igerna (11)
Ignaro (7)
Iseult (11)
Isolde (11)
Jasper (5)

Julian (3)
Kehama (1)
Khawla (4)
Lilian (12)
Llaian (2)
Magued (3)
Mammon (7)
Medina (7)
Merlin (11)
Modred (11)
Moorna (5)
Munera (7)
Newman (5)
Oenone (12)
Oneiza (4)
Orelio (horse) (3)
Oriana (12)
Orraca (Queen) (5)
Paeana (7)
Pelago (3)
Quiara (5)
Romano (3)
Ronald (12)
Senena (2)
Serena (7)
Sergis (7)
Shedad (4)
Terpin (7)
The Cid (5)
Thenot (8)
Theron (dog) (3)
Timias (7)
Turpin (7)
Vivian (12)
Vivien (11)
Witiza (3)

Yeruti (5)
Ygerne (11)
Yseult (11)
Zeinab (4)

7

Acrasia (7)
Adeline (12)
Aemelia (7)
Aladine (7)
Aloadin (4)
Amphion (12)
Aragnol (9)
Argante (7)
Artegal (7)
Arvalan (1)
Aveugle (7)
Cambina (7)
Casyapa (1)
Corydon
Cynetha (2)
Dagonet (11)
Diamond (7)
Egilona (3)
Ereenia (1)
Ettarre (11)
Everard (12)
Favinia (3)
Fidessa (7)
Galahad (11)
Geraint (11)
Gorlois (11)
Ibrahim (3)
Igrayne (11)
Lavaine (11)
Lincoya (2)
Lynette (11)
Lyonors (11)
Maimuna (4)
Maleger (7)
Malinal (2)
Mariana (12)
Marinel (7)
Melibee (7)
Mohareb (4)
Monnema (5)
Mordure (7)
Morrell (8)
Oroglio (7)
Padalon (1)
Penlake (5)
Perissa (7)
Philtra (7)
Pollear (1)

Rudiger (5)
Rusilla (3)
Samient (7)
Sansfoy (7)
Sansjoy (7)
Sansloy (7)
Sir Owen (5)
Thalaba (4)
Ulysses (12)

8

Abdaldar (4)
Adosinda (3)
Alcahman (3)
Alphonso (3)
Amalahta (2)
Annie Lee (10)
Arthegal (7)
Bedivere (11)
Blandina (7)
Bracidas (7)
Busirane (7)
Calepine (7)
Calidore (7)
Claribel (7, 12)
Clarinda (7)
Erillyab (21)
Eurytion (7)
Ferraugh (7)
Florimel (7)
Florinda (3)
Fradubio (7)
Gaudiosa (3)
Gauvaine (11)
Geryoneo (7)
Gloriana (7)
Harpalus (6)
Helinore (7)
Hobbinol (8)
Hodeirak (4)
Hudibras (7)
Jane Grey (12)
Ladurlad (1)
Lancelot (11)
Lucifera (7)
Maccabee (3)
Madeline (12)
Malbecco (7)
Margaret (12)
Mercilla (7)
Meridies (11)
Muscarol (9)
Nealling (1)
Numacian (3)

Occasion (7)
Oliphant (7)
Palinode (8)
Phaedria (7)
Placidas (7)
Pollente (7)
Pyrocles (7)
Radigond (7)
Roderick (King) (3)
Rosalind (8)
Sanglier (7)
Satyrane (7)
Sir Anton (11)
Sir Guyon (7)
Sir Torre (11)
Sisibert (3)
Siverian (3)
Spumador (7)
St. Dubrie (11)
Thomalin (8)
Triamond (7)
Trompart (7)
Wat Tyler (5)

9

Abdalazis (3)
Abulcacem (3)
Amaryllis (6)
Anguisant (11)
Archimage (7)
Archimago (7)
Astrophel (8)
Belphoebe (7)
Bladamour (7)
Brigadore (7)
Britomart (7)
Cadwallon (2)
Charyllis (6)
Corfiambo (7)
Cymochles (7)
Dame Celia (7)
Espriella (5)
Eumnestes (7)
Fourdelis (7)
Grantorto (7)
Grenville (12)
Guinevere (11)
Gwenhidwy (11)
Hermesind (3)
King David (2)
Lady Clare (12)
Llewellyn (2)
Lorrimite (I)
Malecasta (7)

Malengrin (7)
Mirabella (7)
Philip Ray (10)
Philotine (7)
Pithyrian (5)
Portamour (7)
Priscilla (7)
Rosalinda (9)
Ruddymane (7)
Scudamore (7)
Sir Sergis (7)
Sir Terpin (7)
Tezozomoe (2)
The Soldan (7)

10

Blandamour (7)
Bruncheval (7)
Colin Clout (6)
Count Eudon (3)
Count Pedro (3)
Cradlemont (11)
Doctor Dove (5)
Enoch Arden (10)
Kirkrapine (7)
Lady Godiva (12)
Lord Ronald (12)
Marriataby (1)
Pastorella (7)
Sanglamore (7)
Sir Dagonet (11)
Sir Galahad (11)
Sir Geraint (11)
Sir Lavaine (11)
Sir Paridel (7)
Sir Pelleas (11)
Theodofred (3)
Vere de Vere (12)
Waterproof (12)

11

Britomaris (7)
Count Julian (3)
Davie Diggon (8)
Lady Lyonors (11)
Queen Orraca (5)
Saint Dubrie (11)
Sir Bedivere (11)
Sir Calepine (7)
Sir Calidore (7)
Sir Claribel (7)
Sir Ferraugh (7)
Sir Hudibras (7)
Sir Lancelot (11)

Sir Persaunt (11)
Sir Satyrane (7)
Sir Trevisan (7)
Sir Tristram (11)
Yuhidthiton (2)

12

Blatant Beast (The) (7)
Braggadochio (7)
Dame Helinore (7)

King Roderick (3)
Lady Gaudiosa (3)
Lady Jane Grey (12)
Oliver Newman (5)
Prince Pelayo (3)
Sir Percivale (11)
Sir Perimones (11)
Sir Pertolope (11)
Sir Scudamore (7)

13 AND OVER

Chindasuintho (3)
Emma Plantagenet (2)
Father Maccabee (3)
Lady of Shalott (12)
Marian Margaret (6)
Red-Cross Knight (7)
Richard Penlake (5)
Saint Gualberto (5)

Sir Aylmer Aylmer (12)
Sir Richard Grenville
 (12)
Sir Shan Sanglier (7)
Sir Walter Vivian (12)
Squire of Dames, The
 (7)
Will Waterproof (12)

Some characters from **Thackeray**
List of works from which the following characters are taken, with reference numbers.

Ref. No.	Title		Ref. No.	Title	
1.	Adventures of Philip, The	(21 letters)	10.	Major Gahagan, The Adventures of	(27 letters)
2.	Barry Lyndon	(11 letters)	11.	Newcomes, The	(11 letters)
3.	Book of Snobs, The	(14 letters)	12.	Pendennis	(9 letters)
4.	Catherine	(9 letters)	13.	Rebecca and Rowena	(16 letters)
5.	Denis Duval	(10 letters)	14.	Shabby Genteel Story, A	(19 letters)
6.	Fatal Boots, The	(13 letters)	15.	Vanity Fair	(10 letters)
7.	Great Hoggarty Diamond, The	(23 letters)	16.	Virginians, The	(13 letters)
8.	Henry Esmond	(11 letters)	17.	Wolves and the Lamb, The	(19 letters)
9.	Lovel the Widower	(15 letters)			

Note: The numbers in brackets indicate *the works* in which the characters appear

3 AND 4

Bell (12)
Bond (1)
Bows (12)
Bull (3)
'Cat' (4)
Craw (6)
Cuff (15)
Drum (7)
Gann (14)
Gray (3)
Grig (3)
Hall (4)
Holt (8)
Huff (2)
Hunt (1)
Kew (11)
Laws (16)
Legg (3)
Levy (5)
Maw (3)
Moss (15)
Nabb (6)

Page (5, 17)
Pash (7)
Pump (3)
Quin (2)
Ruck (7)
Runt (1, 2)
Sago (3)
Tagg (3)
Tidd (7)
Veal (15)
Ward (16)
Wing (5)
Wirt (3)
Wood (4)

5

Amory (12)
Arbin (5)
Baker (9)
Barry (2)
Bates (6)
Becky (14, 15)
Bevil (5)
Biggs (10)

Bluck (15)
Boots (9)
Bowls (15)
Brady (2)
Brock (4)
Bulbo (15)
'Carry' (14)
Chaff (3)
Clap (15)
Clink (15)
Clump (15)
Crabb (14)
Crump (3)
Daisy (mare) (2)
Denis (5)
Dobbs (4)
Dr. Maw (3)
Duffy (19)
Dumps (3)
Duval (5)
Fagan (2)
Fitch (14)
Flint (5)
Foker (12, 16)

Freny (2)
Gates (7)
Gorer (dog) (15)
Gumbo (16)
Hagan (16)
Hayes (4)
Hicks (3)
Higgs (15)
Hobbs (4)
Hugby (3)
Jowls (2)
Ketch (4)
Kicks (6)
Lovel (9)
Macan (10)
Macer (3)
March (Lord) (16)
Mohun (8)
O'Dowd (3, 15)
Piper (9)
Pippi (2)
Ponto (3)
Prior (9, 17)
Query (7)

Macheath (5)
MacManus (7)
Macmurdo (15)
Malowney (6)
Manasseh (6)
Marchand (10)
Milliken (17)
Miss Bell (12)
Miss Runt (14)
Miss Wirt (3,15)
Mountain (16)
Mrs. Amory (12)
Mrs. Barry (2)
Mrs. Brady (2)
Mrs. Chuff (3)
Mrs. Crabb (14)
Mrs. Dobbs (4)
Mrs. Duval (5)
Mrs. Foker (16)
Mrs. Hayes (4)
Mrs. Lovel (9)
Mrs. Macan (10)
Mrs. O'Dowd (15)
Mrs. Ponto (3)
Mrs. Prior (9, 17)
Mrs. Rowdy (15)
Mrs. Score (4)
Napoleon (10)
Plugwell (9)
Ribstone (12)
Ringwood (1)
Sherrick (9)
Smithers (7)
Sullivan (2)
Talmadge (16)
Titmarsh (7)
Tom Walls (1)
Trestles (5)
Tufthunt (14)
Westbury (8)
Woolcomb (1)

9

Altamount (12)
Augustine (14)
Batchelor (9)
Bell Brady (2)
Bellenden (9)
Bernstein (16)
Bloundell (12)
Bob Stokes (7)
Bob Stubbs (6)
Broadbent (16)
Catherine (4)

Charlotte (1)
Clavering (12)
de la Motte (5)
de Saverne (5)
Dinwiddie (16)
Doctor Maw (3)
Dr. Barnard (5)
Dr. Johnson (2, 16)
Dr. Portman (12)
Dr. Snorter (6)
Dr. Squills (15)
Farintosh (11)
Firebrace (16)
Flowerdew (15)
Geoghegan (16)
Goldsmith (2)
Jack Ketch (4)
James Gann (14)
Joe Swigby (14)
John Hayes (4)
'Jos' Sedley (15)
Lady Baker (9)
Lady Fanny (16)
Lady Maria (16)
Laura Bell (12)
Lightfoot (12)
Lilywhite (10)
Lord Mohun (8)
Macdragon (3)
Mackenzie (11)
Marrowfat (3)
Mary Smith (7)
Miss Brett (12)
Miss Prior (17)
Miss Pybus (12)
Miss Rudge (5)
Montholen (10)
Mrs. Barker (5)
Mrs. Baynes (1)
Mrs. Bonner (12)
Mrs. Brough (7)
Mrs. Fermin (1)
Mrs. Firkin (15)
Mrs. Glowry (15)
Mrs. Gretel (4)
Mrs. Haller (12)
Mrs. Jowler (10)
Mrs. Rummer (12)
Mrs. Scales (5)
Mrs. Sedley (15)
Mrs. Stokes (7)
Mrs. Tinker (15)
Mrs. Tusher (8)
Mrs. Weston (5)

Nora Brady (2)
Pendennis (1, 12)
Pinkerton (15)
Pontypool (12)
Rev. Mr. Holt (8)
Rev. Mr. Runt (2)
Rev. Mr. Veal (15)
Robin Hood (13)
Rory Barry (2)
Roundhand (7)
Sheepskin (8)
Swishtail (6, 15)
Tom Caffin (5)
Tom Esmond (8)
Tom Measom (5)
Tom Parrot (5)
Whitfield (16)

10

Agnes Duval (5)
Athelstane (13)
Becky Sharp (15)
Biddy Brady (2)
Bonnington (9, 17)
Bullingdon (2)
Castlewood (8, 16)
Cissy Lovel (9)
Coplestone (8)
Denis Duval (5)
Dick Steele (8)
Doctor Wing (5)
Eliza Kicks (6)
Fitzboodle (9)
Fred Bayham (12)
Goodenough (1)
Gus Hoskins (7)
Harry Barry (2)
Harry Foker (12)
Henry Foker (12)
Jack Morris (16)
James Wolfe (16)
John Brough (7)
John Howell (17)
Kicklebury (17)
Killblazes (7)
King George (16)
Lady Lyndon (2)
Lady Rowena (13)
Lord Bagwig (2)
Lord Steyne (15)
Mackanulty (10)
Maid Marian (13)
Major Macan (10)
Major Macer (3)

Major O'Dowd (15)
Major Ponto (3)
Mary Barlow (17)
Mary Waters (6)
Miss Clancy (2)
Miss Hunkle (12)
Miss Kiljoy (2)
Miss Pierce (12)
Miss Snobky (2)
Miss Swarby (15)
Mrs. Barnard (5)
Mrs. Brandon (1)
Mrs. Bulcher (10)
Mrs. Lambert (16)
Mrs. Macarty (14)
Mrs. Mugford (1)
Mrs. Penfold (1)
Mrs. Twysden (1)
Mrs. Wapshot (12)
Mrs. Woolsey (1)
Mrs. Worksop (8)
Mysie Brady (2)
Nan Fantail (4)
Peter Brock (4)
Peter Denis (5)
Peter Hobbs (4)
Phil Murphy (2)
Pocahontas (16)
Poly Anthus (3)
Pump Temple (3)
Rev. Mr. Crisp (15)
Rev. Mr. Jowls (2)
Sextonbury (3)
Silverkoop (4)
Solomonson (6)
Sukey Rude (5)
'The Captain' (1)
Tom Hookham (5)
Tom Humbold (16)
Tom Sniffle (3)
Tom Wheeler (7)
Tufton Hunt (1)
Ulick Brady (2)
Warrington (12, 16)
Washington (16)
Will Esmond (16)

11

'Andrea' Fitch (14)
Andrew Fitch (14)
Baron de Barr (6)
Barry Lyndon (2)
Biddlecombe (9)

Black George
  (horse) (2)
Bryan Lyndon (2)
Bute Crawley (15)
Captain Bull (3)
Captain Craw (6)
Captain Grig (3)
Captain Legg (3)
Captain Page (17)
Captain Quin (2)
Captain Wood (4)
Chowder Loll (10)
Claude Duval (5)
Collingwood (15)
Countess Ida (2)
Dick Bedford (9)
Dick Bunting (6)
Doctor Dobbs (4)
Doctor Piper (9)
Dr. Swishtail (6, 15)
Earl of March (16)
Edward Bevil (5)
Eliza Stubbs (6)
Emily Blades (3)
Ensign Hicks (10)
Essex Temple (3)
Fotheringay (12)
General Lake (10)
General Sago (3)
Harry Esmond (8)
Henry Esmond (8)
Jack Spiggot (3)
James Binnie (11)
Julia Jowler (10)
Juliana Gann (14)
King Richard (13)
Lady Crawley (15)
Lady Hawbuck (3)
Lady Scraper (3)
Lady Tiptoff (7)
Lord Buckram (3)
Lucy Hawbuck (3)
Major Thrupp (10)
Mary Pinhorn (9)
Miss Clopper (6)
Miss Crawley (15)
Miss Saltire (15)
Miss Sowerby (1)
Miss Swindle (15)
Montanville (9)
Montfitchet (1)
Mrs. Hoggarty (7)
Mrs. Hollyock (15)
Mrs. Jellicoe (5)

Mrs. Manasseh (6)
Mrs. Mountain (16)
Mrs. Titmarsh (7)
Peggy O'Dwyer (2)
Pitt Crawley (15)
Pompey Hicks (3)
Popham Lovel (9)
Prince Bulbo (15)
Raymond Gray (3)
Robert Gates (7)
Roger Hooker (5)
Roger Lyndon (2)
Samuel Arbin (5)
Simon de Bary (2)
Stiffelkind (6)
Susan Stubbs (6)
Theo Lambert (16)
Thistlewood (12)
Thomas Flint (5)
Tom Tufhunt (14)
Van Den Bosch (16)

12

Agnes Twysden (1)
Alderman Pash (7)
Amelia Sedley (15)
Bella Macarty (14)
Betsy Brisket (6)
Blanche Amory (12)
Captain Baker (9)
Captain Biggs (10)
Captain Denis (5)
Captain Duffy (10)
Captain Fagan (2)
Captain Freny (2)
Captain Prior (9)
Caroline Gann (14)
Cecilia Lovel (9)
Chesterfield (16)
Clive Newcome (11)
Colonel Wolfe (16)
Count Gahagan (10)
Donnerwetter (14)
Dr. Goodenough (1)
Dr. von Glauber (15)
Emily Scraper (3)
Ensign Dobble (6)
Ensign Famish (3)
Ethel Newcome (11)
General Tufto (3)
General Wolfe (16)
George Fermin (1)
George Weston (5)
Hefty Lambert (16)

Helena Flower (2)
Honoria Brady (2)
Jack Costigan (12)
Jack Lockwood (8)
John Jorrocks (15)
Joseph la Rose (4)
Joseph Sedley (15)
Joseph Weston (5)
Lady de Mogyns (3)
Lady Golloper (3)
Lady Ribstone (12)
Linda Macarty (14)
Little Billee (12)
Little Sister (The) (1)
Lord Cinqbars (14)
Lord Ringwood (1)
Major Danvers (16)
Major Gahagan (10)
Mary Malowney (6)
Michael Brady (2)
Mick Hoggarty (7)
Miss Delamere (9)
Miss Tingwood (1)
Morgan Doolan (12)
Mrs. Lightfoot (12)
Mrs. Newbright (15)
Mrs. Pendennis (12)
Philip Fermin (1)
Prince Arthur (13)
Prince Victor (2)
Rachel Esmond (16)
Rebecca Sharp (15)
Redmond Barry (2)
Reginald Cuff (15)
Selina Stokes (7)
Thomas Stubbs (6)
Ulysses Brady (2)

13

Barnes Newcome (11)
Beatrix Esmond (8)
Belinda Brough (7)
Bryan Hawshaw (8)
Captain Dobble (6)
Captain Fizgig (7)
Captain Franks (16)
Captain Punter (2)
Captain Steele (5)
Captain Strong (12)
Captain Waters (6)
Carrickfergus (14)
Catherine Hall (4)
Charles Lyndon (2)
Clarence Baker (9)

Colonel Dobbin (15)
Colonel Esmond (8)
Colonel Jowler (10)
Comte de Florac (11)
Cornet Gahagan (10)
Corporal Brock (4)
Corporal Clink (15)
Count of Chalus (13)
Countess of Kew (11)
Doctor Barnard (5)
Doctor Johnson (16)
Earl of Tiptoff (7)
Emily Costigan (12)
Ensign Macarty (14)
Fanny Mountain (16)
Francis Esmond (8)
General Baynes (1)
George Osborne (15)
Goody Biffings (4)
Hester Lambert (16)
Hon. Poly Anthus (3)
Jack Firebrace (16)
Joseph Addison (8)
Kitty Lorrimer (3)
Lady Clavering (12)
Lady Pontypool (12)
Lefty Lovelace (3)
Lord Firebrace (8)
Lydia den Bosch (16)
Martha Crawley (15)
Martin Lambert (16)
Matilda Briggs (15)
Miss Bellenden (9)
Miss Bonnyface (2)
Miss Pinkerton (15)
Mlle Augustine (14)
Mrs. Blenkinsop (15)
Mrs. Bonnington (9)
Mrs. Goodenough (1)
Mrs. Silverkoop (4)
Parson Sampson (8, 16)
Philip Purcell (2)
Rawdon Crawley (15)
Robert Swinney (7)
Rosa Mackenzie (11)
Sir Peter Denis (5)
Snobley Snobky (3)
Talbot Twysden (1)
Thomas Bullock (4)

Thomas Gregson (5)
Thomas Trippet (4)
Tobias Tickler (2)
Violet Crawley (15)
William Dobbin (15)

14

Agnes de Saverne (5)
Arabella Briggs (15)
Belinda Bulcher (10)
Betty Flannigan (15)
Blanche Twysden (1)
Captain Clopper (6)
Captain Osborne (15)
Captain Pearson (5)
Captain Shandon (12)
Captain Thunder (2)
Captain Touchit (17)
Catherine Hayes (4)
Colonel Cramley (3)
Colonel Lambert (16)
Colonel Newcome (11)
Colonel Snobley (3)
Cornelius Barry (2)
Corporal Steele (8)
Count de Saverne (5)
Dora Warrington (16)
Earl of Ringwood (1)
Elizabeth Prior (9)
Ensign Macshame (4)
Frederick Lovel (9)
General Bulcher (10)
General Tinkler (10)
George Milliken (17)
Godfrey Gahagan (10)
Gregory Gahagan (10)
Helen Pendennis (12)
Horace Milliken (17)
Lady Castlewood (8, 16)
Lady Fanny Rakes (7)
Lady Huntingdon (13)
Lady Kicklebury (17)
Lady Warrington (16)
Laura Pendennis (12)
Lord Bullingdon (2)
Lord Castlewood (8, 16)
Lord Sextonbury (3)
Magdalen Crutty (6)
Major Pendennis (12)

Michael Cassidy (1)
Mrs. Biddlecombe (9)
Mrs. Blackbrooks (15)
Mrs. Juliana Gann (14)
Mrs. Montfitchet (1)
Princess Olivia (2)
Rev. Bute Crawley (15)
Rev. Mr. Flowerdew (15)
Richard Bedford (9)
Samuel Titmarsh (7)
Sir Pitt Crawley (15)
Sir Popham Baker (9)
Thomas Billings (4)
Thomas Clodpole (4)
von Galgenstein (4)
Wilfred Ivanhoe (13)

15

Arthur Pendennis (1, 12)
Captain Costigan (12)
Captain Macheath (5)
Captain Macmurdo (15)
Captain Westbury (8)
Captain Woolcomb (1)
Charles Honeyman (11)
Charlotte Baynes (1)
Dr. Tobias Tickler (2)
Flora Warrington (16)
General Braddock (5)
George Marrowfat (3)
Harry Warrington (16)
Henry Warrington (16)
Isabella Macarty (14)
Jemima Pinkerton (15)
Lady Jane Crawley (15)
Lady Jane Preston (7)
Marquis of Bagwig (3)
Marquis of Steyne (15)
Miss Fotheringay (12)
Miss Montanville (9)
Misses Pinkerton (The) (15)
Mrs. Cecilia Lovel (9)
Queen Berengaria (13)
Ringwood Twysden (1)
Rosalind Macarty (14)
Sir George Esmond (8)
Sir John Hawkshaw (8)

Some characters from **Anthony Trollope**
List of works from which the following characters are taken, with reference numbers.

Ref. No.	Title		Ref. No.	Title	
1.	Alice Dugdale	(12 letters)	10.	Lady of Launay, The	(15 letters)
2.	American Senator, The	(18 letters)	11.	Last Chronicle of Barset, The	(24 letters)
3.	Barchester Towers	(16 letters)	12.	La Vendée	(8 letters)
4.	Dr. Thorne	(8 letters)	13.	Ralph the Heir	(12 letters)
5.	Editor's Tales, An	(14 letters)	14.	Small House at Allington, The	(24 letters)
6.	Eustace Diamonds, The	(18 letters)	15.	Tales of all Countries	(19 letters)
7.	Framley Parsonage	(16 letters)	16.	Telegraph Girl, The	(16 letters)
8.	Frau Frohmann	(12 letters)	17.	Three Clerks, The	(14 letters)
9.	Is He Popenjoy?	(12 letters)	18.	Warden, The	(9 letters)

Note: The numbers in brackets indicate *the works* in which the characters appear

3 AND 4

Bean (2)
Bell (18)
Bold (3, 7, 18)
Bolt (9)
Boom (17)
Bull (8)
Cann (6)
Cox (13)
Dale (11, 14)
Dove (6)
Dunn (11)
Erle (6)
Fawn (6)
Gazy (18)
Grey (6)
Hall (16)
Hoff (8)
Jack (horse) (2)
Knox (9)
Love (14)
Lund (15)
Nogo (17)
Pie (3,4)
Pile (13)
Pole (7)
Ring (15)
Toff (9)
Trow (15)
Watt (5)

5

Anton (8)
Baker (4)
Boyce (11, 14)
Brown (6, 15, 16, 17)

Brush (17)
Bunce (18)
Carey (13)
Croft (11, 14)
Crump (11, 14)
Dandy (horse) (6, 7)
Davis (17)
Denot (12)
Dobbs (14)
Donne (5)
Eames (11, 14)
Fooks (13)
Foret (12)
Fritz (15)
Gager (6)
Glump (13)
Green (2, 4, 9, 11, 16)
Grice (2)
Handy (18)
Hearn (14)
Heine (15)
Hiram (18)
Janet (4)
Jones (7, 9, 15, 17)
Joram (13)
Knowl (10)
Krapp (8)
Lebas (12)
Lupex (14)
M'Ruen (17)
Mason (11)
Miles (10)
Moggs (13)
Moody (18)
Muntz (8)
Nobbs (2)
Oriel (4, 11)

Penge (2)
Plume (12)
Pratt (11, 14)
Price (9)
Pryor (10)
Regan (5)
Ribbs (2)
Robin (7)
Romer (4)
Runce (2)
Sally (16)
Scott (17)
Sharp (5)
Slope (3)
Smith (5, 9, 15)
Snape (9, 17)
Stein (12)
Stemm (13)
Tozer (7, 11)
Tudor (17)
Tweed (1)
Upton (15)
Vigil (17)
Wheal (17)

6

Apjohn (4)
Arabin (3, 7, 9, 14)
Athill (4)
Aunt Ju (9)
Austen (7)
Battle (9)
Bawwah (13)
Baxter (11)
Bergen (15)
Bonner (13)
Boodle (6)

Botsey (2)
Brumby (5)
Buffle (11, 14)
Bunfit (6)
'Caudle' (14)
Clarke (4)
Cobard (8)
Cobble (1)
Conner (14)
Cooper (2)
Currie (2)
D'Elbee (12)
Dr. Bold (18)
Draper (11)
Duplay (12)
Fiasco (14)
Finney (18)
Finnie (3, 4)
Fisher (14)
Flurry (11)
Garrow (15)
Giblet (9)
Glemax (2)
Goarly (2)
Gowran (6)
Graham (16)
Greene (15)
Griggs (6)
Grimes (5)
Gwynne (3)
Hallam (5)
Harter (6)
Holmes (15)
Hoppet (2)
Jemima (7)
Jemima (mare) (2)
Jerome (12)

Joseph (15)
Launay (10)
Lupton (7, 11)
Mewmew (3)
Moffat (4)
Molloy (5)
Morgan (6)
Morris (6, 11, 13)
Morton (2, 15)
'Mrs. Val' (17)
Murray (16)
Nappie (6)
Neefit (13)
Neroni (3)
Newton (13)
Nickem (2)
Norman (17)
Nupper (2)
O'Brien (15)
Onslow (15)
Pabsby (13)
Pepper (13)
Precis (17)
Puffle (5)
Sawyer (9)
Scruby (9)
Seppel (8)
Sludge (11)
Smiler (6)
Soames (11)
Spicer (13)
Spruce (14)
Staple (3)
Stiles (3)
Stokes (9)
Temple (11)
Tendel (8)
Tewett (6)
Thorne (3, 4, 7, 11)
Towers (3, 7, 18)
Trauss (8)
Ushant (2)
Waddle (13)
Walker (7, 9, 11, 13, 15)
Wallop (13)
Weston (15)
Wilson (6, 16)

7

Adolphe (13)
Bangles (11)
Barrère (12)
Bateson (4)
Baumann (9)

Berrier (12)
Bonteen (6)
Boullin (12)
Buggins (7)
Burnaby (13)
Cashett (9)
Century (4)
Chapeau (12)
Chilton (6)
Cloysey (15)
Cobbold (2)
Coelebs (9)
Collins (5)
Conolin (8)
Couthon (12)
Cradell (11, 14)
Crawley (7, 11)
Crosbie (11, 14)
Crumbie (13)
Crumple (18)
De Baron (9)
de Guest (11, 14)
de Salop (17)
Debedin (12)
Dingles (14)
Dugdale (1)
Eardham (13)
Easyman (7)
Emilius (6)
Eustace (6)
Gazebee (4, 11, 14)
Germain (9)
Glossop (2)
Goesler (6)
Gotobed (2)
Grantly (3, 4, 7, 11, 18)
Gregory (10)
Gresham (4, 6, 7)
Gresley (5)
Gruffen (14)
Gushing (4)
Hampton (2)
Harding (3, 7, 11, 14, 18)
Hoffman (2)
Hoggett (11)
Hopkins (2, 11, 14)
Jobbles (17)
Johnson (18)
Judkins (15)
Kissing (11, 14)
'Kit' Dale (14)
M'Buffer (17)
Masters (2)
Mealyer (14)

Mildmay (9)
Minusex (17)
Monsell (7)
Mrs. Bold (3)
Mrs. Dale (11, 14)
Mrs. Gamp (mare) (7)
Mrs. Grey (6)
Mrs. Pole (7)
Mrs. Toff (9)
Mutters (18)
Pawkins (14)
Plomacy (3)
Podgens (7)
Poojean (13)
Porlock (4, 14)
Poulter (15)
Protest (9)
Proudie (3, 4, 7, 11)
Pumpkin (17)
Purefoy (2)
Puttock (2)
Roanoke (6)
Robarts (7, 11)
Rufford (2)
Scalpen (3)
Scrobby (2)
Scuttle (11)
Simkins (1)
Skulpit (18)
Snapper (11)
Sowerby (7)
Spooner (13)
Spriggs (18)
Starbod (17)
Surtees (2)
Talboys (15)
Tankard (2)
Tempest (11)
Thumble (11)
Tickler (7)
Toogood (11)
Trefoil (2, 3)
Trigger (13)
Tuppett (2)
Umbleby (4)
Wanless (1)
Wilkins (11)

8

Abel Ring (15)
Allchops (17)
Anticant (18)
Aunt Jane (6)
Bell Dale (14)

Benjamin (6)
Brabazon (9)
Brownlow (13)
Bumpwell (3)
Caneback (2)
Chadwick (3, 7, 11, 18)
Champion (11)
Charette (12)
Chiltern (6)
Coldfoot (6)
De Courcy (4, 11, 14)
de Laroch (12)
Dr. Crofts (11, 14)
Dr. Gwynne (3)
Dr. Nupper (2)
Dr. Thorne
    (3,4, 7, 11)
Drummond (2)
Dumbello (7, 11, 14)
Fanfaron (14)
Filgrave (11)
Fleabody (9)
Fletcher (11)
Fleurist (12)
Frohmann (8)
Frummage (14)
Geraghty (17)
Groschut (9)
Gumption (7)
Hittaway (6)
Horsball (13)
Houghton (9)
Isa Heine (15)
John Bold (3, 18)
Jolliffe (14)
Lady Dale (14)
Lady Fawn (6)
Lily Dale (11, 14)
Lovelace (9)
Macallum (6)
Mary Bold (3, 18)
Mary Jane (5)
Meredith (7)
Morrison (10)
Mrs. Boyce (11, 14)
Mrs. Croft (11)
Mrs. Crump (14)
Mrs. Davis (17)
Mrs. Eames (14)
Mrs. Green (16)
Mrs. Hearn (14)
Mrs. Knowl (10)
Mrs. Lupex (14)
Mrs. Miles (10)

(3, 4, 7, 18)
Mrs. Gresham (7)
Mrs. Gresley (5)
Mrs. Hopkins (2)
Mrs. Masters (2)
Mrs. Podgers (7)
Mrs. Proudie (3, 4, 7)
Mrs. Robarts (7, 11)
Mrs. Talboys (15)
Mrs. Tickler (7)
Mrs. Umbleby (4)
Musselboro (11)
Nina Cobard (8)
Oldeschole (17)
Omicron Pie (3, 4)
Peter Stein (12)
Rev. Mr. Slope (3)
Scatterall (17)
Sir Jib Boom (17)
Spiveycomb (13)
Thomas Dove (6)
'Turtle' Dove (6)
Twistleton (14)
Uncle Hatto (15)
Walter Watt (5)
Westmacott (13)

11

Abraham Hall (16)
Alaric Tudor (17)
Amelia Roper (14)
Augusta Fawn (6)
Bella Holmes (15)
Bernard Dale (11, 14)
Bertram Dale (11)
Bessy Garrow (15)
Bobby Sludge (11)
Caleb Morton (15)
Captain Dale (11, 14)
Cathelineau (12)
Cecilia Fawn (6)
Clutterbuck (11)
Colonel Dale (14)
Dan Stringer (11)
Dick Hampton (2)
Dr. Fillgrave (4)
Eleanor Bold (3)
Ernest Heine (15)
Farmer Price (9)
Fitzmaurice (6)
Fowler Pratt (11, 14)
Frank Garrow (15)
Gitemthruet (17)
Green Walker (7)

Harold Smith (7)
Harry Garrow (15)
Harry Norman (17)
Henry Norman (17)
Henry Thorne (4)
Jabesh M'Ruen (17)
Jack De Baron (9)
Jane Crawley (11)
Jane Robarts (7)
Jaquêtanape (17)
John Eustace (6)
John Poulter (15)
John Roberts (7)
Johnny Eames (11, 14)
Julia Weston (15)
Kate Masters (2)
Lady Chilton (6)
Lady de Guest (14)
Lady Eardham (13)
Lady Eustace (6)
Lady Germain (9)
Lady Protest (9)
Lady Purefoy (2)
Lady Trefoil (2)
Lady Wanless (1)
Legge Wilson (6)
Lord Chilton (6)
Lord de Guest (14)
Lord Germain (9)
Lord Porlock (4, 14)
Lord Ruffold (2)
Lord Trefoil (2)
Lucy Robarts (7, 11)
Madame Heine (15)
Major Fiasco (14)
Major Garrow (15)
Mark Robarts (7)
Mary Gresley (5)
Mary Masters (2)
Miss Bateson (4)
Miss Collins (5)
Miss De Groat (2)
Miss Gushing (4)
Miss Mealyer (14)
Miss Proudie (3)
Miss Roanoke (6)
Miss Spooner (13)
Miss Trefoil (3)
Miss Wanless (1)
Mountfencer (9)
Mrs. Allchops (17)
Mrs. Brownlow (13)
Mrs. de Courcy (14)
Mrs. Frummage (14)

Mrs. Hittaway (6)
Mrs. Houghton (9)
Mrs. Phillips (3)
Mrs. Richards (3, 17)
Mrs. Robinson (15)
Mrs. Rossiter (1)
Mrs. Stanhope (3)
Mrs. Woodward (17)
Paulo Neroni (3)
Philip Miles (10)
Polly Neefit (13)
Polly Puffle (5)
'Posy' Grantly (11)
Ralph Newton (13)
Rev. Mr. Arabin (7, 14)
Rev. Mr. Clarke (4)
Rev. Mr. Temple (11)
Robespierre (12)
Sophy Greene (15)
Sophy Wilson (16)
Supplehouse (7)
Tony Tuppett (2)
William Gazy (18)
Winterbones (4)
Woolsworthy (15)

12

Adolphe Denot (12)
Alice Dugdale (1)
Andrew Gowran (6)
Aunt Penelope (15)
Baron Crumbie (13)
Chaffonbrass (17)
Charles Tudor (17)
Dean Lovelace (9)
Doctor Thorne
(3, 4, 11)
Dolly Masters (12)
Duke of Omnium
(4, 6, 11)
Edith Wanless (1)
Elias Gotobed (2)
Fanny Gresley (5)
Fanny Monsell (7)
Fanny Robarts (7)
Farmer Walker (13)
Father Gerome (12)
Frank Gresham (4, 7)
Frau Frohmann (8)
Frederic Fawn (6)
George Morris (13)
George Scruby (9)
George Walker (11)
Giles Hoggett (11)

Grace Crawley (7, 11)
Henry Grantly (11, 18)
John Chadwick (11)
John De Courcy (14)
John Robinson (15)
John Rossiter (1)
Judge Crumbie (13)
Julia de Guest (11)
Lady Brabazon (9)
Lady De Courcy
(3, 4, 11, 14)
Lady Dumbello (14)
Lady Meredith (7)
Lady Palliser (6)
Lord De Courcy (3, 4)
Lord Drummond (2)
Lord Dumbello (7, 11, 14)
Lord Gossling (9)
Lord Popenjoy (9)
Major Grantly (11)
Mary Lovelace (9)
Miss Macnulty (6)
Miss Manasseh (17)
Miss Tallowax (9)
Monica Thorne
(3, 4, 11)
Mrs. Arkwright (15)
Mrs. Broughton (11)
Mrs. Carbuncle (6)
Mrs. Crinoline (17)
Mrs. Greystock (6)
Mrs. Lookaloft (3)
Mrs. Mackinnon (15)
Mrs. Opie Green (4)
Mrs. Quiverful (3, 7)
Mrs. St. Quinten (5)
Mrs. Van Siever (11)
Nearthewinde (4)
Netta Proudie (3)
Obadiah Slope (3)
Patmore Green (9)
Patrick Regan (5)
Peter Berrier (12)
Philip Launay (10)
Rev. Evan Jones (7)
Rev. Mr. Crawley (7)
Rev. Mr. Gregory (10)
Rev. Mr. Robarts (11)
Rev. Mr. Surtees (2)
Richard Carey (13)
Samuel Nickem (2)
Sir Simon Bolt (9)
'Soapy' Grantly (18)

Sophy Gresham (4)
Squire Newton (13)
Susan Grantly (11)
Susan Harding (18)
Uncle Gregory (13)
Yates Umbleby (4)

13

Amelia Gregory (10)
Anne Prettyman (11)
Apollo Crosbie (14)
Babette Seppel (8)
Bishop Grantly (3, 18)
Bishop Proudie (4, 7, 11)
Blanch Robarts (7)
Captain Boodle (6)
Captain Glomax (2)
Charles O'Brien (15)
Charles Puffle (5)
Clara Hittaway (6)
de Montmorenci (5)
Dean Greystock (6)
Eleanor Duplay (12)
Farmer Cloysey (15)
Father Conolin (8)
General Bonner (13)
Georgiana Fawn (6)
Gerald Robarts (7)
Godfrey Holmes (15)
Gregory Newton (13)
Griffenbottom (13)
Helena Gresham (4)
Henry Lovelace (9)
Herbert Onslow (15)
Herr Schlessen (8)
Hetta Houghton (9)
Janet Rossiter (1)
John Broughton (15)
Jonathan Brown (5)
Joseph Cradell (14)
Josephine Bull (8)
Josiah Crawley (11)
Kate Coverdale (15)
Katie Woodward (17)
Lady Demalines (11)
Lady Fanny Dale (14)
Lady Hartletop (7, 11, 14)
Lady Penwether (2)
Lady Scatcherd (4)
Lady Underwood (13)
Linda Woodward (17)
Lord Boanerges (7)
Lord Hartletop (11)
Lord Mistletoe (2)

Lord Polperrow (13)
Macasser Jones (17)
Madame Goesler (6)
Major Caneback (2)
Major Rossiter (1)
Mary Jane Wheal (17)
Mathew Spriggs (18)
Michael Molloy (5)
Miss Dunstable (4, 7)
Miss Godolphin (2)
Miss Le Smyrger (15)
Miss Partridge (11)
Mrs. Clantanham (3)
Mrs. Goodenough (18)
Mrs. Mainwaring (2)
North Geraghty (17)
Olivia Proudie (3)
Patience Oriel (4)
Peter Frohmann (8)
Rev. Caleb Oriel (4)
Samuel Grantly (18)
Sarah Thompson (7)
Selina Gresham (4)
Signora Neroni (3)
Sir Omicron Pie (3, 4)
Sophia Wanless (1)
Vesey Stanhope (18)
Wilfred Thorne (3)

14

Alphabet Precis (17)
Amalia Frohmann (8)
Augusta Protest (3)
Bertie Stanhope (3)
Captain De Baron (9)
Churchill Smith (5)
Clara Van Siever (11)
Clary Underwood (13)
Countess of Care (9)
Dick Scatterall (17)
Eleanor Harding (18)
Emily Dunstable (5)
Erle Barrington (6)
Fanny Arkwright (15)
Fidus Neverbend (17)
Francis Gresham (4)
Frank Greystock (6)
Fraulein Tendel (8)
Fritz Schlessen (8)
General Talboys (15)
Gilbert de Salop (17)
Gregory Masters (2)
Grizzel Grantly (18)
Harry Arkwright (15)

Harry Stubbings (2)
Henry Arkwright (15)
Isabella Holmes (15)
Jacques Chapeau (12)
Lady Brotherton (9)
Lady Linlithgow (6)
Lady Margaretta (14)
Larry Twentyman (2)
Lord Brotherton (9)
Lord Carruthers (6)
Lucinda Roanoke (16)
Lydia St. Quinten (5)
Mary Anne Neefit (13)
Maryanne Ruffle (5)
Matilda Johnson (18)
Mrs. Harold Smith (7)
Parry Coverdale (15)
Parry Underwood (13)
Parson Rossiter (1)
Reginald Morton (2)
Rev. Arthur Donne (5)
Rev. Mark Robarts (7)
Senator Gotobed (2)
Sir John Purefoy (2)
Sir Lamda Mewmew (3)
Valentine Scott (17)
Verax Corkscrew (17)

15

Adelaide De Baron (9)
Adolphus Crosbie (11, 14)
Anastasia Bergen (15)
Arabella Trefoil (2)
Archibald Currie (2)
Augusta De Courcy (4)
Baroness Baumann (9)
Beatrice Gresham (4)
Canon Holdenough (9)
Christopher Dale (14)
Conrad Mackinnon (15)
Conway Dalrymple (11)
Dr. Vesey Stanhope (3, 18)
Elizabeth Garrow (15)
Farmer Greenacre (3)
Florinda Grantly (18)
Griselda Grantly (7, 11)
Hon. John De Courcy (4, 14)
Jacintha Pigtail (17)
Jonathan Crumple (18)
Jonathan Oldbuck (15)
Julius Mackenzie (5)
Lady Mountfencer (9)
Lieutenant Smith (9)
Lizzie Greystock (6)

Lord Mountfencer (9)
Madame de Lescure (12)
Major Mackintosh (6)
Malchen Frohmann (8)
Martha Dunstable (7)
Mortimer Gazebee (11, 14)

Mrs. Patmore Green (9)
Olivia Q. Fleabody (9)
Onesiphorus Dunn (11)
Orlando Hittaway (6)
Rev. Caleb Thumble (11)
Rev. Mr. Mainwaring (2)

Septimus Harding (11, 18)
Serjeant Burnaby (13)
Sir George Walker (15)
Sir Raffle Buffle (11)
Violet Effingham (6)

Composers

3 – 5

Adam
Adams
Alkan
Arne
Auber
Auric
Bach
Balfe
Bart
Bax
Berg
Berio
Bizet
Bliss
Bloch
Blow
Boito
Boyce
Brian
Bruch
Bull
Bush
Byrd
Cage
Cowen
Cui
D'Indy
Dufay
Dukas
Dupré
Durey
Elgar
Falla
Fauré
Field
Finck
Friml
Glass
Gluck
Grieg
Haydn
Henze

Holst
Ibert
Ives
Kern
Lalo
Lasso
Lehar
Liszt
Locke
Lully
Mayr
Nono
Orff
Parry
Pärt
Peri
Ravel
Reger
Reich
Rossi
Satie
Senfl
Smyth
Sor
Sousa
Spohr
Suk
Suppé
Tye
Verdi
Weber
Weill
Weir
Widor
Wirén
Wolf
Ysaye
Zorn

6

Arnold
Barber
Bartok
Berlin
Bishop
Boulez
Brahms
Bridge
Busoni
Cardew
Carter
Chopin
Clarke
Coates
Coward
Cowell
Czerny
Davies
Delius
Duparc
Dussek
Dvorák
Enesco
Eötvös
Flotow
Foster

7

Albéniz
Allegri
Antheil
Arriaga
Babbitt
Bantock
Bellini
Bennett
Berlioz
Berners
Berwald
Blacher
Borodin
Britten
Caccini
Campion
Cavalli
Copland
Corelli
Debussy
Delibes
Dowland

Franck
German
Glinka
Gounod
Grétry
Halévy
Handel
Harris
Hummel
Kodály
Krenek
Lassus
Léonin
Liadov
Ligeti
Mahler
Marais
Moeran
Morley
Mozart
Muffat
Parker

Piston
Pleyel
Porter
Quantz
Rameau
Rubbra
Scelsi
Schütz
Searle
Seiber
Stuart
Tallis
Taylor
Varèse
Viotti
Vitali
Wagner
Walton
Webern
Wesley

Feldman
Frankel
Fricker
Galuppi
Gibbons
Górecki
Ireland
Janácek
Joachim
Ketelby
Lambert
Landini
Litolff
Lutyens
Machaut
Martinu
Menotti
Milhaud
Nicolai
Nielsen
Novello
Obrecht
Pérotin
Poulenc
Puccini
Purcell
Quilter
Rodgers
Rodrigo
Rossini
Roussel
Ruggles
Salieri
Schuman
Smetana
Stainer
Stamitz
Strauss
Tartini
Tavener
Thomson
Tippett
Torelli
Vivaldi

Warlock
Weelkes
Wellesz
Xenakis

8

Berkeley
Boughton
Bruckner
Chabrier
Cimarosa
Clementi
Couperin
Dohnanyi
Fletcher
Gabrieli
Gershwin
Gesualdo
Giordano
Glazunov
Grainger
Granados
Honegger
Kreisler
Maconchy
Marcabru
Marcello
Marenzio
Mascagni
Massenet
Messager
Messiaen
Monckton
Musgrave
Ockeghem
Paganini
Palmgren
Panufnik
Petrassi
Pizzetti
Respighi
Schnabel
Schubert
Schumann

Scriabin
Sessions
Sibelius
Sondheim
Stanford
Sullivan
Svendsen
Taverner
Telemann
Victoria
Wagenaar

9 AND 10

Addinsell (9)
Andriessen (10)
Balakirev (9)
Beethoven (9)
Bernstein (9)
Birtwistle (10)
Boccherini (10)
Boieldieu (9)
Buxtehude (9)
Carissimi (9)
Cherubini (9)

Cole Porter (10)
Donizetti (9)
Dunstable (9)
Dutilleux (9)
Hindemith (9)
Kabalevsky (10)
Locatelli (9)
MacDowell (9)
Malipiero (9)
Manfredini (10)
Meyerbeer (9)
Monteverdi (10)
Mussorgsky (10)
Offenbach (9)
Pachelbel (9)
Paisiello (9)
Palestrina (10)
Penderecki (10)
Pergolesi (9)
Ponchielli (10)
Praetorius (10)
Prokofiev (9)
Rawsthorne (10)
Rubinstein (10)

Saint-Saëns (10)
Scarlatti (9)
Schnittke (9)
Schoenberg (10)
Schönberg (9)
Skalkottas (10)
Stravinsky (10)
Sweelinck (9)
Vieuxtemps (10)
Villa-Lobos (10)
Waldteufel (10)

11

Butterworth
Dimitriesen
Dittersdorf
Ferneyhough
Frescobaldi
Humperdinck
Leoncavallo
Lloyd Webber
Lutoslawski
Mendelssohn
Moussorgsky

Rachmaninov
Stockhausen
Szymanowski
Tailleferre
Tchaikovsky
Wolf-Ferrari

12 AND OVER

Coleridge Taylor (15)
Dallapiccola (12)
Hildegard of
    Bingen (17)
Jaques-Dalcroze (14)
Josquin Desprez (14)
Khachaturian (12)
Lennox Berkeley (14)
Maxwell Davies (13)
Rachmaninoff (12)
Racine Fricker (13)
Richard Strauss (14)
Rimsky Korsakov (14)
Shostakovich (12)
Sterndale Bennett (16)
Vaughan Williams (15)

Music, musical instruments and terms

1 – 3

air
alt
bar
bis
bow
cue
dim.
do
doh
duo
f
fa
fah
ff
gju
gu
gue
hum
jig
key
kit
la
lah
lay

mf
mi
p
più
pop
pp.
ray
re
rit.
run
sax
sf
si
soh
sol
ten.
tie
ud
ut
va
vox
zel

4

alta
alto

arco
aria
ayre
band
bard
base
bass
beat
bell
brio
clef
coda
drum
duet
echo
fife
fine
flat
fret
glee
gong
harp
high
hold
horn
hymn

jazz
koto
lead
Lied
lilt
lute
lyre
mass
mode
mood
mort
mute
node
note
oboe
opus
part
peal
pean
pipe
poco
port
raga
rall.
reed
reel

rest
root
sign
sing
slur
solo
song
stop
tace
time
tone
trio
tuba
tuck
tune
vamp
vina
viol
vivo
voce
wind
wood

5

ad lib
adapt

album
arsis
assai
atone
aulos
banjo
basso
basta
baton
bebop
bells
blare
blues
bones
brass
breve
buffo
bugle
canon
canto
carol
cello
cento
chang
chant
chime

choir
chord
cornu
crook
croon
crowd
crwth
dance
dauli
dirge
disco
ditty
dolce
drone
duple
elegy
étude
fifer
flute
folia
forte
fugal
fugue
galop
gamba
gamut
gigue
grace
grave
jodel
knell
kyrie
largo
lento
lyric
major
march
metre
mezzo
minim
minor
molto
mosso
motet
motif
naker
nebel
neume
nodal
nonet
notes
octet
opera
organ

paean
pause
pavan
pedal
piano
pieno
piper
pitch
pluck
polka
primo
proms
psalm
quill
rebec
reeds
regal
resin
rondo
round
scale
scena
score
segno
segue
senza
shake
shalm
sharp
shawm
sitar
sixth
slide
snare
soave
sol-fa
sound
staff
stave
Strad
strum
study
suite
swell
swing
tabla
tabor
tacet
tanto
tardo
tempo
tenor
theme
third

thrum
tonic
tonus
triad
trill
tritone
trope
tuned
tuner
tutti
twang
valse
valve
vibes
viola
vocal
voice
volta
volti
waits
waltz
wrest
yodel
zheng
zinke

6

accent
adagio
al fine
anthem
arghul
arioso
atabal
atonal
attune
aubade
ballad
ballet
bolero
bridge
bugler
cadent
cantor
catgut
chimes
chiuso
choral
choric
chorus
cither
citole
cornet
contra

cymbal
da capo
damper
design
diesis
duetto
dulcet
eighth
encore
fading
fiddle
figure
finale
fluter
fugato
gallop
giusto
ground
guitar
hammer
intone
Ionian
jingle
kettle
kinnor
legato
Lieder
litany
lutist
Lydian
manual
medley
melody
minuet
monody
motive
nobile
oboist
octave
off-key
pavane
phrase
piston
plagal
player
presto
quaver
rattan
rattle
rebeck
record
reggae
rhythm
ritard.

rubato
sancho
scales
second
sempre
sennet
septet
serial
sestet
sextet
shanty
shofar
singer
sonata
spinet
stanza
string
subito
syrinx
tabour
tabret
tam-tam
tenuto
tercet
thesis
tierce
timbal
timbre
tirade
tom-tom
treble
trigon
troppo
tucket
tune up
tuning
tymbal
unison
up-beat
vamper
veloce
ventil
vielle
violin
vivace
volume
warble
zincke
zither

7

agitato
al segno
allegro

alphorn
alt-horn
amoroso
andante
angelot
animato
arietta
ariette
Ars Nova
attacca
attuned
bagpipe
ballade
bandore
Baroque
baryton
bassist
bassoon
battuta
bazooka
bellows
bitonal
bravura
cadence
cadency
cadenza
calando
calypso
cantata
canzona
canzone
caprice
celeste
'cellist
cembalo
chamade
chanson
chanter
chantry
chorale
cithara
cittern
clapper
clarion
clavier
codetta
con brio
concert
conduct
cornett
counter
courant
Cremona
crooner

cymbals
czardas
descant
descend
descent
diagram
discord
distune
dolente
drummer
episode
euphony
fagotto
fanfare
fantasy
fermata
fiddler
flatten
flutist
furioso
G-string
gavotte
giocoso
gittern
harmony
harpist
hautboy
juke-box
karaoke
keynote
kithara
Locrian
lullaby
maestro
maracas
marimba
mazurka
measure
mediant
melisma
melodic
middle C
mistune
mordent
musette
musical
natural
ocarina
octette
offbeat
organum
pan-pipe
pandora
pesante

pianist
pianola
pibroch
piccolo
piffaro
pomposo
pop song
pop tune
posaune
prelude
quartet
quintet
ragtime
recital
refrain
reprise
requiem
rescore
ripieno
romance
rondeau
rondino
rosalia
roulade
sackbut
sambuca
samisen
sarangi
saxhorn
scherzo
sciolto
scoring
serpent
seventh
sfogato
singing
sistrum
skiffle
slurred
soloist
soprano
sordino
spinnet
stopped
stretto
strophe
sub-bass
subject
syncope
taboret
tambour
theorbo
timbrel
timpani

timpano
toccata
tone-row
tremolo
triplet
trumpet
tuneful
ukelele
ukulele
up-tempo
upright
vespers
vibrato
vihuela
violist
violone
warbler
wassail
whistle
zithern

8

absonant
addition
alto horn
altoclef
antiphon
arch-lute
arpeggio
autoharp
bagpiper
bagpipes
baritone
base clef
bass drum
bass note
bass oboe
bass viol
bass-horn
beat time
bell harp
berceuse
canticle
canzonet
carillon
castanet
castrato
cavatina
chaconne
cheville
choirboy
cimbalon
clappers
clarinet

clarsach
clavecin
clavicor
col legno
composer
con amore
con anima
con fuoco
concerto
continuo
courante
cromorne
crotales
crotchet
crumhorn
dal segno
demi-tone
diapason
diatonic
diminish
ding-dong
distance
doloroso
dominant
down beat
drum-head
drumbeat
duettist
dulcimer
eleventh
ensemble
entr'acte
euphonic
exercise
faburden
falsetto
fandango
fantasia
fantasie
flautist
folk-song
forzando
galliard
gemshorn
glee club
grazioso
half-note
handbell
harmonic
harp-lute
hornpipe
interval
intonate
isotonic

jew's-harp
jongleur
key bugle
keyboard
lentando
libretto
ligature
lutanist
lutenist
madrigal
maestoso
major key
mandolin
melodeon
melodics
melodist
melodize
minor key
minstrel
mirliton
miserere
moderato
modulate
monotone
movement
musician
nocturne
notation
notturno
obligato
operatic
operetta
oratorio
organist
ostinato
overture
pan-pipes
part-song
pastoral
phorminx
phrasing
Phrygian
pianette
plectrum
post horn
psaltery
quantity
recorder
reed pipe
register
resonant
response
rhapsody
rigadoon

ritenuto
Romantic
saraband
semitone
septette
sequence
serenade
serenata
sestetto
sextette
sforzato
shamisen
side drum
smorzato
sonatina
song book
songster
spiccato
spinette
staccato
subtonic
symphony
syntonic
tabouret
tamboura
tenorino
terzetto
threnody
timoroso
tonality
tone down
tone poem
triangle
trichord
trigonon
trombone
trouvere
tympanum
vigoroso
virginal
virtuosi
virtuoso
vocalion
vocalist
warbling
woodwind
zambomba

9

accordion
acoustics
adagietto
alla breve
allemande

alto viola	Gregorian	resonance	**10**	grand piano	suspension
andamento	guitarist	rhythmics	accidental	ground bass	symphonist
andantino	half-shift	ricercare	adaptation	harmonicon	syncopated
antiphony	hand organ	roundelay	affettuoso	harp-string	tambourine
arabesque	harmonica	sarabande	alla caccia	homophonic	tarantella
atonality	harmonics	saxophone	allargando	hurdy-gurdy	tetrachord
bagatelle	harmonium	semibreve	allegretto	incidental	tin whistle
balalaika	harmonize	semitonic	antiphonal	instrument	tonic sol-fa
banjolele	hexachord	septimole	appoggiato	intermezzo	triple time
banjoline	high pitch	seraphina	arpeggione	intonation	trombonist
barcarole	high-toned	seraphine	attunement	kettledrum	troubador
bombardon	homophony	serialism	background	lentamente	tuning fork
bow-string	impromptu	sforzando	bandmaster	light opera	twelve-tone
brass band	improvise	Siciliana	barcarolle	major chord	undulation
brillante	in harmony	signature	bass guitar	major scale	vibraphone
bugle-horn	interlude	slow march	basset-horn	melismatic	vocal music
cacophony	inversion	snaredrum	bassoonist	mezzoforte	Zumpe piano
cantabile	irregular	soft pedal	bull fiddle	microtonal	
cantilena	jazz music	solfeggio	cantillate	minimalism	**11**
capriccio	lagrimoso	sopranino	canzonetta	minor chord	accelerando
castanets	larghetto	sostenuto	chitarrone	minor scale	Aeolian harp
celestina	leger-line	sottovoce	chorus girl	minstrelsy	Aeolian mode
charivari	leitmotif	sound-post	clairseach	modulation	arrangement
chromatic	mandoline	spiritoso	clarabella	monotonous	ballad opera
clarionet	melodious	spiritual	clavichord	mouth-organ	barrel-organ
classical	metronome	succentor	coloratura	mouthpiece	broken chord
coach-horn	mezza-voce	symphonic	con spirito	musica viva	canned music
conductor	microtone	syncopate	concertina	musicology	capriccioso
contralto	modulator	tablature	continuato	nobilmente	church music
cornemuse	monochord	tail-piece	contrabass	opera buffa	clarion note
cornopean	monophony	tambourin	cor anglais	opera music	composition
crescendo	monotonic	tenor clef	cornettist	ophicleide	concertante
crookhorn	mouth harp	tenor horn	dance-music	orchestral	contratenor
cymbalist	music-book	tenor tuba	didgeridoo	pentachord	counterpart
danceband	nose flute	tenor viol	diminuendo	percussion	decrescendo
dead-march	obbligato	tessitura	discordant	pianissimo	demi-cadence
decachord	octachord	theorbist	disharmony	pianoforte	diatessaron
deep-toned	orchestra	time-table	dissonance	plainchant	discordance
dissonant	orpharion	timpanist	dissonancy	polychoral	discordancy
dithyramb	part music	trumpeter	dolcemente	polyphonic	extemporize
drone-pipe	pastorale	tympanist	double bass	prima donna	fiddlestick
drumstick	pitch-pipe	union pipe	double time	recitative	figured bass
elbow-pipe	pizzicato	untunable	embouchure	ritardando	finger-board
euphonium	plainsong	variation	enharmonic	ritornello	first violin
extempore	polonaise	violinist	Eolian harp	scherzando	harmonizing
fiddle-bow	polychord	voluntary	Eolian mode	semiquaver	harpsichord
flageolet	polyphony	vox humana	euphonicon	sousaphone	high-pitched
flute-stop	polytonal	whistling	euphonious	Stradivari	hunting-horn
gallopade	quadrille	whole tone	flügelhorn	strathspey	incantation
generator	quartette	xylophone	folk singer	strepitoso	madrigalist
glissando	quintette	xylorimba	fortissimo	string-band	mandolinist
grace-note	recording		French horn	stringendo	minnesinger
gradation	reed organ		gramophone	submediant	music master
grandioso	rehearsal		grand opera	supertonic	nickelodeon

opera bouffe
orchestrate
passing note
piano player
polyphonism
polyphonist
prestissimo
progression
quarter note
quarter-tone
rallentando
rock and roll
sacred music
saxophonist
senza rigore
solmization
subsemitone
symphonious
syncopation
synthesizer
transposing
tridiapason
viola d'amore
violoncello
vivacissimo
voce di petto
voce di testa
volti subito

12

accordionist
acoustic bass
allegrissimo
allegro assai
appassionata
appoggiatura
augmentation
bass baritone
boogie-woogie
cembal d'amour
chamber music

chromaticism
clarinettist
clavicembalo
comedy ballet
concert grand
concert pitch
conservatory
contrapuntal
cottage piano
countertenor
counterpoint
divertimento
dotted quaver
double-octave
extravaganza
false cadence
fiddle string
funeral march
glockenspiel
instrumental
key signature
leggeramente
marcatissimo
mezzo-soprano
military band
musicologist
natural notes
opéra comique
orchestrator
organ recital
organ-grinder
pandean pipes
passion music
penny whistle
philharmonic
philomusical
Phrygian mode
polytonality
pralltriller
repercussion
sesquialtera

Stradivarius
thoroughbass
tuning hammer
viola da gamba
vocalization

13

accompaniment
acoustic guitar
alto saxophone
bagpipe player
basso continuo
choral singing
conservatoire
contrabassoon
cornet-à-piston
disharmonious
harmonic chord
Kapellmeister
music festival
musical comedy
Neoclassicism
operatic music
orchestration
piano concerto
Postmodernism
ranz des vaches
slide trombone
sol-fa notation
staff notation
string quartet
string quintet
superdominant
swanee whistle
symphonic poem
terpsichorean
time signature
transposition
unaccompanied
violin concerto (14)
violoncellist

14 AND OVER

Ambrosian chant (14)
brass instrument(s)
  (15, 16)
chromatic scale (14)
classical music (14)
concerto grosso (14)
demisemiquaver (14)
direct interval (14)
double stopping (14)
double-tonguing (14)
electric guitar (14)
electronic music (15)
fife-and-drum band (15)
fiute-flageolet (14)
Gregorian chant (14)
Highland bagpipe (15)
incidental music (15)
instrumentalist (15)
instrumentation (15)
inverted mordent (15)
Lowland bagpipe (14)
musique concrète (15)
piano accordion (14)
promenade concert
  (16)
reed instrument (14)
regimental band (14)
string orchestra (15)
symphony concert (15)
tintinnabulary (14)
tintinnabulate (14)
tintinnabulation (16)
triple-tongueing (15)
twelve-note music (15)
twelve-tone music (15)
wind instrument(s)
  (14, 15)

Poetry, prose and grammar

2 AND 3	set	case	hack	noun
	tag	coda	hymn	past
lay	wit	copy	iamb	play
MS.		dual	idyl	plot
No	**4**	epic	mime	poem
ode	agon	epos	mode	poet
pen	anon.	foot	mood	puff
pun	bard	form	muse	quip
saw	book	gest	myth	read

rime	lyric	bathos	pathos	context	poetize
root	maxim	chorus	period	couplet	polemic
rule	metre	clause	person	decline	preface
rune	motif	cliché	phrase	descant	present
saga	novel	climax	pidgin	dialect	pronoun
scan	paean	comedy	plural	diction	prosaic
song	parse	copula	poetic	digraph	prosody
stem	poesy	crisis	poetry	distich	proverb
text	proem	critic	précis	eclogue	psalter
tone	prose	dactyl	prefix	edition	pyrrhic
verb	prosy	dative	primer	elegiac	refrain
weak	quill	define	résumé	elision	regular
word	quote	derive	review	epicene	requiem
yarn	rebus	dictum	rhythm	epigram	romance
	recto	diesis	riddle	epistle	rondeau

5

	rhyme	digest	rondel	epitaph	Sapphic
acute	rondo	dipody	satire	euphony	sarcasm
adage	runic	ending	series	extract	scholia
affix	scald	epopee	sestet	fantasy	sestina
argot	scene	errata	simile	fiction	setting
blurb	sci fi	etymon	sketch	georgic	sextain
canto	shift	eulogy	sonnet	grammar	spondee
caret	skald	exposé	stanza	harmony	stichic
carol	slang	finite	stress	Homeric	strophe
codex	stich	future	strong	homonym	subject
colon	story	gender	suffix	idyllic	summary
comma	study	genius	symbol	imagery	syncope
diary	style	gerund	syntax	inflect	synonym
dirge	summa	gnomic	thesis	introit	systole
ditty	tense	govern	umlaut	journal	tiercet
drama	theme	heroic	verbal	jussive	tragedy
elegy	tilde	hiatus	zeugma	lampoon	trilogy
elide	tract	homily		leonine	triolet
envoi	triad	hubris	**7**	lexicon	triplet
envoy	usage	humour		library	trochee
epode	verse	hybris	abridge	literal	versify
essay	verso	hymnal	adjunct	litotes	virelay
fable	vowel	hyphen	anagram	lyrical	vocable
farce		iambic	analogy	memoirs	western
folio	**6**	iambus	analyse	metonym	
genre		jacket	anapest	mimesis	**8**
geste	abrégé	jargon	antonym	mystery	
ghost	accent	lacuna	apocope	nemesis	ablative
gloss	active	legend	apology	novella	absolute
gnome	adonic	lyrist	article	paradox	abstract
haiku	adverb	macron	ballade	parsing	acrostic
humor	Aeneid	mantra	berhyme	passage	allegory
ictus	alcaic	memoir	bucolic	passive	allusion
idiom	annals	monody	cadence	pen-name	alphabet
idyll	annual	neuter	caesura	perfect	amoebean
image	anthem	number	cantata	phoneme	analects
index	aorist	object	cedilla	playlet	analysis
Ionic	aperçu	octave	chanson	poetess	anapaest
irony	author	parody	collate	poetics	anaphora
	ballad		content		anecdote

anti-hero
antiphon
aphorism
apodosis
apologia
apothegm
appendix
archaism
assonant
asterisk
Augustan
bacchius
balladry
brackets
caesural
Calliope
canticle
chiasmus
choriamb
clerihew
construe
contrast
critique
dactylic
definite
dialogue
didactic
dieresis
discrete
doggerel
dramatic
ellipsis
enclitic
epic poem
epigraph
epilogue
essayist
euphuism
exegesis
eye rhyme
fabulist
feminine
folktale
footnote
full stop
genitive
glossary
guttural
handbook
Horatian
hornbook
language
laureate
libretto

ligature
limerick
logogram
lyricism
madrigal
metaphor
metonomy
metrical
modifier
morpheme
narrator
negative
nonsense
novelist
optative
opuscule
Ossianic
oxymoron
paradigm
particle
pastoral
personal
phonetic
Pindaric
pleonasm
poetical
positive
prologue
quantity
quatrain
relative
revision
rhapsody
rhetoric
romantic
root word
satirist
scanning
scansion
scenario
scholium
sentence
singular
solecism
spelling
stanzaic
suspense
swan song
syllable
synopsis
synoptic
systolic
temporal
textbook

thematic
threnody
thriller
treatise
tribrach
trimeter
trochaic
trouvère
unpoetic
versicle
vignette
vocative
whodunit
word play
yearbook

9

accidence
acrostics
adjective
adverbial
ambiguity
amoebaean
ampersand
anacrusis
anapestic
Anglicism
annotator
anonymous
anthology
antinovel
apocopate
archetype
assonance
authoress
autograph
biography
broadside
burlesque
cacophony
catalogue
catharsis
chronicle
classical
comic book
conjugate
consonant
copyright
criticism
diaeresis
diphthong
dithyramb
dramatist
elegiacal

epic verse
etymology
euphemism
exegetics
facsimile
fairy tale
fictional
flashback
formative
free verse
Gallicism
gazetteer
gerundive
guidebook
hemistich
hendiadys
hexameter
hexastich
hypallage
hyperbole
hypotaxis
idiomatic
imperfect
inflexion
inversion
irregular
leitmotiv
love story
lyric poem
masculine
melodrama
metaplasm
minor poet
monometer
monorhyme
monostich
narration
narrative
neologism
nonce word
novelette
objective
pararhyme
parataxis
partitive
past tense
philippic
philology
phonemics
platitude
poetaster
potboiler
potential
predicate

preterite
privative
prolepsis
prose poem
prosodist
pseudonym
quotation
recension
reflexive
rhymester
roundelay
semantics
semicolon
semivowel
soliloquy
sonneteer
syllabary
syllepsis
symbolism
symposium
symptosis
synalepha
syntactic
terza rima
tetrapody
trimetric
verse form
versifier
Virgilian
vulgarism
whodunnit

10

accusative
adjectival
amphibrach
amphimacer
anapaestic
anarthrous
anastrophe
Anglo-Saxon
antepenult
anticlimax
antithesis
apostrophe
apposition
avant-garde
bestseller
blank verse
bowdlerize
caricature
choriambus
circumflex
colloquial

common noun
comparison
compendium
declension
definition
definitive
denouement
derivation
derivative
dissonance
disyllabic
disyllable
epenthesis
epenthetic
epic poetry
fairy story
figurative
finite verb
ghost story
government
grammarian
heptameter
hexametric
hyphenated
imperative
impersonal
incunabula
indefinite
indicative
infinitive
inflection
intonation
involution
lexicology
linguistic
manuscript
metathesis
miscellany
mock heroic
morphology
naturalism
neuter verb
nom de plume
nominative
non-fiction
noun clause
ottava rima
palindrome
paraphrase
participle
pentameter
Petrarchan
picaresque
plagiarism

pleonastic
pluperfect
possessive
pronominal
proper noun
reciprocal
short story
similitude
spoonerism
subjective
synaeresis
synaloepha
synecdoche
tetracolon
tetrameter
tetrastich
transitive
unpoetical
vernacular
vocabulary

11

abridgement
acute accent
Alexandrine
amphibology
anacoluthon
antiphrasis
antistrophe
aposiopesis
association
ballad style
bibliomancy
catachresis
catastrophe
chansonette
cliff-hanger
comic relief
comparative
compilation
concordance
conditional
conjugation
conjunction
conjunctive
connotation

constituent
declination
descriptive
disjunctive
dissyllabic
dissyllable
dithyrambic
dithyrambus
engrossment
enjambement
first person
future tense
ghost writer
glottal stop
grammatical
grave accent
hemistichal
heroic verse
heteroclite
Horatian ode
hudibrastic
linguistics
lyric poetry
malapropism
miracle play
nom de guerre
novelettish
oblique case
parenthesis
passion play
passive verb
pastoralism
portmanteau
preposition
punctuation
regular verb
reiterative
subjunctive
subordinate
substantive
superlative
suppression
syntactical
third person
tragicomedy
trimetrical

12

abbreviation
abstract noun
alliteration
alliterative
alphabetical
antibacchius
antimetrical
antiphrastic
antistrophic
Asclepiadean
bibliography
condensation
deponent verb
direct object
direct speech
dissyllabify
distributive
epigrammatic
episodically
epithalamium
etymological
grammaticism
grammaticize
heteroclitic
hexametrical
indeclinable
interjection
intransitive
introduction
lexicography
man of letters
metaphorical
nursery rhyme
onomatopoeia
part of speech
passive voice
perfect tense
poet laureate
polysyllable
postposition
prescriptive
present tense
prothalamion
prothalamium

question mark

13 AND OVER

antepenultimate (15)
autobiography (13)
back formation (13)
colloquialism (13)
creative writing (15)
definite article (15)
detective story (14)
epigrammatical (14)
exclamation mark (15)
figure of speech (14)
frequentative (13)
future perfect (13)
heroic couplet (13)
historic present (15)
hysteron proteron (16)
indicative mood (14)
indirect object (14)
indirect speech (14)
interrogative (13)
inverted commas (14)
irregular verb (13)
lexicographer (13)
lyrical poetry (13)
mixed metaphor (13)
nonsense verse (13)
objective case (13)
past participle (14)
personal pronoun (15)
personification (15)
Petrarchan sonnet (16)
poetic licence (13)
positive degree (14)
possessive case (14)
principal parts (14)
relative clause (14)
relative pronoun (15)
reported speech (14)
rhyming couplet (14)
science fiction (14)
socialist realism (16)
split infinitive (15)
transformation (14)
ungrammatical (13)

Theatre, opera, ballet, cinema, television and radio

2 AND 3	ASM	box	gag	mug	rag
	BBC	cue	ham	No	rep
act	bit	dub	hit	pan	run
arc	bow	fan	ITV	pit	set

tag
TV
wig

4

bill
book
boom
busk
cast
clap
clip
crew
dais
diva
duet
Emmy
epic
exit
film
flop
foil
gaff
gala
gods
grid
hero
idol
jeté
joke
lead
line
live
mask
mike
mime
mute
part
play
plié
prop
rake
role
rush
shot
show
skit
sock
solo
spot
star
take
team
turn

tutu
unit
wing

5

actor
ad lib
agent
angel
apron
arena
aside
barre
baton
break
cable
cloth
clown
comic
debut
decor
drama
dry up
enact
exode
extra
farce
flies
focus
foyer
halls
heavy
hoist
hokum
house
inset
lines
manet
mimer
mimic
movie
odeum
on cue
opera
Oscar
piece
props
radio
revue
scene
scrim
slips
sound
stage

stall
stunt
telly
usher
video
wings

6

acting
action
appear
backer
ballet
barker
big top
boards
busker
buskin
camera
Ceefax
chassé
chorus
cinema
circle
circus
claque
comedy
critic
dancer
dimmer
direct
dubbed
effect
encore
finale
floats
flyman
kabuki
lights
lyrics
make-up
masque
method
motley
movies
mummer
nautch
number
on tour
one act
parody
patron
patter
player

podium
poster
prompt
puppet
recite
repeat
return
ring up
rushes
satire
screen
script
season
serial
series
singer
sitcom
sketch
speech
stalls
stooge
studio
talent
talkie
ticket
tights
timing
tinsel
troupe
TV show
viewer
walk-on
warm-up
writer

7

acrobat
actress
all-star
amateur
balcony
benefit
bit part
booking
box seat
buffoon
cabaret
callboy
cartoon
casting
catcall
catwalk
channel
charade

chorine
circuit
clapper
close-up
commère
company
compère
concert
console
costume
curtain
dancing
danseur
deadpan
diorama
dress up
drive in
dubbing
fan club
fantasy
farceur
feature
film set
fouetté
gallery
heroine
ingenue
juggler
leg show
leotard
long run
maillot
manager
matinée
mimicry
mummery
musical
mystery
network
new wave
on stage
overact
pageant
perform
phone-in
Pierrot
players
playing
playlet
pop star
portray
prelude
present
preview

produce
program
re-enact
recital
reciter
resting
revival
rostrum
royalty
scenery
show biz
showman
sponsor
stadium
stagery
staging
stand-in
stardom
starlet
support
tableau
talkies
the gods
theatre
tragedy
trailer
trilogy
trouper
tumbler
upstage
variety
vehicle
viewing
western

8

applause
arthouse
artistry
audience
audition
backdrop
bioscope
blackout
Broadway
burletta
cabriole
carnival
chat show
Cinerama
clapping
clowning
coliseum
comeback

comedian
conjurer
coryphée
costumer
coulisse
crush bar
danseuse
designer
dialogue
director
disguise
dramadoc
dramatic
dumb show
duologue
entr'acte
entrance
epilogue
exit line
farceuse
fauteuil
festival
figurant
film crew
film star
film unit
filmgoer
first act
funny man
glissade
ham actor
interval
juggling
juvenile
libretto
lighting
live show
location
magician
male lead
morality
newsreel
offstage
operatic
operetta
overture
parterre
pastoral
peep show
pictures
pit stall
platform
playbill
playgoer

première
producer
prologue
prompter
protasis
quiz show
rehearse
ring down
scenario
set piece
showbill
side show
smash hit
stagebox
star turn
straight
stripper
subtitle
tapedeck
telecast
Thespian
third act
tragical
travesty
typecast
wardrobe
wigmaker

9

acoustics
animation
announcer
arabesque
backcloth
backstage
ballerina
bandstand
barnstorm
bit player
blue movie
box office
broadcast
burlesque
cameraman
character
chorus boy
cinematic
clip joint
cloakroom
Columbine
conjuring
costumier
coulisses
criticism

cyclorama
discovery
double act
downstage
dramatics
dramatist
dramatize
drop scene
elevation
entertain
entrechat
exhibitor
figurante
film actor
film extra
filmstrip
first lead
flashback
floorshow
folk dance
footlight
full house
gala night
gogglebox
green room
guest star
Harlequin
home movie
impromptu
interlude
limelight
love scene
low comedy
major role
melodrama
minor role
monodrama
monologue
movie star
movie-goer
music hall
night club
noises off
orchestra
panel game
pantaloon
pantomime
pas de deux
performer
photoplay
Pierrette
pirouette
pit-stalls
play-actor

playhouse
portrayal
programme
projector
promenade
prompt-box
publicity
punch-line
quartette
recording
régisseur
rehearsal
repertory
represent
second act
sight line
slapstick
soap opera
soliloquy
soubrette
spectacle
spectator
spotlight
stage door
stage left
stage play
stagehand
stage-name
take a part
tap dancer
teledrama
the boards
title role
tormentor
tragedian
usherette
voiceover
wisecrack

10

afterpiece
appearance
auditorium
chorus girl
clapper-boy
comedienne
comedietta
comic opera
commercial
continuity
coryphaeus
crowd scene
denouement
disc jockey

drag artist
drama group
dramaturge
dramaturgy
fantoccini
film house
film script
first house
first night
floodlight
footlights
get the bird
high comedy
hippodrome
histrionic
horror film
horse opera
impresario
in the round
in the wings
intermezzo
junior lead
lap dancing
leading man
legitimate
librettist
marionette
masquerade
microphone
movie actor
music drama
newscaster
newsreader
on location
opera buffa
opera house
performing
play-acting
playwright
prima donna
production
prompt-book
properties
proscenium
Pulcinella
puppet-show
rave notice
rave review
recitation
repertoire
repetiteur
ringmaster
screenplay
silent film

sound track
stage fever
stage right
stagecraft
star player
striptease
substitute
sword-dance
tap dancing
tear-jerker
television
theatre box
theatrical
torchdance
travelogue
understudy
variety act
vaudeville
walk-on part
wide screen

11

accompanist
all-star cast
art director
balletomane
barnstormer
black comedy
broadcaster
cap and bells
charity show
Cinemascope
circus-rider
cliff-hanger
comedy drama
comic relief
commentator
concert hall
credit title
curtain call
cutting room
dance troupe
documentary
drama critic
drama school
dramatic art
dress circle
electrician
entertainer
equilibrist
exeunt omnes
feature film
film theatre
fire curtain

folk dancing
funambulist
greasepaint
Greek chorus
histrionics
house lights
illusionist
impersonate
kitchen-sink
leading lady
legerdemain
light comedy
matinée idol
method actor
miracle play
off-Broadway
opera bouffe
opera singer
pantomimist
Passion play
performance
picture show
problem play
protagonist
psychodrama
Punchinello
scene change
set designer
set the scene
show-stopper
showmanship
sound effect
spectacular
stage design
stage effect
stage fright
stage player
stage school
stage-struck
star billing
star quality
star vehicle
star-studded
straight man
stripteaser
strobe light
talent scout
Technicolor
terpsichore
thaumaturgy
theatregoer
theatreland
theatricals
Thespian art

tragedienne
tragicomedy
trick riding
unrehearsed
upper circle
variety show
ventriloquy
wind-machine
word-perfect

12

academy award
actor-manager
amphitheatre
ballet-dancer
balletomania
choreography
cinema studio
clapperboard
comedy ballet
concert party
costume drama
credit titles
dramaturgist
dressing-room
exotic dancer
extravaganza
film director
film festival
film producer
first-nighter
Grand Guignol
harlequinade
impersonator
introduction
juvenile lead
make-up artist
melodramatic
method acting
minstrel show
modern ballet
morality play
name in lights
natural break
opera glasses
orchestra pit
picture house
principal boy
Punch and Judy
puppet-player
scene-painter
scene-shifter
scene-stealer
screenwriter

scriptwriter
show business
silver screen
song and dance
sound effects
stage manager
stage whisper
standing room
starring role
steal the show
stock company
straight part
top of the bill

13

ballet dancing
burlesque show
choreographer
cine projector
cinematograph
contortionist
corps de ballet
curtain-raiser
dance festival
emergency exit
entertainment
musical comedy
Nouvelle Vague
pantomime dame
projectionist
Russian ballet
safety curtain
sleight-of-hand
sound engineer
stage lighting
studio manager
thaumaturgics
theatre school
ventriloquist
video cassette
video recorder

14 AND 15

acrobatic troupe (15)
ballet-mistress (14)
cable television (15)
character actor (14)
classical ballet (15)
continuity girl (14)
dancing academy (14)
divertissement (14)
domestic comedy (14)
dramatic critic (14)
dramatic society (15)

dress rehearsal (14)
features editor (14)
gala performance (15)
incidental music (15)
orchestra stalls (15)
prima ballerina (14)
property master (14)

proscenium arch (14)
revolving stage (14)
school of acting (14)
school of dancing (15)
shooting script (14)
situation comedy (15)
slide projector (14)

smoking concert (14)
sound-projector (14)
stage carpenter (14)
stage direction (14)
stage properties (15)
strolling player (15)
supporting cast (14)

tableaux vivants (15)
talking pictures (15)
tightrope-walker (15)
touring company (14)
variety theatre (14)

MEASUREMENT
Coins and currency

2 AND 3

as
at
bit
bob
cob
dam
ecu
far
fen
fin
jon
lac
lat
lek
leu
lev
mag
mil
mna
oof
öre
pie
pya
red
ree
rei
sen
sho
sol
sou
tin
won
yen
zac
zuz

4

anna
baht
bean
beka
biga
buck
cash
cedi
cent
chip
chon
daum
dawm
dime
doit
dong
dosh
duro
euro
geld
joey
kick
kran
kuna
kyat
lipa
lira
lire
loot
lwei
mail
mark
merk
mina
mite
note
obol
para
peag
peak
peso
pice
pony
punt
quid
rand
real
reis
rial
riel
ryal
sent
tael
taka
thou
unik
yuan
zack

5

agora
angel
asper
aurei
belga
betso
boole
brass
bread
chiao
colón
conto
copec
crore
crown
daric
dinar
dobra
dough
ducat
eagle
fanam
fiver
franc
grand
groat
haler
koban
kopek
krona
krone
kroon
leone
liard
libra
litas
livre
locho
lolly
louis
lucre
medio
mohar
mohur
moola
naira
noble
obang
ochre
oncer
paisa
paolo
pence
pengo
penny
piece
plack
pound
ready
rhino
riyal
royal
ruble
rupee
rupia
sceat
scudi
scudo
semis
soldi
soldo
stica
styca
sucre
sugar
sycee
tical
ticcy
tizzy
toman
uncia
unite
verso
zloty

6

amania
aureus
balboa
bawbee
bezant
bodole
boodle
change
condor
copang
copeck
copper
couter
DauDee
deaner
décime
denier
dirham
dirhem
doblon
dollar
drachm
escudo
florin
forint
fuorte
gourde
groszy
guinea
gulden
halala
heller
kobang
kopeck
koruna
kwacha
lepton
markka
monkey
nickel
obolus
pagoda
pagode
peseta
pesewa
rosser
rouble
rupiah
sceatt
sequin
shekel
souran
specie
stater
stiver
talari
talent
tanner
tenner
tester
teston
thaler
tickey
tizzie
tomaun
valuta
zechin

7

afghani
angelot
bolivar
carolus
centava
centavo
centime
cordoba
crusado
denarii
drachma
exergue
guaraní
guilder
ha'penny
jacobus
kopiyka
lempira
manilla
millime
milreis
moidore
ngusang
nummary
obverse
pfennig
piastre
pistole
quarter
quetzal
reverse
ringgit
sawbuck
sextans
smacker
solidus
stooter
testoon
testril
thrymsa
unicorn

8

ambrosin
assignat
cruzeiro
denarius
didrachm
doubloon
ducatoon
farthing
florence
groschen
half anna
half mark
imperial
johannes
kreutzer
louis d'or
maravedi
megabuck
napoleon
new pence
new penny
picayune
planchet
portague
quadrans
quetzale
sesterce
shilling
sixpence
stotinka
tuppence
twopence
zecchino

9

boliviano
centésimo
cuartillo
didrachma
dupondius
fourpence
gold broad

gold noble
gold penny
half ackey
half angel
half broad
half eagle
half groat
halfcrown
halfpenny
lilang-eni
pistareen
rixdollar
rose-noble
schilling
sestertii
sovereign
spur royal
yellow boy

10

broad piece
crown piece
double
easterling
emalangeni
first brass
gold stater
half florin
half guinea
half laurel
quadrussis
Reichsmark
sestertium
silverling
stour-royal
threepence
threepenny
tripondius
venezolano

11

Deutschmark
double crown
double eagle

george noble
guinea piece
half guilder
half thistle
silver penny
spade guinea
tetradrachm
twelvepenny

12 AND 13

antoninianus (12)
Deutsche Mark (12)
double sequin (12)
folding money (12)
half farthing (12)
half rose-noble (13)
half sovereign (13)
mill sixpence (12)
piece of eight (12)
quarter angel (12)
quarter dollar (13)
quarter florin (13)
quarter laurel (13)
quarter noble (12)
silver dollar (12)
silver-stater (12)
sixpenny piece (13)
threepenny bit (13)
twenty dollars (13)
two pound coin (12)
twopenny piece (13)

14 AND OVER

fifty pence piece (15)
five-guinea piece (15)
Hong Kong dollar (14)
Maria Theresa dollar
  (18)
three farthings (14)
threepenny piece (15)
twenty shillings (15)
two-guilder piece (15)
two-guinea piece (14)

Time (including specific dates, periods, seasons, annual festivals, etc.)

(H.) = Hindu; (I) = Islam; (J.) = Jewish months (variously spelt); (R.) = Roman

2 – 4

A.D.
A.M.

Ab (J.)
Adar (J.)
aeon
age

ages
ago
B.C.
B.S.T.

date
dawn
day
dusk

Elul (J.)
eon
Eos
era

ere
eve
ever
fall

fast	epoch	dotage	sudden	harvest	undated
G.M.T.	Fasti (R.)	Easter	summer	Heshvan (J.)	wartime
Holi (H.)	flash	elapse	Sunday	high day	weekday
hour	horal	extant	sunset	holiday	weekend
Ides (R.)	jiffy	faster	Tammuz (J.)	holy day	Whitsun
Iyar (J.)	Kalpa (H.)	feriae	Tebeth (J.)	holy day	workday
July	later	ferial	termly	instant	Xmas day
June	March	Friday	timely	interim	
last	matin	future	Tishri (J.)	Iron Age	**8**
late	month	gnomon	to date	January	
Lent	never	heyday	ultimo	journal	aestival
May	night	hiemal	jubilee	annually
morn	Nisan (J.)	hourly	update	Kalends	antecede
Noel	nonce	Ice Age	vernal	lady day	antedate
noon	nones	Jet Age	vesper	long ago	anterior
now	of old	Julian	weekly	long run	biannual
N.S.	often	Kislev (J.)	whilom	lustrum	biennial
O.S.	passé	Lammas	whilst	midweek	bimensal
oft	pause	lapsed	winter	monthly	birthday
old	prime	lately	yearly	morning	biweekly
once	prior	latest		new moon	blue moon
past	Purim (J.)	latish	**7**	New Year	calendar
P.M.	quick	latish		nightly	carnival
slow	reign	Lenaea	ageless	noonday	chiliasm
soon	short	May Day	almanac	October	chiliast
span	Sivan (J.)	memory	already	overdue	date line
term	so far	mensal	ancient	postwar	day by day
then	spell	midday	antique	proximo	daybreak
tick	sunup	minute	archaic	quartan	deadline
tide	teens	modern	bedtime	quarter	December
time	Tevet (J.)	moment	belated	quicker	Dionysia
week	times	Monday	betimes	quickly	dogwatch
when	today	morrow	by and by	quintan	domesday
Xmas	trice	New Age	Calends (R.)	quondam	doomsday
year	until	o'clock	century	Ramadan (I.)	duration
yore	watch	off-day	chiliad	regency	earliest
Yuga (H.)	while	old age	Chisleu (J.)	rent day	eggtimer
Yule	years	pay-day	current	sabbath	enduring
	young	period	dawning	shortly	Epiphany
5	youth	prewar	daytime	sine die	estivate
		pro tem	diurnal	slowest	eternity
after	**6**	prompt	dog days	some day	eventide
again		pronto	earlier	sundial	evermore
alway	actual	rarely	elapsed	sundown	every day
April	always	recent	endless	sunrise	feast day
bells	annual	record	epochal	tea time	February
brief	August	rhythm	equinox	teenage	festival
clock	autumn	season	estival	tertian	fleeting
cycle	before	second	eternal	Thammuz (J.)	forenoon
daily	betime	seldom	etesian	time gun	formerly
dated	brumal	Shebat (J.)	evening	time lag	frequent
delay	coeval	slower	extinct	time was	futurist
diary	curfew	slowly	fast day	timeous	futurity
early	decade	sooner	fête day	tonight	Georgian
epact	Diwali (H.)	spring	for ever	Tuesday	gloaming
			half-day		

209

half-hour
half-past
half-term
half-time
half-year
Hannukah (J.)
hibernal
high noon
high time
hitherto
Hogmanay
holidays
Holy Week
in future
in no time
in season
infinity
interval
keep time
kill time
last time
last week
lateness
latterly
leap year
lifelong
lifespan
lifetime
long time
Lord's Day
lose time
make time
mark time
mealtime
meantime
medieval
menology
midnight
minutely
natal day
New Style
next week
noon-time
noontide
November
nowadays
oft-times
Old Style
old times
Olympics
our times
overtime
Passover (J.)
past time

periodic
postdate
postpone
previous
punctual
quickest
right now
Saturday
se'nnight
seasonal
seed time
semester
sidereal
sometime
Space Age
speedily
Stone Age
suddenly
temporal
Thursday
timeless
tomorrow
twilight
until now
untimely
up to date
vacation
weeklong
whenever
yearbook
yearlong
Yuletide
zero hour

9

Adar Shani (J.)
aforetime
afternoon
afterward
all at once
anciently
antedated
antiquity
bimonthly
Boxing Day
Bronze Age
Candlemas
centenary
childhood
Christmas
chronicle
clepsydra
continual
decennary

decennial
decennium
diurnally
Easter Day
Edwardian
Ember days
ephemeral
ephemeris
erstwhile
eternally
feast days
flexitime
forthwith
fortnight
fruit time
Golden Age
Gregorian
Halloween
hard times
hereafter
hodiernal
honeymoon
hourglass
immediacy
immediate
in the past
indiction
instantly
interlude
latterday
lean years
light year
local time
long since
long-lived
longevity
lunar year
lunchtime
market day
Martinmas
matutinal
menstrual
metronome
middle age
midsummer
midwinter
night-time
nightfall
nightlong
octennial
out of date
overnight
past times
peace time

Pentecost
perennial
permanent
postponed
premature
presently
quarterly
quick time
quotidian
recurrent
regularly
right away
Saint's day
salad days
September
sexennial
short-term
sometimes
spare time
speech day
spend time
time flies
timepiece
times past
timetable
transient
triennial
trimester
Victorian
waste time
Wednesday
whole time
yesterday
Yom Kippur (J.)

10

afterwards
All Hallows
Anno Domini
antecedent
anticipate
at all times
before long
before time
beforehand
behind time
biennially
bimestrial
break of day
bygone days
centennial
chiliastic
chronogram

chronology
close of day
continuous
days of yore
dinner time
Easter term
Easter time
estivation
evanescent
Father Time
frequently
Good Friday
half-yearly
hebdomadal
henceforth
Hilary term
historical
immemorial
in good time
isochronal
Lammastide
lunar cycle
lunar month
Lupercalia
Michaelmas
Middle Ages
millennium
nick of time
occasional
oftentimes
olden times
Palm Sunday
posthumous
prehistory
present day
quarter day
Quirinalia
record time
ripe old age
Saturnalia
seasonable
septennial
sexagesima
sextennial
Shrovetide
solar month
springtime
summer term
summertime
synchronal
Theban year
thereafter
time enough
time server

time signal
timekeeper
transitory
triple time
ultimately
unpunctual
vespertine
watch night
wedding day
Whit Monday
Whit Sunday
wintertime
working day
yesteryear

11

adolescence
All Fools' Day
All Souls' Day
anachronism
anniversary
antecedence
antemundane
anteriority
Bacchanalia
Bank Holiday
behindtimes
bicentenary
bygone times
chronograph
chronometer
closing time
continually
cosmic clock
crack of dawn
cuckoo clock
day and night
day in day out
Elizabethan
everlasting
fashionable
fin de siècle
fortnightly
good old days
half holiday
harvest home
harvest time
hebdomadary
immediately
interregnum
isochronism
isochronous
Judgment Day
lapse of time

leisure time
little while
long-lasting
march of time
millenarian
modern times
never-ending
New Year's Day
New Year's Eve
night and day
Passion Week
perennially
perpetually
point of time
prehistoric
prematurely
present time
prime of life
pudding time
punctuality
quadrennial
quartz clock
sands of time
seeding time
settling day
synchronism
synchronize
synchronous
tempus fugit
thenceforth
time and tide
time bargain
time to spare
Tudor period
twelvemonth
ultramodern
waiting time

Whitsuntide

12

afterthought
All Saints' Day
antediluvial
antediluvian
antemeridian
anticipation
Armistice Day
Ascension Day
Ash Wednesday
auld lang syne
betrothal day
bicentennial
carbon dating
Christmas Day
Christmas Eve
contemporary
continuously
course of time
duodecennial
early closing
Easter Sunday
eleventh hour
following day
Midsummer Day
Midsummer Eve
occasionally
old-fashioned
once in a while
post-diluvian
postmeridian
postponement
postprandial
Quadragesima
quinquennial

red-letter day
Rogation days
Rosh Hashanah (J.)
sidereal year
simultaneous
standard time
synchronized
tercentenary
time and again
time will tell
time-honoured
tricentenary
tropical year
Twelfth Night
unseasonable

13

All Hallowmass
All Hallowtide
April Fools' Day
breakfast time
calendar month
Christmastide
Christmastime
chronological
everlastingly
every other day
golden jubilee
golden wedding
holiday season
lunisolar year
Michaelmas Day
once upon a time
Passion Sunday
retrospective
Shrove Tuesday
silver jubilee

silver wedding
St. Swithin's Day
summer holiday
thenceforward
Trinity Sunday
vernal equinox

14 AND 15

behind the times (14)
biological clock (15)
early closing day (15)
early Victorian (14)
Holy Innocents'
    Day (16)
in the nick of time (15)
Julian calendar (15)
lunisolar cycle (14)
Maundy Thursday (14)
Michaelmas term (14)
Mothering Sunday (15)
once in a blue moon
    (15)
once in a lifetime (15)
quatercentenary (15)
Remembrance Day (14)
Rogation Sunday (14)
sabbatical year (14)
St. Valentine's Day (15)
synchronization (15)
synodical month (14)
Thanksgiving Day (15)
tomorrow morning (15)
Walpurgis night (14)
world without end (15)

Weights and measures

(A.) = Argentina
(B.) = Brazil
(b.) = bread
(C.) = Canada
(c.) = coal
(Ch.) = China
(E.) = Egypt
(elec.) = electricity
(Eth.) = Ethiopa
(F.) = France
(f.) = fish
(G.) = Greece

(H.) = Hebrew
(Hon.) = Honduras
(I.) = India
(Ice.) = Iceland
(Indo.) = Indonesia
(Ire.) = Ireland
(It.) = Italy
(J.) = Japan
(liq.) = liquids
(M.) = Malta
(Malay.) = Malaysia
(min.) = minimg

(Mor.) = Morocco
(N.) = Norway
(O.) = Oriental
(P.) = Portugal
(pap.) = paper
(print.) = printing
(R.) = Russia
(Rom.) = Roman
(S.) = Spain
(s.) = silk or cotton
(S.A.) = South Africa
(S. Am.) = South America

(SI) = Système
    Internationale: metric
    system
(T.) = Turkey
(Thai.) = Thailand
(U.S.) = United States
(v.) = various
    commodities
(w.) = wool
(w.y.) = worsted yarn

1 – 3

A4 (pap.)
aam
amp (elec.)
amu
are (SI)
as (Rom.)
aum (S.A.)
bar
bel
bit
B.S.I.
B.T.U.
cab (H.)
cho (J.)
cm (SI)
cor (H.)
cwt.
day
DIN
dwt.
el
ell
em (print.)
en (print.)
erg
fen (Ch.)
fou
ft.
g (SI)
hin (H.)
in.
keg
ken (J.)
kg
kin (J. and Ch.)
km
lb.

lea (s.)
li (Ch.)
log (H.)
lux (SI)
m.
mho (elec.)
mil
min.
mou (Ch.)
mu
nit (SI)
niu (Thai.)
ohm (elec.)
oka (F.)
oke (T.)
oz.
pic (G.)
pin
piu (It.)
pot
rad
rai (Thai.)
rem
ri (J.)
rio (J.)
rod
sen (Thai.)
sho (J.)
SI
sun (J.)
tan (Ch.)
to (J.)
tod (w.)
tog
ton
tot
tun (liq.)
vat (liq.)
wah (Thai.)

wey (w.)
yd.

4

acre
atom
bale (v.)
barn
bath (H.)
boll
bolt
B.Th.U.
butt (liq.)
byte
cade (f.)
case (v.)
cask (liq.)
ch'ih (Ch.)
comb
cord
coss (I.)
cran (f.)
darg
demy (pap.)
dose
drah (Mor.)
dram
drop
dyne
epha (H.)
feet
flint (R.)
foot
gill
gram (SI)
gray
hand (horses)
hank (w.y.)
hath (I.)

hide
hour
inch
iota
keel (c.)
kela (E.)
kilo (SI)
knot
koku (J.)
koss (I.)
kwan (J.)
last (f., w.)
line
link
load (min.)
mile
mina (G.)
moio (P.)
mole (SI)
mudd
muid (S.A.)
nail
natr (Eth.)
obol (G.)
oket (Eth.)
omer (H.)
onza (A.)
paal
pace
pack
palm
peck
phon
phot
pica
pint
pipe (liq.)
pole
pood (R)

post (pap.)
pott (pap.)
pund (N.)
raik (I.)
ream (pap.)
reed (H.)
reel (s.)
rood
rotl (E.)
sack (c., w.)
sawk
seah (H.)
seam
seer (I.)
slug
span
tael (Ch., J.)
tare
tola (I.)
torr
tret
tron
troy
ts'un (Ch.)
unit
vara (S. Am.)
volt (elec.)
watt (elec.)
yard

5

almud (T.)
angle
anker (S.A.)
ardeb (E.)
bahar (Ar.)
bekah (H.)
cable
candy (I.)

canna
carat
catty (Ch.)
cawny (I.)
ch'ien (Ch.)
chain
chang (Ch.)
cheki (T.)
clove
coomb
count (w.y.)
crown (pap.)
cubic
cubit
curie
cusec
cycle
debye
ephah (H.)
farad
fermi
gauge
gauss
gerah (H.)
grain
gross
henry
hertz (elec.)
homer (H.)
joule
kaneh
kikeh (T.)
legua
liang (Ch.)
libra (B.)
ligne
lippy
litre (SI)
livre (F. and G.)
lumen (SI)
maund (I.)
meter (SI)
metre (SI)
minim (liq.)
month
neper
obole (G.)
ocque (G.)
okieh (E.)
ounce
pearl (print.)
pecul (Ch.)
perch
picul (Ch.)

piede (M.)
point (print.)
poise (SI)
pound
proof
pugil
purse (T.)
qirat (E.)
quart
quire (pap.)
quota
royal (pap.)
sabin
sajen (R.)
shaku (J.)
sheet (pap.)
shock
skein (s.)
stade
stere (SI)
stone
stoup (liq.)
tesla
therm
tithe
toise (F.)
token (pap.)
tonne
truss
tsubo (J.)
ungul (I.)
vedro (R.)
verst (R.)
weber
yojan (I.)

6

ampère (elec.)
archin (T.)
armful
aroura (E. and G.)
arpent
arroba (S., P. and S. Am.)
assize
bandle (Ire.)
barrel (v.)
batman (T.)
bundle (v.)
bushel
calory
candle
cantar (E. and T.)
casing (pap.)

cental (C. and U.S.)
cental (B. and G.)
chopin (liq.)
dalton
decare
degree
denier
dirham (E.)
dirhem (E.)
djerib (T.)
double
drachm
endaze (T.)
fanega (S. and S. Am.)
fathom
feddan (E.)
firkin
firlot
fother
gallon (liq.)
gramme (SI)
kantar (Eth.)
kelvin
kilerg
league
libbra (I.)
medium (pap.)
megohm (elec.)
metric
micron (SI)
minute
moiety
morgen (S.A.)
newton
noggin
obolus (G.)
octant
octave
octavo (pap.)
oxgang
parsec
pascal
photon
pocket (hops)
pottle (liq.)
proton
quarto (pap.)
radian
rotolo
sajene (R)
schene (E.)
second

shekel (H.)
shtoff (R)
stokes
suttle
talent (G.)
thrave (Ice.)
tierce (liq.)
vishan (I.)
weight
yojana (I.)

7

acreage
boiling
braccio (I.)
calorie
candela (SI)
Celsius
centner
century
chalder
chiliad
chronon
coulomb (elec.)
dangall (L)
deciare (F.)
decibel
dioptre
drachma (G.)
ellwand
faraday
fresnel
furlong
geodesy
gilbert
gravity
half-aum (S.A.)
half-ton
hectare (SI)
kilobar
lambert
maximum
maxwell
measure
mega-erg
megaton
mileage
miller
minimum
modicum
oersted
outsize
pailful
per cent

poundal
quantar (E.)
quantum
quartan
quarter
quinary
quintal
röntgen
rottolo
scruple
sea mile
siemens (SI)
sievert (SI)
spindle (s.)
stadium (G.)
stature
stremma (G.)
ternary
ternion
tonnage
virgate

8

angstrom
centiare (F.)
centibar
chaldron (c.)
chaudron (c.)
chetvert (R.)
cubic ton
decagram
decigram
distance
division
elephant (pap.)
foolscap (pap.)
footrule
freezing
graviton
half-hour
half-inch
half-mile
hogshead (liq.)
imperial (pap.)
infinity
kassabah (E.)
kilodyne
kilogram
kilovolt
kilowatt (elec.)
magneton
megadyne
megavolt
megawatt

metrical
millibar
molecule
mutchkin (liq.)
parasang
plateful
puncheon (liq.)
quadrant
quantity
quartern (b.)
roentgen
sarplier (w.)
serplath
ship-load (c.)
short ton (C. and U.S.)
spoonful
tonelada (S. and S. Am.)
watt-hour
yardland
yardwand
zolotnik (R)

9

altimetry
amplitude
areometry
becquerel
bisegment
board foot
centigram
cuartilla (S. and S. Am.)
cubic foot
cubic inch
cubic yard
decalitre (SI)
decametre (SI)
decilitre (SI)
decimetre (SI)
decistere (F.)
dekalitre (SI)
dekametre (SI)
dimension
foot-pound
half-ounce
half-pound
hectogram (SI)
isometric
kilderkin
kilocycle

kilohertz (elec.)
kilolitre (SI)
kilometre (SI)
large sack (c.)
light year
long dozen
megacycle
megahertz (elec.)
metric ton
microgram
microwatt
milestone
milligram (SI)
nanometre (SI)
net weight
quadruple
quarterly
quintuple
scantling
steradian
threefold
troy ounce
yardstick

10

araeometry
barleycorn
barrel-bulk
centesimal
centigrade
centilitre (SI)
centimetre (SI)
centistere (F.)
cubic metre (SI)
deadweight
decagramme (SI)
decigramme (SI)
dessiatine (R)
double-demy (pap.)
double-post (pap.)
dry measure
eighth part
Fahrenheit
fifty-fifty
fluid ounce
hectolitre (SI)
hectometre (SI)
horsepower
kilogramme (SI)

lunar month
microfarad (elec.)
micrometre
millesimal
millilitre (SI)
millimetre (SI)
nanosecond
quadrantal (Rom.)
rutherford
square foot
square inch
square mile
square yard
super-royal (pap.)
tripartite
tron weight
troy weight

11

antiquarian (pap.)
avoirdupois
baker's dozen
candlepower
centigramme (SI)
day's journey
double-crown (pap.)
double-royal (pap.)
equidistant
fluid drachm
half and half
hand-breadth
heavyweight
hectogramme (SI)
imperial cap (pap.)
long hundred
   (eggs and f.)
long measure
milligramme (SI)
millimicron
millisecond
pennyweight
short weight
square metre (SI)
tape measure
teaspoonful
thermal unit
thermometer
two-foot rule

wine-measure
yard-measure

12

angstrom unit
areometrical
bantamweight
boiling point
cable's length
cubic measure
electronvolt
equidistance
hair's breadth
half-quartern
hand's-breadth
kilowatt-hour
measured mile
metric system
printer's ream (pap.)
quantitative
quartern loaf (b.)
Réaumur scale

13

calendar month
decimal system
featherweight
freezing point
hundredweight
hypermetrical
inside measure
linear measure
medicine glass
square measure
tablespoonful
three-foot rule

14

atomic mass unit
cubic decimetre (SI)
double elephant (pap.)
outside measure
zenith distance

15

centigrade scale
cubic centimetre (SI)
square decimetre (SI)
square kilometre (SI)

NATURAL HISTORY (I) LIVING CREATURES
Birds

2 AND 3

auk
cob
daw
emu
ern
fop
fum
hen
jay
kae
kea
mew
moa
owl
pen
pie
poe
ree
roc
ruc
tit
tui

4

alca
anas
ayes
barb
bird
bubo
chat
cock
coly
coot
crax
crow
dodo
dove
duck
erne
eyas
fowl
gier
guan
gull
hawk
hern
huia

ibis
kaka
kite
kiwi
knot
koel
lark
loom
loon
lory
lung
mina
myna
otus
pavo
pern
pica
piet
poll
rail
rhea
rook
ruff
shag
skua
smew
sora
sord
spot
swan
taha
teal
tern
tody
wren
yite
yunx

5

agami
ajaia
amzel
ardea
biddy
booby
brant
brent
capon
chick
crake

crane
didus
diver
drake
eagle
egret
eider
finch
galah
geese
glede
goose
goura
grebe
harpy
heron
hobby
junco
larus
lowan
macaw
madge
mavis
merle
miner
murre
mynah
nandu
noddy
ornis
ousel
ouzel
owlet
pewet
pewit
picus
pipit
pitta
poaka
poult
quail
raven
reeve
robin
rodge
saker
scaup
scops
scray
senex

serin
shama
sitta
skite
snipe
solan
spink
squab
stilt
stint
stork
strix
swift
terek
twite
urubu
veery
vireo
wader
wavey
whaup

6

alcedo
alcyon
ancona
anklet
argala
avocet
avoset
bantam
barbet
brolga
bulbul
canary
chewet
chough
chukar
citril
condor
corbie
corvus
coucal
cuckoo
culver
curlew
cushat
cygnet
cygnus
darter

dipper
drongo
dunlin
eaglet
falcon
fulmar
gambet
gander
gannet
garrot
godwit
gooney
gorhen
goslet
grakle
grouse
hoopoe
howlet
jabiru
jacana
jaeger
jerkin
kakapo
lanner
leipoa
linnet
loriot
magpie
martin
merlin
missel
mistle
mopoke
motmot
musket
nestor
oriole
osprey
parrot
pavone
peahen
pecker
peewit
petrel
pigeon
plover
pouter
puffin
pullet
pygarg

quelea
quezal
ratite
redcap
roller
runner
scobby
scoter
sea-bar
sea-cob
sea-pie
seamew
shrike
simurg
siskin
sultan
takabe
tercel
thrush
tirwit
tomtit
toucan
tringa
trogon
turaco
turbit
turdus
turkey
turner
weaver
whydah
wigeon
willet
yaffle
yowley
zivola

7

apteryx
awl-bird
babbler
barn owl
bee-bird
bittern
bluecap
bluetit
boobook
buceros
bullbat
bunting

buphaga	jacamar	seagull	dinornis	nightjar	whistler
bustard	jackass	sea-hawk	dipchick	notornis	white-eye
buzzard	jackdaw	seriema	dotterel	nuthatch	wildfowl
cariama	jacobin	sirgang	duck hawk	ovenbird	wood ibis
cat-bird	kamichi	skimmer	duckling	oxpecker	wood wren
cheeper	kestrel	skylark	dun-diver	parakeet	woodchat
chicken	killdee	sparrow	eagle-owl	paraquet	woodcock
ciconia	kinglet	squacco	fauvette	peesweep	woodlark
coaltit	lapwing	staniel	fern-bird	peetweet	yeldring
cobswan	largopus	sunbird	fish-hawk	phaethon	yoldring
colibri	leghorn	swallow	flamingo	pheasant	zopilote
columba	lich-owl	tadorna	gairfowl	podargus	
corella	limpkin	tanager	game-bird	popinjay	**9**
cotinga	mallard	tarrock	gamecock	prunella	accipiter
courlan	manakin	tattler	gang-gang	puff bird	aepyornis
courser	manikin	tiercel	garefowl	redshank	albatross
cow-bird	marabou	tinamou	garganey	redstart	ant-thrush
creeper	martlet	titlark	great auk	reed wren	bald eagle
cropper	migrant	titling	great tit	reedling	Baltimore
culculus	moorhen	titmice	greenlet	ricebird	bean goose
dorhawk	motacil	touraco	grey duck	rifleman	beccafico
dorking	moth owl	tree tit	grey teal	ringdove	beefeater
dottrel	mudlark	trochil	grosbeak	ringtail	black cock
dovekie	oil bird	tumbler	guacharo	rock dove	black swan
dovelet	ortolan	vulture	hamerkop	sagecock	blackbird
dum bird	oscines	vulturn	hawfinch	sakabula	blacktail
dunnock	ostrich	wagtail	hemipode	screamer	bower-bird
egg-bird	pandeon	wapacut	hernshaw	scrub-tit	brambling
emu wren	partlet		hickwall	sea-drake	broadbill
fantail	peacock	**8**	hornbill	sea-eagle	bullfinch
fen duck	peafowl	accentor	hula-bird	shelduck	campanero
fern owl	pelican	adjutant	killdeer	shoebill	cassowary
finfoot	penguin	aigrette	kingbird	shoveler	chaffinch
gadwall	percher	amadavat	landrail	snowbird	chatterer
galeeny	phoenix	avadavat	langshan	snowy owl	church owl
gobbler	pinnock	barnacle	lanneret	songbird	cockatiel
gorcock	pintado	bee-eater	laverock	songlark	columbine
gorcrow	pintail	bellbird	lorikeet	songster	cormorant
goshawk	poe-bird	blackcap	love-bird	starling	corncrake
gosling	poshard	bluebird	lyrebird	struthio	crossbill
grackle	poultry	boat-bill	mandarin	swamphen	currawong
grallae	puttock	bobolink	marabout	tantalus	dandy-cock
greyhen	quetzal	bob-white	marsh tit	tawny owl	dowitcher
greylag	redpoll	brancher	megapode	tercelet	eagle-hawk
griffin	redwing	bush hawk	mire crow	thrasher	eider duck
haggard	rooster	caracara	moorbird	throstle	field wren
halcyon	rosella	cardinal	moorcock	titmouse	field-duck
harrier	ruddock	cockatoo	moorfowl	tomnoddy	fieldfare
hawk owl	sakaret	cockerel	moorgame	tragopan	firecrest
hickway	sawbill	curassow	morillon	umbrette	fledgling
hoatzin	sea-crow	cursores	musk duck	waterhen	francolin
horn owl	sea-dove	dabchick	mute swan	wheatear	friar-bird
ice-bird	sea-duck	dandy-hen	myna bird	whimbrel	fringilla
impeyan	sea-fowl	didapper	nestling	whinchat	frogmouth

gallinazo
gallinule
gerfalcon
gier-eagle
goldcrest
goldeneye
goldfinch
goosander
great skua
grenadier
grey goose
grey heron
grossbeak
guillemot
guinea-hen
gyrfalcon
hammerkop
heathbird
heathcock
heath-fowl
heath-game
horned owl
jacksnipe
jenny-wren
jerfalcon
kittiwake
lint-white
little auk
macartney
mallee hen
mallemuck
marsh bird
marsh hawk
marsh wren
merganser
merulidan
mousebird
natatores
night hawk
ossifrage
paradisea
partridge
passerine
peregrine
phalarope
ptarmigan
quail-call
quail-hawk
razorbill
red grouse
redbreast
rifle-bird
ring-ouzel
rossignol

salangane
sandpiper
scaup duck
scrub-bird
scrub-fowl
scrub-wren
sedge-bird
sedge-wren
shearbill
sheldrake
shorebird
shoveller
shrike-tit
silver-eye
skunk-bird
snake-bird
snow goose
sooty tern
spinebill
spoonbill
stilt-bird
stock-dove
stonechat
storm-bird
strigidae
swamp-hawk
talegalla
tetraonid
thickhead
thornbill
tiercelet
trochilus
trumpeter
turnstone
waterbird
waterfowl
water-rail
wedgebill
wheat-bird
whiteface
whitetail
widow-bird
wild goose
willow tit
windhover
woodspite
wyandotte

10

aberdevine
ant-catcher
Arctic skua
Arctic tern
bearded tit

bell-magpie
bird of prey
blight-bird
blue-throat
boobook owl
brent goose
bronzewing
budgerigar
burrow-duck
butter-bird
canary bird
canvasback
chiffchaff
crested tit
demoiselle
didunculus
dishwasher
dusky minah
dusky robin
ember goose
eurylaimus
fledgeling
flycatcher
fratercula
goatmilker
goatsucker
grassfinch
greenfinch
greenshank
grey falcon
grey parrot
grey plover
ground dove
ground lark
guinea-fowl
hammerhead
harpy eagle
hen-harrier
honey-guide
honeyeater
hooded crow
jungle-fowl
king parrot
kingfisher
kookaburra
magpie-lark
mallee bird
mallee-fowl
meadowlark
mutton-bird
night heron
night raven
nutcracker
parson-bird

prairie hen
pratincole
ramphastos
regent-bird
rock parrot
rock pigeon
rock thrush
rockjumper
sacred ibis
saddleback
sagegrouse
sanderling
sandgrouse
sandmartin
screech-owl
sea-swallow
shearwater
sheathbill
shovelbill
silver gull
solan goose
song thrush
sun-bittern
tailor-bird
tit-warbler
tree-runner
tropic-bird
turkey-cock
turtle dove
water crake
water-ouzel
wattlebird
weaverbird
whidah-bird
white egret
whydah-bird
willow wren
wonga-wonga
wood-pigeon
woodgrouse
woodpecker
yellow-bird
yellowlegs
zebra finch

11

apostle-bird
banded stilt
barn swallow
black falcon
black grouse
black martin
bonebreaker
booby gannet

brush-turkey
bush-creeper
butcher-bird
button quail
Canada goose
carrion crow
chanticleer
citril finch
cochinchina
cock-sparrow
corn bunting
dentiroster
Dorking fowl
dragoon-bird
fairy martin
flock pigeon
frigate-bird
fruit-pigeon
golden eagle
grallatores
grey wagtail
ground robin
herring gull
house martin
humming-bird
king penguin
king vulture
lammergeier
lammergeyer
leatherhead
leptodactyl
lily-trotter
magpie-goose
meadow-pipit
mocking-bird
Muscovy duck
nightingale
pied wagtail
pintail duck
procellaria
reed babbler
reed bunting
reed sparrow
reed warbler
rhamphastos
rock warbler
scarlet ibis
scissor beak
scissor bird
scissor tail
scissor-bill
screech hawk
sea-pheasant
snow-bunting

song sparrow
sparrowhawk
stilt plover
stone curlew
stone plover
tenuiroster
tree sparrow
tree-creeper
wall-creeper
whitethroat
whooper swan
wood warbler
wood-swallow

12

adjutant bird
burrowing-owl
capercaillie
capercailzie
cardinal-bird
collared dove
common turkey

crested grebe
Dentirostres
fairy penguin
Fissirostres
golden oriole
golden plover
grass warbler
greater skaup
ground thrush
hedge sparrow
honey-buzzard
house sparrow
mandarin duck
marsh harrier
marsh warbler
missel-thrush
mistle-thrush
mourning-dove
pink cockatoo
red-head finch
sea cormorant
sedge warbler

serpent-eater
stone-chatter
stormy petrel
swamp sparrow
swamp-harrier
tenuirosters
turbit-pigeon
umbrella bird
water-wagtail
wattle turkey
whippoorwill
white goshawk
yellowhammer

13

Adélie penguin
adjutant crane
adjutant stork
American eagle
argus pheasant
Baltimore bird
barnacle goose

carrier pigeon
crested pigeon
crocodile bird
fantail pigeon
harlequin duck
little bustard
long-tailed tit
northern diver
oystercatcher
plain-wanderer
recurviroster
screech martin
secretary bird
spider-catcher
swallow-shrike
tumbler-pigeon
turkey vulture
turkey-buzzard
whistling duck
whistling swan
willow warbler
yellow bunting

yellow wagtall

14

bearded vulture
bird of paradise
canvasback duck
emperor penguin
golden pheasant
griffon vulture
horned screamer
king-lory parrot
Manx shearwater
prairie-chicken
red-headed finch
rhinoceros-bird
Rhode Island Red
robin redbreast
tawny frogmouth
whistling eagle

Dogs

3 AND 4

chow
cur
peke
pom
pug
pup
Skye
tike
toy
tyke

5

bitch
boxer
brach
cairn
corgi
dhole
dingo
hound
husky
pooch
puppy
shock
spitz
whelp

6

Afghan
bandog
barbet
basset
beagle
borzoi
bowwow
canine
cocker
collie
Eskimo
gundog
jowler
kelpie
lapdog
pariah
poodle
pugdog
pye-dog
ranger
ratter
saluki
setter
shough
talbot
toy dog

7

basenji
bird-dog
brachet
bulldog
clumber
griffon
harrier
lurcher
Maltese
mastiff
mongrel
pointer
samoyed
sheltie
spaniel
terrier
tumbler
whippet
wolf-dog

8

Aberdeen
Airedale
Alsatian
Blenheim
chowchow

coachdog
Doberman
elkhound
foxhound
hound-dog
housedog
keeshond
Labrador
otter dog
papillon
Pekinese
Sealyham
sheepdog
spitz dog
Springer
turnspit
watchdog
water-dog

9

badger dog
boarhound
buckhound
chihuahua
dachshund
Dalmatian
deerhound
Eskimo dog

gazehound
Great Dane
greyhound
Kerry blue
limehound
lyamhound
Pekingese
police dog
red setter
retriever
schnauzer
St. Bernard
staghound
wolfhound

10

Bedlington
bloodhound
Clydesdale
fox terrier
Maltese dog
otter hound
Pomeranian
Rottweiler
schipperke
Weimaraner
Welsh corgi

11

Afghan hound
basset hound
bull mastiff
bull terrier
carriage dog
Irish setter
Jack Russell
King Charles
shepherd dog
Skye terrier

12

Belvoir hound
Border collie
cairn terrier
Gordon setter
Irish terrier
Newfoundland
Saint Bernard
water spaniel
Welsh terrier

13

Border terrier
Boston terrier
cocker spaniel
Dandie Dinmont
English setter
Scotch terrier
Sussex spaniel

OVER 14

Aberdeen terrier (15)
Airedale terrier (15)
Blenheim spaniel (15)

clumber spaniel (14)
English springer (15)
German shepherd (14)
golden retriever (15)
Highland terrier (15)
Irish wolfhound (14)
Lakeland terrier (15)
Norfolk spaniel (14)
pitbull terrier (14)
Pyrenean mastiff (15)
Scottish terrier (15)
Shetland sheepdog (16)
springer spaniel (15)
Tibetan mastiff (14)

Fish, crustaceans, etc.

3 AND 4

amia
barb
bass
bib
blay
brit
cale
carp
char
chub
cod
coho
crab
cusk
dab
dace
dory
drum
eel
esox
fin
fugu
gar
ged
goby
grig
hag
hake
huso
huss
ide
jack
kelt
keta

ling
lox
luce
lump
mako
mold
mort
opah
orca
orfe
parr
peal
pike
pope
pout
ray
roe
rudd
ruff
sapo
sar
scad
scar
shad
snig
sole
tau
tope
tuna

5

ablen
ablet
angel
apode
blain

bleak
bleck
bream
brill
charr
cisco
cobia
cohoe
cuddy
doree
dorse
elver
fluke
gaper
grunt
guppy
laker
loach
molly
moray
murry
nacre
nurse
perch
pogge
porgy
powan
prawn
reeve
roach
roker
ruffe
salmo
sargo
saury
scrod

sepia
sewin
shark
skate
smelt
smolt
snoek
snook
solen
sprag
sprat
sprod
squid
tench
tetra
togue
torsk
trout
tunny
umber
whiff
witch

6

alevin
anabas
angler
barbel
belone
beluga
blenny
bonito
bowfin
burbot
caplin
caranx

cheven
chevin
comber
conger
cuttle
darter
Diodon
doctor
dorado
ellops
finnan
gadoid
ganoid
gardon
garvie
ginkin
goramy
grilse
groper
gunnel
gurnet
hermit
kipper
launce
maigre
marlin
milter
minnow
mud-eel
mullet
plaice
pollan
puffer
quahog
red-eye
remora

robalo
rochet
runner
saithe
salmon
samlet
sardel
sauger
saurel
scampi
scarus
sea-ape
sea-bat
sea-cat
sea-eel
sea-egg
sea-fox
sea-hog
sea-owl
sea-pad
sea-pig
sephen
shanny
shiner
shrimp
sucker
tarpon
tautog
tomcod
trygon
turbot
twaite
wapper
weever
wirrah
wrasse

zander
zingel

7

acaleph
actinia
alewife
anchovy
asterid
batfish
bergylt
bloater
box-fish
bubbler
bummalo
capelin
cat-fish
chimera
cichild
cod-fish
codling
cow-fish
croaker
crucian
cusk eel
cyprine
dog-fish
dun-fish
echinus
eel-fare
eel-pout
fiddler
garfish
garpike
garvock
gourami
grouper
grunter
gudgeon
gurnard
gwyniad
haddock
hagfish
halibut
herling
herring
hogfish
homelyn
houting
icefish
jewfish
keeling
lampern
lamprey

latchet
lobster
mahseer
merling
monodon
moon-eye
morwong
mud-fish
Muraena
murexes
oar-fish
octopus
old-wife
osseter
pegasus
pen-fish
piddock
pig-fish
pike eel
piranha
pollack
pollock
polypus
pompano
ragfish
rat-tail
red-fish
rock-cod
rotifer
sand eel
sardine
sawfish
Scomber
sculpin
sea-bass
sea-fish
sea-hare
sea-lion
sea-moth
sea-pike
sea-slug
sea-wolf
Silurus
snapper
sock-eye
sterlet
sunfish
sweeper
teleost
top-knot
torgoch
torpedo
vendace

whiting
worm-eel

8

albacore
Anguilla
arapaima
ascidian
Asterias
asteroid
band-fish
barnacle
bill fish
blue fish
blue-gill
boarfish
brisling
bullhead
calamary
cavefish
characin
chimaera
clupeoid
coalfish
corkwing
cowshark
crawfish
crayfish
dealfish
dragonet
drum-fish
eagle-ray
eulachon
filefish
fire-fish
flatfish
flathead
flounder
forktail
fox-shark
gamefish
Ganoidei
gillaroo
gilt-head
glass-eel
goatfish
goldfish
graining
grayling
green eel
gymnotus
halfbeak
halosaur
horn-beak

horn-fish
John Dory
king crab
king-fish
lancelet
land crab
lemon dab
lump-fish
lung-fish
mackerel
manta ray
menhaden
milkfish
monkfish
moon-fish
moray eel
nannygai
numbfish
ophidion
Physalla
pickerel
pigmy-eel
pilchard
pipefish
polyneme
poor-John
red perch
redbelly
reedfish
rock-bass
rock-fish
rockling
sail-fish
salt-fish
sand-fish
sardelle
saw-shark
scombrid
scopelid
sea bream
sea robin
sea snipe
sea-acorn
sea-devil
sea-horse
sea-lemon
sea-louse
sea-perch
sea-raven
siscowet
skipjack
soapfish
sparling
spelding

spiny eel
springer
starfish
sting-ray
stomapod
sturgeon
swamp-eel
tarwhine
teraglin
testacea
thrasher
thresher
toad-fish
trevally
troutlet
tuna fish
wolf-fish
zoophyte

9

acalephae
angel-fish
argentine
barracuda
black drum
blackfish
blue nurse
blue shark
brandling
bullshark
bulltrout
ceratodus
chaetodon
cling-fish
conger eel
coralfish
crampfish
crustacea
cycloidei
devil fish
dimyarian
Dover sole
echinidan
finny-scad
fire-flair
fish-louse
frost-fish
ganoidean
garden eel
globe-fish
goldsinny
goosefish
grenadier
grey nurse

gulper eel
hippodame
houndfish
jaculator
jellyfish
jollytail
lemon sole
loach goby
mango fish
Murray cod
pike perch
pilot fish
placoderm
porbeagle
pycnodont
razor fish
red mullet
red salmon
ribbon eel
river crab
sand shark
sand-lance
schnapper
sea-mullet
sea-needle
sea-nettle
sheat-fish
silver-eel
snipefish
spear-fish
stargazer
stingaree
stockfish
stomapoda
stone fish
stone-bass
surfperch
surmullet
sweetfish
sword-tail
swordfish
thornback
threadfin
tiger-barb
tigerfish
tittlebat
toothcarp
top minnow
troutling
trumpeter
trunkfish
tunny fish
whitebait
whitefish

wobbegong
yellowfin
zebra fish

10

angelshark
angler fish
archer fish
barracouta
basket fish
black bream
black whale
blue groper
Bombay duck
bottle-nose
brown trout
butterfish
candlefish
Cestracion
clouded eel
clown loach
cock-paddle
coelacanth
coral trout
cornet fish
ctenoidans
cuttlefish
cyclostome
damselfish
doctor fish
dragon-fish
dwarf shark
echinoderm
fingerling
five-finger
flying fish
ganoideans
ghost-shark
great skate
grey mullet
groundling
guitarfish
hammerfish
hammerhead
hermit crab
Holothuria
lizardfish
loggerhead
lumpsucker
maskanonge
maskinonge
midshipman
mirror carp
mudskipper

needlefish
nurse shark
paddlefish
parrot-fish
periwinkle
pufferfish
pycnodonts
pygmy perch
rapier fish
red gurnard
red snapper
ribbon-fish
robber-crab
rudderfish
sand-hopper
sand-launce
sand-mullet
scleroderm
Scopelidae
sea catfish
silver carp
silver dory
silverfish
silverside
squeteague
sucker-fish
surf scoter
tiger shark
tongue-sole
trout perch
tub gurnard
turkey fish
turret-fish
whale-shark
white shark
yellow-tail
zebra shark

11

balance-fish
black-angler
blue catfish
blue-pointer
bluefin tuna
bridled goby
brineshrimp
brown groper
carpet-shark
common skate
crested goby
electric eel
electric ray
fiddler crab
fiddler fish

flying squid
golden trout
gurnet perch
hatchet fish
hippocampus
holothurian
jackass-fish
javelin-fish
lantern fish
lepidosiren
orange perch
peacock-fish
peacock-sole
plectognath
prickleback
rainbow-fish
red fire-fish
salmon-trout
scleroderms
sea-cucumber
sea-elephant
sea-hedgehog
sea-scorpion
silver perch
soldier-crab
soldier-fish
stickleback
surgeon-fish
torpedo fish
trigger fish
trumpet-fish

12

basking shark
cucumber-fish
dogfish shark
European pike
fan-tailed ray
four-eyed fish
Pacific saury
rainbow trout
requiem shark
river garfish
rock flathead
scarlet bream
scorpion fish
sentinel crab
silver mullet
sixgill sharp
spiny lobster
squirrelfish
thornback ray
worm pipefish

13

barred garfish
blacktip shark
butterfly fish
climbing perch
finnan haddock
flying gurnard
giant boar-fish
gilthead bream
greater weaver
horse-mackerel
leafy seahorse
leatherjacket
long-finned eel
mackerel shark
ox-eyed herring
Pacific salmon
porcupine fish
saltwater fish
scarlet angler
snub-nosed dart
sockeye salmon
spiny flathead
spiny seahorse
striped angler
thresher shark
tiger-flathead
zebra firefish

14

banded sea-perch
black stingaree
blue-spotted ray
great barracuda
Greenland whale
Macquarie perch
many-banded sole
purple sea-perch
red gurnet-perch
river blackfish
short-finned eel
shovel-nosed ray
smooth flathead
spotted dogfish
spotted whiting
striped catfish
striped gudgeon
striped sea-pike
white horse-fish
zebra angelfish

15

Australian perch
Australian smelt
beaked coral-fish
blue-spot rock-cod

common stingaree
crusted flounder
electric catfish
frigate mackerel
hairback herring
long-finned perch

marbled flathead
painted dragonet
short sucker-fish
small-headed sole
smooth stingaree
spangled grunter

Spanish mackerel
spotted cat-shark
spotted eagle-ray
spotted pipe-fish
white-spotted ray

Fossils, shells, etc.

(f.s.) = fossil shell; (s.) = shell

4 AND 5

amber
auger
baler
chama (s.)
chank (s.)
conch (s.)
cone (s.)
cowry
drill (s.)
gaper (s.)
murex (s.)
nacre
ormer
peuce
razor (s.)
snail (s.)
tooth (s.)
tulip (s.)
whelk (s.)

6

buckie (s.)
chiton (s.)
cockle (s.)
cowrie
fornix (s.)
helmet (s.)
jingle (s.)
limpet (s.)
macoma (s.)
matrix
mussel (s.)
natica (s.)
nerite (s.)
Ogygia
olenus
oyster (s.)
quahog (s.)
seaear
tellin (s.)

triton (s.)
trivea (s.)
turban (s.)
volute (s.)
winkle (s.)

7

abalone (s.)
crabite
crinoid
discoid (s.)
muscite
neptune (s.)
ovulite
piddock (s.)
scallop (s.)
zoolite

8

ammonite (f.s.)
argonaut (s.)
ark shell (s.)
balanite
buccinum (s.)
capstone
ceratite
choanite
cololite
conchite (f.s.)
dogwhelk (s.)
ear shell (s.)
echinite
epiornis
escallop (s.)
fig shell (s.)
galerite
janthina (s.)
mangelia (s.)
muricite
mytilite
nautilus (s.)
penshell (s.)

ram's horn (f.s.)
retinite
scaphite (f.s.)
sea snail
seashell
solenite (f.s.)
strombid (s.)
testacel (s.)
topshell (s.)
trochite
tunshell (s.)
volulite (f.s.)
volutite (f.s.)

9

Aepyornis
alcyonite
belemnite
buccinite (f.s.)
cancerite
carpolite
clam shell (s.)
cone shell (s.)
coprolite
corallite
crow stone
dicynodon
encrinite
favosites
foot shell (s.)
frog shell (s.)
giant clam (s.)
harp shell (s.)
hippurite
horn shell (s.)
lima shell (s.)
lithocarp
lithophyl
marsupite
miliolite (f.s.)
moon shell (s.)
moon snail (s.)

muscalite (f.s.)
nautilite
nummulite
ostracite (f.s.)
palmacite
patellite (f.s.)
reliquiae
rock-borer (s.)
serpulite (f.s.)
slip shell (s.)
star shell (s.)
stone lily
strombite (f.s.)
tellinite (f.s.)
trilobite
turbinate (f.s.)
turrilite (f.s.)
tusk shell (s.)

10

agate shell
batrachite
canoe shell (s.)
confervite
dendrolite
dicynodont
entomolite
entrochite
gyrogonite
mosasaurus
odontolite
periwinkle (s.)
razor shell (s.)
screw shell (s.)
snake stone (f.s.)
tiger shell (s.)
tubiporite
ulodendron
wentletrap (s.)
wing oyster (s.)
xanthidium

11

amphibolite
asterolepis
cetotolites
dinotherium
fairy stones
finger shell (s.)
finger stone
furrowshell (s.)
gongiatites (f.s.)
helmet shell (s.)
ichthyolite
madreporite
margin shell
milleporite
mohair shell (s.)
needle shell (s.)
needle whelk (s.)
ornitholite
oyster drill (s.)
rhyncholite
sting winide (s.)
strobilites
sunset shell (s.)
tiger cowrie (s.)
trough shell (s.)
turtle shell (s.)

12

brocade shell (s.)
Chinaman's
  hat (s.)
holoptychis
Hungarian cap (s.)
lantern shell (s.)
macrotherium
megalichthys
pandora shell (s.)
pelican's foot (s.)
pentacrinite
saddle oyster (s.)

serpentstone
slipper shell (s.)
spindle shell (s.)
sundial shell (s.)
trumpet conch
trumpet shell (s.)
zamiostrobus

13 AND 14

bothrodendron (13)
carboniferous (13)
conchyliaceous (f.s.) (14)
dolichosaurus (13)
lepidodendron (13)
lithoglyphite (13)

nacreous shells (s.) (14)
necklace shell (s.) (13)
palaeontology (13)
porphyry shell (s.) (13)
staircase shell (s.) (14)
syringodendron (14)
woodcock shell (s.) (13)

Insects, etc.

3 AND 4

ant
bee
bot
bug
cleg
cob
dor
flea
fly
frit
gnat
grig
grub
ked
lice
mawk
mite
moth
nit
pupa
slug
tick
wasp
worm
zimb

5

acera
aphid
aphis
borer
brize
cimex
comma
culex
drake
drone
egger
emmet
fluke

imago
larva
louse
midge
musca
pulex
satyr
snail
thea

6

acarid
acarus
ant cow
bedbug
bee fly
beetle
blatta
botfly
breeze
burnet
buzzer
caddis
capsid
chafer
chigoe
chinch
cicada
cicala
cigala
coccus
cocoon
dayfly
dobson
earwig
elater
gadfly
hop-fly
hopper
hornet
Io moth
jigger

lappet
larvae
locust
looper
maggot
mantis
maybug
mayfly
mygale
sawfly
scarab
sow-bug
sphinx
spider
termes
thrips
Tipula
tsetse
weevil
worker
woubit

7

annelid
ant-hill
ant-lion
antenna
aphides
army ant
bagworm
bean fly
bee moth
beehive
blowfly
boat fly
cestoid
chalcid
chigger
cricket
culicid
cutworm
daphnia

Diptera
epizoon
firefly
frit-fly
gallfly
greyfly
hexapod
June bug
katydid
lady-cow
lobworm
lugworm
mawworm
microbe
monarch
noctuid
peacock
pismire
pyralid
rose-bug
rotifer
sandfly
satyrid
skipper
stylops
termite
tortrix
Vanessa
wasp bee
wasp-fly
wax-moth
wood-ant

8

acaridan
alder-fly
antennae
arachnid
army worm
blackfly
bookworm
caseworm

cheilfer
cinnabar
cocktail
cranefly
dipteran
doglouse
drone-fly
ephemera
firebrat
flatworm
flesh-fly
fossores
fruitfly
gall-wasp
geometer
glow worm
goat-moth
greenfly
hawkmoth
honey-bee
hop-louse
horntail
horsefly
housefly
hoverfly
Isoptera
itch-mite
lacewing
ladybird
luna moth
mason bee
mealworm
mealy bug
mosquito
multiped
myriapod
night-fly
nocturna
parasite
pedipalp
Pupipara
puss moth

queen-bee
rotifera
sand-flea
sand-wasp
sandworm
scolytus
scorpion
sheep ked
shipworm
silkworm
stone-fly
tapeworm
tetrapod
water-bug
water-fly
wheat-fly
white ant
white-fly
wireworm
wood wasp
woodlice

9

acaridean
Amazon ant
Anopheles
Arachnida
arthropod
atlas moth
auger worm
bloodworm
book louse
brimstone
bumble-bee
burnet fly
butterfly
caddis fly
canker fly
cantharis
centipede
cheesefly
chinch bug

chrysalis
clavicorn
cochineal
cockroach
coleopter
corn borer
crab-louse
cynipides
damsel fly
dorbeetle
dragonfly
driver-ant
dumbledor
earthworm
egger moth
ephemerid
ephemeron
flying-ant
forest-fly
gall louse
gall-midge
geometrid
ghost-moth
gipsy moth
hemiptera
hornet fly
humble-bee
ichneumon
isopteran
lac insect
longicorn
millipede
Myriapoda
nymphalid
oil beetle
orange-tip
owlet moth
plant-lice
potato bug
robber fly
saturniid
screw worm
sheep-lice
sheep-tick
shield bug
squash-bug
sugar-mite
tarantula
thysanura
tiger moth
tumblebug
turnip-fly
warble-fly
water-flea

wax-insect
wheat-moth
whirligig
wood-borer
wood-louse
worker ant
worker bee

10

arachnidan
arthropods
bark-beetle
bird-spider
black widow
blister-fly
bluebottle
boll-weevil
bombardier
burnet moth
cabbage-fly
caddice fly
caddisworm
cankerworm
carpet moth
chalcid fly
cheese-mite
coccinella
cockchafer
Coleoptera
corn-beetle
corn-weevil
crab spider
cuckoospit
death's-head
death-watch
digger wasp
dolphin-fly
dorr-beetle
drosophila
dumbledore
dung beetle
entomolite
flea-beetle
fritillary
froghopper
gall insect
green-drake
hairstreak
harvest bug
harvest man
hessian-fly
June beetle
lantern-fly
lappet moth

leaf beetle
leaf cutter
leaf hopper
leaf-insect
looper-moth
musk beetle
Neuroptera
Orthoptera
palmerworm
phylloxera
pine-weevil
plant-louse
pond skater
potter wasp
red admiral
ribbonworm
rice-weevil
rose beetle
rosechafer
rove beetle
saltigrade
scarabaeus
sheep-louse
silver-fish
soldier ant
Spanish fly
spider wasp
spittlebug
springtail
stag beetle
thysanuran
timber-moth
treehopper
trichopter
turnip-flea
wasp beetle
web-spinner
wheat-midge
wolf-spider
woolly-bear
xylophagan

11

arachnidans
assassin bug
atlas beetle
auger beetle
bagworm moth
balm-cricket
beehawk moth
black beetle
bloodsucker
bristletail
bush cricket

cabbage moth
cabbage worm
cantharides
camel spider
capharis bug
caterpillar
chalcia wasp
click beetle
clothes moth
codling moth
coprophagan
drumbledore
emperor moth
entomophaga
Ephemeridae
flour weevil
grain beetle
grasshopper
Hymenoptera
Lepidoptera
mole-cricket
noctuid moth
painted lady
pyralid moth
saprophagan
scale insect
scolopendra
scorpion-fly
snout-beetle
stick-insect
swallow-tail
tetrapteran
thysanurans
tiger-beetle
Trichoptera
tussock-moth
vine-fretter
water beetle
water spider
wood-fretter

12

bent-wing moth
book-scorpion
cabbage white
carpenter ant
carpenter bee
carpet beetle
cecropia moth
cinnabar moth
clerid-beetle
diadem spider
diving beetle
flower-beetle

geometer moth
ground beetle
horned clerid
horse-stinger
ichneumon fly
money-spinner
nightcrawler
potato beetle
Rhynchophera
scarab beetle
sexton beetle
spruce sawfly
sycamore moth
trichopteran
walking-stick
water-boatman
water-strider
white admiral

13

blister beetle
burying beetle
carpenter moth
clearwing moth
clouded yellow
daddy-longlegs
diamond beetle
elm bark beetle
fig-leaf beetle
giant wood-moth
goliath beetle
green wood-moth
ichneumon-wasp
leaf-cutter ant
leaf-cutter bee
leather-jacket
praying mantis
purple emperor
saturniid moth
soldier beetle
tortoiseshell
underwing moth
water scorpion

14

ambrosia beetle
cabbage-root fly
Colorado beetle
death's-head moth
elephant-beetle
Hercules beetle
ironbark saw-fly

15

funnel-web spider
serricorn beetle

striped hawkmoth
wheel-animalcule
whirligig beetle

Mammals

2 AND 3	4				
ai	ure	moke	apery	horse	rasse
ape	wat	mole	ariel	hound	ratel
ass	yak	mule	beast	husky	rhino
bat	zho	musk	bidet	hutia	royal
cat	zo	mutt	billy	hyena	sable
cob		neat	biped	hyrax	saiga
cow	**4**	nowt	bison	indri	sajou
cub	anoa	oryx	bitch	izard	sasin
cur	Arab	oxen	bongo	jocko	screw
dam	arni	paca	brach	jumbo	serow
doe	barb	paco	brock	kaama	sheep
dog	bear	pard	bruin	kiang	shire
dso	beef	pika	bubal	koala	shoat
dzo	boar	pony	bunny	kulan	shote
elk	buck	prad	burro	kyloe	shott
ewe	bull	puma	camel	lemur	shrew
fox	calf	puss	caple	liger	simia
gam	cavy	quey	capra	llama	skunk
gnu	colt	roan	capul	loris	sloth
goa	cony	runt	cavey	magot	sorel
hob	coon	rusa	civet	manis	sorex
hog	deer	saki	coati	manul	spitz
kid	douc	seal	coney	maral	steed
kob	dray	sika	coypu	meles	steer
man	euro	stag	crone	moggy	stirk
mog	eyra	stot	cuddy	moose	stoat
nag	fawn	stud	daman	morse	swine
orc	foal	suni	dhole	mount	tabby
ox	gaur	tahr	dicky	mouse	takin
pad	goat	tait	dingo	nagor	talpa
pig	hack	tatu	dogie	nandu	tapir
pod	hare	tike	drill	nanny	tatou
pug	hart	titi	eland	nyala	taxel
ram	hind	topi	equus	okapi	tayra
rat	ibex	tyke	fauna	oribi	tiger
roe	jade	unau	felis	otter	tigon
sal	joey	urus	filly	ounce	urial
seg	kine	vole	fitch	panda	urson
sow	kudu	wolf	fossa	pekan	ursus
teg	lamb	zati	gayal	phoca	vixen
tit	lion	zebu	genet	pinto	waler
tod	lynx	zobo	goral	pongo	whale
tom	mare		grice	pooch	whelp
tup	mhor	**5**	grise	potto	yapok
	mice	addax	hinny	puppy	zebra
	mink	ammon	hippo	pussy	zerda

zibet	fisher	ovibos	wow-wow	griffon	raccoon
zoril	fox bat	padnag	yapock	grizzly	red deer
zorra	galago	poodle		grysbok	rietbok
zorro	garron	porker	**7**	guanaco	roe buck
	gelada	possum		hackney	roe deer
6	gerbil	pugdog	acouchi	hamster	rorqual
	gibbon	pyedog	ant-bear	harrier	saimiri
agouti	ginnet	pygarg	aurochs	huanaco	sapajou
aliped	gopher	quagga	banteng	hystrix	sassaby
alpaca	grison	quokka	bettong	jacchus	sciurus
Angora	grivet	rabbit	bighorn	jackass	sea-bear
aoudad	guenon	racoon	blesbok	jumbuck	sea-calf
argali	hacker	ranger	blue cat	karakul	sea-lion
aye-aye	he goat	red fox	blue fox	lambkin	sheltie
baboon	heifer	reebok	Bovidae	lemming	siamang
badger	hogget	renard	brawner	leopard	Siamese
bandog	howler	rhesus	brocket	leveret	spaniel
barrow	hunter	roarer	bubalis	linsang	spanker
bayard	hyaena	rodent	buffalo	lioness	sumpter
beagle	hybrid	saluki	bulldog	lurcher	tamarau
beaver	impala	sambar	bullock	macaque	tamarin
beeves	inyala	sambur	Burmese	mammoth	tarsier
bharal	jackal	sea cow	bushcat	manatee	tatouay
bobcat	jaguar	serval	bushpig	Manx cat	terrier
boomer	jennet	setter	cane rat	mariput	testudo
bovine	jerboa	shammy	caracal	markhor	thiller
bronco	Jersey	she ass	caribou	marmose	tigress
brumby	jument	shelty	cattalo	meerkat	toxodon
castor	kalong	simian	cervine	megamys	trotter
catalo	kelpie	sleuth	cetacea	mole-rat	twinter
cattle	kitten	sorrel	chamois	mongrel	urocyon
cayuse	Kodiak	suslik	charger	moon rat	vampire
cervus	koodoo	taguan	cheetah	moschus	viverra
chacma	langur	talbot	Cheviot	mouflon	wallaby
chetah	lapdog	tanrec	clumber	muntjak	wart-hog
coaiti	lechwe	tarpan	colobus	musk-rat	wheeler
cocker	lionet	taurus	courser	mustang	wild ass
colugo	litter	teledu	dasyure	mustela	wild dog
cosset	macaco	tenrec	dinmont	narwhal	wildcat
cougar	mammal	thamin	dolphin	nasalis	wistiti
coyote	margay	theave	Echidna	noctule	wolf-dog
cuscus	marmot	tomcat	ermelin	nylghai	zamouse
dassie	marten	tupaia	fatling	nylghau	zorilla
desman	mataco	tusker	finback	opossum	
dickey	merino	urchin	fitchew	pack rat	**8**
dik-dik	monkey	vermin	foumart	palfrey	
dobbin	morkin	vervet	fur seal	panther	aardvark
dog fox	mouser	vicuña	gazelle	peccary	aardwolf
dogape	musk ox	walrus	gelding	polecat	anteater
donkey	musmon	wapiti	gemsbok	potoroo	antelope
entire	nilgai	weasel	gerenuk	prancer	axis deer
ermine	ocelot	wether	giraffe	pricket	babirusa
farrow	olingo	wisent	glutton	primate	Bactrian
fennec	onager	wombat	gorilla	primate	behemoth
ferret			grampus	procyon	bontebok

brown rat
bull-calf
bushbaby
bushbuck
cachalot
capuchin
capucine
capybara
carcajou
cariacou
cavebear
cavicorn
chipmunk
civet-cat
Cotswold
creodont
cricetus
dormouse
duckbill
elephant
entellus
eohippus
foxhound
Galloway
gin-horse
grey wolf
grysbock
Guernsey
hair seal
hedgehog
hoggerel
hylobate
kangaroo
kinkajou
kolinsky
lamantin
landrace
macropus
Mammalia
mandrill
mangabey
mantiger
marmoset
mastodon
maverick
meriones
mongoose
moufflon
milch-cow
musk deer
musquash
ouistiti
pack mule
pangolin

physeter
platypus
polo pony
porkling
porpoise
pteropus
reedbuck
reindeer
river-hog
Rodentia
ruminant
sea-otter
sei whale
serotine
sewellel
sewer-rat
shorling
sirenian
springer
squirrel
staggard
stallion
steenbok
suilline
suricate
tabby-cat
talapoin
tamandua
tetrapod
tiger cat
twinling
ungulata
viscacha
wallaroo
wanderoo
war-horse
warrigal
water-hog
water-rat
weanling
wild boar
wild goat
yeanling
yearling

9

Angora cat
arctic fox
armadillo
babacoote
babirussa
bandicoot
bezantler
binturong

black bear
black buck
blue whale
brood-mare
brown bear
buckhound
carnivore
cart-horse
catamount
chevrotin
chickaree
dachshund
deer-mouse
desert rat
Didelphys
Didelphia
Dinoceras
draught-ox
dray-horse
dromedary
dziggetai
eared seal
flying-fox
glyptodon
golden cat
greyhound
grimalkin
ground-hog
gruntling
guinea-pig
hamadryad
honey-bear
ichneumon
lagomorph
leviathan
livestock
malt-horse
marsupial
monotreme
mouse-hare
mousedeer
orang-utan
pachyderm
pack-horse
palm civet
percheron
petaurist
phalanger
pipistrel
polar bear
porcupine
post-horse
predacean
prongbuck

pronghorn
prosimian
quadruped
racehorse
retriever
rock hyrax
rosinante
rosmarine
shearling
shorthorn
shrew-mole
silver fox
sitatunga
sloth-bear
solenodon
southdown
springbok
steerling
steinbock
stud-horse
thylacine
tragelaph
tree hyrax
tree shrew
waterbuck
watermole
watervole
white bear
wild horse
wolverene
wolverine
woodchuck
woodshock
youngling
zoophagan

10

Angora goat
angwantibo
anthropoid
babiroussa
barasingha
Barbary ape
bloodhound
bottlenose
buckjumper
cacomistle
camelopard
catarrhine
chevrotain
chimpanzee
chinchilla
Chiroptera
chousingha

Clydesdale
coach-horse
coatimundi
cottontail
dolichotis
fallow deer
fieldmouse
giant panda
hartebeest
honey mouse
hooded seal
housemouse
human being
jack rabbit
Kodiak bear
Malay tapir
marsupials
monotremes
muscardine
musk beaver
otter shrew
paddymelon
pantheress
paradoxure
Persian cat
pichiciago
pilot whale
pine marten
prairie dog
pygmy shrew
quadricorn
quadrumane
raccoon dog
rhinoceros
right whale
river horse
rock badger
rock rabbit
Ruminantia
saki monkey
sea-unicorn
shrew-mouse
sperm whale
springhaas
timber wolf
vampire bat
water shrew
white whale
wildebeest

11

American elk
barbastelle
brown hyaena

bull terrier
Cape buffalo
Cheiroptera
digitigrade
douroucouli
flying lemur
Grevy's zebra
grizzly bear
harbour seal
horned horse
Insectivora
jumping deer
kangaroo dog
kangaroo rat
killer whale
Megatherium
mountain cat
orang-outang
pipistrelle
prairie wolf
Pterodactyl
red kangaroo
red squirrel
sea elephant
sleuthhound
snow leopard
vespertilio
wishtonwish

12

Angora rabbit
Barbary sheep
catamountain
cinnamon bear
draught horse
elephant seal
flittermouse
goat antelope
grey squirrel
harvest mouse
hippopotamus
horseshoe bat
howler monkey
jumping mouse
klipspringer
mountain goat
mountain ibex
mountain lion
Pachydermata
Paleotherium
pouched mouse
rhesus monkey
rock squirrel
Shetland pony
snowshoe hare
spider monkey
spotted hyena

striped hyena
tree kangaroo
water buffalo
water spaniel

13

Abyssinian cat
Australian cat
Bactrian camel
carriage horse
Chapman's zebra
European bison
Galeopithecus
golden hamster
Indian buffalo
laughing hyena
mountain sheep
Palaeotherium
Parry's wallaby
ring-tail coati
sable antelope
Semnopithecus
shorthorn bull
spiny anteater
sulphur bottom
Tasmanian wolf
tree porcupine

14

bridled wallaby
Burchell's zebra
capuchin monkey
crab-eating seal
flying squirrel
ground squirrel
hunting leopard
Indian elephant
Indian pangolin
laughing hyaena
Patagonian cavy
snowshoe rabbit
Tasmanian devil

15

African elephant
American buffalo
American leopard
Bennett's wallaby
flying phalanger
laughing jackass
ring-tailed coati
sabretooth tiger
springer spaniel
Tasmanian possum
Thomson's gazelle
white rhinoceros

Marine growths, etc.

4 – 6

algae (5)
astrea (6)
coral (5)
dulse (5)
fungia (6)
kelp (4)
laver (5)
limpet (6)
mussel (6)
polyp (5)
sponge (6)
tang (4)
tangle (6)
varec (5)
ware (4)
wrack (5)

7 AND 8

actinia (7)
agar agar (8)
alcyonic (8)
astraea (7)
badioga (7)
blubber (7)
calycle (7)
eschara (7)
fungite (7)
gulf weed (8)
naiades (7)
polypary (8)
porifera (8)
red algae (8)
red coral (8)
sea moss (7)
seaweed (7)
seawrack (8)

tubipora (8)
zoophyte (8)

9

Alcyoneae
alcyonite
bathybius
blue algae
blue coral
carrageen
ecardines
Irish moss
madrepore
millepore
nullipore
pink coral
sea nettle

10 AND OVER

abrotanoid (10)
acorn barnacle (13)
Alcyonacea (10)
alva marina (10)
animal flower (12)
bladder kelp (11)
bladder wrack (12)
brown algae (10)
carragheen (10)
coral zoophytes (14)
goose barnacle (13)
lithodendron (12)
lithogenous (11)
lithophyte (10)
marine plants (12)
sea anemone (10)
tubiporite (10)
utricularia (11)

Molluscs, tunicates, etc.

3 – 5

bulla
chank
clam
clio
ensis
fusus
gaper
helix
murex
mya
naiad
sepia
slug
snail
solen
spat
Unio
venus
whelk

6

anodon
buckie
chiton
cockle
cuttle
dodman
dolium
limpet
loligo
mantle
mussel
naiads

nerite
ostrea
oyster
pecten
quahog
sea ear
teredo
triton
volute
winkle

7

acerans
actaeon
aplysia
balanus
bivalve
diceras
eschera
etheria
glaucus
mollusc
mytilus
octopus
patella
piddock
polyzoa
purpura
quahaug
scallop
scollop
sea hare
spirula
taccata

teffina
toheroa

8

argonaut
ascidian
buccinum
decapoda
limnaeid
Mollusca
nautilus
pedireme
pteropod
sea lemon
sea snail
shipworm
spirifer
strombus
teredine
tridacna

9

acephalan
gastropod
giant clam
heteropod
hodmandod
lithodome
ostracean
pteropods
rock borer
scaphopod
shellfish
spondylus

10

acorn shell
amphineura
amphitrite
brachiopod
cephalopod
conchifera
cuttlefish
date-mussel
Haliotidae
Heteropoda
periwinkle
razorshell
stone borer
stone eater

11

dragon shell
fasciolaria
Gasteropoda
pearl oyster
river oyster
rock scallop
terebratula

12 AND OVER

boring mussel (12)
cyclobranchiata (15)
entomostomata (13)
lamellibranch (13)
pelican's foot (12)
spindleshell (12)
tectibranchiata (15)

Reptiles and amphibians

3 – 5

adder
agama
anole
apod
asp
aspic
boa
cobra
draco
eft
ernys

frog
gecko
guana
hydra
krait
kufi
mamba
newt
olm
pipa
rana
seps
siren

skink
snake
toad
tokay
viper
worm

6

anolis
caiman
cayman
dipsas
dragon

gavial
iguana
lizard
moloch
mugger
python
Sauria
taipan
triton
turtle
uraeus
worral
zonure

7

agamids
axolotl
coluber
gharial
ghavial
hicatee
lacerta
monitor
ophidia
paddock
rattler

reptile
saurian
scincus
serpent
snapper
tadpole
testudo
tuatara
urodele
varanus

8

amphibia
anaconda
asp viper
basilisk
bullfrog
cerastes
chelonia
Congo eel
dinosaur
hiccatee
keelback
lachesis
matamata
moccasin
mud puppy
ophidian
pit viper
platanna
rat snake
ringhals
scincoid
seasnake
slow-worm
terrapin
tortoise
treefrog
typhlops

9

alligator
amphibian
batrachia
blind-worm
blue krait
boomslang
box turtle
caecilian
chameleon
chelonian
coach-whip

corn snake
crocodile
dart snake
eyed skink
galliwasp
giant frog
giant toad
green toad
hairy frog
hamadryad
hawk's-bill
horned asp
king cobra
king snake
marsh frog
ophidians
pine snake
pterosaur
puff adder
ring snake
rock snake
spadefoot
stegosaur
tree snake
vine snake
wall gecko
whip snake
wolf snake

10

black mamba
black snake
blind snake
bushmaster
chuckwalla
clawed frog
cockatrice
Congo snake
copperhead
coral snake
death adder
diplodocus
eyed lizard
fer-de-lance
glass snake
grass snake
green anole
green mamba
green snake
hellbender
horned frog
horned toad

mosasaurus
natterjack
plesiosaur
pond turtle
river snake
rock python
salamander
sand lizard
sea serpent
sidewinder
tiger snake
wall lizard
water snake
worm lizard

11

amphisbaena
banded krait
black cayman
black iguana
bloodsucker
carpet snake
cottonmouth
crested newt
diamondback
draco lizard
flying snake
forest cobra
Gaboon viper
gartersnake
gila monster
goliath frog
gopher snake
green lizard
green turtle
horned snake
horned viper
ichthyosaur
leatherback
midwife toad
pterodactyl
rattlesnake
royal python
smooth snake
stegosaurus
Surinam toad
thorny devil
triceratops

12

brontosaurus
chicken snake

flying lizard
herpetofauna
horned lizard
Komodo dragon
leopard gecko
marine iguana
pond tortoise
spring lizard

13 AND OVER

alligator lizard (15)
bearded dragon (13)
blue-tongued skink (16)
boa constrictor (14)
brown tree snake (14)
coach-whip snake (14)
cobra de capello (14)
dolichosaurus (13)
egg-eating snake (14)
fire salamander (14)
five-lined snake (14)
frilled lizard (13)
giant tortoise (13)
golden tree frog (14)
golden tree snake (15)
green pit viper (13)
green tree frog (13)
hawk's-bill turtle (15)
Himalayan viper (14)
hog-nosed snake (13)
horn-nosed viper (14)
ichthyosaurus (13)
legless lizard (13)
long-nosed viper (14)
mangrove snake (13)
Nile crocodile (13)
painted terrapin (15)
painted turtle (13)
rat-tailed snake (14)
rhinoceros viper (15)
ringhals cobra (13)
Russell's viper (13)
snapping turtle (14)
spadefoot toad (13)
stump-tailed skink (16)
tiger salamander (15)
Tyrannosaurus) (13
water moccasin (13)

NATURAL HISTORY (2) PLANTS
Cereals, etc.

3 AND 4

bere
bran
brigg
corn
dari
dohl
dura
far
gram
malt
meal
oats
oca
poar
rabi
rice
rye
sago
teff
zea

5

bajra
bajri

brank
durra
durum
emmer
ervum
fundi
grain
grama
grist
grout
maize
paddy
panic
pulse
rivet
short
spelt
straw
typha
wheat

6 AND 7

barley (6)
cassava (6)
corncob (7)
dhurra (6)

farina (6)
groats (6)
hominy (6)
mealie (6)
meslin (6)
millet (6)
muesli (6)
nocake (6)
raggee (6)
rokeage (7)
sorghum (7)
tapioca (7)
wild oat (7)
Zea mays (7)

8 AND 9

arrowroot (9)
buckwheat (9)
espiotte (8)
garavance (9)
mangcorn (8)
middlings (9)
pearl rice (9)
pot barley (9)
seed corn (8)
seed grain (9)

semolina (8)
sweetcorn (9)
wild rice (8)

10 AND OVER

barleycorn (10)
barleymeal (10)
basmati rice (11)
cracked wheat (12)
German millet (12)
gramma grass (11)
Guinea corn (10)
Indian corn (10)
Indian meal (10)
Indian millet (12)
Indian rice (10)
long-grain rice (13)
mountain rice (12)
pearl barley (11)
pearl millet (11)
Scotch barley (12)
spring wheat (11)
summer wheat (11)
turkey wheat (11)
winter barley (11)
winter wheat (11)

Flowers

3 AND 4

aloe
arum
balm
flag
geum
iris
ixia
lei
lily
may
musk
pink
rose
sego
weld
whin
wold

5

agave
aspic
aster
avens
blite
briar
broom
canna
daisy
erica
faham
flora
gilia
gorse
gowan
henna
lilac
linum

lotus
lupin
orris
ox-eye
oxlip
padma
pagle
pansy
peony
petal
phlox
poppy
sepal
spray
stock
tansy
thyme
tulip
viola

yucca
yulan

6

acacia
acaena
acorus
alisma
alpine
alsike
arnica
azalea
balsam
bellis
bennet
borage
cactus
camass
cistus
clover

coleus
cosmea
cosmos
crants
crocus
dahlia
datura
fennel
henbit
iberis
kochia
lupine
lychis
madder
mallow
malope
mimosa
myrtle
nerine
nuphar

opulus
orchid
orchis
oxalis
paigle
privet
reseda
rocket
salvia
scilla
sesame
silene
sundew
thrift
torana
violet
wattle
yarrow
zinnia

7

aconite
alonsoa
aloysia
althaea
alyssum
anchusa
anemone
begonia
blawort
blewert
blossom
bouquet
bugloss
campion
candock
catmint
chaplet
chelone
chicory
clarkia
cowslip
cup rose
cytisus
day lily
deutzia
dittany
dog rose
festoon
figwort
freesia
fuchsia
gazania
genista
gentian
gerbera
godetia
heather
honesty
jasmine
jessamy
jonquil
kingcup
lantana
linaria
lobelia
lupinus
marybud
may-lily
melissa
milfoil
mimulus
nelumbo

nemesia
nigella
nosegay
opuntia
papaver
petunia
picotee
primula
ragwort
rambler
rampion
sea-pink
seringa
spiraea
statice
succory
syringa
tagetes
tea rose
thistle
tritoma
ursinia
verbena
vervain
witloof

8

abutilon
acanthus
achillea
ageratum
amaranth
angelica
arum lily
asphodel
aubretia
auricula
bear's ear
bedstraw
bignonia
bindweed
bluebell
buddleia
calamint
camellia
camomile
capsicum
catchfly
cattleya
clematis
cockspur
cornflag
crowfoot
cyclamen

daffodil
dianthus
dicentra
dropwort
erigeron
feverfew
fleabane
foxglove
gardenia
geranium
gladiola
gladioli
glaucium
gloriosa
gloxinia
goat's rue
hare's ear
harebell
hawkweed
helenium
hepatica
hibiscus
hottonia
hyacinth
japonica
laburnum
larkspur
lavatera
lavender
lent-lily
magnolia
marigold
martagon
moss rose
musk rose
myosotis
nenuphar
noisette
nymphaea
oleander
phacelia
phormium
plumbago
pond lily
primrose
rock-rose
scabious
sea-heath
skull-cap
snowdrop
stapelia
starwort
sweet-pea
tigridia

toad-flax
trillium
tuberose
turnsole
valerian
veronica
viscaria
wild rose
wistaria
wisteria
wood sage
woodbind
woodbine
xanthium

9

Aaron's-rod
achimines
amaryllis
anagallis
aquilegia
bear's foot
buttercup
calendula
campanula
candytuft
carnation
carthamus
celandine
cherry pie
China rose
cineraria
clove pink
cockscomb
colchicum
colt's foot
columbine
composite
coreopsis
corn-poppy
dandelion
digitalis
dog violet
dove's foot
edelweiss
eglantine
forsythia
gelsemium
gladiolus
golden rod
hellebore
hollyhock
hydrangea
jessamine

kniphofia
lady-smock
lotus lily
mayflower
meadowrue
moneywort
monkshood
moon daisy
naked lady
narcissus
nemophila
oenothera
pimpernel
polygonum
pyrethrum
remontant
rudbeckia
saxifrage
snowflake
speedwell
spikenard
sunflower
tiger lily
twayblade
verbascum
wake robin
water flag
water-lily
wolf's-bane

10

agapanthus
amaranthus
aspidistra
bell flower
belladonna
blue-bottle
burnet rose
caffre lily
calliopsis
China aster
chionodoxa
cinquefoil
coquelicot
corn violet
corncockle
cornflower
crane's-bill
crow flower
cuckoopint
damask rose
delphinium
Easter lily
fritillary

gaillardia
gelder rose
goat's-beard
golden drop
gypsophila
heart's-ease
helianthus
heliophila
heliotrope
immortelle
king's spear
lady's-smock
limnanthes
marguerite
mayblossom
mignonette
mock orange
montbretia
moonflower
nasturtium
nightshade
orange lily
ox-eye daisy
passiflora
pennyroyal
pentstemon
periwinkle
poinsettia
polyanthus
potentilla
ranunculus
snapdragon
spiderwort
stork's bill
sweetbriar
sweetbrier
thalictrum
wallflower
white poppy
willow herb

wind flower
wood sorrel
yellow wort

11

Aaron's beard
antirrhinum
bittersweet
bladderwort
blood flower
cabbage rose
calandrinia
calceolaria
cheiranthus
convallaria
convolvulus
cotoneaster
everlasting
fig marigold
forget-me-not
gillyflower
globeflower
green dragon
guelder rose
heather bell
helichrysum
honey-flower
honeysuckle
Indian cress
kidney-vetch
lady's mantle
London pride
loosestrife
love-in-a-mist
Madonna lily
meadowsweet
Nancy pretty
night flower
pelargonium
pepper elder

poppy mallow
ragged robin
rambler rose
red-hot poker
rose campion
schizanthus
sea lavender
spear flower
St. John's wort
sweet rocket
sweet sultan
tiger flower
wild flowers
wood anemone
xeranthemum

12

apple blossom
autumn crocus
bougainvilia
century plant
cuckoo-flower
heather bells
Iceland poppy
Jacob's ladder
lady's slipper
morning glory
none-so-pretty
old man's-beard
orange flower
pasque flower
peach blossom
pheasant's eye
rhododendron
rose of Sharon
salpiglossis
Shirley poppy
snow in summer
Solomon's seal
sweet william

tradescantia
virgin's bower

13

African violet
alpine flowers
blanket flower
bleeding heart
bougainvillea
Bristol flower
cherry blossom
Christmas rose
chrysanthemum
creeping jenny
crown imperial
eschscholtzia
grape-hyacinth
huntsman's horn
marsh marigold
meadow saffron
orange blossom
passion flower
sweet calabash
traveller's joy
trumpet flower
water hyacinth

14 AND 15

bougainvillaea (14)
Canterbury bell (14)
cardinal flower (14)
Christmas flower (15)
evening primrose (15)
lily of the valley (15)
lords-and-ladies (14)
love-in-idleness (14)
Michaelmas daisy (15)
shepherd's purse (14)
star of Bethlehem (15)

Fruit

3 AND 4

akee
bito
Cox's
crab
date
fig
gage
gean

haw
hep
hip
kaki
kiwi
lime
mare
mast
musa
nut

ogen
pear
pepo
plum
pome
rasp
skeg
sloe
ugli
uva

5

abhal
agava
agave
akena
anana
apple
arnot
betel

carob
cubeb
drupe
eleot
grape
grout
guava
lemon
lichi
mango

melon
merry
morel
morus
naras
olive
papaw
peach
pecan
prune

regma
ribes
rubus
whort
whurt

6

achene
almond
ananas
banana
biffin
cashew
cedrat
cherry
citron
citrus
cobnut
colmar
damson
drupel
durian
egriot
elk nut
ginger
groser
lichee
linden
longan
loquat
lychee
mammee
medlar
narras
nelies
nutmeg
orange
papaya
pawpaw
peanut
pignut
pippin
pomelo
prunus
punica
quince
raisin
rennet
russet
samara
squash
tomato
walnut
zapote

7

apricot
avocado
bilimbi
bramble
buckeye
bullace
capulin
cassava
catawba
cedrate
cheston
coconut
codling
corinth
costard
cumquat
currant
deal-nut
dessert
dogwood
etaerio
filbert
genipap
golding
hautboy
hog-plum
karatas
kumquat
litchee
mahaleb
mayduke
mineola
morello
naartje
pompion
pumpkin
quashey
rizzart
rosehip
satsuma
soursop
sultana
tangelo
wilding
winesap

8

allspice
barberry
bayberry
beechnut
bergamot

betel-nut
bilberry
breadnut
buckmast
calabash
cat's-head
chestnut
citrange
coquilla
cream-nut
date-plum
dewberry
dogberry
drupelet
earthnut
earthpea
fenberry
fig-apple
fox grape
hastings
hazelnut
japonica
jonathan
mandarin
may apple
minneola
mulberry
muscadel
muscatel
musk pear
nonesuch
oleaster
pearmain
plantain
prunello
quandong
queening
rambutan
shaddock
spondias
sweeting
tamarind
Valencia
whitsour
windfall

9

alkekengi
apple-john
aubergine
beechmast
blueberry
brazil nut
butternut

cantaloup
canteloup
carmelite
cherimoya
chokepear
corozo nut
crab-apple
cranberry
crowberry
damascene
drupaceae
elvas plum
greengage
groundnut
haanepoot
king apple
kiwi fruit
melocoton
mirabelle
monkey nut
muscadine
muskapple
muskmelon
nectarine
nonpareil
Ogen melon
ortanique
oxycoccus
persimmon
pineapple
pistachio
raspberry
redstreak
sapodilla
sorbapple
star-apple
tangerine
ugli fruit
victorine
Worcester

10

adam's apple
bird-cherry
blackberry
blackheart
breadfruit
cantaloupe
charentais
china berry
chokeberry
cider apple
clementine
clingstone

cream-fruit
damask plum
dried fruit
elderberry
florentine
gooseberry
granadilla
grapefruit
Indian date
loganberry
Madeira nut
mangosteen
marking nut
orange musk
pompelmous
queen-apple
redcurrant
stone fruit
strawberry
waterlemon
watermelon
wild cherry
winter pear

11

anchovy pear
bitter apple
blood orange
boysenberry
candleberry
China orange
chokecherry
coquilla nut
French berry
granny smith
huckleberry
hurtleberry
Jaffa orange
leathercoat
mammee apple
monkey bread
myrtleberry
navel orange
pomegranate
quarrington
russet apple
scuppernong
winter apple
winter berry

12

bitter almond
blackcurrant
chaumontelle

Chester grape
chocolate nut
cooking apple
custard apple
mammee-sapota
passion fruit
pistachio nut

serviceberry
Victoria plum
white currant
whortleberry
winter cherry
winter citron

13 AND OVER

alligator pear (13)
Barbados cherry (14)
Blenheim orange (14)
Cape gooseberry (14)
Catherine pear (13)
conference pear (14)

cornelian cherry (16)
golden delicious (15)
mandarin orange (14)
morello cherry (13)
preserved fruit (14)
Seville orange (13)
water chestnut

Herbs and spices

3 – 5

ani se
balm
basil
bay
chive
clary
clove
cress
cumin
dill
mace
mint
myrrh
rape
rue
sage
senna
tansy
thyme
woad

6

bennet
betony
borage
burnet
capers
chilli
chives
cicely
cloves
endive
fennel
galega
garlic
ginger
hyssop
isatis
lovage
lunary
nutmeg

orpine
pepper
rocket
savory
sesame
simple
sorrel

7

aconite
burdock
caraway
catmint
cayenne
chervil
chicory
comfrey
dittany
frasera
gentian
henbane
juniper
lettuce
milfoil
mustard
oregano
panicum
paprika
parsley
pimento
pot herb
rampion
saffron
salsify
spignel
succory
tabasco
turpeth
vanilla
zedoary

8

agrimony

allspice
angelica
camomile
cardamom
centaury
cinnamon
costmary
feverfew
fumitory
hog's-bean
lavender
lungwort
marigold
marjoram
mouse ear
origanum
plantain
purslane
reedmace
rosemary
samphire
spicknel
tarragon
turmeric
waybread
wormwood

9

baneberry
bear's foot
chickweed
colocynth
coriander
coronopus
dittander
eyebright
fenugreek
fever-root
finocchio
goose foot
groundsel
hellebore
horehound

liquorice
patchouli
sea fennel
spearmint
sweet herb
tormentil

10

asafoetida
cassumunar
lemon thyme
motherwort
penny royal
peppermint
watercress
willow herb

11

dog's cabbage
dragon's head
hedge hyssop
horseradish
hyoscyamine
oyster plant
pot marigold
pot marjoram
sweet rocket
swine's cress
winter cress
wintergreen

12 AND OVER

adder's tongue (12)
Florence fennel (14)
medicinal herb (13)
mournful widow (13)
mustard and cress (15)
southernwood (12)
summer savory (12)
sweet marjoram (13)
thoroughwort (12)
winter savory (12)

Plants

3

box
cos
ers
fog
hay
hop
ivy
nep
oat
oca
pea
pia
poa
rue
rye
seg
tea
tod
yam
zea

4

aira
akee
alfa
aloe
anil
arum
balm
bean
beet
bent
bigg
bulb
cane
coca
coco
coix
cole
corn
crab
culm
dari
dill
diss
dock
doob
dora
ecad
fern

flag
flax
gale
gama
geum
hemp
herb
holm
ilex
iris
jute
kale
kali
kans
leek
ling
mint
moly
moss
musa
musk
nard
okra
peat
pipi
ragi
rape
reed
rhea
rice
root
rush
sage
sago
sida
sium
sloe
soma
star
tara
tare
taro
teff
thea
tree
tule
turf
tutu
ulex
vine
wald
weed

weld
whin
woad
wort

5

abaca
agave
ajuga
algae
alpia
anise
apium
arnut
aspic
aster
avena
basil
brake
brank
briar
broom
bugle
cacao
calla
camas
canna
chive
cicer
clary
clote
clove
couch
cress
cumin
cycad
dagga
daisy
dicot
dryas
dulse
durra
dwale
erica
eruca
ficus
fitch
fucus
fungi
furze
glaux
goman

gorse
gourd
grama
grass
grias
henna
holly
hosta
kunai
ledum
liana
liane
lotus
loufa
lupin
madia
maize
medic
morel
moril
mucor
mudar
musci
napal
olive
orach
orpin
orris
oryza
oshac
osier
oxlip
paddy
palas
palea
panic
poker
radix
ramie
reate
rheum
roosa
rubia
rubus
runch
savin
savoy
scrog
sedge
shrub
sison
solah

starr
stipa
stole
sumac
swede
tacca
tamus
tansy
thorn
thyme
trapa
tucum
urena
vetch
vicia
vinca
viola
vitis
wahoo
wapon
wheat
whort
withy
wrack
yerba
yucca
yupon
zamia

6

acorus
agaric
albino
alisma
amomum
aninga
annual
arabis
aralia
azalea
bamboo
barley
batata
bejuco
betony
biblus
borage
bryony
burnet
cactus
caltha
camass

cassia
catnip
cicely
cicuta
cissus
cistus
clover
cockle
conium
conyza
cosmos
cotton
cowage
croton
cynara
darnel
daphne
dodder
elaeis
endive
eringo
exogen
fathen
fennel
ferula
fescue
filago
fiorin
frutex
fucoid
fungus
funkia
gallum
garlic
garrya
gervan
gnetum
gromel
guills
hedera
henbit
hervea
hyssop
iberis
indigo
jawari
jujube
juncus
kalmia
kiekie
knawel
kousso

lichen	scilla	bulrush	fumaria	quamash	**8**
locust	secale	burdock	funaria	ragwort	
lolium	sesame	bur-reed	genista	rambler	abutilon
lupine	sesban	calamus	gentian	rampion	acanthus
luzula	seseli	caltrop	gerbera	redroot	adiantum
madder	smilax	calypso	ginseng	rhatany	agrimony
maguey	sorrel	campion	gladwyn	rhubarb	air plant
mallee	spurge	canella	guayule	saffron	amaranth
mallow	spurry	cannach	gunnera	saguaro	amphigen
manioc	squash	caraway	gutwort	saligot	angelica
marram	squill	carduus	hardock	salsify	anthemis
matico	stolon	carline	hawkbit	salsola	asphodel
medick	styrax	cassada	heather	sampire	banewort
milium	sumach	cassado	hemlock	sanicle	barometz
millet	sundew	cassava	henbane	sarcina	bear's ear
mimosa	teasel	cat's-ear	hogweed	sawwort	bearbind
myrica	teazel	catmint	honesty	sea tang	bedstraw
myrtle	thrift	chicory	hop-bind	seaweed	bellwort
nardoo	tutsan	clarkia	hop-bine	sencion	bignonia
nerium	twitch	clotbur	hop-vine	senecio	bindweed
nettle	urtica	columba	humulus	seringa	blueweed
nostoc	viscum	comfrey	ipomaea	solanum	bogberry
nubbin	yamboo	cowbane	jasmine	sonchus	bogwhort
oilnut	yarrow	cowhage	Jew's ear	sorghum	boxthorn
orache		cow-itch	jonquil	sourock	brassica
orchid	**7**	cowslip	juniper	soybean	buckweed
orchis	absinth	cow-weed	karatas	spignel	bullweed
origan	aconite	creeper	kedlack	spiraea	bullwort
orpine	alcanna	crottle	lobelia	sporule	calamint
osmund	alecost	cudbear	lucerne	statice	camomile
oxalis	alfalfa	cudweed	lychnis	syringa	cannabis
paigle	alhenna	cup moss	lycopod	tagetes	capsicum
pampas	alkanet	curcuma	madwort	talipot	carraway
peanut	all-good	cytisus	mahonia	tannier	cassweed
peplis	all-heal	dasheen	melilot	thistle	cat's foot
pepper	althaea	dionaea	milfoil	tobacco	cat's tail
phleum	amanita	dittany	monocot	trefoil	catchfly
potato	aquatic	dogbane	mudwort	truffle	centaury
privet	arabine	dog's rue	munjeet	turpeth	cerealia
protea	arbutus	ear-wort	mustard	uncaria	cetraria
quinoa	awlwort	ehretia	nonsuch	vanilla	charlock
quitch	azarole	elatine	opuntia	verbena	cinchona
radish	barilla	epacris	oregano	vervain	cleavers
raffia	bartram	esparto	osmunda	vetiver	clematis
raggee	begonia	eugenia	panicum	waratah	clubmoss
ramson	bistort	euryale	papyrus	wcorara	clubrush
rattan	bogbean	euterpe	pareira	zalacca	cocculus
redtop	bogmass	felwort	parella	zanonia	cockspur
reseda	bogrush	festuca	parelle	zizania	cockweed
rocket	bracken	ficaria	parsley		conferva
ruscus	bramble	figwort	pinguin		cornflag
sabine	bugloss	fitweed	primula		cornrose
savine	bugwort	foxtail	pumpion		costmary
savory	bulbule	frogbit	pumpkin		cow-wheat

cowberry
cowgrass
crithmum
crow silk
cunjevoi
danewort
death-cap
death-cup
dewberry
diadelph
diandria
dicentra
dog briar
dog grass
dog's bane
dolichos
downweed
dropwort
duckmeat
duckweed
dumb-cane
earth nut
earth-pea
echinops
eelgrass
eggplant
eglatere
eleusine
epiphyte
erigeron
erisimum
feverfew
finochio
fireweed
flaxweed
fleabane
fleawort
flixweed
foalfoot
foxglove
fragaria
fussball
garcinia
gillenia
glory pea
gloxinia
glumales
glumella
glyceria
goutweed
goutwort
gratiola
gromwell
gulfweed

hagtaper
hare's ear
harebell
hartwort
hawkweed
hawthorn
hepatica
hibiscus
hockherb
ice plant
isnardina
knapweed
knotweed
laceleaf
ladyfern
larkspur
lavender
lungwort
lustwort
male fern
mandrake
marjoram
mat grass
matfelon
may bloom
mezereon
milkweed
milkwort
monocarp
moonseed
moonwort
mulewort
mushroom
myosotis
nut grass
oenanthe
oleander
orchanet
oreganum
paspalum
peat moss
phormium
pillwort
pinkroot
plantlet
plantule
plumbago
pokeweed
polygala
pond weed
prunella
puffball
purslane
putchock

red algae
reedrace
rib grass
roccella
rock-rose
rockweed
rosebush
rosemary
rye grass
sainfoin
saltwort
samphire
sargasso
scammony
sea holly
seawrack
seedling
sengreen
septfoil
shamrock
simaruba
skull-cap
smallage
soapwort
stapelia
starwort
sun-plant
sweetsop
tara fern
tarragon
tea plant
tentwort
tickweed
toad-flax
tree-fern
tremella
triticum
tuberose
turk's cap
turmeric
turnsole
valerian
veratrum
veronica
victoria
wait-a-bit
wall-moss
wall-wort
wartwort
water-poa
wild oats
wild rose
wind seed
wistaria

wisteria
with-wine
woodbine
woodroof
woodruff
woodsage
woodwart
wrightia
xanthium
zhigiber

9

abrotanum
aerophyte
alpargata
amaryllis
arbor-vine
arracacha
arrowhead
arrowroot
artemisia
asclepiad
balsamine
basil weed
bean caper
bearberry
beech fern
bent grass
bird's foot
birthwort
bloodroot
bloodwort
blue algae
blue grass
bog myrtle
brooklime
brookmint
brookweed
broomcorn
broomrape
burstwort
butterbur
candytuft
canebrake
caprifole
cardamine
carrageen
catchweed
celandine
cetrarine
chickweed
cineraria
club-grass
coal plant

cock's head
cockscomb
colchicum
colocynth
colt's foot
columbine
coralwort
coriander
corn poppy
corn salad
cotyledon
crabgrass
cramp-bark
crosswort
crowberry
cuckoo bud
culver key
cup lichen
cyclamine
decagynia
decandria
desert rod
didynamia
digitalis
digitaria
dittander
dockcress
doob grass
duck's foot
duck's meat
dulcamara
dyer's weed
earthstar
eglantine
elaeagnus
entophyte
equisetum
euphorbia
euphrasia
evergreen
evolvulus
eyebright
fenugreek
fever root
feverwort
fly agaric
forsythia
galingale
gama grass
gelanthus
germander
glasswort
golden cup
golden rod

goose corn
goosefoot
gramineae
grapewort
grasspoly
greenweed
ground ivy
groundnut
groundsel
hair grass
hellebore
helophyte
hoarhound
holly fern
holy-grass
honeywort
horehound
horsefoot
horsetail
houseleek
hypericum
Indian fig
Irish moss
jessamine
Job's tears
kite's foot
knee holly
knotgrass
ladysmock
lark's heel
laserwort
liquorice
liverwort
lyme grass
mare's tail
marsh fern
meadow rue
milk vetch
mistletoe
monk's-hood
moschatel
mousetail
navelwort
nelumbium
nepenthes
nicotiana
patchouli
pellitory
pennywort
penstemon
pilularia
pimpernel
planticle
poison ivy

polygonum
portulaca
pyracanth
pyrethrum
quillwort
rafflesia
red clover
red pepper
reed-grass
rocambole
rock-plant
rockcress
royal fern
safflower
saintfoin
saxifrage
sea-tangle
smartweed
snakeroot
snakeweed
snowberry
soap plant
socotrine
spearmint
spearwort
speedwell
spikenard
spirogyra
spoonwort
stellaria
stinkweed
stonecrop
sugar cane
sugarbeet
sun spurge
sweet flag
sweet gale
sweet john
sweet rush
taraxacum
thallogen
theobroma
toadstool
toothwort
tormentil
trifolium
twayblade
villarsia
wakerobin
wall cress
waterlath
waterlily
waterweed
waterwort

wax myrtle
whitecrop
widow wail
wincopipe
wolf's claw
wolfsbane
wormgrass
woundwort
xanthosia

10

Adam's apple
Adam-and-Eve
adder grass
agrostemma
alabastrus
alexanders
amaranthus
ampelopsis
angiosperm
arbor vitae
arrow grass
asarabacca
aspidistra
beard grass
beccabunga
belladonna
bitterwort
brome grass
brown algae
butterbush
butterweed
butterwood
butterwort
Canada lily
candelilla
cassumunar
cellulares
cinquefoil
cloudberry
corn rocket
corncockle
cotton rose
cottonweed
couch grass
cow parsley
cow parsnip
crake berry
crotalaria
cuckoopint
dead nettle
devil's club
dog's fennel
dog's poison

dog's tongue
dracontium
elaeococca
elecampane
eriocaulon
eriophoron
escallonia
eupatorium
fimble-hemp
friar's cowl
fritillary
gaultheria
globe daisy
globularia
goat's-beard
golden seal
goldenhair
goldilocks
goose grass
granadilla
grass-wrack
green algae
gymnosperm
heart's-ease
helianthus
hemp nettle
herb robert
herds grass
honey stalk
Indian corn
Indian hemp
Indian reed
Indian shot
Jew's mallow
jimson weed
kidney-wort
king's spear
lemon grass
lycopodium
maidenhair
mandragora
manila hemp
may blossom
mock orange
mock privet
motherwort
muscardine
nasturtium
nightshade
nipplewort
panic grass
passiflora
penny-cress
pennyroyal

pentstemon
peppermint
pepperwort
periwinkle
poker plant
potentilla
race ginger
ranunculus
rest harrow
rhein berry
rhinanthus
rose mallow
salicornia
sand-binder
saprophyte
sarracenia
sea lettuce
setterwort
shave grass
shield fern
silver weed
sneezewort
sow thistle
Spanish nut
speargrass
spiderwort
spleenwort
stavesacre
stitchwort
stonebreak
stork's bill
sweetbriar
sweetbrier
swine bread
swinecress
swinegrass
swordgrass
thalecress
throatwort
tiger's foot
touch-me-not
tragacanth
tropaeolum
tumbleweed
Venus's comb
wall pepper
water plant
way thistle
whitethorn
wild indigo
willow herb
willow weed
witch hazel
wolf's peach

wood sorrel
yellow wort
yellow-root

11

Adam's needle
bear's breech
bell heather
bishop's weed
blackbonnet
bottle gourd
brank ursine
bur marigold
calceolaria
calcyanthus
canary grass
chanterelle
chive garlic
coffee plant
contrayerva
convolvulus
corn parsley
cotton grass
cotton plant
crest marine
cuckoo's meat
dame's violet
dog's cabbage
dog's mercury
dracunculus
dragon's head
dragon's wort
Dutch clover
dyer's rocket
erythronium
everlasting
false acacia
fescue grass
fig marigold
finger grass
fuller's weed
gentianella
giant cactus
giant fennel
gramma grass
green dragon
guelder rose
hart's tongue
holy thistle
honeysuckle
horseradish
humble plant
Iceland moss
Indian berry

Indian cress
indigo plant
ipecacuanha
kidney vetch
lady's-finger
latticeleaf
laurustinus
London pride
marram grass
marsh mallow
meadowsweet
melon cactus
milk thistle
millet grass
moon trefoil
moving plant
myoporaceae
oyster plant
pampas grass
pedicedaris
pelargonium
pepper grass
prickly pear
red-hot poker
ribbon grass
ripple grass
Roman nettle
rubber plant
scurvy grass
sea lavender
sea milkwort
sempervivum
serpentaria
snail clover
snail flower
sparrow wort
spergularia
stagger bush
star thistle
sulphur-wort
swallow wort
swallow-wort
sweet cicely
sweet cistus
sweet potato
thorough wax
tonquin bean
tree creeper
tussac grass
twitch grass
viper's grass
water pepper
water radish
water violet

water-nymph
welwitschia
white clover
white darnel
winter berry
winter bloom
winter cress
wintergreen
wood anemone
xanthoxylum

12

adder's-tongue
adderstoupie
aerial plants
bladderwrack
buffalo grass
Christ's thorn
compass plant
corn marigold
cow's lungwort
deadly carrot
echinocactus
erythroxylon
esparto grass
feather grass
fennel flower
fool's parsley
German millet
globe thistle
hemp-agrimony
hound's tongue
Indian millet
Indian turnip
Jacob's ladder
leopard's bane
mangel wurzel
marsileaceae
melon thistle
palma christi
pickerel weed
pitcher plant
poison sumach
quaking grass
reindeer moss
rhododendron
sarsaparilla
sheep's fescue
skunk cabbage
snail trefoil
Solomon's seal
southern wood
Spanish broom
Spanish grass

sparrow-grass
spear thistle
strangleweed
swine thistle
telentospore
timothy grass
tobacco plant
torch thistle
tussock grass
Venus flytrap
Venus's sumach
vinegar plant
virgin's bower
water hemlock
water milfoil
water parsnip
water pitcher
water soldier
white campion
whitlow grass
whortleberry
wild williams
winter cherry
xanthorrhiza
yellow rattle

13

chrysanthemum
crown imperial
dog's-tail grass
elephant grass
elephant's foot
eschscholtzia
flowering fern
flowering rush
globe amaranth
golden thistle
horse mushroom
Indian tobacco
lady's bedstraw
meadow saffron
noli-me-tangere
raspberry bush
Scotch thistle
spike lavender
stag's-horn moss
summer cypress
sweet marjoram
traveller's joy
Venus's fly trap
vervain mallow
viper's bugloss
wall pellitory
wall pennywort

water calamint
water crowfoot
water hyacinth
wayfaring tree

14

blackberry bush
blue couch grass
carline thistle

distaff thistle
fuller's thistle
giant groundsel
golden lungwort
golden mouse-ear
gooseberry bush
lords and ladies
mountain sorrel
prince's feather

reindeer lichen
sensitive plant
shepherd's pouch
shepherd's purse
shepherd's staff
snake's-head iris
Spanish bayonet
starch hyacinth
treacle mustard

15

golden saxifrage
Italian rye grass
shepherd's needle
Venus's navelwort
Virginia creeper
woody nightshade

Trees, shrubs, etc.

2 AND 3

asa
ash
bay
bel
ben
bo
box
elm
fig
fir
gum
haw
hip
hop
ita
ivy
kin
may
nut
oak
sal
sap
tea
ti
tod
yew

4

acer
akee
aloe
amla
arar
arum
atap
bael
balm
bark
bass

bast
bead
beam
bhel
bito
bixa
bole
bosk
bush
cone
cork
dari
dan
date
deal
dhak
dita
doob
holm
huon
hura
ilex
jaca
kina
lana
leaf
lime
milk
mowa
nipa
ombu
palm
pear
pine
pipe
plum
pole
rata
rimu
roan
root

rose
shea
sloe
sorb
teak
teil
toon
tree
twig
ulex
upas
vine
whin

5

abele
abies
acorn
afara
agave
agila
alder
algum
almug
amber
anise
anona
apple
arbor
areca
Argan
aspen
assai
balsa
Banga
beech
belah
belar
birch
bough
briar

brier
brush
bunya
butea
cacao
caper
carob
cedar
China
clove
copse
coral
cubeb
durio
dwarf
ebony
elder
fagus
fruit
furze
glade
gorse
grove
guava
hazel
henna
holly
hurst
iroko
jambu
judas
karri
kauri
kokra
kunal
larch
lemon
lilac
mahwa
mango
maple

mulga
myall
myrrh
ngaio
nyssa
olive
osier
palas
palay
papaw
peach
pecan
picea
pinon
pipal
plane
plank
quina
roble
roots
rowan
salal
salix
sally
saman
sapan
scrog
shrub
sumac
taxus
thorn
tilia
tingi
trunk
tsuga
tuart
ulmus
walan
yucca
yulan
zamia

6

abroma
acacia
acajou
alerce
almond
antiar
aralla
arbute
arolla
balsam
bamboo
banana
banyan
baobab
bo-tree
bog-oak
bombax
bottle
branch
brazil
buriti
busket
butter
button
carapa
carica
cashew
catkin
caudex
cedrat
cembra
cerris
cerrus
cherry
citron
coffee
cornel
daphne
deodar

241

durian
durion
elaeis
emblic
fustet
fustic
gatten
ginkgo
gomuti
gomuto
illipe
jarool
jarrah
jujube
kalmia
kittul
kumbuk
kunari
laurel
lignum
linden
locust
loquat
macoya
mallee
manuka
mastic
medlar
mimosa
miriti
myrtle
nargil
obeche
orange
papaya
pawpaw
pepper
pinery
platan
poplar
privet
quince
red bud
red fir
red gum
ricker
rubber
sallal
sallow
sapota
sappan
saxaul
she-oak
sissoo

sorrel
souari
spruce
sumach
sylvan
tallow
tamanu
tewart
timber
titoki
touart
tupelo
veneer
vinery
walnut
wampee
wattle
wicken
willow
yampon

7

ailanto
ambatch
amboyna
aniseed
arbutus
ash tree
avocado
banksia
bay tree
bebeeru
blossom
blue gum
boxwood *Drawble*
bubinga
buckeye
bullace
bursera
cabbage
cajaput
camphor
camwood
catalpa
champac
coconut
conifer
coppice
coquito
cork-oak
corylus
cowtree
cypress
daddock

dammara
determa
deutzia
dogwood
dottard
duramen
elk-wood
elm tree
emblica
enterpe
fan palm
fig tree
fir cone
fir tree
genipap
gum tree
hemlock
hickory
hog palm
holm oak
hop tree
jugians
juniper
king gum
lentisk
logwood
lumbang
madroña
madroño
margosa
mastich
mesquit
moriche
moringa
nut palm
nut pine
oak tree
oakling
oil palm
orchard
palmyra
pinetum
pollard
quercus
quillai
red pine
redwood
robinia
saksaul
sandbox
sanders
sapling
sapwood
sequoia

seringa
service
shallon
shittah
shittim
silk oak
snow-gum
sour-sop
spindle
sundari
syringa
tanghin
tea-tree
varnish
wallaba
wax palm
wax tree
wych-elm

8

agalloch
agalwood
alburnum
algaroba
allspice
arbuscle
ash grove
barberry
bass wood
beachnut
beam tree
beef-wood
benjamin
berberis
berberry
bilberry
black gum
box elder
bud-scale
calabash
carnauba
castanea
chestnut
cinchona
coco-palm
coco-tree
coolabah
cork tree
crab-tree
date palm
date plum
date-tree
doom-palm
eucalypt

euonymus
fraxinus
gardenia
giant gum
glory pea
groo-groo
guaiacum
hardbeam
hardwood
hawthorn
hemp palm
holly-oak
hornbeam
ironbark
ironwood
jack tree
jack wood
kingwood
laburnum
lacebark
lavender
lima wood
long jack
magnolia
mahogany
mangrove
manna-ash
mezereon
milk tree
mulberry
musk wood
mustaiba
oiticica
oleander
oleaster
palm tree
palmetto
pandanus
pear tree
piassava
pichurim
pinaster
pine cone
pine tree
pistacia
plantain
pockwood
quillaia
raintree
red cedar
red maple
rosemary
rosewood
royal oak

sago palm
sandarac
sapindus
scrub-oak
searwood
seedling
shadbush
silky oak
softwood
sugar gum
swamp oak
sweet gum
sweet sop
sweet-bay
sycamine
sycamore
tamarack
tamarind
tamarisk
taxodium
teil-tree
toon-wood
tungtree
upas tree
viburnum
white ash
white fir
white gum
white oak
wistaria
witch-elm

9

adansonia
ailanthus
algarroba
aloes wood
alpine fir
Andromeda
angophora
araucaria
areca palm
balsam fir
blackwood
bodhi tree
brown pine
buckthorn
bully tree
butternut
calambour
caliatour
caliature
casuarina
chaparral

China tree
chincapin
coniferae
courbaril
crab apple
crowberry
Cupressus
deciduous
dwarf tree
eaglewood
erythrine
evergreen
forest oak
forsythia
fruit tree
grapevine
greenwood
ground ash
ground oak
hackberry
hydrangea
ivory palm
jacaranda
Judas tree
Juneberry
kokra wood
lance wood
lentiscus
lilac tree
macaw tree
maracauba
mustahiba
paper bark
paulownia
persimmon
pistachio
pitchpine
plane tree
poison oak
pyracanth
quebracho
quickbeam
rose apple
rowan tree
royal palm
sagebrush
sandarach
sapan wood
sapodilla
saskatoon
sassafras
satinwood
Scotch elm
Scotch fir

Scots pine
screw-pine
scrogbush
shade tree
shell-bark
silver fir
sloethorn
smoke tree
snake-wood
snowberry
soapberry
sour-gourd
spicewood
star anise
stonepine
suradanni
sweetwood
terebinth
thorn tree
tigerwood
toothache
touch-wood
tulip tree
wax myrtle
white pine
whitebeam
whitewood
woodlayer
wych-hazel
yacca wood
zebrawood

10

African oak
agollochum
almond tree
artocarpus
balaustine
blackthorn
blue spruce
bottle tree
brazilwood
breadfruit
bunji-bunji
bunya-bunya
burra-murra
butter tree
button bush
button tree
buttonwood
chinquapin
coastal-tea
coccomilia
coniferous

cotton tree
cottonwood
Douglas fir
dragon tree
durmast oak
eucalyptus
fiddle wood
flindersia
flooded gum
garlic-pear
goat's thorn
gomuti palm
greenheart
ground pine
hackmatack
holly berry
Indian date
japati palm
kunai grass
laurestine
letter wood
lilly-pilly
locust tree
manchineel
mangosteen
orange wood
orange-ball
palisander
paper birch
pine needle
prickly ash
quercitron
rain forest
redsanders
rose acacia
sand-cherry
sand-myrtle
sandalwood
sappanwood
Scotch pine
silverbell
sneeze-wood
Spanish fir
strawberry
sugar-maple
swamp maple
tall wattle
tallow tree
thyine wood
tree of life
weeping ash
white cedar
whitethorn
wild cherry

witch-hazel
woolly butt
yellow-wood

11

African teak
Algerian fir
bald cypress
bean trefoil
black walnut
black wattle
black willow
bladder tree
blue-gum tree
bottle-brush
cabbage palm
cabbage tree
camel's thorn
camphor tree
cedar wattle
chrysobalan
coconut palm
cootamundra
copper beech
cotoneaster
cypress pine
elaeocarpus
eriodendron
glory flower
golden chain
golden mohur
hoary poplar
honey locust
Japan laurel
juniper tree
laurustinus
leper-wattle
lignum vitae
mountain ash
pandanaceae
phoenix-palm
pomegranate
pussy willow
quicken tree
red mahogany
red-iron bark
sandbox tree
sea-purslane
service tree
sideroxylon
silver birch
slippery elm
spindle tree
stringybark

243

sweet willow
varnish tree
white poplar
white spruce
white willow
xanthozylum
zygophyllum

12

almond willow
balsam poplar
balsam spruce
benjamin-tree
betel-nut palm
calabash tree
caryophyllus
chesnut tree

Christ's-thorn
crow's-foot elm
cucumber tree
custard apple
flowering ash
golden wattle
monkey-puzzle
Norway spruce
rhododendron
sea buckthorn
serviceberry
silver-wattle
Spanish broom
Spanish cedar
spurge laurel
tree of heaven
umbrella tree

virgin's-bower
weeping birch
welllngtonia
white cypress
winter cherry
xylobalsamum

13 AND OVER

bird's-eye maple (13)
campeachy wood (13)
Cedar of Lebanon (14)
Christmas tree (13)
cornus florida (13)
dog-wood wattle (13)
galactodendron (14)
horse-chestnut (13)
Japanese cedar (13)

Lombardy poplar (14)
maidenhair tree (14)
partridge wood (13)
red sandalwood (13)
Spanish chestnut (15)
strawberry shrub (15)
sweet chestnut (13)
sunshine wattle (14)
toothache tree (13)
toxicodendron (13)
trembling poplar (15)
turpentine tree (14)
weeping willow (13)
white sandalwood (15)

Vegetables

3 AND 4

bean
beet
cole
corn
faba
kale
leek
lima
neep
oca
okra
pea
sage
slaw
spud
tuber
urd
yam

5

caper
chard
chick
chive
cibol
cress
cubeb
fitch
maize
navew
onion

orach
pease
pulse
savoy
swede

6

borage
carrot
celery
chilli
cowpea
daucus
endive
fennel
garlic
girkin
greens
legume
lentil
marrow
murphy
nettle
orache
porret
potato
pratie
radish
rocket
runner
savory
sprout
squash

tomato
turnip

7

batatas
bay leaf
blewits
cabbage
cardoon
chervil
chicory
collard
frijole
gherkin
haricot
hasting
hotspur
lactuca
lettuce
mustard
parsley
parsnip
pea bean
peppers
pimento
pumpkin
salsify
seakale
shallot
skirret
soybean
spinach

sprouts
zanonia

8

allspice
beetrave
beetroot
borecole
brassica
broccoli
capsicum
celeriac
chickpea
coleslaw
colewort
cucumber
eggplant
eschalot
kohlrabi
lima bean
mirepoix
mushroom
plantain
rutabaga
scallion
smallage
soyabean
split pea
tickbean
zucchini

9

aduki bean

artichoke
asparagus
aubergine
broad bean
calabrese
courgette
curly kale
dandelion
dried peas
green peas
horsebean
mangetout
marrowfat
new potato
radicchio
red pepper
split peas
sweetcorn
turban-top
turnip top

10

adsuki bean
alexanders
beet radish
butter bean
cos lettuce
cow parsnip
French bean
green beans
kidney bean
King Edward
petits pois

red cabbage
runner bean
salad onion
sauerkraut
scorzonera
stringbean
turnip tops
watercress
Welsh onion

11

cauliflower
French beans

green pepper
haricot bean
horseradish
ratatouille
scarlet bean
spinach beet
sweet potato
water radish

12

bamboo shoots
chat potatoes
chilli pepper

corn on the cob
giant shallot
lamb's lettuce
savoy cabbage
Spanish onion
spring greens
spring onions
white cabbage

13 AND OVER

broccoli sprouts (15)
Brussels sprouts (15)
Chinese cabbage (14)

globe artichoke (14)
green vegetables (15)
horse cucumber (13)
ladies' fingers (13)
marrowfat peas (13)
purple broccoli (14)
scarlet runner (13)
spring cabbage (13)
tankard turnip (13)
vegetable marrow (15)
water chestnut (13)

PEOPLES AND LANGUAGES
African peoples

3

Edo
Ewe
Fon
Ibo
Ijo
Iru
Luo
Rif
San
Suk
Tiv
Vai
Yao

4

Afar
Agni
Alut
Anyi
Baga
Bena
Bete
Bini
Bisa
Bubi
Efik
Fang
Fula
Guro
Haya
Hehe
Hirna
Hutu
Igbo

Ijaw
Khoi
Lala
Lozi
Mali
Meru
Nama
Nupe
Nyao
Oran
Pedi
Riff
Teso
Toro
Yako
Ziba
Zulu

5

Anuak
Bamum
Bantu
Bassa
Baule
Bemba
Chaga
Chewa
Chopi
Dinka
Dogon
Dyula
Galla
Ganda
Gissi
Grebo
Hausa

Iraqu
Kamba
Luhya
Lulua
Lunda
Lwena
Makua
Mande
Masai
Mende
Mongo
Mossi
Nandi
Ngoni
Nguni
Nguru
Oromo
Pygmy
Rundi
Shona
Sotho
Swazi
Tonga
Tussi
Tutsi
Xhosa

6

Acholi
Angoni
Anywak
Awemba
Bakota
Balega
Bamoun
Bapedi

Basuto
Bateke
Batusi
Batoro
Bayaka
Berber
Chagga
Fulani
Griqua
Herero
Ibibio
Kikuyu
Kpwesi
Lumbwa
Luvale
Malozi
Maravi
Murozi
Ngqika
Ngwato
Rolong
Sambaa
Senufo
Somali
Sukuma
Thonga
Tlokwa
Tsonga
Tswana
Tuareg
Veddah
Wahaya
Warega
Yoruba

7

Ashanti
Baganda
Bakweii
Bambara
Bangala
Bapende
Barotse
Barundi
Basonge
Batonka
Berbers
Bunduka
Bushmen
Dagamba
Dagomba
Gcaleka
Haranga
Kalanga
Khoisan
Kipsigi
Makonde
Malinde
Manyika
Mashona
Namaqua
Ndebele
Nilotes
Samburu
Shilluk
Songhai
Soninke
Turkana
Watutsi

8
Bergdama
Bushongo
Kipsikis
Mamprusi

Mandingo
Matabele
Nyakyusa
Nyamwezi

Tallensi
Vhavenda

9 AND OVER
Bangarwanda (11)
Bathlaping (10)

Hottentots (10)
Karamojong (10)
Karimojong (10)
Kgalagedi (9)

Languages, nationalities and races

2 AND 3				5	
Dan	Alur	Kelt	Puyi	Bassa	Hindi
Edo	Ambo	Khmu'	Remi	Batak	Idoma
Ewe	Anyi	Kisi	Riff	Bemba	Igala
Fon	Arab	Ko'ho	Samo	Benga	Iloko
Fur	Avar	Komi	Scot	Berta	Indic
Ga	Bali	Kono	Sena	Bhili	Inuit
Gur	Bari	Kota	Serb	Bikol	Ionic
Ha	Basa	Koya	Sgaw	Bulom	Iraqi
Hun	Beja	Krio	Shan	Burra	Iraqw
Ibo	Bena	Kurd	Sikh	Bussi	Irish
Ido	Bete	Laki	Slav	Carib	Jarai
Ijo	Bini	Lala	Sobo	Chaga	Kabre
Ila	Bisa	Lapp	Soga	Chopi	Kadai
Jew	Bobo	Lari	Sora	Croat	Kafir
Kam	Bodo	Lett	Susu	Cuban	Kamba
Kru	Boer	Lisi	Tara	Cymry	Karen
Kua	Buja	Lobi	Teke	Czech	Kazak
Kui	Bulu	Loma	Teso	Dagur	Khasi
Kwa	Buol	Lore	Thai	Dayak	Khmer
Lao	Caga	Lozi	Toba	Dinka	Kisii
Li	Celt	Luba	Toda	Diola	Konde
Luo	Chad	Lubu	Toro	Dogon	Kongo
Mam	Cham	Luwu'	Tswa	Doric	Konzo
Mon	Ciga	Madi	Tulu	Duala	Krahn
Pai	Copt	Mame	Tupí	Dutch	Kumyk
Pho	Dane	Mano	Turk	Dyold	Kurku
San	Efik	Manx	Tuva	Dyula	Kusal
Shi	Embo	Margi	Urdu	Fante	Kweni
Sui	Enga	Mende	Wend	Farsi	Lahya
Tem	Erse	Mero	Zend	Frank	Lamba
Tho	Eton	Miao	Ziba	Galla	Lango
Tiv	Fang	Moor	Zulu	Ganda	Latin
Twi	Finn	Moxu	**5**	Gbari	Lenda
Vai	Garo	Naga		Gbaya	Lendu
Wa	Gaul	Naha	Akoli	Gipsy	Lenge
Wu	Gaya	Nuba	Aleut	Gondi	Limba
Yao	Ge'ez	Nuer	Aryan	Greek	Lomwe
Zan	Gogo	Nung	Asian	Gurma	Makua
4	Gola	Nupe	Attic	Gusii	Malay
	Gond	Pali	Azeri	Gwere	Malvi
Afar	Grig	Palu	Banda	Gypsy	Mande
Akan	Igbo	Pedi	Bantu	Hadya	Maori
	Ijaw	Pict	Bare'e	Hadza	Masai
	Kafa	Pole	Bargu	Hausa	Mongo

Mossi	Yupik	Hebrew	Pashto	**7**	Illongo
Mu'òng	Zande	Herero	patois		Ilocano
Munda		Ibanag	Polish	Acadian	Iranian
Mwera	**6**	Ibibio	Pushto	African	Israeli
Nandi	Abkhas	Indian	Pushtu	Amharic	Italian
Naron	Acholi	Inupik	Quiché	Angolan	Kambata
Negro	Aeolic	Ionian	Rajput	Arabian	Kannada
Ngaju	Afghan	Italic	Romaic	Aramaic	Karanga
Ngala	Altaic	Jewess	Romany	Aramean	Khoisan
Ngoni	Arabic	Jewish	Ruguru	Armoric	Khorcin
Nguni	Arawak	Judaic	Rwanda	Asiatic	Kikamba
Nkore	Argive	Kabyle	Ryukyu	Avestan	Kirghiz
Norse	Aymará	Kaffir	Saamia	Bagirmi	Konkani
Nyole	Baltic	Kalmuk	Sabine	Balanta	Kumauni
Nyong	Bangba	Kalmyk	Samoan	Balochi	Kurdish
Nyoro	Baoule	Kanuri	Senari	Baluchi	Kuwaiti
Oirat	Basque	Kazakh	Sérère	Bambara	Lampung
Ordos	Berber	Kekchí	Sidamo	Banggai	Laotian
Oriya	Bihari	Khalka	Sindhi	Bashkir	Laotien
Oromo	Bokmal	Kikuyu	Slavic	Bedouin	Lappish
Oscan	Bolewa	Kirgiz	Slovak	Belgian	Latvian
Otomi	Brahui	Korean	Somali	Bengali	Lingala
Punic	Breton	Kosali	Soviet	Bisayan	Loinang
Roman	Briton	Kpelle	Sranan	Bislama	Lombard
Ronga	Bulgar	Kpessi	Sukuma	British	Losengo
Rundi	Bungku	Kurukh	Syriac	Burmese	Lugbara
Sango	Buryat	Lahnda	Syrian	Bushmen	Maduran
Santa	Celtic	Libyan	Talysh	Butung	Makonde
Saudi	Chamba	Lobiri	Tangsa	Catalan	Malinka
Saxon	Chimbu	Luvale	Telegu	Chechen	Malinke
Scots	Chokwe	Maasai	Teuton	Chilean	Maltese
Serer	Ciokwe	Magahi	Theban	Chinese	Mandyak
Shilh	Coptic	Manchu	Thonga	Chuvash	Manxman
Shluh	Creole	Masaba	Tobote	Cornish	Marathi
Shona	Cymric	Mbundu	Tongan	Cypriot	Masalit
Sinic	Dagari	Mixtec	Trojan	Dagbani	Meithei
Songe	Daghur	Mongol	Tsonga	Dagomba	Mexican
Sotho	Danish	Mumuye	Tswana	Dalicad	Moorish
Swazi	Dargwa	Navaho	Tuareg	dialect	Mordvin
Swede	Derasa	Ndandi	Tungus	English	Morisco
Swiss	Dorian	Ndonga	Turkic	Finnish	Mozareb
Tajik	Eskimo	Neners	Tuscan	Fleming	Mulatto
Tamil	Fijian	Nepali	Udmurt	Flemish	Mundari
Tatar	Frafra	Newari	Uighur	Frisian	Nahuatl
Temne	French	Ngbaka	Viking	Gambian	Nauruan
Tigré	Fulani	Ngombe	Votyak	Gaulish	Ndebele
Tikar	Gaelic	Norman	Walamo	Guarani	Negrito
Tonga	Gagauz	Nsenga	Yankee	Haitian	Ngbandi
Uigur	Gallic	Nubian	Yemeni	Hamitic	Nilamba
Uzbek	Gambai	Nyanja	Yoruba	Hebraic	Nilotic
Venda	Gascon	Ostman	Zenaga	Hessian	Nynorsk
Welsh	German	Papuan	Zigula	Hittite	Occitan
Wolof	Gothic	Parian		Iberian	Ossetic
Xhosa	Gurage	Parsee		Igbirra	Ottoman

Pahiavi
Palaung
Panjabi
Persian
Prakrit
Punjabi
Quechua
Quekchí
Redjang
Romance
Romansh
Russian
Rwandan
Samiote
Samoyed
Sandawe
Santali
Sebuano
Semitic
Serbian
Shambaa
Shilluk
Siamese
Slovene
Songhai
Soninke
Sorbian
Spanish
Spartan
Swahili
Swedish
Tadzhik
Tagalog
Tibetan
Tigrina
Tinombo
Totonac
Tripuri
Turkana
Turkish
Turkmen
Ugandan
Umbrian
Umbundu
Venetic
Walloon
Yiddish
Zairese
Zambian
Zapotec

8

Abderite
Achinese

Akkadian
Albanian
Algerian
American
Andorran
Antiguan
Aramaean
Armenian
Assamese
Assyrian
Austrian
Balantak
Balinese
Bamileke
Bavarian
Bermudan
Bhojpuri
Biginese
Bohemian
Bolivian
Cambrian
Canadian
Chaldaic
Chaldean
Chamorro
Cheremis
Cherokee
Chingpaw
Corsican
Cushitic
Cyrenaic
Delphian
Dutchman
Dzongkha
Egyptian
Estonian
Ethiopic
Etruscan
Eurasian
Filipino
Frankish
Friulian
Gallican
Garhwali
Georgian
Germanic
Ghanaian
Gujarati
Guyanese
Hawaiian
Hellenic
Helvetic
Honduran
Illyrian

Irishman
Japanese
Javanese
Kanarese
Karachay
Karelian
Kashmiri
Kasimbar
Kerintji
Kimbundu
Kingwana
Konkomba
Kuki-Chin
Kukuruku
Kwanyama
Lebanese
Lezghian
Liberian
Madurese
Maithili
Makassar
Malagasy
Malawian
Mandarin
Mandingo
Mandinka
Mangbetu
Memphian
Moroccan
Moru-Madi
Negrillo
Nepalese
Nigerian
Nyamwesi
Nyankole
octoroon
Old Norse
Old Saxon
Parthian
Pelasgic
Peruvian
Phrygian
Prussian
Romanian
Romansch
Rumanian
Sanskrit
Scotsman
Scottish
Sicilian
Slavonic
Spaniard
Sudanese
Sumerian

Tamashek
Taungthu
Teutonic
Tigrinya
Tunisian
Turanian
Turkomen
Tuvinian
Vandalic
Visigoth
Welshman

9

Abkhazian
Afrikaans
Afrikaner
Afro-Asian
Anatolian
Armorican
Barbadian
Bengalese
Brazilian
Bulgarian
Byzantian
Byzantine
Cambodian
Cantonese
Caucasian
Ceylonese
Cimmerian
Colombian
Congolese
Dravidian
Esperanto
Ethiopian
Frenchman
Gorontalo
Hanseatic
Hibernian
Hottentot
Hungarian
Icelander
Icelandic
Israelite
Jordanian
Kabardian
Kannarese
Khandeshi
Low German
Malayalam
Malaysian
Maldivian
Mauritian
Mongolian

Norwegian
Ostrogoth
Pakistani
Provençal
Red Indian
Rhodesian
Roumanian
Samaritan
Sardinian
Sinhalese
Sri Lankan
Sundanese
Taiwanese
Tanzanian
Tocharian
Ukrainian
Uruguayan

10

Abyssinian
Algonquian
Amerindian
Anglo-Saxon
Araucanian
Australian
autochthon
Babylonian
Cakchiquel
Circassian
Costa Rican
Ecuadorian
Englishman
Finno-Ugric
Florentine
Guatemalan
High German
Hindustani
Indonesian
Karakalpak
Karamojong
Lithuanian
Macedonian
Melanesian
Monegasque
Neapolitan
Nicaraguan
Nicobarese
Panamanian
Pangasinan
Paraguayan
Patagonian
Philippine
Philistine
Phoenician

Polynesian
Pomeranian
Portuguese
Rajasthani
Scots Irish
Senegalese
Serbo-Croat
Singhalese
Venezuelan
vernacular
Vietnamese

11

Argentinian
Azerbaijani
Bangladeshi
Belorussian
Greenlander
Indo-Hittite
Indo-Iranian
Irish Gaelic
Mauretanian

Minangkabau
Palestinian
Scots Gaelic
Sino-Tibetan
Trinidadian

12

Afro-American
basic English
Byelorussian
Chattis-garhi

Indo-European
King's English
Luxemburgish
Moru-Mangbetu
mother tongue
New Zealander
Plattdeutsch
Scandinavian
Tibeto-Burman

13

Irish American
pidgin English
Queen's English
Rhaeto-Romanic
Serbo-Croatian

Native American peoples

3 AND 4

Cree
Crow
Fox
Hopi
Hupa
Inca
Iowa
Maya
Mold
Pima
Sac
Sauk
Ute
Yuma
Zuñi

5

Aztec
Blood
Caddo
Campa
Carib
Creek
Haida
Huron
Kansa
Kiowa
Konza
Lipan
Miami
Moqui

Nahua
Omaha
Osage
Piman
Sioux
Teton
Wappo
Yaqui
Yuchi
Yunca

6

Abnaki
Apache
Aymara
Aztecs
Biloxi
Caribs
Cayuga
Cocopa
Dakota
Dogrib
Kichai
Mandan
Micmac
Mixtec
Mohave
Mohawk
Navaho
Navajo
Nootka
Ojibwa
Oneida

Ostiak
Ottawa
Paiute
Pawnee
Pequot
Pericu
Piegan
Pueblo
Quakaw
Salish
Santee
Sarcee
Seneca
Toltec
Warrau

7

Amerind
Arapaho
Arikara
Catawba
Chilcal
Chinook
Choctaw
Hidatsa
Mapuche
Mohegan
Mohican
Nahuatl
Naskapi
Natchez
Ojibway
Orejone

Quechua
Serrano
Shawnee
Stonies
Tlingit
Tlinkit
Tonkawa
Wichita
Wyandot
Yucatec

8

Aguaruna
Algonkin
Cherokee
Cheyenne
Chippewa
Comanche
Delaware
Flathead
Illinois
Iroquois
Kickapoo
Kootenay
Kwakiutl
Menomini
Muskogee
Nez Percé
Onondaga
Powhatan
Seminole
Shoshone
Shushwap

9

Algonquin
Apalachee
Ashochimi
Blackfoot
Chickasaw
Karankawa
Menominee
Muskogean
Penobscot
Tuscarora
Wappinger
Winnebago

10

Amerindian
Araucanian
Assiniboin
Athabascan
Bella Coola
Leni-Lenapé
Minnetaree
Montagnais
Shoshonean

11 AND OVER

Narragansett (12)
Passamaquoddy
　(13)
Root-diggers (11)
Susquehanna (11)

RELIGION AND MYTHOLOGY
Biblical characters

3

Asa
Eve
God
Ham
Job
Lot

4

Abel
Adam
Agag
Ahab
Amos
Baal
Boaz
Cain
Esau
Ezra
Jael
Jehu
Joab
Joel
John
Jude
Leah
Levi
Luke
Magi (The)
Mark
Mary
Moab
Noah
Paul
Ruth
Saul
Shem

5

Aaron
Annas
Caleb

David
Demas
Devil (The)
Elihu
Enoch
Herod
Hiram
Hosea
Isaac
Jacob
James
Jesse
Jesus
Joash
Jonah
Judah
Judas
Laban
Linus
Micah
Moses
Nahum
Naomi
Peter
Satan
Sihon
Silas
Simon
Titus
Uriah
Uriel
Zadok

6

Abijah
Andrew
Balaam
Christ
Daniel
Darius
Dorcas
Elijah
Elisha

Esther
Festus
Gehazi
Gideon
Haggai
Isaiah
Jahweh
Jairus
Jethro
Joseph
Joshua
Judith
Kohath
Martha
Miriam
Naaman
Naboth
Nathan
Philip
Pilate
Rachel
Reuben
Salome
Samson
Samuel
Simeon
Sisera
Thomas
Uzziah
Yahweh

7

Abraham
Absalom
Ananias
Azariah
Clement
Delilah
Eleazar
Ephraim
Ezekiel
Gabriel
Goliath

Ishmael
Japheth
Jehovah
Jezebel
Joiakim
Lazarus
Lucifer
Malachi
Matthew
Meshach
Michael
Obadiah
Pharaoh
Raphael
Rebekah
Shallum
Solomon
Stephen
Thadeus
Timothy
Zebulun

8

Abednego
Barnabas
Barrabas
Benjamin
Caiaphas
Gamaliel
Habakkuk
Hezekiah
Issachar
Jeremiah
Jeroboam
Jonathan
Matthias
Mordecai
Nehemiah
Philemon
Rehoboam
Sapphira
Shadrach

Thaddeus
Zedekiah

9

Abimelech
Ahasuerus
Bathsheba
Jehoiakim
Maccabees
Nathanael
Nicodemus
Thaddaeus
Zacchaeus
Zachariah
Zacharias
Zechariah
Zephaniah

10

Bartimaeus
Belshazzar
Holofernes
Methuselah
Theophilus

11

Bartholomew
Jehoshaphat
Melchizedek
Sennacherib

13 AND 14

Herod the Great
   (13)
John the
   Baptist (14)
Judas Iscariot (13)
Mary Magdalene
   (13)
Nebuchadnezzar
   (14)
Pontius Pilate (13)

Mythology

2 AND 3	Aea	Amt	Aon	Ate	Bes
	Ahi	Ana	As	Aya	Bor
Aah	Ali	Anu	Ask	Bel	Con

Cos
Dis
Ea
elf
Ens
Eos
Eru
fay
Fum
Ge
Geb
god
Gog
Heh
Hel
hob
Höd
Ida
imp
Io
Ira
Kay
Lar
Ler
Lif
Lot
Lug
Mab
Min
mo
Mot
Mut
Neo
Nix
Nox
Nun
Nut
On
Ops
Orc
Pan
Pax
Ra
Ran
Roc
Roe
Seb
Set
Shu
Sif
Sol
Sri
Sua
Tiw

Tum
Tyr
Ull
Uma
Urd
Urt
Van
Ve
Ziu

4

Abae
Abas
Abia
Abii
Acis
Adad
Agni
Ajax
Amam
Amen
Amor
Amsi
Amsu
Amun
Anit
Ankh
Annu
Anpu
Apia
Apis
Area
Ares
Argo
Asia
Askr
Aten
Atys
Auge
Baal
Bakh
Bali
Bast
Beda
Beli
Bias
Bilé
Bran
Buri
Buto
Ceto
Ceyx
Chac
Chin

Clio
Core
Dana
Danu
Deva
Devi
Dice
Dido
Dike
Dino
Donu
Duse
Dwyn
Echo
Eden
Elli
Enna
Enyo
Eros
Esus
Fama
Fate
Faun
Frey
Fury
Gaea
Gerd
gods
Gwyn
Gyes
Hapi
Hebe
hell
Heno
Hera
hero
Hest
Idas
Idun
Iila
Ikto
Ilus
Inar
Iole
Iris
Irus
Isis
Issa
Itys
Iynx
jinn
Jove
Juno
Kali

Kama
Kami
Lear
Leda
Leto
Llyr
Lofn
Loki
Ludd
Maat
Maia
Mana
Mara
Mark
Mars
Math
Medb
Moly
Mont
Mors
muse
myth
Nabu
Naga
Nebu
Nick
Nike
Nila
Nubu
Nudd
Odin
Ogma
ogre
Pasi
Peri
Pero
pixy
Ptah
Puck
Rahu
Raji
Rama
Rhea
Roma
saga
Sati
Selk
Shai
Shri
Sita
Siva
Soma
Spes
Styx

Surt
Susa
tabu
Tadg
Tara
Thia
Thor
Tiki
Tros
Troy
Tupa
Tyro
Upis
Vali
Vata
Vayu
Vili
Wasi
Xulu
Yama
Yeti
Yggr
Ymir
Yoga
Yuga
yule
Zemi
Zeus
Zume

5

Abila
Acron
Actor
Aditi
Aedon
Aegir
Aegis
Aegle
Aello
Aenea
Aesir
Aeson
Aesop
Aetna
Agave
Ahura
Alope
Amata
Ament
Ammon
Amset
Anava
angel

Anher
Anhur
Anius
Antea
Anxor
Anxur
Apepi
Arawn
Arcas
Arete
Arges
Argos
Argus
Ariel
Arimi
Arion
Armes
Artio
Ashur
Asius
Atlas
Atman
Attis
Aulis
Bacis
Barce
Belus
Bennu
Beroe
Bitol
Biton
Boann
Bogie
Borvo
Bragi
Butis
Byrsa
Cacus
Cales
Canis
Capra
Capys
Caria
Carna
Carpo
Ceres
Chaos
Cilix
Circe
Coeus
Creon
Crete
Crius
Cupid

Cyane	Galli	Jotun	Nuada	Thoas	Africa
Dagda	Garme	Kaboi	nymph	Thoth	Agenor
Dagon	Gauri	Kabul	Ogina	Thrym	Aglaia
Damon	genie	Khnum	Orcus	Thule	Agrius
Danaë	Gerda	Khons	Oread	Thyia	Aithea
Dares	Getae	Kurma	Orion	Thyus	Alecto
deity	ghost	Ladon	Paean	Titan	Aletes
Delos	ghoul	Laius	Pales	Tohil	Aleuas
demon	giant	Lamia	Panes	Tonan	Aloeus
Deuce	Gibil	Lamus	Paris	totem	Amazon
Deuse	gnome	lares	Pavan	Troad	Amen-Ra
devas	golem	Lethe	Perse	Troll	Amon-Ra
devil	Gorge	Liber	Phaon	Tyche	Ampyse
Diana	Grail	Linus	Phyto	Uazit	Amrita
Dione	Gwyar	Lludd	Picus	Uller	Amycus
Dirce	Gyges	Lotis	pigmy	Urien	Amydon
djinn	Gymir	Lugus	pisky	Ushas	Anapus
Dolon	Hadad	Lycus	Pitys	Uther	Andros
Donar	Hades	Macar	pixie	Vanir	Angont
Doris	Harpy	Macha	Pluto	Venti	Antium
Dorus	Heket	Maera	Poeas	Venus	Anubis
dryad	Helen	Magog	Preta	Vesta	Anukit
Durga	Helle	Manes	Priam	Vidar	Aphaca
dwarf	Herse	Maron	Pwyll	Wodan	Apollo
Dyaus	Homer	Mazda	Remus	Woden	Aquila
Dylan	Honor	Medea	Rimac	Wotan	Araxes
Dymas	Horae	Medon	Rudra	Xquiq	Arctos
Edoni	Horta	Melia	Sakra	Yasna	Arjuna
Egypt	Horus	Metis	Sakti	Zarnna	Arthur
elfin	houri	Midas	Salus	Zelia	Asgard
elves	Hydra	Mimas	Santa	Zetes	Asopus
Embla	Hylas	Mimir	Satan		Athena
Enlil	Hymen	Minos	satyr	**6**	Athene
Epeus	Hymir	Mitra	Sebek	Abaris	Athens
Epona	Iamus	Moira	Seker	Abdera	Atreus
Erato	Iapyx	Molus	Sesha	Abeona	Augeas
Estas	Iason	Momus	Shiva	Abydos	Aurora
Etana	Iasus	Monan	Sibyl	Acamus	Avalon
Eurus	Ichor	Mothi	Sinis	Achaei	avatar
Evius	Idmon	Mullo	Sinon	Achaia	Baalim
faery	Idyia	Muses	Siren	Actaea	Bacabs
fairy	Ilama	naiad	Skuld	Admeta	Balder
Fates	Iliad	Nanda	Sulis	Adonai	Baldur
Fauna	Ilium	Nandi	Supay	Adonis	Balius
Fides	Indra	Neheh	Surya	Aeacus	Battus
fiend	Ionia	Nemon	sylph	Aeetes	Baucis
Flora	Iphis	Nerio	Syren	Aegeus	Befana
Freya	Irene	Niobe	Ta-urt	Aegina	Bendis
Freyr	Istar	Nisus	taboo	Aegypt	Benshi
Frigg	Iulus	Nixie	Tages	Aeneas	Bestla
Frija	Ixion	Njord	Talos	Aeneid	Bitias
Fulla	Janus	Norna	Tanen	Aeolus	Boanna
Gades	Jason	norns	tarot	Aerope	Boreas
Galar	Jorth	Notus	Theia	Aethra	Brahma

Brigit
Buddha
Byblis
Byblus
Cabiri
Cadmus
Calais
Canens
Cardea
Caryae
Castor
Caurus
Celeus
Charis
Charon
cherub
Chione
Chiron
Chryse
Clotho
Clytie
Codrus
Comana
Consus
Cratos
Creios
Creusa
Crissa
Crocus
Cronos
Cybele
Cycnus
Cyrene
daemon
Damona
Danaus
Daphne
Daulis
Daunus
Dea Dia
Delius
Delphi
Dictys
Dipsas
Dirona
Dodona
dragon
Dryads
Dryope
Dumuzi
Durinn
dybbuk
Echion
Egeria

Egesta
Eirene
Elaine
Elatus
Elymus
Empusa
Eostre
Eponae
Erebus
Erinys
Euneus
Europa
Evadne
Evenus
faerie
Fafnir
Faunus
Febris
Fenrir
Fenris
fetish
Fidius
Fimila
Fjalar
Foliot
Fornax
Freyja
Frigga
Furies
Furnia
Galeus
Ganesa
Garuda
Gawain
Gemini
genius
Geryon
Ghanna
Glance
goblin
Gobniu
Gorgon
Graces
Graeae
Haemon
Haemus
Hafgan
Hamhit
Haokah
Hathor
heaven
Hebrus
Hecale
Hecate

Hector
Hecuba
Helice
Helios
Hellen
Hermes
Hesiod
Hestia
Heyoka
Hoenir
Hroptr
Huginn
Hyades
Hygeia
Hyllus
Hypnos
Ianthe
Iarbas
Iasion
Iasius
Icarus
Ilaira
Iliona
Inferi
Iolaus
Iolcus
Iphias
Iseult
Ishtar
Ismene
Isolde
Italus
Ithaca
Ithunn
Itonia
Khensu
Khepri
Kobold
Kraken
Kronos
Kubera
Kvasir
Larvae
Latona
Lilith
Locris
Lucina
Lycaon
Lyceus
Maenad
Mamers
Mammon
Manasa
Marduk

Marica
Matsya
Medusa
Megara
Memnon
Mentor
Merlin
merman
Merope
Merops
Mestra
Mictla
Milcom
Miming
Mintha
Minyas
Mithra
Moccos
Modred
Moerae
Moirae
Moloch
Mopsus
Munnin
Mygdon
Myrrha
mythic
naiads
Narada
Natose
nectar
Neleus
Nereid
Nereus
Nergal
Nessus
Nestor
Ninlil
Nireus
Niskai
Nomius
Nornas
nymphs
Oberon
Oeneus
Oenone
Oeonus
Ogmios
ogress
Ogyges
Ogygia
Oileus
Olenus
ondine

Ophion
oracle
Ormuzd
Orphic
Orthia
Orthus
Osiris
Ossian
Palici
Pallas
Pallos
Panope
Paphus
Parcae
Peleus
Pelias
Pelion
Pelops
Peneus
Perdix
Peryda
Phenix
Pheres
Phocis
Phoebe
Pholus
Phylas
Pirene
Pistor
Plutus
Polias
Pollux
Pomona
Pontus
Pothos
Prithi
Prithu
Pronax
Psyche
Puchan
Pulaha
Pushan
Pyrrha
Pythia
Python
Ravana
Renpet
Rhenea
Rhesus
Rhodes
Rhodos
Rumina
Safekh
Samana

Sancus
Sappho
Saturn
Satyrs
Sciron
Scylla
Scyros
sea god
Selene
Selket
Semele
Semnai
Seshat
Sestus
Sethon
Sibyls
Sigeum
Simois
Sirens
Sirius
Sirona
Skanda
sky god
Somnus
Sothis
Sphinx
spirit
sprite
Stheno
sun god
Syrinx
Talaus
Tammuz
Tarvos
Tefnut
Tellus
Tereus
Tethys
Teucer
Thalia
Thallo
Theano
Themis
Thetis
Thisbe
Thunor
Thyone
Tiamat
Titans
Tlaloc
Tmolus
Triton
Tydeus
Typhon

Ulixes	Amphion	Brauron	Elysian	Hurakan	Minerva
Umbria	Ampycus	Briseis	Elysium	Hydriad	Mithras
undine	Amymone	Bromius	Epaphus	Hygieia	Mjolnir
Upuaut	Amyntor	Brontes	Epigoni	Hylaeus	Mordred
Urania	Anaburn	brownie	Erginus	Iacchus	Morrigu
Uranus	Anagnia	Busiris	Erigone	Ialemus	Musaeus
Utgard	Anaphae	Cabeiri	erl-king	Iapetus	Myrddin
Utopia	Anaurus	Caeneus	Eumaeus	Icarius	Nauplia
Vacuna	Ancaeus	Calchas	Eumelus	Idalium	Nemesis
Valkyr	Angitia	Calypso	Eunomia	Idothea	Nephele
Vamana	Anigrus	Camelot	Euryale	Iguvium	Neptune
Varaha	Antaeus	Camenae	Eurybia	Imhotep	Nereids
Varuna	Antenor	Camilla	Eurytus	Inarime	Niflhel
Vishnu	Anteros	Canopus	Euterpe	incubus	Nokomis
Vulcan	Anthene	Capella	Evander	Inferno	Nycteus
Xangti	Antiope	Caranus	evil eye	Iobates	Nysaeus
Xelhua	Antissa	Carneus	Exadius	Ioskeha	Oceanus
Xolotl	Aphetae	Cecrops	Februus	Ismenos	Ocyrhoe
Xuthus	Aphytos	Celaeno	Feronia	Itzamna	Oeagrus
Yaksha	Arachne	centaur	Formiae	Iztal Ix	Oedipus
Zancle	Arcadia	Cepheus	Fortuna	Iztat Ix	Ogygian
Zethus	Arestor	Cercyon	Fylgjur	Jocasta	Old Nick
zombie	Argolis	Cessair	Gabriel	Jupiter	Olympia
	Ariadne	Chelone	Galahad	Juturna	Olympus
7	Arsinoë	chimera	Galatea	Khepera	Omphale
	Artemis	Chloris	Galleus	Krishna	Onniont
Abderus	Asathor	Chryses	Gargara	Laeradh	oracles
Acarnam	Astarte	Cinyras	Gelanor	Laertes	Orestes
Acastus	Asteria	Cleobis	Glaucus	Lakshmi	Ormenus
Acerbas	Astraea	Clymene	Gnossos	Laocoon	Orphean
Acestes	Astrope	Cocytus	goddess	Laodice	Orpheus
Achaeus	Ataguju	Copreus	Goibniu	Lapiths	Orthrus
Achates	Athamas	Coronis	Gordius	Larunda	Ortygia
Acheron	Atropos	Creteus	Gorgons	Latinus	Ouranos
Acoetes	Audumla	Curetes	Grannus	Lavinia	Pandion
Actaeon	Autonoë	Cyaneae	gremlin	Leander	Pandora
Admetus	Auxesia	Cyclops	Grendel	Lemures	Parvati
Aegaeon	Avallon	Cythera	griffin	Limnads	Pegasus
Aegiale	avatars	Dactyls	Grimnir	Lorelei	Penates
Aenaria	Avernus	Danaids	gryphon	Lothurr	Perseis
Aepytus	Bacchae	Daphnis	Gungnir	Lynceus	Perseus
Aesacus	Bacchus	Delphus	Halesus	Macaria	Petasus
Aetolus	banshee	Demeter	Hamoneu	Machaon	Phaedra
Agamede	banshie	demi-god	Hanuman	Maenads	Phegeus
Agyieus	Behdety	Diomede	Harpies	Maponos	Phemius
Ahriman	Belenos	Discord	Harpina	Marsyas	Phineus
Alastor	Bellona	Dwynwen	Helenus	Megaera	Phoebus
Alcides	Beltane	Echemus	Helicone	Menippe	Phoenix
Alcmene	Bifrost	Echidna	Hesione	Mercury	Phorcys
Alcyone	Bochica	Ehecatl	Hilaira	mermaid	Phrixus
Alpheus	bogyman	Electra	Himeros	Metylto	Phyllis
Aluberi	Bona Dea	Eleusis	Hor-Amen	Michabo	Pierian
Amathus	Brahman	Elicius	Hun-Ahpu	Michael	Pleiads
Amazons	Branwen	Elpenor	Hunbatz	Midgard	Pleione
Ampelus					

Plouton
Pluvius
Polites
Priapus
Procles
Procris
Proetus
Proteus
Pryderi
Purusha
Pylades
Pyramus
Pyrrhus
Pythias
Qabanil
Racumon
rain god
Raphael
Renenet
Rhamnus
Rhoecus
Rhoetus
Rig-Veda
Robigus
Romulus
Rubicon
Rukmini
Samblin
Saranya
Savitar
Savitri
Scandea
Scaptia
Scheria
Scythia
Segesta
Sekhmet
Selleis
Serapis
serpent
Sesheta
Setebos
Shamash
Sicinus
Sigmund
Silenus
Skirnir
Soranus
Spright
sprites
Stentor
Stimula
sylphid
Talarea

Taueret
Taygete
Telamon
Telemus
Temenus
Thaumas
Theonoe
Theseus
Thialfi
Titania
Triopas
Tristan
Troilus
Ubertas
Ubitina
Ulysses
unicorn
Unktahe
vampire
Veionis
Venilia
vestals
Vintios
Virbius
Vitharr
Walkyrs
Wayland
Wieland
wood god
Xanthus
Xibalba
Xmucane
Yakshas
Yolcuat
Zagreus
Zipacna

8

Abantias
Absyrtus
Academus
Achelous
Achilles
Acidalla
Aconteus
Acontius
Acrisius
Adrastia
Adrastus
Aeacides
Aegimius
Aegyptus
Aeneades
Agamedes

Aganippe
Aglauros
Aidoneus
Alberich
Albiorix
Alcathoe
Alcestis
Alcimede
Alcinous
Alcmaeon
Alsaeids
Amaethon
Amaithea
ambrosia
Anacreon
Anatarho
Anchiale
Anchises
Anemotis
Angharad
Antemnae
Anthedon
Anthemus
Anthylla
Anticlea
Antigone
Antiphus
Apaturia
Apidonus
Apollyon
Appareus
Arcesius
Arethusa
Argonaut
Arianrod
Ascanius
Asmodeus
Asterion
Astraeus
Astyanax
Ataensic
Atalanta
Atlantis
Avernian
Baba Yaga
basilisk
Bebryces
Bedivere
Belisama
Bhairavi
bogeyman
Bolthorn
Branchus
Briareus

Brynhild
Bubastis
Bylazora
caduceus
Caeculus
Calliope
Callisto
Camaxtli
Camazotz
Carmenta
Castalla
Celaenae
centaurs
Centeotl
Cephalus
Cerberus
Cercopes
Chalybes
Chantico
Charites
Chimaera
Chrysaor
Chryseis
Cimmeril
Cipactli
Cocidius
Coroebus
Cretheus
Crommyon
Cyclades
Cyclopes
Cyllarus
Cynosura
Cytherea
Daedalus
Damascus
Damastes
Damocles
Dardanus
Delanira
demiurge
Dervones
Despoena
Diomedes
Dionysos
Dionysus
Dioscuri
Dodonian
Doybayba
Draupnir
El Dorado
Elivager
Endymion
Enigorio

Entellus
Enyalius
Epicaste
Epidanus
Eriphyle
Erynnyes
Erytheis
Eteocles
Eteoclus
Eumolpus
Euphemus
Euryabus
Euryclea
Eurydice
Eurynome
Faesulae
Farbauti
Favonius
folklore
Fornjotr
Ganymede
giantess
Gigantes
Gilgames
good folk
Govannon
Gucumatz
Halcyone
Harmonia
Haroeris
Heimdall
Heliadae
Heracles
Hercules
Hermione
Hersilia
Hesperus
Hyperion
Ilithyia
Illatici
Iphicles
Jarnsaxa
Jurupari
Juventas
Kalevala
Keridwen
Kukulcan
Labdacus
Lachesis
Lampetie
Lancelot
Laodamas
Laodamia
Laomedon

Lapithae
Iardanes
Lupercus
Lycurgus
Maeander
Mama Nono
Manannan
Marpessa
Megareus
Melampus
Meleager
Menelaus
Merodach
Merseger
Meshkent
Messenia
Minotaur
Morpheus
Mulciber
Myrtilus
Narayana
Nauplius
Nausicaa
Nefertum
Nekhebit
Nephthys
Nibelung
Niflheim
Nin-Lilla
Oceanids
Odysseus
Oenomaus
Olympian
Orithyia
Othrerir
Pacarina
Palaemon
Pandarus
Panopeus
Pantheon
Panthous
paradise
Parjanya
Pasiphaë
Pasithea
Pelasgus
Pelopids
Penelope
Pentheus
Pephredo
Perceval
Percival
Periphas
Perseids

Pessinus
Phaethon
Philemon
Phintias
Phlegyas
Phoronis
Picumnus
Pierides
Pilumnus
Pisander
Pittheus
Pleiades
Podarces
Polyxena
Porthaon
Portunus
Poseidon
Prithivi
Proximae
Psamathe
Pulastya
Queen Mab
Quiateot
Quirinal
Quirinus
Ragnarok
Rakshasa
Rhiannon
Rhodopis
Rosmerta
Rubezahl
Sabazius
Sahadeva
Sarawati
Sarpedon
Schedius
Sciathus
Seriphos
Silvanus
Sipontum
Sisyphus
Sleipnir
Sparsana
Srikanta
Steropus
succubus
Summanus
Talassio
talisman
Tantalus
Tartarus
Tecmessa
Telephus
Terminus

Thamyris
Thanatos
Theogony
Thyestes
Tiresias
Tithonus
Tonatiuh
Tristram
Tvashtar
Ucalegon
Valhalla
Valkyrie
Vasudeva
Verdandi
Vesuvius
Victoria
Virginia
Visvampa
Wakinyan
water god
Waukkeon
werewolf
Xpiyacoc
Yadapati
Zalmoxis
Zephyrus

9

Achilleum
Acmonides
Adsullata
Aegialeus
Aegisthus
Aethiopia
Agamemnon
Agathyrsi
Akha-Kanet
Alcathous
Alcyoneus
Amalivaca
Ambrosial
Amphrysus
Anaxarete
Andraemon
Androclus
Androgeus
Andromeda
Antandrus
Antevorta
Aphrodite
Areithous
Areopagus
Argonauts
Aristaeus

Ascalabus
Asclepios
Asclepius
Ashtoreth
Assoracus
Autolycus
Automeden
Aventinus
Bacchante
Bosphorus
Brunhilde
Bucentaur
Byzantium
Cassandra
Cephissus
Cerberean
Cernunnos
Chalcodon
Charybdis
Chthonius
Clitumnus
Coatilcue
Cockaigne
Concordia
Cytherean
Davy Jones
Deianeira
Deiphobus
Demophoon
Dervonnae
Deucalion
Dian Cécht
Diespiter
Dionysius
Domdaniel
Enceladus
Epidaurus
Eumenides
Euphorbus
Eurybates
Eurypylus
Eurysaces
Excalibur
Fabia Gens
fairy tale
Fairyland
Faustulus
Ferentina
Feretrius
Fjawrgynn
Friar Tuck
Gagurathe
Gargaphin
Ghisdubar

Gilgamesh
Guinivere
Hamadryad
Harakhtes
Harmakhis
Harsaphes
Heimdallr
Hippocoon
Hippolyta
Hippolyte
hobgoblin
Holy Grail
Hypsipyle
Idacanzas
Idomeneus
Ilmarinen
Immortals
Indigetes
Iphigenia
Iphimedia
Ixiomides
Jotunheim
labyrinth
Launcelot
Lycomedes
Lyonnesse
Melanthus
Melisande
Melpomene
Menoeceus
Menoetius
Mertseger
Metaneira
Missibizi
Mnemosyne
Mnestheus
Myrmidons
Nanahuatl
Narasimha
Narcissus
Noncomala
Nyctimene
Oceanides
orgiastic
Palamedes
Pandareus
Pandrosos
Parnassus
Patroclus
Pelopidae
Periander
Philammon
Philomela
Phoroneus

Tezcatlipoca
Theoclymenus
Trismegistus
Wandering Jew
white goddess
Xochiquetzal
Yohualticiti
Yudhishthira

13 AND OVER

Achilleus Dromos (15)
Apochquiahuayan (15)
Apple of Discord (14)
Augean stables (13)
Calydonian Hunt (14)
Ceryneian Hind (13)

Colonus Hippius (14)
Damocles' sword (13)
Elysian Fields (13)
Father Christmas (15)
Halirrhathius (13)
Hermaphroditus (14)
Huitzilopochtli (15)
Itsikamahidis (13)
Jupiter Elicius (14)
Jupiter Pluvius (14)
Jupiter Victor (13)
Laestrygonians (14)
Lernaean Hydra (13)
Llew Llaw Gyffes (14)
Mayan mythology (14)
Never Never Land (14)

Oonawieh Unggi (13)
Phoebus Apollo (13)
Quetzalcohuatl (14)
Robin Goodfellow (15)
Stymphalian Birds (16)
Sword of Damocles (15)
Thesmophoriae (13)
Tioque Nahuaque (14)
Tonacatecutli (13)
Tuatha De Danann (14)
Uther Pendragon (14)
Walpurgis Night (14)
Wayland the Smith (15)
Yoalli Ehecati (13)

Ecclesiastical terms, etc.

2 – 4	guni	pyre	amice	dulia	manse
	guru	pyx	Amish	elder	matin
abbé	hadj	R.I.P.	angel	ephod	Mecca
alb	hajj	rite	apron	exeat	mitre
alms	halo	robe	Arian	faith	morse
ambo	hell	rood	banns	fakir	motet
amen	holy	sect	beads	fanon	myrrh
apse	host	see	Bible	friar	nones
ark	hymn	seer	bigot	glebe	Omega
ave	icon	sext	bless	glory	padre
Baal	idol	sin	burse	godly	paean
bema	IHS	Siva	canon	goyim	pagan
bier	imam	soul	carol	grace	papal
bon	I.N.R.I.	Sufi	cella	Grail	pasch
bull	Jah	text	chant	grave	paten
cant	Jain	Toc H	chela	guild	piety
cell	Jew	tomb	choir	Hades	pious
chan	joss	Veda	cotta	hafiz	prior
cope	kirk	veil	credo	Hindu	psalm
Copt	lama	vow	creed	image	purim
cowl	lay	Xmas	cross	Islam	rabbi
curé	Lent	yoga	cruet	Jewry	relic
dana	mass	Zen	crypt	Kaaba	saint
dean	monk	Zion	curia	karma	Satan
Ebor	naos		Dagon	knell	selah
Eden	nave	**5**	deify	Koran	stole
Eve	nun		deism	laity	stoup
evil	obit	abbey	deist	lauds	stupa
ewer	pall	abbot	deity	laver	Sudra
fane	pew	agape	demon	limbo	Sunna
fast	pie	aisle	devil	Logos	Sunni
font	pome	Allah	dirge	Magus	sutra
God	pope	Alpha	dogma	Maker	synod
goy	pray	altar	druid	manna	taboo
		ambry			

terce
Torah
tract
Vedic
vicar
vigil

6

abbacy
abbess
Advent
adytum
anoint
anthem
ashram
aumbry
Babism
beadle
Beguin
Belial
bishop
Brahma
Buddha
burial
cantor
casket
censer
chapel
cherub
chimer
chrism
Christ
church
cierge
clergy
cleric
coffin
corban
Culdee
curacy
curate
datary
deacon
decani
deific
devout
dharma
diadem
divine
dossal
double
Dunker
Easter
Elohim

embalm
Essene
Exodus
Father
ferial
flamen
friary
Gloria
Gospel
gradin
hallow
hearse
heaven
Hebrew
Hegira
heresy
hermit
homily
hymnal
I-ching
intone
Israel
Jesuit
Jewess
Jewish
Jordan
Judaic
keblah
latria
lavabo
lector
legate
Levite
litany
living
mantra
martyr
matins
maundy
missal
Mormon
mosaic
Moslem
mosque
mullah
Muslim
mystic
nimbus
novena
novice
nuncio
oblate
octave
office

ordain
orders
orison
pagoda
painim
palace
palmer
papacy
papism
papist
parish
Parsee
parson
pastor
popery
prayer
preach
priest
primus
priory
proper
psalms
pulpit
purana
Quaker
rector
repent
ritual
rochet
rosary
rubric
sacred
Saddhu
santon
schism
scribe
sedile
seraph
sermon
server
sexton
Shaker
shaman
Shiite
Shinto
shrine
shrive
shroud
sinful
sinner
sister
solemn
spirit
stalls

Sufism
Sunday
suttee
tablet
Talmud
tantra
Taoism
Te Deum
temple
theism
tierce
tippet
trance
triune
verger
vestry
virgin
Vishnu
voodoo
votive
Wahabi
zealot

7

Aaronic
Abaddon
acolyte
Adamite
advowee
Alcoran
Alkoran
almoner
ampulla
angelic
Angelus
animism
apostle
atheism
atheist
Bahaism
baptism
baptist
baptize
beatify
Beghard
Beguine
bigotry
biretta
blessed
Brahman
Brahmin
brother
cabbala
calotte

calvary
capuche
cassock
chalice
chancel
chantry
chaplet
chapter
charity
chrisom
Cluniac
collect
complin
confirm
convent
convert
crosier
crozier
crusade
dataria
deanery
decanal
defrock
deified
dervish
diocese
diptych
diviner
Elohist
epistle
Essenes
eternal
evangel
exegete
faculty
fanatic
fasting
frontal
Galilee
gaudete
Gehenna
Genesis
Genevan
gentile
glorify
gnostic
goddess
godhead
godless
gradine
gradual
gremial
hassock
heathen

heretic
hexapla
holy day
hosanna
impiety
impious
incense
infidel
introit
Jainism
Jehovah
jubilee
Judaism
Judaize
Lady Day
lamaism
Lateran
lectern
lection
liturgy
Lollard
low mass
madonna
maniple
mattins
Messiah
mid-Lent
minaret
minster
miracle
mission
muezzin
mystics
narthex
nirvana
nocturn
nunnery
oratory
ordinal
orphrey
Our Lady
pallium
parable
paschal
penance
peshito
pietism
pietist
pilgrim
piscina
pontiff
prayers
prebend
prelate

prester
primacy
primate
profane
prophet
Psalter
Puritan
Quakers
Ramadan
rebirth
rectory
requiem
reredos
retable
retreat
Sabbath
sacring
sainted
saintly
sanctum
Saracen
satanic
Saviour
secular
sedilia
serpent
service
Shakers
Shaster
Shastra
Sivaism
Sivaist
Sivaite
soutane
steeple
stipend
sub-dean
Sunnite
synodal
Tantric
Tempter
tonsure
Trinity
tunicle
unction
unfrock
Vatican
Vedanta
vespers
Vulgate
worship
Xmas day
Zionism

8

ablution
aceldama
acephali
acephali
advowson
agnostic
Agnus Dei
alleluia
almighty
anathema
anchoret
Anglican
anointed
antiphon
antipope
apostasy
apostate
Arianism
Arminian
Ave Maria
basilica
beadroll
beadsman
beatific
bedesman
believer
benifice
bénitier
biblical
blessing
brethren
breviary
Buddhism
Buddhist
canonize
canticle
cantoris
capuchin
cardinal
catacomb
Catholic
celibacy
cemetery
cenobite
cenotaph
chaplain
chasuble
cherubim
chimere
choirboy
chrismal
christen
ciborium

cincture
clerical
cloister
compline
conclave
corporal
covenant
creation
credence
crucifer
crucifix
Crusader
dalmatic
deaconry
devotion
diaconal
Dies Irae
diocesan
disciple
ditheism
ditheist
divinity
divinize
doctrine
Donatism
Donatist
doxology
druidess
druidism
Ebionism
Ebionite
elements
Ember Day
embolism
Emmanuel
epiphany
epistler
Erastian
Essenian
eternity
Eusebian
evensong
exegesis
exorcism
exorcist
faithful
feretory
frontlet
futurist
God's acre
Good Book
Hail Mary
hallowed
hellfire

hierarch
high mass
holiness
holy city
Holy Land
holy rood
Holy Week
Holy Writ
Huguenot
hymn book
idolater
idolatry
Immanuel
immortal
Jesuitic
Jesuitry
Judaizer
lamasery
laywoman
libation
lichgate
literate
Lord's Day
Lutheran
lychgate
marabout
mass book
menology
minister
ministry
Minorite
Miserere
Mohammed
monachal
monastic
Moravian
mozzetta
nativity
Nazarene
neophyte
obituary
oblation
offering
ordinary
orthodox
paganism
pantheon
papistry
Paradise
pardoner
parousia
Passover
penitent
Pharisee

pontifex
preacher
predella
prie-dieu
priestly
prioress
prophecy
prophesy
Proverbs
province

9

psalmist
psalmody
psaltery
Puseyism
Puseyite
quietism
quietist
Ramadhan
recollet
Redeemer
religion
response
reverend
reverent
rogation
Romanism
Romanist
Romanize
rood loft
sacristy
Sadducee
sanctify
sanctity
satanism
scapular
sequence
seraphic
seraphim
Shepherd
sidesman
skullcap
Socinian
suffrage
superior
surplice
synoptic
Tantrism
Tenebrae
theology
thurible
thurifer
transept
Trimurti
triptych

unbelief
venerate
versicle
vestment
viaticum
vicarage
Wesleyan
zoolatry

9

ablutions
adoration
Adventist
All Saints
alleluiah
allelujah
anchorite
anointing
antipapal
Apocrypha
apostolic
archangel
archenemy
archfiend
Ascension
atonement
Ayatollah
baldachin
baldaquin
baptismal
barbarian
beatitude
Beelzebub
beneficed
bishopric
bismillah
black mass
blasphemy
born-again
cabbalism
Calvinism
Calvinist
Candlemas
canonical
Carmelite
catechism
cathedral
celebrant
celestial
cerecloth
cerements
Christian
Christmas
churching

claustral
clergyman
cloisters
co-eternal
coadjutor
communion
confessor
converted
Cordelier
credendum
cremation
dalmatica
Dalai Lama
damnation
deaconess
Decalogue
dedicated
Dei gratia
desecrate
devotions
diaconate
dissenter
dissident
dog collar
Dominican
Easter Day
Ember days
Ember week
episcopal
epistoler
Eucharist
godfather
godliness
godmother
godparent
good works
gospeller
Gregorian
hagiarchy
hagiology
Halloween
hereafter
Hexateuch
hierarchy
hierogram
hierology
High Altar
Holocaust
Holy Ghost
Holy Grail
holy water
incumbent
induction
interdict

interment
Jansenism
Jansenist
Jesuitism
joss-stick
Lamb of God
Lammas Day
last rites
lay reader
Levitical
Leviticus
Low Church
Low Sunday
Magdalene
Mahomedan
Maronites
martyrdom
Methodism
Methodist
moderator
monachism
monastery
Monsignor
Mormonism
Mosaic Law
mundatory
Mussulman
mysticism
Nestorian
obeisance
offertory
orthodoxy
ostensory
pantheism
pantheist
papal bull
Paraclete
Parseeism
patriarch
Pentecost
pharisaic
plainsong
prayer mat
prayer rug
preaching
precentor
presbyter
priestess
profanity
proselyte
prothesis
purgatory
Quakerism
reconvert

religieux
religious
reliquary
repentant
responses
reverence
righteous
ritualism
ritualist
rural dean
sabbatism
Sabellian
sackcloth
sacrament
sacrarium
sacrifice
sacrilege
sacristan
sainthood
salvation
sanctuary
scapegoat
scapulary
Scripture
semi-Arian
sepulchre
shamanism
Shintoist
solemnity
solemnize
spiritual
sub-beadle
subdeacon
subrector
succentor
suffragan
sutteeism
synagogue
synergism
synodical
teleology
Testament
Theatines
theocracy
theomachy
theopathy
theophany
theosophy
triforium
tritheism
unfrocked
Unitarian
venerable
vestments

Waldenses
Yom Kippur
zucchetto

10

absolution
abstinence
Albigenses
All Hallows
almsgiving
altar bread
altar cloth
altar front
altar plate
altar rails
altar table
altarpiece
amen corner
Anabaptism
Anabaptist
anointment
Antichrist
Apocalypse
apostolate
apotheosis
arch-priest
archbishop
archdeacon
archflamen
archimagus
Armageddon
Assumption
Athanasian
baldachino
baptistery
bar mitzvah
Benedicite
Bernardine
bible class
black friar
Brahminism
Buddhistic
canonicals
Carthusian
catechumen
ceremonial
Church Army
church bell
churchgoer
churchyard
Cistercian
clearstory
clerestory
cloistered

confession
conformist
consecrate
consistory
conversion
Covenanter
dedication
devotional
diaconicon
ditheistic
divination
doctrinism
Dominicans
dragonnade
Eastertide
ecumenical
Eleusinian
Ember weeks
encyclical
episcopacy
episcopate
episcopize
evangelism
evangelist
evangelize
Evil Spirit
fellowship
Franciscan
free chapel
Free Church
Geneva gown
gnosticism
God-fearing
golden calf
Good Friday
gospel side
gymnosophy
hagiolatry
halleluiah
hallelujah
heathenism
heliolater
heliolatry
Heptateuch
hierocracy
hierophant
High Church
high priest
holy orders
Holy Spirit
House of God
hylotheism
hyperdulia
iconoclasm

iconoclast
iconolater
iconolatry
idolatress
idolatrous
impanation
incumbency
indulgence
infallible
invocation
irreligion
irreverent
juggernaut
Lady chapel
Last Supper
lay brother
lectionary
Magnificat
Mariolatry
meditation
ministrant
missionary
Mohammedan
monotheism
monotheist
monstrance
omnipotent
ophiolatry
ordination
Palm Sunday
papal court
papal cross
Passionist
Pentateuch
pharisaism
phylactery
pilgrimage
pontifical
prayer book
prayer flag
prebendary
presbytery
priesthood
procession
prophetess
Protestant
Providence
puritanism
rectorship
redemption
repentance
revelation
rock temple
Roman Curia

rood screen
sacerdotal
sacrosanct
sanctified
sanctifier
schismatic
scholastic
scriptural
Scriptures
Septuagint
sepulchral
Sexagesima
Shrovetide
subdeanery
syncretism
tabernacle
temptation
theologian
Tridentine
unanointed
unbaptized
unbeliever
unorthodox
veneration
visitation
Whit Sunday
white friar
worshipper
Zend-Avesta

11

abbreviator
agnosticism
All Souls' Day
altar screen
antependium
antiphonary
apologetics
apotheosize
arch-heretic
arch-prelate
archdiocese
Arches Court
Arminianism
aspergillum
aspersorium
Augustinian
Benedictine
benediction
benedictory
bibliolatry
bibliomancy
blasphemous
Bodhisattva

burning bush
Catholicism
celebration
chrismatory
Christendom
christening
church house
commandment
commination
communicant
consecrator
conventicle
convocation
crematorium
crucifixion
decanal side
deification
desecration
devotionist
divine light
doxological
ecclesiarch
epistle side
Erastianism
eschatology
eternal life
evangelical
evening hymn
everlasting
exhortation
fire-worship
freethinker
Geneva bands
Geneva Bible
genuflection
graven image
hagiography
hagiologist
Hare Krishna
hierarchism
hierography
humeral veil
immortality
incarnation
Inquisition
intercessor
investiture
irreligious
irreverence
Judgment Day
Latin Church
lawn sleeves
Lord of Hosts
Lord's Prayer

Lord's Supper
Lutheranism
miracle play
Mohammedism
Nicene Creed
œcumenical
original sin
parish clerk
parishioner
paschal lamb
passing bell
Passion play
Passion Week
paternoster
patron saint
pedobaptism
pharisaical
pontificals
pontificate
prayer wheel
priestcraft
Prodigal Son
proselytism
proselytize
protomartyr
purificator
Rastafarian
Reformation
religionary
religionism
religionist
religiosity
requiem mass
reservation
ritualistic
Roman Church
Sabbatarian
sacramental
sacring bell
Sadduceeism
saintliness
Sanctus bell
sarcophagus
Scientology
Socinianism
theosophist
Trinitarian
triple crown
unbeneficed
uncanonical
unorthodoxy
unrighteous
vicar forane
Wesleyanism

Whitsuntide
Zen Buddhism
Zoroastrian

12

All Saints' Day
altar frontal
Annunciation
Apostolic See
archdeaconry
Ascension Day
Ash Wednesday
Augustinians
Bible Society
bishop's court
chapel of ease
chapterhouse
Charterhouse
choir service
chosen people
Christianity
Christmas Day
Christmas Eve
church living
church parade
churchwarden
confessional
confirmation
Confucianism
congregation
consecration
consistorial
Coptic Church
denomination
devil worship
Disciplinant
disestablish
dispensation
ditheistical
Easter Sunday
Ecclesiastes
ecclesiastic
ecclesiology
enthronement
Episcopalian
evangelicism
frankincense
Good Shepherd
hagiographer
hot gospeller
image worship
intercession
interdiction
Jacob's ladder

Last Judgment
Low Churchman
Major Prophet
metropolitan
Minor Prophet
mission house
New Testament
Nunc Dimittis
Old Testament
omnipresence
paedobaptism
Presbyterian
Promised Land
purification
Quadragesima
reconsecrate
reconversion
red letter day
Redemptorist
residentiary
Resurrection
Rogation days
Sabellianism
sacrilegious
Salvationist
Sanctus bell
Second Coming
spiritualism
Sunday school
superfrontal
thanksgiving
Three Wise Men
Tower of Babel
ultramontane
Unitarianism
Universalism
Universalist
unscriptural
vicar-general

13

Allhallowmass

Allhallows Eve
Allhallowtide
Anglo-Catholic
Antichristian
antiepiscopal
Apostles' Creed
archbishopric
archdeaconate
beatification
bidding prayer
burial service
burnt offering
canonical hour
church service
confessionary
convocational
coreligionist
Corpus Christi
Court of Arches
credence table
Day of Judgment
devotionalist
divine service
Eastern Church
ecumenicalism
eschatologist
excommunicate
glorification
High Churchman
holy innocents
Last Judgement
Lord Spiritual
miracle worker
mission church
Mohammedanism
morning prayer
Nonconformist
Nonconformity
paschal candle
pectoral cross
prayer-meeting
Protestantism

Quinquagesima
reincarnation
Roman Catholic
Sacerdotalism
Salvation Army
scripturalist
Shrove Tuesday
Swedenborgian
Tractarianism
Trinity Sunday
unconsecrated
Vicar of Christ
way of the cross
Zarathustrian

14

Anglican Church
antiscriptural
archiepiscopal
church assembly
communion table
crutched friars
denominational
Easter offering
ecclesiastical
Ecclesiasticus
ecclesiologist

eschatological
evangelicalism
evangelization
extreme unction
fire-worshipper
fundamentalism
fundamentalist
Gregorian chant
high priesthood
intercommunion
Maundy Thursday
morning service
mother superior
Orthodox Church

Oxford Movement
psilanthropism
psilanthropist
Rastafarianism
reconsecration
Recording Angel
Reformed Church
Revised Version
Rogation Sunday
Sabbatarianism
Sacramentarian
sanctification
sign of the cross
Society of Jesus
transmigration
Tridentine Mass
Trinitarianism
vicar apostolic
Zoroastrianism

15

anticlericalism
antitrinitarian
archiepiscopate
articles of faith
Athanasian Creed
cardinal virtues
chapter and verse
Church of England
Episcopalianism
excommunication
General Assembly
harvest festival
infernal regions
Jehovah's Witness
metropolitanate
Moral Rearmament
Mothering Sunday
Presbyterianism
suffragan bishop
Ten Commandments
Transfiguration

Saints

3 AND 4

Abb
Anne
Bede
Bee
Bega
Chad

Cyr
Ebba
Eloi
Gall
Joan
John
Jude
Leo

Luce
Lucy
Luke
Mark
Mary
Olaf
Paul
Roch

Rose
Zeno

5

Agnes
Aidan
Alban
Amand

Asaph
Basil
Bride
Bruno
Clare
Cyril
David
Denis

Elias
Genny
Giles
Hilda
James
Kilda
Louis
Lucia

Peter
Simon

6

Albert
Andrea
Andrew
Anselm
Ansgar
Blaise
Cosmas
Fabian
Fergus
George
Heiler
Helena
Hilary
Hubert
Jerome
Joseph
Justin
Magnus
Martha
Martin
Maurus
Michel
Monica
Philip
Teresa
Thomas
Ursula
Xavier

7

Ambrose
Anthony
Austell

Barbara
Bernard
Bridget
Casimir
Cecilia
Charles
Clement
Crispin
Dominic
Dorothy
Dunstan
Eustace
Francis
Gregory
Isidore
Joachim
Leonard
Matthew
Maurice
Michael
Pancras
Patrick
Raphael
Raymond
Romuald
Saviour
Stephen
Swithin
Swithun
Thérèse
Vincent
William

8

Aloysius
Barnabas
Benedict

Boniface
Cuthbert
Damianus
Donatian
Eusebius
Germanus
Hyacinth
Ignatius
Lawrence
Longinus
Mamertus
Margaret
Nicholas
Paulinus
Polycarp
Veronica
Walpurga
Winifred
Zenobius

9

Apollonia
Augustine
Catherine
Demetrius
Elizabeth
Exuperius
Fredewith
Joan of Arc
Sebastian
Servatius
Sylvester
Valentine
Walpurgis

10 AND 11

Apollinaris (11)
Athanasius (10)
Bartholomew (11)
Bonaventura (11)
Christopher (11)
Ethelburga (10)
Eustathius (10)
Gallo Abbato (11)
Gaudentius (10)
Hippolytus (10)
Jeanne d'Arc (10)
Mercuriale (10)
Peter Martyr (11)
Philip Neri (10)
Scholastica (11)
Thomas More (10)
Zaccharias (10)

12 AND OVER

Anthony of Padua (14)
Bridget of Sweden (15)
Catherine of Siena (16)
Francis of Assisi (15)
Francis Xavier (13)
James the Great (13)
James the Less (12)
John the Baptist (14)
Justin Martyr (12)
Mary Magdalene (13)
Simon Stylites (13)
Teresa of Avila (13)
Thomas Aquinas (13)
Thomas Becket (12)
Vincent de Paul (13)
Vincent Ferrer (13)

SCIENCE AND TECHNOLOGY
Agriculture

3

awn
bin
cob
cod
cow
cub
dam
dig
ear
ewe

fen
gid
hay
hoe
hog
hop
ket
kid
kip
lea
ley
moo

mow
pig
pip
ram
rut
rye
sow
ted
teg
tup

4

acre
bale
barn
beam
beef
beet
bent
bere
bigg
bran

bull
byre
calf
cart
clay
corn
cote
crop
culim
curb
dock
dung

farm
fell
foal
gait
herd
hind
holt
hops
hull
husk
kine
lamb

lime	**5**	ovine	dobbin	punner	drought
loam		plant	drover	raggee	droving
mare	aphid	ranch	eatage	rancho	eanling
marl	araba	rumen	écurie	realty	erosion
meal	auger	sheep	fallow	reaper	farming
milk	avena	shoat	farina	roller	fee-tail
neat	baler	shuck	farmer	runrig	fertile
neep	beans	spelt	farrow	scythe	foaling
oast	biddy	spuds	fescue	sheave	foldage
oats	borax	staig	fleece	sickle	foot rot
odal	bothy	stall	fodder	silage	forcing
pale	braxy	stead	forage	socage	fox trap
peat	brize	stich	furrow	sowans	gadsman
pest	calve	stipa	gargol	sowing	granary
pone	carse	stook	garron	spruit	granger
quey	cavie	straw	gaucho	stable	grazing
rabi	chaff	swill	gimmer	steppe	hallier
rake	churn	tilth	gluten	stover	harvest
rape	clamp	tithe	grains	tanist	haycart
root	clone	tiver	grange	tedder	haycock
roup	couch	tuber	harrow	tomand	hayrick
runt	croft	veldt	heifer	travis	hedging
rust	crone	vimen	hogget	trough	herding
ryot	crops	vives	hogsty	turnip	hogcote
sand	dairy	vomer	hopper	turves	hop pole
scab	ditch	wagon	huller	warble	hunkers
sear	drill	wheat	hurdle	weevil	implant
seed	drove	withe	incult		infield
shaw	durum	withy	inning	**7**	innings
silo	ergot	worms	inspan		kidling
silt	farcy	yield	intine	acidity	lamb-ale
skep	flail		jument	aerator	lambing
slob	fruit	**6**	linhay	alfalfa	laniary
sock	fungi		litter	amidine	layland
soil	gebur	angora	llanos	anthrax	leasowe
soya	glume	animal	manger	avenage	lucerne
span	grain	arable	manure	binding	maizena
stot	grass	barley	meadow	boscage	malting
teff	graze	beeves	mealie	budding	marlite
till	guano	binder	merino	bulchin	milk can
toft	haugh	botfly	milium	bullock	milking
tope	haulm	butter	millet	buttery	misyoke
tore	hedge	carney	milsey	cabbage	morling
udal	hilum	cattle	mowing	calving	multure
vale	hoove	cereal	nubbin	combine	murrain
vega	horse	cloche	padnag	compost	nest box
weed	humus	clover	pampas	copland	novalia
wold	kulak	colter	piglet	cornage	nursery
yean	lande	corral	pigsty	coulter	orchard
zebu	llano	cotter	plough	cowherd	organic
	maize	cowman	podsol	cowshed	pabular
	mower	cratch	polder	demesne	paddock
	mulch	cutter	porker	digging	panicum
	mummy	digger	potato	dipping	pannage
		disbud		docking	

pasture	threave	hopfield	herbicide	swine fever
peonage	thwaite	kohlrabi	hop-picker	transplant
piggery	tillage	landgirl	horserake	weedkiller
pinetum	tilling	loosebox	husbandry	wheatfield
pinfold	topsoil	milkcart	implement	
polders	tractor	Paraquat	incubator	**11**
poultry	trammel	pedigree	livestock	agriculture
prairie	trekker	pigswill	pasturage	agrobiology
praties	trotter	plougher	pesticide	brucellosis
predial	udaller	root crop	phosphate	cake crusher
provine	vaquero	rotation	pig trough	chaff cutter
pruning	vitular	rotovate	ploughing	chicken farm
pulping	wagoner	ruminant	rice field	cultivation
pummace	windrow	sainfoin	Rotovator	fertilizing
radicle	yardman	shearing	screening	germination
raking		sheepdip	separator	insecticide
rancher	**8**	vineyard	shorthorn	pastureland
reaping	acid soil	watering	sugar beet	poultry farm
rearing	agronomy	wireworm	sugar cane	reclamation
retting	bone meal		swineherd	stock-taking
rhizome	branding	**9**	thrashing	swath turner
rokeage	breeding		threshing	viticulture
rundale	cash crop	agrimotor	trenching	weed control
rustler	clipping	agroville	warble fly	
ryotwar	cropping	allotment	winnowing	**12**
savanna	ditching	black rust		agribusiness
sickled	drainage	butterfat	**10**	agricultural
slanket	elevator	cold frame		feeding-stock
spancel	ensilage	cornfield	agronomics	fermentation
spinner	farmyard	dairyfarm	agronomist	horticulture
stacker	fat stock	dairymaid	battery hen	insemination
station	forestry	disc drill	cattle cake	market garden
stooker	fowl pest	fertility	cultivator	mixed farming
stubble	gleaning	free-range	fertilizer	silviculture
stuckle	grafting	fungicide	harvesting	smallholding
subsoil	hayfield	gathering	husbandman	turnip cutter
swinery	haymaker	grassland	irrigation	
tantony	haystack	harrowing	mouldboard	
tax cart	haywagon	harvester	plantation	
		haymaking	selfbinder	

Astronomy

(a.) = asteroid; (c.) = constellation; (c.p.) = constellation (popular name);
(g.) = group of stars; (p.) = planet; (s.) = noted star; (sa.) = large satellite

2 – 4	coma	Fox (c.p.)	Keel (c.p.)	Mira (s.)	Ram (c.p.)
	Crab (c.p.)	Goat (c.p.)	Leo (c.)	Moon	Rhea (sa.)
Amor (a.)	Crow (c.p.)	Grus (c.)	limb	Net (c.p.)	Sol
Apus (c.)	Crux (c.)	halo	Lion (c.p.)	node	Star
Ara (c.)	Cup (c.p.)	Hare (c.p.)	Lynx (c.) (c.p.)	nova	Sun
Argo (c.)	Dove (c.p.)	Hebe (a.)	Lyra (c.)	orb.	Swan (c.p.)
belt	Eros (a.)	Io (sa.)	Lyre (c.p..).	Pavo (c.)	Vega (s.)
Bull (c.p.)	Fly (c.p.)	Juno (a.)	Mars (p.)	pole	

Vela (c.)
Wolf (c.p.)

5

Algol (s.)
Altar (c.p.)
apsis
Aries (c.)
Arrow (c.p.)
Ceres (a.)
Cetus (c.)
Clock (c.p.)
comet
Crane (c.p.)
Deneb (s.)
Digit
Dione (sa.)
Draco (c.)
dwarf
Eagle (c.p.)
Earth (p.)
epact
epoch
error
flare
giant
Hamal (s.)
Hyads (g.)
Hydra (c.)
Indus (c.)
Janus (sa.)
Lepus (c.)
Level (c.p.)
Libra (c.)
lunar
Lupus (c.)
Mensa (c.)
Metis (sa.)
Mimas (sa.)
Musca (c.)
nadir
Norma (c.)
orbit
Orion (c.)
phase
Pluto (p.)
polar
Pyxis (c.)
Regel (s.)
Rigel (s.)
River (c.p.)
Sails (c.p.)
Saros
Shield (c.p.)

solar
space
Spica (s.)
stars
Stern (c.p.)
Table (c.p.)
Titan (sa.)
Twins (c.p.)
umbra
Venus (p.)
Vesta (a.)
Virgo (c.)
Whale (c.p.)

6

albedo
Altair (s.)
Antlia (c.)
apogee
Apollo
Aquila (c.)
Archer (c.p.)
astral
Auriga (c.)
aurora
binary
Bolide
Boötes (c.)
Caelum (c.)
Cancer (c.)
Carina (c.)
Castor (s.)
Charon (sa.)
Chiron (a.)
Chisel (c.p.)
colure
corona
Corvus (c.)
cosmic
cosmos
crater
Crater (c.)
Cybele (a.)
Cygnus (c.)
Davida (a.)
Deimos (sa.)
Dipper (c.p.)
Dorado (c.)
Dragon (c.p.)
Europa (sa.)
Fishes (c.p.)
Fornax (c.)
galaxy
Gemini (c.)

gnomon
Hermes (a.)
Hunter (c.p.)
Hyades (g.)
Hydrus (c.)
Hygeia (a.)
Icarus (a.)
Indian (c.p.)
Leonid
Lizard (c.p.)
lunary
meteor
nebula
Nereid (sa.)
Oberon (sa.)
Octans (c.)
Octant (c.p.)
Pallas (a.)
parsec
Persei (g.)
Phobos (sa.)
Phoebe (sa.)
Pictor (c.)
Pisces (c.)
planet
Pleiad (g.)
Plough (g.)
Pollux (s.)
pulsar
Puppis (c.)
quasar
Saturn (p.)
Scales (c.p.)
Scutum (c.)
Sirius (s.)
sphere
Square (c.p.)
sundog
syzygy
Taurus (c.)
Tethys (sa.)
Toucan (c.p.)
Triton (sa.)
Tucana (c.)
Uranus (p.)
vector
vertex
Viking
Virgin (c.p.)
Volans (c.)
zenith
zodiac

7

Airpump (c.p.)
Alphard (s.)
anomaly
Antares (s.)
apogean
appulse
apsides
Astraea (a.)
auroral
azimuth
big bang
Canopus (s.)
Capella (s.)
Centaur (c.p.)
Cepheid
Cepheus (c.)
  (c.p.)
cluster
Columba (c.)
cometic
Dog Star (s.)
Dolphin (c.p.)
eclipse
equator
equinox
Eunomia (a.)
faculae
Furnace (c.p.)
gibbous
Giraffe (c.p.)
Hidalgo (a.)
Iapetus (sa.)
Jupiter (p.)
Lacerta (c.)
Mariner
Mercury (p.)
Miranda (sa.)
mock Sun
nebulae
nebular
Neptune (p.)
new moon
Peacock (c.p.)
Pegasus (c.)
perigee
Perseus (c.)
Phoenix (c.) (c.p.)
Polaris (s.)
Procyon (s.)
Proxima (s.)
radiant
Regulus (s.)

Sagitta (c.)
Scorpio (c.)
Sea goat (c.p.)
Serpens (c.)
Serpent (c.p.)
Sextans (c.)
Sextant (c.p.)
sextile
spectra
Sputnik
stellar
sunspot
Thania (sa.)
transit
Trojans (a.)
Umbriel (sa.)
Unicorn (c.p.)

8

Achernar (s.)
aerolite
aerolith
Aipherat (s.)
Almagest
altitude
Amalthea (sa.)
aphelion
Aquarius (c.)
Arcturus (s.)
asterism
asteroid
Callisto (sa.)
Canicula
Circinus (c.)
cometary
Cynosure (c.)
Denebola (s.)
ecliptic
epicycle
Equuleus (c.)
Eridanus (c.)
evection
Explorer
fireball
flocculi
free fall
full moon
galactic
Ganymede (sa.)
Great Dog (c.p.)
half moon
Hercules (c.)
  (c.p.)
Herdsman (c.p.)

Hesperus
Hyperion (sa.)
isostasy
latitude
Leo Minor (c.)
Loadstar (s.)
Lodestar (s.)
lunation
meridian
meteoric
Milky Way
mock moon
night sky
nutation
occulted
parallax
parhelia
penumbra
perigean
Pleiades (g.)
Pointers
Pole Star (s.)
quadrant
red dwarf
red giant
red shift
Scorpion (c.p.)
Scorpius (c.)
Sculptor (c.)
Ship Argo (c.p.)
sidereal
solstice
spectrum
spheroid
starless
stellary
sublunar
sunspots
Triangle (c.p.)
universe
Vanguard
variable
zodiacal

9

aerolitic
Aldebaran (s.)
Andromeda (c.) (c.p.)
anthelion
ascendant
ascension
astrolabe
astrology
astronomy

azimuthal
black hole
canicular
celestial
Centaurus (c.)
Chameleon (c.p.)
coelostat
Compasses (c.p.)
cosmogony
cosmology
Delphinus (c.)
elevation
Enceladus (sa.)
ephemeris
epicyclic
firmament
fixed star
Fomaihaut (s.)
giant star
Great Bear (c.p.)
heliostat
hour angle
libration
light year
Little Dog (c.p.)
longitude
lunisolar
magnitude
mesosphere
meteorite
meteoroid
Minuteman
Monoceros (c.)
novilunar
Nubeculae
Ophiuchus (c.)
parhelion
planetary
planetoid
Ploughman (c.p.)
Ptolemaic
radio star
reflector
refractor
Reticulum (c.)
satellite
solar wind
stargazer
starlight
sublunary
supernova
Swordfish (c.p.)
synodical
telescope

Telescope (c.p.)
uranology
Ursa Major (c.)
Ursa Minor (c.)
Via Lactea
Vulpecula (c.)

10

aberration
almucantar
altazimuth
apparition
asteroidal
astrologer
astrometer
astronomer
astronomic
Atlantides (g.)
atmosphere
Betelgeuse (s.)
brightness
Canis Major (c.)
Canis Minor (c.)
Cassiopeia (c.) (c.p.)
Chamaeleon (a.)
Charioteer (c.p.)
collimator
cometarium
Compass Box (c.p.)
Copernican
cosmic dust
cosmic rays
Crab nebula
depression
double star
earthshine
elongation
Euphrosyne (a.)
extrasolar
Flying Fish (c.p.)
green flash
Greyhounds (c.p.)
Horologium (c.)
hour circle
ionosphere
Lesser Bear (c.p.)
Little Bear (c.p.)
Little Lion (c.p.)
lunar cycle
lunar month
lunar probe
Microscope (c.p.)
North Star
opposition

Orion's Belt
outer space
paraselene
perihelion
precession
prominence
quadrature
refraction
retrograde
Sea Serpent (c.p.)
selenology
siderolite
solar cycle
solar flare
stargazing
supergiant
terminator
trajectory
Triangulum (c.)
tropopause
uranoscopy
Water Snake (c.p.)
white dwarf

11

astrography
astronomize
Baily's Beads
blazing star
Capricornus (c.)
conjunction
coronagraph
cosmography
declination
Evening Star (p.)
falling star
Gegenschein
giant planet
Hunting Dogs (c.p.)
last quarter
Little Horse (c.p.)
major planet
metemptosis
meteorolite
minor planet
Morning Star (p.)
neutron star
observatory
occultation
Orion's Sword
photosphere
planetarium
planisphere
radio source

Sagittarius (c.)
solar system
Southern Fly (c.p.)
spectrology
Telescopium (c.)
terrestrial
uranography
Water Bearer (c.p.)
Winged Horse (c.p.)

12

astronautics
astronomical
astrophysics
Charles's Wain (g.)
chromosphere
crescent moon
Doppler shift
eccentricity
first quarter
Halley's comet
heliocentric
interstellar
lunar eclipse
Metonic Cycle
Microscopium (c.)
Saturn's rings
selenography
shooting star
sidereal time
solar eclipse
Southern Fish (c.p.)
spectroscope

spiral galaxy
stratosphere
uranographic
Van Allen Belt
variable star

13

Alpha Centauri (s.)
Berenice's Hair (c.p.)
Canes Venatici (c.)
Coma Berenices (c.)
constellation
Crux Australis (c.)
Doppler effect
draconic month
extragalactic
intergalactic
meteorography
Northern Crown (c.p.)
Painter's Easel (c.p.)
River Eridanus (c.p.)
scintillation
Serpent Bearer (c.p.)
sidereal clock
Southern Cross (c.p.)
Southern Crown (c.p.)
Wolf–Rayet star
zodiacal light

14

annular eclipse
Aurora Borealis
Bird of Paradise (c.p.)

Camelopardalis (c.)
Corona Borealis (c.)
interplanetary
Musca Australis (c.)
northern lights
partial eclipse
radio astronomy
radio telescope
right ascension
Sculptor's Tools (c.p.)
summer solstice
transit of Venus
vertical circle
winter solstice
zenith distance

15 AND 16

Alphonsine tables (16)
armillary sphere (15)
astronomical unit (16)
Aurora Australis (15)
celestial sphere (15)
Corona Australis (c.) (15)
Fraunhofer lines (15)
Hubble's constant (15)
Magellanic Clouds (16)
meteoric showers (15)
Piscis Austrinus (c.) (15)
Proxima Centauri (15)
Rudolphine tables (16)
Sculptor's Chisel (c.) (15)
Southern Triangle (c.p.) (16)

Biology, biochemistry, botany, and zoology

2 AND 3	gut	anus	food	lung	urea
ADH	IAA	apex	foot	milk	vein
ADP	jaw	axil	gall	NADH	wilt
ATP	lip	axon	gene	NADP	wing
bud	NAD	bark	germ	neck	wood
CNS	ova	bile	gill	node	yolk
cud	pod	bird	haem	ovum	
DNA	rib	body	hair	palp	**5**
ear	RNA	bone	hand	pith	actin
egg	rod	bulb	head	pome	akene
ER	sac	burr	hoof	pore	algae
eye	sap	cell	host	root	aorta
FAD	sex	claw	iris	salt	aster
fin	**4**	cone	leaf	seed	auxin
gel	alar	cork	lens	skin	berry
gum	anal	corm	life	stem	bifid
		cyst	limb	tail	birth

blood	ovate	annual	labium	thorax	cuticle
bract	ovoid	anther	labrum	tissue	cutting
brain	ovule	apical	lacuna	tongue	diploid
bursa	penis	artery	lamina	turgor	dormant
calyx	petal	atrium	larynx	ureter	ecdysis
chyle	phage	biceps	leaves	uterus	ecology
chyme	plant	biotic	lignin	vagina	elastin
cilia	pubic	biotin	lipase	vessel	enteron
class	pubis	botany	lysine	vision	entozoa
clime	pupil	branch	mammal	zygote	epiboly
clone	ramus	bulbil	mantle	zymase	epigeal
codon	resin	caecum	marrow		gastric
colon	scale	canine	mucous	**7**	genital
cutin	semen	carpal	muscle		gizzard
cycad	sense	carpet	mutant	abdomen	gliadin
cycle	sepal	caudal	nastic	acyclic	glottis
cyton	shell	chaeta	nectar	adenine	habitat
death	shoot	chitin	nekton	adipose	haploid
digit	sinus	climax	neural	adrenal	hearing
drupe	skull	cloaca	neuron	aerobic	hepatic
druse	slide	coccus	oocyte	albumen	histone
fauna	smell	coccyx	oogamy	albumin	hormone
femur	sperm	cocoon	ovisac	amylase	humerus
fibre	spine	coelum	palate	anatomy	incisor
flora	spore	colony	palpus	annulus	insulin
fruit	stoma	cornea	pappus	antenna	isogamy
gemma	style	cortex	pectin	antigen	jejunum
genus	sweat	dermis	pelvic	asexual	keratin
gland	taste	dormin	pelvis	atavism	lactase
gonad	taxis	embryo	phloem	auricle	lacteal
graft	testa	enamel	phylum	benthos	lamella
group	thigh	energy	pistil	biology	lignose
heart	tibia	enzyme	plasma	biotope	linkage
hilum	touch	facial	pollen	bipolar	mammary
humus	trunk	faeces	purine	bladder	maxilla
hymen	tuber	family	rachis	blubber	medulla
hypha	urine	fibril	radius	bronchi	meiosis
ileum	vagus	fibrin	rectum	cambium	mitosis
imago	villi	fibula	retina	capsule	myotome
labra	virus	floral	runner	cardiac	nectary
larva	whorl	flower	sacrum	carotid	neurone
latex	wrist	foetus	sexual	cell sap	nostril
linin	xylem	forest	spinal	chaetae	nucleus
liver	zooid	fusion	spleen	chalaza	obovate
lymph		gamete	stamen	chiasma	obovoid
lysin	**6**	gemmae	stigma	chorion	oogonia
molar		genome	stolon	cochlea	organic
mouth	achene	girdle	sucker	conifer	osmosis
mucus	aerobe	growth	tactic	cordate	oviduct
nasal	agamic	gullet	tannin	corolla	ovulate
nerve	albino	hybrid	telome	cranial	oxidase
order	allele	hyphae	tendon	cranium	papilla
organ	amnion	joints	tensor	creeper	pedicel
ovary	amoeba	labial	testis	cristae	pedicle
	animal			culture	

petiole
pharynx
pigment
pinnate
plastid
plumule
protein
pyloric
radicle
rhachis
rhizoid
rhizome
root cap
species
spindle
sternum
stomach
stomata
suberin
synapse
syncarp
synergy
syngamy
systole
tap root
tapetum
teleost
tetanus
thallus
thyroid
trachea
triceps
trophic
tropism
trypsin
urethra
vacuole
viscera
vitamin
yolk sac
zoogamy
zoology

8

abductor
abscisin
acoelous
acrosome
adductor
aeration
alkaloid
allogamy
alveolus
amitosis

amoeboid
anaerobe
antibody
apospory
appendix
auditory
autogamy
bacteria
basidium
biennial
bile duct
biomorph
bisexual
blastema
blastula
brachial
carapace
carotene
cell wall
cellular
cerebral
cerebrum
chordate
clavicle
cleavage
clitoris
coenzyme
collagen
cytology
demersal
dendrite
diastase
duodenum
ectoderm
efferent
egestion
endoderm
entozoon
epiblast
feedback
flagella
flatworm
follicle
ganglion
genetics
genitals
genotype
geotaxis
germ cell
holdfast
holozoic
homodont
homogamy
hypogeal

inner ear
involute
isotropy
lamellae
lenticel
life span
ligament
mast cell
maxillae
membrane
meristem
mesoderm
midbrain
moulting
movement
muscular
mutation
mycelium
mycology
nerve net
nucellus
ontogeny
oogonium
organism
pancreas
papillae
parasite
pectoral
perianth
pericarp
perineum
placenta
plankton
polarity
polysome
pregnant
prop root
prophase
protozoa
receptor
ribosome
root hair
ruminant
sclereid
seedling
skeleton
spiracle
symbiont
synapsis
syncarpy
taxonomy
tegument
tentacle
thalamus

thiamine
tracheid
tympanum
vascular
vertebra
virology
xenogamy
zoospore

9

adrenalin
allantois
amino acid
anabolism
anaerobic
aneuploid
anisogamy
antennule
appendage
arteriole
atavistic
autonomic
basal body
bifarious
bionomics
biorhythm
branchial
branching
capillary
carnivore
cartilage
cellulase
cellulose
centriole
chiasmata
chromatid
chromatin
chrysalis
coenobium
coenocyte
commensal
community
convolute
corpuscle
cotyledon
cytoplasm
Darwinism
diaphragm
dichotomy
digestion
dimorphic
dominance
dura mater
ecosystem

ectoplasm
endocrine
endoplasm
endosperm
endospore
endostyle
epidermis
eukaryote
evolution
excretion
excretory
exodermis
fertilize
flagellum
folic acid
forebrain
germinate
gestation
guttation
gynaeceum
gynaecium
gynoecium
haemocoel
halophyte
herbivore
heterosis
hindbrain
histology
homospory
hypocotyl
ingestion
inhibitor
internode
intestine
isotropic
life cycle
life forms
limnology
megaspore
metaplasm
micropyle
microsome
middle ear
migration
morphosis
mutagenic
nephridia
nerve cell
notochord
nucleolus
olfactory
oogenesis
operculum
optic lobe

organelle
organogeny
ovulation
oxidation
pacemaker
perennial
pericycle
Petri dish
phagocyte
phellogen
phenology
phenotype
phycology
phylogeny
pituitary
polar body
polyploid
proboscis
protozoan
pulmonary
pyridoxal
recessive
reflex arc
reticulum
retractor
sclerotic
sebaceous
secretion
secretory
selection
sieve cell
sieve tube
sporangia
sporogony
sterility
substrate
succulent
symbiosis
synecious
synoicous
telophase
tricuspid
umbilical
unisexual
ventricle
xerophyte
zoogamous

10

achromatin
acoelomate
actomyosin
albuminoid
alimentary

androecium
antheridia
archegonia
archespore
autecology
biogenesis
biological
biometrics
biophysics
blastocoel
blastocyst
blastoderm
blastomere
blastopore
bronchiole
catabolism
centromere
centrosome
cerebellum
chemotaxis
chromomere
chromosome
coleoptile
copulation
dehiscence
dermatogen
dimorphism
embryology
entomology
enzymology
epididymis
epiglottis
epithelium
etiolation
fibrinogen
generation
geotropism
glomerulus
grey matter
guard cells
hemocyanin
hemoglobin
herbaceous
hereditary
heterodont
homocercal
homozygote
homozygous
hygrophyte
hypophysis
incubation
inhibition
integument
interferon

involution
Krebs cycle
Lamarckism
leaf sheath
leucoplast
locomotion
lymphocyte
mesenteron
metabolism
monoecious
morphology
mother cell
mycorrhiza
nephridium
nerve fibre
neural tube
nitrifying
nucleotide
oesophagus
omnivorous
osteoblast
osteoclast
parasitism
parenchyma
pathogenic
periosteum
phelloderm
photonasty
phototaxis
physiology
pineal body
polyploidy
population
prokaryote
prothallus
protoplasm
pyridoxine
saprophyte
sarcolemma
schizogony
sieve plate
splanchnic
sporangium
sporophyte
stone cells
strophiole
subspecies
succession
synecology
vegetation
vegetative
vertebrate
viviparity
viviparous

11

aestivation
allelomorph
anisotropic
antheridium
antibiotics
archegonium
archenteron
astrobotany
autotrophic
autotropism
biodynamics
blastocoele
carbon cycle
carboxylase
carnivorous
chlorophyll
chloroplast
chromoplast
collenchyma
competition
conjugation
deamination
desiccation
eccrinology
endothelium
environment
erythrocyte
exoskeleton
facultative
gall bladder
gametophyte
genetic code
germination
Golgi bodies
haemocyanin
haemoglobin
halophilous
heterospory
hibernation
homeostatic
homeostatis
infundibulum
inheritance
lipoprotein
loop of Henle
monoculture
monomorphic
muscle fibre
nematoblast
nucleic acid
orientation
parturition

pericardium
pinocytosis
plasmodesma
plasmolysis
polar bodies
pollination
polypeptide
pseudopodia
pyramidines
respiration
somatic cell
spermatozoa
sub-cellular
tapetal cell
thermotaxis
unicellular
white matter
X chromosome
Y chromosome
zooplankton

12

all-or-nothing
archesporium
astrobiology
back-crossing
bacteriology
basal granule
biochemistry
biosynthesis
buccal cavity
cell division
chondroblast
denitrifying
diploblastic
distribution
ectoparasite
endoparasite
endoskeleton
fermentation
flexor muscle
gastrulation
heliotropism
heterocercal
heterogamete
heterogamous
heterozygous
homoeostasis
homoeostatic
hypothalamus
invagination
invertebrate
keratogenous
mammary gland

medullary ray
microbiology
mitochondria
myelin sheath
nerve impulse
palaeobotany
phospholipid
phototropism
pyridoxamine
radiobiology
red blood cell
reductionism
reproduction
sclerenchyma
smooth muscle
spermatozoid
telolecithal
trace element
zoochemistry

13

accommodation
acotyledonous
bacteriophage
bicuspid valve
binary fission
biodegradable
bioenergetics
blastogenesis
cephalization
chemoreceptor
decomposition
dental formula
erector muscle
extracellular
Fallopian tube
fertilization
hermaphrodite
homoiothermic

insectivorous
intracellular
marine biology
micro-organism
mitochondrion
morphogenesis
multinucleate
organogenesis
ovoviviparity
ovoviviparous
palisade cells
parthenocarpy
photoreceptor
phytoplankton
plasmodesmata
proprioceptor
striped muscle
thermotropism
thigmotropism
translocation

transpiration
triploblastic

14 AND 15

bioengineering (14)
Brunner's glands (14)
chemosynthesis (14)
extensor muscle (14)
Haversian canal (14)
multiple fission (15)
osmoregulation (14)
oxyhaemoglobin (14)
parthenogenesis (15)
photoperiodism (14)
photosynthesis (14)
poikilothermic (14)
polysaccharide (14)
vascular bundle (14)
voluntary muscle (15)

Chemistry and metallurgy

2 AND 3

azo
DDT
DNA
dye
gas
ion
lab
mu
oil
ore
pH
PVA
PVC
RNA
sol
tin
TNT

4

acid
acyl
alum
aryl
atom
base
bond
Buna
calx

cell
clay
coal
coke
dyad
enol
gold
iron
keto
lead
lime
meta
mica
mole
mond
neon
rust
salt
slag
soda
spin
zinc

5

agene
agent
aldol
alkyl
alloy
amide

amine
amino
anion
arene
argon
assay
azote
basic
beryl
borax
boron
brass
braze
ester
ether
ethyl
Freon
group
imine
inert
Invar
ionic
leach
Lysol
metal
model
molal
molar
monad
niton

nitre
nylon
oxide
ozone
phase
poise
radon
redox
resin
roast
salol
salts
smelt
solid
steel
sugar
vinyl
wootz
xenon

6

acetal
acetic
acetyl
acidic
adduct
aerate
alkali
alkane
alkene

alkyne
amatol
ammine
anneal
atomic
barite
barium
baryta
biuret
bleach
borane
borate
bronze
buffer
butane
carbon
cation
cerium
chrome
cobalt
copper
cresol
curium
decane
dilute
dipole
dry ice
energy
erbium
ethane

ferric
galena
halide
helium
indium
iodate
iodide
iodine
iodite
iodize
ionium
isomer
kation
ketone
labile
ligand
liquid
litmus
lysine
methyl
natron
nickel
octane
olefin
osmium
oxygen
period
pewter
phenol
phenyl

273

potash
proton
quartz
radium
reduce
refine
reflux
retort
ribose
rutile
silica
silver
sinter
sodium
solder
solute
starch
sterol
sulfur
tannin
Teflon
thoria
thoron
thymol
xylose

7

acetate
acetone
acidity
aerosol
alchemy
alcohol
alembic
alumina
amalgam
ammonal
ammonia
amylose
analyse
aniline
anodize
antacid
arsenic
aspirin
barytes
bauxite
bell jar
benzene
bismuth
bitumen
bonding
bromate
bromide

bromine
burette
cadmium
caesium
calcium
calomel
camphor
carbide
chemist
chloric
coal tar
cocaine
codeine
colloid
corrode
crystal
cuprite
cyanate
cyanide
dextran
dextrin
dialyse
dibasic
dioxide
ebonite
element
entropy
ferment
fermium
ferrate
ferrite
ferrous
formate
formula
gallium
gelatin
glucose
hafnium
halogen
holmium
hydrate
hydride
iridium
isotope
krypton
leucine
leucite
lithium
menthol
mercury
methane
micelle
mineral
monomer

naphtha
neutral
niobium
nitrate
nitride
nitrite
orbital
organic
osmosis
osmotic
oxidant
oxidize
oxyacid
pentane
pentose
Perspex
pig iron
plastic
polymer
propane
pyrites
quinine
rare gas
reagent
red lead
rhenium
rhodium
silicon
soda-ash
soluble
solvent
sorbite
spectra
spelter
sucrose
sulfate
sulfide
sulfite
sulphur
terbium
terpene
thorium
thulium
titrate
toluene
tritium
uranide
uranium
valence
valency
Veronal
vitriol
wolfram
yttrium

8

actinide
actinism
actinium
aldehyde
alkaline
aluminum
ammonium
analysis
antimony
aromatic
arsenate
arsenide
asbestos
astatine
atropine
Bakelite
benzoate
Bessemer
bivalent
caffeine
carbolic
carbonic
carbonyl
cast iron
catalyse
catalyst
charcoal
chemical
chlorate
chloride
chlorine
chromate
chromite
chromium
cinnabar
corundum
covalent
cryolite
cyanogen
dextrose
dialysis
diatomic
didymium
dissolve
divalent
electron
emission
emulsion
enthalpy
ethylene
europium
firedamp

fluoride
fluorine
francium
fructose
glucinum
glycerin
glycerol
graphite
gunmetal
half-life
haloform
hematite
hydrated
hydrogen
hydroxyl
inert gas
iodoform
isomeric
kerosene
keto form
levulose
litharge
lone pair
lutecium
lutetium
magnesia
Manganin
marsh gas
masurium
melamine
methanal
methanol
molecule
monoxide
Nichrome
nicotine
nitrogen
nobelium
noble gas
non-metal
oxidizer
paraffin
periodic
peroxide
phosgene
platinum
plumbago
polonium
pot metal
reactant
reaction
refining
rock salt
rubidium

samarium
saturate
scandium
selenium
silicane
silicate
silicone
solution
suboxide
sulphate
sulphide
sulphite
tantalum
tartrate
test tube
thallium
titanium
tribasic
trioxide
tungsten
unit cell
unstable
vanadium
water gas

9

acetylene
acylation
alchemist
alcoholic
aliphatic
allotrope
allotropy
aluminate
aluminium
americium
amino acid
anhydride
anhydrous
apparatus
aqua regia
atmolysis
bell metal
berkelium
beryllium
bivalence
black lead
boric acid
brimstone
carbonate
catalysis
catalytic
cellulose
chemistry

chokedamp
cobaltite
copolymer
corrosion
covalence
deuterium
diazonium
digitalin
duralumin
elastomer
erythrite
flotation
fulminate
galactose
galvanize
germanium
glucoside
glyceride
guncotton
gunpowder
haematite
histamine
homolysis
homolytic
hydration
hydrazine
hydroxide
indicator
inorganic
insoluble
ionic bond
isomerism
laevulose
lanthanum
limestone
limewater
magnesium
magnetite
malic acid
manganese
metalloid
millerite
molecular
monatomic
neodymium
neptunium
nitration
oxidation
palladium
permalloy
petroleum
phosphate
phosphide
plutonium

polar bond
polyamide
polybasic
polyester
polythene
polyvinyl
potassium
pyrolysis
quicklime
raffinose
rare earth
rare gases
reductant
reduction
resonance
ruthenium
saltpetre
semimetal
solvation
stability
strontium
sulphuric
synthesis
synthetic
tellurite
tellurium
titration
univalent
verdigris
vulcanite
white lead
ytterbium
zirconium

10

acetic acid
alkalinity
alkyl group
allotropes
amphoteric
analytical
bimetallic
bisulphate
bond energy
bond length
carnallite
catenation
chalybeate
chemically
chloroform
cinchonine
citric acid
constantan
dative bond

dichromate
double bond
dysprosium
electronic
enantiomer
eudiometer
exothermic
formic acid
free energy
gadolinium
heavy water
homocyclic
hydrolysis
ionization
isocyanide
laboratory
lactic acid
lanthanide
lawrencium
metallurgy
metamerism
mischmetal
molybdenum
monovalent
Muntz metal
natural gas
neutralize
nitric acid
oxalic acid
phosphorus
picric acid
polyatomic
polymerize
promethium
rare earths
saccharate
saccharide
solubility
sphalerite
technetium
trivalence
viscometer
white metal
zinc blende
zwitterion

11

accelerator
acetylation
acrylic acid
benzene ring
benzoic acid
bicarbonate
californium

carborundum
cassiterite
chloric acid
cobalt bloom
crystallize
cyclohexane
dehydration
einsteinium
electrolyte
elimination
endothermic
equilibrium
free radical
German steel
Glauber salt
haloid acids
heterolytic
hydrocarbon
hydrocyanic
laughing gas
litmus paper
mendelevium
Mond process
naphthalene
non-metallic
oxidization
paraldehyde
phosphonate
phosphorous
pitchblende
polystyrene
polyvalence
precipitate
prussic acid
quicksilver
radioactive
radiocarbon
ribonucleic
sal ammoniac
Schiff's base
sebacic acid
sublimation
substituent
tautomerism
tetravalent
transuranic
wrought iron
zone melting

12

acetaldehyde
alkali metals
alkyl halides
atomic number

atomic theory
atomic weight
benzaldehyde
blast furnace
Bunsen burner
butanoic acid
carbocations
carbohydrate
carbonic acid
chlorination
condensation
covalent bond
deliquescent
diamagnetism
disaccharide
dissociation
distillation
electrolysis
fermentation
formaldehyde
German silver
Haber process

halogenation
hydrochloric
hydrogen bond
muriatic acid
permanganate
praseodymium
prince's metal
protactinium
radioisotope
rate constant
Rochelle salt
sulphonamide
tartaric acid
zone refining

13

Bessemer steel
carbon dioxide
chain reaction
chromium steel
hydrochloride
hydrosulphate

lattice energy
molecular mass
paramagnetism
periodic table
petrochemical
precipitation
protoactinium
recrystallize
reducing agent
sulphuric acid
trisaccharide

14 AND OVER

aufbau principle (15)
Born–Haber cycle (14)
Britannia metal (14)
carbon monoxide (14)
carboxylic acid (14)
Chile saltpetre (14)
decarbonization (15)
deoxyribonucleic (16)
diazonium salts (14)

electrochemical (15)
esterification (14)
ferro-manganese (14)
ferrous sulphate (15)
giant structures (15)
Grignard reagent (15)
microchemistry (14)
molecular weight (15)
monosaccharide (14)
nitrogen dioxide (15)
nitroglycerine (14)
organo-metallic (14)
oxidizing agent (14)
oxonium compound
  (15)
phosphor bronze (14)
photosynthesis (14)
polysaccharide (14)
reaction kinetics (16)
saponification (14)
trinitrotoluene (15)

Computers

1 AND 2

AI
C
CD
IT
PC
w.p.

3

ADA
alt
APL
Avr
BOS
bug
CAD
CAM
COM
CPL
CPU
DOS
DTP
end
esc
fax
key
OCR

pad
PIN
POP
PSU
RAM
ROM
RSI
tab
VDT
VDU
wpm
zap

4

baud
boot
byte
chip
code
copy
data
disc
disk
down
drag
dump
edit
exit

feed
file
font
hack
home
icon
ikon
JAVA
LISP
load
LOGO
loop
menu
MIDI
move
nest
peek
poll
port
quit
read
save
scan
sort
type
unit
WIMP

5

Algol
ASCII
BASIC
CD-ROM
Cobol
COMAL
CORAL
crash
debug
drive
E-mail
enter
erase
field
FORTH
fount
input
key in
log in
log on
macro
micro
modem
mouse
octal
pixel

queue
reset
slave
store
virus
write

6

access
AZERTY
back up
binary
boot up
cursor
decode
delete
escape
folder
format
hacker
hopper
indent
JOVIAL
keypad
laptop
memory
on-line
ouput

PASCAL
PILOT
Prolog
QWERTY
reboot
return
screen
scroll
sector
server
sign on
SNOBOL
window

7

address
booting
circuit
command
console
corrupt
default
density
desktop
display
emulate
execute
Fortran

gigabit
hot zone
imaging
kilobit
menu bar
monitor
network
off-line
pointer
polling
printer
program
readout
recover
scanner
sort key
storage
surfing
toolbox
toolkit
upgrade
zip disk

8

arrow key
capacity
caps lock
cold boot
databank
database
diskette
document
download
emulator
function
gigabyte
graphics
hard disk
hardware
internet
joystick
key punch
keyboard
kilobyte
language
light pen
megabyte
password
printout
real time
recovery

register
scramble
shift key
shut down
software
space bar
spooling
terminal
typeface
warm boot
word wrap
zip drive

9

alternate
backspace
character
cycle time
deprogram
directory
disk drive
dot matrix
facsimile
half space
hard error
interface
jumbo chip
mail-merge
mainframe
microchip
neurochip
overwrite
paper tray
processor
range left
repeat key
scrambler
soft error
word break

10

alphameric
daisy wheel
de-scramble
file server
floppy disk
memory bank
numeric pad
peripheral
processing
programmer

range right
spellcheck
stand alone
system disk
throughput
wraparound

11

application
circuit card
cut and paste
data capture
diagnostics
display mode
display unit
function key
input device
line printer
machine code
numberic pad
silicon chip
spreadsheet
Trojan Horse
unformatted
visual BASIC
work station

12

addition time
alphanumeric
bubble memory
circuit board
direct access
dumb terminal
home computer
housekeeping
integer BASIC
laser printer
machine cycle
output device
random access
response time
serial access
user friendly

13

alphabetic pad
compatibility
display screen
double density
justified text

microcomputer
postprocessor
query language
remote station
word processor

14

author language
computer dating
data processing
data protection
electronic mail
microprocessor
read-only memory
remote terminal
systems analyst
word processing

15

computer science
computerization
double-sided disk
machine language
natural language
storage capacity
systems analysis

16

assembly language
bubblejet printer
compiler language
computer engineer
computer language
computer literacy
computer operator
computer-literate
control character
dot matrix printer
low-level language
personal computer

17

assembler language
dedicated computer
desk-top publishing
high-level language
satellite computer
satellite terminal
synthetic language

Dyes, paints and colours

3

bay
dun
hue
jet
lac
red
tan
vat

4

acid
anil
ashy
bice
bise
blue
buff
cyan
dark
deep
drab
ecru
fast
fawn
gilt
gold
gray
grey
gris
hoar
jade
kohl
lake
navy
pale
pink
puce
roan
room
rose
ruby
rust
sage
saxe
vert
weld
wine
woad
wold

5

amber
ashen
azure
azurn
basic
beige
black
blond
brown
camel
chica
coral
cream
diazo
ebony
flame
grain
green
gules
hazel
henna
hoary
ivory
jetty
khaki
lemon
light
lilac
livid
lovat
mauve
murex
ocher
ochre
ochry
olive
paint
peach
perse
raven
rouge
ruddy
sable
sandy
sepia
snowy
sooty
stain
taupe
tawny

ulmin
umber
white

6

anatta
anatto
auburn
aureat
aurora
azo dye
azured
bablah
bistre
bluish
bronze
canary
cerise
cherry
chrome
claret
cobalt
copper
damask
direct
enamel
fallow
flaxen
fulvid
fustic
ginger
golden
greeny
indigo
Isabel
kamala
kermes
lac dye
litmus
lustre
madder
mallow
maroon
minium
modena
morone
murrey
orange
orchil
ormulu
pastel
purple

raddle
reddle
reseda
rubian
rubied
rubric
ruddle
rufous
russet
sallow
sanded
sienna
silver
sorrel
spotty
titian
Tyrian
umbery
vat dye
vermil
violet
yellow

7

alkanet
annatto
apricot
aureate
avocado
barwood
bezetta
biscuit
camboge
camwood
carmine
carotin
carroty
cassius
catechu
cerulin
cesious
chermes
citrine
cramesy
crimson
cudbear
cyanine
darkish
emerald
flavine
fulvous
fuscous

gamboge
gentian
grayish
greyish
grizzle
grizzly
hazelly
ingrain
logwood
magenta
mahaleb
minious
mordant
mottled
munjeet
mustard
nacarat
nankeen
nattier
natural
neutral
old gold
olivine
piebald
pigment
pinkish
plunket
red lead
reddish
rubican
ruby red
russety
saffron
scarlet
silvern
silvery
sinopic
sinople
sky blue
solvent
spotted
stammel
streaky
striped
sulphur
swarthy
verdant
vermiel
whiting
whitish
xanthic

xanthin
zaphara

8

alizarin
amaranth
amethyst
ash blond
ashy pale
baby blue
bloncket
blood red
brazilin
brownish
brunette
burgundy
caesious
cardinal
carotene
cerulean
cerulein
chay root
chestnut
chromule
cinnabar
cramoisy
croceate
croceous
dark blue
disperse
dyestuff
eau de Nil
eggshell
glaucous
greenish
gridelin
grizzled
gunmetal
icterine
iron grey
jet black
lavender
litharge
luteolin
mandarin
mazarine
mulberry
navy blue
Nile blue
nut brown
oak stain
ochreous

off-white
orpiment
palomino
pea green
philamot
primrose
purplish
purpurin
raw umber
red ochre
rose pink
rose-hued
rubicund
rubrical
saffrony
sanguine
santalin
sap green
sapphire
saxe blue
sea green
speckled
streaked
tincture
titanium
turmeric
verditer
viridian
xanthine

9

albescent
anthocyan
argentine
aubergine
azure tint
bloodshot
blue-black
boneblack
brilliant
caerulean
calcimine
carnation
carnelian
champagne
chaya root
chocolate
chrome red
cinereous
coal black
cochineal
colcothar
colour box
columbine

coralline
curcumine
double dye
draconine
duck green
dun colour
Dutch pink
dyer's weed
dyestuffs
encrimson
envermeil
erythrean
euchioric
foliomort
Indian red
indigotin
jade green
kalsomine
lampblack
leaf-green
light blue
lily white
lime green
moss green
myrobalan
Nile green
oil colour
olive drab
oxidation
Paris blue
pearl grey
pigmental
pistachio
prasinous
puniceous
purpureal
purpurine
quercetin
royal blue
rufescent
safflower
sallowish
sap colour
sapanwood
sarcoline
Saxon blue
sky colour
snow-white
solferino
steel blue
steel grey
tangerine
turkey red
turquoise

verdigris
verditure
vermilion
vinaceous
virescent
white lead
yellowish
zinc white

10

alutaceous
apple green
aquamarine
Berlin blue
body colour
brazilwood
burnt umber
carthamine
chartreuse
Chinese red
cobalt blue
colour code
coquelicot
coromandel
double-dyed
dove colour
endochrome
erubescent
euchlorine
fiesta pink
flake white
flavescent
florentine
French grey
French navy
giallolina
grass green
heliotrope
indigo blue
ivory black
ivory white
morbidezza
mosaic gold
ochraceous
olivaceous
olive green
Oxford blue
Oxford grey
Paris green
Paris white
petrol blue
pigmentary
powder blue
puce colour

quercitrin
quercitron
roan colour
rose colour
ruby colour
salmon pink
sappanwood
silver grey
smaragdine
snowy white
spadiceous
Spanish red
stone ochre
strawberry
terracotta
terre verte
violaceous
whity-brown

11

anthocyanin
ash-coloured
bombycinous
bottle green
burnt orange
burnt sienna
chlorophyll
chrome green
cineritious
cinnamon red
crimson lake
dun-coloured
ferruginous
flame colour
flesh colour
fluorescent
hunting pink
incarnadine
king's yellow
lateritious
lemon yellow
liver colour
mouse colour
neutral tint
orange tawny
peach colour
peacock blue
stone colour
straw colour
substantive
terra sienna
ultramarine
Venetian red
Vienna white

viridescent
water colour
yellow ochre

12

airforce blue
Avignon berry
canary yellow
cherry colour
Chinese white
chrome colour
chrome yellow
claret colour
copper colour
dragon's blood
Egyptian blue
electric blue
emerald green
ferruginated
feuille morte
golden yellow
grain colours
greenish blue
Indian madder
Indian yellow
Lincoln green
midnight blue
Naples yellow
Persian berry
pillar-box red
Prussian blue
rose-coloured
sapphire blue
Spanish black
Spanish brown
Spanish white
Thenard's blue
Tyrian purple

13

Adrianople red
auripigmentum
Brunswick blue
cadmium yellow
Cambridge blue
chestnut brown
couleur de rose
cream-coloured
flame-coloured
flesh-coloured
monochromatic
peach-coloured
pepper-and-salt
rainbow-tinted

Scheele's green
slate-coloured
straw-coloured
tortoiseshell
trout-coloured
Venetian white

versicoloured

14 AND 15

atramentaceous (14)
Brunswick black (14)
Brunswick green (14)

chocolate colour (15)
copper-coloured (14)
heather-mixture (14)
highly coloured (14)
orange-coloured (14)
quercitron bark (14)

Engineering

2 AND 3

ace
amp
b.h.p.
bit
cam
cog
dam
e.m.f.
erg
fan
fit
gab
h.p.
hob
hub
ion
jib
key
lag
nut
ohm
oil
r.p.m.
ram
rig
sag
tap
taw
tew
tie
u.h.f.
v.h.f.

4

arch
axle
beam
belt
bolt
burr
byte
cast

coak
cone
cowl
flaw
flux
fuel
fuse
gear
glue
hasp
hook
hose
jack
kiln
lens
lift
link
lock
loom
main
mill
mine
nail
nave
oily
pawl
pile
pipe
plan
plug
pump
rack
rail
reel
road
rope
rung
rust
skid
slag
stay
stop
stud
sump

tamp
tank
test
tilt
tire
tool
tram
tube
turn
tyre
unit
vane
vent
void
volt
weir
weld
wire
work
worm

5

alloy
anode
binac
blast
braze
cable
chair
chase
civil
clamp
cleat
compo
crane
crank
crate
deuce
dowel
drill
drive
elbow
emery
felly

flume
flush
force
gauge
girder
H-beam
helix
hinge
hoist
ingot
input
jenny
jewel
joint
joist
keyed
laser
level
lever
lewis
miner
model
motor
mould
oakum
oiler
pedal
pivot
plant
power
press
pylon
quern
radar
radio
ratch
relay
resin
rigid
rivet
rough
rusty
screw
shaft

short
shunt
slack
slide
sling
smelt
spoke
spool
spout
stamp
steam
still
strap
strut
stulm
swage
swape
T-rail
taper
tewel
tommy
tools
tooth
train
valve
video
waste
wedge
wharf
wheel
wiper
works

6

aerial
analog
anneal
barrel
bit-end
blower
bobbin
boiler
bridge
buffer

burner
camber
clutch
column
coppin
cotter
couple
cradle
cut-out
damask
damper
derail
duplex
dynamo
energy
engine
felloe
fitter
flange
flashe
funnel
geyser
gutter
hinged
hooter
ingate
intake
jigger
kibble
lacing
ladder
lamina
latten
magnet
milled
mining
moment
monkey
nipple
nozzle
oilcan
oil-gas
output
petrol

pinion	**7**	lagging	tinning	fireclay	puddling
piston		lockage	torsion	fireplug	pump gear
pulley	adapter	locknut	tracing	flywheel	pump head
rarefy	adaptor	machine	treadle	fracture	purchase
repair	air duct	magneto	trolley	friction	radiator
retard	air pipe	male die	turbine	fuse clip	rag-wheel
rigger	air pump	manhole	turning	galvanic	railroad
rocket	air trap	mill dam	unrivet	gas gauge	recharge
roller	air tube	mill-cog	unscrew	gas mains	refinery
rotary	airfoil	milling	ventage	gasworks	register
rundle	airlock	monitor	viaduct	governor	rheostat
saggar	autovac	moulded	voltage	gradient	rigidity
sagger	battery	moulder	voltaic	hardware	ring bolt
saw pit	bearing	mud hole	welding	hot blast	rotatory
sheave	belting	nuclear	wet dock	hot press	shearing
siding	booster	Ohm's law	wringer	ignition	silk mill
sleeve	bracket	oil lamp	wrought	injecter	skew arch
sluice	caisson	oil pump	**8**	injector	smeltery
smiddy	casting	pattern		ink stone	smelting
smithy	cathode	pig iron	air brake	insulate	soft iron
socket	chamfer	pontoon	air valve	ironwork	split pin
solder	chimney	program	annealed	irrigate	stamping
spigot	cistern	pug mill	aqueduct	Jacquard	standard
static	clacker	rag bolt	axletree	joint box	starling
stoker	conduit	railway	ball cock	junk ring	stone pit
strain	cutting	ratchet	bevelled	laminate	stopcock
stress	derrick	reactor	bridging	land roll	tailrace
strike	digital	riveter	cam wheel	leverage	telotype
sucker	drawbar	road bed	camshaft	limekiln	tempered
switch	drawing	roadway	cassette	linch pin	template
swivel	dry dock	sawmill	cast iron	Linotype	terminal
system	dry pile	sea-bank	castings	lock gate	throttle
tackle	dynamic	sea-wall	catenary	lock sill	tide mill
tappet	exciter	shackle	chauffer	loop line	tide-gate
temper	exhaust	shuttle	cog wheel	magnetic	tilekiln
tender	eye-bolt	sleeper	compound	mechanic	tinplate
thrust	factory	smelter	computer	mill pond	tractile
tie-bar	ferrule	spindle	concrete	mill race	traction
tie-rod	firebox	stamper	contrate	momentum	tractive
tinned	fitting	statics	corn mill	monorail	tram rail
toggle	forging	suction	coupling	monotype	tramroad
torque	founder	sump-pit	cradling	Monotype	velocity
tripod	foundry	support	cylinder	moulding	water gas
trolly	fulcrum	syringe	Davy lamp	movement	wind pump
tubing	furnace	tamping	dead lift	mud valve	windmill
tunnel	fuse box	templet	draw gear	oil stove	wiredraw
tuyere	gas trap	tension	edge rail	oilstone	wireless
uncoil	gearing	test bay	electric	operator	wood mill
vacuum	gimbals	testing	elevator	overshot	workable
washer	gudgeon	thimble	engineer	ozonizer	workshop
welded	hydrant	tie-beam	eolipyle	pendulum	wormgear
welder	inertia	tilting	fan blast	penstock	
willow	jointer	tin mine	feed pipe	pile shoe	
	journal	tinfoil	feed pump	platform	
				pressure	

9

acoustics
aeolipyle
air engine
air filter
air vessel
amplifier
artificer
baseplate
bevel gear
blueprint
brakedrum
brakepipe
brick kiln
cast steel
chain belt
chainpump
clockwork
condenser
conductor
cotter pin
crosshead
cyclotron
datum line
dead level
diaphragm
disc brake
disk brake
dynamical
earthwork
eccentric
electrify
electrode
escalator
female die
fire brick
fish joint
fishplate
floodgate
fog signal
foot valve
force pump
framework
funicular
galvanize
gas engine
gas fitter
gas geyser
gas holder
gas retort
gasometer
gearwheel
horse mill

hydraulic
hydrostat
idle wheel
induction
inductive
inertness
injection
insertion
insulated
insulator
ironsmith
ironworks
jet engine
knife edge
laminated
lewis bolt
Leyden jar
limelight
lubricant
lubricate
machinery
machinist
magnetize
male screw
man engine
master key
mechanics
mechanism
mechanize
mild steel
millstone
mine shaft
mud sluice
nodal line
nose piece
oil geyser
oil-engine
perforate
petrol can
piston rod
pneumatic
polarizer
porous pot
power loom
programme
propeller
prototype
pump brake
pump spear
pump stock
radiation
rectifier
reflector
regulator

reservoir
resultant
rheomotor
rheophore
road metal
roughcast
sandpaper
shunt coil
sleeve nut
slide rule
smack mill
soapworks
soldering
spring box
spur wheel
stanchion
steam pipe
stock lock
stoke hole
structure
superheat
telephone
tempering
tin mining
transform
trunk line
turntable
twin cable
vibration
vulcanite
vulcanize
water tank
watermark
wheelrace
white heat
winepress
wire gauze
wire wheel
worm wheel

10

alternator
automation
automobile
bevel wheel
broad gauge
brush wheel
cantilever
case-harden
centigrade
chain-drive
clack valve
coach screw
combustion

crankshaft
crown wheel
dead weight
dielectric
discharger
diving bell
donkey pump
drawbridge
earthplate
efficiency
electrical
electronic
embankment
emery cloth
emery paper
emery wheel
engine room
escapement
fire escape
flange rail
fluid drive
footbridge
galvanized
gas turbine
glass paper
goods train
goods truck
grid system
gudgeon pin
guillotine
hair spring
heart wheel
hogger pipe
hogger pump
horsepower
hydrophore
idle pulley
Indian fire
instrument
insulating
insulation
iron heater
irrigation
isodynamic
laboratory
lamination
leaf bridge
lewis joint
lock paddle
locomotive
lubricator
macadamize
magnetizer
male thread

manila rope
mechanical
nodal point
paper cable
pentaspast
percolator
petrol tank
piledriver
pneumatics
powder mill
powerhouse
powerplant
programmer
pulverizer
pump handle
recondense
refraction
rejointing
resistance
revolution
safety-lamp
scoop-wheel
self-acting
skew bridge
smokestack
soap boiler
socket pipe
socket pole
solid state
spokeshave
steam gauge
streamline
structural
swing wheel
swivel hook
telegraphy
telescopic
television
telpherage
temper heat
thermopile
thermostat
torque tube
transients
transistor
tunnelling
unsoldered
voltaic arc
voltaplast
water crane
water power
water tower
watertight
waterwheel

waterworks
wave motion
well-boring
wind tunnel
wiped joint

11

accelerator
accumulator
air fountain
anelectrode
atomic clock
bell founder
bell foundry
block system
Bramah press
brush wheels
cable laying
candlepower
compression
computation
coupling box
coupling pin
damask steel
diamagnetic
dished wheel
driving band
driving belt
dynamometer
electrician
electricity
electrolyte
electrolyse
electronics
endless belt
engineering
exhaust pipe
female screw
frame bridge
graving dock
helical gear
incinerator
inking table
iron filings
iron founder
iron foundry
latten-brass
lock chamber
low pressure
lubrication
machine tool
maintenance
manila paper
manufactory

mechanician
narrow gauge
oil purifier
oil strainer
perforation
pile-driving
pillow block
pilot engine
power factor
rack-railway
rarefaction
retardation
revolutions
rolling mill
rubber cable
safety valve
searchlight
series-wound
service pipe
skeleton key
sleeve valve
socket joint
steam boiler
steam engine
steam hammer
stuffing box
stuffing nut
suction pipe
suction pump
summit level
superheater
swing bridge
switchboard
synchronism
synchronize
synchrotron
tappet valve
toggle joint
transformer
transmitter
trundle head
tube railway
underground
uninsulated
voltaic pile
vulcanizing
warping bank
water cement
water engine
water furrow
water hammer
water supply
welding heat
wind furnace

wire drawing
wire grading
workmanship
wrought iron

12

acceleration
aerodynamics
anti-friction
arterial road
artesian well
assembly line
balance wheel
belt fastener
blast furnace
block machine
block signals
buffing wheel
canalization
chain reactor
coaxial cable
counterpoise
danger signal
diamagnetism
diesel engine
differential
disc coupling
donkey engine
double acting
driving shaft
driving wheel
dry-core cable
eccentric rod
eduction pipe
electric fire
electric iron
electrolysis
electromotor
endless screw
exhaust valve
female thread
floating dock
flying bridge
flying pinion
founder's dust
founder's sand
friction gear
gas condenser
gas container
gas regulator
hanging valve
high pressure
hydraulic ram
hydrodynamic

inking roller
installation
jewel bearing
lubrifaction
machine tools
magnetomotor
marine boiler
marine engine
master spring
negative pole
non-conductor
nuclear power
oxyacetylene
petrol engine
petrol filter
plummer block
polarization
pressure pump
ratchet wheel
Réaumur scale
rolling press
rolling stock
service cable
short circuit
shunt winding
single-acting
sleeve button
solar battery
specific heat
spinning mill
stamping mill
steam heating
steam turbine
steam whistle
suction valve
synchronized
terminal post
thermocouple
toothed wheel
transmission
unmechanical
unmechanized
vibratiuncle
water turbine
wheel cutting
wheel-and-axle
working model

13

civil engineer
compound-wound
contrate wheel
control theory
Cornish engine

counterweight
direct current
draught engine
Drummond light
eccentric gear
electric cable
electric clock
electric light
electric motor
electric stove
electrifiable
electromagnet
engine-turning
expansion gear
floodlighting
fluid flywheel
friction balls
friction cones
friction wheel
injection cock
injection pipe
insulated wire
kinetic energy
lifting bridge
lubrification
magnetic fluid
magnetization
non-conducting
overshot wheel
pneumatic tyre

pontoon bridge
pressure gauge
printing press
rack-and-pinion
roller bearing
series winding
shock absorber
sniffing valve
standard gauge
telegraph line
telegraph pole
telegraph wire
telephone line
telephone wire
throttle valve
thrust bearing
water drainage
wave mechanics
whirling table

14

analog computer
blowing machine
diesel-electric
discharge valve
discharging rod
disintegration
eccentric strap
eccentric wheel
electric cooker

electric kettle
electrodynamic
electrostatics
electrothermic
explosive rivet
floating bridge
friction clutch
galvanized iron
hydraulic press
insulated cable
lubricating oil
magnetic needle
multi-core cable
nuclear reactor
pneumatic drill
portable engine
resino-electric
resultant force
shunt regulator
thermo-electric
three-core cable
traction engine
universal joint
voltaic battery
washing machine

15 AND 16

brake horsepower
concentric cable
digital computer

electric battery
electric circuit
electric current
electrification
electrochemical
electrodynamics
electrokinetics
electromagnetic
electronegative
electronic brain
electropositive
expansion engine
friction rollers
galvanic battery
hydraulic cement
insulating paper
irrigation canal
linotype machine
machine language
magnetic battery
magneto-electric
ohmic resistance
perpetual motion
pressure machine
railway engineer
smelting furnace
specific gravity
synchrocyclotron (16)
tensile strength
water-tube boiler

Instruments

2

PC

4 – 6

abacus
camera
clock
dial
dynamo
filter
flange
fleam
funnel
gasket
gauge
grid
lancet
laptop
laser

lens
lever
maser
Megger
meter
nozzle
octant
octile
orrery
pole
probe
relay
rule
ruler
scale
square
style
stylus
tester
toner

tool
trocar
tube
valve

7

aerator
ammeter
aneroid
balance
bellows
binocle
compass
counter
divider
monitor
pH meter
scriber
sextant
sundial

T-square
vernier
wetbulb

8

biograph
bioscope
boot tree
bootjack
calipers
computer
detector
diagraph
gasmeter
horologe
odometer
ohmmeter
otoscope
quadrant
receiver

recorder
rheostat
shoetree
solenoid
spy glass
udometer

9

aeolipyle
aerometer
altimeter
apparatus
arcograph
areometer
astrolabe
atmometer
auxometer
barograph
barometer
baroscope

callipers
clepsydra
compasses
condenser
dip circle
dynameter
dynometer
eidograph
eriometer
gasometer
generator
gyroscope
heliostat
hodometer
holometer
hour glass
litholabe
lithotome
logometer
magnifier

manometer
marigraph
megaphone
megascope
metronome
microtome
microtron
Nilometer
oleometer
optigraph
optometer
pedometer
periscope
polygraph
polyscope
pyrometer
pyroscope
rain gauge
rectifier
retractor
rheometer
rheoscope
rheotrope
rotameter
saccarium
scarifier
set-square
shot gauge
slide rule
steelyard
tasimeter
taximeter
telegraph
telephone
telescope
televisor
tellurion
tide gauge
voltmeter
wind gauge
zoeotrope
zymometer

10

acetimeter
acidimeter
altazimuth
anemograph
anemometer
anemoscope
angioscope
anglemeter
araeometer
astrometer

astroscope
audiometer
audiophone
binoculars
bow compass
calculator
calorifier
chiroplast
clinometer
collimator
cometarium
cryophorus
cyanometer
cyclograph
declinator
diagometer
drosometer
duplicator
ear-trumpet
elaeometer
elaiometer
endiometer
field glass
goniometer
gravimeter
heliograph
heliometer
helioscope
hydrometer
hydrophone
hydroscope
hyetograph
hyetometer
hygrometer
hygroscope
lactometer
lactoscope
macrometer
metrograph
micrometer
microphone
microscope
multimeter
multiplier
night glass
nitrometer
noctograph
ombrometer
pantagraph
pantograph
pantometer
pentagraph
phonograph
phonoscope

photometer
photophone
piezometer
plane-table
planimeter
pleximeter
protractor
pulsimeter
radiometer
respirator
rev counter
spirometer
steam-gauge
tachometer
teinoscope
theodolite
thermostat
transistor
tribometer
tuning-fork
typewriter
viscometer
voltameter
water-clock
water-gauge
water-meter

11

actinograph
actinometer
alkalimeter
auxanometer
beam compass
calorimeter
cardiograph
chlorometer
chronograph
chronometer
chronoscope
comptometer
cosmosphere
craniometer
dendrometer
depth-finder
dynamometer
graphometer
magnetophon
odontograph
optical lens
pluviometer
polarimeter
polariscope
polemoscope
pseudoscope

range-finder
salinometer
seismograph
seismometer
seismoscope
sideroscope
speedometer
spherograph
spherometer
stereometer
stereoscope
stethometer
stethoscope
teleprinter
thaumatrope
thermometer
thermoscope
transformer
transmitter
zymosimeter

12

aethrioscope
arithmometer
assay balance
averruncator
burning glass
camera lucida
chondrometer
control valve
declinometer
ductilimeter
electrometer
electrophone
electroscope
evaporometer
field glasses
galactometer
galvanometer
galvanoscope
harmonometer
inclinometer
kaleidoscope
laryngoscope
machine ruler
magnetograph
magnetometer
night glasses
opera glasses
oscillograph
parallel rule
psychrometer
reading glass
scarificator

sliding scale
spectrometer
spectroscope
sphygmometer
thermocouple
tuning hammer
weatherglass

13

alcoholometer
bubble chamber
burning mirror
camera obscura
chromatometer
diaphanometer
dipleidoscope
dipping needle
electric meter
electrophorus
esthesiometer
Geiger counter
pneumatometer
potentiometer
pressure gauge
probe scissors
pyrheliometer
refractometer
saccharometer
sidereal clock
spring balance
sympiesometer
watt-hour meter

14

aesthesiometer
air thermometer
desk calculator
geothermometer
hydrobarometer
interferometer
manifold writer
ophthalmoscope
radio telescope
sonic altimeter
torsion balance
wire micrometer

15

chemical balance
digital computer
magnifying glass
mariner's
  compass
solar microscope

285

Mathematics

2 AND 3

add
arc
cos
cot
l.c.d.
l.c.m.
log
map
pi
sec
set
sin
sum
tan

4

apex
area
axes
axis
base
cone
cosh
cube
cusp
edge
face
line
loci
lune
math
mean
node
null
plus
ring
root
sine
sinh
surd
term
trig
unit
zero

5

acute
angle
bevel
chord

conic
cosec
cotan
cubed
cubic
curve
digit
equal
field
focal
focus
graph
group
helix
index
lemma
limit
locus
maths
minus
plane
point
power
prime
prism
proof
radii
radix
range
ratio
rhomb
rider
solid
table
unity
value

6

abacus
binary
bisect
centre
choice
circle
conics
conoid
convex
cosine
cuboid
cyclic
degree
denary

divide
domain
equals
factor
figure
finite
height
heptad
isogon
matrix
maxima
median
minima
minute
modulo
moment
normal
number
oblate
oblong
obtuse
octant
origin
pentad
radian
radius
random
result
scalar
secant
sector
senary
series
sphere
square
subset
tables
tensor
tetrad
vector
vertex
volume

7

algebra
aliquot
average
bracket
cissoid
commute
complex
concave

conical
cubical
cycloid
decagon
decimal
divisor
ellipse
evolute
fluxion
formula
fractal
hexagon
indices
integer
inverse
lattice
mapping
maximum
minimum
modulus
nothing
numeral
numeric
oblique
octagon
octuple
ordinal
percent
polygon
problem
product
prolate
pyramid
quinary
rhombic
rhombus
scalene
segment
squared
subtend
surface
tangent
ternary
ternion
theorem
totient
trapeze
unitary
unknown
vernier

8

abscissa
addition
algorism
aliquant
analysis
argument
binomial
bisector
brackets
calculus
centrode
centuple
circular
codomain
conoidal
constant
cosecant
cube root
cubiform
cuboidal
cylinder
diagonal
diameter
dihedral
division
elliptic
equation
exponent
formulae
fraction
frustrum
function
geometer
geometry
gradient
helicoid
heptagon
identity
infinite
infinity
integers
integral
involute
isogonal
mantissa
matrices
monomial
multiple
multiply
negative

new maths
numerary
numerate
octonary
operator
ordinate
osculate
parabola
parallel
pentagon
positive
prismoid
quadrant
quadrate
quantity
quartile
quotient
rational
repetend
rhomboid
rotation
septimal
sequence
sextuple
spheroid
subgroup
subtract
symmetry
tetragon
totitive
triangle
trigonal
trochoid
variable
vicenary
vinculum

9

algebraic
algorithm
asymptote
Cartesian
chi-square
chiliagon
compasses
corollary
cotangent
curvature
decagonal
dimension
directrix
dodecagon

duodenary
eccentric
ellipsoid
Euclidean
expansion
factorize
fluxional
frequency
geometric
hemicycle
hexagonal
hyperbola
imaginary
increment
inflexion
intersect
isosceles
logarithm
Napierian
Newtonian
numerator
numerical
octagonal
parabolic
parameter
perimeter
polygonal
polyhedra
pyramidal
quadratic
quadruple
quintuple
re-entrant
rectangle
remainder
set square
set theory
slide rule
spherical
tetragram
trapezium
trapezoid
trinomial

10

arithmetic
biquadrate
centesimal
co-ordinate
complement
concentric
continuity
conversion
decahedron

derivative
dimensions
duodecimal
eigenvalue
epicycloid
equivalent
expression
fractional
game theory
golden rule
hemisphere
heptagonal
hexahedral
hexahedron
hyperbolic
hypotenuse
hypothesis
inflection
irrational
multiplier
octahedral
octahedron
orthogonal
osculation
paraboloid
pentagonal
percentage
percentile
polyhedral
polyhedron
polynomial
proportion
protractor
quadrangle
quadratics
quadrature
quaternary
real number
reciprocal
right angle
semicircle
square root
statistics
stochastic
subtrahend
tangential
tetragonal
triangular
trilateral
versed sine

11

aliquot part
approximate

binary digit
binary scale
biquadratic
coefficient
combination
commutative
computation
coordinates
denominator
determinant
directrices
dodecagonal
eigenvector
equiangular
equidistant
equilateral
equilibrium
exponential
geometrical
Gödel's proof
heptahedron
hyperboloid
icosahedron
integration
logarithmic
mathematics
mensuration
mixed number
Möbius strip
obtuse angle
orthocentre
pentahedral
pentahedron
permutation
prime number
probability
progression
proposition
real numbers
rectangular
rectilinear
reflex angle
right-angled
round number
rule of three
sesquialter
submultiple
subtraction
symmetrical
tetrahedron
trapezoidal
Venn diagram
whole number

12

alphanumeric
common factor
conic section
decimal point
differential
dodecahedron
eccentricity
harmonic mean
intersection
least squares
long division
metric system
multilateral
multiplicand
Napier's bones
number theory
oblique angle
quadrangular
quadrinomial
semicircular
straight line
substitution
tetrahedroid
trigonometry
vernier scale

13

antilogarithm
approximation
circumference
common divisor
complementary
complex number
concentricity
differentiate
dihedral angle
exterior angle
geometric mean
golden section
interior angle
linear algebra
parallelogram
perfect number
perpendicular
plane geometry
quadrilateral
solid geometry

14 AND 15

alphanumerical (14)
arithmetic mean (14)
axis of symmetry (14)

binomial theorem (15)   decimal notation (15)   multiplication (14)   unknown quantity (15)
cardinal number (14)   differentiation (15)   natural numbers (14)   vulgar fraction (14)
common fraction (14)   harmonic series (14)   proper fraction (14)
common multiple (14)   imaginary number (15)   pure mathematics (15)
complex numbers (14)   linear equation (14)   rational numbers (15)

Medicine

2 AND 3	boil	hypo	sole	botch	helix
	bone	ilia	sore	bowel	hilum
CJD	bubo	iris	spot	brace	hyoid
ear	burn	jowl	stye	brain	ictus
ECG	burp	knee	swab	bulla	ileum
ECT	calf	lame	tent	bursa	iliac
EEG	cast	limb	tolu	canal	ilium
ENT	cell	lint	turn	chafe	incus
eye	chin	lips	ulna	cheek	joint
fat	clap	lisp	vein	chest	lance
fit	clot	lobe	vena	chill	leech
flu	cold	lung	wale	chyle	leper
gum	coma	maim	wall	chyme	liver
gut	corn	mole	ward	cilia	locum
hip	cure	mute	wart	colic	lungs
HIV	cusp	nail	weal	colon	lupus
ill	cyst	nape	welt	cough	lymph
jaw	deaf	neck	womb	cramp	lysis
leg	derm	noma	X-ray	crick	mania
lip	diet	nose	yaws	croup	medic
LSD	disc	numb		death	molar
ME	dope	oral	**5**	decay	mouth
MS	dose	otic		donor	mucus
p.m.	drip	ovum	acute	drain	mumps
p.r.	drug	pain	agony	dress	nasal
pox	duct	palm	algid	drops	navel
pus	dumb	pang	algor	edema	nerve
rib	face	pica	aloes	elbow	nurse
sty	falx	pill	ancon	ether	opium
tic	flux	pock	angst	faint	orbit
toe	foot	pore	ankle	femur	organ
VD	gall	râle	anvil	fetus	ovary
wen	game	rash	aorta	fever	palsy
	gene	rest	apnea	fibre	penis
4	germ	rete	ataxy	flesh	phial
ache	gout	ribs	aural	flush	piles
acne	grip	roof	belch	fossa	pinna
ACTH	guts	root	belly	gauze	plate
ague	hair	scab	birth	gland	plica
AIDS	hand	scan	blain	gonad	polio
axon	head	scar	bleed	graft	polyp
back	heal	shin	blend	graze	probe
balm	heel	sick	blind	gumma	pulse
bile	hips	SIDS	blood	gyrus	pupil
bleb	hurt	skin	bolus	heart	purge
			borax		

quack	virus	cortex	lesion	suture	bandage
rabid	vomit	coryza	lotion	tablet	bedsore
renal	vulva	costal	lumbar	taenia	bifocal
rheum	waist	cowpox	lunacy	tampon	bilious
rigor	wound	crisis	maimed	tannin	bladder
salts	wrist	crutch	malady	tartar	blister
salve	X-rays	deflux	maniac	temple	booster
scald		dengue	matron	tendon	boracic
scalp	**6**	dental	matter	tetany	bromide
scurf	addict	dermis	megrim	thorax	bubonic
semen	ailing	doctor	morbid	throat	bulimia
senna	albino	dorsal	morula	thrush	calomel
serum	amytal	dosage	mucous	ticker	capsule
shock	anemia	dropsy	muscle	tissue	cardiac
sight	anemic	eczema	myopia	tongue	cascara
sinew	angina	elixir	myopic	tonsil	catarrh
sinus	antrum	embryo	oedema	torpor	caustic
skull	apnoea	emetic	opiate	trance	cautery
sleep	areola	eschar	oxygen	trauma	chafing
sling	armpit	eyelid	palate	tremor	chancre
spasm	arnica	fascia	pelvis	trepan	chloral
sperm	artery	fester	pepsin	troche	choking
spine	asthma	fibula	peptic	tumour	cholera
sprue	ataxia	finger	perone	typhus	chronic
stall	aurist	flexor	phenol	unwell	cocaine
sting	autism	foetus	phenyl	uterus	cochlea
stoma	axilla	foment	phobia	vagina	colitis
stone	balsam	fornix	pimple	vomica	coroner
stool	bedpan	gargle	plague		cranium
stupe	bellon	goitre	plasma	**7**	culture
sweat	benign	gravel	pleura	abdomen	cupping
swoon	biceps	gripes	poison	abscess	curable
tabes	biopsy	grippe	potion	acidity	cuticle
talus	bowels	growth	quinsy	aconite	deltoid
teeth	breath	gullet	rabies	adenoid	dentist
thigh	bruise	healer	radium	adipose	dietary
thumb	bunion	health	ranula	adrenal	dieting
tibia	caecum	hernia	reflex	ailment	disease
tonic	callus	heroin	remedy	albumen	dissect
tooth	cancer	herpes	retina	allergy	earache
torso	canker	hiccup	sacrum	amnesia	eardrum
toxin	caries	idiocy	saliva	anaemia	endemic
tract	carpus	immune	scurvy	anaemic	enteric
treat	cavity	infect	sepsis	analyst	eupepsy
trunk	cervix	infirm	septic	anatomy	eyewash
truss	chorea	injury	sister	anodyne	fasting
tummy	clinic	insane	spinal	antacid	febrile
ulcer	clonic	intern	spleen	anthrax	femoral
ulnar	clonus	iodine	splint	antigen	fibroid
unfit	coccyx	iritis	sprain	aphasia	filling
urine	comedo	kidney	squint	aseptic	fistula
uvula	concha	labium	stitch	aspirin	forceps
vagus	corium	labour	stroke	atrophy	forearm
valve	cornea	larynx	stupor	autopsy	formula

gastric
glottis
gumboil
harelip
healing
healthy
heparin
hormone
hospice
humerus
hygiene
illness
inhaler
insulin
invalid
jugular
kneecap
knuckle
lanolin
leprosy
leprous
linctus
lockjaw
lozenge
lumbago
Luminal
lunatic
malaria
massage
masseur
mastoid
measles
medical
menthol
microbe
mixture
morphia
myalgia
nervous
nostrum
obesity
occiput
oculist
operate
organic
ossicle
otalgia
otology
palsied
panacea
patella
patient
pharynx
pillbox

pink-eye
placebo
plaster
podagra
polypus
pustule
pyaemia
pyretic
quinine
recover
relapse
rickets
roseola
rubella
rupture
sarcoma
scabies
scalpel
scanner
seasick
seizure
sick-bay
sickbed
spastic
stamina
stammer
sterile
sternum
steroid
stertor
stomach
stunned
styptic
sunburn
surgeon
surgery
symptom
syncope
syringe
tetanus
theatre
therapy
thyroid
tonsils
trachea
triceps
typhoid
tympana
urethra
vaccine
variola
Veronal
verruca
vertigo

vitamin
wet-pack
whitlow
wryneck

8

abnormal
abortion
abrasion
accident
acidosis
adenoids
adhesion
allergic
alopecia
amputate
aneurysm
antibody
antidote
aperient
apoplexy
appendix
appetite
Asian flu
asphyxia
atheroma
atropine
backache
bacteria
baldness
beri beri
bile duct
blackout
blue pill
botulism
caffeine
carditis
casualty
cataract
catheter
cervical
clinical
club foot
cold sore
collapse
comatose
compress
coronary
critical
cyanosis
cystitis
dandruff
deafness
deathbed

debility
deceased
deformed
delirium
delivery
demented
dementia
dentures
diabetes
diagnose
dialyser
diseased
disorder
diuretic
dressing
drop-foot
dropsied
druggist
dyslexia
emulsion
epidemic
epilepsy
excision
eye salve
eye tooth
eyedrops
fainting
feverish
first aid
flat feet
forehead
formalin
fracture
freckles
fumigate
ganglion
gangrene
glaucoma
grand mal
hard drug
hay fever
headache
heat spot
hiccough
hip joint
hospital
hot flush
hygienic
hypnotic
hysteria
immunity
impetigo
impotent
incision

infected
inflamed
insanity
insomnia
iodoform
iron lung
irritant
jaundice
lameness
laudanum
laxative
lethargy
ligament
ligature
liniment
lobotomy
lordosis
magnesia
mal de mer
malarial
medicine
melanoma
membrane
mescalin
migraine
morphine
narcosis
narcotic
neonatal
neuritis
neurotic
ointment
oncology
otoscope
overdose
paranoia
paranoic
paranoid
paroxysm
pellagra
pharmacy
phthisis
placenta
pleurisy
poisoned
poultice
pregnant
prenatal
progeria
prostate
ptomaine
pulmonic
recovery
Red Cross

remedial
rest cure
revivify
ringworm
sanitary
schizoid
sciatica
scrofula
sedation
sedative
senility
shingles
shoulder
sickness
sickroom
smallpox
sneezing
soft drug
specific
specimen
speculum
stitches
subacute
surgical
swelling
syphilis
tapeworm
terminal
the bends
thoracic
tincture
toxaemia
trachoma
traction
ulcerous
uric acid
varicose
vertebra
vomiting
wheezing
windpipe

9

admission
adrenalin
aetiology
alleviate
allopathy
Alzheimer
ambulance
analgesic
angiogram
ankylosis
antalkali

antenatal
antitoxin
arthritis
asthmatic
bedridden
bilharzia
birthmark
blackhead
blindness
blood test
breakdown
Caesarean
carbuncle
carcinoma
cartilage
castor oil
catalepsy
catatonic
catharsis
cauterize
chilblain
cirrhosis
cold cream
colostomy
complaint
condition
conscious
contagion
contusion
cortisone
curvature
deformity
delirious
dentistry
deodorant
diagnosis
diaphragm
diarrhoea
diathermy
dietetics
dietetist
dietician
digestion
digestive
discharge
disinfect
dislocate
doctoring
dropsical
dysentery
dyspepsia
dystrophy
emaciated
emergency

emollient
emphysema
epileptic
eye lotion
eyestrain
faintness
frost-bite
funnybone
gastritis
gathering
geriatric
germicide
giddiness
glandular
glycerine
halitosis
hartshorn
healthful
heartburn
hepatitis
histamine
hunchback
hygienist
hypnotism
hypnotist
hysterics
ill health
impaction
in plaster
in-patient
incubator
incurable
infection
infirmary
infirmity
influenza
inoculate
invalided
isolation
isoniazid
leukaemia
liquorice
Listerism
liver spot
long sight
malignant
medicated
medicinal
menopause
midwifery
milk teeth
mongolism
mouthwash
nappy rash

narcotics
nebulizer
nephritis
nerve cell
neuralgia
nostalgia
Novocaine
nutrition
nux vomica
nystagmus
open-heart
operation
osteopath
pacemaker
paralysis
paralytic
pathology
phlebitis
physician
pneumonia
poisoning
porphyria
pregnancy
premature
prescribe
psoriasis
psychosis
psychotic
pulmonary
pulsation
purgative
pyorrhoea
radiology
rheumatic
rock-fever
sclerosis
secretion
silicosis
sinusitis
skin graft
soporific
squinting
sterilize
stiff neck
stiffness
still-born
stimulant
stone deaf
stretcher
sunstroke
toothache
treatment
umbilicus
unhealthy

urticaria
vaccinate
vasectomy
water cure
wet nurse

10

amputation
anti-poison
antibiotic
antiseptic
apoplectic
apothecary
aureomycin
barium meal
blood count
blood donor
blood group
brain death
brain fever
breastbone
bronchitis
cardiogram
chicken pox
chloroform
collar bone
concussion
congestion
consultant
contagious
convalesce
convulsion
cotton wool
cough syrup
cystectomy
depressant
depression
dermatitis
diagnostic
diphtheria
dipsomania
disability
dispensary
dispensing
dissecting
dissection
drug addict
Ebola fever
emaciation
enervation
epidemical
epiglottis
Epsom salts
erysipelas

eucalyptus
euthanasia
extraction
false teeth
fibrositis
flatulence
fumigation
gingivitis
gonorrhoea
hearing aid
heat stroke
hemorrhage
homoeopath
hydropathy
hypodermic
incubation
indisposed
infectious
inhalation
insanitary
interferon
ionization
kiss of life
knock-kneed
laparotomy
laryngitis
Lassa fever
lung cancer
mastectomy
medicament
meningitis
metabolism
nettle rash
neuropathy
night nurse
obstetrics
oesophagus
ophthalmia
optic nerve
orthocaine
osteopathy
out-patient
oxygen mask
oxygen tent
paediatric
painkiller
palliative
paraplegic
penicillin
pestilence
pharmacist
post mortem
presbyopia
preventive

psychiatry
quarantine
recuperate
relaxation
rheumatism
salmonella
sanatorium
sanitarium
scarlatina
short sight
sickle-cell
sore throat
specialist
spinal cord
staff nurse
stammering
starvation
sterilizer
strychnine
stuttering
thrombosis
tourniquet
toxic shock
tracheitis
transplant
urethritis
wheel chair

11

abnormality
acupuncture
albuminuria
aminobutene
amphetamine
anaesthetic
angioplasty
anti-pyretic
asthmatical
astigmatism
bactericide
bandy-legged
barbiturate
beta blocker
biliousness
blood vessel
bloodstream
brucellosis
Calabar bean
cardiograph
case history
chiropodist
cholesterol
circulation
cleft palate

cod-liver oil
colour-blind
confinement
consumption
consumptive
contact lens
corn plaster
dengue fever
dermatology
disablement
dislocation
double-blind
embrocation
examination
expectorant
face-lifting
fatty tissue
fibre optics
finger stall
fluoroscope
fomentation
frostbitten
gall bladder
gastrectomy
gerontology
gynaecology
haemoglobin
haemophilia
haemorrhage
heart attack
homoeopathy
hospitalize
hydrophobia
hypothermia
indigestion
inoculation
intercostal
intravenous
jungle fever
kwashiorkor
miscarriage
mustard bath
nursing home
observation
obstruction
orthopaedic
palpitation
pathologist
peptic ulcer
peritonitis
perspiration
pharyngitis
plaster cast
prickly heat

probationer
proctoscope
prophylaxis
psittacosis
radiography
restorative
rigor mortis
sal volatile
seasickness
septicaemia
skin disease
spina bifida
stethoscope
stomach ache
stomach-pump
suppuration
temperature
thalidomide
therapeutic
thermometer
tonsillitis
torticollis
tracheotomy
transfusion
trench fever
typhus fever
unconscious
vaccination
vasodilator
vivisection
wisdom tooth
yellow fever

12

alexipharmic
anaesthetist
appendectomy
appendicitis
aquapuncture
athlete's foot
auscultation
carbolic acid
casualty ward
chemotherapy
chiropractor
complication
constipation
consultation
convalescent
cough mixture
court plaster
critical list
day blindness
decongestant

degeneration
disinfectant
disinfection
Dover's powder
encephalitis
enteric fever
faith healing
fallen arches
family doctor
friar's balsam
gastric fever
group therapy
growing pains
heart disease
heart failure
homoeopathic
hospital case
hypertension
hysterectomy
immune system
immunization
inflammation
malnutrition
menstruation
mesothelioma
neurasthenia
obstetrician
orthodontics
osteoporosis
palpitations
parasitology
pharmaceutic
pharmacology
prescription
preventative
prophylactic
psychiatrist
radiotherapy
recuperation
recuperative
reflex action
sarsaparilla
scarlet fever
sclerodermia
shaking palsy
short-sighted
skin-grafting
sleeping pill
slimming diet
spinal column
streptococci
streptomycin
student nurse
subcutaneous

surgical boot
takadiastase
talcum powder
tartar emetic
tertian fever
thyroid gland
tuberculosis
typhoid fever
varicose vein
Weil's disease
zinc ointment

13

anti-spasmodic
anticoagulant
antihistamine
blood pressure
bubonic plague
cardiac arrest
Chagas' disease
clearing station
contraception
convalescence
Crohn's disease
dental surgery
Down's syndrome
duodenal ulcer
elephantiasis
eucalyptus oil
fever hospital
gamma globulin
gentian violet
German measles
group practice

gynaecologist
health service
health visitor
heat treatment
hydrocephalus
indisposition
intensive care
kidney machine
lead poisoning
malarial fever
materia medica
medical school
medicine glass
mononucleosis
mortification
non-contagious
ophthalmology
osteomyelitis
paediatrician
pharmaceutics
pharmacopoeia
physiotherapy
poliomyelitis
schizophrenia
shooting pains
shoulder blade
smelling salts
social disease
speech therapy
St. Vitus's dance
sterilization
stretcher case
styptic pencil
tonsillectomy

tranquillizer
varicose veins
whooping cough

14

Achilles tendon
blood poisoning
Bright's disease
bulimia nervosa
carcinogenesis
cardiovascular
conjunctivitis
corticosteroid
corticotrophin
cross-infection
cystic fibrosis
family planning
floating kidney
glandular fever
Gregory's powder
hallucinations
hallucinogenic
hole in the heart
housemaid's knee
Kaposi's sarcoma
keyhole surgery
medical officer
medical student
medicine bottle
mucous membrane
mustard plaster
night blindness
operating table
pasteurization

patent medicine
pectoris
phenobarbitone
plastic surgery
pneumoconiosis
psychoanalysis
rheumatic fever
Seidlitz powder
smelling bottle
surgical spirit

15

Addison's disease
adhesive plaster
alimentary canal
anorexia nervosa
antenatal clinic
aversion therapy
blackwater fever
counter-irritant
delirium tremens
dressing station
endocrine glands
Eustachian tubes
gastroenteritis
general practice
Hodgkin's disease
locomotor ataxia
manic depression
morning sickness
physiotherapist
sticking plaster
vasoconstrictor
venereal disease

Minerals (including alloys, metals, ores, precious stones, rocks, etc.)

3 AND 4

alum
bort
caix
cauk
clay
coal
gold
grit
iron
jade
jet
lava
lead
Lias

marl
mica
onyx
opal
rag
rock
ruby
sard
spar
talc
trap
tufa
wad
wadd
zinc

5

agate
albin
alloy
argil
baric
beryl
borax
boron
brass
chalk
chert
emery
erbia
flint

fluor
Invar
macle
magma
nitre
ochre
pitch
prase
shale
silex
slate
steel
topaz
trona
tutty

6

acmite
albite
aplite
aplome
arkose
augite
barite
barium
basalt
blende
bronze
cannel
cerite
cerium

cherty
cobalt
copper
davyne
dipyre
dogger
egeran
erbium
gabbro
galena
gangue
garnet
glance
gneiss
gypsum
halite

humite
indium
iolite
jargon
jasper
kaolin
kunkur
marble
mesole
minium
mundic
nappal
nickel
nosean
ophite
ormolu
osmium
pelite
pewter
pinite
plasma
potash
pumice
pyrite
pyrope
quartz
radium
rutile
schist
schorl
silica
silver
sinter
sodium
speiss
sphene
spinel
thoria
tombac
xylite
yenite
zircon

7

adamant
alumina
alunite
anatase
apatite
aphrite
arsenic
asphalt
axiline
azurite

barytes
bauxite
biotite
bismuth
bitumen
bornite
breccia
cadmium
caesium
calcite
calcium
caliche
calomel
cat's-eye
citrine
cuprite
cyanite
desmine
diamond
diorite
edenite
emerald
epidote
epigene
erinite
euclase
fahlerz
fahlore
felsite
felspar
fuscite
gahnite
gallium
granite
greisen
gummite
hafnium
helvite
hessite
holmium
hyalite
ice spar
iridium
jacinth
jadeite
jargoon
kainite
kernite
kyanite
lead ore
leucite
lignite
lithium
mellite

mercury
mullite
nacrite
niobium
olivine
orthite
peridot
petzite
pycnite
pyrites
realgar
red lead
rhenium
rhodium
romeine
sahlite
silicon
sinoper
sinople
sulphur
syenite
sylvite
talcite
thorite
thorium
thulite
thulium
tripoli
uranium
wolfram
wurgite
yttrium
zeolite
zeuxite
zincite
zoisite
zorgite
zurlite

8

achirite
adularia
aegirite
aerolite
allanite
alquifou
aluminum
amethyst
amiantus
analcime
analcite
andesine
andesite
ankerite

antimony
aphanite
asbestos
basanite
blue john
boracite
braunite
bronzite
brookite
calamine
calcspar
cast iron
cerusite
chabasie
chlorite
chromite
chromium
cinnabar
corundum
crocoite
cryolite
dendrite
diallage
diaspore
diopside
dioptase
dolerite
dolomite
eclogite
embolite
enargite
epsomite
essonite
euxenite
fayalite
feldspar
felstone
fireclay
fluorite
gibbsite
glucinum
goethite
graphite
hematite
hyacinth
idocrase
ilmenite
jarosite
jasponyx
konilite
laterite
lazulite
lazurite
ligurite

limonite
litharge
lomonite
lutecium
lutetium
magnesia
massicot
meionite
melanite
melilite
mesolite
micanite
mimetene
mimetite
monazite
mudstone
mylonite
nemalite
nephrite
noumeite
obsidian
orpiment
pagodite
pea stone
peridote
petalite
pisolite
platinum
plumbago
porphyry
prehnite
psammite
pyroxene
ragstone
rhyolite
rock cork
rock salt
rock soap
rock wood
rubidium
sagenite
samarium
sanidine
sapphire
sardonyx
scandium
selenite
selenium
siberite
siderite
smaltine
sodalite
stannite
steatite

stellite
stibnite
stilbite
tantalum
thallium
tin stone
titanite
titanium
trachyte
traprock
triphane
tungsten
vanadium
vesuvian
voltzite
weissite
wood opal
wood rock
wurtzite
xanthite
xenotime
yanolite
zirconia

9

alabaster
allophane
almandine
alum shale
alum slate
aluminate
aluminium
amianthus
amphibole
anamesite
andradite
anglesite
anhydrite
anorthite
aphrisite
aragonite
argentite
argillite
arquifoux
asphaltum
baikalite
basaltine
beryllium
boltonite
brick-clay
brimstone
brown coal
brown-spar
byssolite

cairngorm
carbonado
carbuncle
carnelian
carnotite
cat-silver
celestite
cerussite
ceylanite
ceylonite
chabazite
chalybite
china clay
chondrite
cobaltine
cobaltite
columbite
cornelian
cornstone
dialogite
diatomite
dripstone
dyprosium
earth flax
elaeolite
elaterite
enstatite
erythrite
eucairite
eudialite
ferberite
fibrolite
firestone
fluorspar
galactite
gehlenite
germanium
glucinium
gmelinite
granitite
granulite
graywacke
greensand
grenatite
greystone
greywacke
haematite
harmotome
heavy spar
hessonite
hornstone
indianite
ironstone
johannite

kaolinite
killinite
laccolith
lanthanum
latrobite
laumonite
lenzinite
limbilite
limestone
lodestone
magnesite
magnesium
magnetite
malachite
manganese
manganite
marcasite
margarite
marmolite
melaphyre
meteorite
mica slate
microdine
microlite
millerite
mispickel
monzonite
moonstone
moorstone
muscovite
nagyagite
natrolite
necronite
needletin
neodymium
nepheline
niccolite
noumeaite
omphacite
ozocerite
ozokerite
palladium
pargasite
pearl spar
pectolite
pegmatite
penninite
periclase
petroleum
phenacite
phenakite
phonolite
physalite
pleonaste

plinthite
potassium
proustite
pyrophane
quartzite
raphilite
rhodonite
rhombspar
rubellite
ruthenium
sandstone
satin spar
scapolite
scheelite
scolecite
scorodite
soapstone
spodumene
streamtin
strontium
sylvanite
sylvinite
tachylite
tantalite
tapiolite
tellurium
theralite
torbanite
torrelite
tremolite
tridymite
turmaline
turnerite
turquoise
uraninite
uvarovite
variscite
veinstone
vivianite
vulcanite
wavellite
wernerite
willemite
withamite
witherite
woodstone
wulfenite
ytterbium
zinc bloom
zirconium

10

actinolite
amianthoid

amygdaloid
andalusite
anthracite
apopyllite
aquamarine
aventurine
azure stone
batrachite
beudantite
bismuthite
bloodstone
bourmonite
calaverite
cannel coal
carnallite
cervantite
chalcedony
chalcocite
chalybeate
chrysolite
clinkstone
colemanite
constantan
cordierite
coupholite
cross-stone
dyscrasite
eagle stone
false topaz
floatstone
forsterite
gabbronite
gadolinium
garnierite
glauberite
glauconite
glottalite
greenstone
heterosite
heulandite
hornblende
hornsilver
hydrophane
indicolite
iridosmine
iron glance
karpholite
Kentish rag
kieselguhr
kimberlite
koupholite
laumontite
lead glance
lepidolite

liriconite
malacolite
melaconite
mica schist
mocha stone
molybdenum
Monel metal
nussierite
nuttallite
orthoclase
osmiridium
peridotite
phosgenite
phosphorus
picrosmine
polyhalite
pyrochlore
pyrolusite
pyrrhotite
redruthite
retinalite
rock butter
rose quartz
rothottite
safflorite
sapphirine
sardachate
saussurite
schalstein
serpentine
smaragdite
sparry iron
sperrylite
sphalerite
stalactite
stalagmite
staurolite
stephanite
talc schist
themardite
thomsonite
thorianite
tiavertine
topazolite
torbernite
tourmaline
triphylite
vanadinite
villarsite
vitrophyre
websterite
wolframite
zinc blende

11

alexandrite
amorthosite
amphibolite
amphiboloid
Babbit metal
black silver
brewsterite
cassiterite
cerargyrite
chondrodite
chromic iron
chrysoberyl
chrysocolla
cobalt bloom
crichtonite
crocidolite
dendrachate
diving stone
epistilbite
feldspathic
figure stone
hypersthene
Iceland spar
iron pyrites
labradorite
lapis lazuli
libethenite
molybdenite
Muschelkalk
napoleonite
needlestone

nephelinite
octahedrite
pentlandite
phillipsite
piedmontite
pitchblende
plagioclase
polymignite
pryallolite
psilomelane
pyrargyrite
pyrochroite
pyrosmalite
rock crystal
sillimanite
smithsonite
smoky quartz
sordavalite
sphaerulite
tetradymite
titanic iron
valentinite
vermiculite
vesuvianite
yttrocerite
zinnwaldite

12

aerosiderite
agalmatolite
arsenopyrite
artvedsonite
bismuthinite

chalcopyrite
cobalt glance
copper glance
feldspathoid
forest marble
fuller's earth
greyweathers
grossularite
hemimorphite
jeffersonite
kupfernickel
mineral black
mineral green
montmartrite
mountain cork
mountain flax
mountain milk
mountain soap
murchisonite
praseodymium
protactinium
puddingstone
pyromorphite
pyrophyllite
quartz schist
red sandstone
senarmontite
silver glance
skutterudite
somervillite
Spanish chalk
specular iron
speisscobalt

sprig crystal
strontianite
tetrahedrite
wollastonite
xanthoconite

13

agaric mineral
anthophyllite
chlorophaeite
cinnamon stone
cleavelandite
copper pyrites
emerald copper
kerosene shale
needle zeolite
rhodochrosite

14 AND 15

antimony glance (14)
arkose sandstone (15)
bituminous coal (14)
Britannia metal (14)
brown haematite (14)
Cairngorm stone (14)
chlorite schist (14)
elastic bitumen (14)
graphic granite (14)
hydromica schist (15)
quartz porphyry (14)

Physics

2 AND 3

a.a.
a.c.
amp
bar
bel
e.m.f.
erg
gas
lux
ohm
ray
r.p.m.
u.h.f.
v.h.f.

4

atom
beam
cell
coil
core
dyne
flux
foci
fuse
heat
kaon
lens
mach
mass
muon

node
phon
pile
pion
pole
rays
spin
tube
unit
volt
watt
wave
work
X-ray

5

anion
anode
curie
cycle
diode
earth
farad
field
fluid
focus
force
gauss
henry
hertz
image

joule
laser
lever
light
lumen
maser
meson
motor
phase
pitch
polar
power
prism
quark
radar
radio
relay

shell
solid
sonic
sound
speed
valve
weber

6

albedo
ampere
atomic
baryon
cation
charge
corona
dipole

energy
fusion
hadron
impact
isobar
kelvin
lepton
liquid
magnet
micron
moment
motion
newton
nuclei
optics
period
photon
plasma
proton
quanta
radome
sensor
torque
triode
vacuum
vector
weight

7

ammeter
aneroid
battery
beta ray
bipolar
breeder
calorie
candela
cathode
Celsius
circuit
coulomb
crystal
current
damping
decibel
density
dry cell
elastic
element
entropy
fallout
fissile
fission
gaseous

gravity
heating
hyperon
impulse
inertia
isochor
isotone
lattice
machine
maxwell
neutron
nuclear
nucleon
nucleus
nuclide
optical
orbital
physics
pi-meson
quantum
radiant
reactor
röntgen
spectra
statics
thermal
torsion
voltage
voltaic

8

adhesion
aerofoil
aerology
alpha ray
angstrom
antinode
armature
betatron
bevatron
Brownian
cohesion
constant
delta ray
detector
deuteron
dynamics
electric
electron
emission
enthalpy
filament
free fall
friction

fuel cell
gamma ray
graviton
half-life
harmonic
hologram
ideal gas
inductor
infrared
isogonic
kilowatt
kinetics
klystron
long wave
magnetic
magneton
molecule
momentum
negative
negatron
neutrino
overtone
particle
pendulum
polarity
Polaroid
positive
positron
pressure
rest mass
rheostat
roentgen
solenoid
spectrum
subshell
velocity
watt-hour
wave-form

9

acoustics
adiabatic
amplifier
amplitude
antimeson
barometer
black body
bolometer
Boyle's law
capacitor
coherence
condenser
conductor
cyclotron

electrode
frequency
gamma rays
generator
impedance
induction
insulator
isoclinic
kilohertz
Leyden jar
magnetism
magnetron
mechanics
plutonium
polarizer
potential
radiation
radio wave
real image
rectifier
resonance
resultant
short wave
spark coil
subatomic
threshold
vibration
viscosity

10

aberration
absorption
achromatic
antilepton
antimatter
antiproton
atomic mass
atomic pile
biophysics
cathode ray
centigrade
conduction
convection
cosmic rays
cryogenics
Dewar flask
dielectric
dispersion
distortion
electrical
electronic
Fahrenheit
geophysics
heavy water

horsepower
inductance
ionization
isodynamic
isothermal
kinematics
latent heat
mass number
nanosecond
nucleonics
omega meson
omega minus
oscillator
precession
reflection
refraction
relativity
resistance
ripple tank
Röntgen ray
scattering
short waves
shunt-wound
solid-state
supersonic
synchroton
thermionic
thermopile
transistor
transition
vacuum tube
wavelength
xerography
zwitterion

11

accelerator
accumulator
actinic rays
atomic clock
capacitance
capillarity
cathode rays
centrifugal
centripetal
coefficient
compression
conductance
declination
diffraction
electricity
electrolyte
electronics
falling body

fast neutron
fibre optics
focal length
gravitation
ground state
hypercharge
interaction
irradiation
nucleophile
oscillation
positronium
radioactive
resistivity
restitution
series-wound
solar energy
spectrogram
synchrotron
temperature
transformer
transuranic
ultraviolet
vacuum flask

12

acceleration
Angstrom unit
antineutrino
antiparticle
atomic energy

atomic number
atomic weight
band spectrum
beta particle
centre of mass
cloud chamber
conductivity
critical mass
deceleration
diamagnetism
disintegrate
displacement
eccentricity
electrolysis
electrophile
electroscope
geomagnetism
interference
kilowatt-hour
oscilloscope
permittivity
polarization
scintillator
selenium cell
specific heat
spectrograph
standing wave
wave equation
wave function

13

alpha particle
bubble chamber
chain reaction
critical angle
direct current
discharge tube
Doppler effect
electric field
electric motor
electric power
electromagnet
electromotive
electrostatic
ferromagnetic
gravitational
induction coil
kinetic energy
magnetic field
magnetic north
magnetic poles
paramagnetism
photoelectric
quantum number
quantum theory
radioactivity
rectification
scintillation
semiconductor

transmutation

14 AND OVER

breeder reactor (14)
Brownian
  movement (16)
cathode ray tube (14)
centre of gravity (15)
disintegration (14)
electric current (15)
electric energy (14)
electrification (15)
electromagnetic (15)
electrostatics (14)
ferromagnetism (14)
ionizing radiation (17)
nuclear physics (14)
nuclear reactor (14)
nuclear-powered (14)
Planck's constant (15)
potential energy (15)
specific gravity (15)
synchrocyclotron (16)
terminal velocity (16)
thermal capacity (15)
thermodynamics (14)
thermoelectric (14)
transformation (14)
Wheatstone bridge (16)

Poisons

4 AND 5

acids
agene
bane
coca
drug
dwale
ergot
fungi
lead
lysol
nitre
opium
toxin
upas
venom

6

alkali
antiar
cicuta
curare
heroin
iodine
ourari
phenol

7

aconite
alcohol
amanita
ammonia
aniline
arsenic
atropia
atropin

bromine
brucina
brucine
cadmium
calomel
caustic
chloral
cocaine
gamboge
henbane
mercury
ptomain
Veronal
vitriol
wourali

8

antimony
atropine
botulism

chlorine
chromium
ergotine
hyoscine
morphine
nicotine
oenanthe
Paraquat
pearl ash
phosgene
ptomaine
ratsbane
selenium

9

baneberry
barbitone
beryllium
chromates
colchicum

colocynth
croton oil
grapewort
hellebore
herbicide
mercurial
monkshood
nux vomica
potassium
rat poison
strychnia
sulphonal
toadstool
veratrine
white lead
wolf's-bane

10

antiseptic
aqua fortis

belladonna
chloroform
cyanic acid
mustard gas
nightshade
nitric acid
oxalic acid
phosphorus
picric acid
salmonella
snake venom
strychnine

thorn apple
weed-killer

11

blue vitriol
boracic acid
caustic soda
dog's mercury
hyoscyamine
insecticide
lead acetate
prussic acid

snake poison
sugar of lead

12

barbiturates
bitter almond
carbolic acid
fool's parsley
lead arsenate
lunar caustic
pharmacolite
water hemlock
white arsenic

13 AND OVER

allantotoxicum (14)
carbon monoxide (14)
carbonic oxide (13)
caustic potash (13)
deadly nightshade (16)
hydrocyanic acid (15)
meadow saffron (13)
sulphuric acid (13)
yellow arsenic (13)

Sciences

5 AND 6

augury (6)
botany (6)
conics (6)
logic (5)
optics (6)

7

algebra
anatomy
biology
cookery
ecology
farming
finance
geodesy
geogony
geology
gunnery
history
hygiene
myology
orology
otology
phonics
physics
science
statics
zoology
zootomy

8

aerology
agronomy
atmology
barology
biometry

bryology
calculus
cytology
dynamics
ethology
etiology
eugenics
forestry
genetics
geometry
glyptics
horology
kinetics
medicine
mycology
nosology
ontology
penology
pharmacy
politics
pomology
posology
rheology
rhetoric
Sinology
sitology
spherics
taxonomy
tocology
topology
typology
virology
zymology

9

acoustics
aerometry
aetiology

allopathy
altimetry
anemology
annealing
areometry
astronomy
barometry
cartology
chemistry
chiropody
chorology
cosmology
dentistry
desmology
dietetics
diplomacy
economics
embalming
engraving
ethnology
gardening
geography
gnomonics
harmonics
histology
horometry
husbandry
hydrology
hygrology
hymnology
ichnology
lithology
mammalogy
mechanics
micrology
neurology
ophiology
orography

osteology
otography
pathology
petrology
philology
phonetics
phonology
phytogeny
phytology
phytotomy
radiology
semiology
sitiology
sociology
surveying
taxidermy
telephony
uranology
zoography

10

aerography
aesthetics
apiculture
araeometry
arithmetic
ballistics
bathymetry
biometrics
biophysics
cardiology
catoptrics
chromatics
cometology
conchology
craniology
demography
dendrology

docimology
Egyptology
embryology
energetics
entomology
enzymology
game theory
gastrology
geophysics
homeopathy
hydraulics
hydrometry
hydropathy
hygrometry
hypsometry
immunology
kinematics
lexicology
metallurgy
microscopy
morphology
nematology
nephrology
nosography
obstetrics
odontology
oneirology
organology
osteopathy
pedagogics
pediatrics
phlebology
photometry
phrenology
physiology
planimetry
pneumatics
potamology

psychiatry
psychology
relativity
seismology
selenology
semeiology
somatology
splenology
splenotomy
statistics
technology
telegraphy
teratology
topography
toxicology
typography

11

aeronautics
aerostatics
agriculture
anemography
arachnology
archaeology
arteriology
arteriotomy
campanology
carcinology
cartography
cell biology
chondrology
chronometry
climatology
cosmography
craniometry
criminology
cupellation

cybernetics
dermatology
diacoustics
electricity
electronics
engineering
entozoology
ethnography
games theory
geomedicine
gynaecology
haematology
heliography
homoeopathy
hydrography
hyetography
ichthyology
lichenology
linguistics
mathematics
methodology
micrography
myodynamics
neurography
ornithology
osteography
paediatrics
paleography
petrography
photography
phytography
probability
prophylaxis
pteridology
radiography
sericulture
skeletology

spectrology
stereometry
stereoscopy
stethoscopy
thanatology
uranography
watch-making

12

aerodynamics
amphibiology
anthropology
architecture
astrophysics
atomic theory
auscultation
biochemistry
biogeography
cytogenetics
econometrics
electropathy
epidemiology
floriculture
geochemistry
horticulture
hydrostatics
lexicography
microbiology
neuroanatomy
neurobiology
number theory
oceanography
organography
ornithoscopy
palaeography
pharmacology
physiography

pisciculture
pneumatology
protozoology
seismography
silviculture
spectroscopy
stratigraphy
sylviculture
synosteology
trigonometry
zoophytology

13

anthropometry
arboriculture
bioenergetics
cephalography
chrematistics
climatography
crustaceology
endocrinology
geochronology
geomorphology
helminthology
hydrodynamics
hydrokinetics
ichthyography
lichenography
linear algebra
marine biology
matrix algebra
meteorography
ophthalmology
palaeontology
pharmaceutics
psychophysics
psychotherapy

quantum theory
splanchnology
stoichiometry
wave mechanics
zoophysiology

14

architectonics
bioclimatology
chromatography
cinematography
electrobiology
electrostatics
fluid mechanics
hippopathology
hydrophytology
macroeconomics
microeconomics
natural history
natural science
parapsychology
photogrammetry
phytopathology
psychonosology
radiochemistry
thermodynamics

15

computer science
crystallography
electrodynamics
electrokinetics
material science
neurophysiology
psychopathology
thermochemistry

Tools and simple machines
See also **Engineering** and **Instruments** (pages 280–288)

3
adz
awl
axe
bit
die
dog
fan
gad
gin

hod
hoe
jig
saw
zax

4
adze
bill
bore
burr

celt
clam
crab
file
fork
gage
hook
hose
jack
last
loom

maul
mule
nail
peel
pick
plow
pump
rake
rasp
rule
spud

tool
trug
vice
whim

5
anvil
auger
bench
besom
bevel

blade
borer
brace
burin
chuck
churn
clamp
clasp
cleat
cramp
crane

croze
cupel
dolly
drill
flail
forge
gauge
gavel
gouge
hoist
jemmy
knife
lathe
level
lever
mower
parer
peavy
plane
plumb
prong
punch
quern
quoin
ratch
razor
sarse
scoop
screw
sieve
spade
spike
spile
spill
swage
tommy
tongs
wedge
winch

6

barrow
beetle
blower
bodkin
bowsaw
brayer
broach
burton
chaser
chisel
colter
dibber
dibble

digger
doffer
dredge
driver
fanner
faucet
flange
folder
gadget
gimlet
grater
graver
hackle
hammer
harrow
jagger
jigger
jig-saw
ladder
laptop
lister
mallet
mortar
muller
oil-can
oliver
pallet
peavey
pencil
pestle
pitsaw
planer
pliers
plough
rammer
ramrod
rasper
reaper
riddle
rip-saw
roller
rubber
sander
saw-set
screen
scribe
scythe
shaver
shears
shovel
sickle
sifter
skewer
sledge

slicer
spigot
square
strike
stylus
tackle
tedder
tenter
trepan
trowel
wrench

7

andiron
arc lamp
bandsaw
boaster
bradawl
buzz-saw
capstan
cautery
chopper
cleaver
cold saw
coulter
crampon
crisper
crowbar
cuvette
derrick
diamond
dog-belt
dredger
drudger
flippers
forceps
fretsaw
gradine
grainer
grapnel
grub hoe
hacksaw
handsaw
hatchet
hayfork
jointer
mandrel
mattock
nut hook
pickaxe
piercer
pincers
plummet
poleaxe

pounder
pricker
salt-pan
scalpel
scauper
scraper
scriber
scuffle
shuttle
spanner
spatula
sprayer
stapler
swingle
T-square
tenoner
thimble
toolbox
trestle
triblet
twibill
whip-saw
whittle
woolder

8

billhook
bistoury
blowlamp
boathook
butteris
calender
calipers
cant-hook
chainsaw
clippers
crow mill
crucible
die stock
dividers
dowel bit
drill bow
Dutch hoe
edge tool
filatory
flashgun
flatiron
flax comb
glass-pot
hand tool
hand-loom
hand-mill
handloom
hayknife

horsehoe
lapstone
mitre-box
molegrip
oilstone
panel saw
penknife
picklock
pinchers
plumb bob
polisher
power saw
prong-hoe
puncheon
reap hook
saw wrest
scissors
shoehorn
spray-gun
stiletto
strickle
Strimmer
tenon saw
throstle
tommy bar
tooth key
tweezers
twist bit
water-ram
weed-hook
windlass
windmill

9

baseplate
belt punch
bench hook
blow torch
can opener
cement gun
centre-bit
compasses
corkscrew
cotton gin
cramp iron
curry comb
die sinker
draw knife
draw-plate
drift bolt
drop forge
drop-drill
excavator
eyeleteer

fining pot
fly-cutter
fork-chuck
grease gun
hair-drier
hair-dryer
handbrace
handscrew
handspike
implement
jackknife
jackplane
jackscrew
lace frame
lawnmower
nail punch
nut wrench
pitchfork
plane iron
planisher
plumb-line
plumb-rule
rotary hoe
screw-jack
secateurs
shear-legs
sheep-hook
steam iron
steelyard
sugar mill
telescope
tin opener
tire lever
try-square
turn-bench
turnscrew
tyre lever
watermill
woodscrew

10

box spanner
bush-harrow
churn staff
claspknife
claw-hammer
coal shovel
cold chisel
compass saw
crane's bill
cultivator
drill-press

drop-hammer
edging tool
emery wheel
fire escape
grindstone
instrument
masonry bit
masticator
mitre block
motor mower
mouldboard
nail drawer
paintbrush
paper knife
perforator
pipe wrench
rotary pump
safety lamp
screw press
spokeshave
steam press
stepladder
tenterhook
thumbscrew
tilt hammer
trip hammer
turf cutter
turn-buckle
twist drill
watercrane
watergauge
water-level
wheel brace

11

brace-and-bit
breast-drill
cheese press
cigar cutter
circular saw
countersink
crazing-mill
crosscut saw
drill barrow
drill harrow
drill-plough
electric saw
fanning mill
glass cutter
grubbing axe
grubbing hoe
helve-hammer

machine tool
monkey block
paint roller
ploughshare
pocket knife
pruning hook
rabbet-plane
reaping-hook
sanding disc
screwdriver
scribing awl
snatchblock
spirit level
steam hammer
steam shovel
sward cutter
swing-plough
tape-measure
touch needle
turfing iron
two-foot rule
warping hook
warping post
watering can
weeding fork
weeding hook
wheelbarrow

12

branding iron
breast-plough
caulking iron
countergauge
cradle-scythe
crimping-iron
curling tongs
driving wheel
flour dresser
garden shears
glass furnace
hedge-trimmer
hydraulic ram
mandrel lathe
marlinespike
masonry drill
monkey wrench
palette knife
pruning knife
pulley blocks
rotary plough
sledgehammer
straightedge

trench plough
trying square
turfing spade
water-bellows
weeding-tongs

13

chopping block
chopping knife
cylinder press
electric drill
grappling-iron
hydraulic jack
mowing machine
packing needle
precision tool
sewing machine
soldering iron
spinning jenny
spinning wheel
stocking frame
subsoil plough
three-foot rule
weeding chisel

14

blowing machine
carding machine
draining engine
draining plough
fillister plane
pneumatic drill
reaping machine
shepherd's crook
smoothing plane
three-metre rule

15

carpenter's bench
crimping machine
dredging machine
drilling machine
entrenching tool
pestle and mortar
pump screwdriver
weighing machine

TRANSPORT
Aviation and space travel

3 AND 4

ace
air
bank
bay
bump
buzz
car
crew
dive
dope
drag
fin
flap
fly
fuel
gap
gas
hull
jet
kite
knot
land
lane
leg
lift
loop
mach
nose
prop
rev
rib
roll
slip
slot
span
spar
spin
tail
taxi
trim
UFO
veer
wash
wind
wing
yaw
york
zoom

5

aloft
apron
bends
blimp
cabin
cargo
chock
chord
cleat
climb
craft
crash
crate
ditch
drift
filer
flaps
float
glide
jumbo
pitch
plane
prang
pylon
radar
range
rev up
rigid
slots
stall
strut
stunt
valve

6

aerial
Airbus
airman
airway
basket
beacon
bomber
camber
canard
cruise
cut out
drogue
fabric

flight
floats
flying
gas-bag
glider
hangar
intake
jet set
jet-lag
launch
module
nose-up
octane
piston
ram jet
refuel
rocket
rudder
runway
Skylab
yawing

7

aerobus
aileron
air base
air foil
air jump
air lane
air rage
air taxi
air-raid
aircrew
airdrop
airflow
airlift
airline
airport
airsick
airsock
aviator
bale out
ballast
balloon
banking
biplane
birdman
bomb bay
capsule
ceiling

charter
chassis
chopper
clipper
co-pilot
cockpit
compass
contact
cowling
descent
ejector
emplane
fairing
fighter
flyover
flypast
gliding
gondola
helibus
hostess
inflate
jump-jet
landing
lift-off
mae west
milk run
nacelle
nose-cap
on board
pancake
payload
Pioneer
re-entry
ripcord
shuttle
sponson
Sputnik
steward
tailfin
take-off
taxiing
Trident
Tristar
twin jet
Voyager
wingtip

8

aerodyne
aerofoil

aeronaut
aerostat
air brake
air force
air route
airborne
aircraft
airfield
airframe
airliner
airplane
airscrew
airspace
airspeed
airstrip
airwoman
altitude
anhedral
approach
autogiro
aviation
aviatrix
ballonet
black box
bomb-rack
buoyancy
carousel
Concorde
corridor
cruising
dihedral
elevator
envelope
flat spin
fuel pipe
fuselage
grounded
gyrostat
heliport
in flight
intercom
jet pilot
jet plane
joystick
jumbo jet
kamikaze
long-haul
moonshot
near miss
non-rigid

nose down
nose-cone
nosedive
pitching
pulse-jet
radiator
seaplane
sideslip
spaceman
squadron
stopover
subsonic
tail unit
tail-skid
tailspin
terminal
throttle
triplane
turbofan
turbojet
twin-tail
volplane
warplane
wind cone
windsock
wing-flap
Zeppelin

9

aerodrome
aeroplane
air bridge
air intake
air pocket
airworthy
altimeter
amphibian
astrodome
astronaut
autopilot
cabin crew
cosmonaut
countdown
crash-land
delta-wing
dirigible
doodlebug
empennage
fuel gauge
gyroplane

jet bomber
launch pad
launching
longerons
low-flying
monocoque
monoplane
navigator
nosewheel
overshoot
parachute
power dive
propeller
rudder bar
sailplane
satellite
semi-rigid
short-haul
sonic boom
spacecrew
spaceship
spacesuit
spacewalk
stability
stratojet
sweepback
swing-wing
tailplane
taxiplane
test pilot
touch down
turboprop
twin-screw
wind gauge

10

aero-engine
aerobatics
aeronautic
aerostatic
air balloon
air control
air defence
air hostess
air service
air steward
air support
air traffic
airfreight
anemometer

ballooning
balloonist
cantilever
cargo plane
Challenger
dive bomber
flight deck
flight path
flight plan
flying boat
fuel intake
ground crew
helicopter
hydroplane
jet fatigue
jet fighter
landing run
Mach number
microlight
outer space
oxygen mask
pathfinder
pilot error
pilot plane
robot plane
rudder-post
slipstream
solo flight
space probe
spacecraft
splashdown
stabilizer
stewardess
supersonic
test flight
turbulence
V-formation

11

aeronautics
aerostatics
afterburner
air corridor
air terminal
air umbrella
blind flying
combat plane
ejector seat
flying speed
free balloon

ground speed
hand luggage
heat barrier
heavy bomber
kite-balloon
laminar flow
landing deck
landing gear
leading edge
loop the loop
moon landing
mooring-mast
ornithopter
parachutist
radio beacon
retractable
retro-rocket
sesquiplane
slotted wing
soft landing
space centre
space flight
space rocket
space travel
stabilizers
stunt flying
vapour trail
weather-vane

12

aerodynamics
air ambulance
air–sea rescue
airfreighter
arrester gear
beacon lights
belly landing
control stick
control tower
crash landing
ejection seat
fighter pilot
flying circus
flying saucer
gliding-angle
hedge-hopping
jet-propelled
landing field
landing light
landing speed

landing strip
launching pad
Lunar Orbiter
maiden flight
manned rocket
night fighter
pilot balloon
pressure suit
pursuit plane
radar scanner
radial engine
reverse thrust
sound barrier
space capsule
space shuttle
space station
space vehicle
trailing edge

13 AND OVER

air stewardess (13)
aircraft-carrier (15)
airworthiness (13)
control-column (13)
cruising speed (13)
decompression (13)
dihedral angle (13)
engine-mounting (14)
escape velocity (14)
excess luggage (13)
fighter-bomber (13)
flight recorder (14)
forced landing (13)
ground control (13)
heavier-than-air (14)
in-line engines (13)
jet propulsion (13)
lighter-than-air (14)
looping the loop (14)
radio-location (13)
semi-retractable (15)
shock-absorber (13)
space traveller (14)
stalling-speed (13)
Stratocruiser (13)
troop-transport (14)
undercarriage (13)
vertical take-off (15)
weightlessness (14)

Boats and ships
See also **Nautical terms** (pages 310–315)

3 AND 4

ark
bark
boat
brig
buss
cog
dhow
dory
duck
four
gig
hoy
hulk
junk
keel
koff
M.T.B.
pair
pram
proa
punt
raft
saic
scow
ship
snow
sub
T.B.D.
tub
tug
yawl

5

aviso
balsa
barge
canoe
coble
cogge
craft
dandy
E-boat
eight
ferry
fleet
float
funny
kayak
ketch

liner
praam
Q-ship
razee
scull
shell
skiff
sloop
smack
tramp
U-boat
umiak
whiff
xebec
yacht

6

argosy
banker
barque
bateau
bawley
bireme
caique
carvel
coggle
cutter
decker
dinghy
dogger
dugout
galeas
galley
gallot
hooker
hopper
launch
lorcha
lugger
mistic
oomiak
packet
pedalo
pirate
PT boat
puffer
randan
sampan
sealer
settee
slaver

tanker
tartan
tender
trader
vessel
whaler
wherry

7

bumboat
caravel
carrack
carrier
catboat
clinker
clipper
coaster
cockler
collier
coracle
corsair
cruiser
currach
curragh
dredger
drifter
drogher
dromond
felucca
flivver
flyboat
four-oar
frigate
galleon
galliot
gondola
gunboat
gunship
ice-boat
lighter
man-o'-war
minisub
mistico
monitor
mud-scow
pair-oar
pinnace
piragua
pirogue
polacca
polacre

pontoon
rowboat
sculler
shallop
steamer
tartane
towboat
trawler
trireme
tugboat
warship

8

bilander
car ferry
coalship
cockboat
corvette
dahabeah
dahabiya
derelict
eight-oar
fireboat
fire-ship
flagship
flat-boat
galleass
galliass
gallivat
hoveller
ice yacht
Indiaman
ironclad
keelboat
lifeboat
longboat
mailboat
man-of-war
sailboat
schooner
showboat
steam-tug
surf-boat
trimaran
waterbus
well-boat

9

bomb-ketch
bucentaur
cable ship

canal boat
cargo boat
catamaran
depot ship
destroyer
ferryboat
freighter
frigatoon
guard boat
guard ship
horse boat
houseboat
hydrofoil
jollyboat
lightship
minelayer
motorboat
oil tanker
outrigger
pilot boat
powerboat
privateer
prize ship
river boat
sand yacht
sheer-hulk
ship's boat
slave ship
speedboat
steamboat
steamship
storeship
submarine
transport
troopship
two-decker
whale-boat

10

banana boat
barkentine
battleship
bomb vessel
brigantine
cattleboat
cockleboat
four-master
hovercraft
hydroplane
icebreaker
monkey-boat

motor yacht
narrow-boat
nuclear sub
ocean liner
ore-carrier
packet-boat
paddleboat
patrol boat
picket boat
pirate ship
prison ship
quadrireme
repair-ship
rivercraft
rowing boat
royal barge
small craft
supply ship
survey ship
tea-clipper
train ferry
turret ship
victualler
Viking ship
watercraft
windjammer

11

barquentine
bulk carrier
capital ship
chasse-marée
cockleshell
dreadnought
factory ship
fishing boat
luxury liner
merchantman
minesweeper
motor launch
motor vessel
naval vessel
pilot cutter
prize vessel
quinquereme
racing shell
sailing boat
sailing ship
sardine boat
slave-trader
steam launch
submersible
supertanker

three-decker
three-master
torpedo boat

12

cabin cruiser
despatch boat
East Indiaman
escort vessel
fishing smack
heavy cruiser
hospital ship
landing barge
landing craft
light cruiser
merchant ship
pleasure boat
police launch
sailing barge
sailing craft
square-rigger
stern-wheeler
supply vessel
survey vessel
training ship
tramp steamer
troop carrier

13

battlecruiser
container ship
double-sculler
four-oared boat
paddle-steamer
passenger-boat
passenger-ship
sailing vessel
ship-of-the-line
trading vessel
transport ship

14 AND 15

aircraft-carrier (15)
cable-laying ship (15)
cable-repair ship (15)
channel steamer (14)
coasting vessel (14)
eight-oared boat (14)
flotilla leader (14)
seaplane tender (14)
submarine chaser (15)
torpedo-gunboat (14)
victualling ship (15)

IVRs (Vehicle Registration)

A Austria
ADN Yemen
AFG Afghanistan
AL Albania
AND Andorra
AUS Australia
B Belgium
BD Bangladesh
BDS Barbados
BG Bulgaria
BH Belize
BR Brazil
BRN Bahrain
BRU Brunei
BS Bahamas
BUR Burma
C Cuba
CDN Canada
CH Switzerland
CI Ivory Coast
CL Sri Lanka
CO Colombia
CS Czech Republic

CY Cyprus
D Germany
DK Denmark
DOM Dominican Republic
DY Benin (formerly Dahomey)
DZ Algeria
E Spain
EAK Kenya
EAT Tanzania
EAU Uganda
EC Ecuador
ES El Salvador
ET Egypt
ETH Ethiopia
EW Estonia
F France
FIN Finland
FJI Fiji
FL Liechtenstein
FR Faroe Islands
GB Great Britain
GBA Alderney
GBG Guernsey

GBJ Jersey
GBM Isle of Man
GBZ Gibraltar
GCA Guatemala
GH Ghana
GR Greece
GUY Guyana
H Hungary
HKJ Jordan
I Italy
IL Israel
IND India
IR Iran
IRL Ireland
IRQ Iraq
IS Iceland
J Japan
JA Jamaica
K Cambodia (formerly
  Kampuchea)
KWT Kuwait
L Luxembourg
LAO Laos

LAR Libya
LB Liberia
LS Lesotho
LT Lithuania
LV Latvia
M Malta
MA Morocco
MAL Malaysia
MC Monaco
MEX Mexico
MS Mauritius
MW Malawi
N Norway
NA Netherlands Antilles
NIC Nicaragua
NL Netherlands
NZ New Zealand
P Portugal
PA Panama
PAK Pakistan
PE Peru
PI Philippines
PL Poland
PY Paraguay
RA Argentina
RB Botswana

RC Taiwan
RCA Central
    African Republic
RCB Congo
RCH Chile
RH Haiti
RI Indonesia
RIM Mauretania
RL Lebanon
RM Madagascar
RMM Mali
RN Niger
RO Romania
ROK South Korea
RSM San Marino
RU Burundi
RUS Russia
RWA Rwanda
S Sweden
SD Swaziland
SGP Singapore
SME Surinam
SN Senegal
SWA Namibia
    (South West Africa)
SY Seychelles

SYR Syria
T Thailand
TG Togo
TN Tunisia
TR Turkey
TT Trinidad and Tobago
U Uruguay
USA United States
V Vatican City
VN Vietnam
WAG Gambia
WAL Sierra Leone
WAN Nigeria
WG Grenada
WL/WV Windward Islands
WS Western Samoa
WV St. Vincent and the
    Grenadines
YU Yugoslavia
YV Venezuela
Z Zambia
ZA South Africa
ZW Zimbabwe

Motoring

2 AND 3

A.A.
air
b.h.p.
c.c.
cam
can
cap
car
cog
fan
fit
G.T.
gas
h.p.
hub
jam
jet
key
lap
lug
M.O.T.
map

nut
oil
pin
pit
R.A.C.
rev
rim
rod
run
ton
top

4

axle
belt
body
bolt
boot
boss
bulb
bush
clip
coil
cowl

dash
disc
door
drum
flat
fuse
gate
gear
hood
hoot
horn
idle
jack
lane
lock
nail
park
pink
plug
pump
road
roll
rope
seat

skid
sump
tail
tank
test
tire
tour
tube
tyre
veer
wing

5

apron
brake
cable
chain
chart
choke
clamp
coupé
cover
crank
cut in

drive
float
frame
gauge
joint
knock
lay-by
level
lever
model
motor
on tow
pedal
rally
rev up
rivet
rotor
route
scale
screw
sedan
servo
shaft
shift

spark
speed
spoke
squab
stall
start
stick
ton up
tools
tread
U-turn
valve
wheel
wiper
works

6

adjust
air bag
big end
bonnet
bumper
bypass
camber

car tax
charge
clutch
cut out
dazzle
de luxe
decoke
de-icer
detour
dickey
divert
driver
dynamo
engine
fender
fitter
flange
funnel
garage
gasket
grease
grille
handle
hooter
hot rod
hub cap
idling
klaxon
lock-up
louvre
mascot
milage
mirror
octane
oilcan
one-way
petrol
pile-up
pinion
piston
rebore
saloon
signal
spokes
spring
swerve
switch
tappet
timing
torque
tow bar
tuning
winker

7

air hose
airlock
axle-box
battery
bearing
blowout
bollard
build-up
bus lane
bus stop
carpark
carport
cat's eye
chassis
contact
control
cooling
dipping
drive-in
driving
exhaust
fan belt
flyover
gearbox
give way
goggles
gudgeon
hardtop
highway
joyride
L driver
L plates
licence
linkage
locknut
log book
luggage
magneto
map-case
mileage
misfire
missing
mixture
MOT test
muffler
no entry
non-skid
off-road
offside
oil seal
oil-feed
parking

pillion
pinking
pull out
reverse
road tax
roadhog
roadmap
rolling
run into
seizing
service
skidpan
spindle
springs
starter
test run
toolkit
top gear
touring
towrope
traffic
trailer
viaduct
warning
wingnut

8

air brake
air inlet
airtight
armature
arterial
Autobahn
back seat
backfire
bodywork
brake pad
brake rod
camshaft
cat's eyes
clearway
coasting
converge
coupling
crankpin
cruising
cul-de-sac
cylinder
declutch
delivery
dipstick
driveway
fast lane
fastback

feed pipe
feed pump
flat tyre
flywheel
foglight
footpump
freezing
friction
fuel pipe
fuel tank
garaging
gasoline
gradient
guide-rod
handpump
ignition
inlet cam
knocking
lead-free
manifold
missfire
motoring
motorist
motorway
mudguard
nearside
oil gauge
oncoming
open road
overhaul
overpass
overtake
overturn
pavement
prowl car
puncture
radiator
rattling
rear axle
rear lamp
ring road
road rage
road sign
road test
roadside
roofrack
rotor arm
rush hour
seat belt
side road
sideslip
silencer
skid mark
skidding

slip road
slow down
slow lane
speeding
squad car
steering
stock car
tail skid
tailgate
taxi rank
throttle
tire pump
track rod
turnpike
two-speed
tyre pump

9

air filter
alignment
anti-glare
autoroute
back wheel
ball-valve
batteries
bench seat
brake drum
brake shoe
breakdown
bus driver
cab driver
car driver
car polish
chain-link
chauffeur
clearance
coachwork
concourse
condenser
cotter pin
crank axle
crankcase
crossroad
cutting in
dashboard
dashlight
defroster
dipswitch
direction
dirt track
disc brake
diversion
drum brake
estate car

filler cap
footbrake
framework
free-wheel
front axle
front seat
fuel gauge
gear lever
generator
Grand Prix
grease-box
grease-gun
guarantee
handbrake
hatchback
headlight
hit-and-run
indicator
inner tube
insurance
limousine
lubricate
monocoque
motor show
motorbike
motorcade
nipple key
oil engine
oil filter
overdrive
oversteer
passenger
patrol car
petrol can
piston rod
point duty
police car
prop shaft
racing car
radial-ply
rear light
reflector
revving up
road sense
road works
saloon car
sidelight
side-valve
spare tire
spare tyre
spark plug
sports car
spotlight
stoplight

switch off
T-junction
tail-light
taximeter
third gear
tire lever
tramlines
trunk road
two-seater
two-stroke
tyre lever
underpass
underseal
wheel spin
wheelbase
white line

10

access road
adjustment
alternator
amber light
anti-dazzle
antifreeze
bevel-wheel
bottom gear
box-spanner
brake fluid
brake pedal
brakeblock
brakelight
broken down
bucket seat
car licence
coachbuilt
combustion
commutator
crankshaft
crossroads
detonation
dickey seat
drive shaft
dry battery
fluid drive
four-seater
four-stroke
front wheel
gear casing
gear change
green light
gudgeon pin
headlights
horsepower
inlet valve

insulation
lighting up
low-tension
lubricator
mileometer
motorcycle
overtaking
petrol pump
petrol tank
piston ring
private car
radial tire
radial tyre
rear mirror
rev counter
right of way
roadworthy
roundabout
safety belt
signalling
spare wheel
speed limit
streamline
suspension
tachograph
tachometer
third-party
three-speed
toll bridge
touring car
traffic cop
traffic jam
two-wheeler
upholstery
ventilator
wheelbrace
windscreen
wing mirror

11

accelerator
accessories
accumulator
anti-roll bar
blind corner
brake lining
built-up area
carburetter
carburettor
carriageway
clutch pedal
compression
convertible
crash helmet

de-luxe model
decarbonize
distributor
driving seat
driving test
exhaust pipe
exhaust port
feeler-gauge
front lights
Highway Code
ignition key
interrupter
lorry driver
lubrication
luggage rack
motor spirit
needle-valve
number plate
oil pressure
over-revving
overhauling
overheating
owner-driver
petrol gauge
pre-ignition
racing model
radiator cap
request stop
reverse gear
reverse turn
rotary valve
screen-wiper
self-starter
sliding roof
speedometer
splashboard
sports model
streamlined
synchromesh
tappet valve
thermometer
through road
ticking over
trafficator
vacuum brake
valve-timing
wheel wobble

12

acceleration
approach road
arterial road
ball-bearings
breakdown van

car insurance
clutch-spring
coachbuilder
contact-screw
countershaft
cylinder head
diesel engine
differential
driving wheel
driving-chain
driving-shaft
exhaust valve
float-chamber
freewheeling
gear changing
hazard lights
lock-up garage
miles per hour
motor scooter
motor vehicle
motorcyclist
parking light
parking meter
parking place
petrol filter
pillion rider
racing driver
ratchet-wheel
registration
repair outfit
road junction
running-board
sparking plug
starter motor
steering gear
sunshine roof
supercharger
transmission
turbocharger
two-speed gear
warning light

13

breakdown gang
connecting rod
cooling system
driving mirror
fluid flywheel
fuel injection
hydraulic jack
induction pipe
inspection pit
licence-holder
overhead valve

309

petrol station
pillion-riding
power steering
pressure-gauge
rack-and-pinion
roller-bearing
servo-assisted
shock absorber
shooting brake
speed merchant
steering wheel
traffic signal

14
adjusting-screw
circuit-breaker
compression tap
contact-breaker
double-declutch
driving licence
exhaust-cam axle
filling station
four-wheel drive
friction-clutch
hydraulic brake

grease-injector
lighting-up time
lubricating oil
luggage-carrier
miles per gallon
off-road vehicle
propeller shaft
reclining seats
service station
starting handle
steering column
third-party risk
three-speed gear

universal joint
15
carriage-builder
front-wheel drive
dual carriageway
instrument panel
insurance policy
reversing lights
road-fund licence
seating capacity
windscreen wiper

Nautical terms

2 AND 3
A.B.
A1
aft
bay
bow
box
cat
cay
C.I.F.
con
cox
ebb
fid
F.O.B.
fog
gam
guy
H.M.S.
hog
jaw
jib
lay
lee
log
man
nut
oar
ply
ram
rig
R.M.
R.N.
rum
run
sag

sea
set
SOS
tar
top
tow
way
yaw

4
ahoy
alee
back
bale
beam
beat
bend
bitt
boom
bows
brig
bunk
bunt
buoy
calk
calm
coak
comb
cott
crew
deck
dive
dock
down
dune
east
eddy

fake
flag
floe
flow
foam
fore
foul
frap
furl
gaff
gale
gang
gear
girt
grog
hank
hard
haul
haze
hazy
head
helm
hold
hove
hulk
jack
junk
keel
knot
land
last
lead
leak
line
list
load
loof

luff
mast
mess
mine
mist
mole
moor
navy
neap
oars
peak
pier
poop
port
prow
punt
quay
raft
rail
rake
rank
rate
rear
reef
ride
road
roll
rope
rove
rung
sail
sand
scud
seam
ship
sink
skid

slip
spar
stay
stem
step
surf
swab
tack
taut
tend
tide
tilt
toss
trim
trip
veer
waft
wake
warp
wave
wear
west
whip
winch
wind
wing
yard
yarn

5
aback
abaft
abeam
afoul
after
ahead
ahull

aloft
apeak
aport
atrip
avast
awash
beach
belay
below
berth
bight
bilge
block
board
bosun
bouse
bower
bowse
brace
brail
bream
briny
cabin
cable
cadet
canal
cargo
caulk
chain
chart
check
chock
clamp
cleat
craft
crank
cuddy

davit	royal	cablet	on deck	towage	counter
depth	sally	canvas	outfit	unbend	cresset
diver	salve	careen	paddle	unbitt	cringle
douse	salvo	comber	parcel	uncoil	cyclone
downs	screw	convoy	patrol	undock	dead-eye
dowse	sheer	course	paunch	unfurl	deep-sea
draft	sheet	crotch	pay off	unlade	degauss
embay	shelf	cruise	pay out	unload	dismast
entry	shoal	crutch	pennon	unmoor	dockage
flake	shore	debark	Pharos	unship	dog-vane
fleet	siren	diving	pillow	vessel	dolphin
float	skeet	double	pintle	voyage	draught
fluke	sling	earing	piracy	yawing	dry dock
foggy	sound	embark	pirate		dunnage
gauge	spirit	engine	piston	**7**	ease off
grave	steer	ensign	pooped		ebb tide
gusty	stern	escort	poppet	aground	embargo
hands	storm	fathom	purser	athwart	eye-bolt
hatch	surge	fender	rating	backing	fairway
haven	swell	fo'c'sle	ratlin	bale out	fishery
hawse	thole	for'ard	reefed	ballast	flotsam
hitch	tidal	fother	reefer	beached	fogbank
hoist	trice	funnel	rigged	bearing	foghorn
horse	truck	furled	rigger	beating	foretop
hound	truss	galley	rocket	boarder	forward
jetty	waist	gasket	rudder	bobstay	founder
kedge	watch	gunnel	sailor	bollard	freight
kevel	weigh	halser	saloon	boomkin	freshen
lay to	wharf	hawser	salute	bow wave	freshet
lay up	wheel	hove-to	salvor	bowline	frogman
leaky	windy	jetsam	sculls	boxhaul	futtock
leech	woold	jigger	sealer	bracing	gangway
ligan	wreck	kedger	seaman	breaker	gimbals
lurch		lading	seaway	bulwark	go about
metal	**6**	lateen	sennit	bunting	go below
misty		launch	sheets	buoyage	grapnel
naval	aboard	lay-off	shroud	caboose	grating
north	adrift	league	signal	calking	graving
oakum	afloat	leeway	sinker	can-buoy	grommet
ocean	anchor	Lloyd's	sinnet	capsize	grummet
order	armada	locker	splice	capstan	gudgeon
orlop	ashore	manned	squall	captain	gun-deck
pitch	astern	marina	square	cast off	gun-port
prick	aweigh	marine	stocks	catfall	gun-room
prize	awning	marker	stormy	cathead	gunnage
radar	bargee	maroon	strake	cat's-paw	gunwale
radio	batten	marque	strand	channel	guy-rope
range	beacon	masted	stream	charter	half pay
refit	becket	mayday	tackle	claw off	halyard
rhumb	billow	mizzen	tender	coaling	harbour
roads	bonnet	moored	thwart	cockpit	harpoon
ropes	bridge	mutiny	tiller	compass	haul off
route	bumkin	needle	timber	conning	head off
rower	bunker	offing	toggle	cordage	head sea
	burton			corsair	

headway
heave to
horizon
iceberg
icefloe
inboard
inshore
Jack Tar
jib boom
jibstay
keelage
keelson
landing
laniard
lanyard
lashing
lastage
latches
leaking
lee side
lee tide
lee-gage
leeward
listing
loading
logbook
log-line
log-reel
lookout
low tide
lugsail
maintop
mariner
marines
marline
marling
matelot
mistral
monsoon
moorage
mooring
mudhook
oarsman
oceanic
old salt
on board
outport
oversea
painter
pennant
pooping
port-bar
quayage
rafting

rations
ratline
reefing
ride out
rigging
rip tide
rollers
rolling
rope-end
rostrum
rowlock
run down
sailing
salvage
scupper
scuttle
sea mile
sea room
sea-card
seafolk
sea-lane
sealegs
sea-mark
seasick
seaward
set sail
sextant
shallow
shelves
shipper
shipway
shrouds
sick-bay
sinking
skipper
skysail
slipway
spanker
spencer
squally
stand-by
steward
stopper
stowage
tacking
tactics
tempest
thimble
tonnage
top deck
top mast
topsail
topside
tornado

torpedo
towline
towpath
towrope
transom
trysail
typhoon
unladen
unsling
unslung
veering
waftage
ward off
warping
wavelet
wet dock
whistle
wrecked
wrecker
yardarm

8

anchored
aplustre
approach
armament
at anchor
aweather
backstay
backwash
barbette
bargeman
barnacle
beam-ends
bearings
becalmed
berthage
berthing
binnacle
boat-deck
boathook
bolt-rope
bowsprit
broach to
bulkhead
bulwarks
buntline
castaway
caulking
claw away
clubhaul
coamings
coasting
coxswain

crossing
cruising
cutwater
dead slow
dead-wood
deckhand
derelict
ditty-bag
ditty-box
dockyard
dog watch
dog-shore
doldrums
doubling
downhaul
drifting
easterly
eastward
even keel
fife-rail
flag-rank
floating
flotilla
fogbound
foot-rope
forefoot
foremast
forepeak
foresail
foreship
forestay
forewind
free-port
gaffsail
go aboard
go ashore
hard alee
hatchway
head into
head wind
headfast
helmless
helmsman
high seas
high tide
hornpipe
hull-down
icebound
icefield
jackstay
jettison
jury mast
keel over
keelhaul

land ahoy!
land wind
landfall
landmark
landsman
landward
larboard
lead-line
lee gauge
lee shore
leeboard
lifebelt
lifebuoy
lifeline
load-line
loblolly
long haul
low water
magazine
main boom
main deck
mainmast
mainsail
mainstay
mainyard
make sail
maritime
martinet
masthead
mastless
messmate
midships
moorings
moulinet
mutineer
mutinous
nautical
navigate
neap tide
ordnance
outboard
overrake
overseas
paravane
periplus
picaroon
pierhead
pilotage
plimsoll
poop deck
porthole
portside
pratique
pumproom

put about
put to sea
quarters
re-embark
reef-knot
ride easy
ride hard
roadster
sail-loft
sail-room
sail-yard
salvable
salvager
sandbank
scudding
sea-chest
sea-rover
seaborne
seafarer
seagoing
shallows
shark-net
sheer off
ship ahoy
ship oars
shipmate
shipment
shipping
shipworm
shipyard
sounding
spy-glass
squadron
stand off
standard
staysail
steerage
sternway
stowaway
stranded
streamer
stunsail
submerge
tackling
tafferel
taffrail
thole-pin
tranship
traverse
unbuoyed
uncoiled
under way
underset
unfurled

vanguard
wall-knot
wardroom
water-rot
waterman
waterway
waveworm
welldeck
west wind
westerly
westward
windlass
windrode
windsail
windward
woolding
wreckage
yachting

9

about-ship
admiralty
affreight
afterdeck
air-funnel
all aboard
alongside
amidships
anchorage
anchoring
bargepole
beaconage
below deck
bilge-keel
bilge-pump
blue peter
boardable
boat drill
broadside
bunkering
captaincy
careenage
chartered
chartroom
close haul
coastwise
companion
corposant
cross-jack
crosswind
crow's nest
Davy Jones
dead-water
deck cargo

demurrage
departure
disanchor
discharge
disembark
doggerman
dress ship
drift-sail
driftwood
false keel
firedrill
flood-tide
floodmark
flying jib
foreshore
foundered
free-board
gangboard
gangplank
gather way
groundage
half-hitch
hard aport
high water
hoist sail
holystone
house-flag
houseline
hurricane
jack-block
jack-staff
kentledge
land ahead
lobscouse
lower deck
loxodrome
maelstrom
mainbrace
mainsheet
manoeuvre
midstream
minefield
minute-gun
mizzentop
naumachia
navicular
navigable
navigator
neptunian
north wind
northerly
northward
ocean lane
orlop deck

outrigger
overboard
parbuckle
periscope
pilot boat
pilot flag
press-gang
privateer
prize-crew
promenade
quicksand
recharter
reckoning
Red Ensign
reef-point
refitment
revictual
rhumb-line
roadstead
rockbound
royal mast
Royal Navy
rum-runner
sailcloth
sea-letter
sea-robber
seafaring
seaworthy
semaphore
sheathing
ship's crew
shipboard
shipowner
shipshape
shipwreck
shoreward
sick-berth
sidelight
sight land
sou'wester
south wind
southerly
southward
spindrift
spinnaker
spritsail
stanchion
starboard
stateroom
steersman
stemfast
sternmost
sternpost
stokehold

storm-beat
stormsail
stormstay
stretcher
tarpaulin
telescope
tide-table
tophamper
trade wind
twin-screw
two-decker
unballast
uncharted
unlighted
upper deck
water-line
water-sail
whirlwind
wind-bound
wring-bolt
yachtsman

10

A1 at Lloyd's
aboard ship
after-guard
after-hatch
after-sails
alongshore
anchor buoy
anchor hold
anchorable
astarboard
ballasting
batten down
Bermuda rig
bilgewater
Blue Ensign
bluejacket
bootlegger
breakwater
cargo space
cast anchor
casting-net
catch a crab
chainplate
charthouse
coal-bunker
cork jacket
cross-piece
crosstrees
deadlights
degaussing
diving-bell

dockmaster
downstream
drop anchor
drop astern
embarkment
engine room
escutcheon
fathomless
fiddle-head
figurehead
fore-and-aft
forecastle
forge ahead
freightage
freshwater
frostbound
full-rigged
gaff-rigged
harbourage
harness tub
heavy-laden
high-and-dry
jigger-mast
Jolly Roger
jury rudder
jury-rigged
landlocked
landlubber
lateen sail
lateen yard
lay a course
liberty-man
life-jacket
lighterage
lighthouse
lookout-man
loxodromic
manoeuvres
marker buoy
martingale
middle deck
midshipman
mizzenmast
mizzensail
mizzenstay
navigating
navigation
night watch
ocean-going
orthodromy
parcelling
pilot house
pipe aboard
port of call

powder-room
prize-court
prize-money
quarantine
raking fire
reduce sail
rendezvous
reshipment
rope-ladder
round-house
rudder post
rudderless
seamanlike
seamanship
ship-broker
ship-rigged
shipmaster
shipwright
signalling
skyscraper
slack-water
spring tide
square-sail
stanchions
stay-tackle
stern-board
stern-frame
sternsheet
submariner
supercargo
take in sail
tally-clerk
thwartship
tidal basin
tidal river
tiller-rope
topgallant
unfathomed
unfordable
upper works
water-borne
waterspout
watertight
wheel-house

11

abandon ship
anchor light
beachcomber
belaying pin
captainship
centre-board
chafing-gear
close-hauled

compass card
compass rose
contact mine
debarkation
depth-charge
dismastment
diving bell
diving suit
dock charges
echo-sounder
embarcation
embarkation
escape hatch
foam-crested
fore-topmast
foul weather
gallows-tops
get under way
go alongside
graving-dock
groundswell
harbour dues
harness-cask
hug the shore
keelhauling
landing deck
lifeboatman
loblolly boy
main-topmast
main-topsail
make headway
marine store
mess steward
middle watch
monkey-block
naval rating
orthodromic
paddle wheel
port charges
port of entry
press of sail
quarterdeck
range-finder
reconnoitre
riding-light
sailing date
Samson's post
searchlight
seasickness
sheet anchor
ship's doctor
ship's papers
shipbreaker
sliding keel

snatchblock
sounding-rod
south-wester
spring a leak
St. Elmo's fire
standing off
steerage-way
stern-chaser
sternsheets
storm signal
three-masted
thwartships
tidal waters
torpedo tube
unballasted
unchartered
under canvas
under-masted
unnavigable
unnavigated
unsheltered
unsoundable
waterlogged
weathermost
weatherside
weigh anchor
white ensign

12

air-sea rescue
between-decks
bill of lading
breeches-buoy
cable's-length
canvas length
caulking iron
change course
collision-mat
companionway
conning tower
counterbrace
displacement
double-banked
double-manned
equinoctials
fishing fleet
floating dock
futtock-plate
ground-tackle
hard-aweather
jack-o'-lantern
Jacob's ladder
lateen-rigged
line of battle

longshoreman
magnetic mine
maiden voyage
man overboard
marine boiler
marine engine
marlinespike
measured mile
minesweeping
mizzen course
nautical mile
naval command
navigability
orthodromics
outmanoeuvre
outward-bound
Plimsoll line
Plimsoll mark
privateering
recommission
ride at anchor
ship's husband
ship-chandler
shipping line
slack in stays
sounding lead
sounding line
spanking boom
spilling line
square-rigged
starboard bow
studding sail
tourist class
training ship
transhipment
Trinity House
undercurrent
unfathomable
weather-gauge
weatherboard
weatherbound
weatherglass
westerly wind
will-o'-the-wisp

13

affreightment
cat-o'-nine-tails
close quarters
compass signal
dead reckoning
deck passenger
fishing-tackle
floating light

grappling-iron
high-water mark
hurricane deck
life-preserver
mizzen rigging
naval dockyard
naval ordnance
navigableness
north-east wind
north-west wind
northerly wind
order of battle
press of canvas
re-embarkation
royal dockyard
ship's articles
ship-of-the-line
south-east wind
south-west wind
southerly wind
spilling lines
starboard beam
starboard side
steering-wheel
weather report

14

circumnavigate
compass bearing
disembarkation
dolphin striker
futtock shrouds
hard astarboard
horse latitudes
letter-of-marque
Lloyd's Register
naval architect
powder magazine
prevailing wind
running rigging
schooner rigged
screw-propeller
ship's-carpenter
superstructure
swivel-rowlocks
topgallant mast

15

Admiralty Office
circumnavigable
command of
  the sea
companion ladder
Davy Jones' locker

loxodromic curve   operation orders
marine insurance   victualling yard
mariner's compass

Vehicles

2 – 4	van	digger	balloon	trailer
Audi	wain	dodgem	Bentley	tramcar
auto	Yugo	doolie	bicycle	trishaw
bier	**5**	drosky	bob-sled	Triumph
biga	araba	engine	britzka	trolley
bike	artic	fiacre	Bugatti	trundle
BMW	bogey	go-cart	caboose	tumbrel
BMX	bogie	hansom	cacolet	turnout
bogy	brake	hearse	caravan	vis-à-vis
bus	buggy	hot rod	caravel	voiture
cab	chair	hurdle	cariole	**8**
car	coach	Jaguar	caroche	aircraft
cart	coupé	jalopy	chariot	barouche
DAF	crate	jingle	chopper	brake van
drag	cycle	jitney	Citroën	brancard
dray	float	Lancia	Daimler	britzska
duck	Honda	landau	dogcart	brougham
Fiat	Lexus	limber	droshky	buck cart
fly	lorry	litter	flivver	cable car
Ford	Lotus	Model-T	fourgon	Cadillac
gig	Mazda	Morgan	growler	carriage
heap	moped	Morris	gyrocar	carriole
HGV	motor	Nissan	hackery	carry-all
JCB	pulka	oxcart	hackney	carrycot
Jeep	Rover	Proton	hardtop	Chrysler
jet	sedan	saloon	haywain	clarence
Lada	Skoda	sledge	Hyundai	curricle
limo	sulky	sleigh	kibitka	dustcart
loco	tonga	Sno-Cat	mail car	equipage
luge	train	spider	mail-van	fleet car
MG	truck	Subaru	minibus	golf cart
mini	Volvo	surrey	minicab	goods van
Opel	wagon	Suzuki	omnibus	handcart
pram	**6**	tandem	pedrail	horse car
PSV	Austin	tanker	Peugeot	ice-yacht
RV	banger	tender	phaeton	jetliner
Saab	barrow	tipper	Porsche	mail-cart
Seat	Berlin	tourer	Pullman	monorail
shay	bowser	Toyota	railcar	motorbus
skis	boxcar	troika	Reliant	motorcar
sled	calash	waggon	Renault	old crock
tank	camper	whisky	scooter	pushbike
taxi	chaise	**7**	sidecar	pushcart
tram	Daiwoo	Amtrack	taxicab	quadriga
trap	diesel	autobus	tilbury	rally car
tube		autocar	tipcart	rickshaw
			tractor	

315

roadster
rockaway
runabout
sociable
staff car
stanhope
stock car
toboggan
tricycle
unicycle
Vauxhall
victoria
Zeppelin

9

aeroplane
Alfa Romeo
ambulance
amphibian
applecart
bandwagon
bath-chair
boat-train
bobsleigh
box-wagon
bubblecar
bulldozer
cabriolet
charabanc
Chevrolet
diligence
dining car
dodgem car
Dormobile
estate car
funicular
guard's van
half-track
hansom cab
hatchback
ice skates
intercity
Land Rover
landaulet
limousine
low loader
mail-coach
mail-train

milkfloat
motorbike
motorcade
muletrain
palanquin
prison van
racing car
rail coach
saloon car
sand yacht
sports car
streetcar
stretcher
tarantass
tin lizzie
two-seater
wagonette
water-cart

10

automobile
beach buggy
Black Maria
boneshaker
conveyance
donkey-cart
fire-engine
four-in-hand
freight van
goods train
goods truck
goods wagon
hackney cab
handbarrow
hovercraft
invalid cab
jinricksha
juggernaut
knockabout
locomotive
luggage van
motor lorry
motorcoach
motorcycle
pedal cycle
pony engine
post-chaise
Pullman car

Range Rover
removal van
Rolls-Royce
sedan chair
smoking car
snowmobile
snowplough
spacecraft
spring-cart
stagecoach
state coach
tip-up lorry
touring car
tramway-car
trolley-bus
trolley-car
troop train
velocipede
Volkswagen
waggonette
wagon train
war chariot
wheelchair

11

armoured car
brewer's dray
bullock cart
Caterpillar
convertible
delivery van
fire balloon
four-wheeler
goods waggon
gun-carriage
horse-lifter
jaunting-car
jinrickshaw
landaulette
magic carpet
mail phaeton
sleeping car
steam engine
steamroller
three-in-hand
transporter
waggon train
wheelbarrow

12

baby carriage
coach-and-four
coach-and-pair
covered wagon
double decker
freight train
furniture van
hackney coach
horse and cart
invalid chair
Mercedes-Benz
motor scooter
mountain bike
pantechnicon
perambulator
railway train
single decker
station wagon
three-wheeler
troop carrier
watering-cart

13

ambulance cart
covered waggon
electric train
fork-lift truck
governess cart
mourning-coach
penny-farthing
people carrier
shooting brake

14 AND 15

ambulance wagon (14)
bathing-machine (14)
hackney carriage (15)
invalid carriage (15)
luggage trailer (14)
passenger train
prairie-schooner (15)
railway carriage (15)
refrigerated van (15)
traction engine (14)

MISCELLANEOUS
Abbreviations

1 AND 2

A-1	first class in Lloyd's Register
A.A.	Automobile Association, anti-aircraft, Alcoholics Anonymous
AB	Alberta
A.B.	able-bodied seaman
A.C.	alternating current, Companion of the Order of Australia, Apellation contrôlée (wine classification)
A.D.	Anno Domini (In the year of our Lord)
A.G.	Adjutant-General, Attorney-General
A.H.	Anno Hegirae
A.I.	Amnesty International, artificial insemination, artificial intelligence
A.K.	Knight of the Order of Australia
A.M.	Master of Arts
a.m.	ante meridiem (before noon)
AO	Officer of the Order of Australia
AS	Anglo-Saxon
at.	atomic
A.V.	Authorized Version
av.	avenue, average
b.	born, bowled
B.A.	Bachelor of Arts, British Academy, British Airways, British Association
B.C.	Before Christ, British Columbia
B.D.	Bachelor of Divinity
B.E.	Bachelor of Engineering, Bachelor of Education
b.f.	bold face
b.l.	bill of lading
B.M.	British Museum

BO	body odour
B.P.	British Pharmacopoeia
b.p.	blood pressure, boiling point
Bp	Bishop
BR	British Rail
br.	branch
B.S.	Bachelor of Surgery, Bachelor of Science
BT	British Telecom
Bt.	Baronet
C.	Celsius, centigrade
c.	caught, cent(s), chapter, circa
C.A.	chartered accountant
CA	California
ca	circa (around, about)
C.B.	citizens' band, Companion of the Bath
c.b.	confined to barracks
C.C.	cricket club, county council
c.c.	carbon copy (copies), cubic centimetre(s)
CD	Civil Defence, compact disc, Corps Diplomatique
C.E.	Church of England, civil engineer, Common Era
cf.	compare
cg	centigram
CH	Companion of Honour, Confédération Helvétique
ch.	chapter, check, church
C.I.	Channel Islands
C.J.	Chief Justice
cm	centimetre
C.O.	commanding officer, conscientious objector
Co.	company, county
c.o.	care of
CP	Communist Party
cr.	councillor, creditor
CT	Connecticut
ct.	cent, court
C.U.	Cambridge University
cu.	cubic

CV	curriculum vitae
d.	daughter, died, old penny, old pence
D.A.	district attorney
D.B.	Bachelor of Divinity
D.C.	detective constable, District of Columbia (U.S.)
d.c.	da capo, direct current
D.D.	Doctor of Divinity
dd	direct debit
dg	decigram
DJ	dinner jacket, disc jockey
dl	decilitre
D.M.	Doctor of Medicine
DM	Deutschmarks
do	ditto
DP	data processing, displaced person
Dr.	Doctor
dr.	dram, debtor, drive
D.S.	Doctor of Science
D.V.	Deo volente (God willing)
E.	east
ea.	each
E.C.	East Central, European Community
ed.	edited, edition, editor
e.g.	exempli gratia (for example)
E.I.	East Indies
E.R.	Elizabeth Regina (Queen)
F	Fahrenheit, franc(s)
f.	feminine, forte
F.A.	Football Association
F.C.	football club
ff.	folios, fortissimo
fl.	floruit (flourished)
F.M.	field-marshal, frequency modulation
F.O.	Field Officer, Flying Officer, Foreign Office
fo.	folio
Fr.	Father, France, French, Friday
ft	foot, feet

g	*gram (s)*	K.G.	*Knight of the Garter*	NB	*New Brunswick*
G.B.	*Great Britain*	kg	*kilogram (s)*	n.b.	*nota bene (note well)*
G.C.	*George Cross*	K.T.	*Knight of the Thistle*	N.E.	*north-east*
G.I.	*government issue (U.S.A.)*	Kt	*knight*	N.F.	*National Front*
Gk	*Greek*	kt.	*knot*	N.I.	*National Insurance, Northern Ireland*
G.M.	*General Manager, George Medal, Grand Master*	kW	*kilowatt*	No.	*number (numero)*
		L.	*lira, Latin, Liberal*	N.P.	*new paragraph*
		l.	*left, litre*	nr.	*near*
G.P.	*General Practitioner*	lb.	*libra (pound)*	NS	*New Style, Nova Scotia*
G.R.	*Georgius Rex (King George)*	l.c.	*lower case (printing)*	N.T.	*New Testament, Northern Territory*
		Ld.	*Lord*		
Gr.	*Greek*	L.F.	*low frequency*	N.W.	*north-west*
gr.	*grain (s), gram (s), gross*	L.P.	*low pressure*	N.Y.	*New York*
GT	*gran turismo*	L.T.	*low tension*	N.Z.	*New Zealand*
Gt.	*great*	Lt.	*Lieutenant*	o	*octavo*
H.C.	*House of Commons*	M.	*Mach, medium, member, Monsieur (Fr.), thousand (mille)*	ob	*obiit (died)*
H.E.	*high explosive, His Eminence, His (Her) Excellency*			OB	*outside broadcast*
				O.C.	*Officer Commanding*
				Oc.	*Ocean*
H.F.	*high frequency*	m.	*metre (s), miles (s), masculine, married, meridian*	OD	*on demand, overdose, overdrawn*
hf.	*half*				
H.H.	*His (Her) Highness*	M.A.	*Master of Arts*	OE	*Old English*
H.M.	*His (Her) Majesty*	M.B.	*Bachelor of Medicine*	OF	*Old French*
h.p.	*high pressure, hire purchase, horsepower*	M.C.	*Master of Ceremonies, Member of Congress (U.S.), Military Cross*	O.M.	*Order of Merit*
				op.	*opus (work)*
H.Q.	*headquarters*			o.p.	*out of print*
hr.	*hour*			OR	*other ranks (mil.)*
H.T.	*high tension*	M.D.	*Doctor of Medicine, Managing Director*	OS	*Old Style, Ordnance Survey*
ht.	*height*				
h.v.	*high velocity, high voltage*	ME	*Middle English, myalgic encephalomyelitis*	O.S.	*old style*
				O.T.	*occupational therapy, Old Testament*
Hz	*hertz*	mf	*mezzoforte*		
IA	*Iowa*	mg	*milligram*	O.U.	*Oxford University, Open University*
ID	*Idaho, identification*	mi.	*mile*		
id.	*idem (the same)*	mk.	*mark*	P	*parking, pawn, peseta, peso*
i.e.	*id est (that is)*	ml	*millilitre*		
IL	*Illinois*	MM.	*Messieurs (Fr.)*	p.	*page, penny, pence, piano*
IN	*Indiana*	M.M.	*Military Medal*		
I.Q.	*intelligence quotient*	M.O.	*medical officer*	PA	*personal assistant, Press Association, Publishers Association*
Is.	*Isaiah, island (s)*	Mo.	*month*		
IT	*information technology*	M.P.	*Member of Parliament, Military Police*		
It.	*Italian, Italy*				
I.W.	*Isle of Wight*	M.R.	*Master of the Rolls*	p.a.	*per annum*
J.	*joule, judge*	Mr.	*mister*	PC	*personal computer, police constable, politically correct, Privy Councillor*
JC	*Jesus Christ*	M.S.	*Master of Science, multiple sclerosis*		
J.P.	*Justice of the Peace*				
Jr.	*junior*	MS	*manuscript*		
Jt.	*joint*	M.T.	*mechanical transport*	p.c.	*per cent, postcard, post cibum (after meals)*
K	*kelvin*	Mt.	*mount*		
k.	*kilo, one thousand*	N.	*newton, north*	pd	*paid*
KB	*kilobyte*	n.	*neuter, noun*	p.d.	*per diem, potential difference*
K.C.	*King's Counsel*	N.A.	*North America, not applicable*		
kc	*kilocycle*			P.E.	*physical education*

P.G.	*paying guest*	S.	*Saint, Schilling, second,*	V.O.	*Victorian Order*
Pg.	*Portugal, Portuguese*		*singular, shilling,*	V.R.	*Victoria Regina*
pg.	*page*		*son, south*		*(Queen)*
pl.	*plural, place*	S.A.	*Salvation Army, South*	W.	*watt, west*
P.M.	*Prime Minister, Provost*		*Africa, South*	W.C.	*water closet, West*
	Marshal, Past		*America, South*		*Central*
	Master, Postmaster		*Australia,*	W.D.	*War Department*
p.m.	*post meridiem, post*		*Sturmabteilung –*	w.f.	*wrong fount (printing)*
	mortem		*(Nazi militia)*	W.I.	*West Indies*
P.O.	*Personnel Officer, Petty*	s.c.	*small capitals*	W.O.	*War Office, Warrant*
	Officer, Pilot Officer,		*(printing)*		*Officer,*
	postal order, post	S.E.	*south-east (ern)*		*Wireless Operator*
	office	SF	*science fiction*	wt.	*weight*
pp	*pages, pianissimo*	sf	*sforzando*	yd.	*yard*
p.p.	*per pro*	s.g.	*specific gravity*	yr.	*year, your*
PR	*proportional*	SI	*Système International*		
	representation,	S.J.	*Society of Jesus*	**3**	
	public relations	S.M.	*Sergeant-Major*	A.A.A.	*Amateur Athletic*
P.S.	*postscript, private*	Sp.	*Spain, Spanish*		*Association,*
	secretary	sp.	*special, specific, spelling*		*American*
Pt.	*part, port*	Sq.	*squadron*		*Automobile*
pt	*pint, point*	sq.	*square*		*Association*
Q.	*quartermaster*	Sr.	*Señor, Sister*	A.B.A.	*Amateur Boxing*
q	*query, question*	sr.	*senior*		*Association,*
Q.B.	*Queen's Bench*	SS	*Saints, Steamship,*		*American Bar*
Q.C.	*Queen's Counsel*		*Schutzstaffel (Nazi*		*Association*
Q.M.	*Quartermaster*		*elite unit)*	A.B.C.	*American Broadcasting*
qr.	*quarter, quarterly*	St.	*Saint, street, stone,*		*Company, Australian*
qt.	*quart*		*stumped*		*Broadcasting*
q.v.	*quod vide (which see)*	S.W.	*south-west (ern)*		*Corporation*
R.	*Réaumur, Royal, Rex,*	Sw.	*Sweden, Swedish*	ABM	*antiballistic missile*
	Regina, right, river,	t	*ton (ne)*	Abp.	*archbishop*
	rouble, rupee	T.A.	*Territorial Army*	A.C.A.	*Associate of the Institute*
R.A.	*Rear Admiral, Royal*	T.B.	*torpedo-boat,*		*of Chartered*
	Academician, Royal		*tuberculosis*		*Accountants*
	Academy, Royal	T.D.	*Territorial Decoration*	A.C.T.	*Australian Capital*
	Artillery,	T.T.	*teetotal, Tourist Trophy*		*Territory*
R.C.	*Roman Catholic*	tr.	*transitive, translated,*	A.D.C.	*aide-de-camp, amateur*
Rd.	*road*		*translator*		*dramatic club*
R.E.	*religious education,*	TU	*trade union*	adj.	*adjective*
	Royal Engineers	TV	*television*	Adm.	*Admiral*
RF	*radio frequency*	u.c.	*uppercase (printing)*	ADP	*automatic data*
rh	*right hand*	U.K.	*United Kingdom*		*processing*
RI	*religious instruction*	U.N.	*United Nations*	adv.	*adverb*
RL	*Rugby League*	U.P.	*Uttar Pradesh*	A.E.A.	*Atomic Energy*
R.M.	*Royal Mail, Royal*	U.S.	*United States*		*Authority*
	Marines	V	*volt, volume, victory*	A.E.C.	*Atomic Energy*
R.N.	*Royal Navy*	v.	*verb, versus (against)*		*Commission*
R.R.	*Right Reverend*	vb.	*verb*	A.E.U.	*Amalgamated*
R.S.	*Royal Society*	V.C.	*Vice Chancellor,*		*Engineering Union*
Rs.	*rupees*		*Victoria Cross*	A.F.C.	*Air Force Cross*
R.U.	*Rugby Union*	V.D.	*venereal disease*	Afg.	*Afghanistan*
ry.	*railway*	v.g.	*very good*	A.F.M.	*Air Force Medal*
		V.I.	*Virgin Islands*	Afr.	*Africa*

AGM	Annual General Meeting	B.D.S.	Bachelor of Dental Surgery	C.N.D.	Campaign for Nuclear Disarmament
AID	artificial insemination by donor	B.Ed.	Bachelor of Education	c.o.d.	cash on delivery
a.k.a.	also known as	B.E.F.	British Expeditionary Force	C.O.I.	Central Office of Information
Alb.	Albania	b.h.p.	brake horsepower	Col.	Colorado, Colossians
Alg.	Algeria	B.I.M.	British Institute of Management	col.	column
alg.	algebra			coy.	company (mil.)
A.L.P.	Australian Labour Party	B.M.A.	British Medical Association	cpl.	corporal
AMU	atomic mass unit	B.M.C.	British Medical Council	CPO	chief petty oficer
A.N.C.	African National Congress	B.M.J.	British Medical Journal	C.P.R.	Canadian Pacific Railway
AOB	any other business	BMX	bicycle motocross	C.P.S.	Crown Prosecution Service
A.O.C.	Air Officer Commanding, Appellation d'origine contrôlée (wine classification)	Bro.	brother	C.R.E.	Commission for Racial Equality
		B.R.S.	British Road Services	CRT	cathode ray tube
		B.Sc.	Bachelor of Science	C.S.E.	Certificate of Secondary Education
		BSE	bovine spongiform encephalopathy	C.S.M.	Company Sergeant-Major
A.O.F.	Ancient Order of Foresters	B.S.I.	British Standards Institution	C.V.O.	Commander of the Victorian Order
A.P.M.	Assistant Provost Marshal	BST	British Standard Time, British Summer Time	C.W.S.	Co-operative Wholesale Society
APR	annual percentage rate	B.V.M.	Blessed Virgin Mary	cwt.	hundredweight
Apr.	April	CAP	common agricultural policy	D.A.G.	Deputy Adjutant-General
APT	Advanced Passenger Train	cap.	capital	D.B.E.	Dame Commander of the British Empire (Order)
A.R.A.	Associate of the Royal Academy	C.B.C.	Canadian Broadcasting Corporation		
A.R.P.	Air Raid Precautions	C.B.E.	Commander of the British Empire (Order)	D.C.B.	Dame Commander of the Bath (Order)
Arg.	Argentina			D.C.L.	Doctor of Civil Law
arr.	arranged, arrival, arrive (s, d)	C.B.I.	Confederation of British Industry	D.C.M.	Distinguished Conduct Medal
A.S.A.	Advertising Standards Authority	C.B.S.	Columbia Broadcasting System	DDR	Deutsche Demokratische Republik (East Germany)
A.S.H.	Action on Smoking and Health	CEO	chief executive officer		
A.T.C.	air-traffic control, Air Training Corps	C.G.T.	Confédération Générale du Travail (French trade union association)		
				D.D.S.	Doctor of Dental Surgery
ATP	adenosine triphosphate			DDT	dichlorodiphenyl-trichloroethane
ATV	all-terrain vehicle, Associated Television	C.I.A.	Central Intelligence Agency	Dec.	December
Aug.	August	C.I.D.	Criminal Investigation Department	dec.	deceased, decimal, decimetre, decrescendo (music)
aux.	auxiliary				
ave.	avenue	c.i.f.	cost, insurance, freight	def.	definite, definition
B.A.A.	British Airports Authority	C.I.O.	Congress of Industrial Organizations (U.S.)	del.	delegate
B.B.C.	British Broadcasting Corporation	CJD	Creutzfeldt–Jacob disease	Den.	Denmark
BCG	Bacillus Calmette Guérin (anti-tuberculosis vaccine)	C.M.G.	Companion of St. Michael and St. George (Order)	Det.	Detective
				D.F.C.	Distinguished Flying Cross
B.C.L.	Bachelor of Civil Law				

D.F.M.	*Distinguished Flying Medal*
Dip.	*Diploma*
div.	*Dividend*
DIY	*do-it-yourself*
DNA	*deoxyribonucleic acid*
D.N.B.	*Dictionary of National Biography*
DOA	*dead on arrival*
doz.	*dozen*
DPP	*Director of Public Prosecutions*
dpt.	*department*
D.S.C.	*Distinguished Service Cross*
D.Sc.	*Doctor of Science*
D.S.M.	*Distinguished Service Medal*
D.S.O.	*Distinguished Service Order*
DST	*Daylight Saving Time*
DTs	*delirium tremens*
D.T.I.	*Department of Trade and Industry*
DTP	*desktop publishing*
ECT	*electroconvulsive therapy*
ECU	*European Currency Unit*
E.D.C.	*European Defence Community*
E.E.C.	*European Economic Community*
EEG	*electroencephalogram, electroencephalograph*
EFL	*English as a Foreign Language*
e.m.f.	*electromotive force*
E.N.E.	*east-north-east*
ENT	*ear, nose and throat*
E.O.C.	*Equal Opportunities Commission*
E.S.E.	*east-south-east*
ESN	*educationally subnormal*
ESP	*extrasensory perception*
esp.	*especially*
Esq.	*Esquire*
EST	*Eastern Standard Time, electric shock treatment*
est.	*estimated*

ETA	*expected time of arrival*
etc.	*et cetera*
ETD	*expected time of departure*
FAO	*Food and Agriculture Organization*
F.B.A.	*Fellow of the British Academy*
F.B.I.	*Federal Bureau of Investigation*
F.C.A.	*Fellow of the Institute of Chartered Accountants*
Feb.	*February*
fem.	*feminine*
F.G.S.	*Fellow of the Geological Society*
F.I.A.	*Fellow of the Institute of Actuaries*
fig.	*figure, figuratively*
Fin.	*Finland, Finnish*
fin.	*finance, financial*
F.L.A.	*Fellow of the Library Association*
f.o.b.	*free on board*
F.P.A.	*Family Planning Association*
Fri.	*Friday*
F.R.S.	*Fellow of the Royal Society*
F.Z.S.	*Fellow of the Zoological Society*
fur.	*furlong*
Gal.	*Galatians*
G.B.E.	*Knight (or Dame) Grand Cross of the British Empire*
GBH	*grievous bodily harm*
G.C.B.	*Knight Grand Cross of the Bath*
G.C.E.	*General Certificate of Education*
GDP	*gross domestic product*
GDR	*German Democratic Republic*
gen.	*gender, general, genitive, genus*
G.H.Q.	*General Headquarters*
Gib.	*Gibraltar*
G.L.C.	*Greater London Council*
Gmc.	*Germanic*
G.M.T.	*Greenwich Mean Time*
GNP	*Gross National Product*

G.O.C.	*General Officer Commanding*
G.O.M.	*grand old man*
Gov.	*government, governor*
G.P.O.	*General Post Office*
gtd.	*guaranteed*
H.A.C.	*Hon. Artillery Company*
H.B.M.	*His (Her) Britannic Majesty*
h.c.f.	*highest common factor*
HGV	*heavy goods vehicle*
H.I.H.	*His (Her) Imperial Highness*
H.I.M.	*His (Her) Imperial Majesty*
HIV	*human immunodeficiency virus*
H.L.I.	*Highland Light Infantry*
H.M.I.	*His (Her) Majesty's Inspector*
H.M.S.	*His (Her) Majesty's Ship or Service*
H.N.C.	*Higher National Certificate*
H.N.D.	*Higher National Diploma*
Hon.	*honorary, Honourable*
Hos.	*Hosea*
H.R.H.	*His (Her) Royal Highness*
hrs.	*hours*
HRT	*hormone replacement therapy*
I.B.A.	*Independent Broadcasting Authority*
I.C.A.	*Institute of Chartered Accountants, Institute of Contemporary Arts*
I.C.E	*Institution of Civil Engineers*
I.C.I.	*Imperial Chemical Industries*
I.E.E.	*Institution of Electrical Engineers*
I.H.S.	*Jesus, Saviour of men (Iesus Hominum Salvator)*
I.L.O.	*International Labour Organization*
I.L.P.	*Independent Labour Party*

I.M.F.	*International Monetary Fund*	K.K.K.	*Ku Klux Klan*	Min.	*Minister, Ministry*
imp.	*imperative, imperfect, imperial*	kWh	*kilowatt-hour*	min.	*mineralogy*
		Lab.	*Labour*	MLR	*minimum lending rate*
Inc.	*incorporated*	lab.	*laboratory*	Mme.	*Madame*
inc.	*including, inclusive, increase*	Lat.	*Latin*	M.O.D.	*Ministry of Defence*
		lat.	*latitude*	mod.	*moderate, modern*
Ind.	*India, Indiana*	l.b.w.	*leg before wicket*	M.O.H.	*Medical Officer of Health*
ind.	*independent, indicative, industrial, industry*	L.C.C.	*London County Council*		
		l.c.d.	*liquid crystal display, lowest common denominator*	Mon.	*Monday*
inf.	*infinitive, informal*			m.p.h.	*miles per hour*
int.	*interest, internal, international*			M.Sc.	*Master of Science*
		L.C.J.	*Lord Chief Justice*	MSS	*manuscripts*
I.O.C.	*International Olympic Committee*	l.c.m.	*lowest common multiple*	M.T.B.	*motor torpedo boat*
		L.D.S.	*Licentiate in Dental Surgery*	M.V.O.	*Member of the Royal Victorian Order*
I.O.F.	*Independent Order of Foresters*				
		L.E.A.	*Local Education Authority*	nat.	*national, native*
I.O.M.	*Isle of Man*			NBA	*Net Book Agreement*
I.O.U.	*(acknowledgment of debt)*	LED	*light-emitting diode*	N.C.B.	*National Coal Board*
		LEM	*lunar excursion module*	N.C.C.	*Nature Conservancy Council*
I.O.W.	*Isle of Wight*	Lev.	*Leviticus*		
IPA	*International Phonetic Alphabet*	LL.B.	*Bachelor of Laws*	N.C.O.	*non-commissioned officer*
		LL.D.	*Doctor of Laws*		
I.R.A.	*Irish Republican Army*	LL.M.	*Master of Laws*	N.C.P.	*National Car Parks*
I.S.O.	*Imperial Service Order, International Standards Organization*	LSD	*lysergic acid diethylamide*	NEB	*New English Bible*
				neg.	*negative*
		l.s.d.	*librae; solidi; denarii (pounds shillings pence)*	N.F.U.	*National Farmers' Union*
ITA	*International Teaching Alphabet*			NHS	*National Health Service*
		L.S.E.	*London School of Economics*	N.N.E.	*north-north-east*
I.T.U.	*International Telecommunications Union*			N.N.W.	*north-north-west*
		LSO	*London Symphony Orchestra*	nos.	*numbers*
				Nov.	*November*
ITV	*Independent Television*	Ltd.	*Limited*	N.P.A.	*Newspaper Publishers Association*
IUD	*intra-uterine device*	Lux.	*Luxembourg*		
IVF	*in vitro fertilization*	mag.	*magazine*	N.P.L.	*National Physical Laboratory*
Jan.	*January*	Maj.	*Major*		
Jas.	*James*	Mar.	*March*	N.R.A.	*National Rifle Association*
Jer.	*Jeremiah*	mar.	*married*		
Jon.	*Jonah*	max.	*maximum*	NSU	*non-specific urethritis*
Jos.	*Joseph*	M.B.A.	*Master of Business Administration*	N.S.W.	*New South Wales*
jun.	*junior*			N.U.J.	*National Union of Journalists*
juv.	*juvenile*	M.B.E.	*Member of the British Empire (Order)*		
K.B.E.	*Knight Commander of the British Empire (Order)*			N.U.M.	*National Union of Mineworkers*
		M.C.C.	*Marylebone Cricket Club*		
				Num.	*Numbers*
K.C.B.	*Knight Commander of the Bath*	MCP	*male chauvinist pig*	N.U.R.	*National Union of Railwaymen*
		M.E.P.	*Member of European Parliament*		
K.G.B.	*Komitet Gosudarstvennoi Bezopasnosti (Committee of State Security)*			N.U.S.	*National Union of Seamen, National Union of Students*
		met.	*meteorological, metropolitan*		
		M.F.H.	*Master of Foxhounds*	N.U.T.	*National Union of Teachers*
		Mgr.	*Manager, Monsignor*		
		MHz	*megahertz*	NYC	*New York City*
kHz	*kilohertz*	mil.	*military*	OAP	*old age pensioner*

O.A.S.	Organisation de l'Armée Secrète (movement violently opposed to Algerian independence), Organization of American States	ppr.	present participle	R.H.S.	Royal Horticultural Society
		PPS	parliamentary private secretary	R.I.P.	requiescat in pace (may he or she rest in peace)
		pps.	post postscriptum	R.M.A.	Royal Military Academy
		P.R.B.	Pre-Raphaelite Brotherhood	RNA	ribonucleic acid
O.B.E.	Officer of the British Empire (Order)	P.R.O.	public relations officer	R.N.R.	Royal Naval Reserve
obs.	obsolete	PSV	public service vehicle	R.O.C.	Royal Observer Corps
OCR	optical character reader (recognition)	PTA	Parent–Teacher Association	ROM	read-only memory
Oct.	October	P.T.O.	please turn over	Rom.	Roman, Romania
oct.	octavo	PVC	polyvinyl chloride	rom.	roman (typeface)
off.	offer, officer, officer	Pvt.	Private	RPI	retail price index
O.F.T.	Office of Fair Trading, Orange Free State	PWR	pressurized water reactor	R.S.A.	Republic of South Africa, Royal Scottish Academy, Royal Society of Arts
O.N.D.	Ordinary National Diploma	q.e.d.	quod erat demonstrandum (which was to be proved)	R.S.C.	Royal Shakespeare Company
o.n.o.	or near(est) offer	Q.M.G.	Quartermaster-General	RSI	repetitive strain injury
Ont.	Ontario	Q.M.S.	Quartermaster-Sergeant	R.S.M.	Regimental Sergeant-Major, Royal Society of Music, Royal Society of Medicine
opp.	opposed, opposite				
ord.	ordained, order, ordinary, ordnance	Que.	Quebec		
O.T.C.	Officers' Training Corps	R.A.C.	Royal Armoured Corps, Royal Automobile Club	RTE	Radio Telefis Eireann
Pac.	Pacific			R.U.C.	Royal Ulster Constabulary
Pal.	Palestine	R.A.F.	Royal Air Force		
Pan.	Panama	R.A.M.	Royal Academy of Music	SAD	seasonal affective disorder
Par.	Paraguay				
par.	paragraph, parallel, parish	RAM	random access memory	s.a.e.	stamped addressed envelope
		R.C.A.	Royal College of Art		
P.B.S.	Public Broadcasting Service	R.C.M.	Royal College of Music	S.Af.	South Africa
		R.C.N.	Royal College of Nursing	SAM	surface to air missile
PBX	Private Branch Exchange			S.Am.	South America
		R.C.P.	Royal College of Physicians	Sam.	Samuel
pen.	peninsula			SAS	Special Air Service
PEP	personal equity plan	R.C.S.	Royal College of Surgeons	Sat.	Saturday, Saturn
Ph.D.	Doctor of Philosophy			Sc.D.	Doctor of Science
P.L.A.	Port of London Authority	rec.	receipt, record	S.C.E.	Scottish Certificate of Education
		ref.	referee, reference		
PLC	Public Limited Company	rel.	religion, religious	sci.	science, scientific
		REM	rapid eye movement	SDI	Strategic Defense Initiative
P.L.O.	Palestine Liberation Organization	rep.	report, reprint		
		ret.	retired	S.D.P.	Social Democratic Party
PLP	Parliamentary Labour Party	Rev.	Reverend		
		rev.	revenue, revision, revolution	sec.	secant, second, secretary
PLR	Public Lending Right			Sen.	senate, senator, senior
P.M.G.	Paymaster-General, Postmaster-General	R.F.C.	Royal Flying Corps, Rugby Football Club	Sep.	September, Septuagint
				seq.	sequens (the following)
PMT	premenstrual tension	R.G.N.	Registered General Nurse	Sgt.	Sergeant
pop.	population			SIB	Securities and Investment Board
POW	prisoner of war	R.G.S.	Royal Geographical Society		
PPE	philosophy, politics and economics			Sib.	Siberia
		R.H.A.	Royal Horse Artillery	Sic.	Sicily

SIS — *Secret Intelligence Service*
Skt. — *Sanskrit*
S.L.D. — *Social and Liberal Democrats*
SLR — *single-lens reflex*
S.N.P. — *Scottish National Party*
snr. — *senior*
Soc. — *Socialist, society*
sop. — *soprano*
S.P.G. — *Society for the Propagation of the Gospel*
S.R.C. — *Science Research Council, Student Representative Council*
S.R.N. — *State Registered Nurse*
S.S.E. — *south-south-east*
S.S.W. — *south-south-west*
STD — *subscriber trunk dialling*
stg. — *sterling*
S.W.G. — *standard wire gauge*
Tas. — *Tasmania*
ten. — *tenor*
TGV — *train à grande vitesse (high-speed passenger train)*
Tim. — *Timothy*
TIR — *Transports Internationaux Routiers (International Road Transport)*
TNT — *trinitrotoluene (explosive)*
T.U.C. — *Trades Union Congress*
typ. — *typographical, typography*
U.A.E. — *United Arab Emirates*
U.A.R. — *United Arab Republic*
U.D.A. — *Ulster Defence Association*
UDC — *Urban District Council*
U.D.I. — *unilateral declaration of independence*
U.D.R. — *Ulster Defence Regiment*
UFO — *unidentified flying object*
uhf — *ultra-high frequency*
ult. — *ultimate, ultimo (last month)*

U.N.O. — *United Nations Organization*
U.P.U. — *Universal Postal Union*
Uru. — *Uruguay*
U.S.A. — *United States of America*
USN — *United States Navy*
USS — *United States Senate, United States Ship*
usw — *ultra-short wave*
U.V.F. — *Ulster Volunteer Force*
V.A.D. — *Voluntary Aid Detachment*
VAT — *value added tax*
VCR — *video cassette recorder*
VDU — *visual display unit*
Ven. — *Venerable*
Vet. — *veterinary surgeon*
vhf — *very high frequency*
V.I.P. — *very important person*
viz. — *videlicet (namely)*
vlf — *very low frequency*
voc. — *vocative*
vol. — *volume, volunteer*
VSO — *very superior old, (brandy) Voluntary Services Overseas*
War. — *Warwickshire*
W.B.A. — *World Boxing Association*
w.e.f. — *with effect from*
WHO — *World Health Organization*
W.N.W. — *west-north-west*
wpb — *wastepaper basket*
W.P.C. — *Woman Police Constable*
wpm — *words per minute*
W.S.W. — *west-south-west*
Y.H.A. — *Youth Hostels Association*
yrs. — *years*
Y.T.S. — *Youth Training Scheme*

4

ABTA — *Association of British Travel Agents*
ACAS — *Advisory Conciliation and Arbitration Service*
ACTH — *adrenocorticotrophic hormone*
Adjt. — *adjutant*
advt. — *advertisement*

AIDS — *Acquired Immune Deficiency Syndrome*
anon. — *anonymous*
APEX — *Advance Purchase Excursion, Association of Professional, Executive, Clerical and Computer Staff*
A.R.A.M. — *Associate of the Royal Academy of Music*
A.R.C.M. — *Associate of the Royal College of Music*
a.s.a.p. — *as soon as possible*
asst. — *assistant*
AWOL — *absent without leave*
B.A.O.R. — *British Army of the Rhine*
Bart. — *baronet*
B.Com. — *Bachelor of Commerce*
Beds. — *Bedfordshire*
Belg. — *Belgian, Belgium*
B.Eng. — *Bachelor of Engineering*
B.F.P.O. — *British Forces Post Office*
Bibl. — *Biblical*
biog. — *biographical, biography*
biol. — *biological, biology*
B.Lit. — *Bachelor of Literature*
B.Mus. — *Bachelor of Music*
Brig. — *Brigadier*
Brit. — *British*
Bros. — *brothers*
B.Th.U. — *British Thermal Unit*
B.U.P.A. — *British United Provident Association*
Cant. — *Canterbury*
caps. — *capital letters*
Capt. — *Captain*
cath. — *cathedral, Catholic*
cent. — *centigrade, century*
C.E.R.N. — *Conseil Européen pour la Recherche Nucléaire*
chem. — *chemical, chemistry*
Chron. — *Chronicles*
C. in C. — *Commander in Chief*
Cllr. — *Councillor*
coll. — *college*

comp.	*company, comparative, composer, composition, composito, comprehensive*
cont.	*contents, continued*
Corp.	*Corporal, corporation*
C.P.R.E.	*Council for the Preservation of Rural England*
dept.	*department*
dict.	*dictionary*
dist.	*district*
D.Lit.	*Doctor of Literature*
D.Mus.	*Doctor of Music*
D.V.L.A.	*Driver and Vehicle Licensing Authority*
Ebor.	*Eboracum (York)*
eccl.	*ecclesiastical*
E.C.S.C.	*European Coal and Steel Community*
Edin.	*Edinburgh*
E.F.T.A.	*European Free Trade Association*
elec.	*electrical, electricity*
E.N.S.A.	*Entertainments National Service Association*
Epis.	*Episcopal, Epistle*
Esth.	*Esther*
et al.	*and elsewhere, and others*
FIFA	*Fédération Internationale de Football Association*
FIFO	*first in, first out*
F.R.A.M.	*Fellow of the Royal Academy of Music*
F.R.A.S.	*Fellow of the Royal Astronomical Society*
F.R.C.P.	*Fellow of the Royal College of Physicians*
F.R.C.S.	*Fellow of the Royal College of Surgeons*
F.R.G.S.	*Fellow of the Royal Geographical Society*
F.R.S.A.	*Fellow of the Royal Society of Arts*
F.R.S.L.	*Fellow of the Royal Society of Literature*
F.R.S.M.	*Fellow of the Royal Society of Medicine*
G.A.T.T.	*General Agreement on Tariffs and Trade*
G.C.M.G.	*Knight Grand Cross of St. Michael and St. George (Order)*
G.C.S.E.	*General Certification of Secondary Education*
G.C.V.O.	*Knight Grand Cross of the Victorian Order*
geog.	*geographical, geography*
geol.	*geological*
geom.	*geometric, geometry*
Glos.	*Gloucestershire*
govt.	*government*
gram.	*grammar, grammatical*
Guat.	*Guatemala*
Guin.	*Guinea*
I.A.T.A.	*International Air Transport Association*
ibid.	*ibidem (in the same place)*
I.B.R.D.	*International Bank for Reconstruction and Development*
ICBM	*Intercontinental Ballistic Missile*
I.L.E.A.	*Inner London Education Authority*
impf.	*imperfect*
incl.	*including, inclusive*
I.N.L.A.	*Irish National Liberation Army*
I. of W.	*Isle of Wight*
INRI	*Iesus Nazarenus Rex Iudaeorum (Jesus of Nazareth King of the Jews)*
inst.	*instant, institution, institute (in the present month)*
intr.	*intransitive*
IRBM	*Intermediate Range Ballistic Missile*
ISBN	*International Standard Book Number*
Ital.	*Italian, Italy*
ital.	*italic*
Josh.	*Joshua*
Judg.	*Judges*
K.A.N.U.	*Kenyan African National Union*
K.C.M.G.	*Knight Commander (of the Order) of St. Michael and St. George*
K.C.V.O.	*Knight Commander of the Royal Victorian Order*
kilo	*kilogram*
LIFO	*last in first out*
Lith.	*Lithuania*
long.	*longitude*
L.R.A.M.	*Licentiate of the Royal Academy of Music*
L.R.C.M.	*Licentiate of the Royal College of Music*
L.R.C.P.	*Licentiate of the Royal College of Physicians*
mach.	*machine, machinery*
masc.	*masculine*
math.	*mathematics*
Matt.	*Matthew*
mech.	*mechanics*
memo.	*memorandum*
Meth.	*Methodist*
M.I.C.E.	*Member of the Institution of Civil Engineers*
M.I.E.E.	*Member of the Institution of Electrical Engineers*
M.I.M.E.	*Member of the Institution of Mechanical Engineers*
MIRV	*multiple independently targeted re-entry vehicle*
Mlle.	*Mademoiselle*
M.O.R.I.	*Market and Opinion Research Institute*
M.R.C.P.	*Member of the Royal College of Physicians*

M.R.C.S.	Member of the Royal College of Surgeons	Prov.	Proverbs, Province, Provost	S.N.C.F.	Société Nationale de Chemins de Fer Français (French National Railways)
Mus.B.	Bachelor of Music	prox.	proximo (next month)		
Mus.D.	Doctor of Music	PSBR	public sector borrowing requirement		
myth.	mythology			S.P.C.K.	Society for Promoting Christian Knowledge
N.A.S.A.	National Aeronautics and Space Administration	R.A.A.F.	Royal Australian Air Force		
				sp. gr.	specific gravity
N.A.T.O.	North Atlantic Treaty Organization	R.A.D.A.	Royal Academy of Dramatic Art	SPQR	Senatus Populusque Romanus (the Senate and the People of Rome)
N.U.P.E.	National Union of Public Employers	R.A.M.C.	Royal Army Medical Corps		
O.E.C.D.	Organization for Economic Cooperation and Development	R.A.O.B.	Royal Antediluvian Order of Buffaloes	STOL	short take-off and landing (aircraft)
		R.A.O.C.	Royal Army Ordnance Corps	Supt.	superintendent
				Surg.	surgeon, surgery, surgical
O.E.E.C.	Organization for European Economic Cooperation	R.A.S.C.	Royal Army Service Corps	TASS	Telegrafnoye Agenstvo Sovetskovo Soyuza (Soviet news agency)
		R.C.M.P.	Royal Canadian Mounted Police		
O.H.M.S.	On Her (His) Majesty's Service	recd.	received		
		Regt.	regiment	T.A.V.R.	Territorial Army and Volunteer Reserve
O.P.E.C.	Organization of Petroleum-Exporting Countries	R.E.M.E.	Royal Electrical and Mechanical Engineers	TEFL	Teaching English as a Foreign Language
		R.I.B.A.	Royal Institute of British Architects	TESL	Teaching English as a Second Language
O.U.D.S.	Oxford University Dramatic Society	R.I.C.S.	Royal Institute of Chartered Surveyors	T.G.W.U.	Transport and General Workers' Union
Oxon.	Oxford, Oxfordshire				
Parl.	Parliament, Parliamentary	R.N.I.B.	Royal National Institute for the Blind	Tues.	Tuesday
				U.C.C.A.	Universities Central Council on Admissions
part.	participle	R.N.L.I.	Royal National Lifeboat Institution		
pass.	passive			U.E.F.A.	Union of European Football Associations
path.	pathological, pathology	R.N.V.R.	Royal Naval Volunteer Reserve		
P.A.Y.E.	pay as you earn	R.S.P.B.	Royal Society for the Protection of Birds	U.S.A.F.	United States Air Force
P.D.S.A.	People's Dispensary for Sick Animals			U.S.S.R.	Union of Soviet Socialist Republics
perf.	perfect	R.S.V.P.	Répondez s'il vous plaît (please reply)	VSOP	very superior old pale (brandy)
pers.	person, personal				
plup.	pluperfect	SALT	Strategic Arms Limitation Talks	VTOL	vertical take-off and landing (aircraft)
plur.	plural				
prec.	preceding	SATB	soprano, alto, tenor, bass (choral music combination)	Vulg.	Vulgate
pred.	predicate			W.A.A.C.	Women's Army Auxiliary Corps
pref.	preference, prefix				
prep.	preparation, preposition	SAYE	save as you earn	W.A.A.F.	Women's Auxiliary Air Force
		Scand.	Scandinavia (n)		
pres.	present	S.D.L.P.	Social Democratic and Labour Party	WASP	White Anglo-Saxon Protestant
Pres.	President				
Prof.	professor	Sept.	September	W.Cdr.	Wing Commander
pron.	pronoun, pronunciation	SIDS	Sudden Infant Death Syndrome	W.F.T.U.	World Federation of
Prot.	Protectorate, Protestant				

	Trade Unions		elect.	*electrical, electricity*
W.R.A.C.	*Women's Royal Army Corps*		ERNIE	*Electronic Random Number Indicator Equipment*
W.R.A.F.	*Women's Royal Air Force*		et seq.	*et sequens (and what follows)*
W.R.N.S.	*Women's Royal Naval Service*		ex div.	*without dividend*
W.R.V.S.	*Women's Royal Voluntary Service*		F.R.I.B.A.	*Fellow of the Royal Institute of British Architects*
Xmas	*Christmas*			
Y.M.C.A.	*Young Men's Christian Association*		F.R.I.C.S.	*Fellow of the Royal Institute of Chartered Surveyors*
Yugo.	*Yugoslavia*		Hants.	*Hampshire*
Y.W.C.A.	*Young Women s Christian Association*		Herts.	*Hertfordshire*
Z.A.N.U.	*Zimbabwe African National Union*		indef.	*indefinite*
Z.A.P.U.	*Zimbabwe African People's Union*		intro.	*introduction*
zool.	*zoology*		Lancs.	*Lancashire*

5

			Leics.	*Leicestershire*
ad lib.	*ad libitum (as much as desired)*		Lieut.	*Lieutenant*
admin.	*administration, administrative*		Lincs.	*Lincolnshire*
Anzac	*Australian and New Zealand Army Corps*		Litt.D.	*Doctor of Letters*
ANZUS	*Australia, New Zealand and the United States (Pacific security alliance)*		L.R.C.V.S.	*Licentiate of the Royal College of Veterinary Surgeons*
			Lt. Col.	*Lieutenant-Colonel*
			Lt. Com.	*Lieutenant-Commander*
A.R.I.B.A.	*Associate of the Royal Institute of British Architects*		Lt. Gen.	*Lieutenant-General*
			Lt. Gov.	*Lieutenant-Governor*
A.S.L.E.F.	*Associated Society of Locomotive Engineers and Firemen*		Middx.	*Middlesex*
			Mlles.	*Mesdemoiselles*
Assoc.	*associate, association*		M.R.C.V.S.	*Member of the Royal College of Veterinary Surgeons*
A.S.T.M.S.	*Association of Scientific, Technical and Managerial Staffs*		N.A.A.F.I.	*Navy, Army and Air Force Institutes*
B.A.F.T.A.	*British Academy of Film and Television Arts*		Notts.	*Nottinghamshire*
			N.S.P.C.C.	*National Society for the Prevention of Cruelty to Children*
B.A.L.P.A.	*British Airline Pilots' Association*			
b. and b.	*bed and breakfast*		op.cit.	*opere citato (in the work cited)*
Berks.	*Berkshire*		P. and O.	*Peninsular and Oriental*
B.Litt.	*Bachelor of Letters*		R.A.F.V.R.	*Royal Air Force Volunteer Reserve*
Bucks.	*Buckinghamshire*		R. and D.	*research and development*
Cambs.	*Cambridgeshire*		R.o.S.P.A.	*Royal Society for the Prevention of Accidents*
CAMRA	*Campaign for Real Ale*			
CENTO	*Central Treaty Organization*		R.S.P.C.A.	*Royal Society for the Prevention of Cruelty to Animals*
Chron.	*Chronicles*			
C.O.H.S.E.	*Confederation of Health Service Employers*		Rt. Hon.	*Right Honourable*
			Rt. Rev.	*Right Reverend*
Comdr.	*Commander*		Salop.	*Shropshire*
Comdt.	*Commandant*		S.E.A.T.O.	*South-East Asia Treaty Organization*
Corpn.	*corporation*		Sergt.	*Sergeant*
C.S.R.I.O.	*Commonwealth Scientific and Industrial Research Organization*		S.H.A.E.F.	*Supreme Headquarters Allied Expeditionary Forces*
D. and C.	*dilation and curettage*		S.H.A.P.E.	*Supreme Headquarters Allied Powers in Europe*
Dip. Ed.	*Diploma in Education*			
D.Litt.	*Doctor of Letters*		S.O.G.A.T.	*Society of Graphical and Allied Trades*
D.Phil.	*Doctor of Philosophy*			
Dr.Iur.	*Doctor of Laws*			

S.W.A.P.O.	*South-West Africa People's Organization*
suppl.	*supplement(ary)*
TESSA	*Tax Exempt Special Savings Account*
trans.	*transitive, translated, translator*
Treas.	*treasurer*
U.N.R.R.A.	*United Nations Relief and Rehabilitation Administration*
vocab.	vocabulary
Wilts.	*Wiltshire*
Worcs.	*Worcestershire*
Xtian	*Christian*
Yorks.	*Yorkshire*

6 AND OVER

approx. (6)	*approximately*
attrib. (6)	*attribute, attributive*
Cantab. (6)	*of Cambridge*
Cantuar. (7)	*of Cambridge*
Col.-Sergt. (8)	*Colour-Sergeant*
COMECON (7)	*Council for Mutual Economic Aid*
Cominform (9)	*Communist Information Bureau*
Comintern (9)	*Communist International*
D.Theol. (6)	*Doctor of Theology*
Dunelm. (6)	*of Durham*
E. and O.E. (6)	*errors and omissions excepted*
Euratom (7)	*European Atomic Energy Community*

intrans. (7)	*intransitive*
Lieut.-Col. (8)	*Lieutenant-Colonel*
Lieut.-Gen. (8)	*Lieutenant-General*
Lieut.-Gov. (8)	*Lieutenant-Governor*
Lit.Hum. (6)	*Literae Humaniores (classics)*
loc. cit. (6)	*in the place cited*
Maj.-Gen. (6)	*Major-General*
matric. (6)	*matriculation*
M.I.Mech.E. (7)	*Member of the Institution of Mechanical Engineers*
M.I.Min.E. (6)	*Member of the Institution of Mining Engineers*
mod. cons. (7)	*modern conveniences*
Mus.Bac. (6)	*Bachelor of Music*
nem. con. (6)	*nemine contradicente (none objecting)*
Non-com. (6)	*non-commissioned officer*
per pro (6)	*per procurationem (by proxy)*
pro tem. (6)	*pro tempore (for the time being)*
Q.A.R.A.N.C. (6)	*Queen Alexandra's Royal Army Nursing Corps*
quango (6)	*quasi-autonomous non-governmental organization*
U.N.E.S.C.O. (6)	*United Nations Educational, Scientific and Cultural Organization*
U.N.I.C.E.F. (6)	*United Nations International Children's Emergency Fund*
verb. sap. (7)	*verbum sapienti (a word to the wise)*

Apostles

Andrew (6)	Judas (5)	Simon (5)
Bartholomew (11)	Jude (4)	Thaddeus (8)
James the Elder (13)	Matthew (7)	Thomas (6)
James the Less (12)	Peter (5)	
John (4)	Philip (6)	

Bibles

Authorized (10)	Gutenberg (9)	Printers' (8)
Bishop's (7)	Indian (6)	Revised (7)
Coverdale (9)	Itala (5)	Taverner (8)
Cranmer (7)	Judas (5)	Tyndale (7)
Cromwell (8)	King James (9)	Vinegar (7)
Douai (5)	Kralitz (7)	Wycliffe (6)
Geneva (6)	Matthew (7)	
Great (5)	Mazarin (7)	

Books of the Apocrypha

Baruch (6)
Bel and the Dragon (15)
Ecclesiasticus (14)
Epistle of Jeremiah (17)
Esdras (6)
Esther (6)

History of Susanna (16)
Judith (6)
Maccabees (9)
Song of the Three Holy
  Children (26)
The Prayer of Manasses (19)

The Wisdom of Solomon (18)
Tobit (5)

Chemical elements

Name	Symbol	Name	Symbol
ACTINIUM	Ac	INDIUM	In
ALUMINIUM	Al	IODINE	I
AMERICIUM	Am	IRIDIUM	Ir
ANTIMONY	Sb	IRON	Fe
ARGON	Ar	KRYPTON	Kr
ARSENIC	As	LANTHANUM	La
ASTATINE	At	LAWRENCIUM	Lr
BARIUM	Ba	LEAD	Pb
BERKELIUM	Bk	LITHIUM	Li
BERYLLIUM	Be	LUTETIUM	Lu
BISMUTH	Bi	MAGNESIUM	Mg
BORON	B	MANGANESE	Mn
BROMINE	Br	MENDELEVIUM	Md
CADMIUM	Cd	MERCURY	Hg
CAESIUM	Cs	MOLYBDENUM	Mo
CALCIUM	Ca	NEODYMIUM	Nd
CALIFORNIUM	Cf	NEON	Ne
CARBON	C	NEPTUNIUM	Np
CERIUM	Ce	NICKEL	Ni
CHLORINE	Cl	NIOBIUM	Nb
CHROMIUM	Cr	NITROGEN	N
COBALT	Co	NOBELIUM	Nb
COLUMBIUM	Cb	OSMIUM	Os
COPPER	Cu	OXYGEN	O
CURIUM	Cm	PALLADIUM	Pd
DUBNIUM	Db	PHOSPHORUS	P
DYSPROSIUM	Dy	PLATINUM	Pt
EINSTEINIUM	Es	PLUTONIUM	Pu
ERBIUM	Er	POLONIUM	Po
EUROPIUM	Eu	POTASSIUM	K
FERMIUM	Fm	PRASEODYMIUM	Pr
FLUORINE	F	RADIUM	Ra
FRANCIUM	Fr	RADON	Rn
GADOLINIUM	Gd	RHENIUM	Rn
GALLIUM	Ga	RHODIUM	Rh
GERMANIUM	Ge	RUBIDIUM	Rb
GOLD	Au	RUTHENIUM	Ru
HAFNIUM	Hf	SAMARIUM	Sm
HELIUM	He	SCANDIUM	Sc
HOLMIUM	Ho	SEABORGIUM	Sg
HYDROGEN	H	SELENIUM	Se

Name	Symbol	Name	Symbol
SILICON	Si	TIN	Sn
SILVER	Ag	TITANIUM	Ti
SODIUM	Na	TUNGSTEN	W
STRONTIUM	Sr	URANIUM	U
SULPHUR	S	VANADIUM	V
TANTALUM	Ta	WOLFRAM	W
TECHNETIUM	Tc	XENON	Xe
TELLURIUM	Te	YTTERBIUM	Yb
TERBIUM	Tb	YTTRIUM	Y
THALLIUM	Tl	ZINC	Zn
THORIUM	Th	ZIRCONIUM	Zr
THULIUM	Tm		

Deserts

Arabian (7)
Atacama (7)
Colorado (8)
Gibson (6)
Gobi (4)
Great Basin (10)
Great Sandy (10)
Great Victoria (13)

Kalahari (8)
Kara Kum (7)
Kyzyl-Kum (8)
Mojave (6)
Nafud (5)
Namib (5)
Negev (5)
Patagonian (10)

Sahara (6)
Sinai (5)
Sonoran (7)
Syrian (6)
Takla Makan (10)
Taklimakan (10)
Thar (4)

French revolutionary calendar

Brumaire (8) fog, Oct.
Floréal (7) blossom, April
Frimaire (8) sleet, Nov.
Fructidor (9) fruit, Aug.

Germinal (8) seed, March
Messidor (8) harvest, June
Nivôse (6) snow, Dec.
Pluviôse (8) rain, Jan.

Prairial (8) pasture, May
Thermidor (9) heat, July
Vendémiaire (11) vintage, Sept.
Ventôse (7) wind, Feb.

Fuels

Alcohol (7)
Anthracite (10)
Argol (5)
Astatki (7)
Benzine (7)
Benzol (6)
Benzole (7)
Calor gas (8)
Coal (4)
Coke (4)
Derv (4)

Diesel (6)
Electricity (11)
Ethyl (5)
Fluothane (9)
Gas (3)
Gascoal (7)
Gascoke (7)
Gasoline (8)
Halothane (9)
Hydrocarbon (11)
Kerosene (8)

Lignite (7)
Methane (7)
Naphtha (7)
Oil (3)
Paraffin (8)
Peat (4)
Petrol (6)
Petroleum (9)
Spirit (6)
Turf (4)
Wood (4)

Group terms

3 AND 4

band (of musicians)
bevy (of larks, quails, roes, or women)
box (of cigars)
brew (of beer)
case (of whisky or wine)
cast (of hawks)
cete (of badgers)
clan (people)
club (people)
crew (oarsmen or sailors)
crop (of farm produce)
down (of hares)
dule (of doves)
fall (of woodcock)
form (at schools)
four (card-players, oarsmen, or polo team)
gang (of elk, hooligans, labourers, slaves or thieves)
hand (at cards)
herd (of asses, buffalo, cattle, cranes, deer, giraffes, goats, or oxen)
host (of angels)
hunt (hounds and hunters)
husk (of hares)
knob (of pochards, teal, toads, or widgeon)
leap (of leopards)
lepe (of leopards)
lot (in auctioneering)
meet (of hounds and hunters)
mess (military and naval)
mute (of hounds)
nest (of machine-guns, mice, rabbits, or wasps)
nide (of pheasants)
nine (baseball team)
pace (of asses)
pack (of grouse, hounds, wolves, or cards)
pair (of oarsmen and various)
park (of guns or cars)
peal (of bells)
pile (of arms)
pod (of whiting or peas)
pony (betting; £25)
pool (various)
posy (of flowers)

rag (of colts)
rope (of onions or pearls)
rout (of wolves)
run (of poultry)
rush (of pochards)
sect (of religious people)
set (of various articles)
show (of agricultural products, dogs, horses, etc.)
side (of players)
six (of cub scouts, sportsmen)
sord (of mallards or wild-fowl)
stud (of horses and mares)
sute (of mallards or wild-fowl)
team (of ducks, horses, oxen, or players)
trio (of musicians)
tuft (of grass)
walk (of snipe)
wing (of plovers)
wisp (of snipe)
wood (trees)
yoke (of oxen)

5

batch (of bread and various)
bench (of bishops or magistrates)
blast (of hunters)
blush (of boys)
board (of directors)
brace (of ducks, partridges, etc.)
brood (of hens)
bunch (of flowers, grapes, teal, or widgeon)
caste (of bread)
charm (of goldfinches)
class (of children at schools)
clump (of trees)
copse (trees)
covey (of grouse, partridges, or other birds)
crowd (of people)
doylt (of tame swine)
draft (of police or soldiers)
drove (of cattle or kine)
eight (oarsmen)
field (hunters, race-horses, or runners)
fleet (of motor-cars or ships)

flock (of birds, pigeons, or sheep)
flush (at cards)
flyer (money; £5)
genus (of animals or plants)
grand (money; £1000 or $1000)
group (photographic and various)
guard (soldiers)
hoard (of gold, etc.)
horde (of savages)
leash (of bucks or hounds)
party (of people)
plump (of wildfowl)
posse (of police)
pride (of lions)
scrum (at rugby football)
sedge (of bitterns or herons)
sheaf (of corn)
shoal (of fish)
siege (of herons)
skein (of geese, silk, or wool)
skulk (of foxes)
sloth (of bears)
squad (of beaters or soldiers)
staff (of officials or servants)
stalk (of foresters)
stand (of arms)
state (of princes)
swarm (of bees and other insects)
table (of bridge or whist players)
tribe (of goats or people)
trick (at cards)
troop (of boy-scouts, brownies, cavalry, kangaroos, lions, or monkeys)
truss (of hay)
twins (people)
watch (of nightingales or sailors)

6

barren (of mules)
basket (of strawberries)
budget (of papers)
bundle (of asparagus, firewood, and various)
caucus (of politicians)
cellar (of wine)
clique (of people)
clutch (of eggs)

colony (of gulls or people)
covert (of coots)
desert (of lapwings)
double (in betting)
eleven (cricket and other teams)
faggot (of sticks)
family (of people or sardines)
flight (of aeroplanes, doves, dunlins, or pigeons)
gaggle (of geese)
galaxy (of beauties)
harras (of horses)
kennel (of dogs)
kindle (of kittens)
labour (of moles)
litter (of cubs, pigs, pups, or whelps)
melody (of harpers)
monkey (in betting; £500)
museum (of antiques, works of art, etc.)
muster (of peacocks or soldiers)
nation (of people)
outfit (of clothes or sails)
packet (of cigarettes)
parade (of soldiers)
punnet (of strawberries)
quorum (minimum number of people)
rayful (of knaves)
rubber (at cards)
school (of porpoises or whales)
sextet (of musicians)
sleuth (of bears)
spring (of teal)
stable (of horses)
string (of pearls or racehorses)
tenner (money; £10)
throng (of people)
trophy (of arms, etc.)
troupe (of actors, dancers, or minstrels)
twelve (lacrosse team)
vestry (parochial assembly)

7

battery (of guns)
bouquet (of flowers)
brigade (of troops)
clamour (of rooks)
clouder (of cats)
cluster (of grapes or stars)
company (of actors, capitalists, or widgeon)
council (advisers or local authorities)
dopping (of sheldrakes)
draught (of butlers)
fifteen (rugby football team)
gallery (of pictures)
library (of books or music)
nosegay (of flowers)
orchard (of fruit trees)
quartet (of musicians)
service (of china or crockery)
sounder (of boars or swine)
spinney (of trees)
thicket (of trees)
vintage (of wine)

8

assembly (of people)
audience (of people)
building (of rooks)
division (of troops)
flotilla (of boats)
jamboree (of boy-scouts)
paddling (of ducks)
partners (in business or games)
regiment (of soldiers)
richesse (of martens)
sequence (at cards)
squadron (of cavalry or ships)
triplets (people)

9

army corps (of troops)
badelynge (of ducks)

committee (people)
community (of people or saints)
cowardice (of curs)
gathering (of people and the clans)
morbidity (of majors)
orchestra (of musicians)
sachemdom (N. American Indians)
shrubbery (of shrubs)
subtiltie (of sergeants)
syndicate (of capitalists)

10

assemblage (of clergy and various)
buttonhole (of flowers)
chattering (of choughs)
collection (of stamps, works of art, etc.)
commission (committee of enquiry)
detachment (of police or soldiers)
exaltation (of larks)
exhibition (of commercial products, pictures, works of art, etc.)
observance (of hermits)
shrewdness (of apes)
simplicity (of subalterns)

11 AND OVER

confraternity (brotherhood, usually religious) (13)
congregation (of birds or worshippers) (12)
constellation (of stars) (13)
convocation (of clergy or university authorities) (11)
murmuration (of starlings) (11)

Hebrew alphabet

Aleph (5)	Koph (4)	Shin (4)
Ayin (4)	Lamedh (6)	Sin (3)
Beth (4)	Mem (3)	Tav (3)
Daleth (6)	Nun (3)	Teth (4)
Gimel (5)	Pe (2)	Vav (3)
He (2)	Resh (4)	Yod (3)
Heth (4)	Sade (4)	Zayin (5)
Kaph (4)	Samekh (6)	

Heraldry

2 – 4

arms
band
bar
bend
boar
coué
dawl
delf
enty
erne
fess
fret
garb
gore
gray
kite
lion
or
orle
pale
pall
paly
pean
pile
posé
rose
semé
vair
vert

5

alant
animé
armed
azure
badge
barry
baton

bendy
bowed
breys
cable
chief
crest
cross
eagle
erect
ermin
fesse
field
fusil
garbe
gorge
gules
gurge
gyron
label
motto
pheon
rebus
rompu
sable
scarp
torse
waved

6

aiglet
apaumy
argent
armory
at gaze
attire
baston
bazant
bendil
bevile
bezant

billet
blazon
border
bouche
buckle
canton
charge
checky
chequy
cleché
cotise
couché
coward
dexter
dragon
ermine
escrol
etoile
falcon
fillet
flanch
fleury
florid
fretty
fylfot
garter
ground
guttée

heater
herald
jessed
knight
manche
mascle
maunch
mullet
naiant
Norroy
pallet
rebate

rustre
sejant
shield
square
timbre
vairée
vested
voided
voider
volant
vorant
wivern
wyvern

7

adorsed
adossed
alberia
annulet
arrière
arrondi
attired
barruly
bearing
bendlet
bevilly
bordure
bottony
brisure
cadency
chapter
chevron
clarion
courant
croslet
dolphin
dormant
emblaze
embowed
embrued

enarmed
endorse
engoulé
engrail
ermelin
estoile
fretted
fructed
gardant
griffin
Ich Dien
leopard
lioncel
lozenge
lozengy
martlet
miniver
nombril
passant
potence
purpure
quarter
raguled
rampant
roundel
salient
saltire
sea-lion
sexfoil
shafted
sinople
statant
swallow
torqued
torteau
trefoil
unicorn

8

affronté
allerion
armorist
aversant
barrulet
bevilled
blazonry
caboched
caboshed
chaperon
couchant
crescent
dancetty
emblazon
englante
enmanché
erminois
escallop
gonfalon
haurient
heraldic
insignia
Lyon King
mantling
naissant
opinicus
ordinary
renverse
roundlet
sea-horse
sinister
standard
tincture
tressure

9

aquilated
arraswise

banderole
blazoning
carbuncle
cartouche
combatant
diapering
displayed
embattled
enveloped
environed
erminites
estoillee
florettée
hatchment
lionceaux
lioncelle
Lyon-Court
regardant
scutcheon

spur-rowel
supporter

10

barry-bendy
barrybendi
bicorporal
blue mantle
cinquefoil
Clarenceux
coat-of-arms
cross-patée
difference
emblazoner
empalement
escalloped
escutcheon
fesse-point
fleur-de-lis
fleur-de-lys

king-at-arms
knighthood
pursuivant
quartering
quatrefoil
quintefoil
rebatement
surmounted

11 AND OVER

bend-sinister (12)
bendy-sinister (13)
bicapitated (11)
College of Arms (13)
counter-paled (12)
counter-passant (14)
countervair (11)
cross-crosslet (13)
cross-fleury (11)
cross-patencée (13)

Earl Marshal (11)
emblazonment (12)
engrailment (11)
escarbuncle (11)
escutcheoned (12)
garde-visure (11)
Garter King of Arms
   (16)
grant of arms (11)
heraldic emblem (14)
honour point (11)
inescutcheon (12)
Lyon King at Arms (14)
marshalling (11)
quarter arms (11)
Somerset herald (14)
transfluent (11)
unscutcheoned (13)

Jewish year

Adar (4)
Av (2)
Elul (4)
Heshvan (7)

Iyar (4)
Kislev (6)
Nisan (5)
Shebat (6)

Sivan (5)
Tammuz (6)
Tevet (5)
Tishri (6)

Law sittings

Easter (6)
Hilary (6)
Michaelmas (10)
Trinity (7)

Musketeers

Aramis (6)
Athos (5)
D'Artagnan (9)
Porthos (7)

Names: boys
Including abbreviations, nicknames, and some common foreign names.

3	Art	Bud	Del	Gil	Hew
	Asa	Col	Des	Gus	Huw
Abe	Ben	Dai	Don	Guy	Ian
Alf	Bob	Dan	Eli	Hal	Ira
Ali	Boy	Dee	Ely	Hay	Ivo

Jan	Wat	Duff	Kane	Ross	Archy
Jay	Win	Duke	Karl	Rudy	Arden
Jed	Zak	Earl	Keir	Russ	Athol
Jem		Eben	Kemp	Ryan	Aubyn
Jim	**4**	Eddy	Kent	Saul	Aymar
Job	Abel	Eden	King	Sean	Baron
Joe	Adam	Emil	Kirk	Seth	Barry
Jon	Alan	Eric	Kris	Shaw	Barty
Jos	Aldo	Erik	Kurt	Stan	Basie
Kay	Alec	Erle	Kyle	Theo	Basil
Ken	Aled	Esau	Lars	Toby	Benjy
Kid	Alex	Esme	Leon	Todd	Benny
Kim	Algy	Esra	Liam	Tony	Berny
Kit	Ally	Euan	Loel	Trev	Berty
Lee	Alun	Evan	Ludo	Troy	Bevis
Len	Amos	Ewan	Luke	Vane	Billy
Leo	Andy	Ewen	Lyle	Vere	Bjorn
Les	Axel	Eyre	Lyle	Wade	Blair
Lew	Bald	Ezra	Marc	Walt	Blake
Lex	Bart	Fred	Mark	Ward	Bobby
Lou	Beau	Gary	Matt	Wilf	Booth
Lyn	Bert	Gene	Merv	Will	Boris
Mac	Bill	Glen	Mick	Winn	Brent
Mat	Bing	Glyn	Mike	Wynn	Brett
Max	Boyd	Gwyn	Milo	Yves	Brian
Mel	Brad	Hank	Mort	Zack	Brice
Nat	Bram	Hans	Moss	Zane	Brock
Ned	Bret	Herb	Muir		Bruce
Nye	Bryn	Huey	Neal	**5**	Bruno
Pat	Buck	Hugh	Neil	Aaron	Bryan
Pip	Burt	Hugo	Nero	Abdul	Bryce
Rab	Cain	Hume	Nick	Abner	Bunny
Ray	Carl	Hyam	Noah	Abram	Byron
Reg	Cary	Iain	Noel	Adolf	Caius
Rex	Cass	Ifor	Norm	Aidan	Caleb
Rob	Ceri	Igor	Olaf	Alain	Calum
Rod	Chad	Ikey	Olav	Alban	Carey
Ron	Chas	Iohn	Orme	Aldis	Carlo
Roy	Chay	Ivan	Ossy	Aldus	Carol
Sam	Ciro	Ivor	Otho	Alfie	Casey
Seb	Clem	Jack	Otis	Algie	Cecil
Sid	Cole	Jake	Otto	Alick	Chris
Sim	Curt	Jean	Owen	Allan	Chuck
Stu	Dale	Jeff	Page	Allen	Clark
Syd	Dana	Jess	Paul	Alvar	Claud
Tam	Dave	Jock	Pete	Alvis	Cliff
Ted	Davy	Joel	Phil	Alwin	Clint
Tel	Dean	Joey	Rafe	Alwyn	Clive
Tex	Dewi	John	René	Amand	Clyde
Tim	Dick	José	Rhys	Amyas	Colin
Tom	Dion	Josh	Rich	André	Conan
Vic	Dirk	Juan	Rick	Angus	Cosmo
Vin	Doug	Judd	Rolf	Anson	Craig
Wal	Drew	Jude	Rory	Anton	Cuddy

Cyril	Geoff	Lewis	Romeo	Alured	Dougal
Cyrus	Gerry	Lisle	Rowan	Andrew	Dudley
Damon	Giles	Lloyd	Rufus	Angelo	Dugald
Danny	Glenn	Louie	Ryder	Anselm	Duggie
Darcy	Glynn	Louis	Sacha	Antony	Duncan
Daryl	Govan	Lucas	Sammy	Archer	Dustin
David	Grant	Luigi	Sandy	Archie	Dwayne
Davie	Gregg	Lyall	Saxon	Armand	Edmond
Denis	Guido	Madoc	Scott	Arnold	Edmund
Denny	Gyles	Manny	Serge	Arthur	Eduard
Denys	Hardy	Marco	Shane	Ashley	Edward
Derby	Harry	Mario	Shaun	Aubrey	Egbert
Derek	Haydn	Marty	Shawn	August	Eldred
Derry	Hebel	Micah	Silas	Austin	Elijah
Dicky	Henri	Micky	Simon	Aylmer	Ellery
Digby	Henry	Miles	Solly	Aylwin	Elliot
Donal	Heron	Mitch	Starr	Balbus	Ernest
Donny	Hervé	Monty	Steve	Barney	Erroll
Dylan	Hiram	Moray	Storm	Bennie	Ervine
Eamon	Homer	Moses	Tabor	Bertie	Esmond
Earle	Humph	Moshe	Taffy	Blaise	Eugene
Eddie	Hyman	Mungo	Teddy	Braham	Evelyn
Edgar	Hymie	Myles	Terry	Brodie	Fabian
Edwin	Hywel	Neill	Timmy	Brutus	Fergal
Edwyn	Idris	Niall	Titus	Bryden	Fergus
Eldon	Inigo	Nicky	Tommy	Bulwer	Finlay
Elias	Innes	Nicol	Tudor	Caesar	Forbes
Eliot	Irvin	Nigel	Ulick	Calvin	Fraser
Ellis	Irwin	Ollie	Upton	Carlos	Freddy
Elmer	Isaac	Orson	Uriah	Caspar	Gareth
Elvin	Jabez	Orval	Vince	Cedric	Garnet
Elvis	Jacky	Oscar	Waldo	Cicero	Garret
Elwyn	Jacob	Osman	Wally	Claude	Gaspar
Emery	Jaime	Oswyn	Wayne	Connor	Gaston
Emile	James	Paddy	Willy	Conrad	Gawain
Emlyn	Jamie	Paolo	Wolfe	Conway	George
Emrys	Jason	Parry	Wyatt	Cormac	Gerald
Enoch	Jemmy	Pedro	Wynne	Dafydd	Gerard
Ernie	Jerry	Percy	Yorke	Dallas	Gideon
Ernst	Jesse	Perry		Damian	Gilroy
Errol	Jimmy	Peter	**6**	Damien	Giulio
Ethan	Johan	Piers	Adolph	Daniel	Godwin
Ewart	Jonah	Punch	Adrian	Darren	Gonvil
Felix	Jonas	Ralph	Aeneas	Darryl	Gordon
Floyd	Jules	Ramon	Alaric	Declan	Graeme
Franc	Karol	Raoul	Albert	Delroy	Graham
Frank	Keith	Ricki	Aldous	Dennis	Gregan
Franz	Kenny	Ricky	Aldred	Denzil	Gregor
Frith	Kevin	Roald	Aldwin	Dermot	Grover
Fritz	Lance	Robin	Aldwyn	Deryck	Gunter
Fulke	Larry	Roddy	Alexis	Dickie	Gustav
Garry	Leigh	Roger	Alfred	Dickon	Gwilym
Garth	Leroy	Rolfe	Alonzo	Donald	Hallam
Gavin	Lewin	Rollo	Alston	Dorian	Hamish

Hamlet	Kieran	Ramsay	Willem	Compton	Hermann
Hamlyn	Kirwan	Ramsey	Willie	Connell	Hewlett
Harley	Launce	Ranald	Willis	Crispin	Hilaire
Harold	Lauren	Randal	Wystan	Cyprian	Hildred
Hassan	Leslie	Rayner	Xavier	Dalziel	Hillary
Hayden	Lionel	Reggie	Yehudi	Darrell	Horatio
Haydon	Loftus	Rendle		Denholm	Humbert
Hector	Lonnie	Reuben	**7**	Denison	Humphry
Hedley	Lucian	Rhodes	Absalom	Derrick	Ibrahim
Henryk	Lucien	Robbie	Adolphe	Desmond	Ichabod
Herbie	Ludwig	Robert	Ainsley	Diggory	Isidore
Herman	Luther	Rodger	Aladdin	Dillwyn	Jackson
Hervey	Lyndon	Rodney	Alberic	Dominic	Jacques
Hilary	Magnus	Roland	Alfonso	Donovan	Jeffrey
Hilton	Malory	Ronald	Alister	Douglas	Joachim
Hobart	Manuel	Ronnie	Almeric	Edouard	Jocelyn
Holden	Marcel	Rowley	Amadeus	Elliott	Johnnie
Holman	Marcus	Royden	Ambrose	Emanuel	Justice
Horace	Marius	Rudolf	Anatole	Emilius	Kenneth
Howard	Marten	Rupert	Andreas	Ephraim	Lachlan
Howell	Martin	Russel	Andries	Etienne	Lambert
Hubert	Marvin	Samson	Aneurin	Eustace	Lazarus
Hughie	Melvin	Samuel	Anthony	Everard	Leander
Hylton	Melvyn	Seamus	Antoine	Ezekiel	Lennard
Ignace	Merlin	Sefton	Antonio	Faraday	Leonard
Illtyd	Mervyn	Selwyn	Artemus	Fielder	Leopold
Irvine	Mickey	Sergei	Auberon	Fitzroy	Lincoln
Irving	Milton	Seumas	Auguste	Florian	Lindsay
Isaiah	Morgan	Shafto	Baldwin	Francis	Lindsey
Israel	Moritz	Sholto	Balfour	Frankie	Lorenzo
Jackie	Morris	Sidney	Barclay	Freddie	Lorimer
Jacomb	Morvyn	Simeon	Barnaby	Gabriel	Lucifer
Japhet	Mostyn	Sinbad	Barnard	Garrett	Ludovic
Jarvis	Murray	St. John	Beaufoi	Gaspard	Malachy
Jasper	Nathan	Steven	Bernard	Gaylord	Malcolm
Jeremy	Nelson	Stevie	Bertram	Geoffry	Mallory
Jerome	Nevile	Stuart	Botolph	Georgie	Matthew
Jervis	Nevill	Sydney	Brandon	Geraint	Maurice
Jethro	Ninian	Taylor	Brendan	Gervais	Maxwell
Johann	Norman	Thomas	Burnard	Gervase	Maynard
Johnny	Norris	Tobias	Calvert	Gilbert	Merrick
Jolyon	Norton	Travis	Cameron	Gilmour	Michael
Jordan	Nowell	Trefor	Caradoc	Gladwyn	Montagu
Joseph	Oliver	Trevor	Carlton	Gloster	Neville
Joshua	Osbert	Vernon	Carlyon	Godfrey	Nicolas
Josiah	Osmond	Victor	Charles	Goronwy	Norbert
Julian	Oswald	Vivian	Charley	Grahame	Orlando
Julien	Pelham	Vyvyan	Charlie	Gregory	Orpheus
Julius	Philip	Wallis	Chester	Gunther	Orville
Justin	Pierre	Walter	Clayton	Gustave	Osborne
Kelvin	Powell	Warner	Cledwyn	Gwynfor	Padraic
Kendal	Prince	Warren	Clement	Hadrian	Padraig
Kenelm	Rabbie	Wesley	Clifton	Hartley	Paladin
Kersey	Rafael	Wilbur	Clinton	Herbert	Patrick

Perseus
Phineas
Pierrot
Quentin
Quintin
Randall
Ranulph
Raphael
Raymond
Raymund
Redvers
Reynard
Ricardo
Richard
Roderic
Rodolph
Rodrigo
Romulus
Rowland
Royston
Rudolph
Rudyard
Russell
Sampson
Sergius
Seymour
Sheldon
Sigmund
Solomon
Spencer
Spenser
Stanley
Stephen
Steuart
Stewart
Tancred
Terence
Tertius
Timothy
Torquil
Travers
Tristan
Ughtred
Ulysses
Umberto
Vaughan
Vincent
Wallace
Warwick
Wendell
Westley
Wilfred
Wilfrid
Wilhelm

Willard
William
Windsor
Winston
Woodrow
Wyndham
Zachary
Zebedee

8

Adolphus
Alasdair
Alastair
Algernon
Alisdair
Alistair
Aloysius
Alphonse
Alphonso
Annesley
Antonius
Aristide
Augustin
Augustus
Aurelius
Barnabas
Bartlemy
Beaumont
Bedivere
Benedict
Benjamin
Bernhard
Berthold
Bertrand
Campbell
Carleton
Champion
Charlton
Christie
Clarence
Claudius
Clemence
Clements
Clifford
Constant
Courtney
Crispian
Crauford
Crawford
Cuthbert
Diarmaid
Dominick
Ebenezer
Emmanuel

Ethelred
FitzHugh
Florizel
François
Franklin
Frederic
Fredrick
Gamaliel
Garfield
Geoffrey
Geoffroy
Giovanni
Giuseppe
Greville
Gustavus
Hamilton
Hannibal
Harcourt
Harrison
Havelock
Herbrand
Hercules
Hereward
Hezekiah
Horatius
Humphrey
Ignatius
Immanuel
Jephthah
Jeremiah
Jonathan
Joscelyn
Josephus
Kingsley
Lancelot
Laurence
Lawrance
Lawrence
Leighton
Leonhard
Leonidas
Llewelyn
Llywelyn
Maitland
Marshall
Melville
Meredith
Montague
Mortimer
Napoleon
Nehemiah
Nicholas
Octavian
Octavius

Oliphant
Oughtred
Paulinus
Perceval
Percival
Peregrin
Peterkin
Philemon
Randolph
Randulph
Reginald
Robinson
Roderick
Ruaraidh
Sandford
Secundus
Septimus
Sheridan
Sherlock
Siegmund
Sinclair
Spensley
Stafford
Stirling
Sylvanus
Thaddeus
Theobald
Theodore
Thornton
Thurstan
Trelawny
Tristram
Vladimir
Winthrop
Wolseley

9

Abernethy
Abimeleck
Alaistair
Alexander
Alphonsus
Ambrosius
Arbuthnot
Archibald
Aristotle
Armstrong
Athelstan
Augustine
Balthasar
Bartimeus
Beauchamp
Broderick
Christian

Christmas
Constable
Cornelius
Courtenay
Courteney
Creighton
Demetrius
Dionysius
Ethelbert
Ferdinand
Francesco
Francisco
Frederick
Gascoigne
Glanville
Granville

Josceline
Launcelot
Llewellyn
Mackenzie
Marcellus
Marmaduke
Nathaniel
Peregrine
Philibert
Rodriguez
Rupprecht
Sackville
Salvatore
Sebastian
Siegfried
Sigismund

Stanislas
Sylvester
Thaddaeus
Theodoric
Valentine
Valentino
Wilbraham
Zachariah
Zechariah

10 AND OVER

Athanasius (10)
Athelstane (10)
Barrington (10)
Bartholomew (11)
Cadwallader (11)

Carmichael (10)
Christopher (11)
Constantine (11)
Hieronymus (10)
Hildebrand (10)
Hippolytus (10)
Maximilian (10)
Montgomery (10)
Sacheverell (11)
Somerville (10)
Stanislaus (10)
Theodosius (10)
Theophilus (10)
Washington (10)
Willoughby (10)

Names: girls

Including abbreviations, nicknames, and some common foreign names.

3

3	4				
Ada	Liz	Alys	Faye	Kate	Neva
Amy	Lot	Anna	Fern	Kath	Niki
Ann	Lou	Anne	Fifi	Katy	Nina
Ava	Mae	Anya	Fran	Kaye	Nita
Bea	May	Avis	Gaby	Keri	Nona
Bee	Meg	Babs	Gail	Lala	Nora
Bel	Mia	Bess	Gale	Leah	Olga
Deb	Nan	Beth	Gaye	Lena	Oona
Dee	Pam	Cary	Gert	Lila	Pola
Dot	Pat	Cath	Gina	Lily	Poll
Eda	Peg	Ceri	Gwen	Lina	Prue
Ena	Pen	Ciss	Gwyn	Lisa	Rena
Eth	Pia	Clem	Hebe	Lita	Rene
Eva	Pru	Cleo	Hedy	Liza	Rita
Eve	Rae	Cora	Hope	Lois	Rosa
Fay	Ria	Dawn	Ilse	Lola	Rose
Flo	Ros	Dido	Inez	Lori	Rosy
Gay	Sal	Dora	Inge	Lorn	Ruby
Gus	Sam	Edie	Iona	Lucy	Ruth
Ida	Sue	Edna	Iris	Lulu	Sara
Ina	Una	Ella	Irma	Lynn	Sian
Isa	Val	Elle	Isla	Mair	Sile
Ivy	Viv	Elma	Isma	Mara	Sita
Jan	Win	Elsa	Jade	Mary	Suky
Jay	Zoë	Else	Jane	Maud	Suzy
Jen	**4**	Emma	Jean	Meta	Tess
Joy	Abby	Emmy	Jess	Mimi	Tina
Kay	Alex	Enid	Jill	Mina	Toni
Kim	Alix	Erna	Joan	Moll	Trix
Kit	Ally	Esmé	Jody	Mona	Vera
Lil	Alma	Etta	Judi	Myra	Vida
	Alva	Etty	Judy	Nell	Vita
		Eye	June	Nena	Viva

Wynn	Cathy	Gerry	Lizzy	Norah	Tilda
Zara	Cecil	Gerty	Lorna	Norma	Tonia
Zena	Celia	Ginny	Lorne	Nuala	Topsy
Zita	Chloe	Gisela	Lotte	Nyree	Tracy
5	Cilla	Grace	Lotty	Odile	Trudy
	Cindy	Greer	Lucia	Olive	Unity
Abbie	Circe	Greta	Lucie	Olwen	Valda
Adela	Cissy	Gussy	Lydia	Oriel	Venus
Adele	Clair	Hazel	Lynne	Pansy	Vesta
Aggie	Clara	Hedda	Mabel	Patsy	Vicki
Agnes	Clare	Heidi	Madge	Patti	Viola
Ailsa	Coral	Helen	Maeve	Patty	Wanda
Aimée	Daisy	Helga	Magda	Paula	Wendy
Alana	Delia	Henny	Maggy	Pearl	Willa
Alexa	Della	Hetty	Mamie	Peggy	Wilma
Alice	Diana	Hilda	Mandy	Penny	Xenia
Aline	Diane	Holly	Manon	Petra	Zelda
Altha	Dilys	Honor	Marge	Phebe	Zelma
Amber	Dinah	Hulda	Margo	Pippa	
Angel	Dodie	Hylda	Maria	Pixie	**6**
Angie	Dolly	Ilona	Marie	Polly	Agatha
Anita	Donna	Irene	Marni	Poppy	Agneta
Annie	Doris	Jacky	Matty	Queen	Aileen
Anona	Dulce	Janet	Maude	Raine	Alexia
Aphra	Edith	Janey	Mavis	Renée	Alexis
April	Effie	Janie	Megan	Rhian	Alicia
Arbel	Eilsa	Janis	Mercy	Rhoda	Alison
Ariel	Elena	Jayne	Merle	Rhona	Althea
Astra	Elfie	Jemma	Merry	Robin	Amabel
Avice	Elisa	Jenny	Meryl	Robyn	Amalie
Avril	Elise	Joann	Milly	Rosie	Amanda
Beata	Eliza	Jodie	Minna	Sadie	Amelia
Becky	Ellen	Joely	Mitzi	Sally	Amelie
Bella	Ellie	Josie	Moira	Sandy	Aminta
Belle	Elsie	Joyce	Molly	Sarah	Anabel
Berta	Emily	Julia	Morag	Selma	Andrea
Beryl	Emmie	Julie	Moyna	Shena	Andrée
Bessy	Erica	Karen	Moyra	Shona	Angela
Betsy	Essie	Karin	Myrna	Sonia	Annika
Bette	Ethel	Kathy	Nadia	Sonja	Annwen
Betty	Ethne	Katie	Nancy	Sophy	Anthea
Biddy	Ettie	Kelly	Nanny	Sukey	Arlene
Bobby	Evita	Kerry	Naomi	Susan	Armyne
Bonny	Faith	Kitty	Nelly	Susie	Astrid
Bride	Fanny	Kylie	Nerys	Sybil	Athene
Brita	Filia	Laila	Nessa	Tammy	Audrey
Britt	Fiona	Laura	Nesta	Tania	Auriol
Bunny	Flavia	Leila	Netta	Tanis	Aurora
Bunty	Fleur	Letty	Nicky	Tansy	Averil
Candy	Flora	Libby	Nikky	Tanya	Barbie
Carey	Freda	Lilia	Ninie	Terri	Barbra
Carla	Freya	Lilly	Ninny	Terry	Beatie
Carly	Gemma	Linda	Niobe	Tessa	Benita
Carol	Gerda	Lindy	Noele	Thora	Bertha

Bessie	Elvira	Jennie	Miriam	Sophia	Aurelia
Bethan	Emilia	Jessie	Mollie	Sophie	Babette
Bettie	Esther	Joanna	Monica	Sorcha	Barbara
Beulah	Eunice	Joanne	Muriel	Stella	Barbary
Bianca	Evadne	Joleen	Myrtle	Stevie	Beatrix
Biddie	Evelyn	Jolene	Nadine	Sybell	Bedelia
Binnie	Fannie	Judith	Nellie	Sylvia	Belinda
Birdie	Fatima	Juliet	Nerina	Tamsin	Bernice
Birgit	Felice	Kirsty	Nessie	Teresa	Bethany
Blanch	Franca	Lalage	Nettie	Tertia	Bettina
Bobbie	Franny	Lallie	Nicola	Tessie	Billy Jo
Bonita	Frieda	Laurel	Nicole	Thalia	Blanche
Bonnie	Galena	Lauren	Noelle	Thelma	Blodwen
Brenda	Gerrie	Lavina	Noreen	Tootie	Blossom
Bridie	Gertie	Leanne	Odette	Tracey	Bridget
Brigid	Gladys	Leonie	Olivia	Tricia	Caitlin
Briony	Glenda	Lesley	Oonagh	Trisha	Camilla
Candis	Glenys	Leslie	Oriana	Trixie	Candice
Carina	Gloria	Lettie	Paddie	Ulrica	Candida
Carmen	Glynis	Lilian	Pamela	Ursula	Carolyn
Carola	Godiva	Lilias	Pattie	Verity	Cecilia
Carole	Goldie	Lilith	Pegeen	Verona	Celeste
Carrie	Gracie	Lillah	Peggie	Vickie	Charity
Cassie	Gretel	Lillie	Pepita	Violet	Charley
Catrin	Grizel	Lizzie	Petula	Vivian	Charlie
Cecile	Gussie	Lolita	Phoebe	Vivien	Chrissy
Cecily	Gwenda	Lorina	Portia	Vyvyen	Christy
Celina	Gwynne	Lottie	Psyche	Wallis	Clarice
Cherie	Hannah	Louisa	Rachel	Winnie	Claudia
Cherry	Hattie	Louise	Ramona	Xanthe	Clodagh
Cicely	Hayley	Luella	Regina	Yvette	Colette
Cissie	Hedwig	Maggie	Renata	Yvonne	Colleen
Claire	Helena	Maidie	Rhonda	Zandra	Coralie
Connie	Helene	Maisie	Richie		Crystal
Dagmar	Hermia	Marcia	Robina	**7**	Cynthia
Daphne	Hester	Margie	Roisin		Damaris
Davina	Hilary	Margot	Rosita	Abigail	Deborah
Debbie	Honora	Marian	Rowena	Adeline	Deirdre
Denise	Honour	Marina	Roxana	Adriana	Delilah
Dorcas	Ileana	Marion	Roxane	Ainsley	Delysia
Doreen	Imelda	Marisa	Sabina	Alberta	Diamond
Dorice	Imogen	Marnie	Sabine	Alethea	Dolores
Dorita	Ingrid	Marsha	Salome	Alfrida	Dorinda
Dulcie	Ioanna	Martha	Sandie	Allegra	Dorothy
Eartha	Isabel	Marthe	Sandra	Allison	Dulcima
Editha	Ishbel	Mattie	Sappho	Ameline	Dymphna
Edwina	Isobel	Maxine	Selina	Annabel	Eleanor
Edythe	Isolde	Melita	Seonad	Annette	Elfreda
Egeria	Jackie	Mercia	Serena	Anouska	Elfrida
Eileen	Jacqui	Meriel	Sharon	Anstice	Ellenor
Elaine	Janice	Mignon	Sheena	Antonia	Ellinor
Elinor	Jeanie	Millie	Sheila	Ariadne	Elspeth
Elissa	Jeanne	Mimosa	Silvia	Arianna	Emerald
Eloise	Jemima	Minnie	Simone	Athenia	Emiline
				Augusta	

Estelle	Lillias	Rebecca	Brigitta	Julianne	Violette
Eudoxia	Lindsay	Rebekah	Brigitte	Julietta	Virginia
Eugenia	Lisbeth	Rhodena	Calliope	Juliette	Vivienne
Eugenie	Lisette	Ricarda	Callista	Kathleen	Wilfrida
Eulalia	Lizbeth	Roberta	Carlotta	Kimberly	Winifred
Evaline	Loraine	Rosalia	Carolina	Laetitia	
Eveline	Loretta	Rosalie	Caroline	Lavender	**9**
Fabiana	Lorinda	Rosetta	Cathleen	Lorraine	Albertina
Felicia	Lucasta	Sabrina	Catriona	Lucretia	Albertine
Fenella	Lucilla	Sheilah	Charlene	Madeline	Alexandra
Feodora	Lucille	Shelagh	Charmian	Magdalen	Amaryllis
Florrie	Lucinda	Shelley	Chrissie	Marcella	Ambrosine
Flossie	Lurleen	Shirley	Christie	Marcelle	Anastasia
Frances	Mahalia	Sibilla	Chrystal	Margaret	Angelique
Frannie	Manuela	Sidonia	Clarinda	Marianne	Annabella
Georgia	Margery	Sidonie	Clarissa	Mariette	Annabelle
Gertrud	Marilyn	Silvana	Claudine	Marigold	Anneliese
Gillian	Marjory	Siobhan	Clemency	Marjorie	Artemisia
Giselle	Martina	Susanna	Clotilda	Mercedes	Bathsheba
Grainne	Martine	Susanne	Consuelo	Meredith	Britannia
Gwladys	Matilda	Suzanne	Cordelia	Michaela	Cassandra
Gwynedd	Maureen	Suzette	Cornelia	Michelle	Catherine
Gwyneth	Meirion	Sybilla	Cressida	Mireille	Celestine
Harriet	Melanie	Tabitha	Daniella	Morwenna	Charlotte
Heather	Melinda	Tatiana	Danielle	Murielle	Charmaine
Héloïse	Melissa	Theresa	Delphine	Nathalie	Christina
Hillary	Michèle	Thérèse	Dorothea	Patience	Christine
Honoria	Mildred	Tiffany	Drusilla	Patricia	Cleopatra
Horatia	Minerva	Titania	Dulcinia	Paulette	Clothilde
Hypatia	Mirabel	Valerie	Eleanora	Penelope	Columbine
Isadora	Miranda	Valetta	Eleanore	Perpetua	Constance
Janette	Modesty	Vanessa	Elfriede	Petronel	Desdemona
Jasmine	Monique	Venetia	Ellaline	Philippa	Eglantine
Jeannie	Myfanwy	Yolanda	Emanuela	Phyllida	Elisabeth
Jessica	Nanette	Yolande	Emmeline	Primrose	Elizabeth
Jillian	Natalia	Zenobia	Euphemia	Prudence	Emmanuela
Jocasta	Natalie	Zuleika	Evelinda	Prunella	Ermengard
Jocelyn	Natasha		Everalda	Raymonde	Ernestine
Johanna	Nerissa	**8**	Felicity	Rhiannon	Esmeralda
Josette	Nigella	Adelaide	Filomena	Rosalind	Esperance
Juanita	Ninette	Adelheid	Florence	Rosamond	Esperanza
Juliana	Octavia	Adrienne	Francine	Rosamund	Francesca
Kathryn	Olympia	Angelica	Georgina	Roseanna	Francisca
Katrina	Ophelia	Angelina	Germaine	Rosemary	Frederica
Kirsten	Ottilie	Angeline	Gertrude	Samantha	Gabrielle
Kristen	Palmyra	Angharad	Gretchen	Sapphire	Georgiana
Kristin	Pandora	Antonina	Grizelda	Sheelagh	Geraldine
Laraine	Paulina	Arabella	Grizelle	Stefanie	Ghislaine
Larissa	Pauline	Araminta	Hepzibah	Susannah	Guglielma
Lavinia	Perdita	Atalanta	Hermione	Tallulah	Guinevere
Leonora	Phillis	Beatrice	Hortense	Theodora	Gwendolen
Letitia	Phyllis	Berenice	Isabella	Veronica	Harriette
Lettice	Queenie	Beverley	Jeanette	Victoria	Henrietta
Lillian	Rafaela	Birgitta	Jennifer	Violetta	Henriette

Hildegard	Millicent	Victorine	Dulcibella (10)
Hippolyta	Mirabelle	Winefride	Ermintrude (10)
Hortensia	Philomena		Ethelwynne (10)
Hyacinthe	Pierrette	**10 AND 11**	Evangelina (10)
Iphigenia	Pollyanna	Alexandrina (11)	Evangeline (10)
Josephine	Priscilla	Antoinette (10)	Fredericka (10)
Kathailin	Rosabelle	Berengaria (10)	Gwendoline (10)
Katharine	Rosalinda	Bernadette (10)	Hildegarde (10)
Katherine	Rosemarie	Christabel (10)	Irmentrude (10)
Kimberley	Seraphina	Christiana (10)	Jacqueline (10)
Madeleine	Sophronia	Christiania (11)	Margaretta (10)
Magdalena	Stephanie	Christobel (10)	Margherita (10)
Magdalene	Theodosia	Cinderella (10)	Marguerite (10)
Margareta	Thomasina	Clementina (10)	Petronella (10)
Margarita	Valentine	Clementine (10)	Philippina (10)
Melisande	Véronique	Constantia (10)	Wilhelmina (10)

Nine Muses

Calliope (8) *epic*
Clio (4) *history*
Erato (5) *love songs*
Euterpe (7) *lyric poetry*
Melpomene (9) *tragedy*

Polyhymnia (10) *sacred poetry*
Terpsichore (11) *choral song and dance*
Thalia (6) *comedy and idyllic poetry*
Urania (6) *astronomy*

Nine Virtues

charity (7)
faith (5)
fortitude (9)

hope (4)
justice (7)
love (4) *charity*

modesty (7)
prudence (8)
temperance (10)

Palindromes

3	eve	pop	ma'am	rotor
aba	ewe	pup	noon	sagas
aga	eye	s.o.s.	otto	sexes
aha!	gag	tat	peep	shahs
ala	gig	tit	poop	sohos
ama	hah!	tot	sees	solos
ana	huh!	tut!	toot	tenet
asa	mam	wow!		
ava	mom	zuz	**5**	**6 AND OVER**
bab	mum		alula	Able was I ere I
bib	nan	**4**	civic	saw Elba (19)
bob	non	abba	kayak	deified (7)
bub	nun	anna	level	Hannah
dad	oho!	boob	madam	marram (6)
did	Oxo	deed	minim	pull-up (6)
dud	pap	dood	put-up	redder (6)
eke	pep	ecce	radar	reifier (7)
ere	pip	keek	refer	repaper (7)

343

reviver (7)   rotator (7)   terret (6)

Rivers of Hell

Acheron (7)   Lethe (5)
Avernus (7)   Phlegethon (10)
Cocytus (7)   Styx (4)

Roman emperors: a selection

Antoninus Pius (13)   Gordian (7)   Pertinax (8)
Augustus (8)   Hadrian (7)   Probus (6)
Aurelian (8)   Honorius (8)   Septimius Severus (16)
Caligula (8)   Jovian (6)   Tiberius (8)
Caracalla (9)   Julian (6)   Titus (5)
Claudius (8)   Lucius Verus (11)   Trajan (6)
Commodus (8)   Marcus Aurelius (14)   Valerian (8)
Constantine (11)   Maximian (8)   Vespasian (9)
Diocletian (10)   Nero (4)   Vitellius (9)
Elagabalus (10)   Nerva (5)
Galba (5)   Otho (4)

Seven against Thebes

Adrastus (8)   Parthenopaeus (13)
Amphiaraus (10)   Polynices (9)
Capaneus (8)   Tydeus (6)
Hippomedon (10)

Seven deadly sins

anger (5)   lust (4)
covetousness (12)   pride (5)
envy (4)   sloth (5)
gluttony (8)

Seven sages

Bias (4)   Pittacus (8)
Chilon (6)   Solon (5)
Cleobonlos (10)   Thales (6)
Periander (9)

Seven Wonders of the World

The Colossus of Rhodes
The Hanging Gardens of Babylon
The Pharos of Alexandria
    or
The Palace of Cyrus (cemented with gold)

The Pyramids of Egypt
The Statue of Zeus by Phidias
The Temple of Artemis (Diana) at Ephesus
The Tomb of Mausolus

Signs of the Zodiac

Aquarius (8), *Water-bearer*
Aries (5), *Ram*
Cancer (6), *Crab*
Capricorn (9), *Goat*

Gemini (6), *Twins*
Leo (3), *Lion*
Libra (5), *Balance*
Pisces (6), *Fishes*

Sagittarius (11), *Archer*
Scorpio (7), *Scorpion*
Taurus (6), *Bull*
Virgo (5), *Virgin*

Three Fates

Atropos (7)   Clotho (6)   Lachesis (8)

Three Furies

Alecto (6)   Megaera (7)   Tisiphone (9)

Three Gorgons

Euryale (7)   Medusa (6)   Stheno (6)

Three Graces

Aglaia (6)   Euphrosyne (10)   Thalia (6)

Three Harpies

Aello (5)   Celaeno/Podarge (7)   Ocypete (7)

Typefaces

Baskerville (11)
Bembo (5)
Bodoni (6)
Bookman (7)
Caslon (6)
Century (7)
Chicago (7)
Clarendon (9)
Courier (7)
Doric (5)

Elzevir (7)
Garamond (8)
Geneva (6)
Gill (4)
Gill Sans (8)
Gothic (6)
Goudy (5)
Helvetica (9)
Ionic (5)
New Century (10)

New York (7)
Optima (6)
Palatino (8)
Perpetua (8)
Times (5)
Times New Roman (13)
Zapf (4)

Index